*Figures in the Carpet*

# Figures in the Carpet

## Finding the Human Person
## in the American Past

*Edited by*

Wilfred M. McClay

WILLIAM B. EERDMANS PUBLISHING COMPANY

GRAND RAPIDS, MICHIGAN / CAMBRIDGE, U.K.

BT
WITHDRAWN
F54
2007

© 2007 William B. Eerdmans Publishing Company

All rights reserved

Published 2007 by

Wm. B. Eerdmans Publishing Co.

2140 Oak Industrial Drive N.E., Grand Rapids, Michigan 49505 /

P.O. Box 163, Cambridge CB3 9PU U.K.

Printed in the United States of America

12  11  10  09  08  07        7  6  5  4  3  2  1

**Library of Congress Cataloging-in-Publication Data**

McClay, Wilfred M.

    Figures in the carpet: finding the human person in the American past /
    edited by Wilfred M. McClay.

        p.        cm.

    ISBN 978-0-8028-6311-9 (pbk.: alk. paper)

    1. Theological anthropology — Christianity.    2. United States — History.

    3. Theological anthropology.    I. Title.

BT701.3.M36    2007

126.0973 — dc22

                                    2006029022

www.eerdmans.com

*For Mike Lacey*

*Not only witty in himself,*
    *but the cause that wit is in others*

# Contents

## III. SEEKERS

## IV. STRUCTURES

# Acknowledgments

This book, perhaps more than most, is a product of many more hands than are indicated on the title page or the table of contents. It is the result of a unique project in collaborative scholarship supported by The Pew Charitable Trusts, administered through the University of Notre Dame, and sited at the Woodrow Wilson International Center for Scholars, Washington, DC. All three of these institutions played an indispensable role in making our work possible, and each warrants our gratitude.

This project was a small part of a much larger undertaking, a Pew-supported multidisciplinary inquiry into the nature and concept of "the human person." Most of the contributors to this book took part in a three-year process, which included three collaborative workshops and two public programs, each of which played a role in the conception and gestation of this book. Calling the undertaking "collaborative" is not mere window-dressing in this case, but an accurate description of the way we actually worked together. Rather than assigning topics to participants who had been selected strictly by reference to their specialized field, we sought something more genuinely dialectical and open-ended. We assembled a team of unusually thoughtful and morally reflective scholars, and placed them in conversation with one another, with the chosen topics and papers to emerge gradually out of these conversations. In several cases, the authors took advantage of an opportunity to move beyond their customary professional niches, and take chances with fresh subjects and approaches. The resulting essays cover a wide array of subjects, and some were solicited independently of the collaborative process. But each conveys the spirit of that extended conversation, and we hope that the book as a whole will serve to perpetuate and multiply such conversations. We are grateful that The Pew Charitable Trusts, and particularly Rebecca Rimel and Luis Lugo, showed such confidence in such an unusual process, and hope that the results justify their confidence.

At Notre Dame, special thanks should go to Nathan Hatch, then the university's Provost, now President of Wake Forest University, who masterminded the entire grant and administered it through the university's Christian Scholars Program, providing just the right combination of directiveness and freedom, creating the kind of environment in which exciting scholarship can flourish. And it is hard to find superlatives sufficient to describe Kurt Berends, whose sharp insights and gentle administrative hand kept us on track, both logistically and substantively. He was fully one of the collaborators in this process, and it is hard to imagine what the final product would have looked like without his helpful, and often crucial, input. Linda Bergling made the financial aspects of the project easy and pleasant.

At the Wilson Center, first of all thanks must go to Director and President, the Honorable Lee Hamilton, who was unstinting in his generosity, and even attended our public functions when his busy schedule permitted. Similar thanks are due to Philippa Strum, the director of the United States Studies Division, to Steven Lagerfeld, editor of the *Wilson Quarterly*, and to Joe Brinley of the Wilson Center's publication office, each of whom was helpful in numerous ways. Huge thanks go to Susan Nugent of the United States Studies Division, who is in a class by herself, both as an extravagantly generous human being and as a smart and graceful coordinator of a thousand details. All of us were enriched by the honor of working with her.

Special mention should also be made of Casey Nelson Blake and Matthew Berke, both of whom participated in our collaborative discussions, and made valuable contributions to the end result. And *Grazie mille* to Rebekah Forman, who helped in many ways, intellectual and logistical.

Finally, one of the magnets drawing this project to the Wilson Center had to do with the participation of Michael Lacey, the longtime director (now retired) of the United States Studies Division at the Center, and an inspiration to a whole generation of scholars who have come through the Wilson Center as fellows and visitors. Everyone who has ever met Mike knows that there is no keener mind, no better listener, and no more indefatigable talker on the face of the planet. In three decades of service he made the Wilson Center into an important venue for serious reflection, not only on foreign affairs and Washingtonian politics, but on the deepest questions of intellectual life and moral existence. In the process, he changed the lives of countless scholars who had the good fortune to cross his path. The dedication of this book to him is but a small down payment on a debt that can never be fully paid.

# Introduction:
# From Self to Person —
# Some Preliminary Thoughts

Wilfred M. McClay

The question of the "human person" which flows through the essays in this book may sound formidably abstract and high-flown, the sort of speculation that good, solid, fact-oriented historians tend to avoid. Let me try to dispel that impression at the outset, then, with an example that I hope brings the question down to earth, where all fruitful inquiry ought to begin.

Consider the humble obituary column in your local newspaper. Not the obituary of a famous politician, soldier, or show-business celebrity. Just an obituary of an ordinary member of an ordinary community. Consider it first from the point of view of a surviving spouse or other family member or friend, the one who has to gather the information for the obituary and select out those facts that are appropriate for presentation in a public and permanent setting. Many of us have had this experience, and know how difficult and unsatisfying the process can be. The right balance between the competing demands of tenderness, respect, justice, loyalty, and candor is hard to find — particularly since we all tend to have genuinely different views of any person, and different ideas about what it means to memorialize that person properly. But still, there are important choices that must be made and emphases to be stressed, or avoided, in constructing the text.

And now let me bring the problem to a point. What photograph of the deceased should be used to accompany the text? Choosing the right words is easy by comparison. But rightly or wrongly, we grant enormous weight to the *image* in forming our enduring sense of the person. What image of that person, in what setting and at what age — at what moment in the trajectory of his or her life — should be provided? This is a newspaper, after all, so there is room for only one photograph, and no room for elaboration. So which will it be? Which period of life would be most representative of that man or woman in his or her fullness — a visual expression, so to speak, of a life's totality or essence? Should

1

the photograph be formal and artful, soberly and self-consciously posed? Or casual and spontaneous, a blithe and impromptu slice of life? Should it record a time of youth, or maturity, or old age?

The sophisticated postmodern response to this string of questions is, of course, to assert that there is no such thing as a human totality or essence, and leave it at that. There is no unitary self, only a series of surfaces, as Emerson once put it, upon which we skate. But such a glib and weightless jibe is no help. Obituaries must still be written, and photographs provided, because one's respects must be paid, and there are better and worse ways of going about it. The roughness of the judgments that life forces upon us does not excuse us from responsibility for making them well and honorably.

This commonplace event presents us with a poignant decision, then. Should one choose a relatively recent photograph? Some would say so. There is commendable honesty in selecting a picture that doesn't try to erase the signs of age, one that presents the deceased's face in a form that will be at least immediately recognizable to the community of family, friends, and acquaintances with whom he or she shared the final days and years. Indeed, there may be a particular virtue in this approach. Perhaps the conditions of our steadily advancing age represent us more fully than our youth, depicting the meaning of our lives as a culmination of all that has come before.

Maybe so, but generally the truth is much less comfortable. And we all know that. Life rarely resembles a Hollywood movie, in which the hero goes out in a blaze of glory, leaving a trail of smiles, admiration, harmony, and contentment in his wake. The actual end of most human lives is a sad, painful, sometimes grueling, profoundly embarrassing, and pathetic matter, often leaving emptiness, loss, regret, relief, and other contradictory and disturbing emotions in its wake. One would never pick a deathbed photograph to accompany an obituary. (Indeed, it probably reveals something important about our age's sensibilities that we have come to find unthinkably ghoulish and unpleasant the once-venerable idea of creating a death mask as a memento of the departed.) So why should one feel bound to use an old-age photograph? Why not make the photograph stand as an idealized representation of the departed, not in a state of decline or debility, but at the pinnacle of his or her physical strength and beauty — even if the face being rendered thereby is a face from thirty or forty years ago, a face much more attractive and cheerful, but one that almost no one still living would recognize?

One can see the logic and respectfulness in that choice, and yet ask: what is such a photograph really memorializing? Does such a choice imply that the aged are merely living on the downhill slope of life, and that one's essential nature was actually realized *in medias res,* in one's youth or early adulthood — even if one didn't know it — and that nothing worth representing or acknowledging is gained by the subsequent experience of aging? Are we to imagine that there was some brief and shining moment, at around the age of thirty-five, that one was at one's peak, was fully oneself, even if it hardly seemed thus at the time? One sometimes notices that women who die in their seventies and eighties are nevertheless represented in their obituaries by their college graduation pictures, or pictures taken in their twenties or early thirties, such as their wedding pictures. Is this merely an example of all-too-human vanity at work? Or is there an implicit judgment about when a woman is most fully herself? When we judge that a man is "past his prime," does that statement carry a larger significance about the way we understand the relative dignity of life's passages?

Of course, neither of these approaches to the photo selection, nor any of those that one might imagine in between them, is ever going to be entirely adequate. A picture may be worth many words — but there are many things a picture simply can never do. A photograph cannot render a life. It can only render a particular instant, the relatively brief unit of time required to form a film or digital image. No single moment is ever going to be sufficient to capture the essence of a human being. No one can translate four dimensions into two — or imagine what the individual looks like *sub specie aeternitatis,* as he or she must appear in the eyes of God, so to speak. Great portraiture, such as that of Rembrandt, might gesture toward the larger frame within which an individual life moves and has its being.[1] But plain and straightforward obituary photographs claim no such ingenuity. Indeed, what makes them so poignant is precisely their artlessness. It is as if their subjects make a silent plea to us, a modern restatement of Gray's *Elegy,* asking us to keep faith with them by remembering the unrendered reality of their lives, filling in the silences, completing their stories in our hearts and our imaginations.

So the obituary always falls far short of what we would like it to be, though it is far better than nothing. In any event, my point in this extended meditation on one of life's small and ordinary events is this: that when we properly celebrate and memorialize a particular life, we believe that we are remembering something discrete, and are doing something more than recording a list of items on a *curriculum vitae.* We are, in some sense, striving for a God's-eye view, one that abstracts from the particulars, stripping away incidentals to reveal and pay homage to the core of this individual. Not just X at a particular moment in his life, but X in his distilled essence, both as he was known and as he knew himself. We are attempting to represent a soul, and a person, something whose nature is greater and deeper than any particular instance can adequately show forth.

1. Marilyn Chandler McEntyre, *Drawn to the Light: Poems on Rembrandt's Religious Paintings* (Grand Rapids: Eerdmans, 2003).

\*     \*     \*

Our age, of course, speaks of selves and not souls. The latter is considered a term too laden with metaphysical implications to pass through postmodern customs. But it is striking to note how poorly the word "self," even though it is one of the cardinal terms of our discourse, serves us as a marker for that thread of essential continuity in the individual life that we acknowledge and commemorate in the obituary. An obituary is not, or not only, about a "self." The "self" is too changeable and contingent and interior a thing for that, and too tied to a romantic and subjective view of the isolated and autonomous individual, to tell us adequately about the individual in the full panoply of his or her relations with others. The self is a movable and malleable target, one that adapts to changing circumstances, revising its constitution repeatedly over the course of an individual life, taking on strikingly different colorations at different times.

And it is, in some fundamental way, unreachable. It divides so as to be unconquered. For although much of modern thought places heavy emphasis on the act of introspection, it enjoins what is frankly a near-impossible task, for the self always manages to elude any final examination — there being always another self that, as the ground of the examination, is not itself examinable. (And perhaps a "higher self" that one already is, in a sense, and yet that one also aspires to conform oneself to.) To add to the complexity, the self can even be thought of as something that, within the termini of an individual life, both comes into being, as in the psychological development of a very young child, and ceases to exist, as in cases of severe dementia or other mental impairment. Yet even when a sense of "self" seems to have departed entirely from an individual we know — and this disappearance itself is often hard to ascertain, since the self is so irreducibly a subjective and interior phenomenon, and is so remarkably protean and resilient — there is something else that remains. What is one to call it?

That something else, I would contend, is better described by the term *person*. It is the person, not merely the self, that we attempt to capture in the obituary. It is the person, not the self, that is not only the home address of our consciousness, but the nexus of our social relations, the chief object of our society's legal protections, the bearer of its political rights, and the communicant in its religious life. To put it another way, it is the person, not the self, whose nature is inextricably bound up in the web of obligations and duties that characterize our actual lives in history, in human society — child, parent, sibling, spouse, associate, friend, and citizen — the positions in which we find ourselves functioning both as agents and acted-upon. The concept of the "self," so steeped for us in romantic individualism, once seemed the most stable thing of all, the resting place of the Cartesian *cogito* and the seat of conscience. The young Emerson could still believe that introspection was the royal road to the universe's secrets, so that the commands to "know thyself" and "study nature" were different ways of saying the same thing.[2] But in the years since the link between self and nature broke down, leaving the self to soldier on alone in exploring the dim and misty marshlands of ungrounded subjectivity, it has proven a highly unstable concept, having a tendency to dissolve on closer examination into a kaleidoscopic whirl of unrelated colors and moods, an ensemble of social roles, a play of elements undirected by any integrative force standing behind them all.[3]

The concept of person, however, extending all the way back to its Latin roots *(persona)*, accepts the social nature of the human individual, and the necessity of social recognition, without ever regarding the individual as reducible to these things. In a word, it stands nearer to the facts of social existence. It is a less vivid but more fundamental concept. A self is what I experience. A person is what I am.

$$*\qquad*\qquad*$$

"The person" has not fared especially well at the hands of modern historiography, which has generally sought to locate historical explanations in the workings of large structures, impersonal forces, and social groups rather than the vagaries and razor-edged contingencies of individual character and agency. Some of this has to do with the enduring quest to make history resemble a science, a vision that took hold in earnest in the nineteenth century and has never entirely lost its appeal among academic historians. And as Alexis de Tocqueville observed, some of this has to do with the profound intellectual changes characteristic of a democratizing world, changes that alter both the subject matter of history and the historian's manner of approach to it. Historians who write in an aristocratic age tend, Tocqueville believed, "to refer all occurrences to the particular will and character of certain individuals." But those historians who write in and about a large modern democracy tend, he thought, to make "general facts serve to explain more things," so that "fewer things are then assignable to individual influences." Ironically, the same democratic age that exalted the value of the individual also rendered that individual

2. Ralph Waldo Emerson, "The American Scholar," in Larzer Ziff, ed., *Selected Essays* (New York: Penguin, 1982).

3. Kenneth J. Gergen, *The Saturated Self: Dilemmas of Identity in Contemporary Life* (New York: Basic, 1991); Walter Truett Anderson, *The Future of the Self* (New York: Tarcher, 1997).

a prisoner of aggregate forces, with little or no power to control or affect the events of his day.[4]

Tocqueville's comments seem especially germane in the present context, for he was very concerned that the democratic historian's emphasis on "general facts," while not entirely wrong, was prone to exaggeration, and therefore could become dangerously misleading. Although the change in historical circumstances made necessary a change in the manner of historical analysis, the extent of that change could easily be overstated. The historians who devoted all their attention to general causes were, he thought, wrong to deny the special influence of individuals simply because such influence was more difficult to track than had been the case in earlier times.

He saw this not only as an explanatory problem, but as a psychological and spiritual one. By promoting such distortions, these writers were creating false images of the human situation in both past and present, which could have the disastrous effect of depriving "the people themselves of the power of modifying their condition," thereby encouraging a kind of fatalism and paralysis of will, and a steady contraction of the human prospect. Such concerns reflected Tocqueville's chief and recurring fears about the dangers to which democratic society was particularly prone, dangers that were as apparent in historical writing as anyplace else. While the historians of antiquity "taught how to command," those in our own time, he complained, "teach only how to obey." They produce works in which "the author often appears great, but humanity is always diminutive." The belief that individual human agency should be factored out of history was, he feared, a self-fulfilling dictum, since the factored-out would come to believe it themselves.[5]

Interesting, too, that this generalizing tendency Tocqueville described was gathering strength at the same time that the main currents of modern Western thought in other disciplines, such as philosophy and literary studies, were moving in a completely opposite direction, toward an ever-tighter embrace of antinomianism and radical subjectivity, as epitomized in the figure of Friedrich Nietzsche. Yet the paradox was only a seeming one, for the two opposites went together. What, after all, could be more logical, in a sense, than the impulse to resist the coercive, domineering force of the increasingly organized and mechanized external world of the nineteenth century, ordered and disciplined and measured on every side by clocks, factories, whistles, telephones, maps, telegraphs, railroads, state bureaucracies, large business corporations, and Stan-

4. Alexis de Tocqueville, "Some Characteristics of Historians in Democratic Times," in *Democracy in America,* ed. Phillips Bradley (New York: Vintage, 1990), 85-88.
5. Tocqueville, "Some Characteristics of Historians in Democratic Times," 85-88.

dard Time Zones, by withdrawing into a zone of inner freedom, by cultivating and furnishing a large and luxuriant interior space, insulated from the world's tightening grip?[6] It is no paradox that we use the term "modern" to refer both to the external material and social forces that transformed the world and to the internal intellectual and expressive movements that wrestled with, and often deplored, the human costs of that same transformation. They were two facets of the same phenomenon.

The seeming gulf of this opposition, though, helps explain much about the unconstructive way in which the dualism of "individualism" and "collectivism" came to be understood for much of the twentieth century, and how it continues to be seen today. It helps explain why so much of the energy of American social and cultural criticism, past and present, has been devoted to the sustained critique of nearly any effective force of political power or social conformism — power elites, corporate magnates, hidden persuaders, would-be "traditions," and other suspect cultural hegemonies — that might inhibit the full expression of the self as an autonomous or relatively unconditioned historical actor. Our age has lost none of its appetite for fables of personal liberation, and it tends to side with the rebels Roger Williams and Anne Hutchinson, or with the precepts of Emersonian self-reliance, or with the antinomian moral fables offered in movies like *One Flew over the Cuckoo's Nest, Dead Poets Society,* or even the seemingly exotic (but thoroughly modern and American) *Fiddler on the Roof.* We are asked to side with the put-upon individual, cast as an unjustly thwarted soul yearning to breathe free, and we are instructed to hiss at the figures of social or political authority, the John Winthrops and Nurse Ratcheds of life, whose efforts to maintain order establish them instead as monsters and enemies of humanity.

Yet autonomy, like the "self" that purports to exercise it, turns out to be an elusive and unreliable god, which never delivers what it promises. Even the most energetically "unencumbered self" is always already a "person" enmeshed in social, intellectual, and institutional frameworks that are not neutral, but instead structure and enable the ideal of autonomy.[7] The liberatory preoccupations of so much modern scholarship and thought has made it very difficult, however, to move beyond the amorphous and untenable concept of "self" to the sturdier and more tenable concept of "person." Indeed, one could argue, following the historian Christopher Shannon (a contributor to this book), that

6. Stephen Kern, *The Culture of Time and Space, 1880-1918* (Cambridge: Harvard University Press, 1983).

7. Michael Sandel, *Democracy's Discontent: America in Search of a Public Philosophy* (Cambridge: Harvard University Press, 1996),

the agenda of modern cultural criticism, relentlessly intent as it has been upon "the destabilization of received social meanings," has served only to further the very social trends it deplores, including the reduction of an ever-widening range of human activities and relations to the status of commodities and instruments, rather than ends in themselves.[8] Given the need to start out in such radically denatured categories of analysis, how can one work backward toward the construction of something that commands our respect, let alone reverence? Small wonder that the present-day communitarian movement, which was launched as a corrective to the excesses of the culture's liberatory impulses, has been so unsuccessful; its task is as challenging as that of reassembling Humpty Dumpty.

One would be a bold prophet indeed to predict that this tendency in our thought and expression will exhaust itself anytime soon. But the present volume points us toward the riches that might lie in store for those who are intrepid enough to venture into such relatively unexplored territory. The authors, to be clear, have not set out to restore the grand and personalizing style of the aristocratic historians. That would be neither possible nor desirable. Nor do these essays seek merely to reaffirm an older humanistic understanding of history, though that certainly is a worthy goal, and inseparable from what is going on in these pages. The intention here is rather to insist upon seeing the human person as the focal and teleological point of historical inquiry, the cynosure of historical meaning, the barely visible figure standing out (for those with eyes to see) in history's lush and lavish carpet. The authors of these essays all take to heart the centrality of the idea of personality, and the recognition that history is arid and incomplete unless it is understood as a work of (and upon) individual human beings, and moreover a story whose substance and manner of telling are both matters of moral significance. Although not all the essays follow the same terminological lead, it's clear that a shift from "self" to "person" can strengthen that endeavor. It can rescue the individual from being smothered by giant structural explanations, the prospect that Tocqueville feared. But it also can rescue the individual from being thrust, in reaction, into a whirling limbo of subjectivism and indeterminacy, a prospect even more inimical to historical understanding.

Many of the essays point toward the possibility that the recovery of the idea of the human person, including careful consideration of how the human person is formed and sustained in American society, yesterday and today, may necessarily entail a reappropriation of neglected religious and other longstanding

8. Christopher Shannon, *Conspicuous Criticism: Tradition, the Individual, and Culture in American Social Thought, from Veblen to Mills* (Baltimore: Johns Hopkins, 1996), xi-xvi.

moral and spiritual normative traditions. "Self" is, to repeat, a strictly psychological term, deliberately stripped of the moral and metaphysical implications attaching to "the soul," one that asks to be evaluated strictly by the non-judgmental therapeutic standard of "health." Yet that standard seems to reflect, in the end, a mistaken understanding of the psyche. As Charles Taylor argued in his magisterial study, *Sources of the Self,* the coherence and integrity of the human person rest upon a moral foundation, on a set of presuppositions about the structure and teleology of the moral universe.[9] In other words, a moral disposition toward one's world, and a prior assent to certain moral criteria, are the preconditions of there being any psychological order and consistency at all in a human personality. If he is right in this analysis, then health is built upon morality, and not vice versa.

So the concept of moral responsibility, which therapy would seek to banish or marginalize, turns out to be essential and inescapable. There is no value-neutral way of being happy and whole, and no way of finding the human person in the American past without remembering that fact — remembering that there are, and have been, other premises about the predispositions of human nature than the ones under which we operate. Which in turn implies that those premises we now possess came into being at some point, and have to be inculcated and reinculcated, generation after generation, if they are to persist.

Accordingly, although there is a vast theoretical literature on historical and sociological conceptions of the self one could draw on, I have found it particularly useful to draw us back to the insights of two older writers, each of whom had an understanding of the distinction between self and person, and whose vision was ultimately grounded in the West's most venerable religious traditions. Martin Buber's long essay "What Is Man?" from his *Between Man and Man* would not be titled today as it was then; but it is still otherwise remarkably fresh and clarifying, stressing the "dialogic" and relational qualities for which Buber had become famous with his great 1936 book *Ich und Du (I and Thou).*[10] For Buber, the human person was reducible neither to the discrete features of individualism nor the collective ones of social aggregates, let alone the vagaries of language and discourse. The study of man, Buber asserted instead, must start with the consideration of "man with man." If you begin there, considering man *with* man, "you see human life, dynamic, twofold, the giver and the receiver, he who does and he who endures, the attacking force and the defending force, the

---

9. Charles Taylor, *Sources of the Self: The Making of the Modern Identity* (Cambridge: Harvard University Press, 1989); and *The Ethics of Authenticity* (Cambridge: Harvard University Press, 1991).

10. Martin Buber, *Between Man and Man,* trans. Ronald Gregor Smith (New York: Macmillan, 1965), 118-205.

nature which investigates and the nature which supplies information, the request begged and granted — and always both together, completing one another in mutual contribution, together showing forth man."[11] Or, as the French neo-Thomist and advocate of "personalism," philosopher Jacques Maritain, put it about a decade later, "There is nothing more illusory than to pose the problem of the person and the common good in terms of opposition," for in reality, it is "in the nature of things that man, as part of society, should be ordained to the common good," and that the problem of the person "is posed in terms of reciprocal subordination and mutual implication."[12] Here, then, one finds no concession either to the romance of the heroic atomic self or to the historiography of vast impersonal forces, or to the putative opposition between them; but rather an insistence upon the fundamental centrality of the person-in-relationship, of the "I and Thou," in defining what "man" is.

One might go even further, and point out that the concept of "person" helps us to understand human dignity as something deriving from the fact of one's intrinsic being, rather than from the extent of freestanding autonomy — what is sometimes called one's "quality of life" — that he or she can demonstrate. Such a view would stand in the longer Western tradition of individualism, affirming the diversity of legitimate human roles and ranks in society as we find it. At the same time, it would stand in direct competition to the increasingly influential view that the dignity and standing of any individual life is dependent upon the competency of the individual in question. How such debates will be resolved in the future is hard to discern. We can anticipate too that our growing knowledge of the biogenetic bases for human psychology and behavior in years to come will have a profound, and equally unpredictable, effect upon our view of the individual, and therefore its own influence on the outcome.

One thing seems clear, however: that is the need to rescue the idea of individual dignity from its captivity in the realms of individual psychology and postmodernist subjectivity, by returning it to the public realm, where it may be able to find a firmer footing and deeper roots. And this, the word "person" accomplishes. It reaffirms that the core meaning of individualism is its insistence upon the ultimate value of the individual human being. But it would also embrace the core insight of communitarianism: the recognition that the self is made in relationship and culture, and the richest forms of individuality cannot be achieved without the sustained company of others. And it would build upon Tocqueville's further insight that it is in the school of public life, and in the em-

---

11. Buber, *Between Man and Man*, 205.

12. Jacques Maritain, *The Person and the Common Good*, translated by John J. Fitzgerald (New York: Scribner's, 1947), 65.

brace and exercise of the title of "citizen," that the selves of men and women become most meaningfully equal, individuated, and free — not in those fleeting, and often illusory, moments when they escape the constraints of society, and retreat into a zone of privacy, subjectivity, and endlessly reconstructed narratives of the "self."

The universal range of the term "personality" encompasses and corrects for the imperfections and inequalities inherent in the endowments of nature and the accidents of culture. (Even the noxious *Dred Scott* decision, which consigned African Americans to the status of noncitizens, could not deny that "negroes" were "a class of persons.")[13] It takes into account not merely self-recognition, but the recognition of others; our personhood is, in some sense, a public fact as well as a private one. In addition, the concept grounds itself in something that the social-scientific view of human nature has sorely neglected: the human ability to initiate, to deliberate, to act, and in so doing to transform the very conditions of action. Accordingly, the most fruitful response to the present-day concerns regarding the disintegration of the self may be a movement away from the characteristic preoccupations of modern sociology and psychology, and toward a fresh reconsideration of our political natures, in all their complexity, contingency, and promise. The Western Christian tradition has always taught that the fractured soul is healed not by drawing in upon itself, but by being poured out into relationship with the things outside itself. That insight still has much to commend it in the twenty-first century.

*     *     *

A final word remains to be said about this book's title, which is taken from Henry James's celebrated story called "The Figure in the Carpet."[14] In a characteristically multilayered and inscrutable tale, James relates the quest of a green and earnest young literary critic for the hidden meaning, "the undiscovered, not to say undiscoverable, secret," behind the work of an eminent novelist called Hugh Vereker. What was sought by all, but known by none, was "the general intention" behind all of Vereker's books, their unifying meaning. The critics and Vereker's other readers, though consistently mystified, were yet certain that "the thing we were all so blank about was vividly there. It was something . . . in the primal plan, something like a complex figure in a Persian carpet."

The story is too elaborate to be told here, but suffice it to say that it is a clas-

13. Dred Scott v. Sandford, 60 U.S. 393, 417, 450-451 (1857).

14. Henry James, *The Figure in the Carpet and Other Stories*, ed. Frank Kermode (New York: Penguin, 1986), 355-400.

sic Jamesian masterpiece of ambiguity, impossible to reduce to a single stable interpretation. Indeed, it can even be read as a mockery of the whole literary exchange, pairing dull and uncomprehending readers who ploddingly manage to miss the obvious, with clever and superior-minded authors (both the fictional Vereker and the actual James), who delight in playing the trickster, and taunting their readers with the hint that there is something — indeed, the whole "point" of it all — that they don't "get." There are moments when one suspects that all the elaborate concealments exist to conceal precisely nothing, and the story is therefore a parable of mockery, dispensed by an author who felt perpetually misunderstood and undervalued. Yet even that bitter and nihilistic interpretation is very hard to sustain in the end, and one is left instead with the sense that the search for that unifying idea behind the fictions — for that figure in the carpet, for that string on which Vereker's pearls were strung — however exasperating and elusive and costly it may be, and however complicated the motives of those doing the searching, is a quest so compelling that one cannot refuse it.

And the story perhaps teaches us something about how to look for such things, and to know what secrets are worth pursuing. As the critic Frank Kermode has written about "The Figure in the Carpet,"

> Vereker's secret — "the thing for the critic to find" — is not, we infer, the sort of thing the celibate and impotent may look for when they speculate about sex. It is a triumph of patience, a quality pervading the life of the subject, like marriage. It is not the subject but the treatment, which is why it is a suffusing presence in all Vereker's work, and not a nugget hidden here or there. It is a matter of life and death and a matter of jokes and games. The error of criticism is a ludicrous one; it is also tragic.[15]

Not a fact-nugget, not a single dark secret, pulled from a personal diary or a police file or a divorce testimony or how-to manual, but a secret in plain view, an abiding condition that can be seen, if at all, only by standing still and looking long and hard at it in the right way, until the pattern emerges, and makes meaningful the life of the subject. It may be as hard to see as the atmosphere, and yet just as necessary a presence. Or as hard to see as the light that rings that ordinary image of an ordinary face on the local paper's obituary page, or the shadowy depths beneath its surface. Yet such are the figures for which these essays search.

---

15. Kermode in James, *The Figure in the Carpet and Other Stories*, 28.

# I. FOUNDATIONS

# Human Depravity:
# A Neglected Explanatory Category

GEORGE M. MARSDEN

Probe deeply enough beneath the surface of any historical explanation, and you soon strike against the hard rock of anthropology. By that term I mean not the academic discipline, but rather the largely unstated assumptions we make about just what sort of beings we are, and are not. Historians being a notoriously business-like bunch, most of them prefer to avoid attacking such issues head-on. Better to leave all such quixotic undertakings to others. But this is an avoidance reflex we can ill afford. For like it or not, we always presume some conception of human nature, if only a rough and ready one, in all the work we do. Any particular account of historical change and development that we put forward will not be judged credible unless it comports with prevailing conceptions of the human person, and our projective anticipations of what may motivate such persons to do the things they do. We won't find an explanation plausible if it is out of phase with what we know, or believe that we know, about the kind of beings we are. Clearly, though, this is a double-edged problem, since it is not hard to see how the conceptions of human nature that prevail in a particular era may also erect a powerful barrier to fresh insight, thus becoming the proverbial boxes outside of which none is able to think. Consider, for example, the limits upon our understanding that were imposed by the conception of "economic man."

It is just such an exercise in rethinking one of the deepest assumptions of modernity that George Marsden urges upon us in this essay. What, he wonders, if we were to reverse our era's usual assumptions — namely, that man is essentially either good or morally neutral and malleable — and instead postulated a darker conception of human nature, one that recalls assumptions that were prevalent in early American history, and that still command respect in many quarters today? After all, it is not as if we lack for evidence of human depravity. What, then, if we were to try looking at American history through that very different lens? What fresh things might we see? At the very least, according to Marsden, by recognizing the value of this "explanatory category," we may achieve a more balanced understanding of both the human person and the history he or she creates. Such a chastened perspective on the human prospect might also serve as a useful brake on the dangerous individualism so characteristic of our times. Marsden is the Francis A. McAnaney Professor of History at the University of Notre Dame, and author of, among many other distinguished works, *Jonathan Edwards: A Life* (Oxford, 1993), which won the Bancroft Prize in American History.

*From the moment they emerged upon the earth, human beings have systematically injured, plundered and enslaved one another. Our own century has been easily the bloodiest on record. . . . This is not of course to deny that there has also been a great deal of resplendent goodness, just that part of what we admire about that goodness is that it comes as something of a surprise. And most of it has belonged to the private rather than the public sphere.*

*This whole condition poses no problem for the Christian, who explains it with reference to original sin. But it ought to pose more of a theoretical challenge to the liberal or postmodernist than it seems to, assuming that they have bothered to reflect on the matter at all.*

Terry Eagleton, *The Illusions of Postmodernism*

Of all traditional Christian teachings the doctrine of original sin or of pervasive human depravity has the most empirical verification. The modern world, rather than undercutting this doctrine, seems increasingly to confirm it. Despite all the optimism about human nature and about moral and social progress that has been proclaimed since the eighteenth century, human beings' ruthlessness, tribalism, cruelty, unrestrained selfishness, and capacity for self-destruction seem only to have enlarged. The twentieth century, notable as it is for all its advances in medicine, technology, and programs to do good, seems all the more remarkable for its surpassing horrors.

My thesis — which I here explore in only a preliminary way — is that, despite such overwhelming evidence, American public commentators on culture have been largely unable or unwilling to face the reality of human depravity. In failing to confront frankly the truth that we and all our neighbors are in significant ways naturally corrupt (even if often doing good), social commentators, historians, and social scientists have neglected an important explanatory category. Only a handful of social critics, political pundits, or media analysts would dare suggest that inborn selfishness, greed, or lust is at the heart of a national problem. Historians seldom employ human depravity as the basis of their explanations. Americans are by no means the only ones to display these unrealistic attitudes toward the human character, but I'll confine my examples to American culture, since that is what I know best, and because these traits may be accentuated there.

In proposing this thesis, I must hasten to clarify a number of aspects of it. The first is that while the *source* of my formulations is my own Augustinian Reformed Christian heritage, the *basis* for my argument is a set of considerations that people from many perspectives might recognize. Furthermore, what I am arguing for is not the full set of particulars of a theological perspective, but only some aspects of that perspective that might be widely useful. For instance, I am not here making specific claims about the original fall of the human race, about the subsequent failure of human beings to love and worship God as they ought, about their becoming unworthy in God's eyes, or about Satan leading people into sin. Rather, I am here only pointing out readily recognizable human tendencies to act in their own interests at the expense of others, often using, condoning, or taking for granted, violent or otherwise oppressive means to do so. Moreover, despite our best intentions, all of us have tendencies toward pride, envy, covetousness, anger, sloth, gluttony, and lust (the "seven deadly sins") and give in to some of these more often than we would like to admit.

At the same time, as soon as I mention terms like original sin and depravity, I need to head off widespread misunderstandings about what these mean in the Augustinian Reformed heritage, and hence what I mean in advocating them. Since the Christian tradition starts with the creation of humans in the image of a loving God, it provides a strong basis (stronger than in naturalistic philosophies that exclude God) for affirming the infinite worth of each individual. In Christianity (as in many other theistic views) the universe is personal, and its most important dimension is personal relationships. Each human being is designed for the highest imaginable destiny of a personal loving relationship with the Creator of the universe, and to truly love the Creator means we should love each of God's creatures.[1] No matter how small, how weak, how foreign, how repulsive to our natural inclinations, how morally corrupted, we must love and value each person (even if not all of their acts) as God's own.

At the same time Christians traditionally believe that these invaluable individuals are fallen and morally corrupted. As Glenn Tinder says, "the principle that a human being is sacred yet morally degraded is hard for common sense to

---

1. Cornelius Plantinga Jr., *Not the Way It's Supposed to Be: A Breviary of Sin* (Grand Rapids: Wm. B. Eerdmans, 1995), provides a lucid and insightful account of this outlook.

grasp." Most people tend to divide the human race between more-or-less good people whom we are to treat with the greatest respect and evil people — whether foreigners, the poor, the rich, the bourgeoisie, political opponents, religious fanatics, secularists, or selected others — whom they treat with less respect. In the ideal Christian view, by contrast, every individual is to be exalted as God's creature even though everyone, including ourselves, is corrupted by the deceptions of evil.[2] Secularists have their own bases for affirming the worth of each individual, yet they usually fail to balance that with a realistic account of human proclivities to evil.

In asserting that few American mainstream commentators factor in inherent moral flaws in human nature in their analyses of what ails our society, I need to underscore that I am not calling for the opposite: an emphasis on depravity that would deny any widespread American or general human virtues. Clearly there is much to celebrate about America, as there is about humans in general. In America, as elsewhere, there are countless acts of charity, generous efforts to help the poor or contribute to world relief, concern for welfare of others, wonderful acts of love and self-sacrifice, progress in accepting formerly alien peoples, and lives guided by classic virtues.

That being granted, the rarity in the American public domain of systematic analysis of human depravity is all the more remarkable because the corrupted human condition is a standard topic in literature, theater, and film. Themes of inherited or pervasive sin are familiar to wide audiences in works such as those of William Faulkner, Tennessee Williams, Flannery O'Connor, Edward Albee, or Tom Wolfe. Film directors and writers such as Martin Scorcese, Paul Schrader, Quentin Tarantino, and Woody Allen often explore such motifs. Vast conspiracies reaching to the highest places (even if typically exempting one or two innocent protagonists) are standard fare in mysteries and thrillers at all levels. Part of the immense popularity of *Seinfeld* was based on viewers' recognizing something of themselves in characters who have no moral compass. Tony Soprano is sometimes seen as a portrait of everyman.

In addition to exposure to the theme in the arts and entertainment, huge numbers of Americans have been taught Christian doctrines of human sinfulness and need for salvation. Although not all churches teach human depravity and many church-trained Americans will describe human nature as "basically good," most will say, in the context of religious discourse, that people are "both

2. Glenn Tinder, "Can We Be Good Without God?" *The Atlantic Monthly* (December 1989), pp. 72-78. This paragraph follows Tinder closely. The publication of Tinder's article in *The Atlantic Monthly* is one of the relatively rare instance of which I am aware of a theoretical discussion of universal human depravity in the mainstream America media.

good *and* sinful" or even "basically sinful." At the least, the large majority of them have been exposed to some doctrine of universal sinfulness.[3] Although such doctrines, or their equivalents, are seldom given serious attention in the mainstream academy, a fair number of well-educated Americans have heard of Reinhold Niebuhr, and might know that his teachings on "original sin" were briefly in vogue after World War II.

Americans' lack of sustained mainstream public discussion of human depravity in recent decades is all the more striking in contrast to the vast literature on the sources of widespread German complicity in the Holocaust. While one school of thought argues that something peculiar to German history explains the willingness of ordinary German citizens to act as Hitler's executioners, the more common view is that the German experience only exacerbated traits that might be widely found in any human society, given the right circumstances.[4] Although there has been some discussion of the general principle involved in this latter view,[5] I do not believe that the principle has often been invoked in American social commentary or history writing.

It may be that one of the practical functions of much of our discussion of radical evil, such as the Holocaust or other incidents of genocide, is to make us feel relatively good about ourselves, by way of contrast.[6] Alan Wolfe, a thoughtful social commentator, illustrates just that tendency in his criticism of the thesis suggested by James Waller, a social psychologist, in his recent title, *Becoming Evil: How Ordinary People Commit Genocide and Mass Killing.* "Forgive me," Wolfe rejoins, "but I do not consider myself evil, nor would I apply that term to most people I know. (I have no doubt harmed people in the course of my life, sometimes deliberately, and people have done the same to me, but this does not make any of us evil.) Some concepts are useful only to the degree they are rarely used, and evil is one of them."[7] In denying that most ordinary people have ca-

3. Christian Smith, *American Evangelicalism: Embattled and Thriving* (Chicago: University of Chicago, 1998), 23, 264.

4. A sample of the immense literature and debates on this can be found in *Unwilling Germans? The Goldhagen Debate,* ed. Frederick M. Schweitzer (Minneapolis: University of Minnesota Press, 1998), commenting on Daniel Golhagen's controversial *Hitler's Willing Executioners: Ordinary Germans and the Holocaust* (1996).

5. One recent example is James Waller, *Becoming Evil: How Ordinary People Commit Genocide and Mass Killing* (New York: Oxford University Press, 2002).

6. Another version of this point is made by Alain Badiou, *Ethics: An Essay on the Understanding of Evil* (Verso, 2001), who suggests that analogies to radical evils such as the Holocaust are often used politically to justify lesser iniquities by states, such as imperialism. Review by Eugene McCarraher, *In These Times.com, August 6, 2001.*

7. Alan Wolfe, "Desperately Wicked: Reckoning with Evil," *Books and Culture* 9:2 (March/April 2003), 27. Wolfe is responding to Waller, *Becoming Evil,* cited in the previous note above.

pacity to participate in radical evil (aside from whether he is correct in that denial), Wolfe is arguing that it is incorrect to apply the term "evil" in any sense to
most of us. In part this may be an issue of semantics. I would argue, contrary to
Wolfe, that there are many small evils as well as the notorious large ones. Furthermore, the many basic flaws that we can find in our hearts, often all the more
insidious because they are so subtle, are indeed "evils" — what else should they
be called? The universality of basic flaws is well characterized as "depravity."
Wolfe, to the contrary, argues from an apparent lack of radical evil in most people, to what I take to be the typical American outlook, that most of us and our
neighbors are essentially good, despite occasional failings.

Although I am confident that the point I am making would apply to public
social analysis and history writing in any western country, I also think it is safe
to say that tendencies to be optimistic about human nature are accentuated in
the United States. During the 1950s (the era of Reinhold Niebuhr), for instance,
a favorite way to contrast America to Europe was in terms of "the myth of
American innocence." Historians were fond of pointing out the persistence,
since at least the American Revolution, of an American story that told of America's relative purity versus European corruption. Literary critics spoke of "The
American Adam" as a figure that recurred in the history of American fiction.
European writers of the time, such as Albert Camus, Jean-Paul Sartre, or Franz
Kafka, were far more likely to explore the depths of the human predicament. Of
the American writers who explored such themes it was no accident that the
most profound were Southerners, who lived in a culture that had experienced
collective guilt and defeat.[8]

Since Vietnam, even if most Americans have not begun to suffer anything
like the calamities experienced in much of the rest of the world, American innocence and the contrast with Europe seem less pronounced.[9] Nonetheless, once
again excepting the arts, mainstream commentators on American public life
have seldom taken seriously the possibility that universal flaws in the human
character might be at the root of many of the nation's most significant problems.
Some theological conservatives and some political conservatives in the Burkean
tradition have, of course, challenged the dominant opinions, but they have had
little impact on the mainstream of social commentators or academia.

8. See, for instance, R. W. B. Lewis, *The American Adam: Innocence, Tragedy, and Tradition
in the Nineteenth Century* (Chicago: University of Chicago Press, 1955); C. Vann Woodward,
"The Irony of Southern History," in *The Burden of Southern History* (New York: Vintage, 1961),
pp. 167-91.

9. So I am not here asserting that European or British social commentators are much more
likely to use human depravity or its equivalent as an analytical category. I suspect that they usually neglect the topic for many of the same reasons that Americans do.

The closest we have to a mainstream analysis of universal human depravity is in sociobiology, such as advocated in E. O. Wilson, *On Human Nature* or in Richard Dawkins, *The Selfish Gene,* and their successors.[10] At least some versions of this viewpoint argue for universal selfish tendencies among all people that are much like the Christian doctrine of original sin.[11] Such views are based on taking seriously the implications of a thoroughgoing evolutionary naturalism. While the plausible logic of their scientific arguments has given these views some popularity, they have also generated great resistance both from those who see them as underwriting conservative politics and those who wish to preserve more room for free will. Biological determinism, however, does not seem to have much impact on cultural analysts outside the realms of that specific debate.[12]

The persistence of talking in the cultural mainstream as though "we" (however defined) are essentially good is all the more striking since it can hardly be argued that America's public commentators of recent decades have not recognized the many dimensions of American evil. American public life is in fact teeming with cultural critics and prophets who condemn American immorality. The problem is that most of these do not include in their analysis some consideration of general traits in human nature, but rather blame the problems solely on someone or something other than themselves or their kind of people. Displacing blame is, of course, as ancient a human trait as is sin itself, and it should not surprise us. Our cultural commentators have three favorite ways of explaining human evil: they blame persons or groups other than themselves; they blame impersonal social and economic forces; and they blame psychological or social-psychological circumstances.

Political liberals use all three of these strategies in explaining the many things they see wrong with American society. America, they point out, is one of the most violent of societies, with more murders per capita than almost any other. That is consistent, they continue, with a long history of violence and cruelty, beginning with that against Native Americans and African slaves. As a nation, they observe, the United States has not especially distinguished from other

10. Edward O. Wilson, *On Human Nature* (New York: Bantam Books, 1978); Richard Dawkins, *The Selfish Gene* (New York: Oxford University Press, 1976).

11. Robert Wright, *The Moral Animal: Evolutionary Psychology and Everyday Life* (London: Abacus, 1994), observes that "the idea that John Stuart Mill ridiculed — of a corrupt human nature, of 'original sin' — doesn't deserve such summary dismissal" (p. 13). Wright also observes that "The title of this book is not wholly without irony," since we have splendid moral equipment that is tragically misused.

12. Ted Peters, in *Sin: Radical Evil in Soul and Society* (Grand Rapids: William B. Eerdmans, 1994), 294-302, summarizes the debates up to that time.

nations with respect to following criteria for just wars. Mention of Hiroshima and Vietnam and of various violent interventions on behalf of dictatorships is sufficient to evidence the point. At home America is plagued by racism, sexism, ethnocentrism, immoral disparities between rich and poor, corporate greed, and rampant acquisitive individualism. If there is personal blame for these conditions, they argue, it lies largely with more conservative Americans who are unwilling to address these issues.

Conservatives, who defend the relative virtue of America, counter that it is political liberals who have allowed traditional principles of personal morality to fall apart at the seams. Divorce rates are higher than ever before, and the ideal of the traditional family is in a state of disintegration. Abortions kill millions of tiny human beings each year. Sexual promiscuity is rampant and celebrated. All these trends reflect a wider breakdown in all sense of moral responsibility and respect for authority. People expect something for nothing. Liberals and the popular culture they support flout traditional values and encourage self-indulgence and a culture of irresponsibility.

In general liberals and conservatives blame each other for the crimes that they see as endemic to American culture. Both sides usually exempt themselves and other "right-thinking" people from responsibility fo the culture's widespread moral failings.

Political liberals, who of the two groups have maintained more optimistic views about human beings' collective abilities to solve their own problems, are especially prone to blame American failings not only on conservatives but also on impersonal and correctable social forces. Most social problems are explained not by some defect in human nature, but by some mistakes in the way the social system, especially as connected to the capitalist economy, is arranged that constrain some people to behave badly. An article of faith is that if the social conditions would improve, the problems would disappear.[13]

Today's political conservatives, shaped as they often are by nineteenth-century liberalism, typically defend capitalism with an optimism about human nature comparable to that of their twenty-first-century liberal counterparts. The principal difference is that today's conservatives focus their optimism on individuals' abilities to help themselves through personal discipline and hard work, in contrast to political liberals' focus on collective ability to correct eco-

13. One strand of the European lineage of such views is suggested by Robert Wright, who quotes Émile Durkheim, the father of modern sociology, as saying at the beginning of the twentieth century that human nature is "merely the indeterminate material that the social factor molds and transforms." Durkheim believed that even such things as sexual jealousy or a father's love of a child were "far from being inherent in human nature." Sociobiologists refer to such views as "the standard social science model." Wright, The Moral Animal, 5, 6.

nomic and social problems. Those political conservatives who are also religiously conservative, however, are more likely than are their secular allies to believe that some sort of religious transformation may be necessary to overcome the defects that keep many individuals from discipline and virtue.

Religiously motivated political conservatives, despite their general distrust of human nature, are not likely to apply that distrust to themselves or to others of their own religious persuasion.[14] Even though they may recognize that human history is filled with instances when religious beliefs have been used to justify selfish and immoral behavior, they tend to speak as though there is a simple distinction between truly religious people such as themselves, who are virtuous, and other people, who promote wrong moral principles, evil, or regimes that lead people astray. That tendency is most pronounced when in foreign affairs many religious conservatives (seemingly forgetting their own critiques of American corruption) unhesitatingly identify America as a whole as "good" versus the "evil" found in other nations or ideologies. Ronald Reagan's remarks about an "evil empire" or George W. Bush's about an "axis of evil" are cases in point.

Cutting across political allegiances are immensely popular psychological explanations for why so many essentially good people do bad things. Much has been written critical of "the therapeutic society." The point most relevant for our purposes is the one made by Philip Rieff in *The Triumph of the Therapeutic*,[15] who argues that many behaviors that used to be designated as sin are now explained as psychological maladjustment. Paul C. Vitz argues even more pointedly that psychology has become the prevailing religion of modern America, a "cult of self worship."[16] Self-adjustment and self-esteem are the ultimate values, not only in frankly liberal culture, but even in many churches, including some that profess most traditional doctrines. One common critique of psychotherapy is that it is a way, in the name of science, to blame one's fault on persons other than oneself. To mention that critique in the present context is, of course, not to suggest that the blame on others is generally without some basis. It is simply to suggest that such blaming is dangerously misleading if it is used, as it so often is, in building self-esteem as a way of exonerating oneself. Much of our culture is built on exploiting the primordial human trait of blaming others.

Christopher Lasch, who was more willing than most to question American

14. Evangelical traditions of the holiness and Pentecostal heritages that teach some doctrine of perfectionism, or triumph over sin by believers, most frankly teach such doctrines.

15. Philip Rieff, *The Triumph of the Therapeutic: The Uses of Faith after Freud* (New York: Harper & Row, 1966).

16. Paul C. Vitz, *Psychology as Religion: The Cult of Self-Worship* (Grand Rapids: William B. Eerdmans, 1977).

optimism, explored with considerable subtlety the interaction of economic and psychological themes. "Economic man himself," he wrote in the late 1970s, "has given way to the psychological man of our times — the final product of bourgeois individualism. The new narcissist is haunted not by guilt but by anxiety." In a culture where people are taught to expect immediate gratification, people live empty lives "in a state of restless, perpetually unsatisfied desire."[17] Robert Bellah and his research team documented similar themes in their analysis of *Habits of the Heart* in the 1980s. The two primary definers of American life, they concluded, are the managers and the therapists. Managers guide people in an essentially depersonalized technological world that values "utilitarian individualism," based only on success measured in monetary terms. The therapists, whose ideals are dominant in the popular media, promote "expressive individualism" which offers ways to find personal "meaning" or at least gratification in a social system that fosters many hollow and disconnected lives.[18]

## The Culture of "Whatever"

Andrew Delbanco, in *The Death of Satan: How Americans Have Lost the Sense of Evil,* provides a most helpful account of the stages in twentieth-century public discourse on human depravity. During the early decades of the century, he points out, scapegoating was especially popular. Human failings were often blamed on those of inferior races, inferior genetic makeup, foreigners, those of inferior education, those of inferior religious belief, the poor, the capitalists, or the communists.[19] Mid-century, after World War II and the Holocaust, there was a brief revival of serious public discussion of evil. But the 1960s introduced what Delbanco well describes as "The Culture of Irony." Symbolized most baldly by the Batman television series of 1966 to 1968, much of our public culture has adopted the stance that most traditional categories, including any distinction between "good" and "evil," must be presented inside quotation marks.[20]

The high culture manifestation of this trend is the postmodern denial of any general human nature. Afraid that any admission that humans share a

17. Christopher Lasch, *The Culture of Narcissism: American Life in an Age of Diminishing Expectations* (New York: W. W. Norton, Warner Books Edition, 1979), 22-23.

18. Robert Bellah, et al., *Habits of the Heart: Individualism and Commitment in American Life* (Berkeley: University of California Press, 1985).

19. Andrew Delbanco, *The Death of Satan: How Americans Have Lost the Sense of Evil* (New York: Farrar, Straus and Giroux, 1995), 155-84. My list is slightly different from his.

20. Delbanco, *The Death of Satan*, 185-218.

common essential nature will reinforce conventional power structures, mores, or sexual categories or restrictions, many interpreters for the past generation have insisted that all human traits are social constructions. Despite the manifest difficulties inherent in maintaining such a position consistently (such as that it undercuts its own trans-cultural claims about universal human rights or that all persons should be treated equally),[21] the anti-essentialist doctrine is so useful to certain immediate causes that it is often maintained as an essential dogma. As Delbanco puts it, "in the undifferentiated world we now live in . . . anyone who makes assertions about 'natural' differences between 'male' and 'female,' say, sounds like a fundamentalist raver."[22]

In more popular culture and social analysis the counterpart is what might be called "the culture of 'whatever.'" That phrase seems particularly apt in the youth culture and the popular media. Rule number one seems to be that no one should judge anyone else (excepting those who hold certain laughably old-fashioned attitudes). More widely considered, however, the culture of "whatever" reflects a combination of two sometimes contradictory tendencies: the non-committal, non-judgmental "cool" stance of the popular culture of irony, and a wider "culture of affirmation" that dominates politics and business. In any case, the effect is to avoid making most traditional moral judgments.

In the political world, the culture of affirmation prevails with no room for irony. All partisan political talk must emphasize the irrepressibly virtuous qualities of "the American people." Jimmy Carter learned this to his regret. In his infamous "malaise" speech, Carter merely chided against "a mistaken idea of freedom" [as] "the right to grasp for ourselves some advantage over others." Such views, he said, lead to "fragmentation" and "failure." He also warned that "owning things and consuming things does not satisfy our longing for meaning." Even though he balanced his criticism with the requisite optimistic assurance that Americans could once again choose the common good and the way of progress, he was shouted down.[23]

What is true of politics is true of most of the practical activities that depend on public support. They are market driven, and so must cater to their audiences. Even most of American religious culture, not only liberal but also much that is more traditional in theology, is likewise shaped by the culture of

21. See, for instance, Barbara Johnson, ed., *Freedom and Interpretation: The Oxford Amnesty Lectures 1992* (New York: Basic Books, 1993), where contributors struggle with this dilemma. Terry Eagleton, in the epigraph for this essay (which shows, of course, that my topic is occasionally, even if rarely, discussed) points out a version of the problem.

22. Delbanco, *The Death of Satan*, 206.

23. Jimmy Carter's 1979 Malaise Speech, available at http://www.rightwingnews.com/speeches/carter.php.

affirmation. Dependent as most religious organizations are on their audiences, they usually tell their potential constituents pretty much what they want to hear. Business and advertising are more frankly based on flattering their customers. Even though in its private councils a business may work on the premise that "a sucker is born every minute," its public image must be that "the customer is always right."

Perhaps the most striking illustration of the difference between our culture of affirmation (with a good bit of cool irony thrown in) and a full-fledged Christian view of human nature is found in the field of advertising. The average American is likely to encounter millions of advertisements in a lifetime.[24] Advertisers are realistic about human nature. They are not shaped by abstract principles of what we might like to believe about human traits. Rather, they scientifically look at human behavior and predict on that basis. What traits do they find as most universal? Near the top of almost any list will be traits that could be well described as six of the traditional "seven deadly sins." These are pride, envy, covetousness, sloth, gluttony, and lust (the seventh, anger, is not good for sales).[25] If we recognize that advertising research provides us with a mirror of our collective desires, then it seems hard to maintain that human beings are essentially virtuous in any traditional sense. In fact, what we find is that we accept as a matter of course this celebration of human traits that we ought to deplore.

Understanding our culture's routine, economically driven approbation of human self-centeredness can help us see why we seem so helpless to resist consumerism. Most of us are ready to agree that it is wrong to define ourselves or our priorities by the things we have, by the fashions we follow, by the neighborhoods in which we live, by the foods and drinks we can offer, or the places we can afford to travel. Yet almost all of us are practitioners of consumerism to a greater extent than we would like to admit. The reason is that consumerism and materialism appeal to traits in us that are nearly irresistible, especially if we are unwilling to recognize them for what they are. As Pogo said prophetically long ago, "We have met the enemy and it is us."

24. Neil Postman, *Amusing Ourselves to Death: Public Discourse in the Age of Show Business* (New York: Penguin Books, 1984), p. 126, reports that average Americans are likely to see a million television commercials by the time they are forty.

25. One of the more subtle ways of covering their deplorable exploitation of human materialism is when advertisers themselves allude to the problem. One of the most successful has been the long-running series of ads that say "there are some things that money can not buy" (usually great personal moments or relationships) even if for "everything else there is Mastercard." Less subtle is an ad run in the winter of 2003 that showed an SUV being used to save a baby seal.

## Human Depravity as an Explanatory Category

What then, by way of summation, are reasons to reintroduce universal human depravity as one of our explanatory tools in cultural analysis?

The first reason is because it is true. Overwhelming evidence indicates that there are broad tendencies in human nature that cut across cultures, even if they may manifest themselves in very different ways, depending on the context. One has only to look again at the list of seven deadly sins, which originated in the Middle Ages[26] in a culture vastly different than our own, to recognize the point. No culture in history has been exempt from these tendencies. No individual is immune from all of them. Even if we can think of rare individuals who seem to have triumphed over most of these tendencies, we know that it has only been with heroic effort that is against many of their most basic inclinations.

For understanding the root of universal human depravity we can do no better than to begin with a simple Augustinian analysis of the human situation. According to Augustine, there are two cities based on two types of love. The earthly city into which we are all born is built on love or desires for created things. Although many such loves or desires may be good and commendable in themselves, they are inevitably destructive of universal love, since there are not enough created things to go around without rancor. Humans are divided, even by their legitimate loves, so that the earthly city is ultimately built on love to self and cupidity. Only mutual love to the creator, as in the heavenly city, could unite humans.[27]

Observers as diverse as Jonathan Edwards and Richard Rorty have suggested the problem of the limits of humans' affections to each other. Both Edwards and many liberal observers today, of whom Rorty is an example, point out that even relatively good people usually act virtuously toward a limited community. Starting with the observation that members of a pirate band may act virtuously toward each other, Edwards argues that human affections are never naturally extended widely enough. Love to family or love to nation is often admired as true virtue, but in each case love and loyalty to one's own means we do not love others as we should.[28] Richard Rorty identifies more or less the

---

26. Lists have varied slightly over the years, but that does not change the point.

27. Augustine, *The City of God*, bk. 14, c. 28. Cf. the commentary by Thomas Merton, in his Introduction to The Modern Library edition (New York: Random House), xii-xiv.

Although Augustine's idea of two cities has sometimes been appropriated to justify a supposedly righteous church versus an evil world, in more realistic versions of the doctrine Christians recognize the imperfection of their sanctification in this life and that, as the Apostle Paul suggests in Romans 7, corruption still plagues them.

28. Jonathan Edwards, *The Nature of True Virtue*, ed. Paul Ramsey, *Ethical Writings, The Works of Jonathan Edwards*, Vol. 8 (New Haven: Yale University Press, 1989), 611.

same problem, but he thinks that it can be resolved by progressive moral enlightenment. "Moral progress," he writes, "on a world-historical scale consists in enlarging the range of people whom we think of as people like us." Rorty thinks great advances have been made in the past century in this regard, as it surely has within some liberal cultures.[29]

Although there is much to be said for views such as Rorty's as perhaps the most commendable attitude one might take in a world without God, his outlook pales beside Edwards's more realistic Augustinian view of human nature, even if viewed in purely secular terms. If one did not know better, one might suppose that it was Edwards who had had the opportunities to read twentieth-century newspapers and histories before presenting his analysis. Although it is a noble dream that liberal ideas of inclusiveness will spread throughout the world as the waters cover the sea, that is a secular millennial vision that is just not going to happen.[30] It simply fails to provide a way to deal with human religious and ideological differences, differences over views of marriage, family, and sexuality, differences in views of rights and loyalties, differences in national, local, and tribal loyalties, inevitable conflicts in economic interests, and propensities to violence and counter-violence — to name only some of the most obvious problems. Moreover, liberal progressivism cannot deal with the problem that liberal inclusiveness, for all its virtues, is always rooted in the interests of persons of particular social classes, ideological and political persuasion, views on religion, family, sexuality, and so forth. In short, the view fails to take into account built-in limits in the human condition that inevitably lead to conflict.

Reinhold Niebuhr, the American public commentator who most influen-

---

29. John Rawls, perhaps the most influential political philosopher of the recent era, seems to suggest the possibility of a similar solution in his *A Theory of Justice* (Cambridge: Harvard University Press, 1971). If everyone could be persuaded to think about a just society with no reference to their own status or interests, then not only could we arrive at reliable principles of justice, but members of such a society "are not much affected by envy and jealousy, and for the most part they do what seems best to them as judged by their own plan of life without being dismayed by the greater amenities and enjoyments of others" (p. 544). Rawls' apparent naïveté regarding human nature is in a way reminiscent of the utopianism of B. F. Skinner, as in *Walden II* (New York: Macmillan, 1962), which reflected the behaviorist Skinner's belief that human nature was correctable if people, although lacking freedom, were subjected to the right scientifically-controlled conditions. Rawls, however, seems to suggest that humans might voluntarily mend their ways.

30. Christian millenarians have often suffered from similar problems. Edwards himself, despite a realistic view of so-called "Christian" nations and of most professed Christians, nonetheless was an uncritical heir to a Constantinianism that viewed Christ's work toward establishing the millennium as involving political conquest by "Christian" powers.

tially critiqued earlier liberal progressivism and defended the concept of "original sin" a half century ago, modified Augustinian realism in a slightly humanistic direction.[31] Addressing the issue in the modern framework of the tension between nature and freedom, Niebuhr saw sin as arising out of the very factors that allow humans to rise above the determining forces of nature. Humans are endowed with powers of freedom, creativity, and ability partially to control their environments, but they inevitably turn these accomplishments toward a too high estimate of themselves, toward the illusion that they can be "as gods."[32]

Niebuhr's analysis is a valuable modern way of explaining human propensity to sin, and his realistic political analysis disposes of any illusions that nations can act out of purely virtuous motives, but it can be argued that he did not go far enough. Niebuhr offers excellent insights on human pride and self-love, but has relatively little to say about some others of the deadly sins, such as envy, anger, covetousness, sloth, gluttony, and lust. When he does discuss sins of sensuality, such as sexual license, drunkenness, gluttony, or love of luxury, he argues cogently that they ought to be subsumed under either misguided self-love or escape from self through worship of an artificial god. Niebuhr's interest is to counter the recurrent Christian tendency to identify sin with sensuality alone; instead he wants people to recognize their pride and self-aggrandizement that is at the root of their rebellion against God.[33] His indictment of modern sinfulness might have more teeth in it, however, if he more often followed the logic of this analysis and pointed out how the sins of sensuality and consumption, so often celebrated in our culture, are symptoms that ought to alert us to our deeper pride and rebellion.

Concentrating only on the themes of nature, freedom, and misguided freedom, Niebuhr lacks a robust doctrine of creation. In a more full-fledged Augustinian view, God has created all things to be used in their proper way, ultimately as reflections of the love and will of God. God's creation and God's law go hand

---

31. H. Richard Niebuhr and a number of other commentators at mid-century, responding especially to National Socialism and Marxism, reflected some Augustinian themes by emphasizing that humans are prone to worship as their highest value something less than the ultimate, whether it be family, race, nation, or one of the "isms" of the day. See, for instance, H. Richard Niebuhr, *Radical Monotheism and Western Culture: With Supplemental Essays* (New York: Harper & Row, 1943), 24-25.

32. See, for instance, *The Essential Reinhold Niebuhr: Selected Essays and Addresses*, ed. Robert McAfee Brown (New Haven: Yale University Press, 1986). On Niebuhr's view of Augustine, see pp. 123-41, "Augustine's Political Realism."

33. Reinhold Niebuhr, *The Nature and Destiny of Man: A Christian Interpretation*, Vol. 1, *Human Nature* (London: Nisbet & Co., 1941), 242-55.

in hand. Human rebellion against God involves thinking that we can be a law unto ourselves. Niebuhr's insights on the nature of that rebellion, pride, and self-aggrandizement are profound. Nonetheless, by minimizing the traditional Christian language of the law (which indeed has often been abused in legalism), Niebuhr neglected one of the surest guides to recognizing the extent of our sinfulness. All things are created by God for good purposes, but fallen due to sin. They are, in the words of Cornelius Plantinga, "not the way they ought to be."[34] Such a consciousness alerts us to the consequences of sin on every side and of the immensity of the task of setting things right, including within our own recalcitrant selves.

While the principal argument for the use of human depravity as an explanatory category is that it fits the evidence, a second reason to employ it is for its moral value. Its chief use in this regard is that it puts us on the same level with those we tend to blame. Rather than suggesting that social problems are simply the fault of others (for instance, in blaming the rich or blaming the poor), we can acknowledge that we ourselves are part of the problem and that everyone shares in the fault, even if in differing ways.

We can apply this principle to the field of history. The first point to be made in this regard is that a realistic or Augustinian view of human nature ought to give us sympathy with many of the insights of postmodernists and their Marxist forebears, who have done so much to shape contemporary academia. Their emphases on power, dominance, exploitation, class struggle, hegemony, false consciousness, hermeneutics of suspicion, corrupt structures, and the like all reflect robust suspicions of human tendencies, especially through power structures, to exploit each other. Often such analyses are accompanied by naïve beliefs that those who recognize the problems can create structures, programs, or attitudes that would lead the human race beyond such tendencies. But that is another issue. Augustinians and others who recognize human depravity can learn much from contemporary analyses of the social dynamics of human exploitation of humans. Christians and other religious believers can also sympathize with the moral instinct that says the last shall be first.

At the same time, a frank recognition of innate human depravity can help us see that such contemporary analyses seldom go far enough. Many historians today, driven by commendable interests in giving the oppressed or the neglected their due, distort the historical record by presenting it as though all the blame in a conflict is on one side. That is, in effect, to put much of the real complexity of human motivation and experience on the side of the powerful, or the

---

34. Plantinga, *Not the Way It's Supposed to Be: A Breviary of Sin.*

oppressors. It is, of course, appropriate to recognize that blame is not distributed equally, and that often the oppressed are acting in extenuating circumstances. Yet the best history is, like the best fiction, that which recognizes the complexities of human motivations, the bad as well as the good on both sides of a conflict. Historians who paint the oppressed or the previously neglected only in glowing terms are patronizing them. Sometimes historians representing a previously disparaged group will attempt to balance the record by writing histories that celebrate only the group's virtues and achievements. Perhaps that may be useful for a time, especially in popular presentations, to redress earlier misrepresentations and damaging images. Nonetheless, as seems to be increasingly recognized, a sign of maturity is when representatives of a group can write history that takes into account that members of that group are flawed humans like everyone else. In the long run the most convincing histories will be those that portray their protagonists with faults as well as virtues. The best histories already do that, but few articulate the principle involved.

It is sometimes suggested that pessimistic or realistic views of human nature tend to inhibit social reform and hence are endorsements of the status quo. That is, of course, a danger, given our natural perversity. Yet there is no reason why realistic views should be especially conducive to such tendencies, so long as we recognize that humans also have immense capacities to do good. Being realistic about how much we are surrounded by and implicated in evil may give us all the more reason to work for the good. It may be true that humans are often better motivated to act on the basis of illusions about themselves than on the basis of reality. Yet even if we wanted to justify illusions on such a basis, we would have to recognize that, while in the short run they may be effective, in the long run they are likely to lead to disillusion and cynicism. Today's widespread cynicism regarding social reform may be a case in point. Realistic analyses of our problems, including our own complicity in them, have better potential to produce realistic and lasting solutions.

Optimistic views of human nature also can contribute to moral complacency. If we each think that we are essentially good, then it is easy to think that when we become relatively well-to-do or blessed in other ways we are just getting what we deserve. That exacerbates our natural tendency not to be concerned for others. If, on the other hand, we had a stronger sense that we are not entitled to any of the good gifts that we have, we should be at least a little more open to overcoming our natural inclinations and to sharing with others.

Crucial to applying the principle of human depravity as a heuristic device is to recognize that we, the observers, are not exempt from the flaws in human nature. Historians and social commentators often speak as though they and their readers stand on a moral pinnacle from which they can freely condemn the moral foibles of the past. In American history it is particularly easy to claim the high moral ground in condemning, for instance, slavery or Indian removal. In an essay on depravity, I am not in the least suggesting that such practices should not be condemned. Rather I am saying that when they are condemned it should be done in such a way as to recognize the moral complexities of the historical situations, and that we probably would not have done better than our ancestors if we had been in their situations. Further, we can point out that we ourselves probably have similar blind spots and that, even though our mistreatment or neglect of our neighbors may not be as notorious or spectacular, we share a common humanity with those whose actions we deplore.

That brings us to the issue of why we should want to write or read history in the first place. If what we are doing primarily is using the past to reinforce our views on current issues, then our histories will be impoverished by special pleadings and we might better analyze present issues directly. If, on the other hand, our goal is truly to learn from the past, then we would best start by looking for how we share a common humanity with our subjects on both sides of any divide. If we are alert to our own faults, we will be better able to see and learn from the faults of the people with whom we identify. At the same time, we may better appreciate the virtues of those whom we instinctively blame.

Such an Augustinian approach to history, recognizing that both virtues and vices are found on both sides of partisan lines (even if some causes are clearly better than others), can help us provide richer portraits of the past. In art and literature, one-dimensionality is one of the principal things to be avoided. In great photography or cinematography the artist plays with light or multiple camera angles, casting the face of the subject in shadows, or the like.[35] Novelists and playwrights present their most compelling portrayals of their protagonists by showing their struggles with light and darkness. Much history writing, by contrast, is moralistic and one-dimensional. An Augustinian alertness to complexities of good and evil in each person can thus help advance the state of the art.

35. I am grateful to Michael DeGruccio for this image as well as for his other astute comments on this essay. I am also grateful to other participants in the Colloquium on Religion and History (CORAH) at the University of Notre Dame for their comments on this paper, some of which I have adopted.

# Losing and Finding the Modern Self: Neglected Resources from the Golden Age of American Pragmatism

Michael J. Lacey

As the intellectual and moral appeal of Marxism continues to fade, the rather more diffuse tradition of American pragmatism has often been pressed into service, as a new and relatively unsullied philosophical basis for the coming generations of democratic social reform. The impulse to do so is understandable. But this substitutionary effort has enjoyed limited success at best, and has not really provided a cogent basis for challenging the hypertrophy of the self in modern Western thought and culture. Marxism at least sought to challenge the ideological primacy of what it called "bourgeois" individualism. But it often seems that pragmatism has, in practice, merely underwritten the pathologies of the modern self, privileging the vantage point of individual consciousness and offering, especially in the hands of some of its postmodern interpreters, a justification for an ungrounded perspectivalism — hardly the stuff of which powerful and enduring human solidarities are likely to be made.

Michael J. Lacey contends that this reading of pragmatism represents a misunderstanding and a missed opportunity. Because of it, we have failed to consider the ways in which a fuller understanding of pragmatism might cut in precisely the opposite direction, and serve us as a way of regrounding "self" as "person." Pragmatism, as arguably the single greatest American contribution to the Western philosophical tradition, confronted the tradition of Western thought at the turn of the twentieth century with the principle of epistemic uncertainty, a realization of the need for wariness, toleration, and tentativeness in the rendering of individual judgments. In Lacey's view, this intellectual and moral breakthrough is properly understood not as a carte blanche empowerment of the unencumbered self, but instead as the groundwork for a new politics of human relations, one in which the optimal human prospect was one not of furthering atomic individualism but of cultivating a deeper awareness of social embeddedness and mutuality. Hence, he argues, a recovery of the neglected resources of pragmatism will necessarily entail a rediscovery of pragmatism's largely forgotten communitarian and religious roots. Michael J. Lacey served for thirty years as the director of the Division of United States Studies at the Woodrow Wilson International Center for Scholars in Washington, DC, and is now an affiliate professor at the Jackson School of International Studies at the University of Washington in Seattle. His many publications include *Religion and Twentieth-Century American Intellectual Life* (Cambridge, 1991), and *The State and Social Investigation in Britain and the United States* (Cambridge, 1993).

"Pragmatism explains everything about ideas except why a person would be willing to die for one." Though a rather sad commentary on America's most distinctive contribution to the world's philosophy, this is the judgment of Louis Menand, and it is a fair one if the meanings of pragmatism are limited to those developed in his Pulitzer prize-winning account of its origins in the late nineteenth century. There is no good reason to stay within these limits however, as the sources invite alternative readings. There is a strain of thinking more challenging and philosophically ambitious to be found there. Menand stresses the wariness of pragmatism, its suspicion of all abstractions for the violence that might be hidden within them should they win unfettered allegiance. For him the chief virtues of the pragmatist tradition are its skepticism and the spirit of toleration that he believes to go along with it. The cultural role of pragmatism has been to help dissolve old metaphysical certainties and to usher in modernity. Its chief achievements in the history of culture have been a jurisprudence protective of civil liberties and the doctrine of academic freedom.[1]

The pragmatist tradition itself, now entering its second century, is in the midst of a great and quarrelsome revival that engages many of the country's leading academic intellectuals and ranges in its manifestation across most disciplines in the humanities and social sciences. Philosophy and history, literary and cultural studies, moral and social theory, legal and religious thought — all have been engaged and affected. Menand's book is an important document in the life history of the revival, and is especially congenial to the outlook developed in recent decades by one segment of the neo-pragmatist movement, the postmodernist wing represented most notably by the work of Richard Rorty

---

1. Louis Menand, *The Metaphysical Club: A Story of Ideas in America* (New York: Farrar, Straus, and Giroux, 2001), 375. For critical scholarly responses to Menand's book and his reply to the criticisms, see the roundtable discussion in *Intellectual History Newsletter* 24 (2002): 84-125.

and, to a lesser degree, Stanley Fish, who favor what they call an "anti-foundational" style of reasoning about reason. It is a style heavily dependent on irony and implicit argument that takes academic skepticism to new levels of resourcefulness and application.[2] While of some usefulness, no doubt, in the first

2. A good deal of information on pragmatism and its revival is available on the Internet, and a good starting point would be the website of The Pragmatism Cybrary at http://pragmatism.org. A touchstone text for the beginnings of the neo-pragmatist revival is Richard Rorty, *Consequences of Pragmatism: Essays, 1972-1980* (Minneapolis: University of Minnesota Press, 1982). Rorty's *Philosophy and the Mirror of Nature* (Princeton: Princeton University Press, 1979) presents his criticisms of epistemology as a traditional concern of philosophers. His *Contingency, Irony, and Solidarity* (New York: Cambridge University Press, 1989) contains two chapters especially pertinent to the themes of the present essay: (1) "The Contingency of Selfhood," and (2) "The Contingency of Liberal Community." For a wide-ranging and well-focused critique of Rorty's work by leading contemporary philosophers and his response to the criticisms, see *Rorty and His Critics,* ed. Robert B. Brandom (Oxford: Blackwell Publishers, 2000). For a sample of Stanley Fish's outlook, see the essays in his *The Trouble with Principle* (Cambridge, Mass.: Harvard University Press, 1999). Fish's last chapter in that volume, "Truth and Toilets," offers a good starting point for his approach to the "anti-philosophy" of neo-pragmatism.

The reader unfamiliar with the scope and depth of the pragmatist revival will benefit from consulting Morris Dickstein, ed., *The Revival of Pragmatism: New Essays on Social Thought, Law, and Culture* (Durham: Duke University Press, 1998), where Dickstein writes a very thoughtful and balanced introduction to the whole phenomenon, "Pragmatism Then and Now." Another useful collection of essays is to be found in Sandra B. Rosenthal, Carl Hausman and Douglas Anderson, eds., *Classical American Pragmatism: Its Contemporary Vitality* (Urbana: University of Illinois Press, 1999). John J. Stuhr's edited volume, *Pragmatism and Classical American Philosophy: Essential Readings and Interpretive Essays* (Second edition, New York: Oxford University Press, 2000) is a handbook well worth consulting. Stuhr's *Pragmatism, Postmodernism, and the Future of Philosophy* (New York: Routledge, 2003) develops from within the postmodernist frame of reference the argument that "pragmatism's tolerance and pluralism must acquire a more critical edge, an edge that will allow it not only to recognize and appreciate plural human natures, choices and lifestyles, but also to assess critically what is better and what is worse in this plurality."

There is an uneasiness within postmodernist pragmatism about the apparent need for rational foundations for a progressive politics of the sort called for by many contemporary feminists and others on the academic left. Perhaps we are getting to the bottom of its anti-foundationalism! For the gist of the criticisms leveled against the political bearings of postmodernism in the pragmatist vein by those sympathetic with its anti-foundational posture but worried about the solipsism it seems to justify, see Cornell West's "The Limits of Neopragmatism," in Michael Brint and William Weaver, eds., *Pragmatism in Law and Society* (Boulder: Westview Press, 1991), pp. 121-126, and in the same volume, Joan C. Williams, "Rorty, Radicalism, and Romanticism: The Politics of the Gaze," pp. 155-180. Cornell West's *The American Evasion of Philosophy: A Genealogy of Pragmatism* (Madison: University of Wisconsin Press, 1989) is an important perspective on the tradition and a critique of its current emphases together with the introduction of West's own sensibility of "prophetic pragmatism." On the question of genealogies for pragmatism, which would be a matter of some dispute in contemporary

phases of cultural criticism, where a sense of distance and independence is in order, the skeptical ethos so central to the postmodern outlook on things is a handicap when it comes to working out in explicit fashion an ethics and a politics. Wariness has its limits.

The postmodern viewpoint is only one among many, however, and its staying power and general road-worthiness have yet to be demonstrated. Many remain stubbornly *within* modernity, at home with its idioms, and not quite ready for the promised liberation from all its questing in art, philosophy, and religion. So far as today's perspectives on the legacy of pragmatism are concerned, it should come as no surprise that postmodernists find in the tradition what they look for. Their treatment of the cultural meanings of the pragmatism of the golden age has been remarkably selective in terms of the authors, themes, and texts that are singled out for attention and approval. One can easily get the impression in sampling their works in the literature of the revival that the founders of the tradition must have been rather diffident thinkers, averse or indifferent to the teachings of tradition in ethics, politics and religion, comfortable in espousing a rather unexacting form of humanism along naturalist lines.

Granted there have been from the beginning various understandings as to what the new movement was all about. Within the first decade of the launching of the term, by William James in a lecture at Berkeley in 1898, the philosopher Arthur O. Lovejoy counted thirteen different pragmatisms, and James is said characteristically to have rejoiced at this plentitude of meanings and accepted all thirteen.[3] In looking back on the writings of the originating pragmatists of the Golden Age — here understood to include Charles S. Peirce, William James, Josiah Royce, John Dewey, and George Santayana — one encounters a complication of opinions on many issues that is difficult to sort out fairly. In my view, however, the postmodernists' reading of classical pragmatism misses a great deal. It filters out far too much that was vital to the founders and remains so to-

---

debates, Rorty's own sense of the subject is reflected in his introduction to John P. Murphy's *Pragmatism: From Peirce to Davidson* (Boulder: Westview Press, 1990), where he says, "Because we do not think of 'finding out how things are' or 'discovering truth' as a distinct human project, Peirce's and Putnam's 'end of inquiry' versions of absolutism seem to us misguided" (p. 4). Finally, note should be taken of James Livingston's *Pragmatism, Feminism, and Democracy: Rethinking the Politics of American History* (New York: Routledge, 2001), which develops the argument that classical pragmatism and contemporary feminism have much more in common than is normally appreciated due to their similar critiques of the idea of the abstraction of the unencumbered self.

3. Arthur O. Lovejoy, *The Thirteen Pragmatisms and Other Essays* (Baltimore: Johns Hopkins University Press, 1963), pp. 1-29. It was Clarence Irving Lewis who made the remark about James in his "Pragmatism and Current Thought," *Journal of Philosophy* 27, No. 9: 238.

day. I would like to argue for a different perspective — modernist rather than postmodernist, one might say — on what the founders were trying to articulate in their more hortatory moods. I will stress the importance of those elements in their work that buttress a distinctively modern, post-scientific-revolution viewpoint on the human self as inherently normative, and indicate its connections to ethical reasoning, communitarian public philosophy, and to modern religious thought.

## Idealism, Pragmatism, and the New Psychology

Perhaps the most important thing to note about pragmatism at its birth is the connection it sustained with the idealist and romantic philosophy of the nineteenth century. While the sources of pragmatism were manifold, none was more important than this German link. Kant and his successors were very much alive in the minds of the classical pragmatists. The basic idealist convictions that mind and spiritual values are grounded realities of a fundamental kind in the universe, in no way subordinate to matter, that knowledge and freedom are not finally opposed but interdependent, that determinism has a place in the natural sciences that is out of place when taken to extremes in the human sciences: these were the themes that carried a special resonance for the pragmatists.

Royce got to the heart of what was most vital in classical pragmatism when he observed that he was both a pragmatist *and* an idealist, and that there was no contradiction in the claim. The choice was not either/or, since "each of these doctrines involves the other and therefore I regard them not only as reconcilable, but as truth reconciled."[4] Precisely how the two involve each other is *the*

---

4. Josiah Royce, *Lectures on Modern Idealism* (New Haven: Yale University Press, 1919), 258. These lectures were given at Johns Hopkins University in 1906 and were not published until after Royce's death. They contain Royce's appraisal of the key figures in the history of modern idealism and his argument that the pragmatism emerging in his own lifetime was one form of post-Kantian idealism as based on the assertion that "Truth meets needs; truth is also true. Of these two propositions I conceive idealism to be constituted" (p. 257). This viewpoint is developed in Royce's later work. From the perspective of pragmatic idealism, Dewey can be read, as he has been by many, as one who naturalized Hegel and the absolute. Perhaps the most distinguished proponent of the pragmatist-idealist viewpoint as truth reconciled after Royce was William Ernest Hocking, a student of both Royce and James and a successor of Royce's in the Alford Professorship at Harvard. Hocking's works in the philosophy of religion and political philosophy are outstanding achievements in the tradition, oddly neglected in the rediscoveries of recent decades. See particularly his *The Meaning of God in Human Experience: A Philosophic Study of Religion* (1912) and *Man and the State* (1926).

Another primary source on the influence of the romantic idealists on the pragmatists is

great question in logic and epistemology — indeed, in the human sciences more generally. It is the question that drives the modern concern with both the merits and limits of historicism and cultural relativism. It has never been fully resolved or abandoned, except perhaps by postmodernists. All the originating pragmatists, however, were agreed that ideals were latent in human experience, and that life was to be lived in light of the ideals. It was the duty of intelligence to bring them to the surface, to criticize them, and to uphold them.

One of the important conclusions reached in William James's scientific masterpiece, *The Principles of Psychology,* vindicated a basic building block of modern idealist philosophy, the notion of necessary, a priori elements in the structure of intellectual experience. These hard-wired elements pointed to the need for an interpretive metaphysics that could go beyond the world of phenomenal appearances and approach the world of noumenal reality, to use Kant's categories, and provided some psychological grounding for it. James agreed with the idealists "that the mind is filled with necessary and eternal relations which it finds between certain of its ideal conceptions, and which form a determinate system, independent of the order of frequency in which experience may have associated the conception's originals in time and space." He called these necessary and eternal relations "postulates of rationality" as distinct from propositions of fact. While the postulates were not sensible realities, they could not be evaded analytically and they had sensible effects: "they have a fertility as ideals, and keep us uneasy and striving always to recast the world of sense until its lines become more congruent with theirs." Here one finds the linkage, epistemologically speaking, to questions of art, ethics, and politics. "The world of aesthetics and ethics is an ideal world, a Utopia, a world which the outer relations persist in contradicting, but which we as stubbornly persist in striving to make actual."[5]

Royce called a properly blended mixture of idealist and pragmatic elements "pragmatic absolutism," a phrase that James rather famously could not accept, given his reservations about the idea of the absolute. The purport of the mixture, however (and this James did accept wholeheartedly), was the conviction that any form of pragmatism that disavows its idealist roots and aspira-

---

George Herbert Mead's lectures on Kant and romantic philosophy in his *Movements of Thought in the Nineteenth Century,* Vol. 2 in *The Works of George Herbert Mead,* ed. and intro. by Merritt H. Moore (Chicago: University of Chicago Press, 1936). Murray G. Murphey's "Kant's Children: The Cambridge Pragmatists," *Transactions of the Charles S. Peirce Society* 4 (1968): 3-33, is the basic article in postwar historical scholarship to develop insight into the idealist connection and its importance.

5. William James, *The Principles of Psychology* (New York: Dover Publications, 1980), Vol. 2, pp. 660-71 passim.

tions is fated to be barren, and any form of idealism that cannot survive trial by experience, as pragmatism challenges it to do, will suffer the same fate. Put differently, the pragmatists hoped their work would be of some special use in coming to terms with all the problems and possibilities entailed in the process of *realizing* ideals.

From the start it has been difficult to formulate pragmatism as a systematic, architectonic philosophy, and yet its proponents have never been content to view it simply as a method, either.[6] Classical pragmatism is anti-formalist in spirit. Its architects were determined to break away from the inherited rationalisms of the Enlightenment. They aimed to shift the attention of philosophy from mind to self, away from abstract truth considered as a thing in itself and towards meanings experienced in the mind and heart of the subject. For this reason, their pragmatism is an attacker of abstractions. The attacks are carried out in the interrogation of intellectual experience, however, and not with the hope of liberating the mind from its own processes of abstraction and generalization, which it cannot do without.

There is no thinking without generalizing and abstracting, and it is the working of these processes in experience that is under investigation. James remarked in this vein that pragmatism "has no objection whatever to the realizing of abstractions, so long as you get about particulars with their aid and they actually carry you somewhere."[7] The appeal to the experience of the ordinary reader, her wish to go somewhere in thinking, is characteristic of the rhetoric of pragmatism and its approach to language. As James famously put the point: "You must bring out of each word its practical cash value, set it at work within the stream of your experience. It appears less a solution, then, than as a pro-

---

6. None of the founders attempted a fully systematic formulation, although Dewey's *Experience and Nature* (1925), the most metaphysical book of this anti-metaphysical philosopher, moves in that direction. Santayana's *The Life of Reason: Or, The Phases of Human Progress,* 5 vols. (1905-06), is another candidate. While some commentators do not regard Santayana as a pragmatist at all, others regard him as the source of one of the most significant streams in the pragmatist tradition — pragmatic naturalism. The case for pragmatic naturalism is explored in Henry Levinson's *Santayana, Pragmatism, and the Spiritual Life* (Chapel Hill: University of North Carolina Press, 1992). Levinson sees pragmatic naturalism as a wide-ranging philosophy of cultural criticism that anticipates the work of many contemporary philosophers and critics, among them Richard Rorty, Cornell West, Giles Gunn, Richard Poirier, and Benjamin Barber. For a contemporary attempt at formulating systematically the core insights of the pragmatist tradition, it should be noted that Sandra B. Rosenthal's *Speculative Pragmatism* (Amherst: University of Massachusetts Press, 1986) is a cogent presentation in the form of a unified, metaphysical vision.

7. William James, *Pragmatism* and *The Meaning of Truth* in one volume, with an introduction by A. J. Ayer (Cambridge, Mass.: Harvard University Press, 1978), 40.

gram for more work, and more particularly as an indication of the ways in which existing realities may be changed."[8]

The idea that to realize an abstraction the experiencing self must undertake a program of work points to something fundamental in the pragmatist ethos. Among the abstractions they wished to know more about and to see better realized were most of the evergreen topics of the philosophical tradition — goodness, truth, objectivity, community, and others of that difficult kind. It may be helpful in this connection to recall that the founding pragmatists were deeply involved in formulating and criticizing the "new psychology" of the late nineteenth century. James's monumental, two-volume *The Principles of Psychology* (1891), at once a great work of science and philosophy, was known chapter and verse by each member of the founding group. Peirce and Royce, for example, are among those acknowledged in the introduction as sources of inspiration. "The reader will seek in vain for any closed system in this book," James noted in its introduction, but the reader would witness the steps involved in reworking and going beyond the inherited theories of cognition that were available in the received intellectual tradition.

What was new about the new psychology was its aspiration to become a trustworthy scientific enterprise, and the pragmatists were averse, not to science, but to "closed systems" of science, which was the point of James's remark. James knew as much as anyone of his day about the merits of laboratory research, and he respected the undertaking — indeed, he gave it roots and reputation in America — but he had no great hopes for what he called "brass instrument psychology." From the start the pragmatists were opposed to restrictive understandings of the human subject. They resisted "nothing-buttery," those positivist and reductionist currents of thought about scientific method that would eventually come to prevail in some of the more narrow-gauged behavioralism of mid-twentieth-century American social science. *The Principles of Psychology* was certainly *not* a behaviorist treatise, unless one thinks of behavior in very broad and philosophical fashion, which the pragmatists encouraged them to do. James's book aimed to set up new terms of reference for the apprehension and analysis of the modern self, and thus contribute to the development of both social science and philosophy.

As "the Science of Mental Life, both of its phenomena and their conditions," James's approach to psychology as a field of knowledge grew out of his command of the *philosophical* tradition, particularly its epistemological and metaphysical branches. It was this philosophical literature that dealt in various but disciplined fashion with the ways in which feelings, desires, cog-

8. James, *Pragmatism* and *The Meaning of Truth*, 31-32.

nitions, reasonings, decisions, and other phenomena of consciousness were understood and described. There were two major streams of the received tradition that James wished to transcend and to bridge. Both had to do with basic ways of classifying experience and accounting for the contents of consciousness.

"The most natural and consequently the earliest way of unifying the material," James observed, "was, first, to classify it as well as might be, and secondly, to affiliate the diverse mental modes thus found, upon a simple entity, the personal Soul, of which they are taken to be so many manifestations." By way of example, he pointed to the way in which "Now, for instance, the Soul manifests its faculty of Memory, now of Reasoning, now of Volition, or again its Imagination or its Appetite." This scheme of classification by faculties, "faculty psychology" as it was known, had a long and distinguished ancestry, going back to Plato and Aristotle. It had been most carefully and systematically developed as an account of the ingredients of the human mind by medieval scholastic theologians and philosophers. As a popular apprehension of the component parts of subjectivity it was pervasive in the taken-for-granted cultural premises of the nineteenth century, and James referred to it as "the orthodox, 'spiritualistic' theory of Scholasticism and common sense."[9]

The second stream of philosophical tradition of special interest to James was that of empiricism, both British and Continental, with its "associationist" account of ideas. Here one explained the process of thinking, James remarked, as one explains houses by reference to stones and bricks. "The 'associationist' schools of Herbart in Germany, and of Hume, the Mills, and Bain in Britain," he observed, "have constructed a *psychology without a soul* [italics his] by taking discrete ideas, faint or vivid, and showing how, by their cohesions, repulsions, and forms of succession, such things as reminiscences, perceptions, emotions, volitions, passions, theories, and all the other furnishings of an individual's mind may be engendered. The very Self or *ego* of the individual comes in this

---

9. William James, *The Principles of Psychology*, Vol. 1 (New York: Dover Publications, 1980), 13. For a brief discussion of the new psychology, see Mitchell Ash, "Psychology," chapter 15 in Theodore M. Porter and Dorothy Ross, eds., *The Cambridge History of Science*, Volume 7, *The Modern Social Sciences* (New York: Cambridge University Press, 2003), particularly pp. 259-62, which describes the common features of the new psychology. For Ash the new psychology that mattered was the "brass instrument psychology" of the kind that James and the pragmatists subjected to criticism. Pragmatism does not appear in the index to the volume, although James's *Principles of Psychology* gets a paragraph for its opposition to narrow experimentalism. According to Ash, James "is rightly cited both as a founder and as a perpetual embarrassment to the new psychology" due to his proposals that the experience of psychics and mystics be given the same objective study as the experience of "normal adults." There is no embarrassment in that for those interested in his contributions to the psychology and philosophy of religion.

way to be viewed no longer as the pre-existing source of the representations, but rather as their last and most complex fruit."[10]

The basic aim of *The Principles of Psychology,* sustained throughout, was to show the reasons for rejecting "both the associationist and the spiritualist theories" of the nature of subjectivity. There was to be no choice between materialism and immaterialism. The treatise worked against the grain of determinism from either direction, and situated the modern self accordingly. The new psychology as developed by the pragmatists acknowledged the dependence of the subject upon its physical, biological, and social conditions. But it also acknowledged the self-transcending character of subjectivity, the experienced freedom of the subject, and the capacity of the self to stand in judgment on all the conditions upon which it depended. The textbooks on psychology written by Dewey and by Royce reflect the same basic orientation.[11] The perspective on the modern self the pragmatists presented was that of an active, dynamic, purposeful subjectivity, a self-in-motion and in motion towards ends, necessarily social in its orientation and dependencies but also chafing against them. It was a self that boiled over. Restlessness was its innermost essence. It was a self subject to development and decline, and necessarily, given its self-transcending character, it was a participant in broader cultural and social processes of development or decline.

It is important to note that while the psychologies of the pragmatists arose out of their philosophical work, and while they hoped to see a satisfactory, scientific, free-standing field of psychology develop in the modern university, they did not believe that the study of human psychology would (or even could, as a matter of principle) outgrow its need for philosophy. The most difficult issues raised by psychological research were philosophical issues, and none of the human sciences could be totally free of philosophy and its traditional concerns. As James said of the scientific perspective on subjectivity opened up in his *Principles of Psychology:* "Of course this point of view is anything but ultimate. Men must keep thinking; and the data assumed by psychology, just like those assumed by physics and the other natural sciences, must some time be over-

---

10. James, *The Principles of Psychology,* Vol. 1, 1-2.

11. See Josiah Royce, *Outlines of Psychology: An Elementary Treatise with Some Practical Applications* (New York: Macmillan Company, 1903), and John Dewey, *Psychology* (New York: Harper and Brothers, 1887), together with his "The New Psychology," *Andover Review* 2 (September 1884), reprinted in *The Early Works,* Vol. 1, pp. 48-60. See also, as a development within the tradition, George Herbert Mead, *Mind, Self, and Society: From the Standpoint of a Social Behaviorist* (Chicago: University of Chicago Press, 1934), published posthumously, and also his *The Individual and the Social Self: Unpublished Works of George Herbert Mead,* ed. David L. Miller (Chicago: University of Chicago Press, 1982).

hauled. The effort to overhaul them clearly and thoroughly is metaphysics; but metaphysics can only perform her task well when distinctly conscious of its great extent. Metaphysics fragmentary, irresponsible, and half-awake, and unconscious that she is metaphysical, spoils two good things when she injects herself into natural science."[12]

## The Ethics of Pragmatism

From the beginning pragmatism was accused by its critics of harboring a corrosive moral relativism, and from the beginning the pragmatists denied the charge. Broadly speaking, theirs was an ethics of self-realization, as distinct from the duty ethics of the Kantian tradition or the utilitarian ethics of rational calculation. Their ethical thinking arose against the background of their psychological investigation, which was oriented to exploring the social nature of the self. There was for them no such thing as an unencumbered self, no abstract, preexisting self, complete with blanks to be filled in by experience, but there was at birth a potential self in the form of a limited set of natural tendencies and dispositions. That potential self was to become an actual self as a consequence of moral action, and no other way. "Every good act," as Dewey put it, "realizes the selfhood of the agent who performs it; every bad act tends to the lowering or destruction of selfhood."

The quality of happiness or satisfaction one could hope to achieve in life was bound up with devotion to moral ideals, and that fidelity might well exact heavy personal costs. To turn to Dewey again: "whatever harm or loss a right act may bring to the self in some of its aspects, — even extending to destruction of the bodily self, — the inmost moral self finds fulfillment and consequent happiness in the good." Moral integrity did not come cheap or easily. James noted on this point that "the most characteristic and peculiarly moral judgments that a man is ever called on to make are in unprecedented cases and lonely emergencies, where no popular rhetorical maxims can avail, and the hidden oracle alone can speak; and it speaks often in favor of conduct quite unusual, and suicidal as far as gaining popular approbation goes."[13] To revert for a

12. Op. cit., p. vi.

13. Quotations attributed to Dewey are from Dewey and James H. Tufts, *Ethics* (New York: Henry Holt and Company, 1908), pp. 391-94 passim. The James quotation is from *Principles*, Vol. 2, 672. The literature on pragmatism and ethics is very extensive. The major recent achievements in pragmatist social and moral theory include Philip Selznick, *The Moral Commonwealth: Social Theory and the Promise of Community* (Berkeley: University of California Press, 1992), and Hans Joas, *The Genesis of Values* (Chicago: University of Chicago Press, 2000). Also

moment to Louis Menand's reading of pragmatism, the tolerant philosophy of civil liberty that "explains everything about ideas except why a person would be willing to die for one," it is in *this* vein of their thought, the ethical vein, that the pragmatists try to make clear why a person might be willing to sacrifice everything for an idea. The "self-sense" of personal integrity might require it as a test of fidelity that vindicates the power of the insensible world of ideals.

Despite this stoic note of indifference to popular approval, however, the ideal of moral self-realization was not a simple matter of asserting the wants or needs of the subject against the conventions of the community. Far more complex transactions of personal appropriation and commitment to universal values were involved. The pragmatists distinguished between self-assertion and self-realization. Dewey noted with reference to self-realization that while it is "Like self-assertion in some respects, it differs in conceiving the self to be realized as universal and ultimate, involving the fulfillment of *all* capacities and *all* relations." What was universal and ultimate was in tension with the particular and the proximate, and to get at this tension the pragmatists resorted to a traditional distinction. The distinction between a lower and higher self was common in pragmatist writing on morals — though, it must be noted, given their opposition to dualism in traditional moral thought, the higher and lower appear as aspects of the same unitary, experiencing self, and the tensions between the two were understood to be tensions within natural inclinations and feelings.

Thus moral development was presented as a process of gradually achieving mastery of the self. The aim was self-control through discipline and repression of the lower self, not simply in the interests of others, but in the interest of the higher self. "The problem of morality, upon the intellectual side," Dewey insists, "is the discovery of, the finding of, the self, in the objective end to be striven for; and then upon the overt, practical side, it is the losing of the self in the endeavor for the objective realization. This is the lasting truth in the conception of self-abnegation, self-forgetfulness, disinterested interest." The old Christian para-

---

important is Joas's *The Creativity of Action* (Chicago: University of Chicago Press, 1996). Helpful studies of the ethical thought of the classical pragmatists include Steven Fesmire, *John Dewey and Moral Imagination: Pragmatism in Ethics* (Bloomington: Indiana University Press, 2003); Robert J. Roth, *John Dewey and Self-Realization* (Englewood Cliffs, N.J.: Prentice Hall, 1962); J. Harry Cotton, *Royce on the Human Self* (Cambridge, Mass.: Harvard University Press, 1954); Peter Fuss, *The Moral Philosophy of Josiah Royce* (Cambridge, Mass.: Harvard University Press, 1965); Frank M. Oppenheim, *Royce's Mature Ethics* (Notre Dame: University of Notre Dame Press, 1993); James Campbell, *The Community Reconstructs: The Meaning of Pragmatic Social Thought* (Urbana: University of Illinois Press, 1992); and his introduction in James Campbell's *Selected Writings of James Hayden Tufts* (Carbondale: University of Southern Illinois Press, 1992).

dox that to find the self one must lose the self in service of what is beyond the self is the bedrock of their thinking on self-realization.[14]

The struggle to shape the natural inclinations and tendencies of human nature in light of ideals latent in them is the basic stuff of pragmatist ethics. Independent of its social relations, the self is nothing. Actual selves are the results of discipline, commitment, and sacrifice of various kinds, and the responsible individuality of the mature self is the fruit of the process. Moral autonomy is the goal but not the beginning of experience. As Royce put it, "Conscience is the flower, not the root of moral life."[15] It is the result of a long process of learning. It is a certain kind of skill that hardly exists apart from its training. Considered as a process of moral development, self-realization is conceived as dynamic and open-ended, requiring the subject always to look outward to the particular frictions, conflicts, and problems of interpersonal life and engage them in an incessant flow of appropriate responses.

These responses build and define subjectivity. They accumulate into patterns of determinate character, and the pragmatists describe the ingredients of the patterns as traits of virtue. Though the point is often neglected in contemporary, neo-pragmatist debates, the ethics of the classical pragmatists was a type of *virtue ethics,* comparable to those of Aristotle and Aquinas. In his most accessible and influential work on ethics, for example, Dewey devotes a chapter to the moral virtues, arguing that "the habits of character whose effect is to sustain and spread the rational or common good are virtues; the traits of character which have the opposite effect are vices."

It should be noted, too, that not all virtues are equal; some are "cardinal," that is, more important than others, in fact building blocks for others. Given their aversion to any form of moral rationalism, the abstract ethics of the textbooks, the pragmatists were leery of listing the virtues and arranging them in hierarchies. Something of the sort was necessary to convey their viewpoint, however. Turning to Dewey again, we find the assertion that there are traits essential to all morality: "we have the 'cardinal virtues' of moral theory. As whole-hearted, as complete interest, any habit or attitude of character involves justice and love; as persistently active, it is courage, fortitude or vigor; as unmixed and single, it is temperance — in the classic sense. And since no habitual interest can be integral, enduring, or sincere, save as it is reasonable, . . . interest in the good is also wisdom or conscientiousness: — interest in the discovery of the true good of the situation." As of old, in pragmatist ethics a

14. Dewey and Tufts, op. cit., 391-94.
15. Josiah Royce, *The Philosophy of Loyalty* (New York: The Macmillan Company, 1908), 260.

prudent wisdom in the active search for good is described as "the nurse of all the virtues."[16]

Ethical values in the writings of the founders typically appear as forms of *knowledge,* as opposed to forms of mere *feeling.* The pragmatists are not "emotivists," in other words, who hold that facts are one thing, about which we can develop valid knowledge, while values, for which we might harbor personal feelings of approval or disapproval, are another matter. Each of them would resist the dichotomy between facts and values that became common in subsequent philosophical debates and often influenced for the worse developments in social science.[17] Values for the founders are facts of a peculiar kind that arise out of natural tendencies and dispositions. Feelings of attraction, repulsion, approval, and disapproval are the data of moral consciousness that are to be interpreted and deliberated upon. While they are different from the data of physics or geology, for example, they are data nonetheless. They are patterned realities, and the patterns are intelligible. They are not to be dismissed as arbitrary or merely subjective. When satisfactorily interpreted, the result is ethical knowledge.

The term *introspection* is suspect in pragmatist circles. It suggests the existence of an oracle within, to be consulted on moral matters, and despite his remark about the hidden oracle, James did not mean to be taken literally on this point. For the pragmatists the self is not a datum of consciousness, to be found by looking within; it is instead the locus of a process of interpretation, linking past and future in the present, and dealing incessantly with what is happening without. Royce speaks of these interpretations as plans of action, and argues that the self *is* an ongoing, living plan of action, constantly reading its environment and editing its own orientation to it. Peirce pointed out that what people call introspection is actually a form of inference, the stuff of thinking rather than looking, and making a moral judgment is an act of deciding, an office of thought. This is what Dewey had in mind when he touched on the paradox of

---

16. Dewey and Tufts, op. cit., 399-405, passim.

17. Opposition to the fact/value dichotomy has been a staple in pragmatist writing from early on, and it continues to be a major theme. On this question, see Hilary Putnam, *The Collapse of the Fact/Value Dichotomy and Other Essays* (Cambridge, Mass.: Harvard University Press, 2002). Perhaps the most profound and challenging ethical thinking in the pragmatist tradition since the work of those in the classical period is the pragmatic naturalism in the work of Clarence Irving Lewis, whose insistent theme is that right thinking and right doing cannot be separated. See his monumental *An Analysis of Knowledge and Valuation* (LaSalle, Ill.: The Open Court Publishing Company, 1946). Three short and accessible books by Lewis bring home the richness of his thinking on society and ethics: (1) *Our Social Inheritance* (Bloomington: Indiana University Press, 1957); (2) *The Ground and Nature of Right* (New York: Columbia University Press, 1955); and (3) *Values and Imperatives: Studies in Ethics,* ed. John Lange (Palo Alto: Stanford University Press, 1969).

self-discovery. As he put it, "the very nature of right action forbids that the self should be an end in the sense of being the conscious aim of moral activity. For there is no way of discovering the nature of the self except in terms of objective ends which fulfill its capacities, and there is no way of realizing the self except as it is forgotten in devotion to these objective ends."[18]

A final point worth noting about the pragmatist approach to ethics is its acknowledgement that conflict and disagreement are ineradicable in human life. They are rooted in human nature and managing them is necessary for self-development. Kant had spoken of man's "unsocial sociability," and the pragmatists knew just what he meant. The social self of the pragmatists was not necessarily a diffident or tranquil self. It was unlikely to be at rest for long. Royce shows how moral development is the outcome of psychic processes of contrast and comparison, ongoing assessments within the mind and heart of the subject that necessarily generate from time to time feelings of embarrassment, inadequacy, conflict and strain. As he put it, "Our fellows train us to all our higher grades of practical self-knowledge, and they do so by giving us certain sorts of social trouble." Self-realization, in other words, is a continuing process of stressful growth, so much so that Peirce suggested it would be appropriate in prayer to "bless God for the law of growth and all the fighting it imposes."[19]

## Pragmatism, Community and Politics

One of the most important features in the ethical thought of the pragmatists is its orientation to community, its well-known emphasis on the social nature of the self. "A man's Social Self," said James, "is the recognition which he gets from his mates." "We are not only gregarious animals," he notes, "liking to be in sight of our fellows, but we have an innate propensity to get ourselves noticed, and noticed favorably by our kind. No more fiendish punishment could be devised, were such a thing physically possible, than that one could be turned loose in society and remain absolutely unnoticed by all the members thereof." The propensity doing the work here is universal because it is innate, and its exercise has both social and subjective consequences.[20]

18. Dewey and Tufts, op. cit, p. 392.

19. Josiah Royce, *The Problem of Christianity* (Chicago: University of Chicago Press, 1968), 107. The Peirce remark is in Charles Hartshorne and Paul Weiss, editors, *Collected Papers of Charles Sanders Peirce*, Vol. 6 (Cambridge, Mass.: Harvard University Press, 1934), 327. Royce's account of contrast, comparison, and conflict in self-development is given in his *The Philosophy of Loyalty* (New York: The Macmillan Company, 1908), 30-40.

20. James, *Principles*, Vol. 1, 293.

Self-realization and the realization of the common good are inherently bound up with one another in the pragmatist perspective. The overarching goal of pragmatist ethics is the responsible use of liberty: "It wants men and women who habitually form their purposes after consideration of the social consequences of their execution," as Dewey puts it. More than shame, blame, and mimicry are at work in the moral formation of the responsible agent. The process calls upon more creative elements of mind and will. "Dislike of disapprobation, fear of penalty, play a part in generating this responsive habit; but fear, operating directly, occasions only cunning and servility. Fused, through reflection, with other motives which prompt to action, it helps bring about that apprehensiveness, or susceptibility to the rights of others, which is the essence of responsibility, which in turn is the sole *ultimate* guarantee of social order."[21]

The other motives are those that come to light in the actual functioning of the higher self; they are expressed in habits of virtue. From the empirical standpoint of social description, these habits are of course variable individual achievements, ways of acting more or less well developed and reliable, but their importance goes well beyond the functions they serve for the virtuous individual. Others have a valid natural interest in the habits, and count on their performance in the transactions of daily life. From the perspective of community life, shared habits of virtue are among the bonds of community, working elements in its "social capital." They comprise its moral code, which gives shape and direction to society and culture.

The notion of the moral act, then, as developed in the pragmatist tradition is a complex one. It is not relativist in the popular sense of the term. It is not the expression of variable personal preferences in the face of which we are justly indifferent. Instead it is the maker of selves and the shaper of cultures, and the pragmatists were not indifferent about the kinds of selves they or those around them became. As students of morals in society they understood that moral codes have varied with time and place, and have been relative to their times and places. But they have been relative also to the functioning of the same set of psychic tendencies and dispositions, and the pragmatists did not believe that *these* have varied over the course of recorded history. They were the elements of a common human nature that made possible the scientific study of psychology and the other human sciences.

Though none of the classical pragmatists wrote a primer on the philosophy of history or on social science method, the common-sense premises each would endorse for these purposes include the premises that (1) there is a real world, of which true knowledge is possible; (2) that human action, the action of selves in

21. Dewey and Tufts, op. cit., 437.

community, past or present, is causally explainable; and (3) that members of one culture can understand members of other cultures, past or present, because there is a psychic unity to humankind undergirding the diversity of belief and behavior to be observed across time and place.[22]

The political bearings of pragmatism follow from its ethics. In their philosophy of human action, the pragmatists stressed three points: (1) the connection between rights and duties, (2) the obligation of the modern state to establish through law and regulation conditions in which responsible liberty could flourish, and (3) an open-ended, positive orientation towards gradual reform. Since the disposition to conflict was ineradicable in human nature, it followed that the work of politics was never really finished. *Semper reformanda* would be an appropriate motto for their attitude towards the state and its relation to society. Theirs was a politics of improvement — melioration, as James preferred to say — the need for which arose out of the incessant flow of creative acts and responses to them within the social order. Acts have consequences, and those who experience the consequences of action — from the determinate one to the indeterminate many — make up the public. As Dewey put it, "The moral act is one which sustains a whole complex system of values; one which keeps vital and progressive the industrial order, science, art, and the State."[23]

In terms of political history, the pragmatists of the classical period were living in the midst of a transition from one type of governance to another. On the one side was the classical liberalism of laissez faire and the kind of individualism in public philosophy associated with it. It was a social order in which the institutions of private property and contract provided the basic framework of life. On the other side was the "new liberalism" of the modern, interventionist, regulatory state, based on the notion of collective responsibility for the overall

---

22. These three premises are adapted and compressed from a list of eight dealt with in depth by Murray G. Murphey in his *Philosophical Foundations of Historical Knowledge* (Albany: State University of New York Press, 1994), a pragmatist account of the foundations of historical knowledge that has application to many areas of social science knowledge as well. Though Murphey does not make a fuss about it in his book, the anti-foundational, anti-representational, anti-realist convictions of some of the contemporary postmodernist neo-pragmatists would undermine the premises he is here defending, and challenge the assertion that genuine knowledge — in the strong sense he is developing — of past or present cultures is possible. One of the handicaps of the "anti-foundationalism" of the postmodernist program is that it cannot be stated in terms of its foundations, a serious shortcoming when it comes to the need for self-criticism within the perspective. The topics covered by Murphey include meaning and reference, other minds and intersubjectivity, causation and explanation, the idea of human action, rules, truth and reality, and the validity of knowledge of the past.

23. Dewey and Tufts, op. cit., 393.

quality of social, cultural, and economic life. Development of a public philoso-phy suitable for the new liberalism of the social self was a pragmatist goal, as was the construction of a government capable of sustaining it.[24]

All of the pragmatists were critics of the old individualism, which seemed to them a dangerous abstraction if ever there was one. Here they would find the possibility of violence and social disorder in the form of unfettered commit-ment to the notion of the modern corporation as a legal individual and the in-dividual property owner as the bearer of immutable rights, an understanding of moral absolutes that was reflected and endorsed in some of the late century

24. On the origins and development of the new liberalism, see Mary O. Furner, "Policy Knowledge: The New Liberalism" in *International Encyclopedia of the Social and Behavioral Sci-ences*, ed. Neil J. Smelser and Paul B. Baltes (Oxford: Elsevier, 2001). The important point in Furner's work on the new liberalism in America is the identification of two forms of it: not only the "corporate liberalism" identified by Martin Sklar, James Weinstein, and Ellis Hawley and others in the 1960s, which, as the name implies, cedes the fundamental initiative in economic and social matters to the leadership elites of the modern corporation, but in addition, and in fact preceding this corporatist innovation and contesting it through the early decades of the twentieth century, a form of statist liberalism, more democratic in origins and objectives, which insisted on public oversight and direction of economic and social trends in the interest of social justice, defined to include a more equitable distribution of the national product and political voice, and a greater measure of individual and family control over the circumstances of living. See Furner, "Knowing Capitalism: Public Investigation and the Labor Question in the Long Progressive Era," in Mary O. Furner and Barry Supple, eds., *The State and Economic Knowledge: The British and American Experiences* (New York: Cambridge University Press, 1990), 241-86. See also Furner, "The Republican Tradition and the New Liberalism: Social Investigation, Social Learning, and State Building in the Gilded Age," in *The State and Social Investigation in Britain and the United States*, ed. Michael J. Lacey and Mary O. Furner (New York: Cambridge Univer-sity Press, 1993) 171-241, and in the same volume my own "The World of the Bureaus: Govern-ment and the Positivist Project in the Late Nineteenth Century," pp. 127-70.

An important exploration of the tension between the stress on individualism and the need for social cohesion in American culture is provided in Wilfred McClay's *The Masterless: Self and Society in Modern America* (Chapel Hill: University of North Carolina Press, 1994). Casey Blake's *Beloved Community: The Cultural Criticism of Randolph Bourne, Van Wyck Brooks, Waldo Frank, and Lewis Mumford* (Chapel Hill: University of North Carolina Press, 1990) explores the cul-tural criticism of these writers and their calls for a culture of personality and self-fulfillment. See also Jeffrey Sklansky, *The Soul's Economy: Market Society and Selfhood in American Thought, 1820-1920* (Chapel Hill: University of North Carolina Press, 2002), for a thought-provoking study of the structural and economic context for the emergence of social psychology. Another important study focused on the interplay of social, cultural and economic factors is James Livingston's *Pragmatism and the Political Economy of Cultural Revolution, 1850-1940* (Chapel Hill: University of North Carolina Press, 1994). Finally on pragmatism and politics, see Andrew Feffer, *The Chicago Pragmatists and American Progressivism* (Ithaca: Cornell University Press, 1993), and Matthew Festenstein, *Pragmatism and Political Theory: From Dewey to Rorty* (Chi-cago: University of Chicago Press, 1997).

rulings of the Supreme Court against the background of bloody conflict over the emergence of organized labor.

It was the immutability that gave them pause, not the rights. The ethics of self-realization was necessarily an ethics of rights, but rights were conceived as social in origin and in need of social regulation. The master ideal of responsible freedom required close analysis of rights claims and their consequences, a process that began with breaking down the various dimensions of meaning attached to the idea of freedom. As Dewey noted, "That which, taken at large or in a lump, is called freedom breaks up in detail into a number of specific, concrete abilities to act in particular ways. These are termed *rights*." As powers to act in certain ways, the actual meanings of rights were brought home in the way they were used, that is in their consequences for others. "A right is never a claim to wholesale, indefinite activity," Dewey insisted, "but to a *defined* activity; *to one carried on under certain conditions*." Not all conditions could be specified or anticipated and social conditions changed, and so there was an implicit dimension to the idea of rights as powers to act. The upshot was that rights were to be used rightly, and the test would be the benefits of their use to society as a whole.[25]

Thus rights and obligations were correlative, and the precise meanings of rights changed over time. "Absolute rights," Dewey insisted, "if we mean by absolute those not relative to any social order and hence exempt from any social restriction, there are none." The emphasis on correlating rights and responsibilities meant that for the pragmatists there was a moral standard to be invoked in all questions of political development. Its purpose was to keep the claims of the individual and of the community in balance. "The moral criterion by which to try social institutions and political measures may be summed up as follows," Dewey explained: "The test is whether a given custom or law sets free individual capacities in such a way as to make them available for the development of the general common good. This formula states the test with the emphasis falling upon the side of the individual. It may be stated on the side of associated life as follows: the test is whether the general, the public, organization and order are promoted in such a way as to equalize opportunity for all."[26]

Perhaps the most important distinction in the legacy of pragmatist political theory is the distinction between formal and real freedom, freedom *from* versus freedom *to*. "The freedom of an agent who is merely released from direct, external obstructions is formal and empty," according to Dewey. Real freedom or effective freedom required a good deal more, and promoting the condi-

---

25. Dewey and Tufts, op. cit., 439-40.

26. Dewey and Tufts, op. cit. The quotation on absolute rights is on p. 441. The statement of the moral criterion of political activity is on pp. 482-83.

tions necessary for effective freedom was the goal of new liberal politics. Liberation was not enough. Exemption from restraint was a necessary but not sufficient condition for effective liberty. In Dewey's formulation, "The latter requires 1) positive control of the resources necessary to carry purposes into effect, possession of the means to satisfy desires; and 2) mental equipment with the trained powers of initiative and reflection requisite for free preference and for circumspect and far seeing desires."[27]

The thrust of the distinction between formal and real freedom is to call attention to the need to narrow the gap between them, and doing so is the work of a meliorist (to use James's term), gradualist, progressive politics. Who is responsible for insuring that the conditions for effective freedom exist? To this question the pragmatists would respond that we all are, and building up the capacities of modern government was a step in that direction. In pragmatist theory the state is the agent of the people — the servant, not the master — and it is to be used in coping with problems that threaten to undermine the common good.[28]

## Pragmatism and Religion

For a long time pragmatism was treated by many of its commentators as a kind of vanguard for the secular tendencies in modern thought, and there is

27. Dewey and Tufts, op. cit., 438.

28. Classic pragmatist texts on the state would include Dewey's *The Public and Its Problems* (New York: Henry Holt and Company, 1927) and also William Ernest Hocking's *Man and the State* (New Haven: Yale University Press, 1926). Hocking writes from the pragmatist/idealist point of view, and his treatment of the idea of the state and its role in modern culture is among the most sophisticated renderings in American philosophy. For this reader he has more of interest to say on the subject than Dewey does. Though he seems a bit nonplussed by Hocking's theism and insistence that pragmatism and idealism belong together, John Stuhr appreciates the value of what Hocking has to say for problems in contemporary public philosophy and calls for a revival of interest in Hocking and his work. See Stuhr, "The Defects of Liberalism: Lasting Elements of Negative Pragmatism," in his *Pragmatism, Postmodernism, and the Future of Philosophy*, 22-44. Evidence that a revival of interest may be beginning is provided in John Lachs and D. Micah Hester, eds., *A William Ernest Hocking Reader, with Commentary* (Nashville: Vanderbilt University Press, 2004), which includes a selection from his work and the discussions of ten contemporary philosophers on its significance. Useful studies of the public philosophies of the classical pragmatists include George Cotkin, *William James: Public Philosopher* (Urbana: University of Illinois Press, 1994); Jacquelyn Ann K. Kegley, *Genuine Individuals and Genuine Communities: A Roycean Public Philosophy* (Nashville: Vanderbilt University Press, 1997); and James Hoopes, *Community Denied: The Wrong Turn of Pragmatic Liberalism* (Ithaca: Cornell University Press, 1998), which argues for the superiority of Peirce's liberal communitarian orientation to the liberal thinking of James and Dewey.

no doubt that its skeptical approach to the abstractions of philosophy and theology contributed some impetus to the pace of secularization in American life and thought. Classical pragmatism was deeply sympathetic to scientific inquiry and hostile to any forms of cultural commitment that claimed exemption from critical inquiry. "Orthodoxy" and "doctrine" and "dogma" are generally terms of abuse in pragmatist writing. In their day both James and Dewey were notoriously suspicious of institutionalized religion as reliquaries for defunct ideas. For them the orthodox conventions of religious practice seemed to offer at best inauthentic, secondhand — and therefore second-rate — kinds of personal experience.

Nonetheless, there was deep ambiguity in the naturalism of the classical pragmatists, in their emphasis on the natural, biologically rooted character of the psychic tendencies and dispositions of human nature. For each of them, that emphasis required close attention to the actual deliverances of experience. And for some of them, reflection on natural experience, particularly the experience of thinking itself, suggested the reality of a supernatural, transcendent God, while for others that suggestion made no sense, and threatened the return of the old dualism of a pre-scientific worldview that all of them had done so much to resist.

James remarked about this dichotomy: "If one should make a division of all thinkers into naturalists and super-naturalists, I should undoubtedly have to go, along with most philosophers, into the super-naturalist branch. But there is a crasser and a more refined supernaturalism, and it is to the refined division that most philosophers of the present day belong."[29] With characteristic modesty James placed himself among "super-naturalists of the piecemeal or crasser type," those who were unable to accept "either popular Christianity or scholastic theism," but were nonetheless convinced that "in communion with the Ideal new force comes into the world, and new departures are made here below." On the basis of his knowledge of their views, James would have placed Peirce and Royce in the more refined division of supernaturalism, while Dewey and Santayana would have been placed in the naturalist branch, with Dewey perhaps among the crasser types.

It should be noted that the modern self as presented in James's *Principles of Psychology* is not only a social self, but a *spiritual* self as well, the latter being a part of the higher self that is trained up in experience. "By the Spiritual Self," James noted, "I mean a man's inner or subjective being, his psychic faculties and dispositions, taken concretely." Unlike the bare principle of personal unity,

---

29. William James, *The Varieties of Religious Experience: A Study in Human Nature* (New York: Vintage Books/The Library of America Edition, 1990), 464.

the "Ego," a person's spiritual self had a sense of depth and dimension to it. "These psychic dispositions are the most enduring and intimate part of the self, that which we most verily seem to be. We take a purer self-satisfaction when we think of our ability to argue and discriminate, of our moral sensibility and conscience, of our indomitable will, than when we survey any of our other possessions. Only when these are altered is a man said to be *alienatus a se*."[30]

There was much in the culture of America during the last third of the nineteenth century to encourage the alienation of the spiritual self, and pragmatists of both types, naturalists and supernaturalists, were committed to the resistance in the battles that mattered. None of these was more important than the battle of science and religion symbolized in the multi-faceted evolutionary controversy. The traditional Christian cosmology with its starry skies above and the moral law within was challenged profoundly in its fundamentals by the implications of Darwin's account of the workings of nature and its history. The old cosmology had been manifest in the folk psychology of common sense (a spiritualistic psychology of the human soul with roots going back to Aristotelian and scholastic philosophy, as James had argued) as a pool of shared traits of popular belief and behavior. It had been supported and articulated at the elite or learned level of the culture in renderings of natural law in the Protestant tradition that took the form of treatises on the moral law and its sources in philosophical theology. As gradually it was assimilated, the new doctrine on natural history and the new types of the higher criticism of scripture with which it was associated forced alterations in the links between the common sense world of folk culture and the elite world of books and learned disputation. The old, loosely jointed Protestant coalition that had dominated American culture from its beginning broke up into two main branches: liberal Protestantism on the one hand, and the evangelically oriented fundamentalist communities on the other.

Broadly speaking, the cultural pattern that emerged on this side of the evolutionary controversy is the one we live in to this day. In response to the inroads of the new scientific and critical methods and their associated institutions, the modern university chief among them, three broad types of worldview emerged: those of fundamentalism, naturalism, and religious modernism. The pragmatists contributed importantly to opening up and exploring the latter two. And ironically, while none of the classical pragmatists could feel at home with modern fundamentalism, with its anti-modernist outlook, its rejection of scientific and critical methods, and its dogged fidelity to a common sense apprehension of the meaning of sacred texts, the mere fact that such an outlook "worked" for

30. James, op. cit., Vol. I, 296.

so many people was a challenge to the pragmatist understanding of truth and a spur to its thinking about religion and culture.

The naturalist outlook was something of a newcomer, historically speaking, to the American scene, and the resourcefulness of John Dewey and George Santayana in elaborating it, each in his unique way, had much to do with giving it strong roots in the culture. "There is room for celebration, consecration, and clarification of human goals," within naturalism, one of its spokesmen noted, "there is room — *pace* Mr. Dewey — for man's concern with the eternal and with what Plato calls 'the deathless and divine.' But for naturalism eternity is no attribute of authentic Being, but a quality of human vision; and divinity belongs, not to what is existent, but to what man discerns in imagination. Thus naturalism finds itself in thoroughgoing opposition," he noted, "to all forms of thought which assert the existence of a supernatural or transcendent Realm of Being and make knowledge of that realm of fundamental importance to human living."[31]

Pragmatic naturalism offered a new, secular understanding of society and culture, history and religion, which was especially useful in university life. There it promised a kind of ecumenical approach to understanding the problems of modern culture that the religious communities, with their doctrines and dogmas and divisions, seemed incapable of mounting. The naturalists agreed that the modern self was a spiritual self, and they acknowledged the religious dimension of human experience. They pioneered in developing psychological, sociological, and aesthetic accounts for the workings of religious consciousness. Santayana's *Life of Reason* has been called "the charter of American naturalism," and its third volume, *Reason in Religion,* has been singled out as committing naturalism to a constructive theory of religious life. As a theory it holds that religion is the poetry of moral consciousness, a product of the human imagination that mediates between nature and the ideal. Religion and poetry are close relatives, and in Santayana's terminology, religion intervenes in human life while poetry supervenes upon it. Both idealize human experience

31. John Herman Randall, "The Nature of Naturalism," in Yervant H. Krikorian, ed., *Naturalism and the Human Spirit* (New York: Columbia University Press, 1944), 358. Some of the most imaginative and wide-ranging literary and cultural criticism written from within a naturalist, neo-pragmatist point of view is Giles Gunn's *Thinking Across the American Grain: Ideology, Intellect, and the New Pragmatism* (Chicago: University of Chicago Press, 1992), and his *Beyond Solidarity: Pragmatism and Difference in a Globalized World* (Chicago: University of Chicago Press, 2001). Gunn discusses the unfortunate neglect of religion in contemporary neo-pragmatism in his "Religion and the Recent Revival of Pragmatism," in the important collection of essays edited by Morris Dickstein, *The Revival of Pragmatism: New Essays on Social Thought, Law, and Culture.*

and attempt to express its meanings and values, tasks which scientific method cannot perform.[32]

32. William Shea, *The Naturalists and the Supernatural: Studies in Horizon and an American Philosophy of Religion* (Macon, Ga.: Mercer University Press, 1984), 92. Shea provides a sympathetic but critical account of naturalist thinking on religion from the standpoint of Bernard Lonergan's cognitional theory. No one has done more to revive interest in the classical pragmatists generally and in their religious thought, too, than John E. Smith. He has written a good deal on the subject, but a convenient starting point is his *Purpose and Thought: The Meaning of Pragmatism* (Chicago: University of Chicago Press, 1978). Smith's own work as a philosopher of religion is an important achievement in the supernaturalist line of descent within pragmatism. See his *The Analogy of Experience: An Approach to Understanding Religious Truth* (New York: Harper and Row, 1973), together with his *Experience and God* (New York: Oxford University Press, 1968), and his *Reason and God: Encounters of Philosophy with Religion* (New Haven: Yale University Press, 1961). His last book, *Quasi-Religions: Humanism, Marxism, and Nationalism* (New York: St. Martin's Press, 1994), is a critique of these naturalist, secular religions from the standpoint of theist, pragmatic idealism.

Important studies bearing on relations between pragmatism and religion include Stuart Rosenbaum, ed., *Religion and Pragmatism: Classical Sources and Original Essays* (Urbana: University of Illinois Press, 2003). The selections and essays here are predominantly naturalist in orientation (sometimes it is hard to tell), and in his introduction Rosenbaum stresses the latter in arguing that, "to put the matter baldly, pragmatists, existentialists, and postmodernists all conceive humans as animals, . . . pragmatists have turned their backs on the idea that humans are ontologically special in the natural world. For pragmatists, humans have no natural telos, no natural eternal destiny, no special faculty of cognition that when properly exercised enables them to know independent reality, and they have no moral law within. Humans are animals, clever animals to be sure, but animals nonetheless" (p. 2). The volume includes a recent essay by Rorty entitled "Pragmatism as Romantic Polytheism," which some say marks a shift in this thinking, though it is unclear just how. Perhaps from a restrained but edgy atheism to a naturalism of the more refined type, as James might put it?

Both naturalists and supernaturalists claim James as one of their own, and no doubt he would be comfortable with this. A naturalist reading of his religious thought is Bennett Ramsey's *Submitting to Freedom: The Religious Vision of William James* (New York: Oxford University Press, 1993). For an account of Dewey's religious naturalism and a critique to the effect that it was not secular and naturalistic enough, see Michael Eldridge, *Transforming Experience: John Dewey's Cultural Instrumentalism* (Nashville: Vanderbilt University Press, 1998). The best study of pragmatic naturalism, as mentioned before, is Henry Samuel Levinson's *Santayana, Pragmatism, and the Spiritual Life.* Levinson provides an excellent overview of the pragmatists (excepting Royce, whom he does not consider a proper pragmatist) from his naturalist perspective in his "Stuck Between Debility and Demand: Religion and Enlightenment Traditions Among the Pragmatists," in William M. Shea and Peter A. Huff, eds., *Knowledge and Belief in America: Enlightenment Traditions and Modern Religious Thought* (New York: Cambridge University Press, 1995), 270-98. An important path-breaking study in the naturalist vein is Robert S. Corrington's *The Community of Interpreters: On the Hermeneutics of Nature and the Bible in the American Philosophical Tradition* (Macon: Mercer University Press, 1987). Corrington treats Peirce and Royce not only as founders of pragmatism, but as founders of American hermeneu-

In his own thinking about religion and its object, Dewey would find it difficult to make out the poetry of the denominations, but he was committed to what he called the religious quality of human experience, which he spoke of as a sense of the significance of the whole of it, and he wanted to see that quality enhanced in modern life. Dewey failed to think through the relations between religious and aesthetic phenomena, and in part for that reason many have found his approach to religion in *A Common Faith* a bit too common, as the quip goes. Like Santayana, however, Dewey sees the office of religious faith as "the unification of the self through allegiance to inclusive ideal ends, which imagination presents to us and to which human will responds as worthy of controlling our desires and choices."[33]

Unquestionably there is such a thing as the truth of fiction, but naturalists and supernaturalists within the pragmatist camp would find it impossible to agree on how this truth should be formulated. Here they are in thoroughgoing opposition, and the differences between them are subtle and perplexing, involving distinctions between the truth of symbolism and the "merely symbolic" as encountered in everyday speech. Where the naturalists would say that man has drawn upon his powers of imagination to make God in his own image, the supernaturalists would say he has made *only the image* of God in his own image, and what else could he do, feeling prompted to make sense of things, as naturally he was, and of course working with the materials that were closest to hand?

For supernaturalists, the idea that religious commitment means giving oneself to the healing fiction makes no sense. It is wishful thinking, and subject to all the shortcomings of wishful thinking as a guide to action. Unless the felt truth of fiction can be accounted for as plausible by reference to some broader, metaphysical vision of the meaning of reality as a whole, it fails to satisfy the mind. For supernaturalists, such an account grounds the conviction that the symbols of religion point to the reality of a transcendent realm of being, and thus underwrite their value as worthy of commitment. The works of T. S. Eliot or W. H. Auden or Czeslaw Milosz reflect the sensibilities of poets informed by the spirit of religious modernism.

For naturalists, on the other hand, the notion that there is a transcendent realm of being is wishful thinking. We have to do the best we can in light of our

---

tics, and argues that the American approach is preferable to the better-known European approaches to the subject by virtue of the communitarian orientation of Royce and Peirce, which differs from the unexamined individualist bias of Heidigger, Gadamer, and others. Royce's religious thinking is very carefully and sympathetically analyzed in Frank M. Oppenheim, *Royce's Mature Philosophy of Religion* (Notre Dame: University of Notre Dame Press, 1987).

33. John Dewey, *A Common Faith* (New Haven: Yale University Press, 1934), p. 33.

finitude, and finitude is not without joys and sorrows of its own, meaningful in their own terms, without reference to any infinities more real or troublesome than those of mathematical theory. Art and religion are among these, and the poetry of Wallace Stevens or Philip Larkin (who claimed that despair did for him what daffodils did for Wordsworth) speaks to their enduring significance as joys and sorrows. In the face of our natural finitude, a stance that is at once ironic and heroic, reminiscent of ancient Stoicism, is at the core of modern spirituality from the standpoint of pragmatic naturalism. Metaphysics without the transcendent, of the sort offered by Santayana or Dewey or Heidegger or Sartre, expresses well enough the meaning of modern reality as a whole.[34]

The underlying differences between the two kinds of pragmatists have to do with what goes on, analytically, in interpreting the psychological experience of transcendence. Both sides agree that the phenomenon of transcendence, the sense of going beyond without leaving behind which is at the heart of those cognitive processes of growth and development that were under study in the pragmatists' psychologies, is a natural experience. The dynamic, purposeful, ends-oriented character of subjectivity and its self-transcending character amount to the same thing. It reflects the biologically rooted restlessness of the psyche. But does reflection on transcending imply the need for the transcendent? The differences between the naturalists and super-naturalists within the pragmatist camp turn on this question. For both sides nature includes human nature. For the super-naturalists, however, nature is a fraction. For the naturalists it is an integer.[35]

As James saw it, the God of philosophers past was not so much false, but barren. He needled Royce on this point, insisting that his Absolute, the God of the modern idealists, was absolutely barren unless it could be shown to be at work in human experience. Royce chafed at this but came to agree with him, and the criticism inspired his best work. Royce needled James to the effect that his piecemeal supernaturalism was too piecemeal and fragmentary to be theologically coherent. The truth had to be true for everybody, whatever the pluralism of truths proclaimed at the surface level of life — the pluralism of first im-

34. Richard Rorty's essay on "The Contingency of Selfhood" in his *Contingency, Irony, and Solidarity* is a meditation on Larkin's way of working with despair, his way of rendering what Rorty calls "the pathos of finitude." For an analysis of contrasting naturalist and religious modernist sensibilities in poetry, see Denis Donoghue's "Wallace Stevens, T. S. Eliot, and the Space Between Them," in Shea and Huff, eds., *Knowledge and Belief in America: Enlightenment Traditions and Modern Religious Thought*, 299-318.

35. The theologian Horace Bushnell used the contrast between fraction and integer to develop his account of relations between the natural and the transcendent in his *Nature and the Supernatural as Together Constituting One System of God* (New York: Charles Scribner, 1858).

pressions, one might say. I think James secretly agreed with him, and would have said it was the best he could do right now. The criticism inspired his best work, and kept him from falling into solipsism. Peirce was something of a specialist at fragments, and never really came close to finishing his architectonic perennial philosophy. The fragments he did complete, however, inspired both James and Royce, because these brilliant bits suggested that the obstacles to religious belief in modern culture were not cognitive in character. In reasoning there was an ethics of belief to be encountered and acknowledged, Peirce knew, and belief in God did not violate it.

The arrival of modernity did not mean the end of religious truth for Peirce, James, or Royce. All were convinced of the reality of God, if not agreed on how best to speak about it. They were agreed that the criteria involved in attempting to speak about God would have to be rooted in experience and tested in it. They were agreed that when it comes to modern religious thought, "what you want," as James told his readers, "is a philosophy that will not only exercise your powers of intellectual abstraction, but will make some positive connection with this actual world of finite human lives." This was the program for religious modernism to which those in the supernaturalist division of the pragmatist group wanted to contribute. For each of them, what they agreed to in their various pragmatisms was a start.[36]

"Rationalism sticks to logic and the empyrean," James noted; "Empiricism sticks to the external senses. Pragmatism is willing to take anything, to follow either logic or the senses, and to count the humblest and most personal experiences. She will count mystical experiences if they have practical consequences. She will take a God who lives in the very dirt of private fact — if that should seem a likely place to find him." For these pragmatists of supernaturalist inclination, the spiritual life was inherently bound up with creativity. Authentic religion had to show the way in a way that science, given the limits of its methods, could not do. Whatever the source of religious experience in modern life, however variously the religious dimension of experience is conceived, the test of its truth was to be experiential. To be true, religious insight had to help in path finding. It had to speak to "what works best in the way of leading us, what fits every part of life best and combines with the collectivity of experience's demands, nothing being omitted."[37]

The God of these pragmatists was real but incomprehensible, necessarily so, and no less important for that. Thomas Aquinas had argued in the thirteenth century that reason unaided can discover *that* God is, but not *what* God

---

36. William James, *Pragmatism* and *The Meaning of Truth*, 17.
37. James, *Pragmatism* and *The Meaning of Truth*, 44.

is. This assertion is the foundation for *natural* theology, the grounding for any philosophical theology that would start out independent of scripture and its interpretation. The pragmatists of supernaturalist bent would have agreed; they were searching for the grounds of natural theology in its post-Kantian, post-scientific revolution, modern guise. It seems clear enough that the finite and temporal cannot comprehend the infinite and eternal, a theologically significant assertion that would not trouble an Anselm or Aquinas. Still, the finite mind can be aware of infinity and wrestle with the problems of that awareness. Religiously speaking, that insight leaves the possibility of an incomprehensible apprehension within the horizon of experience, one that differs from the ordinary puzzle in that it cannot in principle be solved. Perhaps the incomprehensible can be lived with, however, as all the world's religious communities in their different ways have insisted.

Peirce wrestled with this kind of problem, the problem of intelligibility in its various kinds and its limits, in his logic. For him, the only distinctively *human* instinct was the instinct to understand. The others were shared with the rest of creation. Logic was an expression of that instinct, and our psychic reactions to the exercise of our own logic were expressions of the inherent normativeness of the self. A personal encounter with the principle of contradiction could be painful, as he knew. About his own obsession with logic Peirce once remarked, "Every attempt to understand anything — every research — supposes, or at least *hopes,* that the very objects of study themselves are subject to a logic more or less identical with that which we employ." James made a similar point in connection with his postulates of rationality, gateways to the world of noumenal reality, when he said that "the widest postulate of rationality is that the world is rationally intelligible throughout, after the pattern of some ideal system. The whole war of philosophies is over that point of faith."[38]

---

38. Charles Hartshorne and Paul Weiss, eds., *The Collected Papers of Charles Sanders Peirce,* Vol. 6 (Cambridge, Mass.: Harvard University Press, 1934), 134. The quotation attributed to James is from *The Principles of Psychology,* Vol. 2, 670. On the connection between the development of formal logic in the pragmatist tradition from Peirce and Royce through Lewis and Quine as that development bears upon theology and religious thought, Murray Murphey notes, "Thus the sternest modern empiricism turns out to involve a widening of the domain of the empirical to include even the religious. It is certain that neither Quine nor Goodman was moved to this result by any personal religious motives, but rather by the impossibility of constructing an adequate theory of knowledge on any other basis. Nevertheless, their espousal of the pragmatic position confirms the conclusion that the historical role of pragmatism within the empiricist tradition has been to insist that what we call knowledge is a conceptual structure which interprets experience in the interests of order, stability, simplicity, and beauty, and that any such system, whether a science or a theology, has a cognitive function" ("Kant's Children: The Cambridge Pragmatists," 29).

The God of the pragmatists was a presupposition or hope of this kind. It was a "working hypothesis," not the conclusion of a knock-down argument. "The hypothesis of God is a peculiar one," Peirce noted, "in that it supposes an infinitely incomprehensible object." Entertaining the hypothesis was purely voluntary, and there were no penalties for failure to entertain. It was a reasonable hypothesis — in fact, Peirce believed that numerous reasons could be lodged in its favor — but it could not be proved as the less difficult questions of science, dealing with things in their relations to one another, could be proved or at least agreed upon. As a hypothesis it eluded scientific method, but the invention of scientific method itself had been dependent on hypotheses as flashes of creative imagination and insight that scientific method could neither predict or account for within the limits of its own rules of evidence and inference. It could not predict poetry, either, or wit, or the insights of pragmatism. That thought about the character of hypotheses-in-general gave some comfort to religious modernists.

The hypothesis of God could be reasoned about, but the awareness of it was among the implicits of experience, things taken for granted, and no less real for that reason. Peirce believed the hypothesis literally to be instinctive, and thus to account for the fact that religion was a universal cultural trait. "God is a vernacular word and, like all such words, but more than almost any, is *vague.* No words are so well understood as vernacular words, in one way; yet they are invariably vague; and of many of them it is true that, let the logician do his best to substitute precise equivalents in their places, still the vernacular words alone, for all their vagueness, answer the principal purposes."[39]

That the thinker who ignited pragmatism with a paper on how to make our ideas clear should have such respect for the vague is an important clue to the religious thought of the pragmatists.[40] James in *The Principles of Psychology* re-

39. Peirce, *Collected Papers*, Vol. 6, 340. On Peirce's theism, see Vincent Potter, "'Vaguely Like A Man': The Theism of Charles S. Peirce," in his *Peirce's Philosophical Perspectives*, ed. Vincent M. Colapietro (New York: Fordham University Press, 1996), 155-68. See also in the same volume Potter's "C. S. Peirce's Argument for God's Reality: A Pragmatist's View," 167-94. Potter's *Charles S. Peirce on Norms and Ideals*, with a new introduction by Stanley Harrison (originally published 1967; this edition, New York: Fordham University Press, 1997), is also well worth consulting. Vincent Colapietro's *Peirce's Approach to the Self: A Semiotic Perspective on Human Subjectivity*, is a helpful analysis. Finally, the reader interested in Peirce's understanding of the idea of God should consult Donna M. Orange, *Peirce's Conception of God: A Developmental Study* (Lubbock, Tex.: Institute for Studies in Pragmatism, 1984). William Joseph Gavin's *William James and the Reinstatement of the Vague* (Philadelphia: Temple University Press, 1992) is a cogent and wide-ranging treatment of the importance of the vague in James's thinking.

40. Peirce's "How to Make Our Ideas Clear," *Popular Science Monthly* 12 (1878), is the locus classicus for the first presentation of the pragmatic criteria of truth, though the term pragma-

marked that "the reinstatement of the vague to its proper place in our mental life" was one of his chief aims. Human experience is not limited to things clear and distinct or satisfied by them. Their point was that the vague and indeterminate may be no less real than the clear and precise, and those who believe otherwise may be on a positivist path that will cause them to miss an idea that was important to the pragmatists. Vagueness can be reasoned about if not dispelled. Abstractions are vague in a way that particularities are not. Vagueness is a property of general terms, and generalization aims at universals, such as the four transcendentals identified as the qualities of being *as such* in the metaphysics of the medieval scholastics — the one, the true, the good, and the beautiful. These expressed the apprehension of the ideal in medieval philosophy, an apprehension for which Peirce had great respect. Peirce claimed that anyone who followed what he called the logic of continuity "with scientific singleness of heart" would eventually stumble onto the hypothesis of God, and entertaining it "would come to be stirred to the depths of his nature by the beauty of the idea and by its august practicality, even to the point of earnestly loving and adoring his strictly hypothetical God, and to that of desiring above all things to shape the whole conduct of life and all the springs of action into conformity with the hypothesis."[41]

Royce was the most distinguished American philosopher of religion of his day, and together with Peirce, among the most formidable logicians of his day. For him too the mind was inherently normative, and logic was an expression, perhaps a primitive expression, of its norms. For him too logic was bound up with the hope that questions have answers and that the universe reflects the same kind of logic the human mind does. Royce's most important contribution to religious modernism, however, was not his work in logic but rather his analysis of the nature of religious community and its roles in history and culture. His thinking in this area was indebted to both Peirce and James, and was inspired by his disagreements as well as his agreements with them. So inspiration seems to work.

Royce's *The Problem of Christianity* is the most cogent presentation in the literature of American philosophy on the idea of community as the pervasive medium in which the human self develops. It is his response to James's classic *Varieties of Religious Experience,* which focused on the experience of individuals. James's suspicion of institutional religions and his feeling that participation in them was a secondhand, second-rate kind of experience is one of the points

---

tism does not appear in the article. The introduction of the term was the work of James, with acknowledgement of Peirce's work, in his Berkeley lecture of 1898.

41. Peirce, *Collected Papers,* Vol. 6, 319.

of disagreement between the two. The notion that conventional religion, *because conventional*, must be lacking in depth and authenticity, was the main point at issue. James's refusal to take the conventions of ordinary life seriously was for Royce a matter of great consequence, and Peirce would have agreed. "To my mind," said Royce, "it was a profound and momentous error in the whole religious philosophy of our greatest American master in the study of the psychology of religious experience. All experiences must be *at least* individual experience; but unless it is *also* social experience, and unless the whole religious community which is in question unites to share it, the experience is but as sounding brass, and as a tinkling cymbal."[42]

Royce is the most communitarian of the pragmatists. The stressful interplay of self and community in interpreting the promptings of the spirit towards loyalty to ideal ends is for him the essence of Christianity and, indeed, of all religious traditions. He wanted to put the pragmatic tests of truth to work in understanding the meanings and importance of loyalty as a social bond. "I want to put loyalty — this love of the individual for the community — where it actually belongs, not only at the heart of the virtues, not only at the summit of the mountains which the spirit of man must climb if man is really to be saved, but also (where it equally belongs) at the turning point of human history, — at the point when the Christian ideal was first defined, — and when the Church Universal, — that still invisible Community of all the faithful . . . was first introduced as a vision, as a hope, as a conscious longing to mankind. I want to show what loyalty is, and that all this is true of the loyal spirit."[43]

The key process in the development, maintenance, and change of community is the process of *interpretation*, and for his understanding of interpretation as a distinctive kind of cognitive process Royce was borrowing from Peirce's work on semiotics. The important insight here is that the process of interpretation is not a voluntary act, like reading a book or even writing one. It is something more basic and, in a sense, involuntary. It is an aspect or dimension of every act of understanding. Put differently, every act of understanding is an act of interpretation. As such it is a compound act of evaluation and judgment that is always at work within cognition. Perception and conception are not the only processes that make up personal intellectual experience. An ongoing process or flow of interpretation is a third one, on a par, epistemologically speaking, with the others. Where Peirce's initial insights into the nature of interpretation were developed in relation to the idea that a scientific community was the paradigm

42. Josiah Royce, *The Problem of Christianity* (Chicago: University of Chicago Press, 1968), edited and with an introduction by John E. Smith, 41.
43. Royce, *The Problem of Christianity*, 41-42.

case for the study of a self-correcting community of inquiry at work in the pursuit of truth, Royce generalized the idea and applied it to the broader field of moral and religious community — communities of memory, hope, and loyalty.

As treated within these terms of reference, the problem of Christianity is the problem that applies equally well to Judaism, Hinduism, Islam, and to the secular religions of modernity as well. It would apply to Marxism and to Dewey's naturalist humanism. It is the tension in experience between the particular circumstances of specific persons in particular communities and the pull of the universal, between commitment to and participation in the visible church of actual experience and the apprehension of the invisible church of ideal experience and unity in the spirit, which necessarily includes the loyal selves in all traditions. Neither pole, the actual or the ideal, exists meaningfully without the other.

Dewey's mistake in his thinking about religion in culture was to conclude that the ideal could get along without the actual in the case of religious institutions, that the religious quality of experience could be severed from particular religions that had given it form and expression. Once so severed, Dewey thought, the religious quality of life would flourish. The result of this kind of transference in his naturalist pragmatism was the ideal of a sacred democracy, a universal church very much like the Congregational church of his boyhood, which bypassed the conflicts and imperfections of the actual ones. This was the ideal of the cosmopolitan and tolerant "great community" that inspired Dewey's ethics and politics. For Royce, by way of contrast, one could not be cosmopolitan without also being provincial in a principled way. Loyalty in Roycean terms is the bond between self and community that is under stress in this tension. It is betrayed when the pull of the universal is neglected. It is also betrayed when the particular is neglected or abandoned. There is no safe haven in a heartless world, even in religion.

The realization of the value of loyalty requires a demanding ethical and religious discipline. It entails willed subordination, not servitude. It is a form of participation in the life of the ideal that would satisfy the conflicting pressures of both the particular and the universal. The master precept for Royce's ethics — be loyal to loyalty — is not as simple-minded as it might appear. It is designed to counter drift and evasion. For Royce, when loyalties conflict, as they invariably do, the conscience says *"Decide.* If one asks, *How decide?* Conscience further urges, *Decide as I, your conscience, the ideal expression of your whole personal nature, conscious and unconscious, find best.* If one persists, *But you and I may be wrong,* the last word of conscience is, *We are fallible, but we can be decisive and faithful; and this is loyalty."*

It is this master precept that makes Royce's an ethic of solidarity with those whose loyalties differ. It requires respect for the loyalties of groups other than one's own, and in that sense it is a call for toleration. But loyalty cannot be served by toleration alone. There is the pull of the universal to be dealt with as well. By the very nature of cognition, the particular attachments of loyalty, be they ethnic, religious, nationalist, those of class, gender or any other type, will be interpreted as trustworthy or not, reliable in this circumstance or not. If not, revision is in order. Interpretation is always at work in sifting the incessant claims made upon the modern self. The movements of history from Royce's point of view are ultimately the work of communities of interpretation. What changes is the way of seeing and evaluating things, and such movements as there are pivot on alterations in the meaning of loyalty and its demands.

## Summary and Conclusion

A paradox is a truth that seems to be a contradiction. The pragmatists' understanding of the modern self concludes with one: to find yourself, lose yourself in devotion to something outside your self. Their psychology is a moral psychology through and through. Its aim is moral autonomy, but as paradox would have it, individual moral autonomy is a *social* ideal. One cannot be autonomous by oneself. Autonomy cannot flourish without the right kind of cultural surroundings. It has to be learned and socially supported. As Royce put it, "the only way to be practically autonomous is to be freely loyal."[44]

The ethics of the pragmatists is an ethics of virtue. The virtues are rooted in natural dispositions but are trained up in community. They are learned and can be unlearned, so must be kept up in practice. The community counts on them. The goal of a pragmatist ethics is self-realization, and self-realization turns on development of the virtues. Ethical values are not arbitrary, nor are they merely objects of feeling. Moral feelings must be read and reasoned out. Ethics must make sense. Right thinking and right doing are reciprocals. While moral development is personal development, it is not a private matter. One cannot be good by oneself. Pursuit of the good is a collective enterprise.

The politics of pragmatism are the politics of liberal communitarianism that arose out of the political history of the late nineteenth century in the form of the "new liberalism" of that day. In America the new kind of liberalism, collectivist in its orientation as distinct from the individualism of laissez faire in opposition to which it emerged, was known as progressivism, and the pragmatists were the philosophers of moral progress. The goal of liberal communi-

---

44. Josiah Royce, *The Philosophy of Loyalty* (New York: The Macmillan Company, 1908), 95.

tarian politics is being autonomous together, to put it paradoxically. Being autonomous together has its implicit moral criteria. These coalesce in the notion and the pragmatic problem that the common good must be good for everyone. Being autonomous together requires a social architecture of rights, and all rights entail responsibilities. It requires extensive and expensive public infrastructure, hard and soft. It requires a knowledgeable modern state with powers proportionate to the problems of society and economy. Building these up has been the work of the past century, and it is unfinished. As long as there are conflict and change there will be politics, and the ideal for government in the pragmatist tradition is responsiveness. The ideal for politics is improvement or amelioration.

Religion was something about which the pragmatists fruitfully disagreed. Those who became full-fledged philosophical naturalists developed and inspired an important body of work on the social, psychological, and aesthetic functions of religion in culture. They understood something about the spiritual dimension of the modern self. They developed and expressed a naturalist spirituality that was thoroughly at home in the capitalist, scientific, technological culture of modernity, but still reminiscent of pre-Christian philosophy in the Greco-Roman tradition. They celebrated the salt and savor of ordinary experience, the goodness of the secular and its sufficiency. They cultivated a sensibility of ironic heroism and commitment to human ideals in the face of their finitude and in the midst of a nature that was amenable to scientific study but profoundly indifferent to human aims and purposes. They knew what Dylan Thomas meant when in *Fern Hill* he sang, "time held me green and dying, though I sang in my chains like the sea."

Pragmatists of the supernaturalist persuasion left a different legacy. If the reality of God matters in the capitalist, scientific, technologically driven culture of modernity, they tried to make room for it in their thinking. They pioneered in developing the outlook of religious modernism in American intellectual life. Their work foreshadowed the philosophical theologies of experience of the later twentieth century. They offered an alternative to the naturalist humanism of their colleagues, with whom they shared a great deal in their perspective on life. They offered a theistic humanism and defended its integrity as a responsible reading of experience in their philosophical work. They showed that religious belief and modernity could get along. One did not have to abandon the faith of the fathers to participate in good faith in the life of modern culture.[45]

45. For a discussion in this vein of what he calls a "neo-classical" contemporary conception of God, see Schubert M. Ogden, *The Reality of God and Other Essays* (Dallas: Southern Methodist University Press, 1992). Ogden argues that among the most significant intellectual achieve-

Like the naturalists in the pragmatist school, they too celebrated the secular as good in itself, full of joys and sorrows meaningful in their own terms. Like the naturalists, they knew that true freedom consists in being bound by ideals. Moral autonomy can be developed only by commitment to something outside the self. Unlike the naturalists, however, for the religious modernists that something was the sense of a God who was both immanent and transcendent, and for them the ideal modern self was a theonomous self. They did not believe the universe was finally indifferent to their aims and purposes, but rather that it somehow cooperated with them when they were at their best. They felt they needed help, and that help would be provided for those who knew they needed it. They knew what Gerard Manley Hopkins meant when he spoke of himself as "Time's eunuch" and prayed, "Mine, O Thou Lord of Life, Send My Roots Rain."

---

ments of the twentieth century has been the creation of a neo-classical alternative to the classical theism of the scholastic philosophers and theologians. Sometimes called "panentheism," it is a "dipolar" conception of God as both absolute and relative, immanent and transcendent, apart from human beings but, like them, dependent on persons with whom to cooperate. As treated by Ogden, the neoclassical conception is inspired by the process philosophy of Alfred North Whitehead and by the modern natural theology of Charles Hartshorne, the philosopher and editor of the Peirce papers. Hartshorne's panentheism was strongly influenced by Peirce. See Hartshorne's *The Divine Relativity: A Social Conception of God* (New Haven: Yale University Press, 1948), and also his *Aquinas to Whitehead: Seven Centuries of Metaphysics of Religion* (Milwaukee: Marquette University Publications, 1976), and his *A Natural Theology for Our Time* (Lasalle, Ill.: Open Court Publishing Company, 1967). For an experience-based understanding of modern theology and its applications in the criticism of modern culture, see David Tracy's *Blessed Rage for Order: The New Pluralism in Theology* (1975; this edition, Chicago: University of Chicago Press, 1996), with a new preface by the author. See also Tracy's *The Analogical Imagination: Christian Theology and the Culture of Pluralism* (New York: Crossroad Publishing Company, 1981).

# II. FIGURATIONS

# Mirror Images: Framing the Self
# in Early New England Material Piety

Sally M. Promey

In any serious study of the larger shape of American cultural history, and of its characteristic conceptions of selfhood and individualism, all roads are likely to lead one back, eventually, to a consideration of the New England Puritans. One need not go to the extent of crediting the Puritans with "the origins of the American self" to recognize their enormous and defining influence. But for many years, scholars have understood New England Puritanism almost entirely as a culture of the Word — the expression of an intense, religiously animated, and highly literate population that produced a profusion of self-scrutinizing diaries, elaborate and learned expository sermons, and other remarkably sophisticated written works, all of them taking their direction from what was for them the sacramental Text of Texts, the Christian Bible — including a distrust of visual culture and graven images.

But our understanding of American Puritanism has been deepened and complicated in recent years by the careful attention paid by a new generation of scholars to the plentiful elements of visual and material culture that surrounded and enveloped these early colonists. As Sally M. Promey shows in this essay, attention to visual sources can yield surprising and even transformative insights. While the Puritans have never been known for the use of art and artifacts for devotional purposes, Promey shows that the art of the Puritan era provides an unexpectedly valuable window onto Puritan piety. By examining the development of Puritan portraiture and gravestones produced in and around Boston from 1660-1720, she transforms our understanding of the way that selfhood emerged in seventeenth-century New England, in a manner continuous with typological conventions. Such evidence not only uncovers points of profound ambivalence in Puritan culture, but it presents a formidable challenge to much of our longstanding conventional wisdom about the clear disjuncture between the religious and the secular in the Puritan worldview. Sally M. Promey is Chair and Professor in the Department of Art History and Archaeology at the University of Maryland and the author of *Painting Religion in Public* (Princeton, 1999), as well as coeditor (with David Morgan) of *The Visual Culture of American Religions* (California, 2001). In January 2007 she joins the faculty of Yale University as Professor of Religion and Visual Culture and Professor of American Studies.

*"In these Exercises, my Heart was rapt into those heavenly Frames, which would have turned a Dungeon into a Paradise."*

Cotton Mather (1686)

I offer here a set of observations about the use of pictures in, and in relation to, the Puritan devotional practice of self-examination. Specifically, I consider a cluster of seventeenth- and early eighteenth-century gravestone carvings (e.g., fig. 1) and one oil painting, the Thomas Smith *Self-Portrait* (c. 1670-1691; fig. 2). I focus my attention on a set of objects, on stone and canvas, produced in and around Boston between 1660 and 1720.[1] Both kinds of artifacts might well be

1. The cluster of stones around which I build this essay are located in and around Boston in burial grounds that the Charlestown carver and the Joseph Lamson family of carvers served. For these burial grounds, I can demonstrate a large Puritan presence substantiated by genealogical

In shorter form, this chapter first appeared as "Seeing the Self 'in Frame': Early New England Material Practice and Puritan Piety," *Material Religion* 1, no. 1 (Spring 2005): 4-41. It is revised and reproduced here with permission. In November 2003, the community of fellows and colloquium participants at the Center for Advanced Study in the Visual Arts provided warm reception and thoughtful responses to a first draft of the essay; Wendy Bellion did the same for a later version. I am, further, grateful to Richard Ford, Melanie Gifford, and Catherine Metzger (National Gallery of Art); Georgia Barnhill (American Antiquarian Society); and Philip Klausmeyer (Worcester Art Museum) for material and technical expertise regarding the Thomas Smith *Self-Portrait*; to Roger Stein, whose scholarship introduced me to the painting; to Catherine Brekus for insights on Puritan devotional writing practices; to Wilfred McClay, who in 2001 encouraged me to pursue my longstanding interest in the subject of "self-representation" in the material pieties of seventeenth- and early eighteenth-century New England; and to the readers engaged by *Material Religion*. Both iterations of my essay owe much to University of Maryland graduate students Guy Jordan and Jason LaFountain; my thanks to them for generous research assistance and good conversation about visual practice in colonial New England. LaFountain's outstanding master's thesis, "Reflections on the Funerary Monuments and Burying Grounds of Early New England" (University of Maryland, December 2004) makes numerous important contributions to the literature on the subject.

1. **Jonathan Pierpont stone, Wakefield, Massachusetts, 1709.**
   Photo: Sally M. Promey

described as means of "framing" the godly self. Indeed, if Puritan diaries and journals, elegies and meditative poetry, biographies and autobiographies are literatures of and about the self, the gravestones and portrait painting that constitute my subject facilitate the performance of similar introspective labor. These pictures participate in the formation of a "self-image," the mental visualization of a spiritual self-portrait, in conformity with metaphorical images of the godly self and, thus, ultimately in conformity with the "Image" of the Puri-

---

data. The Thomas Smith *Self-Portrait* also belongs to this milieu. I use a number of somewhat later stones from Connecticut burial grounds for purposes of interpreting subject matter, where overlap (based on common scriptural appropriation), can be shown to exist. While I focus my investigation on a relatively small number of mostly Boston-area burying grounds and acknowledge a rich variety of pictorial stones as well as significant local and regional variation, major aspects of my argument withstand scrutiny for other New England gravestones beyond these geographical limits. I wish to emphasize here, however, that mine is not an exclusivist interpretation; additional meanings can be ascribed to the same stones. For example, this essay does not explore the important significance of gravestones as symbolic of doorways and/or beds (taking footstones as well as headstones into account); neither does it consider connections between material artistry and early print culture in New England, nor between notions of figuration in gravestone carving and the sorts of figural objects associated with image-magic in this period. These questions I intend to pursue elsewhere.

**2. Thomas Smith
*Self-Portrait,* oil
on canvas.**
Worcester Art Museum, Worcester,
Massachusetts, museum purchase,
1948.19.

tan Christ. Painting and stones encouraged the imaginative engagement of a certain kind of Christian self otherwise unseen and presently deferred. This transaction involved a visual "objectification" of the self, for purposes of discerning, examining, performing, and re-appropriating a new and newly sanctified subject anchored in a divine moral economy of grace.

The fact that Thomas Smith likely painted his own resemblance while looking in a mirror represents only the most literal assertion of relations between his picture and the Puritan piety of self-examination. In these practices, Puritan aesthetics embraced Christian scripture as pattern-book and style guide, mining the text for typological content, for the mindset of ambivalences and tensions it incorporated, and for the rich metaphorical redundancy that I understand to inform the aesthetic constellation Puritans called "plain style." Approaching these material objects as "technologies of the self" (to adopt a phrasing used by Tom Webster with respect to Puritan diaries), I also resituate them in particular environments and contexts and in relation to common practices and patterns of vision and behavior.[2] I begin to suggest, furthermore, a subject I will explore elsewhere in more detail: the intimate connections, a sophisticated inter-media

2. Tom Webster, "Writing to Redundancy: Approaches to Spiritual Journals and Early Modern Spirituality," *The Historical Journal* 39, no. 1 (1996): 40.

artistry, between these objects-in-place and other pictorial and textual forms of contemporary Puritan manufacture and imagination.[3]

## Historiography and the Qualification of Puritan Iconoclasm

For some readers, the use of art and artifacts in Puritan devotional exercises will seem a contradiction in terms, so customary is the notion of American Puritanism as a uniformly iconoclastic system of belief and behavior. Confusion regarding the extent and nature of American Puritan iconoclasm has constituted a serious obstacle to the study of seventeenth- and early eighteenth-century visual production and consumption. While some scholars, most recently Mark Peterson and Jason LaFountain, have challenged earlier misleading renderings and acknowledged the roles of material objects in Puritan culture, most (including Peterson) continue to construe *pictures* in this context to have been aberrations of one sort or another.[4] The conventional vision of stark whitewashed walls and unadorned beams owes more, however, to the nineteenth century's fictive reconstructions than to careful archaeological and artifactual study. Compelling textual evidence indicates that New Englanders likely displayed the sort of decorative "painted cloths" or wall hangings in households that Tessa Watt has described for English Protestantism in the sixteenth and seventeenth centuries; that English colonists pasted numerous illustrated broadsides to their interior walls, made use of elaborate Bible boxes and Bible covers, carved the paired guardian cherubim of Solomon's temple into their gateposts, and sometimes even inscribed elegies on the window glass of houses. As in contemporary English usage, then, the surfaces of walls and windows could be deployed as spaces for writing, and pictures too.[5] These exam-

3. To different conclusions Robert Blair St. George also productively explores potential visual and semiotic relations between stones and portraiture; Robert Blair St. George, *Conversing by Signs: Poetics of Implication in Colonial New England Culture* (Chapel Hill: University of North Carolina Press, 1998).

4. Mark A. Peterson, "Puritanism and Refinement in Early New England: Reflections on Communion Silver," *William and Mary Quarterly* 58 (April 2001): 307-46; Jason David LaFountain, "Reflections on the Funerary Monuments and Burying Grounds of Early New England," M.A. Thesis, University of Maryland, December 2004.

5. Tessa Watt's illuminating *Cheap Print and Popular Piety* (Cambridge: Cambridge University Press, 1991) examines the visual culture of Protestantism in sixteenth- and seventeenth-century England. She focuses attention on such highly ephemeral objects as illustrated ballads and broadsides, frontispieces, wall paintings in inns and domestic spaces, and a category of imagery called painted cloths which were often, like the prints, sold by stationers and booksellers. See, e.g., Edward Taylor, *Christographia*, ed. Norman S. Grabo (New Haven: Yale University

ples present a cluster of (often religious) early New England domestic pictorial possibilities that compete with the visual appearance of Puritanism long ensconced in American historical "memory."

The view of Puritanism that emerges here accommodates a rich and densely metaphorical material and sensory universe. My aim in this revisionist investigation of Puritan material practice is neither to dismiss Reformation iconoclastic impulses nor to overlook subsequent colonial iconoclastic tensions. At issue is not whether, but when and where and in what senses, these Puritans might be considered iconoclasts. I wish to suggest that pictures and decorated objects occupied a carefully modulated conceptual space of unresolved ambivalence within colonial Puritan culture. Deep-seated suspicion of important categories of (especially religious) images, based on Calvinist applications

---

Press, 1962), "Sermon XIV," 467. According to Watt, "The real poor man's picture was the painted cloth" (192-99). Juliet Fleming's *Graffiti and the Writing Arts in Early Modern England* (Philadelphia: University of Pennsylvania Press, 2001) pursued the subject further with a fascinating study of the material culture of writing, including the use of window panes as a surface for inscription of verses (53-55). The use of a window as a writing surface for an elegy is especially intriguing, given the parallel symbolism of gravestones as portals or window and the conviction that the windows and doors of houses constituted points of special vulnerability to witches and spirits. On this last point see Robert Blair St. George, "Witchcraft, Bodily Affliction, and Domestic Space in Seventeenth-Century New England," in *A Centre of Wonders: The Body in Early America,* ed. Janet Moore Lindman and Michele Lise Tarter (Ithaca, N.Y.: Cornell University Press, 2001), 20-23. Over the last two decades (starting perhaps with two exhibitions and their catalogues, Peter Benes and Phillip D. Zimmerman, *New England Meeting House and Church: 1630-1850,* exh. cat., Boston University, 1979; and the landmark Jonathan L. Fairbanks and Robert F. Trent, *New England Begins: The Seventeenth Century,* exh. cat., 3 vols., Museum of Fine Arts Boston, 1982) a generous handful of scholars have offered compelling revisions to conventional understandings of early New England culture. See, for example, Peterson, "Puritanism and Refinement," 307-46; David D. Hall, *Worlds of Wonder, Days of Judgment: Popular Religious Belief in Early New England* (Cambridge, Mass.: Harvard University Press, 1989); Charles E. Hambrick-Stowe, *The Practice of Piety: Puritan Devotional Disciplines in Seventeenth-Century New England* (Chapel Hill: University of North Carolina Press, 1982); Peter Benes, "Sky Colors and Scattered Clouds: The Decorative and Architectural Painting of New England Meeting Houses, 1738-1834," in *New England Meeting House and Church, 1630-1850, Dublin Seminar for New England Folklife Annual Proceedings, 1979* (Boston: Boston University, 1980), 51-69; Ann Kibbey, *The Interpretation of Material Shapes in Puritanism* (Cambridge: Cambridge University Press, 1986); David H. Watters, *"With Bodilie Eyes": Eschatological Themes in Puritan Literature and Gravestone Art* (Ann Arbor: UMI Research Press, 1981); St. George, *Conversing by Signs;* Max Cavitch, "Interiority and Artifact: Death and Self-Inscription in Thomas Smith's *Self-Portrait,*" *Early American Literature* 37, 2 (2002): 89-117; and Wendy Katz, "Portraits and the Production of the Civil Self in Seventeenth-Century Boston," *Winterthur Portfolio* 39, nos. 2/3 (Summer/Autumn 2004): 101-28. These revisionist histories, however, have not reshaped Puritanism in popular imagination.

of second commandment proscriptions and Reformation engagement with the "Word," formed one ever-present polarity of Puritan material culture. In constant conversation with this assessment of the negative and subsidiary potential of pictures, however, was another equally Puritan use of images, as well as texts, as entities of a sort not deemed subject to the biblical proscription and even as instruments of proper piety.[6]

For the Puritan instrumentalist, all the things of the world, including products of human manufacture and artistry, could be enthusiastically embraced as long as they did not stand between the soul and God. In Samuel Mather's words:

> All the Arts are nothing else but the beams and rays of the Wisdom of the *first Being* in the Creatures, shining, and reflecting thence, upon the glass of man's understanding; and as from Him they come, so to Him they tend: the circle of Arts is *a Deo ad Deum*. Hence there is an affinity and kindred of Arts . . . which is according to the reference and subordination of their particular ends, to the utmost and last end: One makes use of another, one serves to another, till they all reach and return to *Him,* as Rivers to the Sea, whence they flow.[7]

From this preacher's perspective, "All the Arts," including both pictorial and textual forms, inhabit relations of "affinity" and kinship, each "makes use of the other," each one "serves to another." These allied "Arts" are, most essentially, the light of divine wisdom reflecting back to deity off the "looking-glass" of human understanding; the arts come from God and return to God as a reflection of

---

6. Suspended between second commandment rejection of "graven images" as idols, on the one hand, and a highly visual theological imagination, on the other, Puritan pictures were both carefully bounded *and* highly charged by the multivalent context of evaluation. Whether consciously or not, ambivalence was maintained by a constant oscillation of position on the subject, an oscillation both within and between different individuals. While there was agreement about the sinfulness of idolatry, there was less consensus about the precise conditions under which images (or words or even people) became idols. Samuel Mather's definition of pictorial idolatry is a good case in point: no sooner does he justify the pious use of pictures than he takes back with one hand what he has offered with the other; see Samuel Mather, *A Testimony from the Scriptures Against Idolatry and Superstition* (Cambridge, Mass., 1672), 6. This Mather (1626-71), the older brother of Increase, graduated from Harvard College in 1643, entered the ministry, and soon returned to England and then Dublin, Ireland, for the duration of his clerical career, remaining in correspondence with members of his family in the American colonies. His thinking on matters of idolatry and metaphorical pattern is consistent with usage elsewhere in Puritan diaspora.

7. Samuel Mather, "To the Reader," preface to Samuel Stone, *A Congregational Church Is a Catholike Visible Church* (London, 1652), n.p.

God's own brilliance. This justification of arts implies, in its very articulation, "art's" own insubordinate opposite. Images and texts that refused to subordinate themselves, that competed with God for the soul's attention, constituted idols and represented a serious threat. It was the perceived potential of pictures *and* texts to become idols that charged and occasionally complicated reception.

Violently iconoclastic episodes in England generally concerned religious images (painted and sculpted) as the idols most often subject to destruction. Importantly, however, the Rev. John Cotton's anguish over the use of textual "set prayers" as "vain idols" in public worship ultimately precipitated his emigration from the old Boston to the new one. The "idolatry" that brought this eminent Calvinist divine to American shores was thus textual rather than pictorial. In the sense that a prepared prayer (from the Anglican *Book of Common Prayer*, in this case) prevented the speaker's openness to the present action of the Holy Spirit, Cotton believed that this human invention stood between the one delivering the prayer and God.[8]

Moving from the art of the pastor to the arts of poet and painter, the poet as easily as the painter might be subject to vanity, a form of idolatry that put both things and self ahead of God. Furthermore, in considering here the mutual susceptibility of texts and images to idolatry — and the contemporary uses of both in the practice of Puritan piety — it is worth noting that Puritan theology reserved a special place for image as well as word. A chief outcome of the Christian process of glorification, Calvinist theologians asserted, was the cherished possibility of seeing God face to face, of looking directly upon the divine image. Following the biblical example, clergy and laity addressed the Christian savior as both the "Word" of God and the true "Image" of the invisible God. With the second person of the Christian trinity simultaneously construed as "true *Word*" and "true *Image,*" image and text were always implicated, at least theoretically and through this shared authoritative referent, in the other's every presence. This fluid theological relation, even conflation, of image, word, and being had its material counterparts. A complex fabric, a delicate balance, of images and texts and conflicted ideas about them thus motivated the interpretive culture of seventeenth-century Puritan material practices of the self.

The analogical fluidity of Christian scripture, apparent in its treatment of the Christian savior as both picture ("image") and text ("word"), extended to highly flexible metaphorical understandings of human life and formation as well. Among colonial Puritans the multi-layered use of analogy invited the

---

8. Larzer Ziff, *The Career of John Cotton: Puritanism and the American Experience* (Princeton, N.J.: Princeton University Press, 1962), 51, and 247-49; and see John Cotton, *A Modest and Cleare Answer to Mr. Balls Discourse of set formes of Prayer* (London, 1642).

building up of a richly polysemic "picture" of the faithful self — as, for example, an architectural structure, more specifically, a "temple" or "house" of God; a "lively stone" in this larger divine edifice; and a mirror, ideally a "Mirrour of Piety."[9] One set of meanings inflected and reinforced another, providing, through the repetitive, meditative practice of self-examination, a highly textured articulation of the individual's place in a narrative genealogy of redemption. The godly self thus constituted a subject formed over time and with reference to various differentiated reiterative practices of seeing and imagination. In relation to this Puritan hermeneutical strategy, I suggest a twofold significance for the images under consideration. First, these material forms (with their combination of pictures and texts) represented an emblematical and typological portraiture or material biography of the particular self, asserting the specific individual's resemblance to godliness. And, second, through this character of representation, the depicted "saint" (the mirror of piety) was offered as a ready pattern or model, an invitation to imagine the beholder's own life in a saintly "frame" and to bring this self into closer conformity to the divine image. What is original to my account concerns less these two levels of significance and more the particular symbolic and metaphorical strategies of operation represented in the Puritan arts I examine and the material practices of piety that informed them.

In the past, visually attuned research on the objects under consideration here has been complicated not just by an apparent consensus on the ubiquity of Puritan pictorial iconoclasm but also by other disciplinary biases in the American academy. Speaking from the perspective of my own discipline, art historians, for their part, have left the heavy lifting of early American Puritan aesthetics and material culture investigation to literary scholars like Max Cavitch, Juliet Fleming, Ann Kibbey, and David Watters and to folklorists and historians like Peter Benes, Richard Godbeer, David Hall, Charles Hambrick-Stowe, Alan Ludwig, Mark Peterson, and Robert Blair St. George.[10] Most seventeenth-century images and objects in colonial America, in terms of their bid for *art historical* attention, have awaited the turn to visual culture studies, with its methodological commitments to reception and use and its disinclination to dispro-

9. Cotton Mather, "On the *Graves* of *My* young brethren," in *Cotton Mather's Verse in English*, ed. D. D. Knight (Newark, Del.: University of Delaware Press, 1989), 84.

10. In addition to studies already cited in note 5, see Allan I. Ludwig, *Graven Images: New England Stonecarving and Its Symbols* (Middletown, Conn.: Wesleyan University Press, 1966); Peter Benes, *The Masks of Orthodoxy: Folk Gravestone Carving in Plymouth County, Massachusetts, 1689-1805* (Amherst: University of Massachusetts Press, 1977); and Richard Godbeer, *The Devil's Dominion: Magic and Religion in Early New England* (Cambridge: Cambridge University Press, 1992).

portionately privilege unique production. Puritan artifacts come mostly out of artisan traditions (of wood and stone-carving, early print book illustration, funerary ornaments, pictorial broadsides); like colonial practices of literacy, they represent an aesthetic of repetition. Theirs was a visual universe less sensitive to the rhetoric of originality than to the vocabulary of reiteration; such terms as "model," "pattern," "copy," "likeness," "resemblance," "emblem," and "type" are common to contemporary accounts. To the extent that Thomas Smith's painting has claimed serious art historical attention, incidentally, it is largely because it does appear to be an "original": it is "the only seventeenth-century New England portrait by an identified colonial painter and the only extant self-portrait from that period."[11]

A related hurdle has been a compensatory one; its origins appear to lie in an attempt to give gravestone carvings their due by looking at them as "sculptures," from the perspective of training in the culture of the fine arts. Given the nature of the objects themselves, this approach has produced awkward and obscuring strategies that have hampered the dissemination of useful information. For example, the stones have been photographed individually, in uniform lighting, often in details that separate image from text, that separate objects from practices that engage them, that ignore the physical and material characteristics of the stones, and that isolate them from each other and the burial ground context that is so important to their meaningful interpretation.[12]

To bring these introductory historiographical remarks to a conclusion, let me say that my larger goals and aims in this research are threefold: to join scholars in several disciplines in expanding and complicating the visual universe of the early colonial period; to claim devotional practice as a meaningful category of Puritan image production and reception (not something relinquished to post-Reformation Catholicism); and to attend to links between the formal organization of the objects I examine and metaphorical patterns in contemporary Puritan documents of many sorts.

---

11. See entry in Fairbanks and Trent, *New England Begins,* 474-75; the *Self-Portrait* is an unusual document, but its provenance is secure.

12. LaFountain's master's thesis persuasively addresses the siting of these objects and their material character; see LaFountain, "Reflections on the Funerary Monuments and Burying Grounds," especially the second chapter, "The Burying Ground as Colonial Landscape," 33-65. And see Mary Elaine Gage and James E. Gage, *Stories Carved in Stone: The Story of the Dummer Family, the Merrimac Valley Gravestone Carvers, and the Newbury Carved Stones, 1636-1735* (Amesbury, Mass.: Powwow Books, 2003).

## Framing the Self

The first three words of this essay's subtitle, "framing the self," derive from one frequent descriptive terminology used by Puritan New Englanders. The verb asserts the *spiritual* work of the objects in question as it simultaneously indicates an important part of the actual *formal* work that they accomplish: they set the self in a godly *frame*. Several Puritan pictorial forms surround a "vacancy" in the center with images around the "outside." While this visual labor is initially most apparent in the gravestone carvings, I will argue that it is also a key aspect of the Smith *Self-Portrait*. The painter, as he paints, is aware that, from the perspective of most of his mortal audience, the body he depicts in the center of his picture has already been translated out of this world. Like gravestone carving, portraiture is an art form haunted (literally as well as theoretically) by absence — and Smith's painting might fruitfully be considered in concert with the

**3. Title page of Geneva Bible.**
Courtesy of Peter Stallybrass.
Photo: Sally M. Promey

**4. Title Page, Lewis Bayly, *The Practise of Pietie*, 1620.**
The Folger Shakespeare Library, STC 1604. By Permission of the Folger Shakespeare Library.

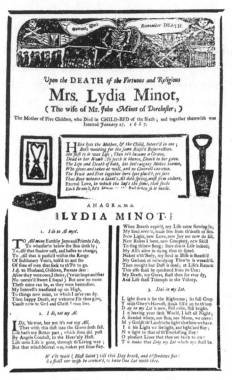

**5.** *Upon the death of the virtuous and religious Mrs. Lydia Minot . . . 1667,* Cambridge, Mass.: Samuel Green, 1668.
Massachusetts Historical Society, 0533.

**6.** *A neighbour's tears sprinkled on the dust of the amiable virgin, Mrs. Rebekah Sewall . . . 1710,* Boston: [Bartholomew Green?], 1710.
Massachusetts Historical Society, 0850.

stones and other formally and conceptually related pictorial objects where the pictures tend to migrate toward the frame, such items as the emblematic title pages or frontispieces of Bibles (fig. 3) and devotional texts (fig. 4) and the illustrated broadsides (figs. 5 and 6) that circulated funeral elegies, decorated the pillars of the belfries from which tolls rang out for the dead, remained pinned to the body or tacked to the coffin at burial, and adorned the walls of New England homes.

The Puritan notion of "framing" that I take up here was rooted in scriptural and ecclesial usage where "to frame" could mean to enclose, to embrace, to describe, to bound, to contain, to fence, to fortify, to encircle, to create, to construct. It was used to refer to the frame of a building (Ephesians 2:21); the frame of Solomon's temple (Ephesians 2:19-21); the frame of a door or window; the "frame" or physical stature of the human body; framing or fencing (and thus "improving") a field or lot or other "vacancy"; framing a question (in such a way that the answer could be found, as in the Protestant catechism); and framing the human self, especially the heart.[13] Most important for our purposes here: the ability to see the self "in frame" (and especially "in a heavenly frame") was a desired outcome of Puritan devotional exercises. Edward Trelawney, a young merchant, for example, wrote about the importance and difficulty of bringing the "heart into frame," of conforming to a Christian pattern.[14] For Richard Sibbes, Christ was the "frame of heaven," the "most excellent frame of all."[15] John Cotton advised: "grow up in a Lambe-like [i.e., Christ-like] frame of spirit and way, until the mystery of God be finished in you."[16] Elsewhere William Morton, in his preface to Cotton's *Way of Life,* asserted the necessity of faith "to fence [and, earlier on the same page, to "frame"] both graces and comforts, to subdue those corruptions, to scatter those clouds, to dispel that smoak, to beat back those oppositions, and so secure the soule from all invasions and incursions of the enemy."[17] Thomas Shepard insisted that his meditations "gave me much light and set my heart in a sweet frame."[18] Jonathan Pierpont, whose gravestone appears here as Figure 1, discovered consola-

13. On Protestant catechizing in this context, see Stanley Fish, *The Living Temple: George Herbert and Catechizing* (Berkeley: University of California Press, 1978), esp. 23; Puritan Jonathan Mitchell admonished those engaged in spiritual self-examination to "take advantage of special seasons of Meditation when your heart is in a feeling frame"; Jonathan Mitchell, *A Discourse of the Glory to Which God hath called Believers by Jesus Christ* (Boston, 1721), 282. LaFountain's argument with respect to fences and improvements is relevant here; see "Reflections on the Funerary Monuments and Burying Grounds," especially 33-50. I am grateful to Guy Jordan for calling to my attention a very useful set of mostly theoretical essays on "framing" in the history of art; see Paul Duro, ed., *The Rhetoric of the Frame: Essays on the Boundaries of the Artwork* (Cambridge: Cambridge University Press, 1996).

14. Edward Trelawney to Robert Trelawney, 10 October 1635, in *Letters from New England: The Massachusetts Bay Colony, 1629-1638,* ed. Everett Emerson (Amherst: University of Massachusetts Press, 1976), 176.

15. Richard Sibbes, *The Excellency of the Gospel above the Law* (London, 1639); reprinted in *Works of Richard Sibbes,* vol. 4, ed. Alexander B. Grosart (Cambridge: University Press, 2001), 259.

16. Quoted in Hambrick-Stowe, *Practice of Piety,* 25.

17. William Morton, in preface to John Cotton, *The Way of Life, Or, God's Way and Course, in Bringing the Soule into, Keeping it in, and Carrying it on, in the wayes of life and peace* (London, 1641), [iii].

18. Thomas Shepard, *God's Plot: The Paradoxes of Puritan Piety Being the Autobiography and Journal of Thomas Shepard,* ed. Michael McGiffert (Amherst: University of Massachusetts Press, 1972), 88.

tion, while visiting his ailing father, in witnessing the older man's "very heavenly frame."[19] Harvard College student John Brock rejoiced in his conviction that "my Frame is heavenly and chearly."[20]

Framing the godly self, as a form of mental and spiritual self-visualization, was a tool of the most common and important of Puritan meditative practices, the spiritual discipline of self-examination, taken up from the Augustinians and modified for Protestant use.[21] Following Reformer John Calvin on the role of the human person in the process of redemption, seventeenth-century American Puritans held not only that God elected only some of his human creatures to salvation but that their salvation depended entirely on God's work of election in them. Despite their utter powerlessness to influence God's will in this regard, however, Christians were nonetheless duty-bound to search their lives for signs of God's saving grace.[22] It was this belief and practice that earned the system the label "experimental Calvinism."[23] As one prominent pastor observed, "Frequent SELF-EXAMINATION, is the duty and the prudence, of all that would *know themselves,* or would not *lose themselves.*"[24] This mandate to introspection urged constant scrutiny, most especially of one's inner self or "heart."[25] Edward Pearse called this exercise "Soul-work."[26]

As Richard Baxter maintained, "the great means to conquer . . . Uncertainty is Self-Examination — or the serious and Diligent trying of a man's heart and state by the Rule of Scripture."[27] This process involved matching the self to

19. "Extracts from the Diary of Rev. Jonathan Pierpont," *New England Historical and Genealogical Register* 13, no. 3 (July 1859): 257. As a young man in 1682, Pierpont had been tutored by that "pious, learned man," John Cotton (255).

20. Clifford K. Shipton, ed., "The Autobiographical Memoranda of John Brock, 1636-1659," *Proceedings of the American Antiquarian Society* 53, part 1 (21 April 1943): 100.

21. Charles Taylor, *Sources of the Self: The Making of Modern Identity* (Cambridge, Mass.: Harvard University Press, 1989), 184.

22. Catherine A. Brekus's illuminating discussion of devotional writing practices is highly relevant here; see Brekus, "Devotional Writing and the Creation of Evangelicalism in Eighteenth-Century America," in *Practicing Protestants: Histories of the Christian Life in America* (Baltimore: Johns Hopkins University Press, 2006), 19-34.

23. See on this subject, for example, Tom Webster, "Writing to Redundancy," 33, 36.

24. Cotton Mather, *Bonifacius: An Essay Upon the Good*, ed. David Levin (Cambridge, Mass.: Harvard University Press, 1966), 35.

25. See Hambrick-Stowe, *Practice of Piety*, 21-22, 26-28; see also Taylor, *Sources of the Self*, 184.

26. Edward Pearse, *The Great Concern: Or, A Serious Warning to a timely and thorough Preparation for Death: With Helps and Directions in order thereunto* (London, 1678), 110.

27. Richard Baxter, *The Saints Everlasting Rest* (London, 1650), part III, 137, quoted in Sacvan Bercovitch, *The Puritan Origins of the American Self* (New Haven: Yale University Press, 1975), 28; see also 34.

a scriptural model, a set of images and analogies, and a search for "likeness" to them. "Resemblance" occupied a key position in this spiritual practice and aesthetic. The conversion experience initiated the Puritan believer into the lifelong task of self-examination.[28] In the words of Puritan writer William Morton, "A Christian never wants [for] work, his work lies mainly within doores [inside the self/heart/soul]; He that knows his heart, knows how hardly it is brought into a good frame, and how soon it is out againe; . . . nor can be repaired in a day, in a month, in a yeare."[29]

Given death's situation as the "culminating exercise" of Puritan devotions, a "final test of faith," all Puritan activity of self-examination was ultimately preparation for death.[30] Despite the fact that Puritans had no formal liturgy for funerals, Puritan death was a highly ritualized and scripted performance. Contemporary manuals of preparation preached the significance of dying well — and of living one's way toward the "good" death.[31] Rejecting the notion of purgatory, Puritans maintained that individuals knew, at the precise moment of death, whether they were elect or damned. For the true saints death was the moment of transformation, the event of ultimate consequence that connected life on earth to a process of celestial glorification that would take place in two distinct steps: the ascent of the sanctified soul to heaven immediately following earthly death; and the re-union of soul and the individual's renewed corporeal body at the Resurrection of the Dead and the establishment of the New Jerusalem. Freighted with metamorphic significance, the actual deathbed scene was a carefully observed and frequently recorded "public" event — public in the sense that family, friends, and acquaintances gathered, hopeful that they would witness a righteous death, one attended by signs that granted them assurance of a loved one's election and functioned, at the same time, as a model for their own personal, future encounter with death. Loss, never a warrant for excessive grief, constituted instead an invitation to self-scrutiny.[32] The goal was to progressively shift the focus from the survivor's grief to the commemorated person

28. On this subject, see Hambrick-Stowe, *Practice of Piety,* esp. ix, 200-203.

29. Morton, preface to Cotton, *Way of Life,* [ii].

30. Hambrick-Stowe, *Practice of Piety,* 229; see also 216-19; and David D. Hall, "Literacy, Religion, and the Plain Style," in Fairbanks and Trent, *New England Begins,* 102-12, esp. 106.

31. See, for example, Cotton Mather, *Bonifacius,* 36, 51-52.

32. According to Cotton Mather, in *Awakening Thoughts on the Sleep of Death* (Boston, 1712), 4-5: "To have *no Sorrow at all,* Or to be *without Natural Affection* is to be *worse than Infidels.*" Still, "To indulge *too much Sorrow,* and the fall into *Extravagant* and *Exorbitant* Ejaculations, this is to be *as bad as Infidels,*" as quoted in Jeffrey A. Hammond, *The American Puritan Elegy: A Literary and Cultural Study* (Cambridge: Cambridge University Press, 2000), 120. Idolatry was also called "spiritual adultery": like pictures and words, people, if loved too much or mourned too grievously, could become idols.

*as a model of the sanctified self,* thus making the individual death exemplary and consequently of use to all who might find in themselves signs of resemblance to the saintly model.[33]

In their article on "Family Strategies and Religious Practice," Anne Brown and David Hall have demonstrated the extent to which two contradictory notions of covenant competed for the attention of New England Puritans from the time of colonization to the Great Awakening: an inclusive Abrahamic covenant (based on Genesis 17:7) according to which blessings descended genealogically along family lines; and an exclusive covenant of limited atonement that protected the purity of the visible saints by seeking to gather only the regenerate into the church. The splits produced by the two covenantal systems emerged not only between different individuals and groups but also within particular individuals at various points in their lives.[34] In the burial ground, and especially as represented in the school of stone carvers I consider in this essay, the Genesis covenant worked hand in hand with experimental Calvinism. Familial clusters of stones both asserted the salvation of loved ones and elicited in survivors a search for assurance of their own inheritance.[35]

Gravestone carvings, like the printed artifacts of poetic elegies for example, did not simply honor and commemorate the dead. They also (and perhaps more importantly) provided a means to make survivors more like them, at least more like their now idealized, sanctified selves. What the aged Rev. John Higginson had to say in 1697 of Cotton Mather's *Magnalia Christi Americana* could as easily be said of these stone carvings: the stones "embalmed and preserved, for the *knowledge and imitation* of posterity, the virtues of the blessed just."[36] Gravestone carvers represented the dead symbolically, in this case emblematically and typologically — and viewers who knew to see *themselves* in these terms appropriated the emblematic images of the dead as their own, facilitating, as Jeffrey Hammond has claimed for the elegiac form, a "redistribution of the deceased's piety throughout the community."[37]

33. I am indebted to Hammond's argument with regard to elegy and the exemplary death; Hammond, *American Puritan Elegy,* 134-37.

34. Anne S. Brown and David D. Hall, "Family Strategies and Religious Practice: Baptism and the Lord's Supper in Early New England," in David D. Hall, ed., *Lived Religion in America: Toward a History of Practice* (Princeton: Princeton University Press, 1997), esp. 42-45, 53-56.

35. The fact that they knew some of these individuals to be reprobates did not dislodge the overall power of the symbolism — and in fact might reinforce it: if God saved such sinners, perhaps there was hope for those uncertain of their own sanctity.

36. John Higginson, "An Attestation to this Church-History of New England," in Cotton Mather, *Magnalia Christi Americana: or, the Ecclesiastical History of New England* (London, 1702), rpt. ed. Kenneth B. Murdock (Cambridge, Mass.: Harvard University Press, 1977), 69.

37. Hammond, *American Puritan Elegy,* 169; see also 141.

Spiritual biography (in both pictorial and literary forms) could function as a model in this fashion because, as Cotton Mather's elegy for Sarah Leverett made explicit, in the sense that they all shared the Image of Christ, all saints "looked alike." In his poem, Mather first lamented that human manufacture did not invent portrait painting early enough to capture the faces of biblical women on canvas ("long did I vex in vain at Stupid Man, that ere Men found out Painting, so long Ages ran. Fair would I *Painted* to the Life have seen The Heroines that in past Times have been"). Still, he contained his disappointment because Leverett made "an end of all complaints"; in her "ONE Matron gives a sight of *all* the *Saints*."[38] Richard Sibbes agreed: "The liker pictures are to the first pattern [Christ], the liker they are to one another."[39]

In theory, Puritans prohibited overly ritualized funerary observances; the evidence suggests, however, that the rules were frequently bent if not broken altogether. Even in early times of strictest compliance, the funeral elegy apparently flourished.[40] Broadside publication of the elegiac text (sometimes before and sometimes after the burial) was the common medium of dissemination beyond the oral performance at the gravesite. Broadsides might communicate the

38. Cotton Mather, "A Lacrymatory: Designed for the Tears let fall at the Funeral of Mrs. Sarah Leverett," lines 3-6 and 21-22 in *Cotton Mather's Verse in English*, ed. Denise D. Knight (Newark: University of Delaware Press, 1989), 80. Interestingly, and as others have already noted, the word biographer entered the English language in 1663, preceded by biographist in 1662, and succeeded by biography in 1683; see Kenneth B. Murdock, "Clio in the Wilderness: History and Biography in Puritan New England," *Church History* 24 (1955): 223-24; see also Webster, "Writing to Redundancy," 44, on "the biographical explosion of the 1650s and onwards." Sacvan Bercovitch identifies Cotton Mather as the first American to use the term "biography" in print. For Mather's employ of "exemplary biography" aimed to instruct by the use of example, see Bercovitch, *Puritan Origins*, 3-5.

39. Sibbes, *Excellency of the Gospel*, 264.

40. Much has been made of the fact that burial grounds were the responsibility of civil society — and they certainly were so in terms of authority, administration, and upkeep. It cannot be presumed from this, however, that these grounds were thus secular spaces rather than religious territory. See, e.g., Matthew Pentland Brown, "Orbits of Reading: The Presence of the Text in Early New England" (Ph.D. dissertation, University of Virginia, 1996), 13, 120-28. In practical application to the spaces of Puritan religious experience, the argument for secularity becomes fairly nonsensical, especially since it rests on the opposition of "civil" burial grounds and "religious" church building. Seventeenth-century meetinghouses sustained multiple civil functions. The more helpful question would be: how did people use and understand the burial grounds? Here one might better allow for multiple perspectives and commitments at once. While his argument differs from my own, Dickran Tashjian's 1978 essay on this subject lays useful groundwork; Dickran Tashjian, "Puritan Attitudes Toward Iconoclasm, *Puritan Gravestone Art II, Dublin Seminar for New England Folklife Annual Proceedings, 1978* (Boston: Boston University, 1979), 37-45. See also Dickran and Ann Tashjian, *Memorials for Children of Change: The Art of Early New England Stonecarving* (Middletown, Conn.: Wesleyan University Press, 1974).

death in advance of the funeral, represent the voice of the deceased at the observance itself, and commemorate the dead after burial. Elegies, read aloud at the house of the primary survivors and/or at graveside, and represented in either broadside reproduction or manuscript form, were frequently tacked or pinned to the hearse or coffin, and often buried with the body.[41] It is in this context that Cotton Mather's poetic description of funeral elegies as "Paper winding-sheets" makes material sense.[42]

Certainly we know that people spent time in the graveyards when they went there in solemn procession with other members of the community for a burial. The literature also indicates that pastors and providers of spiritual advice construed the burial ground as a place of periodic repetitive meditation. Guidelines for reception surface in contemporary devotional manuals. In a book that was itself a part of the material culture of funerary practices (the title page indicated that it was "recommended as proper to be given at funerals"), Edward Pearse advised, "*The meditation of Death . . . is Life;* it is that which greatly promotes our Spiritual Life; therefore walk much among the Tombs, and converse much and frequently with the thoughts of a Dying-hour."[43]

Frequent visitation, however (walking *much* among the tombs), raised the likelihood, and even necessity, of seeing the graveyard, of being present in it, at different hours of the day and seasons of the year, in multiple conditions of weather — as well as visiting it in different psychological moods and spiritual states — and in different stages of the individual's internal conversion narrative. In the latter instance, this would mean that the stones elicited different spiritual meanings and possibilities of identification at different times. The stones themselves would have presented dramatically different viewing experiences with relatively minor changes in time of day, lighting, temperature, and humidity. With seasonal shifts, bright sun virtually obliterated the carving on some slate or granite stones, replacing it with a dazzling, shining flat expanse; rain, on glistening on slate especially, made most of the carving virtually invisible; snow covered the bases so that only a portion of the surface could be seen, and sometimes snow-pack or frost filled the inscriptions, making the graven marks more insistently apparent than was ordinarily the case (fig. 7); icy ground created a reflec-

41. Brown, "Orbits of Reading," 130.

42. Cotton Mather, "An Elegy on . . . the Reverend Nathanael Collins" (Boston, 1685), in James F. Hunnewell, ed., *A Poem and an Elegy by Cotton Mather* (Boston: The Club of Odd Volumes, 1896), (2).

43. Pearse, *Great Concern*, 86-87. Pearse's book appeared in numerous London (beginning in 1671) and Boston editions. Edward Taylor's copy of *Great Concern* is listed in the inventory of his library in *The Poetical Works of Edward Taylor*, ed. Thomas H. Johnson (New York, 1939), 216, item 144.

7. **Mary Long stone, Charlestown, Massachusetts, 1681.**
Photo: Sally M. Promey

8. **Ephraim Tinkham stone, Middleborough, Massachusetts, showing shadows "doubling" stones.**
Photo: Sally M. Promey

9. **Hannah Hubert stone, Cambridge, Massachusetts, 1690.**
   Photo: Sally M. Promey

10. **General view, Plympton, Massachusetts.**
    Photo: Sally M. Promey

**11. Sibyll Wigglesworth stone, Cambridge, Massachusetts, 1708, showing context.**
Photo: Sally M. Promey

tive surface that supplied the stones with "twins"; shadows also "doubled" and "revised" the stones (fig. 8). An important part of the environmental message, then, as changing, fleeting light (fig. 9) and moisture played over the surface of obdurate stone, surely concerned transience and duration, the operations of evanescence and eternity. The numbers of stones (figs. 10-11), consequent multiplication of imagery, and reiteration of subtly varying shapes, sizes, and appearances registered, moreover, as an important aspect of the experience. If "plain style" was a desired aesthetic quality, repetition based on "resemblance" and on layering of multiple, reinforcing, pictorial and formal metaphors was an important aspect of what made plain style "plain." The tension between uniformity and variety animated this artistic vocabulary.

The recommendation to "walk much" did not just encourage visitation of one's own family sites in times of bereavement or commemoration, but rather gave preference to a more comprehensive and general kind of transit as meditative practice. In terms of the actual material/physical context of the graveyard, the individual would be presented with a fluctuating set of extreme contrasts. On one hand were the elaborately carved stones representing Christian ideals and saintly spiritual progress. On the other hand, visitors to the burial grounds might well be sharing the space with renegade rutting pigs that dug up graves — and, less troublesome, with sheep and cattle pastured there to keep down the briars and brambles. This was an emotionally and viscerally charged territory, where assertions of spiritual metamorphosis took place in the context of hard, inscribed surfaces interacting with light and weather, where visitors might contort their bodies and endure physical discomfort to maximize vision, where one was likely to be confronted by turned-up bones and standing water, where it was sometimes very hard to ignore the sensory realities of rotting bodies.[44]

The process of self-scrutiny, of the sort evoked in the burial grounds, involved a fundamental activity of matching aspects of the individual life to an internalized visual and verbal glossary of biblical types and emblems, with recourse to Christian scripture as a kind of pattern or sourcebook of metaphors. Following a biblical admonition to search creation for evidence of sacred history, Puritan practitioners of the period were accustomed to seeing both pictures and words as "signs."[45] The vocabulary of emblem and type was one in which the Puritan population of seventeenth-century New England was well versed. The use of scriptural types and analogies, understood to be divinely instituted and to refer the beholder always back to the antitype, or Christ, as-

44. On the material realities of burying grounds, see Gordon E. Geddes, *Welcome Joy: Death in Puritan New England* (Ann Arbor: UMI Research Press, 1981), 147-51; see Sewall, 24 Dec. 1685, 89-90; 9 July 1689, 227; 11 Dec. 1703, 493; and 1, 2, and 25 August 1712, 696-97. In some New England burial grounds "wolf stones" were laid across graves to keep the pigs and wolves away; on this subject, see LaFountain, "Reflections on the Funerary Monuments and Burying Grounds," 50-65. Dealing with objects on site is a tricky proposition, however. Stones have been moved, over the centuries, to accommodate changing aesthetics and to make space for lawnmowers. Landscaping, too, has changed rather dramatically. During the course of my research for this essay, Jason LaFountain reminded me that seventeenth-century patterns of settlement would have meant the deforestation of many of the sites where burying grounds were located. On this subject see, for example, William Cronon, *Changes in the Land: Indians, Colonists, and the Ecology of New England* (New York: Hill and Wang, 1983).

45. Samuel Mather (1626-1671) explained that "there is in a Type some *outward* or *sensible* thing, that represents an higher spiritual thing, which may be called a *Sign* or a Resemblance, a *Pattern* or a *Figure*, or the like"; Samuel Mather, *The Figures or Types of the Old Testament, By which Christ and the Heavenly Things of the Gospel were Preached and Shadowed to the People of God of Old. Explain'd and Improved in Sundry Sermons* (London, 1705), 52. This volume was published in London and Dublin; while it was not widely available in New England, the Massachusetts Mather family possessed a copy.

serted the insufficiency of human language or art to adequately convey the glory of God in any direct fashion. In a theological system predicated on God's utter transcendence, typological and emblematic constructs worked through indirection, depending on metaphorical modes of thinking.[46] According to art historian Barbara Stafford, the analogical imagination, with its "double avoidance of self-sameness and total estrangement," encourages a conviction of connection across distinction, an intimate relation bridging an insurmountable gulf, between persons and God — and between persons and objects that elaborate the condition of relation and separation. The experience of ambivalence, born of the simultaneous assertion of continuity and difference, undergirds this equation.[47]

Seventeenth-century Puritans explicitly acknowledged the gap: "As there is a Similitude, a resemblance and Analogy between the Type and the Antitype in some things: *So there is ever a dissimilitude and a disparity between them in other things.* It is so in all similitudes. . . . There is a mixture of Consentaneity and Dissentaneity; or else instead of Similitude, there would be Identity. So here in these sacred Similes, it is not to be expected, that the *Type* and *Antitype* should . . . agree in all things."[48] The perceiving self was always still suspended some distance from that with which it sought union — and, in the Puritan case, certainty of the outcome was deferred to the grave. Furthermore, in the sense that analogy displays the capacity to temporarily "materialize" things unseen, it represents an "incarnational" performance. In Edward Taylor's poetry this exchange renders the Christian God a kind of great magician: Taylor describes him as one who "dost use This Metaphor to make [Him]selfe appeare."[49]

---

46. On Puritan convictions regarding the insufficiency of language, see Hammond, *American Puritan Elegy*, 133.

47. Barbara Maria Stafford, *Visual Analogy: Consciousness as the Art of Connecting* (Cambridge, Mass.: MIT Press, 1999), 10, see also 8-9.

48. Mather, *Figures or Types*, 57.

49. *The Poems of Edward Taylor,* ed. Donald E. Stanford, Second Series, Number 101 (New Haven: Yale University Press, 1960), 229. In Puritan devotional practice, analogy thus recapitulated, in each instance of use, a central mystery of the faith: the visible appearance of the invisible; see Stafford, *Visual Analogy,* 24. Like the Christian scriptures upon which Puritan analogical imagination depended, Christ's incarnation and sacrifice (and their reiteration in the celebration of the Lord's Supper) demonstrated the unity of the visible and invisible worlds, the very possibility of "representing" a true image. See Michael Clark, "The Honeyed Knot of Puritan Aesthetics," in Peter White, ed., *Puritan Poets and Poetics: Seventeenth-Century American Poetry in Theory and Practice* (University Park: Pennsylvania State University Press, 1985), 70-71.

## "Portrait" Stones

The question to which I now turn, then, concerns how it was that gravestones might function as "portraits." One of the most direct claims for this interpretation comes from contemporary epitaphs, that of William Pole (d. 1674 at age 81) for example: "which he himself made while he was still living . . . and left it to be ingraven upon his tomb y[e]t so being dead he might warn posterity." By this means the stone then became, as Pole asserted, the "resemblance of the dead man bespeaking ye reader."[50]

Beyond such explicit arguments for a gravestone's "resemblance" to the person whose grave it marked, a more nuanced answer lies essentially in the Puritan typological imagination and, in the case of the cluster of stones I examine here, most particularly in Puritan appropriation and uses of the Hebrew scriptural imagery of Solomon's temple and its typological linkage to Christian scriptural extensions of the temple of the New Jerusalem. Samuel Mather left no doubt as to the significance of this imagery: "Now the Temple is the Church of God; and we may apply this type in three ways: 1. To God and Christ. 2. To the Church. 3. To particular Saints."[51] According to Samuel's influential younger brother Increase, Christ was "the elect cornerstone in [the temple of] Sion," and the saints, at the moment of death, became the "lively stones" that built up God's spiritual temple on this foundation (cf. I Peter 2:4-7). Literary scholar David Watters, who first pursued the subject of temple imagery and personal analogy, charted the saint's four-stage metamorphosis into a lively stone: "the heart [became] a temple for the spirit of Christ through grace, the person [became] a living pillar in the church on earth, at death he or she [was] made into a living stone in the heavenly temple, and finally, in the Resurrection [of the corporeal body at the end of time] he or she return[ed] to earth as a living stone in the New Jerusalem."[52] In a funeral sermon for John Hull, Samuel Willard lamented that when a saint like Hull died, "there is then a Pillar pluckt out of the Building, a Foundation Stone taken out of the Wall, a Man removed out of the Gap."[53] Hull could be pillar, stone, and person simultaneously. Rather

---

50. William Pole epitaph, recorded in "Epitaphs at Dorchester," *New England Historical and Genealogical Register* 2 (1848): 381.

51. Mather, *Figures or Types,* 455-56; also 427.

52. Watters, *"With Bodilie Eyes,"* 90; see also David H. Watters, "A Priest to the Temple," *Puritan Gravestone Art II, Dublin Seminar for New England Folklife Annual Proceedings, 1978* (Boston: Boston University, 1979), 25-36.

53. Samuel Willard, "Sermon Preached October 7, 1683. Occasioned by the Death of the Worshipful John Hull, Esq." (Boston: Printed by Samuel Green for Samuel Sewall, 1683), 14.

than producing any felt disparity, the various reiterative analogues worked together to provide a more complete and complex "picture" of the faithful self.

Puritan stone carvers, too, articulated multiple facets of this temple equation. Perhaps most importantly, grave markers were themselves "*lively* stones," enlivened by their association with a particular saint, and signaling the passage or translation of this person (who was, biblically and figuratively speaking, also a "lively stone") from the earthly to the heavenly temple at the time of death. The inscriptions on the Thomas Kendel and Edmund Angier grave markers, for example, make clear this connection: Kendel (fig. 12) is a "Patarn of Piati" and "Zion's stone." He is also "one of ye 7 of this Church Foundation," a reference to the seven pillars of Wisdom's house in Proverbs 9:1; and Kendel is represented here as a skull atop a pillar (in a "picture" that would have been recognized, simultaneously, as an emblem of death). Angier (fig. 13) "left his earthly, and entred into his heavenly house" (i.e., his temple) upon his death in 1692. The Kendel stone pictured the two cherubim who guarded the temple and its sacred treasures; the Sarah and Mary Long stones did likewise (figs. 14 and 7). In many instances, the pictures cut into stone tympana asserted the ascent of the grave's occupant (most often depicted as winged skull or as soul effigy) through the veil of the temple (figs. 15, 9, and 11), represented by a drape or scallop across the top of the tympanum. Christ was the antitype of Solomon's temple and its high priest. His sacrifice made the holy of holies, or heaven, accessible to the elect who themselves, in his image, might don the garb of the high priest ascending, as in the Abraham Nott stone of 1756 at Essex, Connecticut (fig. 16). Tassels, like those that adorned contemporary pulpit cloths in the meetinghouse and the pall over the coffin in funeral processions, decorated this temple curtain and appeared in a number of slightly later gravestones (fig. 17). At least one of these, the Silas Bigelow stone of Paxton, Massachusetts (fig. 18), depicted tassels in the context of both pulpit drape and temple veil. Typologically, the temple veil represented the flesh of Christ (rent on Good Friday with the crucifixion of Jesus) and thus also the sacrament of the Lord's Supper.[54] The carver of the Matthew Rockwell stone (fig. 19; South Windsor, Connecticut, 1782) juxtaposed the tasseled veil (the flesh of Christ or bread of the Last Supper) with a row of communion vessels. Significantly, for New England Puritans, the sacrality of neither the earthly church nor the heavenly temple depended on a particularly consecrated *space* but rather on converted *human beings*, the saints, the lively stones that most

---

54. See Edward Taylor, *Upon the Types of the Old Testament*, Vol. 1, ed. Charles W. Mignon (Lincoln, Neb.: University of Nebraska Press, 1989), 410-11; and Samuel Mather, *Figures or Types*, 448. See also Watters, "A Priest to the Temple"; and *"With Bodilie Eyes."*

**12. Thomas Kendel stone, Wakefield, Massachusetts, 1678, detail.**
Photo: Sally M. Promey

**13. Edmund Angier stone, Cambridge, Massachusetts, 1692, detail.**
Photo: Sally M. Promey

14. **Sarah Long stone, Charlestown, Massachusetts, 1674.**
Photo: Sally M. Promey

15. **Katharine Greenleafe stone, Cambridge, Massachusetts, 1712.**
Photo: Sally M. Promey

**16. Abraham Nott stone,
Essex, Connecticut, 1756.**
Photo: Sally M. Promey

**17. Augustos Mills stone,
South Windsor, Connecti-
cut, 1759, detail.**
Photo: Sally M. Promey

**18. Silas Bigelow stone, Paxton, Massachusetts, 1769, detail.**
Photo: Sally M. Promey

**19. Matthew Rockwell stone, South Windsor, Connecticut, 1782, detail.**
Photo: Sally M. Promey

fundamentally constituted the celestial temple — whose image was restored in the burial grounds.[55]

Among the visual features of the temple most often represented in the stones were the two famous pillars, said to stand in the temple porch. Texts by Samuel Mather and Samuel Lee described these pillars in detail. In the course of his lengthy disquisition, Mather declared,

> Particular saints are compared to *Pillars in the House of God, Rev.* 3:12. . . . There be two properties of a good Pillar, it must be straight and strong . . . upright and steady. . . . These Pillars [in Solomon's temple] were broken in pieces and carried away to Babylon, but living Pillars in the spiritual Temple shall go out no more, *Rev.* 3.12. but abide in the house forever, *Job* 8.35. . . . Is there this rectitude and straightness, this strength and firmness in the ways of God? Thou art then a Pillar in the House of God, and shalt go no more out.[56]

Lee's large-format illustrated text pictured the two pillars (fig. 20), as did the Geneva Bible, which, along with the more intellectual Authorized Version of 1611, remained a popular translation among Puritan New Englanders.[57] As shown in Lee and other contemporary books and prints, these double pillars topped with spheres bear a striking resemblance to the two "pillars" flanking the gravestones examined here (fig. 21). Given the tendency of the carvers, beginning in the seventeenth century, to represent the spheres topping the pillars as portrait heads of the deceased (e.g., figs. 22 and 23), it is useful to know that the scriptural text named the two pillars as though they were human: "Jachin" and "Boaz" then represented (respectively, and based on the translation of their Hebrew names) fixedness or firmness; and strength.[58]

Like the named pillars in the scriptural temple, named believers took the place of these upright and up-righteous supports. This devotional context for early carved portrait heads qualifies the claims of scholars who assert a connection between the appearance of portraits in gravestone carving and a decline in

---

55. With their own interests in Solomon's temple, eighteenth- and nineteenth-century Freemasons in New England appropriated this stone type and elaborated it to their particular purposes.

56. Mather, *Figures or Types,* 457. Samuel Lee, *Orbis Miraculum, or the Temple of Solomon* (London, 1659), 70, expresses the same conviction. For various and useful pictorial representations of the temple and its parts, see Stefania Tuzi, *Le Colonne e il Tempio di Salomone: La storia, la leggenda, la fortuna* (Roma: Gangemi Editore, 2002).

57. Harry S. Stout, *The New England Soul: Preaching and Religious Culture in Colonial New England* (New York: Oxford University Press, 1986), 25-26. See also David Daniel, *The Bible in English* (New Haven: Yale University Press, 2003), esp. chapters 17, 20, 24, and 25.

58. Lee, *Orbis Miraculum,* 69-70; Mather, *Figures or Types,* 453-55.

68    *The Temple* of Solomon.    Chap. 4.

*The two Pillars standing in the Porch of* the Temple.

1 *King.* 7. 15.
*Jer.* 52. 21.
1 *King.* 7. 19.

NExt in view, come the two famous Pillars which stood in the Porch of the *Temple*; and were, for Matter, Brass; for Form, Cylinders; for Height, 18 Cubits a piece; for Compass, twelve Cubits; for Diameter, about four Cubits, which is conceived to be the meaning of that expression, *That they were four Cubits in the Porch*, that is, the Chapiters were four Cubits Diameter.

**20. Pillars, from Samuel Lee,**
***Orbis Miraculum, or the***
***Temple of Solomon, 1659.***
The Folger Shakespeare Library,
L903.2. By Permission of the
Folger Shakespeare Library.

Puritan piety.[59] Interestingly, the Samuel Mather text described carved decorations of flowers and fruits on these named scriptural pillars, and Cotton Mather's *Bonifacius* connected devotional practices concerning self-scrutiny and meditation on death to Christian fruitfulness: "And if such an exercise were often attended, Oh! How much would we regulate our lives, how watchfully, how fruitfully would it cause us to live."[60] Gravestone carvers pictured this ideal in symbols of spiritual fruitfulness and abundance, including female breasts, in some cases doubling as figs, gourds, or melons, among visual emblems of sacred nourishment (see figs. 9, 11, and 15).[61] The Pierpont stone (fig. 1) explicitly

59. See, for example, Ludwig, *Graven Images,* 316-22; Benes, *Masks of Orthodoxy,* 132, 166-69, 192-94.

60. Cotton Mather, *Bonifacius,* 36.

61. On the spiritual significance of breasts, see, for example, Elizabeth Maddock Dillon, "Nursing Fathers and Brides of Christ: The Feminized Body of the Puritan Convert," in *A Centre of Wonders: The Body in Early America,* ed. Janet Moore Lindman and Michele Lise Tarter

21. **John Brown stone,
    Wakefield, Massachusetts,
    1717.** Photo: Sally M. Promey

22. **Pierpont portrait (detail of
    Fig. 1).** Photo: Sally M. Promey

**23. Pyam and Elizabeth Blower stone, Cambridge, Massachusetts, 1709.**
Photo: Sally M. Promey

praised the Wakefield pastor as a "Fruitful Christian." The Edmund Angier stone (fig. 13) depicted two sets of pillars: an inner "plain" set and an outer set of ornamented portrait pillars.

## Mirror Images

Gravestones enjoined living beholders, walking among the tombs, to examine themselves to discover the fruits of their own faith. The move from the decorated spiritual appearance of the deceased to resemblance in the survivor was facilitated by an aesthetic of imitation that prized reiteration. In a sermon Edward Taylor explained typology in relation to this aesthetic: "God doth as it were pensill out in fair Colours and [engrave] and portray Christ" in the He-

(Ithaca, N.Y.: Cornell University Press, 2001), 129-44. John Cotton titled his popular seventeenth-century catechism *Spiritual Milk for Babes.*

Mark A. Peterson explicates the imagery of temple and garden in a context that meaningfully separates the two. In the work of stone carvers, the two sets of metaphors came together, reinforcing the image of the faithful Christian; see Peterson, *The Price of Redemption: The Spiritual Economy of Puritan New England* (Stanford: Stanford University Press, 1997).

brew scriptures. The image as it appears in these types is imperfect; in Christ this image is perfected. According to Taylor:

> We were made, and formed with an Imitating Principle in our Nature, which cannot be Suffocated, or Stifled, but will act in Imitating Some Example; God to prevent us from taking wrong Patterns to follow, hath presented us with a perfect Pattern of right practice in our own nature in Christ, which is most Examplary, being a most Exact Coppy. . . . Hence our Imitation of him is His due, and our Duty, and to leave this Pattern, is to dishonour him, deform our Lives, to Deviate from our Pattern, and to Disgrace [dis-grace?] our Selves.[62]

Because the saints most effectively imitated the pattern offered by Christ, they too became patterns worthy of imitation, "living" types of the antitypical (original) Christ. "Visible Holiness in everyone," Taylor asserted, "is exemplary, and gives forth influences of holiness attractive to draw others on to the Same."[63] In pictorial form: "Thou [God] portrai'd art in Colours bright, that stick Their Glory on the Choicest Saints, Whereby They are thy Pictures made."[64] In a related metaphorical usage, Puritan writers also equated both "saints" and scriptural "types" (as well as the Bible itself) with mirrors or looking-glasses (and it pays to recall here Samuel Mather's explanation of "all the Arts" as the reflection of God's wisdom "upon the glass of man's understanding," as quoted in the first pages of this essay). Titles of numerous emblem books designated as "mirrors" or "glasses" of godliness the emblems contained therein. In 1706, Cotton Mather, for example, referred to the sanctified dead as "Mirrours of Piety." Thirty-four years earlier, just after poet Anne Bradstreet's death, John Norton II described her as a "Pattern and Patron of Virtue," a "Mirror of Her Age."[65] The images carved into the stones thus provided not only "figurative" portraits of deceased saints but also, by "reflection" and analogy, exemplary spiritual visages that survivors might appropriate as their own. Looking at the godly images

---

62. Edward Taylor, *Christographia, or a Discourse To[u]ching Christ's Person . . . in Several Sermons*, ed. Norman S. Grabo (New Haven: Yale University Press, 1962), "Sermon I," 34.

63. Taylor, *Christographia*, "Sermon VIII," 244.

64. Taylor, *Poems*, 99 (Second Series, Number 11).

65. Cotton Mather, "On the GRAVES of MY Young Brethren," line 45, [1706], *Cotton Mather's Verse in English*, 84; John Norton II, "A FUNERAL ELOGY," [1672], in Harrison T. Meserole, *Seventeenth-Century American Poetry* (New York: New York University Press, 1968), 460. Elsewhere, authors of devotional texts likewise held up "[looking] glasses of godliness," lists of desirable attributes, and encouraged readers to discern in them their own improved "reflection," to see themselves in these "heavenly frames"; see Philip Benedict, *Christ's Churches Purely Reformed: A Social History of Calvinism* (New Haven: Yale University Press, 2002), 321.

**24. John Person stone, Wakefield, Massachusetts, 1679.** Photo: Sally M. Promey

carved on the saints' stones, believers saw themselves — their own spiritualized selves — looking back.

The amenability of the stones to the task of eliciting *self*-visualization was surely enhanced by the fact that the bilateral symmetry of the stones reiterated a formal analogy to the human body. In terms of their shape and appearance the "living" stones might be said to re-*member* the dead as a way of imagining the sanctified self. This "temple" was also a body: its pilasters or pillars the appendages or arms, its tympanum a head, the temple interior, the central, framed space or "vacancy" of the stone, upon which the person's name was written, was the "heart" — and on some gravestones this was literally the case (figs. 7 and 14; on others it was implied — cf. fig. 24). That the death's head or soul effigy could be imagined as an actual visage of a person is apparent in a number of contemporary texts, including an elegy written for Thomas Dudley eight years before his death. With an anagram of Dudley's name as its title: "Thomas Dudley/Ah! Old must dye," the poem included the lines: "A death's head on your hand you neede not weare! A dying head you on your shoulders

**25. General view, South Windsor, Connecticut.**    Photo: Sally M. Promey

beare. You neede not one [a death's head] to mind you, you must dye, You in your [very] name may spell mortalitye."[66]

If one stone signified the bodily person of the individual saint, grouped together, as they were in context (fig. 25), the stones represented the bodily self as part of a community of saints that breached the bounds of time, connecting past to present, and present to future, and future to eternity. The invitation to see the self not only in relation to the familial inheritance of the Abrahamic covenant but also as one of the gathered saints would have been especially important in the 1670s to 1720s, just the years for which there are fairly dramatic increases in the numbers of carved stones. These were times of particular anxiety for Puritan clergy, who feared a waning of piety (with or without demographic evidence). A monumental set of genealogical ancestors thus enlivened the church's past and asserted its connection to the present at a moment of perceived generational crisis.

With the pictures pushed to the frames, the centers of the stones provided a surface for reflection (and projection), a place to imagine one's own name inscribed — for, while there is a fair degree of variation in inscription, the one constant is the most stripped-down of biographical sketches.[67] With the typo-

66. Anonymous, "Thomas Dudley Ah! old must dye," 1645, in Meserole, *Seventeenth-Century American Poetry,* 505.

67. In addition to name and dates of birth and death, many stones included some recita-

logical, emblematical self on the outside, the named individual and the chronological span of their mortal existence appeared on the inside in the registration of names and dates. The stones thus incorporated both generalized saintly pattern *and* biographical specificity.[68] The activity of inscribing names, however, could also be linked to scriptural sources and, in particular, to temple imagery. Samuel Mather's gloss on the biblical texts elaborated this theme. Christ, as high priest, would enter the heavenly temple with the names of the saints carved into the precious stones ornamenting his priestly garments. The names on the stones would be "in everlasting remembrance" before God: "their names are engraven in his sight, that he cannot look off from them."[69]

Puritan poet Anne Bradstreet, at the end of a long piece titled "Contemplations," counted on another scriptural context for interpreting stone inscriptions like these: "O Time the fatal wrack of mortal things/That draws oblivions curtains over kings, . . . But he whose name is grav'd in the white stone//Shall last and shine when all of these are gone." Her "white stone" was taken from the Book of Revelation 2:17; the Geneva Bible that she might have used glossed the stone as "a token of God's favor and grace; . . . a sign that one was cleared in judgment." With quiet and final authority, the white stone signified the named individual's sure election to grace.[70]

For Puritan Samuel Sewall, choosing names for his children was no small task. Names had to be carefully selected and considered for their possible significance, especially with respect to scriptural precedents.[71] Names, further, bore a special sort of likeness to the individual, such that the name was understood to carry hidden spiritual messages relevant to the person — these secret meanings were often evoked to greatest effect around the time of death in elegiac anagrams, acrostics, and puns on names in funeral broadsides.[72] Edward Taylor arranged his elegy for Charles Chauncy, president of Harvard, in the shape of a tombstone, and called the text "A Quadruble Acrostick whose Trible is an Anagram." The anagram, a form that rearranged the letters of an individ-

---

tion of familial relationships, lines or verse praising the deceased or listing their virtues, exhortations to the living (generally in the "voice" of the deceased) regarding death, and/or a scriptural quotation. My thanks to Wendy Bellion for her e-mail correspondence on the self-projective facility of the stones' surfaces.

68. Hammond, *American Puritan Elegy*, 158-59.

69. Mather, *Figures or Types*, 505-9; compare Taylor, Sermon 14, in *Upon the types*, 281-83; and Lee, *Orbis Miraculum*, 89. See also Watters, "A Priest to the Temple," 33.

70. Anne Bradstreet, "Contemplations," verse 33, in *The Complete Works of Anne Bradstreet*, ed. Joseph R. McElrath, Jr., and Allan P. Robb (Boston: Twayne Publishers, 1981), 174.

71. Hall, *Worlds of Wonder*, 218; Sewall, I:324; and see especially LaFountain, "Reflections on the Funerary Monuments and Burying Grounds," 80-93.

72. Webster, "Writing to Redundancy," 46-47.

**26. Nathaniel Goodwine stone, Wakefield, Massachusetts, 1693.**
Photo: Sally M. Promey

ual's name to reveal hidden sacred messages, "became the signature formal device of New England elegies."[73] The anonymous author of Lydia Minot's broadside elegy (fig. 5) found three anagrams in Minot's name ("I di to Al myn," "I di, not my Al," and "Dai is my Lot"), building a short poem around each of the three; the last poem was also an acrostic of her name.[74] Acrostics, in which the letters of an individual's name registered as a vertical column providing the first letter of each line of a verse or poem, also appeared on gravestones; the Dorchester, Massachusetts, stone for James Humfrey is one example.[75] The judgment represented in the inscription of names could be negative as well as positive. A passage that appeared frequently on gravestones all over New England: "The memory of ye just is blessed" (figs. 26 and 13) was but the first part of a verse from the book of Proverbs. While the stone carvers did not usually provide the citation, any contemporary viewer could have supplied the second line from Proverbs 10:7: "The memory of the just is blessed[76] — but the names

73. Hammond, *American Puritan Elegy*, 173.

74. Hammond, *American Puritan Elegy*, 176; see catalogue entry in Fairbanks and Trent, *New England Begins*, 129-31.

75. Jason LaFountain pointed me toward this acrostic stone.

76. The memory of the just is blessed because it brings the living to self-examination and

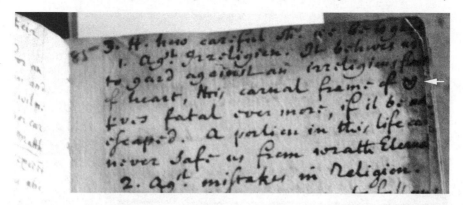

**27. Page 85 from John Leverett Commonplace-Book, showing "carnal frame of heart" phrase with heart pictogram.**
Massachusetts Historical Society. Photo: Sally M. Promey

of the wicked shall rot."[77] Looking on these saintly "mirrors" could be a sobering, even frightening experience as well as a reassuring one.

## Heart Religion

In the terms of its practitioners, Puritanism was "Heart Religion": personal religious experience constituted its core.[78] Richard Baxter described the aim of his own exercise of self-examination in these terms. He searched himself to see or "trace the workings of the spirit upon my heart." He called his spiritual autobiography his "Book of Heart Accounts."[79] Cotton Mather defined Puritan

preparation for their own (presumably good) death. Memory here is about moral injunction as well as commemoration.

*77*. Because of the significance of names, slander and defamation carried stiff punishments, one of which included a kind of shaming or humiliation in the form of a negative reversal of the practice of pinning elegies to coffins: pieces of paper identifying the person and their infraction were attached to them, and especially over their heart or mind. Thus "bad" words as well as good ones could be "written" on bodies. See Robert St. George, "'Heated Speech' and Literacy in Seventeenth-Century New England," in *Seventeenth-Century New England,* Proceedings of a Conference Held by The Colonial Society of Massachusetts, 18 and 19 June 1982 (Boston: Colonial Society of Massachusetts, 1984), 275-322.

78. Thomas Hooker to John Cotton, c. April 1633, in *Thomas Hooker: Writings in England and Holland, 1626-1633,* ed. George H. Williams, Norman Pettit, Winifred Herget, and Sargent Bush, Jr. (Cambridge, Mass.: Harvard University Press, 1975), 297-98.

79. Richard Baxter, *Reliquiae Baxterianae: or, Mr. Baxter's Narrative of the Most Memorable Passages of His Life and Times. Faithfully publish'd from his own original manuscript, by Matthew*

**28. Seventeenth-century Bible Box with carved hearts**
Private Collection. Photo: Sally M. Promey

practice as "the Art of managing our Hearts."[80] John Leverett pictured these hearts in the context of his commonplace book (fig. 27; 1680-1711), which he may well have kept with his Bible and writing implements in a box like this seventeenth-century example decorated with carved hearts (fig. 28). A critical task of Puritan meditative exercises was the transfer of knowledge of God's truth in one's head to faith in that truth in one's heart.[81] The admonition was scriptural, and its scriptural foundation featured hearts in company with stones: the righteous have God's laws inscribed on their hearts instead of on tablets of stone (Ezekiel 11:19; Jeremiah 31:33; Hebrews 8:10 and 10:16). The carver, cutting a heart into stone, rehearsed the anticipated transformation: he wrote and drew on stone, but God would write and draw on the living, beating human heart. The Decalogue, on tablets of stone, became, by Christian metamorphosis, the vital, pulsing engine of life. The heart was, furthermore, God's spiritual temple. With the destruction of the historical temple of Solomon, the

---

*Sylvester* (London: T. Parkhurst, 1696), 6; and Baxter, *The Mis-chiefs of Self-ignorance, and the Benefits of Self-acquaintance* (London, 1662), 304. See also Webster, "Writing to Redundancy," 43.

80. Cotton Mather, "Lacrymatory," line 84, p. 82.
81. Hambrick-Stowe, *Practice of Piety,* 163.

Embleme 26,

CORDIS TABVLA LEGES.

Dabo legem meam in uiſcebus eorum,
et in CORDE eorum ſcribam eam *Jerem. 31. 33.*

Scribo nouam teneri nunc CORDIS in æquore legem,
Cum vetus in duris fit mihi ſcripta petris.

26   *Michel van lochom excu*

O let my heart be ſound in thy
Statutes, that I be not aſhamed.
*Psal. 119. 80.*    *P. 104*

**29. Emblem book, "The Table of the Heart,"** *The School of the Heart,* **showing the law being inscribed upon the heart.** The Folger Shakespeare Library, H184. By Permission of the Folger Shakespeare Library.

**30. Emblem book,** *Pia Desideria: or Divine Addresses,* **showing the trying of the heart in the mirror of scriptural law, which has been substituted for the mirror of vanity.** The Folger Shakespeare Library, H3351. By Permission of the Folger Shakespeare Library.

deity took up residence in the believing heart.[82] This metaphoric set of associations (Decalogue, gravestone, temple, heart) found expression in popular Protestant emblem books (figs. 29 and 30), various editions of the *New England Primer,* several title pages produced for the Geneva Bible (fig. 3), and on the stones themselves (and cf. figs. 7, 14, and 24).[83] In this context, the com-

82. See, for example, Fish, *Living Temple,* 69-73, 84-85; and Edward Taylor, *Christographia,* 370-71.

83. In the *New England Primer,* see especially the letter "H" ("heart") in, for example, the 1727 and 1777 editions. In 1777 the verse reads "My Book [Bible] and Heart/Must never part" and

31. **Lydia Peaslee stone,
Haverhill, Massachu-
setts, 1741.**
Photo: Sally M. Promey

mon phrase "tables of our hearts" made the connection even more explicit and informed its pictorial expression on, for example, the Lydia Peaslee stone (fig. 31) where the heart and the tablets of the Decalogue become one. These grave-stones are, perhaps most essentially, about metamorphosis — about the trans-formation of the self from one state to another, an orthodox and beneficent form of image-magic in which the image of the self in the self becomes the im-age of Christ in the self. The unidentified artisan of the "BW" stone at First Church, Windsor, Connecticut, made it perfectly clear in the poetic inscrip-tion he carved that he cared little for the shape of his words on stone: what he

---

is illustrated by an open Bible, with lines of text indicated across both visible pages, the whole inscribed on a heart, surrounded by flourishes of vegetation like those appearing on numerous gravestones; *The New England Primer* (Boston: Edward Draper, 1777; Aledo, TX: WallBuilder Press, 1991, reprint).

intended was that his message be interiorized, impressed upon the "REDERS MINDE" and heart.[84] The "softened," "melted," or "broken" heart was, in Puritan terms, the preferable spiritual alternative to the hardened, cold, or inflexible heart. Taylor once described his own "rocky heart."[85] The goal was to be pliable, shapeable, amenable to union with Christ; the souls of both men and women, in this context, were gendered female.

The heart, the generally agreed upon location of the soul, provided the ideal surface or ground for both text and image. The human heart became God's tablet for inscription (figs. 29 and 31), the mirror for Christ's reflection, and the canvas for the divine "portrait" — and these equations (the heart as God's tablet, mirror, and canvas) belonged to the seventeenth century. In a sermon preached by Edward Taylor, God's work of regeneration involved "a renewal of his holy Image on man . . . afresh upon his Soule in Evangellical Colours."[86] The divine image or portrait, banned from Puritan churches, was reinscribed on the Puritan heart: "the transplendent Glorious Image of the Son of God in Sparkling-glorious Colours is portrayed again upon the Soule." This Christ was not just the artist, he was the self-portraitist: "It is Christ's Workmanship in portraying his *own* image upon the Soule." And God's work was first "drawing out" "the Portraiture of Christ" in scriptural types: "[God] draws out the very Effigies of his Son upon so many glorious Types and sets them before our eyes to behold him in."[87] "Christ as it were is God's masterpiece."[88]

God, the ultimate artist, was a portraitist who painted, drew, inscribed his image, and the image of his divine son/self, on lively stones and human hearts *as* the believer's own true portrait. This view of divine activity is particularly revealing of a culture in which the most frequently surviving paintings are portraits. In any and all "types," the spiritually conversant viewer could see the image — the "portrait" — of Christ. With an astonishing degree of uniformity, contemporary writers agreed that while mortals see "through a glass darkly," in

---

84. Quoted in Watters, *"With Bodilie Eyes,"* 1.

85. Taylor, *Poems of Edward Taylor,* 57 (First Series, Number 36); and cf. Ezekiel 11:19.

86. Taylor, *Christographia,* 314. Adam, the original creature in the "Image of God," was a "Sparkling Looking Glass, representing the Glorious Image of his Maker"; Taylor, *Upon the Types of the Old Testament,* 53. The original image, stained, compromised, even destroyed, by Satan's design in original sin, would be restored to the godly self.

87. Taylor, *Christographia,* 97; *Edward Taylor's Treatise Concerning the Lord's Supper,* ed. Norman S. Grabo (East Lansing: Michigan State University Press, 1966), 201; Taylor, *Upon the Types of the Old Testament,* 106-7, 53; Taylor, *Christographia,* 453; and Taylor, *Upon the Types of the Old Testament,* 311-12.

88. Sibbes, "Excellency of the Gospel," 259-60.

heaven "we shall have full views of his face, full visions of his Glory."[89] In heaven God would no longer be represented by his name only, the lettered Hebrew acronym YHWH (see fig. 4, upper right hand corner), but by his own clear shining countenance, a brightness reputedly so intense that the sun grew dim by comparison.

The heart on the stone asserted the soul (and the face of God reflected upon it) in its absence. Calvin's thoughts on representing the visible aside, much of New England Puritan aesthetics is involved with indirectly representing what is *not* there, or what is presumed to be present but invisible. The "frame" contains the absent or invisible element. Both the winged death's head and the soul effigy represent the transformation wrought by death, a transformation marked by the soul's ascent to heaven and its subsequent absence from earth (and from the body) until the end of time. The paired contrast of vacancy and indwelling, emptying and filling, describes a constant tension and ambivalence that marks the richly analogical world of Puritan imagination. The task at hand was to empty the self of "self."[90] The contours of this vacancy then allowed space for the image of Christ, provided a frame for the divine portrait. Sin was, most basically here, the fundamental iconoclast. Sin "[destroyed] the image of God upon thee,"[91] creating "a greate Vacancy as to . . . the Image of God on man."[92]

Increase Mather encouraged self-examination in order to see, to recover, the Image of Christ in the self and, through seeing this image, to experience what he called a *"Facial Vision"* of God. Furthermore, he continued, "This *Meditation* should [make those who practiced it] willing to be absent from the Body, so that they may be present with the Lord" — thus simulating what was believed to happen at Puritan death. Mather expected that this spiritual exercise would be "attended with a *Transformative Power,* changing them [practition-

89. Pearse, *The Great Concern,* 213-14: In mortal life, faithful Puritans saw God by faith: "when Death comes, they shall see him face to face, that is fully, clearly, immediately, I Cor. 12.12."

90. Thomas H. Luxon, *Literal Figures: Puritan Allegory and the Reformation Crisis of Representation* (Chicago: University of Chicago Press, 1995), 104: "Reading the self correctly . . . is also a process of reading the old self out of existence, and the new self . . . is a self perpetually deferred, a self that has its being elsewhere" (p. 104). See also Lewis Bayly, *The Practise of Pietie, Directing a Christian how to walke that he may please God,* third edition (London, 1613).

91. Taylor, *Treatise Concerning the Lord's Supper,* 201.

92. Taylor, *Christographia,* 315; see also 314. See, further, Sibbes, "Excellency of the Gospel," 260. When it was not God's paintbrush, or his shining reflection in a mirror, it was the *vision* of God that inscribed the divine face on the soul: "Lord Cleare my Sight, thy Glory then out dart. And let thy Rayes beame Glory in mine eye And stick thy Loveliness upon my heart"; Taylor, *Poems of Edward Taylor,* 57 (First Series, Number 35).

ers] into the same Image" as Christ himself.[93] Thomas Shepard pleaded: "O Lord, imprint this image on me"; and Taylor prayed that Christ would "Begin to draw afresh thine Image out In shining Colours, on my Life, and Heart."[94] In this way, Richard Sibbes maintained, "Christ is alive" in the world "in the hearts of gracious Christians, that carry the picture and resemblance of Christ in them."[95] The heart or soul was both canvas and reflective surface, the looking-glass that "displayed" the image of Christ.

Seeing the self in frame was a way to locate a useful "reflection" in time and space. As a mirror of piety, the saint was a glass turned heavenward to reflect the divine, to resemble the divine in terms of typological attributes — then turned back toward earth as the "ideal" reflected image of the ordinary believer. The object of pious self-examination was eventually to discern or discover the image of Christ in the self. This was a sort of Protestant pictorial *imitatio Christi*. "My Heart shall be thy [Christ's] Chrystall looking Glass," Taylor wrote.[96] In the "mirror of election," the Puritan sought not his or her own image but Christ's image; use of this *"Prospective-Glass for Saints"* transformed the self into the image of Christ.[97] Again, the source was a scriptural one, taken from II Cor. 3:18: "We all with open face beholding, as in a glass, the Glory of the Lord; are changed into the same image."[98] This exercise of self-examination allowed the practitioner to imagine the self as Christ, and to bring the self into conformity with a true image and a true icon. A contemporary glossed the text:

> The *Reflexion* of his Beauty shall be *imprinted* upon our persons, whilst we *behold* him. As for *Example* . . . when we look upon a Glass, which by being *Polite* [i.e., polished], but not *transparent,* reflects the Image of our persons, 'Tis called a *"Looking-Glass"* very fitly; because in our *looking* upon *It,* It seems to be *looking* upon *Us* too. . . . Now our Persons in Heaven will be so

93. Increase Mather, *Meditations on the Glory of the Lord Jesus Christ: Delivered in Several Sermons* (Boston, 1705), ii-iv.

94. Edward Taylor, Meditation 38, lines 32-33, 1700, in Daniel Patterson, ed., *Edward Taylor's* God's Determinations *and* Preparatory Meditations: A Critical Edition (Kent, Ohio: Kent State University Press, 2003), 277.

95. Sibbes, *Excellency of the Gospel,* 264.

96. Edward Taylor, Meditation 132, line 32, in Patterson, ed., *Edward Taylor's* God's Determinations, 452. Taylor as quoted in Watters, *"With Bodilie Eyes,"* 173.

97. Phrases quoted from Bercovitch, *Puritan Origins,* 14; Bercovitch quotes the words of Richard Baxter, William Dell, and Richard Mather.

98. Richard Mather, *The Summe of Certain Sermons Upon Genes[is] 15:6* (Cambridge, Mass., 1652), 23 (referring to II Cor. 3:18). Mirrors were ultimately about the transformation of the individual, the construction of a godly self which was, in fact, finally the self's transformation into the "Image" of Christ.

polished, *(when this Corruptible shall have put on Incorruption,)* that we shall be in respect of *God,* what Looking-Glasses are in respect of *Us;* we receiving *his* likeness, as they do *ours.* . . . We shall be Mirrors exactly made; a kind of Looking-glasses with Eyes; whilst by *seeing* as we are *seen,* and *representing* the *Image* of what we *see,* we shall therefore be *like* unto God himself, because *we shall see him as he Is.*[99]

Given this historical context, it is not difficult to imagine emblematic grave-stones that represented individual saints (though only some included physiognomic portraits) and their virtues as mirrors framed with the typologi-cal ornaments of the fruitful self. Walking among the tombs in the burial grounds, believers might find "looking glasses" that brought their own "reflec-tions" into conformity with the image of the godly saint and in which they were expected to imagine their own names inscribed.[100] As Jason LaFountain has observed, in some cases the symbolic capacities of a stone's particular material qualities reinforced this meaning. Glorified selves, as looking-glasses reflecting the dazzling "lustre" of God's own face, would "shine" and "sparkle," like the sun-struck surfaces of the mica-flecked rough-hewn granite stone, for example, that marked Israel Smith's grave (1793) in the Glastonbury, Connecticut, burial grounds.[101]

99. Thomas Pierce, *Death Consider'd as a Door to a Life of Glory* (London, n.d.), 115.

100. A motif carved in reverse or "mirror" image into a later eighteenth-century stone, the 1790 Margarett Cumings stone of Billerica, Massachusetts, with the same scriptural "Corrupt-ible/Incorruption" passage from I Cor. 15:43-44 and 53-54 at its foot, suggests that contemporary viewers were conversant with this metaphorical assessment. Jason LaFountain brought this stone and its implications for my argument to my attention; see LaFountain, "Reflections on the Funerary Monuments and Burying Grounds," 14-15. Furthermore, in and after rain (and ice in some conditions, too) horizontal slab markers (e.g., tablestones and tombstones, which I do not discuss in this chapter but which were in use in the seventeenth-century burying grounds I ex-plore) became literal surfaces of reflection. Given the horizontal disposition and size of the stones (which approximated the length of an adult corpse) and the orientation of the text across the stones' short axis, these objects in these circumstances invited viewers to glimpse their own reflections "framed," laid out over the biographical inscription, and thus to imagine their own bodies in the grave and, simultaneously (because the sky reflected, too), in the heavens. In bright sun, with the beholder's shadow cast across stone, a similar dynamic relation of be-holder's body to stone prevailed. The stones' shadows further augmented this choreography of materiality, movement, and engagement. An elaborate Puritan theology of shadows suggests further intriguing possibilities for the material reception and interpretive context of the stones.

101. LaFountain, "Reflections on the Funerary Monuments and Burying Grounds," 73-74; and cf. Pierce, *Death Consider'd as a Door to a Life of Glory,* 112-13.

## The *Self-Portrait* of Thomas Smith

I want to redirect attention now to the Thomas Smith *Self-Portrait* (fig. 2) and to consider the painting in relation to what I have said about gravestone carving and Puritan meditative practices of the self. In this painted artifact, Smith is, in fact, an artist working in the genre of spiritual autobiography or self-presentation. He is also an artist observing his own features in a mirror; so the image is, quite literally, about self-examination. The formal organization of this work reveals something of the process of its production. That is to say, with the important exception of the carefully articulated face, the canvas might be imagined as the vacant space of the mirror's reflective surface surrounded or framed by objects, emblems, and types. Thomas Smith is not only painting in a mirror; he is literally and figuratively painting his life "in frame." Were we standing before the painting, we would see that he does so in almost perfect life-scale: he is the beholder's mirror image. We know very little about Smith's actual biography. There were at least a dozen men of the same name who *might* have been the artist. Only two pieces of evidence seem firmly attributable: the painting itself (it is signed); and a record indicating that Harvard College hired "Major" Thomas Smith in 1680 to produce a copy of a 1633 painting of Puritan minister William Ames. The original by Dutch artist Willem van der Vliet crossed the Atlantic with Ames's widow a few years after its completion. Smith's copy has disappeared, and is thought to have been destroyed in a fire in 1764.[102] The original now belongs to Harvard University. With so little definite biographical information available, scholars cannot be absolutely certain that Smith was Puritan. The content of his poem, his dress and comportment, his hairstyle, his employ by (Puritan) Harvard College to copy the painting of the Puritan divine Ames, and the fact that other portraits by the same hand depict eminent Puritans, however, provide substantial ballast for my identification of Smith as Puritan. A document discovered by Jason LaFountain in the course of his master's thesis research provides further corroboration, identifying Smith with militant Puritanism in seventeenth-century England. In a commonplace book entry dated 18 September 1792, Samuel Dexter (1726-1810) remarked, "My mother has the [coat of] arms of an ancestor of her's, of the name of Smith. She has his portrait too, daubed by himself, with some lines in verse at the bottom, of his

---

102. Louisa Dresser, *Seventeenth-Century Painting in New England: A Catalogue of an Exhibition Held at the Worcester Art Museum in Collaboration with the American Antiquarian Society, July and August 1934* (Worcester: Worcester Art Museum, 1935), 133-38; see also Thomas Smith pages on the Worcester Art Museum website.

**32. Frontispiece, John Bunyan, *Pilgrim's Progress*, 1749.** The William Andrews Clark Memorial Library, University of California, Los Angeles, PR3330.A1 1749.

Mr IOHN BUNYAN

own composing, in the style of the day. He was an officer in Cromwell's army, and had also the command of a fort, or garrison."[103]

When I began my research, I was struck by the loose similarity between the Smith *Self-Portrait* and the frontispiece of John Bunyan's *Pilgrim's Progress* (fig. 32). Bunyan published the first edition of his book in 1678 — the volume was

103. Quoted in LaFountain, "Reflections on the Funerary Monuments and Burying Grounds," 200, n.321; see also *Samuel Dexter Commonplace Book*, Massachusetts Historical Society, Ms. SB-219; mfm P-201, 18 September 1792, 276-77.

immensely popular, exported widely, immediately, and, importantly, to Boston. Numerous editions followed in rapid succession, with a first Boston imprint in 1681. But the frontispiece that caught my eye was a 1728 version (similar to the 1749 image shown in figure 32). When I began to do some background checking, I discovered that the 1684 version lacked the prominent skull, which seems not to have appeared before 1695, where it showed up as a small skull and crossbones on a coffin. Here I wish only to suggest (and I feel secure in doing so) that the Smith *Self-Portrait* exhibits some of the same habits of imagination, vision, and thought as the Bunyan frontispiece and the story it summarizes.[104] The Bunyan picture too, based on English artist Robert White's so-called *Sleeping Portrait of Bunyan*, surrounds a portrait bust with emblems of Christian pilgrimage — and Bunyan, too, tells a tale of the progress of the Puritan Christian soul.[105] Bunyan and Smith were both deeply engaged in artistic projects that involved searching the self for resemblance to types of Christian piety and to patterns of Christian life trajectory; both inhabited a culture that described this sort of "progress" as pilgrimage.[106]

The Smith *Self-Portrait*, the carved gravestones, and the Bunyan frontispiece all feature a named self in the center, surrounded and framed by typological or emblematic life-references. In Smith's case the emblems include a maritime battle scene out the "imaginary" window in the painting's upper left corner, the poem and the skull upon which Smith's proper right hand rests, and the curtain with tassel in the painting's upper right corner.

Of the Boston-area Thomas Smiths who might most likely have been the painter, several had maritime careers — and a number of historians who have written about this image in the past have attempted to identify the battle represented in the window. This is a worthwhile task (in its particularity this fight does seem to indicate a specific historic referent), but it is not the one I undertake in this essay. Despite the painter's elusive earthly biography, he almost certainly shared his contemporaries' estimation of the faithful Protestant life as spiritual warfare. Popular devotional writer Edward Pearse maintained his own certainty that "this life is little else but a perpetual war and conflict with Lusts, with Devils, with Afflictions, and with Temptations; hence 'tis call'd *a fight, a warfare,* and the like: and the enemies with which they in this warfare have to

104. See Hall, *Worlds of Wonder*, 120, on Bunyan in this context; see also Hall, *Worlds of Wonder*, 128, on biography and exemplary lives.

105. Interestingly, note the visual similarity between the overall form of the stones under discussion and the configuration of the gates of paradise at the upper right hand corner of figure 32.

106. LaFountain productively pursued for these and similar objects the idea of life as pilgrimage; LaFountain, "Reflections on the Funerary Monuments and Burying Grounds," 120-36.

**33. Thomas Smith *Self-Portrait*, detail of Fig. 2, showing skull, poem, and heart in lace.**

grapple, are formidable enemies: *We wrestle not,* says the Apostle, *with flesh and blood, but with principalities and Powers, and Spiritual wickednesses,* Eph. 6, 12,13."[107] John Foxe's ever popular Book of Martyrs concurred: life was "perpetual warfare on earth."[108] Only God's gracious gift of faith provided any fortification or defense for the soul. "Death, when ever it comes," continued Pearse, "will turn your Conflicts into Victory; this . . . Field of Blood (for such is this world) into a . . . Throne of Glory."[109]

The poem that Smith painted at the lower left communicates a similar worldview:

Why why should I the World be minding
therein a world of Evils Finding.
  Then Farwell World: Farwell thy Jarres
  thy Joies thy Toies thy Wiles thy Warrs,

107. Pearse, *The Great Concern,* 203-4.

108. In the words of martyr John Bradford: ". . . forasmuch as the life of man is a perpetual warfare upon earth, let us run with you to the battle that is set before us, and like good warriors of Jesus Christ, please him who hath chosen us to be soldiers"; Foxe, *Acts and Monuments* 6:58-65.

109. Pearse, *The Great Concern,* 203.

Truth Sounds Retreat: I am not sorye.
   The Eternal Drawes to him my heart
    By Faith (which can thy Force Subvert)
To Crowne me (after Grace) with Glory.

Here death, the skull, as Max Cavitch has recently pointed out, literally consumes "the World" (fig. 33).[110] The poet Smith maintains, however, that faith subverts the world's "Force" and glory sustains the soul.

The appropriation of a skull in this fashion was by this time, of course, a familiar device on both sides of the Atlantic. In Smith's own Boston community, Puritan minister John Cotton had commented, in a passage that recalls the hazards of visiting seventeenth-century burial grounds, on the uses and abuses of obtaining such things as skulls for memento mori objects: "A man passing through a burying place may see a dead man's scalpe cast up, and thereby [justifiably] take occasion from the present object to meditate (for the present) on his mortality, and to prepare for like change." Despite Cotton's subsequent cautionary remarks against taking the skull back home to be used repeatedly, to be depended upon as such an aid, Calvinist Protestants clearly did employ skulls and other death objects in the practice of meditation on death, or at least they were happy to represent themselves doing so.[111]

I will return to the skull, but first a few words about the drapery in the upper right-hand corner of the painting. Like the view out the window and the memento mori arrangement of skull and poem, the drape or swag in the background was a conventional standard of western portrait painting by the seventeenth century. Smith's drape, while entirely ordinary, served several functions. Its sense of "staging" heightened the drama of the scene; it implied (as in the Bradstreet poem quoted earlier) "oblivions curtains," the curtain drawn by death over all mortal beings. It also represented the veil of the temple, signaled so frequently in gravestone carving of Smith's time and place, through which the elect entered into heavenly glory. The golden tassel, as drapery tie, thus had both general and specific significance — which comes into focus when considered in the context of this essay's earlier discussion of tassels on pulpit drapings,

---

110. Cavitch, "Interiority and Artifact," 100.

111. John Cotton, *Modest and Cleare Answer*, 20: "If he . . . keepe that dead mans scalpe in his Closet, or Bed-chamber, to be an ordinary helpe to him, to put him in minde dayly of his mortality: Now in so doing he make an Image of it." Cotton discussed this subject in the context of his criticism of "set formes of prayer." Hambrick-Stowe (*Practice of Piety*, 234-36) concludes that there is evidence that New Englanders nonetheless did regularly use "death objects" in their meditative practices and even "in their devotional Closets," as depicted, for example, in the frontispiece of Williamson's *Sword of the Spirit* (London: 1613).

**34. Jabez Fuller stone, Middleborough, Massachusetts, 1728, detail, showing skull with inverted heart nose.** Photo: Sally M. Promey

palls, and gravestones (figs. 17-19). While such tassels were common features of portraits elsewhere in the colonies and in Europe, this painting is the only seventeenth-century Boston portrait to depict such a prominent golden tassel. In addition to its standard domestic signification, here it also indicates the temple veil, the sacramental veil of flesh opening into the heavens. Diagonally across the painting, Smith opposes this veil's flesh of Christ (consumed by earthly Christians in every celebration of the Lord's Supper) with death's consumption of the World.

This painting might be justifiably considered as a double self-portrait. Smith is represented both by his mortal visage and by the skull he grasps. The skull speaks in the first person *as* Smith: "Why should I [Smith] the world be minding. . . ." And yet, as others have observed, this skull, with its too-round eyes, its inverted heart nose, and its regular row of way-too-many tiny teeth, is not a "real" skull, but a deliberately stylized one.[112] This skull is the skull of the stone carvers (cf. figs. 34 and 8), not the remains of a human body. Furthermore, as Roger Stein first pointed out, the odd tilt of the poem on the table

112. This stylization has already been noted by historians such as Roger Stein and, most recently, Max Cavitch.

35. **Thomas Smith *Self-Portrait*, detail of Fig. 2, showing Smith and lace.**

serves another purpose besides allowing the beholder to read the words inscribed on the sheet. Smith's stylized skull with framed text below announces its visual correlation with the carvers' stones in the burial grounds. A part of the eeriness of this painting resides in the fact that death (the skull) and not Thomas Smith most directly addresses the viewer. The aging artist assumed posthumous beholding. And the visual rhyming of skull/inscription and head/ lace is striking enough (to the extent even of the "twin" inverted heart in the lace itself; see fig. 33) to suggest conscious analogy, a visual parallel between one and the other.[113] Like Thomas Dudley, Smith already carries a death's head on

113. Joy Heyrman, in a response to my first public presentation of this research in 2003, brought this detail in the painting to my attention.

his shoulders.[114] *Lively* stones (in the burial ground) and the speaking dead (Smith) catch the eye and activate both remembrance and self-examination.

Smith's visual punning expands upon the two hearts (in skull nose-hole and lace) and draws attention to the dark-on-light, light-on-dark reversal of text and lace. The picture links writing on a page, or stone, with "writing" on Smith, inscribing his body or "heart" (fig. 35). The lace also shares certain visual characteristics of the floral motifs carved on gravestones. Though Smith speaks, through the skull, like a ventriloquist, from beyond the grave, he claims authorship and voice in the elegiac mode, in which, customarily, the words of the deceased address survivors at the graveside in poetic form.[115] Under ultraviolet illumination, we can see that Smith has "corrected" the more usual identification of the sitter by name and age, inserting his own TS monogram on the finished canvas instead. This emendation highlights the painting's departure from expected "portrait" conventions; and, in a related strategy, it provided Smith with an opportunity to sign both painting and poem at once. For whatever else this painting is, it is also a visual assertion of artistic vocation. As the poem and vanitas skull suggest, Smith is not without ambivalence about his art — and the mirror metaphor contains and reflects a similar tension. The painter might, in his ambivalence, be profitably compared with preacher/poet Edward Taylor's anxieties about his literary art and with John Cotton in the latter's explicit efforts to balance "arte and prophecy" in sermon writing.[116] Smith affixed his name to — he "signed" — both painting and poem, which in themselves ultimately functioned as "signs" of his own Christian pilgrimage and election by grace.

In fact, if the reader assents to the skull-and-tilted-page tombstone analogy, Smith signs painting, poem, *and* carved stone. He thus sanctifies all three arts in the service of a godly ideal, and he demonstrates his own proficiency in two of them. (In this context, it seems useful to point out that carvers some-

114. According to Josiah Flint's epitaph, stones *did* speak, implicating readers/listeners: the "lamenting stone doth speake/his tomb stone crys repent and souls to save/doth preach repentance from his very grave" to those who walk among the tombs; "Epitaphs at Dorchester," 382. A viewing context in which the portrait was likely seen in a domestic space incorporating tomb-shaped broadside elegies supports this interpretation. Portraits in New England were often associated with the absence of the one depicted; family members sent portraits across the Atlantic, often when the one depicted did not travel. Death was here the final absence. Contemporary portraitists, furthermore, would also have been familiar with the iconography of death. In addition to their other tasks, they were employed, for example, to paint death's heads on coffins, design funerary broadsides, and paint funerary hatchments with coats of arms.

115. On elegy and "ventriloquism," see Brown, "Orbits of Reading," 132.

116. Lisa M. Gordis, *Opening Scripture: Biblical Reading and Interpretive Authority in Puritan New England* (Chicago: University of Chicago Press, 2003), 7.

**36.** **Pierpont stone (detail of Fig. 1), showing carver's initials at top left and right of celestial floral motif (NL for Nathaniel Lamson).** Photo: Sally M. Promey

times added their initials to the stones they produced, as in the Pierpont stone on which a youthful Nathaniel Lamson collaborated with his father; fig. 36.) Furthermore, not only has Smith, painter, "stone carver," *and* poet, composed these verses, he has also written them out in his own hand on the painting's surface. Literacy in the seventeenth century did not necessarily carry the assumption that the reader could also write. Handwriting was an additional skill, not acquired by everyone. It carried elevated associations of art and learning as well as commerce, since merchants were among those who needed to learn to write.[117]

More than simply the frame of the mirror into which he peers so intently, more even than the "frame" of life emblems he paints around his mirror image, Smith's "frame," as his poem suggests, is a frame of "Glory." The artist construes as his own both heavenly glory and the glory of his artistry in its service, salvation coexisting in balanced tension with a measure of earthly fame, self-examination with self-display. Like his contemporary John Bunyan, Smith gives us a Puritan pilgrim's "allegory" of vision and creativity, human and divine.

117. See Tamara Plakins Thornton, *Handwriting in America: A Cultural History* (New Haven: Yale University Press, 1996), 3-18.

125

Eyes, as organs of vision and as portholes or windows of the soul, loom large in this picture — and Smith underscores his interest in this visual sensory organ by painting his piercing blue eyes with costly ultramarine pigment.[118]

Smith painted himself "contained." Placing art in the frame of Puritan belief, he looked at his reflection, not at the beholder (only his reflection looked back at the descendants he assumed would stand before the painting). In his mirror, Smith examined himself as Puritan and as artist: this was both a spiritual and an artistic exercise. Given the Puritan theology of mirrors that the man of letters who wrote this poem and painted this picture likely knew, it is tempting to speculate about the actual object of Smith's sight. Looking in the mirror of piety, the saint ultimately and ideally saw not his own countenance but the Image of Christ looking back. This vision would have assured — and empowered — Thomas Smith the artist and Puritan, as well as his familial beholders.

Increase Mather was typical in writing his spiritual autobiography for his descendants as he neared the end of his life. The text he produced was also typical in its representation of the practice of the self embedding itself, framing itself, in time and eternity. "Writing of your former and present life," Puritan Jonathan Mitchell maintained, "is *a thing of endless use.*"[119] Likewise the aging Thomas Smith, painting his self-portrait, observed and recorded his former and present life, his spiritual pilgrimage. In the process, he set his own image in a godly frame and he offered this pattern to his family as part of their inheritance.[120] Simultaneously an assertion of Smith's sanctification (and the sanctity of his vocation as an artist) *and* an invitation to repeated introspection extended to members and generations of his household, Smith's painting remained among his descendants into the twentieth century. Having first made a brief stop at the American Antiquarian Society, it is now part of the collection of the Worcester Art Museum.[121]

The Thomas Smith *Self-Portrait* belongs to a larger context of devotional

118. Ultramarine would have been a highly unusual pigment in a colonial context. Sign paint was standard; ultramarine, by contrast, was a costly import.

119. Jonathan Mitchell, *A Discourse of the Glory to Which God hath called Believers by Jesus Christ* (Boston, 1721), 282. Juliet Fleming has analyzed the "physical properties of language" for this period and the century earlier in her book on writing practices in early modern England and the "social and physical materiality of texts" (Fleming, *Graffiti and the Writing Arts,* 12-13). "[T]he poetic line was a visual as well as an aural unit, which is to say that all poems were, at least potentially, 'ocular representations'" (p. 18).

120. See Mather's address to his children, "The Autobiography of Increase Mather," ed. M. G. Hall, *Proceedings of the American Antiquarian Society* 79 (1962): 277.

121. As a work addressed to the beholder, and because Smith himself "speaks" to the (familial) beholder, the text reads "forward," from the perspective of the person standing in front of the painting, and not in mirror image.

**37. Thomas Smith *Self-Portrait*, in 1934 pre-restoration photograph**
Worcester Art Museum, Worcester, Massachusetts, conservation files.

practices that relied on a fluid relationship between image and text and on multimedia and intermedia reiteration: *re*-reading, wandering *often* among the tombs, looking again and again. Puritan "plain style," in pictures as in texts, concerned neither artlessness nor overt stripped-down simplicity. The key, instead, was correlation with the stylistic conventions of Christian scripture.[122] Overlapping metaphors and interconnected narratives, verbally and visually expressed, constituted, in Jonathan Mitchell's terms, "thing[s] of endless use."

122. Cf. Bercovitch, *Puritan Origins of the American Self,* 29-30.

Their layered, inclusive referents contributed to the "plainness" of plain style: "plain" in the sense of clarity achieved by reiteration and redundancy.[123]

The faint trace of a familiar shape shows up in a 1934 pre-restoration photograph (fig. 37) of the Thomas Smith *Self-Portrait* — and perhaps someone among his relations at one time or another, in wit or wisdom or both, deciphered the painting as Smith's tombstone. More likely, a mid-nineteenth-century family member applied a bit of historicism in the form of a frame with a rounded-arched, probably gilded, liner in an effort to "update" the painting to suit a new décor. Though rounded-arch tabernacle frames were certainly available in the seventeenth century (for mirrors as well as painted portraits), it would be entirely too extravagant to imagine that the elusive ghost painter himself framed his proleptic picture to accentuate its formal and conceptual association with contemporary gravestones.

123. Mitchell, *Discourse of the Glory*, 282.

# The Sympathetic Self in
# American Culture: 1750-1920

DANIEL WICKBERG

Is there a more universally admired and acclaimed sentiment in our culture than sympathy? We send sympathy cards, give sympathy hugs, lend a sympathetic ear, seek out men and women who possess sympathetic personalities. This intersubjective ability to "feel with" the pains and joys and yearnings of others seems to provide what is missing in the fragmented and lonely regime of modern individualism. The capacity for sympathy counteracts our tendency toward isolation, reaching across the chasm of our separate selfhoods to link sensitive souls in a bond that is a kind of foretaste of universal brotherhood. How appropriate, then, that we have come to regard the capacity for sympathy as one of the defining features of a decent, civilized, and morally complete human being, and an important indicator of psychological and spiritual wholeness. Indeed, today we are likely to regard the capacity for sympathy as a far greater good than the capacity for cogent moral and ethical reasoning.

Yet in extolling it in this way, are we perhaps revealing the extent to which a fuller understanding of "sympathy" eludes us? For one thing, as Daniel Wickberg shows in this essay, our high valuation of sympathy is a relatively new phenomenon in Western history. We have not always esteemed sympathy as we do today. It was not considered a virtue in ancient or medieval times, and has had to undergo several stages of dramatic transformation in its cultural meaning since the eighteenth century in order to achieve the high standing it enjoys today. Obvious as the virtue of sympathy now seems to us, it was not obvious to most of our forebears. What then does the prominent role played today by sympathy in our assessment of human actions and experiences tell us about our conceptions of the human person then and now? What assumptions and presuppositions about the nature of the human person lie behind and beneath our culture's emphasis upon the centrality of sympathy? Daniel Wickberg is Associate Professor of History at the University of Texas at Dallas, and author of *The Senses of Humor: Self and Laughter in Modern America* (Ithaca, N.Y.: Cornell University Press, 1998).

*"One's range of sympathy is a measure of his personality, indicating how much or how little of a man he is. . . . [W]hat a person is and what he can understand or enter into through the life of others are very much the same thing."*

Charles Horton Cooley, *Human Nature
and the Social Order* (1902)[1]

In his landmark *The Souls of Black Folk* (1903), W. E. B. Du Bois wrote, "The nineteenth was the first century of human sympathy, — the age when half wonderingly we began to descry in others that transfigured spark of divinity which we call Myself."[2] *Souls* is itself a lengthy experiment in form dedicated to both an analysis of the workings of that human sympathy in creating African American identity (the famous concept of "double consciousness," for instance, is based on the self-alienation involved in seeing oneself through the eyes of others), and to the instantiation of the dynamics of the sympathetic imagination in its form. It is a plea for sympathy across what Du Bois called, variously, the color line, the veil, the outer world. The oppositions of skins and souls, objects and subjects, exterior conditions and interior states, material life and ideal purpose, self and other, structure the text, as Du Bois alternately documents the external historical conditions of black life and then seeks to peel away that visible material world to draw his readers into a sympathetic identification with the inner lives of a people. Its surface concerns are those of race, equality, and black identity in post-Reconstruction America, but the terms in which it views those concerns owe much to a modern liberal conception of personhood that is quite independent of specific racial content. That model of personhood brings together the boundless self of liberal individualism — atomistic, self-conscious, autonomous, unique — with the capacity for the dissolution of that self in its identification with others. The mechanism of that dissolution of self has, for the past two and a half centuries, been conceptualized as something called "sympathy." Human sympathy, as Du Bois described it — even as he misplaced its origins in the nineteenth rather than the eighteenth century — brought to-

1. Charles Horton Cooley, *Human Nature and the Social Order* (New York: Schocken Books, 1964), 140.

2. W. E. B. Du Bois, *The Souls of Black Folk* (New York: Signet, 1995), 235. Future references parenthetically abbreviated SFB in text.

gether the Emersonian idea of the divine self and its boundless interior depth, with the heightened consciousness of the interiority of other people.[3]

Modern Western individualism — and particularly its American variant — developed simultaneously with the ideology of sympathy. The consciousness of self and the consciousness of the selves of others are part of the same historical formation, shaping what I am calling "the sympathetic self" — the ubiquitous but unheralded understanding of the person characteristic of modern liberal thought. This historical formation has been difficult to see, because individualism and sympathy have frequently been associated with diametrically opposed and separate value systems. When we think of individualism, we picture the atomistic self of Lockean philosophy; the abstract person independent of social relations; antistate laissez-faire liberalism; modern economics; the free and rational agent.[4] When we invoke sympathy, on the other hand, we think of the primacy of the social bond; the obligation to others above self-interest; emotional identification over rational and empirical perception; socialism and humanitarianism; solidarity and group consciousness. To the fierce partisans of either free-market capitalism or humanitarian socialism, the idea that they share an ideological outlook with their bitterest political enemies is difficult, if not impossible, to see. Individualism, we might imagine, emphasizes the specific concrete difference of persons from one another; sympathy, on the other hand, seems to be the great solvent of difference, predicated on a shared common nature. But if we were really all alike in every way that mattered, we would scarcely need the instrument of sympathy to overcome our differences. Sympathy, as Du Bois indicated, is based on a projected consciousness of the self, an ascription of selfhood to others; it finds the "me" in the life of others, and so begins with a conception of individual selfhood — "the transfigured spark of divinity which we call Myself." But it also starts with a consciousness of

3. The best source for understanding the intellectual lineage of Du Bois's concept of sympathy — one that identifies both the psychology of William James, American Transcendentalism, and the Scottish tradition leading back to Adam Smith, on the one hand, and the German idealism of the Hegelian tradition, on the other — is Shamoon Zamir, *Dark Voices: W. E. B. Du Bois and American Thought, 1888-1903* (Chicago: University of Chicago Press, 1995), 42-45, 105-106.

4. On individualism, see Steven Lukes, *Individualism* (New York: Harper and Row, 1973); Louis Dumont, *From Mandeville to Marx: The Genesis and Triumph of Economic Ideology* (Chicago: University of Chicago Press, 1977); Dumont, *Essays on Individualism: Modern Ideology in Anthropological Perspective* (Chicago: University of Chicago Press, 1986); Thomas C. Heller, Morton Sosna, and David E. Wellbery, eds., *Reconstructing Individualism: Autonomy, Individuality, and the Self in Western Thought* (Stanford: Stanford University Press, 1986). On the conception of the self as a form of personhood, the most important work is Charles Taylor, *Sources of the Self: The Making of the Modern Identity* (Cambridge: Harvard University Press, 1989).

difference, that a barrier is being both overcome and emphasized at the same time, that, in Du Bois's words, "clodhoppers and peasants, and tramps and thieves, and millionaires and — sometimes — Negroes, became throbbing souls," to be identified with the "myself" (SBF, p. 135). But that "myself" is identified as neither peasant nor millionaire, but somehow free of all external classificatory markings.[5]

Historians have given a great deal of attention to the idea of sympathy, particularly in the nineteenth century, but have tended to view it primarily in terms of sentimentalism, or in its eighteenth-century form, as part of the culture of sensibility.[6] That is, the concern has been with an understanding of sympathy as non-intellectual, emotional, a foregrounding of intuitive emotional response to particulars over commitment to rationality, principle, and universality. To the extent that sentimentalism has replaced or supplemented "romanticism" as a category used by historians, it has been figured as a reaction

5. It is common in much current cultural studies literature to see the lack of marking as a false universalism concealing a particular social identity which then becomes the invisible norm by which deviation is defined. Such, for instance, is the position taken by much of the current literature on whiteness or masculinity as a social category or identity. My point here is not to deny this, but to focus attention on the way the lack of marking is more than just a smokescreen for racial, class, or gender privilege; it is also an attempt to find a subjective identity free of all external markings, a pre-social autonomous being.

6. The literature on sympathy and sentimentalism is voluminous. The best starting place for the current understanding of sentimentalism is the so-called Douglas-Tompkins debate. See Ann Douglas, *The Feminization of American Culture* (New York: Knopf, 1977), and Jane P. Tompkins, *Sensational Designs: The Cultural Work of American Fiction, 1790-1860* (New York: Oxford University Press, 1985). Recent work on the late eighteenth century includes Andrew Burstein, *Sentimental Democracy: The Evolution of America's Romantic Self-Image* (New York: Hill and Wang, 1999); Julia Stern, *The Plight of Feeling: Sympathy and Dissent in the Early American Novel* (Chicago: University of Chicago Press, 1997); Elizabeth Barnes, *States of Sympathy: Democracy and Feeling in the Early American Novel* (New York: Columbia University Press, 1997); Julie Ellison, *Cato's Tears and the Making of Anglo-American Emotion* (Chicago: University of Chicago Press, 1999); and Bruce Burgett, *Sentimental Bodies: Sex, Gender, and Citizenship in the Early Republic* (Princeton: Princeton University Press, 1998). On the notion of sensibility and its relation to sentimentalism, see Janet Todd, *Sensibility: An Introduction* (New York: Methuen, 1986); G. J. Barker-Benfield, *The Culture of Sensibility: Sex and Society in Eighteenth-Century Britain* (Chicago: University of Chicago Press, 1992); Markman Ellis, *The Politics of Sensibility* (New York: Cambridge University Press, 1996). On nineteenth-century sentimentalism, see Shirley Samuels, ed., *The Culture of Sentiment: Race, Gender, and Sentimentality in Nineteenth-Century America* (New York: Oxford University Press, 1992); Kristin Boudreau, *Sympathy in American Literature: American Sentiments from Jefferson to the Jameses* (Gainesville: University Press of Florida, 2002); Glenn Hendler, *Public Sentiments: Structures of Feeling in Nineteenth-Century American Literature* (Chapel Hill: University of North Carolina Press, 2001).

to the inadequacies of Enlightenment rationalism. In much recent historical and social thought, individualism and sympathy have been seen as parts of opposed systems of values. If individualism, for instance, is viewed as characteristic of antebellum market capitalism and the centrality of self-interest as a mechanism of economic life, sympathy is viewed as characteristic of the socialistic and cooperative efforts of late-nineteenth-century reformers who rejected the terms of market capitalism, or the humanitarian movements of the era that elevated concern with suffering and cruelty over abstract moral principle. Sympathy, in this view, was a response to the corrosive effects of untrammeled individualism, a rejection of laissez-faire ideology and an embrace of social solidarity.[7] Similarly, historians have constructed the gender system of antebellum society in terms of the ideology of separate spheres. The masculine world of public life, market society, and political action was figured as aggressive, competitive, and driven by self-interest, all attributes associated with masculine nature; the feminine world of the home, on the other hand, was based on nurture, sentiment and sympathy as a counterbalance to the market, a "haven in a heartless world."[8] Even as historians have recently criticized the inadequacy of this gender ideology for understanding nineteenth-century American culture and have moved sentiment and sympathy out into the marketplace and the world of masculine action, they have tended to import the terms of affect and sentiment into the market, rather than understanding sympathy apart from the culture of sentimentalism.[9] The identification of sympathy with sentimentalism has im-

7. See, for example, Bruce Mazlish, *A New Science: The Breakdown of Connections and the Birth of Sociology* (University Park: Pennsylvania State University Press, 1989), in which the rise of sympathy is seen as a response to a market society in which the "cash nexus" has become the sole tie between persons. For a partial challenge to this view, see Jeffrey Sklansky, *The Soul's Economy: Market Society and Selfhood in American Thought, 1830-1920* (Chapel Hill: University of North Carolina Press, 2002).

8. On the ideology of separate spheres, see Barbara Welter, "The Cult of True Womanhood: 1820-1860," *American Quarterly* 18 (1966): 151-74; Nancy F. Cott, *The Bonds of Womanhood: "Woman's Sphere" in New England, 1780-1835* (New Haven: Yale University Press, 1977); Kathryn Kish Sklar, *Catharine Beecher: A Study in American Domesticity* (New York: W. W. Norton, 1973); Christopher Lasch, *Haven in a Heartless World: The Family Besieged* (New York: Basic Books, 1977); Linda Kerber, "Separate Spheres, Female Worlds, Woman's Place: The Rhetoric of Women's History," *Journal of American History* 75 (June 1988): 9-39.

9. On male sentimentality, see Caleb Crain, *American Sympathy: Men, Friendship, and Literature in the New Nation* (New Haven: Yale University Press, 2001), and Mary Chapman and Glenn Hendler, eds., *Sentimental Men: Masculinity and the Politics of Affect in American Culture* (Berkeley: University of California Press, 1999). On sentiment in market culture, see Elizabeth Alice White, "Charitable Calculations: Fancywork, Charity, and the Culture of the Sentimental Market, 1830-1880," in *The Middling Sorts: Explorations in the History of the American Middle Class*, ed. Burton J. Bledstein and Robert D. Johnston (New York: Routledge, 2001), 73-85; Lori

peded the understanding of the broader role of sympathy in spheres of American life not usually associated with sentimentalism: political economy, moral philosophy, medicine, early psychology and social science, nationalism, ethnic and class consciousness, proslavery as well as abolitionist thought.[10]

That the concept of sympathy could give shape to both the emotional subjectivism of sentimental response and the analytical objectivism of social science indicates just how protean a concept it has been. What these diverse spheres of American culture have in common is an underlying model of the person; the same person who can get outside of himself or herself in order to experience and "feel" the pain of others, to commiserate and extend compassion to those who suffer, is also the person who can achieve a sense of distance from the self and its immediate responses by adopting an external point of view, by reflecting upon the world of selves as a world of objects to be analyzed. In other words, greater subjective capacity has functioned as a necessary condition for objective self-transcendence. To enter into the lives and minds of others has required both a deep sense of self and a willingness to distance oneself from an attachment to that self. It has required a "double consciousness." Sympathy has meant both an expansion out of the self and an expansion of the self; self-transcendence and self-fulfillment.

Many of the contradictions of American — and more generally, modern Western — culture can be found in the values and modes of being associated with the sympathetic self. The simultaneous valorization of individual autonomy, on the one hand, and the capacity and willingness to adapt to the needs of others, on the other; the romantic celebration of community and group identification, and the equally romantic celebration of a critical alienation from the conformity of mainstream society; the appreciation of difference and diversity in a society increasingly made culturally homogenous by the forces of market capitalism; the commitment to equality of persons as sharing a common humanity, and the necessary inequality between persons giving and receiving sympathy; sympathy as a stabilizing antidote to a fluctuating world of instrumental market exchange, and sympathy as itself an imaginative form of exchange of feelings and situations. Sympathy, then, has not just been a feature of sentimental culture; it has been one of the key ideas of modern culture more generally. It has allowed for a form of personhood that simultaneously empha-

---

Merish, *Sentimental Materialism: Gender, Commodity Culture, and Nineteenth-Century American Literature* (Durham: Duke University Press, 2000); Joseph Fichtelberg, *Critical Fictions: Sentiment and the American Market 1780-1870* (Athens: University of Georgia Press, 2003).

10. For an exception to this, see Amit S. Rai, *Rule of Sympathy: Sentiment, Race, and Power 1750-1850* (New York: Palgrave, 2002), 18, where, following Markman Ellis, he identifies a wide range of discourses in which the idea of sympathy is central.

sizes individual and group differences between people and the oneness of a common humanity.

One of the keys to understanding the history of the sympathetic self is the recognition that sympathy has had a number of meanings in its modern incarnations; any attempt to fix the meaning of sympathy as, for instance, natural emotional feeling for the suffering of others, is bound to overlook a great deal of what sympathy has meant. Sympathy has sometimes been seen as artificial or theatrical rather than natural, cognitive or imaginative rather than simply emotional, not itself a feeling but a faculty or process by which particular feelings are shared, and concerned with shared happiness and pleasure as well as suffering. A fixed definition of sympathy is fundamentally unhistorical; it runs the risk of converting past meanings into the present and thus obscuring important historical and ideological differences. As a generation of historians of political language has taught us, if one assumes the modern liberal definition of "liberty" in instances in which one finds the word in the past, one is bound to misread eighteenth-century political ideology as liberal, instead of being governed by a set of values at odds with liberalism.[11] So with sympathy. Instead of starting with a fixed definition of sympathy, then, it makes sense to look at the shifting meaning of the term, what definitions have been created historically, and how they act as indices to particular conceptions of personhood and social order. In this sense, sympathy can be understood as a keyword, a term whose changing significations reveal central features of modern culture.[12]

For instance, the distinction between sympathy and empathy — feeling with and feeling "into," with the greater intensity of identification with the object associated with the latter — is a product of early-twentieth-century psychology and aesthetic theory. Prior to Theodor Lipps's invention of the concept of einfühling, translated as empathy by E. B. Tichener in 1909, the idea was folded into the meaning of sympathy.[13] By this it should not be understood that nineteenth-century thinkers had separate concepts of "feeling with" and "feeling into," and simply used one word to indicate both. Rather, they configured the relationship between the psyche and the world of others in such a way that they saw no difference between these two modes of feeling. The invention of the concept of empathy actually redefined the meaning of sympathy by drawing a distinction where there had been none before, in effect defining sympathy as "not empathy." We should be careful, then, not to import the distinction between

11. Joyce Appleby, *Capitalism and a New Social Order: The Republican Vision of the 1790s* (New York: New York University Press, 1984), 15-23.

12. On the notion of keywords, see Raymond Williams, *Keywords: A Vocabulary of Culture and Society* (New York: Oxford University Press, 1983).

13. *OED*, s.v. "empathy."

sympathy and empathy into the nineteenth century, where it was not part of the mental equipment available to those who spoke of sympathy. This is, I think, a fairly obvious example of the cultural redefinition of a word, precisely because we have the coining of a new word to indicate a new concept; most of the ways in which words change their meanings are subtler and less obvious than this, and must be inferred from patterns of use and context. More broadly, this example points to the cultural historian's need to see changing definitions of words such as sympathy as indicators of a changing mental universe, and in this case, a changing understanding of the relationship between selves and others.

The general context for the emergence of sympathy as a social value lay in the challenges to the notion of fixed, rank-ordered or hierarchical societies in early modern Europe and America. The simultaneous rise of commercial wealth and its challenge to landed wealth, the fluidity of identities under new market processes, new forms of intellectual authority based on empiricism or critical reason rather than tradition and established authority, republican ideology and its appeal to natural law, social contract and notions of economic independence over established forms of top-down political order, ongoing Protestant challenges to established religious authority: the list is a familiar one. The most immediate problem for seventeenth- and eighteenth-century social thought was what was to replace traditional forms of order that to many observers seemed to be eroding. One set of responses to the perception of disorder was to emphasize the necessity of a fixed hierarchical order based on absolutist political authority. Such was the response associated with Thomas Hobbes, who attempted to establish a fixed social and political order that was consistent with the new empiricist and scientific modes of thought. Another was to reaffirm in more rigorous terms the Christian view of man, in which political authority was derived from man's fallen state and his consequent incapacity to govern himself. Such was the response developed by Jean Calvin and his followers, including the English Puritans. Both Hobbes and the Calvinists, despite their fundamentally different world views, shared a conception of human nature as irrational, destructive, and driven by selfish motives, a nature in which violent emotions — referred to as "the passions" — and desire for self-aggrandizement were the primary defining features. The disorderly nature of man required an order imposed from without; there was no reliable source of order from within.

The specter of man as an egoistic, passion-driven being inspired a range of responses from those who sought to legitimate new forms of political, economic, and social order. The notion that human nature was fundamentally rational, and therefore capable of being governed by rational desire, defined as "interest," rather than the irrational desire of "passion," was one such response.[14] The notions that rational self-interest could regulate human behavior or, alternatively, that propertied independence could sustain public-minded virtue and secure republican institutions, were two more counters to the image of man as inherently sinful and disorderly. For an understanding of the idea of sympathy, however, the most important attempt to sweep aside the threat of Hobbesian and Calvinist images of humanity was the view of human nature as inherently benevolent. This view has been traced from the latitudinarian thought of British thinkers, such as the Cambridge Platonists, of the seventeenth century, through the writings of Shaftesbury in the early eighteenth century, and to the principle thinkers of the Scottish Enlightenment — Hutcheson, Smith, Kames, and Stewart among them — and on to the American revolutionary generation through figures such as John Witherspoon, Benjamin Rush, and Thomas Jefferson.[15] As opposed to the view that grounded morality and social action in rationality or self-interest, the benevolentist outlook insisted not that man was necessarily more rational than Hobbes or Calvin had suggested, but that his emotions and feelings were not so malignant or disorderly. The benevolent or "social" feelings were, according to this line of thought, the dominant ones in man's nature; man was inherently sociable, kind, and moral. As Jefferson put it, "Morals were too essential to the happiness of man to be risked on the incertain combinations of the head. She laid their foundation therefore in sentiment, not in science."[16] The notion that the morality governing human interaction was a product of intuitive feeling rather than either rational reflection or submission to external political or religious authority represented a revolution in understandings of human nature.

The main concepts associated with the benevolentist school of thought, and the Scottish moral philosophers in particular, were those of the moral sense, and of sympathy or the sympathetic imagination. The notion of the

14. Albert O. Hirschman, *The Passions and the Interests: Political Arguments for Capitalism Before Its Triumph* (Princeton: Princeton University Press, 1977).

15. On the lineage of the benevolent image of man, see T. A. Roberts, *The Concept of Benevolence: Aspects of Eighteenth-Century Moral Philosophy* (London: Macmillan, 1973); John K. Sherriff, *The Good-Natured Man: The Evolution of a Moral Ideal, 1660-1800* (University: University of Alabama Press, 1982). For the influence of the Scottish Enlightenment on American thought, see Richard B. Sher and Jeffrey R. Smitten, eds., *Scotland and America in the Age of Enlightenment* (Edinburgh: Edinburgh University Press, 1990); Terence Martin, *The Instructed Vision: Scottish Common Sense Philosophy and the Origins of American Fiction* (Bloomington: Indiana University Press, 1961); Douglas Sloan, *The Scottish Enlightenment and the American College Ideal* (New York: Teachers College Press, 1971); Garry Wills, *Inventing America: Jefferson's Declaration of Independence* (Garden City, New York: Doubleday, 1978).

16. Thomas Jefferson, Letter to Maria Cosway, Paris, October 12, 1786, in *Writings*, ed. Merrill D. Peterson (New York: Library of America, 1984), p. 874.

moral sense, articulated specifically in the thought of Shaftesbury and Francis Hutcheson, was an extension of the sensationalist and faculty psychology developed by Locke in the *Essay Concerning Human Understanding* (1690); it is important to note that the same blank-slate psychology and empiricism that underlay liberal individualism in the Lockean mode also underwrote the Scottish moral philosophy. Man was not born with an innate understanding of morality or moral principles, but with a faculty of moral perception that allowed him to make immediate intuitive judgments of right and wrong, just as he was not born with knowledge of the external world, but was able to attain such knowledge through his senses. The moral sense acted as a kind of internal guide, independent of moral teachings, rules, or external authority, by which the person could discern the goodness or evil of any particular act. In the thought that followed Hutcheson on this point, the specific content of moral teachings might vary from society to society, but the impulse to morality was not a product of society and its teachings, nor was it dependent upon society in any way. Rather, the reverse was the case: man's natural possession of a moral sense laid the foundation for society by drawing people toward one another, just as human nature in the pre-social state paved the way for the social contract in Lockean political philosophy. Looking inward to the authority of the moral sense pushed man outward to the bonds of society.[17]

Again, Jefferson is instructive, as he inherited and used the weight of the moral sense concept as it had been developed in the eighteenth century. Arguing in 1814 that the Creator had made "the moral principle so much a part of our constitution as that no errors of reasoning or of speculation might lead us astray from its observance in practice," Jefferson describes the moral sense as "a love of others, a sense of duty to them, a moral instinct in short, which prompts us irresistibly to feel and to succour their distresses." He then likens the moral sense to the five senses while at the same time identifying it as a social disposition, thus rooting social feeling in the natural capacity for sensation — moral sensation.

> The creator would indeed have been a bungling artist, had he intended man for a social animal, without planting in him social dispositions. It is true they are not planted in every man; because there is no rule without exceptions; but it is false reasoning which converts exceptions into the general rule. Some men are born without the organs of sight, or of hearing, or without hands. Yet it would be wrong to say that man is born without these faculties; and sight, hearing and hands may with truth enter into the general definition of

17. D. Daiches Raphael, *The Moral Sense* (London: Oxford University Press, 1947); William Frankena, "Hutcheson's Moral Sense Theory," *Journal of the History of Ideas* 16 (1955): 356-75.

Man. The want or imperfection of the moral sense in some men, like the want or imperfection of the senses of sight and hearing in others, is no proof that it is a general characteristic of the species.[18]

What is particularly interesting about Jefferson's use of the concept of the moral sense here is that he describes it as a feeling, a disposition, an instinct, a faculty, and a principle all in the same passage. The faculty of moral perception is equated with an irresistible instinctual feeling for the suffering of others; it is simultaneously a way of experiencing, a capacity for judgment, and a pre-reflective stimulus to action. Importantly, Jefferson blurs the line between the moral sense and sympathy, collapsing the discrimination of good from bad into the ability to identify with the suffering of others.

As the general orientation of benevolentist thought was diffused in the late eighteenth and early nineteenth centuries, and its terms became part of the common coin of educated discourse, the meaning of the key terms — the moral sense, sympathy, the sympathetic imagination, the social feeling, fellow-feeling, sensibility, sentiment, benevolence — tended to bleed into one another. Jefferson, for instance, made no clear distinction between the moral sense and the capacity to feel the distress of others. Hume regularly used the terms "benevolence," "humanity," and "fellow-feeling" as synonyms, thus equating good will toward others with universalism and sympathetic identification.[19] Benjamin Rush casually collapsed sympathy, sensibility, and what he called "the moral faculty" into a single "principle of human nature."[20] The consequence was to conflate immediate perception, moral judgment, and imaginative identification with others. For those steeped in Scottish Common Sense philosophy, which was the dominant school of thought shaping the curriculum of late-eighteenth- and early-nineteenth-century American colleges, the concept of sympathy was infused with meanings associated with sensationalist psychology and moral sense doctrine. The perception of others through the external senses — particularly the sense of sight — seemed to lead immediately to both moral judgment and social feeling.

18. Thomas Jefferson, Letter to Thomas Law, June 13, 1814, in *Writings*, 1337-38.

19. Thomas Schlereth, *The Cosmopolitan Ideal in Enlightenment Thought* (Notre Dame: University of Notre Dame Press, 1977), 60-61.

20. Benjamin Rush, "An Enquiry into the Effects of Public Punishments Upon Criminals, and Upon Society. Read in the Society for Promoting Political Enquiries, Convened at the House of Benjamin Franklin, Esq., in Philadelphia, March 9th, 1787," in *Essays: Literary, Moral and Philosophical*, ed. Michael Meranze (Schenectady: Union College Press, 1988), 82. For good discussions of Rush's concept of sympathy, see Meranze's introduction to this volume as well as Michael Meranze, *Laboratories of Virtue: Punishment, Revolution, and Authority in Philadelphia, 1760-1835* (Chapel Hill: University of North Carolina Press, 1996), 120-27.

If the idea of the moral sense was initially identified most strongly with Hutcheson, the ideas of sympathy and the sympathetic imagination were developed most fully in Adam Smith's *Theory of Moral Sentiments* (1759). Like the moral sense, the idea of sympathy had very broad currency in the late eighteenth and early nineteenth centuries.[21] Its use in the benevolentist philosophy of the era was at once influential in shaping the late-nineteenth- and twentieth-century meanings of sympathy, but also somewhat idiosyncratic in relation to the dominant eighteenth-century meanings of sympathy. In order to make sense of Smith's development of the concept of sympathy — both in relationship to his portrait of market society in the *Wealth of Nations* and to the cultural definitions of selfhood that would stem from it — we need to examine more fully the eighteenth-century meanings of sympathy in which Smith operated.

Because sympathy today is thought of primarily as a feeling associated with a consciousness of the feelings of others, it is difficult to see that in the eighteenth century, and well into the nineteenth as well, the idea of sympathy was grounded in organic and bodily conceptions of personhood and the natural world. Some of these meanings live on in the narrow and technical use of the idea of sympathy in physiology and medicine, but their larger significance has disappeared. The dominant meanings of sympathy in the eighteenth century, in fact, frequently excluded consciousness, will, or motive as ways to understand the connections sympathy drew between persons. Just as our modern conception of empathy was folded into the concept of sympathy before the twentieth century, so were corporeal and occult meanings central to early modern notions of sympathy in ways they are no longer. Those notions are at odds with modern concepts of the dematerialized self and the desacralized world of the scientific imagination. To chart the shift in the meaning of sympathy is to see a gradual dematerialization of personhood, a withdrawal of the sensing, thinking and feeling self from the material and social world, and a reentry into that world on new terms of shared emotion and consciousness.[22]

21. Norman Fiering, "Irresistible Compassion: An Aspect of Eighteenth-Century Sympathy and Humanitarianism," in *Race, Gender, and Rank: Early Modern Ideas of Humanity*, ed. Maryanne Cline Horowitz (Rochester: Rochester University Press, 1992), 387-401; John Stafford, "Sympathy Comes to America," in *Themes and Directions in American Literature*, ed. Ray B. Browne and Donald Pizer (Lafayette, Ind.: Purdue University Studies, 1969), 24-37.

22. I have dealt with this shift from the integration of corporeal, mental, and characterological meanings to the psychological in my discussion of the changing meanings of humor in the modern era; sympathy, like many other terms, follows a similar path. See Daniel Wickberg, *The Senses of Humor: Self and Laughter in Modern America* (Ithaca: Cornell University Press, 1998), 25-34. A very helpful discussion on the dematerialization of modern consumer culture is Jackson Lears, *Fables of Abundance: A Cultural History of Advertising in America* (New York: Basic Books, 1994).

The *Oxford English Dictionary* gives the first definition of sympathy, now obsolete, as "A (real or supposed) affinity between certain things, by virtue of which they are similarly or correspondingly affected by the same influence, affect or influence one another (esp. in some occult way), or attract or tend towards each other." This meaning antedates all later meanings associated with compassion, commiseration, or "fellow-feeling" based on observation of the condition of another by at least a century.[23] There is nothing in this earlier meaning that involves the subjective seeing into the interior life of another; in fact, object-subject relations are configured in an entirely alien way. The attraction that draws persons (or things) toward one another is a force that acts through them, and is not a matter of imagination or mental conception at all. Persons *and* things are held to have attractions (and repulsions — antipathies) in the same kinds of ways. Sympathy in this sense implies a cosmology, an understanding of the world and the things in it as governed by the influence of supernatural forces, harmonies, and unions independent of the intentions or motives of persons. The images of a string vibrating in unison or harmony with that of another, or of objects being drawn to one another by magnetic force, are figures that are invoked again and again into the middle of the nineteenth century to describe sympathy.[24] This notion of sympathy is at odds with the Cartesian dualism that puts consciousness outside a purely material and mechanical world, that rejects the notion of the occult and supernatural influence, that sees sympathy as something in the mind as opposed to in the world.[25]

Closely connected to this idea of a world of influence and affinity — a kind of residual animism — is the medical or physiological understanding of sympathy. Particular bodily organs and parts were held to have a secret or invisible affinity with one another, so that action in one part of the body produced a parallel or corresponding action in another. In particular, irritation or damage to one part of the body was thought to create a similar expression of irritation or

23. *OED*, s.v. "sympathy."

24. The following passage is a good example. "A chord of a musical instrument will vibrate when another in exact unison with it is struck. The human mind may be compared to a finely attuned instrument, upon which the power of sympathy operates in a similar manner." [Anon.], "Sympathy," *Examiner and Hesperian* [Pittsburgh] 2.1 (1840): 9. Note that here the physical vibration has become a metaphor for the activities of the mind, rather than a literal description of the relations of physical affinity.

25. For a good discussion of eighteenth-century meanings of sympathy, see James Rodgers, "Sensibility, Sympathy, Benevolence: Physiology and Moral Philosophy in *Tristram Shandy*," in *Languages of Nature: Critical Essays on Science and Literature*, ed. L. J. Jordanova (New Brunswick: Rutgers University Press, 1986), 117-58; Christopher Lawrence, "The Nervous System and Society in the Scottish Enlightenment," in *Natural Order: Historical Studies of Scientific Culture*, ed. B. Barnes and S. Shapin (London: Sage, 1979), 19-40.

damage in another; the body was a unified system whose parts moved along lines of affinity, just as things and persons in the universe were governed by affinity or sympathy. The organic model of society characteristic of much early modern social thought — probably best known to students of American culture in John Winthrop's famous lay sermon, "A Model of Christian Charity" — saw the relationship of persons to the living social whole as akin to the relationship of body parts to the living organism. The early modern notion of sympathy confirmed this relationship. As late as 1845, even as newer notions of sympathy as interior mental state or feeling were becoming dominant, an anonymous article on sympathy could invoke the notion of physiological sympathy to explain social bonds.

> As the body is a system of organs bound together, and mutually operating by means of animal sympathy, in such a manner that an irritation of one part affects, directly or remotely, in a greater or less degree, every other, so human society is connected, and the happiness or misery of one member has an influence upon his fellows. As naturally as tickling excites laughing, or yawning is produced by seeing another yawn, will sorrow be called forth by the exhibition of grief. Apathy is as unnatural to the soul as insensibility is to the body.[26]

This passage is particularly interesting because it combines the older occult and physiological understandings of sympathy with the newer spectatorial idea of sympathy — that grief is produced in the viewer by the observation of grief in others — that is a product of Scottish moral philosophy and the writing of Adam Smith in particular. It suggests the lasting residual meaning of the occult or supernatural understanding of sympathy in the nineteenth century, even as the newer understandings based on sensation and conscious identification with the feelings of others were becoming dominant.

That the occult and physiological meanings of sympathy were not narrowly technical meanings only subscribed to by would-be alchemists, mystics, or physicians is clear. In fact, the first American novel — the quintessential middle-class literary form — William Hill Brown's *The Power of Sympathy; or the Triumph of Nature* (1789), bases its social relations precisely on this conception of sympathy. Often identified as an early work of American sentimentalism, *The Power of Sympathy* is not primarily concerned with sympathy as a power of commiseration or shared sorrow or conscious identification of any kind. Rather, it is concerned with the force of attraction and affinity grounded in nature and the body independent of consciousness. The plot concerns the

---

26. [Anon.], "Sympathy," *The Ladies' Repository* [Cincinnati] 5 (July 1845): 192.

love between a young man of good station and rank, Harrington, and an orphan of indeterminate background, Harriet. The epistolary form of the novel documents the revelation that Harriet is Harrington's sister, the offspring of his father's seduction of a young woman, and that their relationship is an incestuous one. Things end badly, as one might imagine, but not before the power of sympathy — which is identified with the triumph of nature — is invoked to explain their relationship.

Three relevant passages help unpack what sympathy means in the novel. The first comes from a letter from Mrs. Holmes, who knows Harriet's background, to Harrington's sister, Myra, following the newly revealed fact that Harrington's love for Harriet is really his incestuous love for his sister: "GREAT God! Of what materials hast thou compounded the hearts of thy creatures! Admire, O my friend! the operation of NATURE — and the power of SYMPATHY! — ." The second comes from a letter from Harrington's father to Mr. Holmes: "But how shall we be able — how shall we pretend to investigate the great springs by which we are actuated, or account for the operation of SYMPATHY — my son, who has been at home about eight weeks, has accidentally seen her, and to complete THE TRIUMPH OF NATURE — has loved her." And finally, Harriet writes to Harrington: " — ALLIED by birth, and in mind, and similar in age — and in thought still more intimately connected, the sympathy which bound our souls together, at first sight, is less extraordinary. Shall we any longer wonder at its irresistible impulse? — Shall we strive to oppose the *link of nature* that draws us to each other?"[27] Nature and sympathy are in all these passages controlling forces, overriding and determining the will, drawing the lovers to one another. The "link of nature" is the blood relation itself, operating through nature despite the lack of consciousness of the tie. Sympathy operates not through consciousness, but through biological affinity, for surely if Harriet and Harrington had been conscious of their biological relation, Brown indicates, they would never have been drawn to one another. Sympathy is sparked by an initial visual sensation, and is figured as irresistible, but it is *not* simply the emotional bond between the two; it is the natural biological affinity collapsed into the emotional relationship. The power of sympathy is invoked to explain the relationship, but it is also figured as a mystery, something that cannot be understood by the rational mind, something that controls people rather than being controlled by them.

The same figure of sympathy is repeated in a story published in *The American Magazine* in 1788. "The Force of Sympathy" concerns a naval officer who

27. William Hill Brown, *The Power of Sympathy* (New York: Columbia University Press, 1937), vol. 2, pp. 35, 83-84, 113.

loses his three-year-old daughter in a shipwreck and sinks into a lifelong melancholy. Eighteen years later he saves a young child from drowning at the same spot he lost his daughter, only later to discover that the boy is the son of the daughter, who had survived the earlier accident. The story, like *The Power of Sympathy,* turns on a blood relation that is unknown to its protagonist. He is moved to action not by a concern for the suffering of an unknown child, but by a force that brings him back to the very spot of the original calamity to repeat, this time successfully, his attempt to save the child. The parallel events of children saved from drowning in a vast sea are linked to the controlling power of parallel parent-child relations. There is an order and harmony to events precisely because they are governed by a controlling sympathy.[28]

In the course of the eighteenth and nineteenth centuries, the notion of sympathy as compassion or a shared mental action by which a spectator enters into the life and feelings of another person came to supplant this older occult idea of sympathy. Sympathy became interiorized, a state of mind rather than a way of being that unified mind, body, society and nature into an integrated pattern. Sympathy was less and less the parallel action of two bodies possessing an affinity for one another, and more and more the active mental projection into, or the emotional identification of a spectator with, a suffering other. We can identify at least two clear trajectories in the changing meaning of sympathy during this period: the movement from physical to mental, from sympathy as a mode of being to sympathy as mode of feeling or imagination; and a transformation of the social relation of sympathy from a participatory affinity of two or more people, to a relation of active observer and passive observed. In the latter transformation, sympathy was something felt by one person toward another, rather than a feeling between two persons. Even the idea of mutual sympathy, for instance, was based on the idea that the roles of observer and observed would go both ways, not that sympathy was something outside of the persons involved. The newer idea of sympathy might refer to an action sparked by the senses, but this sympathy originated within a person, and was a mental projection, having no ontological status in the space between persons, as the older sympathy had.

The overlap between these older and newer meanings was present throughout much of the nineteenth century, so that even as the idea of sympathy as a mental activity was developed, the proponents of that understanding

---

28. [Anon.], "the Force of Sympathy," *The American Magazine* (May 1788): 384-86. For another, later example of this fictional theme, but one in which the sentimental idea of compassion for the suffering of others is present, see "Reciprocal Sympathy," *Saturday Evening Post* (October 12, 1850): 4. The very notion that sympathy is "reciprocated" implies the triumph of an exchange model of sympathy, which is not present in the earlier fictional depictions.

still tended to use the occult frame of reference — and the fundamentally different worldview it inhabited — for understanding sympathy. A good example of this overlap can be found in an article entitled "A Dialogue on Sympathies" that appeared in *The Knickerbocker* in 1836. Couched in the language of physiology and medical discovery, this dialogue moved back and forth between the early modern world of cosmological governing sympathy and Victorian notions of sympathy as emotion and mental identification.

> It is quite probably that the body is subject to the same attraction as the waters of the ocean. Like them it is part of a great chain — the universe — and if we reason theoretically it must be influenced and must sympathize with every object in existence. Sun, and moon, and stars, must all affect it. . . . [B]ut there is another sympathy, that between mind and mind, which cannot be attributable to the same cause. . . . Sympathy between mankind is exclusively mental. It is one of the kind ordinances of Providence, that emotions tend to awaken their counterparts, and as virtuous feelings possess greater attractions than vicious, as beauty has a fascination denied to deformity, we should look upon this arrangement as the noblest branch of the social system. But this sympathy most usually demands similar instruments to extract harmony. The coward and the brave have no affinity. You might as well assimilate the war-cry to the whinings of the wretch craving for mercy. To effect unison, the harps must be tuned alike. . . . This is the sympathy of individuals.[29]

I will return to the idea that sympathy requires a similarity or affinity of type between persons — which I take to be a residual holdover from the older occult meaning — and the way in which it was challenged by a newer liberal idea of universal sympathy that acts to unite those who are dissimilar. The point I want to make here about this passage is that it seeks to draw a firm line between the sympathy of matter and the distinctively human sympathy of minds, to put mind into a separate category from the operations of matter. But even in making sympathy a matter of mental and emotional conception it retains the occult notion of an independent governing force drawing mind to mind.[30]

Contrast this passage with an early-nineteenth-century understanding of

29. A., "A Dialogue on Sympathies," *The Knickerbocker or New York Monthly Magazine* 7 (May 1836): 463-64.

30. For other examples of this retention of older meanings in the context of a newer interiorized mental/emotional conception of sympathy, see J. N. B., "Secret Sympathies," *The Knickerbocker or New York Monthly Magazine* 6 (December 1835): 481-84; W. W. S., "Sympathy and Antipathy," *The Boston Miscellany of Literature and Fashion* 2 (1842): 79-88; Speranza, "Sympathy," *Ladies Repository and Gatherings of the West* 6 (January 1846): 9-10.

sympathy in which all references to an occult or mystical force have disappeared, and sympathy is understood as a means of entering into the mental life of others: "Sympathy is that principle in the mind, which enables us to feel the sufferings or participate in the happiness of others."[31] This sounds very much like Benjamin Rush or other Enlightenment figures in the Scottish moral philosophy or benevolentist tradition. In the eighteenth century the idea of sympathy associated with Hume, Smith, and others was emergent, a redefinition of the ways in which persons were drawn to one another that partook of sensationalist psychology, empiricist epistemology, and materialist cosmology. By the end of the nineteenth century, this idea of sympathy would be dominant, and the older notion of a governing sympathy that had been dominant in the eighteenth century would be on its way to obsolescence.

This, then, was the context in which Smith's *Theory of Moral Sentiments* took up the issue of sympathy, and redefined it in such a way that its regulating power would stem from the imaginative exchange of consciousness rather than from an occult order embedded in the material world. The idea of sympathy as compassion or pity was already a familiar one in the mid-eighteenth century, and that notion of sympathy had been developed by Hume, among others, to explain certain moral and psychological phenomena.[32] But sympathy, in Smith's hands, became something more: the basis for all moral evaluation, but more importantly, the very glue of society, providing for concerted social action, consciousness of sameness and difference, and the dynamics of social proximity and distance. From Smith's conception of sympathy as a dynamic and imaginative exchange of consciousness between spectators and actors — every person simultaneously being a social actor and a sympathetic spectator to the social actions of others — stemmed the twentieth-century tradition of social psychology identified with Charles Horton Cooley, George Herbert Mead, and Erving Goffman. In this tradition, sympathy became a hall of mirrors in which self and society were reflected back and forth from countless angles and perspectives; the sharing of the perspective of others meant becoming a spectator of oneself; appearances as well as essences became key to self-definition; and society itself became an internalized fact of consciousness rather than an objective order.[33]

31. [Anon.], "Sympathy," *Ladies' Literary Cabinet* 1, no. 23 (April 15, 1820): 182.

32. David Hume, *A Treatise of Human Nature* (1739-40), 2nd edition, ed. L. A. Selby-Bigge (Oxford: Oxford University Press, 1978).

33. The key texts associated with these authors are Charles Horton Cooley, *Human Nature and the Social Order* (1902; reprint New York: Schocken Books, 1964); George Herbert Mead, *Mind, Self, and Society* (1934; reprint Chicago: University of Chicago Press, 1959); Erving Goffman, *The Presentation of Self in Everyday Life* (New York: Doubleday, 1959). This tradition

Smith's solution to the early modern problem of what was to replace fixed hierarchies of rank, absolutist government, and traditional social relations in regulating the dangerous passions of human beings was sympathy, defined as "our fellow-feeling with any passion whatever."[34] Unlike the sentimentalist tradition that would emphasize shared suffering, tears, and sorrow, Smith construed sympathy as the capacity to share any and all states of feeling, thus opening the possibility for identification along paths other than pity, or from higher to lower in the social order. From this conception of sympathy, Smith built an entire superstructure of law, government, social relations, and morals. Sympathy allowed navigation between one's own interior state and that of others by creating an imaginary third party to those relations, a party Smith dubbed "the impartial spectator." The impartial spectator was only necessary because sympathy was imaginative and projective, and as a consequence was unable to fully overcome the barrier that separated self from other. From the limits of sympathy emerged the theatricality of society as a system of representations of self and other.[35]

In a famous passage at the very beginning of the text, Smith outlined the limits of sympathy. In what followed, those limitations were made the very basis of social order:

> As we have no immediate experience of what other men feel, we can form no idea of the manner in which they are affected, but by conceiving what we ourselves should feel in the like situation. Though our brother is upon the rack, as long as we ourselves are at our ease, our senses will never inform us of what he suffers. They never did, and never can, carry us beyond our own person, and it is by the imagination only that we can form any conception of what are his sensations. Neither can that faculty help us to this any other way, than by representing to us what would be our own, if we were in his case. It is the impressions of our own senses only, not those of his, which our imaginations copy. (TMS, p. 9)

---

of social psychology is discussed in John P. Hewitt, *Dilemmas of the American Self* (Philadelphia: Temple University Press, 1989).

34. Adam Smith, *The Theory of Moral Sentiments*, ed. D. D. Raphael and A. L. Macfie (1976; reprint, Indianapolis: Liberty Fund, 1984), 10. All further references indicated parenthetically in text by TMS. For a good recent discussion of Smith's moral theory, from the point of view of a philosopher rather than a historian, see Charles L. Griswold Jr., *Adam Smith and the Virtues of Enlightenment* (Cambridge: Cambridge University Press, 1999).

35. On the relationship of Smith's notion of sympathy to theatricality, see David Marshall, *The Figure of Theater: Shaftesbury, Defoe, Adam Smith, and George Eliot* (New York: Columbia University Press, 1986); Jean-Christophe Agnew, *Worlds Apart: The Market and the Theater in Anglo-American Thought, 1550-1750* (Cambridge: Cambridge University Press, 1986), 176-88.

Unlike the sentimentalist conception of sympathy, in which excessive identification with the suffering of others was central and sympathy was all emotion, Smith's idea of sympathy focused on the way in which sympathy was an imaginative projection of the self, one that reinforced the barrier between the self and other at the very moment of its bridging. The sympathetic self fails to enter fully into the experience of others because it is limited to the experience of one's own senses, so one imaginatively projects what one would experience if in the place of another. There is an act of exchange, a trading of places, but one in which the experience of the self is the only framework for understanding others. In fact, Smith's concept of self involves a radical isolation from others, an inability to truly know or understand them: the incomplete identification of the sympathetic imagination inscribes others as "not me." Instead of the self being a pre-social atom, a consciousness apart prior to society, the self is here figured as a product of a sympathetic navigation that creates the boundaries separating self from other.

The conclusion Smith drew from this vision of necessary solitude and alienation premised on sympathy as an imaginative representation of self as other was not negative or despairing in any way. Rather, the limits of sympathetic imagination actually drew persons closer to one another, and moderated excessive passions in ways that contained them. Realizing that he can only participate in an imaginative projection and not in the actual feelings of others, the spectator of others' emotions becomes conscious that those others must be similarly limited in their capacities to understand or enter into the spectator's own feelings. In order to elicit sympathy from others, the social actor imagines how he might feel if he were not himself, if he were another person regarding his own situation from the outside; in other words, he sympathizes with those who might potentially sympathize with him, and comes to look upon himself as an object of sympathy. Since he knows that others cannot share his feelings, he moderates those feelings to line up with what an "impartial spectator" might feel in observing him.

> We must . . . view ourselves not so much according to that light in which we may naturally appear to ourselves, as according to that in which we naturally appear to others. Though every man may, according to the proverb, be the whole world to himself, to the rest of mankind he is a most insignificant part of it. . . . When he views himself in the light in which he is conscious that others will view him, he sees that to them he is but one of the multitude in no respect better than any other in it. If he would act so as that the impartial spectator may enter into the principles of his conduct, which is what of all things he has the greatest desire to do, he must, upon this, as upon all other occa-

sions, humble the arrogance of his self-love, and bring it down to something which other men can go along with. (TMS, p. 83)

The figure of the impartial spectator, then, is a product of the dynamics of the sympathetic imagination turned back upon itself. What Smith elsewhere refers to as "the man within the breast," the "great inmate," or simply "conscience," is an internalization of the imaginary external view of the self.

There are several points worth making about the impartial spectator and his relationship to the idea of the sympathetic self. First, it is clear that Smith's vision of sympathy is sharply antisentimentalist, and that the impartial spectator, as a fictive character, is responsible for restraining the dangerous passions of the self. Instead of the excess of emotion associated with sentimentalism, Smith's vision of sympathy is a moderation of excess, and identification with the relative apathy or coolness of distance. Precisely because people desire the sympathy of others, and are capable of a sympathetic imagination of the feelings of others, they put a check upon their own passions. The impartial spectator — aloof, cool, uncommitted — sets the standard of acceptable sympathy. Contrary to those historians and critics who have identified Smith's *Theory of Moral Sentiments* with the dominant forms of nineteenth-century American literary and domestic sentimentalism, a close reading of Smith reveals the calculated control of emotions invoked in the image of a figure doubly aloof: both a spectator rather than an actor, and impartial rather than excessively identified with subjective feeling. Smith's version of the sympathetic self, as one might expect from the author of the founding text of classical economics, *The Wealth of Nations,* turns out to be a market-savvy figure, attuned to the perceptions of others through the sympathetic imagination. Sympathy lessens emotional intensity by creating a dynamic system of exchange, a market in feelings. Intense emotion is priced too high for the impartial buyer, so the seller "cools" his self-representation and his emotions in order to win approbation.

If the regulating figure in *The Wealth of Nations* (1776) is the famous "invisible hand," shaping and balancing economic outcomes for the good of the whole independent of individual motives, the equivalent figure in *The Theory of Moral Sentiments* is the "impartial spectator," an equally invisible and imaginary figure regulating emotional exchange and identification. Smith in effect replaced the occult notion of sympathy as a regulator of unions, affinities, and harmonies through organic, physiological, or magnetic means, with the impartial spectator, who regulated through the dynamics of the sympathetic imagination. Whereas the occult notion of a governing sympathy implied an objective, albeit mysterious, system of natural affinities, Smith's idea of sympathy exerted its regulating or controlling power through consciousness and imagination. The impartial spectator had no objective status, but was a subjective imagination of objectivity. The consequence of sympathy was to draw people to an imaginary impartial standard, to regulate social behaviors through the moderation of the passions, and to prevent antisocial and selfish behavior. Unlike the occult sympathy in which persons were guided to one another by the ontological structures in which they were embedded, Smithian sympathy was a phenomenon of consciousness, imagination, and interior life. Regulation and order from without were replaced by regulation and order from within.

Another critical point concerning the impartial spectator is his fictive or artificial nature. Smith saw the impulse to sympathy, as did the entire benevolentist tradition, as rooted in human nature. Human beings naturally sympathized with the feelings — both painful and pleasurable — of others, and just as naturally sought the sympathies of others with their own feelings. But what began in nature ended in artifice. To the extent that the imaginary figure of the impartial spectator was internalized as "the man within the breast," and thus provided the motives and moral principles underlying action, persons were conceived of as being guided not by the natural impulse to sympathy, but by the artificial standard of the imagination. Moral standards and principles of conduct were not grounded in natural feeling, intuition, or moral sense, but in the perspective of an imaginary person. Instead of associating the power of sympathy with the triumph of nature over convention, and thus setting a transparent and fixed standard of moral judgment, Smith invoked an ever-shifting standard based on imagination, social distance, and capacity for self-alienation. Smith would never have used the term, but morality was "socially constructed" in his scheme, the product of socially-produced imaginary representations rather than the voice of nature.

In fact, the dynamics of the sympathetic imagination — and the model of personhood in which it was based — laid the foundations for an entire way of thinking characteristic of modern liberalism. I have already noted the way in which W. E. B. Du Bois's concept of double consciousness is rooted in the self-objectifying vision of sympathy: "this sense of always looking at one's self through the eyes of others, of measuring one's soul by the tape of a world that looks on in amused concept and pity" (SBF, p. 45). Here is the echo of Adam Smith, filtered through William James. James's own advocacy of a broad and liberal tolerance in essays such as "On a Certain Blindness in Human Beings" (1899) is based on the same demand for imaginative self-transcendence in a world in which the interior life of others is inaccessible, and blindness to others leads to spectatorial or detached reflection upon the self.

We are practical beings, each of us with limited functions and duties to perform. Each is bound to feel intensely the importance of his own duties and the significance of the situations that call these forth. But this feeling is in each of us a vital secret, for sympathy with which we vainly look to others. The others are too much absorbed in their own vital secrets to take an interest in ours. Hence the stupidity and injustice of our opinions, so far as they deal with the significance of alien lives. Hence, the falsity of our judgments, so far as they presume to decide in an absolute way on the value of other persons' conditions or ideals.[36]

The distrust and critique of one's own ideals, motives, desires, and subjectivity based on a consciousness of the impossibility of entering into those of another is a step toward expanding the self by diminishing its particularistic prejudices and feelings. James makes the necessary blindness of human beings, their incapacity for bridging the divide between selves, the condition for the construction of a non-judgmental self; the only legitimate judgments appear to be those directed against the narrowness of the self. As Charles Horton Cooley put it, "the imaginative and sympathetic aims that are commonly spoken of as self-renunciation are more properly an enlargement of the self."[37]

The twentieth-century psychological concept of self-hatred, by which members of disparaged minority groups are depicted as internalizing the negative views of themselves associated with the dominant groups in society, arises out of the same dynamics of the sympathetic imagination.[38] Smith prefigured the logic of self-hatred in his depiction of the ways in which the imagined condemnation of the impartial spectator leads the person to sympathize with those who detest him. "By sympathizing with the hatred and abhorrence which other men must entertain for him, he becomes in some measure the object of his own hatred and abhorrence" (TMS, p. 84). In Smith's depiction, self-hatred is aimed at criminal and immoral behavior, and leads to remorse, a compound of various forms of sympathy. Only in the twentieth century would this process of self-hatred become identified with a social identity or essence rather than a form of behavior. The sympathetic self was thus both a model of liberal toler-

---

36. William James, "On a Certain Blindness in Human Beings," in *Pragmatism and Other Writings,* ed. Giles Gunn (New York: Penguin, 2000), 267.

37. Cooley, *Human Nature and the Social Order,* 164.

38. The concept of self-hatred was first developed in relation to Jews, but was later applied to other groups, particularly African Americans and homosexuals. Kurt Lewin, "Self-Hatred Among Jews," *Contemporary Jewish Record* 4 (June 1941): 219-32. See my discussion in Daniel Wickberg, "Homophobia: On the Cultural History of an Idea," *Critical Inquiry* 27 (Autumn 2000): 42-57.

ance and a source of psychological pathology that the tolerant liberal person could critique. But the model of self and society common to both tolerance and pathology — in which the self is based on the internalization of society, and society is based on an imaginative projection of the self — was already fully developed in *The Theory of Moral Sentiments*. The elements of a liberal, tolerant, relativistic, critical, sociological conception of the person were laid down in Smith in a way that numerous writers through the twentieth century would echo and extend — without necessarily identifying Smith as the basis of that conception.

Smith's *Theory of Moral Sentiments* is less the source of modern conceptions of the sympathetic self than it is a moment in the history of the ideology of sympathy, in which a number of the shifting meanings and implications of the idea of sympathy were instantiated. The cultural meanings of sympathy that Smith drew on and developed were part of a subjectification of the meaning of sympathy that was common to many eighteenth- and nineteenth-century writings, even as those writings diverged on many of the specific features of sympathy. Virtually all definitions of sympathy in the nineteenth century shared a core understanding. Sympathy came to be defined in terms of sensation, the relationship between an active spectator and an object of perception; it was figured as a source of moral authority derived from within; it provided a bridge between the self and others, if only imaginatively. But within this broad consensus, there was much ground for disagreement and diversion — any ideological conception that was central to both abolitionist and proslavery thought, as sympathy was, could hardly have maintained a uniform meaning. There were two broad conflicts or differences in conceptions of sympathy in the nineteenth century: one between what I will call cognitive or intellectual understandings, and emotive or sentimentalist understandings, of sympathy; the other between particularistic and universalistic meanings of sympathetic identification.

Smith's vision of sympathy, for instance, was cognitive and not primarily emotive or sentimentalist.[39] Because sympathy was a matter of imagination, it necessarily involved the formation of representations and ideas in the mind, rather than the immediate force of feeling, compassion, or pity associated with the sentimentalist conception of sympathy. It is not that the cognitive understanding of sympathy rejected feeling or sentiment; it is that feeling was imagined as bound up with cognition and imagination, rather than being a force of its own that was opposed to intellect along the border that divided "head" from "heart." The sentimentalist understanding of sympathy, on the other hand, embraced the distinction between intellect and emotion, elevating the latter, as Jef-

39. This point is made forcefully in Griswold, *Adam Smith and the Virtues of Enlightenment*, 115.

ferson had in the passage earlier quoted. If the cognitive approach stressed sympathy with any and all feeling as a matter of imagination, the sentimentalist approach stressed the overwhelming compassion for those who suffered. If the cognitive understanding of sympathy seemed to involve an endless imaginative process of exchange and negotiation that looked very much like the dynamics of market society, the sentimentalist understanding defined the domestic sphere as an arena of feeling opposed to the intellectual negotiations of the market.

It is important to understand, then, that sympathy was as central to market conceptions of personhood and motive as it was a counter to those conceptions in the form of domestic ideology. One emphasized the imagination of the feelings of others, the other the immediate feeling for the suffering of others. The cognitive concept of sympathy allowed self-interest to function in a sophisticated way: by imagining the interests of others, one could act with greater understanding of the perspectives from which others acted, and adjust one's own behavior in ways that fulfilled one's self-interest. Broad perspective, understanding of the complexity of motives, and a kind of cosmopolitan vision of the world not bound by the narrowness of provincial or personal experience were the results. The emotional or sentimental conception of sympathy, on the other hand, appeared to dissolve self-interest in the emotional identification with others. This sympathy was a counter to market society, not a self-interested system of impression management based on self-objectification, or a use of the sympathetic imagination to achieve one's own ends. Rather, emotional identification was uncalculated, an outpouring of the self, an immersion of the self in the pain of others, a bond between persons rather than a means of navigating in the social order. The one was associated with the masculine world of work and public life, the other with the feminine world of home and private life.[40]

The sentimental conception of sympathy is probably the one most familiar to students of nineteenth-century American culture — it is the sympathy of *Uncle Tom's Cabin* and the domestic fiction tradition from which it stems, the sympathy of humanitarian representations of suffering and pain, the sympathy of "women's sphere," of tears, sorrow, and heart religion. Sympathy in this un-

---

40. The notion that competition, for instance, as a basis of market activity, was at odds with sympathy is a sentimentalist idea. In the cognitivist view of sympathy, competition and the sympathetic imagination are entirely consistent — in fact, necessary to one another. Here is Charles Horton Cooley, for instance: "The idea that competition is always destructive of sympathy will not bear examination. . . . Indeed it is chiefly through competition that we come to know the world, to get a various insight into people's minds, and so to achieve a larger kind of sympathy, while those who lead a protected life generally lack a robust breadth of view and sense of justice." Cooley, *Social Process* (New York: Charles Scribner's Sons, 1918), 127.

derstanding is not simply an outpouring of feeling, but an effectual source of relief of suffering. Again and again, nineteenth-century sentimental writers referred to sympathy as the balm that heals the wounds of the suffering, as if the shared suffering of the observer could ameliorate the suffering of a victim. In dozens and dozens of poems entitled "Sympathy" in middle-class magazines throughout the nineteenth century, a vision of teary sympathy reaching out to comfort the afflicted was repeated over and over again.[41] The following passage is an early representative of this vision of sympathy:

> It is a pure stream that swells the tide of sympathy — It is an excellent heart that interests itself in the feelings of others — It is a heavenlike disposition that engages the affections, and extorts the sympathetick tear for the misfortunes of a friend. Mankind are ever subject to ills, infirmities, and disappointments. Every breast, at some particular period, experiences sorrow and distress. Pains and perplexities are the long lived plagues of human existence: But sympathy is the balm that heals these wounds. . . . Sympathy is a tender passion, the offspring of refinement, fostered in the bosom of friendship, and nurtured by love, compassion, and benevolence.[42]

This "power of sympathy" to heal the sick and help the suffering is, of course, a far cry from the occult influence of sympathy in the older cosmology.[43] Feeling itself, in the sentimentalist conception, is a way of identifying with others: "I feel your pain" is of a different order than "I imagine what your feeling might be if I were you, which I am not and never can be." Sympathy in the sentimentalist understanding is direct, an immediate bridging of the space that divides persons; it involves no third person intermediaries such as Smith's impartial spectator. Such, for instance, is the vision we find in Horace Bushnell's "Unconscious Influences" (1846), which invokes the older notion of a governing sympathy in a sensationalist context: "it is as if one heart were thus going directly into another, and carrying its feelings with it. Beholding, as in a glass, the feelings of our neighbor, we are changed into the same image, by the

41. A brief sample would include, Louisa, "Sympathy," *Saturday Evening Post* 6, no. 295 (March 24, 1827): 1; Ernest Helfenstein, "Sympathy," *Graham's Lady's and Gentlemen's Magazine* 24 (October 1843): 197; Miss Phoebe Carey, "Sympathy," *The Herald of Truth* (Cincinnati) 2, no. 5 (November 1847): 376-77; Rebecca, "Sympathy," *Boston Cultivator* 11, no. 32 (August 11, 1849): 253; Simeon Tucker Clark, "Sympathy," *Current Literature* 18 (December 1895): 480.

42. [Anon.], "On Sympathy," *The Massachusetts Magazine or Monthly Museum* 3 no, 2 (February 1791): 2-3.

43. Contrast the way in which this phrase is used here with the early American novel of the same title. [Anon.], "Sentimental — The Power of Sympathy," *The Methodist Magazine and Quarterly Review* 16, no. 2 (April 1834): 238-40.

assimilating power of sensibility and fellow-feeling."[44] Like the Smithian or cognitive notion of sympathy, the spectator is changed by the act of sympathy upon viewing the emotional expression of another person, but in Bushnell's formulation that change proceeds from a direct fusion of feeling, rather than from the imagination responding to the limits of sympathetic identification. Sentimental sympathy makes the identification of self with other complete, creating bonds based on sameness rather than difference, melting away the external difference of situation and condition to affirm an underlying identity of sentiment.

The two ways of thinking about sympathy — as imagination and as feeling — were not always distinct from one another, and existed side by side and in combination throughout the nineteenth and early twentieth centuries. Nevertheless, one might say that the discourses surrounding moral philosophy, psychology, and in the later nineteenth century evolutionary biology and social science, partook of the cognitive notion of sympathy, while the discourses surrounding humanitarian appeal, domestic fiction, and evangelical religion — including abolition, moral reform, and temperance — partook of the sentimentalist notion of sympathy. But the lineage of these ideas, and their connections with particular social movements, often appear in unexpected ways. Sympathy was a protean idea, and its many meanings spilled over one another in ways that are often surprising. For instance, George Fitzhugh, the proslavery theorist, drew on the older organic, occult notion of sympathy — as one might expect for a conservative thinker of his ilk — but he combined it with a notion of sympathy taken from the Scottish moral philosophy tradition of Adam Smith, and an appeal to compassion and pure feeling of the sentimentalist kind, to argue against the justifications for market capitalism, and to legitimate slavery. Smith and others in the benevolentist tradition had construed sympathy as an inner source of social and moral order so as to reject the necessity of external systems of coercion; Fitzhugh made the natural sympathy of man the basis for legitimating a fixed social order opposed to freedom.

> We are all philanthropists by force of nature, for we are social beings, tied to each other by invisible chords of sympathy. Nature, which makes us members or limbs of the being society, and affects us, pleasantly or painfully, as any of those members or limbs, however distant from us, are affected, would teach us how to promote the well being of each and all, if we would but attend to her lessons. The slaveholder feels quite as sensibly the vibrations of

44. Horace Bushnell, "Unconscious Influence," in *Sermons for the New Life*, rev. ed. (New York: Charles Scribner's Sons, 1886), 192-93.

the nervous system of humanitarian sympathy which makes society one being, as the abolitionist, the socialist, or the Christian. . . . By observing and
studying the habitudes of the bees and the ants, of flocking birds and gregarious animals, we must become satisfied that our social habits and sympathetic feelings are involuntary, a part of our nature, and necessary to our
healthful and natural existence. This induces us to reject the social contract
of Locke . . . and also the philosophy of Adam Smith.[45]

Fitzhugh was, to a great extent, an idiosyncratic figure, but his use of the idea of
sympathy reveals the way in which mixed and contrary meanings could coexist.
His notion of society as an organism in which the differentiation of parts allowed for the sympathetic effect of one part upon another drew on both an
early modern organic theory of society and a medical vision of organic sympathy. He was the first American "sociologist," developing the German romanticism of Herder and others toward a twentieth-century sociological holism that
he used to critique the atomistic individualism he associated with Locke and
Smith. And yet his vision of a "humanitarian sympathy" based on sensation
owes a great deal to Smith and Scottish moral philosophy. Fitzhugh's critique of
capitalism and political economy shared a large substantive content with its object. In Fitzhugh we find the occult notion of sympathy sitting side by side with
both the emotive and cognitive constructions of sympathy.

The other major division between forms of sympathy was between those
that emphasized the way in which sympathy affirmed pre-existing bonds of
shared experience, background, and social identity, and those that saw sympathy as a means of uniting people who were different in kind. The first emphasized the attraction of like to like; the second, the attraction across boundaries
of difference. For convenience, we may refer to these as particularistic and universalistic forms of sympathy. The particularistic form provided the psychological foundation for class, ethnic, racial, and national consciousnesses, on the
one hand, and for new understandings of mass psychology and mob behavior
on the other. It assumed a kind of fixed and particularistic essence, grounded in
heredity, experience, or even physical proximity, and saw sympathy as the
means by which persons became conscious of those already existing identities,
or were moved in concert with those of like kind or proximity. The universalistic form of sympathy provided the psychological foundation, on the other
hand, for a dissolution of particular identities by emphasizing the common elements of a universal human nature that all persons share. Sympathy was a

45. George Fitzhugh, "Southern Thought" (1857), in *The Ideology of Slavery: Proslavery Thought in the Antebellum South, 1830-1860*, ed. Drew Gilpin Faust (Baton Rouge: Louisiana State University Press, 1981), 293-94.

bridge across ethnic, racial, and national barriers rather than the foundation of them. Particularistic sympathy offered the solidarity of the social group, the merging of the self in shared experience, and the rejection of the possibility of sympathetic crossing from one social identity to another. Universalistic sympathy offered the dissolution of narrow identities, liberation from the claims of the primary group, and an appreciation for "diversity" that ultimately undermined itself in the claims of a uniform human nature.

The particularistic form of sympathy was, in many ways, a holdover from the earlier vision of a cosmological governing sympathy. It emphasized the likeness and affinity of persons for one another, and made sympathy the instrument of the union of like with like. By the end of the nineteenth century, however, this union of the similar had become conceptualized as a mental union, a matter of consciousness, rather than an objective affinity. This notion was widely articulated whenever people spoke of national or racial identity in the nineteenth century, but it was probably given its most forceful articulation in one of the founding texts of American sociology, Franklin Giddings's *The Principles of Sociology*. Many writers had seen sympathy as a kind of social cement or glue, some emphasizing the union of the individual and the social whole, others articulating the bonding between different groups within society. But Giddings made what he called "consciousness of kind" the fundamental fact of society, and the beginnings of any sociological analysis. In the preface to the third edition (1896), Giddings explicitly identified Smith's *Theory of Moral Sentiments* as the germ from which he developed the concept of "consciousness of kind." He defined "consciousness of kind" as "A state of consciousness in which any being, whether low or high in the scale of life, recognizes another conscious being as of like kind with itself." For Giddings, "Our conduct towards those whom we feel to be most like ourselves is instinctively and rationally different from our conduct toward others, whom we believe to be less like ourselves." Among the phenomena explained by consciousness of kind: racial animosity and class distinctions, as well as social alliances and broad political movements. "White men do not usually marry black women," said Giddings; "gentlemen do not habitually wed their cooks or ladies their coachmen." Not only did sympathy provide a bond holding like to like; in doing so, it drew lines between those who were like and unlike, and created the divisions, conflicts, and animosities present within society.[46]

The particularistic notion of sympathy, then, both invoked a powerful sentiment of affinity, but also conditioned that affinity on antipathy or alienation

---

46. Franklin Henry Giddings, *The Principles of Sociology: An Analysis of the Phenomena of Association and of Social Organization,* 3rd ed. (New York: Macmillan Co., 1896), x, 17-18, xiii.

from those who were unlike. One might say, like Abraham Lincoln, for instance, that "The strongest bond of human sympathy, outside of the family relation, should be one uniting all working people of all nations, and tongues, and kindreds."[47] Lincoln's advocacy of working-class consciousness was broad and expansive, but rooted in the notion that all workers shared a common experience that made such sympathy possible. And Lincoln warned that such sympathy should not become the basis for animosity against those who were not bound by it. But the flipside of that conception was that those who were not workers could never truly sympathize or enter into their experiences. As the clergyman Peck in William Dean Howells's *Annie Kilburn* (1888) puts it, arguing against the capacity for the wealthy ever to bond with the poor, "Sympathy — common feeling — the sense of fraternity — can spring only from like experiences, like hopes, like fears. And money cannot buy these."[48] The dynamics of particularistic sympathy ended in precisely the primitive group feeling or identity — with all its prejudices, provincialism, and exclusionary practices — that the advocates of a cosmopolitan, universalistic sympathy opposed. Sympathy, it turned out, was not the antidote to a certain blindness in human beings, but the very foundation of that blindness.

Particularistic sympathy took another form, one that would reach its liberal zenith in the twentieth-century critique of mass society. The notion of sympathy as a form of magnetic or imitative attraction based on sensation meant that physical proximity was imagined as the condition for creating a kind of mass conformity. The concern with mob behavior, in which individual rationality was subsumed in the irrationality of the group, was based on the particularistic proximity of individuals to one another. Like the laughter or yawning that spread infectiously, or the tumultuous emotion of religious revivalism, emotion was imagined as a kind of contagion. The shared experience of a common event created a set of shared emotional states. Mobs acted under the influence of sympathy. "Sympathy," said one writer in 1846, "is displayed in one of its most striking manifestations in the vast assembly, when the mighty mass of human life is permeated by one and the same feeling — is swayed and controlled by the thrilling eloquence of the orator."[49] What some called "imitative sympathy," and others called "passive sympathy," shared with other particularistic notions of sympathy the notion that those within its boundaries of opera-

47. Abraham Lincoln, "Reply to New York Workingmen's Democratic Republican Association" (March 21, 1864), in *Collected Works of Abraham Lincoln, 1809-1865*, ed. Roy P. Basler (Springfield, Ill.: Abraham Lincoln Association, 1953-55), vol. 7, p. 259.

48. William Dean Howells, *Annie Kilburn*, in *Novels 1886-1888* (New York: Library of America, 1989), 684, quoted in Kristin Boudreau, *Sympathy in American Literature*, p. 162.

49. Speranza, "Sympathy," *Ladies Repository, and Gatherings of the West* 6 (January 1846): 9.

tion were held together by a set of bonds that differentiated them from those who were not within those boundaries.[50] Even if this sympathy was momentary, based on proximity and particular conditions rather than a shared essential identity, it was at odds with the more universalistic orientation of liberal sympathy.

That universalistic orientation had its historical roots in Enlightenment notions of universal human nature, and can be found in an early version in Smith. "Though our effectual good offices can very seldom be extended to any wider society than that of our own country," said Smith, "our goodwill is circumscribed by no boundary, but may embrace the immensity of the universe. We cannot form the idea of any innocent and sensible being, whose happiness we should not desire, or to whose misery, when distinctly brought home to the imagination, we should not have some degree of aversion" (TMS, p. 235). Proximity and distance, of course, shaped the intensity of sympathetic feeling and imagination, but the sympathetic imagination was not grounded in a fixed identity, but was open to the possibility of identities far removed in time and place. Since the individual was radically isolated from the interior life of any other individual to begin with, he was capable of imagining the experience of all others, and not just those like himself.

Granting that sympathy operated within groups, advocates of universalistic sympathy imagined a process of natural history by which sympathy came to transcend the particular group and immerse itself in the life of others separated by language, custom, religion, or race. In the first half of the nineteenth century, this perspective was driven by evangelical Christianity and its sense of mission. "As our heavenly Father designed his children to be the medium of comfort to each other," said one writer, "we are to reach beyond the limited range of our own experience, and to place ourselves in the condition of others, 'putting our souls in their souls' stead.'"[51] "[I]t is not enough that we enter warmly into the feelings of those closely allied to us," said another. Christian duty requires the "self-renouncing Christian" to "at all times sympathize with his fellow man."[52] By the early twentieth century, this understanding of sympathy as a form of union across social divisions had become part of a modern secular liberalism. Thinkers such as Charles Horton Cooley, John Dewey, and Randolph Bourne were advocates of a broad, expansive, universalistic, and

50. See the distinction between "passive" sympathy — related to the "herd instinct" — and the "active" sympathy of affection between equals, as expressed by William McDougall, *An Introduction to Social Psychology* (Boston: John W. Luce and Co., 1921), 95, 173.

51. [Anon.], "Sympathy," *Ladies Repository, and Gatherings of the West* 5 (August 1845): 246.

52. Mary F___, "Christian Sympathy," *Ladies Repository, and Gatherings of the West* 4 (July 1844): 198.

cosmopolitan sympathy that drew the person into a new relationship with others unlike him- or herself.

The capacity for universal sympathy marked a conception of the person that was at odds with the particularism of fixed identity. Sympathy, in this conception, involved personal growth and an expansion of the self, rather than a limitation. As the early-twentieth-century psychologist Mary Whiton Calkins put it,

> It is interesting to observe that, with the widening of one's sympathy, the limiting circumference of one's own self is pushed further outward. The sympathetic person has always a richer, concreter personality than the self-centered one. He has actually shared in experiences that are not immediately his own; he has seen with others' eyes and heard with their ears, and his pulses have beat high to their hopes and joys: his experience has been enlarged by his sympathies.
>
> There is something abnormal, therefore, in the checking at any point of this outgrowth of sympathy. People whose sympathies embrace only the members of their family, their cult or their class are only incompletely human, for a lack of emotional comprehension, or sympathy, marks a stunted personality.[53]

The only fully human person is the cosmopolitan person capable of an expansive integration of the experience of others into the self through the sympathetic imagination. One might imagine that all that sympathizing with persons who are not fully human would result in a greater appreciation for their humanity, but this is not the conclusion reached by Calkins and other liberal advocates of universal sympathy. The result of the dynamics of universalistic sympathy is not a more abstract person, emptied of the specific contents of a particular identity, but a "richer, concreter personality." The openness to the process of imaginative exchange, of creating a fluid self constantly imagining new experiences and bridging categories of concrete identity, results in a self that is at once appreciative of experiential difference but also a solvent of that difference.

This brings us back to Du Bois. Sympathy of both the particularistic and universalistic kind is at work in *The Souls of Black Folk*. Du Bois asks his reader to imagine the lives, the desires, the spiritual strivings of people different in condition of life, cultural inheritance, and physical appearance. He asks for a dissolution of particularistic identities in the imagination of a world above the

53. Mary Whiton Calkins, *An Introduction to Psychology* (New York: Macmillan Co., 1904), 274-75.

veil, where material conditions, skin color, and the external world of appearances give way to a shared identity across the color line. But Du Bois, like the African Americans he describes, is divided by "double aims." Central to his depiction of a black "folk" is a particularistic sympathy, one that represents a problem for the author: to what extent is racial consciousness and identity a product of the sympathy that binds Du Bois to the folk he documents? In "The Forethought," Du Bois asks, "[N]eed I add that I who speak here am bone of the bone and flesh of the flesh of them that live within the Veil?" (SBF, p. 42). Du Bois's relationship to that folk throughout the text is problematic: he is the observer, the detached sociologist, the historian, as well as the spokesman for the group he purports to describe. The particularistic sympathy that allows him to claim an African American consciousness, a black folk culture, is precisely the sympathy that prevents a sympathetic crossing of the color line. The meanings of sympathy are at odds with themselves in the text. The contradictions of the sympathetic self, seeking solidarity in the lives of others but dissolving any fixed identities, are the contradictions of a modern personhood. We might very well sympathize with Du Bois's predicament.

# The Disenchantment of Women: Gender and Religion at the Turn of the Century (1865-1930)

Margaret Bendroth

One can hardly overstress the extent to which the task of disentangling our conceptions of the human person from our conceptions of gender has emerged as one of the chief challenges of our times. Both the language of traditional Christianity and the language of romantic individualism tend to affirm the infinite worth and dignity of all human beings — yet they frequently tend to regard the quintessential agent as implicitly (and often explicitly) male, a restriction that was, until fairly recently, rigidly codified in many areas of the civil law, where the "unpersonhood" of women was all too unmistakably asserted. The dilemmas faced by those who would alter this state of affairs are many, however. How are we to affirm an egalitarian social ideal that nevertheless recognizes and makes room for the profound and life-shaping differences between and among us? Or, to reverse the question, how are we to affirm the profound "differences" between the sexes without asserting a hierarchy, or consigning individuals to categories to which they may or may not wish to belong? It matters little in the end whether those differences are defined as "essential" or merely culturally and historically constructed, since the problem is the same in the end. Whether one is a man or a woman is, in one sense, a fact felt at the very deepest core of one's identity. And yet, in another sense, it is felt to be entirely irrelevant to one's standing as a human person. How are we to resolve this puzzle?

It is no coincidence that such a conundrum has presented itself with particular force in the West, which is not only the place where cultural modernity is most advanced, but the part of the world decisively formed by the long cultural hegemony of Christianity. The historical phenomenon of Christianity has always contained within itself, and carried along in its historical stream, both sides of the dilemma, featuring teachings that reinforce gender hierarchy as well as teachings that oppose it, asserting a radical equality in which there is "neither male nor female." Nor is it an easy matter to divorce these two sides, or finally choose one over the other. Because Christianity is a uniquely incarnational faith, which preaches the Word made flesh, and envisions a resurrection of the body at the end of time, it will not do to treat the fact of our bodily maleness and femaleness as if it were a mere passing shadow. Even so, though, it remains equally true that, at the core of Christianity, the fact of our common human personhood must trump and transcend all such considerations. How can this be? How can the most important measure of our worth be something so completely distinct from the form of our embodiment?

Small wonder, then, that the subsequent history of feminism has so often struggled with the tension between equality and difference. But the nature of that struggle has too often been oversimplified, particularly where religion is involved. In the present day, when feminism has so often come to be construed as a secularizing movement in opposition to most of the world's traditional religions, it is of crucial importance that we be reminded of how integral a role religion played in challenging earlier understandings of gender. By the end of the nineteenth century, as Margaret Bendroth shows, the view of women had evolved far beyond the confining notions inherited from classical antiquity that had pervaded Christian thought and practice for centuries. With the emergence of the Victorian Christian understanding of "ensoulment," Bendroth argues, the turn of the century also saw a turn in its conception of gender, a breakthrough which at last gave women "the opportunity to be both thoroughly flawed and authentically human." Margaret Bendroth is Executive Director of the American Congregational Association, and the author of, among many other works, the prize-winning study *Fundamentalism and Gender* (Yale, 1993).

In the late nineteenth century, American Protestants took up the "woman question" with dogged intensity. "All over the United States," as Universalist minister Mila Frances Tupper declared with satisfaction in 1891, "there is agitation of the question in some form."[1] A few tantalizingly brief passages in the New Testament provided endless fodder for debate about women's right to participate in denominational assemblies, to be appointed deacons and elders, or to be ordained as ministers. A large tangle of uncertainties surrounded the question of women speaking in church: Might they pray aloud? Did it matter if a woman

---

1. Mila Frances Tupper, "Present Status of Women in the Church," in *Transactions of the National Council of Women of the United States*, ed. Rachel Foster Avery (Philadelphia: J. B. Lippincott Co., 1891), 98.

stood behind or before the pulpit, took one text or several? The debates were complex, wide-ranging, and often tedious, involving long arguments about Greek grammar and the behavior of first-century prostitutes. From time to time the public thrilled to stories of angry exits from floor debates and, in one case, an all-out heresy trial, but the controversy resulted in relatively little formal change. In most cases, women's ordination would have to wait until the late twentieth century. Still, the sheer volume of invective on both sides makes this debate one of the longest and most significant in American Protestant history.[2]

A century or more later, this sustained fervor is a bit hard to understand. Nineteenth-century Protestant churches were not, on the whole, very formal in their understanding of church office, and at least compared with Roman Catholics, they faced relatively few theological hurdles to women's ordination. Even the Bible did not present an insurmountable obstacle: by the end of the nineteenth century all of the relevant texts had been examined and reinterpreted to at least theoretically allow women full exercise of their gifts in Protestant churches.[3] In fact, the real root of the debate was not primarily about the Bible or church polity, but about the nature of women.

Despite their antiquarian feel, the old controversies over women's ecclesiastical role offer a key vantage point for understanding some old and new assumptions about human nature, especially the meaning of gender differences. Behind all of the archeological and semantic debate about Scripture texts, nineteenth-century Protestants wondered whether sex differences were real

---

2. For general treatments see, for example, Carl J. Schneider and Dorothy Schneider, *In Their Own Right: The History of American Clergywomen* (New York: Crossroad Publishing, 1997), and Susan Hill Lindley, *"You Have Stept Out of Your Place": A History of Women and Religion in America* (Louisville: Westminster/John Knox Press, 1996).

3. Most Protestant denominations did not, for example, subscribe to the argument that because Christ was male, all those ordained to the priesthood should be also. And though the range of biblical interpretation in the late nineteenth century supported a case for women's ordination, the arguments over biblical texts were of course still genuinely important. The relevant texts were Genesis 3:16, describing God's curse on Eve; I Corinthians 11 and 14, detailing rules for women's silence and covering in religious assemblies; Ephesians 5, requiring wifely submission; and I Timothy 2, forbidding women to teach. Most often at issue was the question of applicability. The more extreme position argued that the New Testament texts pertained only to local, temporary situations and the need to impose order in worship and family life; the more popular argument, mirroring arguments about the Bible and slavery, was to argue that Christ's death and resurrection abrogated the original curse, and that the broad trajectory of biblical theology and Christian history was toward greater freedom for those oppressed by human custom. On possible biblical arguments, see Margaret Bendroth, *Fundamentalism and Gender, 1875 to the Present* (New Haven: Yale University Press, 1993), 33-53; and on parallels with slavery arguments, see Mark Noll, *America's God: From Jonathan Edwards to Abraham Lincoln* (New York: Oxford University Press, 2002), 386-401.

enough to justify separate treatment for male and female church members. They were, of course, not alone. In the decades that spanned the turn of the century, Americans engaged in intensive speculation about the origins and implications of the differences between the sexes. The more well-known debate over suffrage was only one facet of a much larger discussion that sparked, in the words of one scholar, worries about "sexual anarchy" and "the longing for strict border controls around the definition of gender."[4] New questions about the relationship between soul and body, raised by evolutionary theory and experimental psychology and pursued in an array of mind-cure movements, created a "tapestry of uncertainty" about the real root of human identity. Gender, as either a fundamental aspect of personhood or an arbitrary set of physical characteristics, sat at the center of speculation.[5]

Knotty religious questions lurked just below the surface of the political, scientific, and psychological debate about women's nature. As the opening section of this essay explains, nineteenth-century Protestant ideas were rooted in traditional categories of Christian thought regarding the relationship between the soul and body, but refracted through modern notions about gender and identity. The result was a vigorous, but at times frustratingly circular, debate about women's metaphysical qualifications for church leadership. The latter part of this essay takes the unresolved question of women's religious role into the early twentieth century, where an emerging cultural ethos rendered it slowly irrelevant. Rather than energize the religious debate, the modern drift toward egalitarianism made it, in the end, a bit trivial. Once central to questions of women's social status, religion rather quickly — but I think unnecessarily — devolved into a minor role in shaping twentieth-century feminism.

## Women and Ensoulment in Christian Tradition

Across the broad span of Christian history, the eternally feminine woman of the nineteenth century was an oddity. In fact, theologians rarely imagined the soul

---

4. Elaine Showalter, *Sexual Anarchy: Gender and Culture at the Fin de Siecle* (New York: Viking Press, 1990), 3, 4.

5. Cynthia Eagle Russett, *Sexual Science: The Victorian Construction of Womanhood* (Cambridge: Harvard University Press, 1989), 14. On gender debates see also Rosalind Rosenberg, *Beyond Separate Spheres: The Intellectual Roots of Modern Feminism* (New Haven: Yale University Press, 1982); Beryl Satter, *Each Mind a Kingdom: American Women, Sexual Purity, and the New Thought Movement, 1875-1920* (Berkeley: University of California Press, 1999); George Cotkin, *Reluctant Modernism: American Thought and Culture, 1880-1900* (New York: Twayne Publishers, 1992), 75-83.

as either male or female; more often gender issues arose in regard to the larger philosophical problem of corporeality, that is, the relationship between a person's inner spiritual nature and outward physical form. For Eve's daughters, the question was not so much the presence or absence of a soul, but the undeniable fact of their female bodies. "The purposeful wickedness of women," Margaret Miles explains, "was viewed as coming directly from her body, unlike male sin, which . . . [came] from the spirit."[6]

Christian tradition provided two basic solutions to the problem, both of which played in to the Victorian Protestant understanding of women's religiosity. Platonic dualism, emphasizing the radical divide between body and soul, offered the promise of escape from bodily limitations through spiritual transcendence. The other model, reflecting a more Aristotelian understanding of ensoulment, was that of redemption through the transformation of bodily flesh. As the following two sections show, both constructs rattled in and out of the post–Civil War debates about women's ecclesiastical role, though sometimes managing only an awkward fit with contemporary notions of "true womanhood."

## Transcendence

Platonic categories shaped much early Christian speculation about women and embodiment, specifically the assumption that the body is merely the soul's prison from which it seeks escape. As many observers have noted, this particular construct has left a dubious legacy. Dualisms that equated maleness with higher rational and spiritual qualities and femaleness with lower, irrational forces obviously fed a great deal of misogynism in Christian tradition. At bottom, the platonic model assumed that women's bodies were a burden that set them further apart from the divine than did men's.[7]

But the vast spiritual distance between embodied women and a perfect God also created a powerful possibility — even necessity — of transcendence. Historical records are full of examples of women claiming direct, ecstatic access to God as their souls wrenched free of their bodies. The records also show that in many cases, prophetic authority translated directly into social power. When seventeenth-century Quaker women claimed that their souls separated from

6. Margaret Miles, *Carnal Knowing: Female Nakedness and Religious Meaning in the Christian West* (Boston: Beacon Press, 1989), 121.

7. Denise Riley, *"Am I That Name?" Feminism and the Category of "Women" in History* (Minneapolis: University of Minnesota Press, 1988), 19-20; Margaret Miles, *Carnal Knowing*, 121-22.

their bodies in moments of religious ecstasy, they achieved a measure of institutional power in religious meetings. By the eighteenth century, as historian Phyllis Mack explains, the Quaker idea of a "divine light" within the hearts of all believers gave women an individual authority that legitimized their public leadership in moral causes like temperance and antislavery.[8] Other historians have pointed out that the equal opportunity aspect of spiritual transcendence allowed men to employ heavily feminine metaphors to describe experiences of love, surrender, and ecstasy in the arms of Christ, the soul's heavenly bridegroom. The prime example here is the erotic language characteristic of much seventeenth-century Puritan devotional writing. With the soul unfixed to a body of one gender or the other, it roamed free, allowing for what one historian has described as a "spiritual cross-dressing" almost incomprehensible to later Protestant generations.[9]

In the United States, a robust tradition of female preaching spanned the religious awakenings of the late eighteenth and early nineteenth centuries. These unusual women, who flourished along the margins of Protestant institutions, warded off criticism by invoking the old principle of transcendence and claiming that they were merely mouthpieces of the divine word. Thus, in their dress and demeanor, legendary figures such as Mother Ann Lee of the Shakers and Jemima Wilkinson, an enigmatic figure popularly known as the Public Universal Friend, presented themselves as neither male nor female. The limits of this argument were already becoming clear by the 1830s and 1840s, as Methodists, Free Will Baptists, and other frontier sects aspiring toward social respectability began to raise institutional bars against self-proclaimed prophets. Female preachers, long associated with the disorder of backwoods revivalism, became something of an embarrassment. But something more, beyond the standard dynamics of institutional growth, contributed to the decline. By the mid-nineteenth century, it was no longer possible for a woman, even one with a prophetic gift, to claim the privilege of sexlessness; the "true woman" of the mid-nineteenth century could not, even in moments of religious ecstasy, escape her female body or her feminine nature.[10]

This much seems clear from a well-publicized Presbyterian controversy over women in the pulpit that took place during the 1870s. In 1832 the denomination's General Assembly had condemned female preachers with a pastoral

8. Phyllis Mack, *Visionary Women: Ecstatic Prophecy in Seventeenth-Century England* (Berkeley: University of California Press, 1992), 24-34.

9. Susan Hardman Moore, "Sexing the Soul: Gender and the Rhetoric of Puritan Piety," in *Gender and Christian Religion*, ed. R. N. Swanson (Rochester, N.Y.: Boydell Press, 1998), 175-86.

10. Catherine Brekus, *Saints and Strangers: Female Preaching in America, 1740-1845* (Chapel Hill: University of North Carolina Press, 1998).

letter, an advisory measure that fell far short of an official ruling on the matter. After the Civil War, the application of the pastoral letter became the focus of sharp disagreement, especially as missionary and temperance work increasingly brought talented women into the public forum. In 1872 New York pastor Theodore Cuyler spurred a flurry of controversy in the denominational press when he allowed Quaker preacher Sarah Smiley into his pulpit; in fact, the ensuing hubbub pushed the General Assembly to take up the question of the pastoral letter in 1874. But in a session marked by undignified uproar — in this case sustained clapping and stamping — Presbyterian leaders refused to set a hard and fast rule, preferring to leave the matter up to the discretion of individual churches and pastors.[11]

Not surprisingly, that move only invited further acrimony. In 1876, when New Jersey pastor Rev. Isaac M. See allowed several female temperance organizers into his pulpit, his colleague, the Rev. E. R. Craven, raised a complaint with the Newark presbytery.[12] Although the official charges against See referenced the denomination's 1874 ruling and a variety of biblical texts, the lines of battle did not simply pit conservatives against liberals. As one of See's defenders, the Rev. C. T. Berry, reminded those present, "Every one of us, if living a century ago, would have been ecclesiastically decapitated if we had presumed to hold the views we do now with the first chapter of Genesis."[13] The real issue, according to the conservative denominational press, was See's "mysticism." At the time of the trial, See was affiliated with the Higher Life movement, a popular form of radical piety emphasizing the importance of self-surrender as a means of deeper communion with God. Later he moved a bit further down the mystical path and embraced the more occult theology of the Swedenborgians. "Pressing the scriptural doctrines of the illumination of the soul of the believer by the Spirit of God," the *Presbyterian* complained, See and his female preachers had "emancipated themselves from submission to the written word, or accepted its teachings only as they accorded with the inward revelations made to their own hearts."[14]

11. Lois A. Boyd and R. Douglas Brackenridge, *Presbyterian Women in America: Two Centuries of a Quest for Status* (Westport, Conn.: Greenwood Press, 1983), 98-101. Cuyler invited Smiley for a second time in 1874, but constructed a special podium for her in front of the pulpit.

12. Boyd and Brackenridge, *Presbyterian Women in America*, 101-105; Boyd, "Shall Women Speak? Confrontation in the Church, 1876," *Journal of Presbyterian History* 56 (1978): 281-94; *Case of the Rev. E. R. Craven Against the Rev. I. M. See in the Presbytery of Newark and the Synod of New Jersey* (n.p., n.d.).

13. *Speech of Rev. C. T. Berry, of Caldwell, N.J., Before the Newark Presbytery on the Trial of Isaac M. See* (Newark: J. A. Beecher, 1877), n.p.

14. "The Preaching of Women," *Presbyterian*, January 6, 1877, 9.

Craven rejected even this relatively mild claim of transcendence on several grounds. To begin with, Presbyterian teaching never privileged individual revelation over the infallible word of scripture and the teachings of the church. Direct communication with God, ungoverned by communal sources of authority, opened the door to all kinds of antinomian errors. But at the heart of Craven's protest was the potential for deception. "How am I to know," he demanded, "if a woman is not speaking under her own sinful influences or a delusive spirit?" An even more fundamental duplicity rested in women preachers themselves, whose actions willfully betrayed the ground rules set by their feminine natures. To Craven the "whole question" was "one of subordination," and he insisted that a woman who asserted herself in public committed a deep indecency, "an offense against her own modesty." "It was positively base for a woman to speak in Corinth," he declared, "positively base for her to speak anywhere." A female preacher was, in Craven's view, "a shame and a nuisance."[15] In the end, the presbytery declined to condemn See for misusing the Scriptures, reasoning that "a different interpretation of them may be honestly held"; instead they admonished him for raising what they saw as a far more fundamental problem: the "disorder and mischief" that women preachers would inevitably introduce.[16]

The problem was not the content of their message, which could be presumed to be above moral reproach, but one of personal purity. The charge was not new: since the first century, women who claimed prophetic gifts had often been discredited with charges of sexual immorality.[17] What is interesting, however, is Craven's complaint that in committing an offense against their own modesty, women preachers were fundamentally duplicitous. According to this logic, women who followed an urge to speak publicly on religious subjects risked their moral reputations. Presbyterians were not the only ones with such worries. In 1876 a Congregationalist writer warned against the "debasing of female character" in the pulpit controversy. "Can thinking people really believe," he demanded, "that female virtue will in general be as safe, when the outworks of reserve with which nature has surrounded it are leveled to an equality with man?" At bottom, the preaching issue raised the uncomfortable possibility of a divided female self, harboring secret motivations behind a public persona. It

15. Craven quoted in Matilda Joslyn Gage, "Religious Tyranny," *Ballot Box* 2 (December 1877): 4.

16. *Case of the Rev. E. R. Craven Against the Rev. Isaac M. See,* 1-2.

17. Karen L. King, "Prophetic Power and Women's Authority: The Case of the *Gospel of Mary* (Magdalene)," in *Women Preachers and Prophets Through Two Millennia of Christianity,* ed. Beverly Mayne Kienzle and Pamela J. Walker (Berkeley: University of California Press, 1998), 28-30.

was a prospect that, as the following section describes, defied the nineteenth-century Protestant understanding of woman's nature.[18]

## Continuity

The construction of nineteenth-century womanhood drew from another strand of Christian tradition, following Aristotle's view of the soul as an animating life spirit, which emphasized the unity and fundamental continuity of the inner and outer person.[19] Although in Aristotle's view women were lower in the order of things than men, their embodied souls could at least in theory privilege their access to God. Thus, the miraculously tortured bodies of thirteenth-century female mystics uniquely dramatized an intrinsic tie between flesh and spirit that was at least theoretically true of all women. Indeed, women's bleeding, lactating bodies evidenced a capacity for suffering and nurture that more closely resembled the body of Christ than those of their male counterparts. Thus, argues historian Carolyn Walker Bynum, the "bodiliness of women," especially when associated with mystical achievement, was a powerful "means of approaching God."[20]

In the long history of western Christian thought about gender and embodiment, the post-Enlightenment era tended to affirm Aristotle's model, as more and more the body became the primary source of human identity. Yet it also marked a distinct new stage. Science, especially the growing understanding of the biology of human conception, focused more and more attention on physical bodies — and women's bodies in particular — as the source of unbridgeable differences between the sexes. This marked a break with the past, for in classical and medieval science women were not a separate order of being, but

18. C. W. Clapp, "Is the Ideal Christian Woman a Public Character? IV," *The Advance,* September 14, 1876, 27. It is perhaps worth noting that other women who claimed the right to prophesy, especially in the holiness movement, tended to use the language of "infilling" to describe their experience. In other words, women gained the power to speak not when they transcended bodily limitations, but when their bodies became filled with divine power. See, for example, descriptions in Fannie McDowell Hunter, *Women Preachers* (Dallas: Berachah Printing Co., 1905), reprinted in *Holiness Tracts Defending the Ministry of Women,* ed. Donald W. Dayton (New York: Garland Publishing, Inc., 1985).

19. The third-century theologian Tertullian also believed that the soul was corporeal, to the extent that it even had a distinct human shape. In his view souls were eternally male and female and ranked accordingly: Adam's masculine soul justified his superior social status since it was "more complete than Eve's." See King, "Prophetic Power and Women's Authority: The Case of the *Gospel of Mary* (Magdalene)," 25.

20. Carolyn Walker Bynum, *Fragmentation and Redemption: Essays on Gender and the Human Body in Medieval Religion* (New York: Zone Books, 1991), 227-29, 202-203.

an inferior form of a primary male type. Following the Aristotelian assumption that they were literally colder, physically denser beings than men, pre-modern science saw female reproductive organs as the literal inverse of male genitalia, the same pear-like structure but shriveled into the body cavity. That given, the sexes were not fundamentally or ontologically different from each other; for all practical purposes, being male or female meant holding a particular social rank, not possessing a certain genetic endowment or different body chemistry. But the seventeenth- and eighteenth-century scientists who dissected male and female bodies, or who viewed eggs and sperm under microscopes, began to see sex differences as far more fundamental. As Thomas Laqueur writes, "Women's bodies in their corporeal, scientifically accessible concreteness, in the very nature of their bones, nerves, and, most important, reproductive organs, came to bear an enormous new weight of meaning. Two sexes, in other words, were invented as a new foundation for gender."[21]

By the nineteenth century, gender defined the entire person. A woman was not just someone with a female body or a certain social status, but was "thoroughly sexed through all the regions of [her] being."[22] For Victorian Protestants, there was no question that women were female in every possible way — physically, mentally, and especially spiritually. As Congregational theologian Horace Bushnell argued in his anti-suffrage tract subtitled *The Reform Against Nature*, men and women were so different "that they are a great deal more like two species, than like two varieties." These differences were so fundamental that, said Bushnell, they would continue beyond this world into the next. "For there is a sexhood also in spirits, as truly as in organic life."[23] For most Protestants, that assumption seemed written in the laws of nature. As a Presbyterian pastor reminded the young women in his congregation, nature itself "looks for a correspondence between the outward and the inward and expects that unlike bodies will be found to enshrine unlike souls." For, he said, "if man and woman are spiritually alike, then one or the other has been imprisoned in a fleshy tabernacle unsuited to the spirit that inhabits it."[24]

---

21. Thomas Laqueur, *Making Sex: Body and Gender from the Greeks to Freud* (Cambridge: Harvard University Press, 1990), 150. The emphasis on women's bodies also distanced them from the Enlightenment emphasis on reason, and from the possibilities of citizenship. See Riley, *"Am I That Name?"* 18, 19.

22. Anthony Fletcher, "Beyond the Church: Women's Spiritual Experience at Home and in the Community, 1600-1900," in *Gender and Christian Religion*, 189-190; Riley, *"Am I That Name?"* 18.

23. Bushnell, *Woman Suffrage: The Reform Against Nature* (New York: Charles Scribner, 1869), 51, 83.

24. J. H. Worcester Jr., *Womanhood. Five Sermons to Young Women Preached at the 6th Pres-*

This new notion of femininity drew from many sources, though more heavily weighted toward the romanticism of Rousseau and Goethe's idea of the "eternal feminine" than the Bible or Christian tradition. Marilyn Chapin Massey traces its roots to early-nineteenth-century German attempts to stem rising rates of infanticide and infant morality, reflected in the efforts of influential thinkers like Goethe, Pestalozzi, and Schleiermacher to glorify the bond between mother and child as the source not only of human morality but salvation itself. The female soul, Massey writes, was a unique "psychobiological essence, reaching on one side to the divine and on the other into the female body."[25]

Locked within this tight reciprocal unity, women's bodies were no longer a theological problem. Indeed, a speaker at the Northfield Christian Workers' Conference expressed confidence that the "perfection of womanhood" through Christian faith would not just elevate women's social and intellectual powers, but make them physically more beautiful. Similarly, a British cleric, writing on "what Christianity has done for women" in 1893, cited an archeological study of human skulls around the time of Christ with the startling finding that "the difference in size between the male skull and the female skull is much less in the Christian era than in any previous period of history."[26]

Though nineteenth-century Protestant women could not expect transcendence, except when the soul finally escaped the body at the moment of death, their embodied spirituality afforded them an almost routinized access to God. Thus one admirer described the effortless spiritual power of evangelist Hannah Pearce Reeves: "Without descending from her own serene altitudes she lifted other souls from their cloudier ones."[27] Certainly godly women possessed an uncommon gift for nonverbal communication. As a female evangelist declared in 1893, "Nowhere are the distinctive qualities of woman so indispensable as in dealing with the soul." "As she sits by the penitent Magdalene or the poor sot who feels better impulses stirring in him, she does not require that the shameful facts of a degraded past be retailed to her. All the meaning that lies behind a

---

byterian Church, Chicago (Philadelphia: Presbyterian Board of Publications, 1885), 13. Significantly, Victorians used the term "inversion" to describe male homosexuality. A homosexual was, literally, a female soul trapped in a male body. An attraction for other men was not simply a matter of sexual desire, but a reversal of every aspect of the self, fundamentally unnatural and deeply immoral. See Sandra Bem, *The Lenses of Gender: Transforming the Debate on Sexual Inequality* (New Haven: Yale University Press, 1993), 82-87.

25. Massey, *Feminine Soul: The Fate of an Ideal* (Boston: Beacon Press, 1985), 83.

26. E. K. Price, "The Perfection of Womanhood," *Northfield Echoes* 3 (1896): 314-20; Hugh Price Hughes, "What Christianity Has Done for Women," *Independent*, September 28, 1893, 3.

27. Mary Stevens Robinson, "Mrs. Hannah Pearce Reeves, Preacher of the Gospel," *Methodist Quarterly Review* 59 (1877): 444.

furtive glance, an involuntary gesture or an ejaculation of despair, her intuitive power grasps at once."[28]

Women's superior claim to religion rested not on a higher soul, but on a greater level of ontological purity, in their fundamental continuity of character. In that sense, women exemplified the Victorian enthusiasm for formal systems of thought, and models of smooth, developmental progress. "Nineteenth-century minds disagreed about almost everything," one scholar has observed, "except how much they disliked hard edges."[29] For practical reasons, middle-class Americans also worried a great deal about hypocrisy. In their increasingly urban, pluralized social world, perpetual danger lurked in the ability of a "confidence man" to project a deceptively honest image. In contrast, the true woman was "constitutionally transparent," fundamentally pure and unadulterated by alien feelings or desires. Indeed, her physical form invariably involuntarily betrayed her inner emotions, through sudden tears, swoons, and illness.[30] Even masculine moral fortitude required a degree of internal simplicity; what to modern ears might ring a bit false was for Victorians clear evidence of authenticity. In an essay on "character," a Baptist author praised the dying President McKinley's final gasping queries after the wellbeing of his attacker, and his apology for having been "a cause of trouble to the Exposition." "A man can simulate much for pious effect," this admirer wrote, "but no man can receive a fatal shot and stand in full view of the Eternal World and extemporize such sentiments." The expiring president's courteous conduct was clear evidence "of a deep and genuine Christian character."[31]

In its nineteenth-century definition, "manliness" was self-restraint, the ability to control conflicting internal impulses for the sake of a higher good. True womanliness, however, presupposed a certain lack of self-awareness, the absence of an inner critical voice. This purity occasioned high praise. Woman's

28. Mrs. George B. Frost, "Woman's Part in Evangelization," in *Addresses Delivered During the Ladies' Hour at the Sixth Annual Convention of the Evangelistic Association of New England* (Lynn, Mass., 1893), 12, 14. In a somewhat similar fashion, the intuitive powers of women and their essential passivity allowed them to excel as spiritualist mediums, to allow others to speak through them. As trance speaker Lizzie Doten declared, "Woman does not need to cultivate her intellect in order to perceive spiritual truths. Let her live, only, true to her Divine nature and her spiritual perceptions." Doten quoted in Ann Braude, *Radical Spirits: Spiritualism and Women's Rights in Nineteenth-Century America*, 2nd ed. (Bloomington: Indiana University Press, 2001), 85.

29. William R. Everdell, *The First Moderns: Profiles in the Origins of Twentieth-Century Thought* (Chicago: University of Chicago Press, 1997), 9.

30. Karen Halttunen, *Confidence Men and Painted Women: A Study of Middle-Class Culture in America, 1830-1870* (New Haven: Yale University Press, 1982), 57.

31. "The Legacy of Character," *Watchman*, September 26, 1901, 8-9.

"moral perceptions are clearer, and her intuitions of what is pure, good, and right are far more unerring," a Presbyterian wrote in 1895. "Her mind is well-nigh a stranger to doubt."[32] Similarly, Methodist bishop Gilbert Haven declared, "Man feels the gentle touch of the Gospel only when some of the dross of his character has been purged away; woman, in a nature more refined and spiritual, is reached directly through the heart."[33]

This high regard for women's moral character did not necessarily translate into institutional power. Among northern Methodists, the controversy over women's role spread across three decades, beginning with an 1868 ruling that "laymen" would be eligible to attend the General Conference, the main deliberative body of the Methodist Episcopal Church. This democratizing move allowed local associations to elect not just clergy, but ordinary church members to represent them in the national meeting. Though only men attended the next General Conference in 1872, the ambiguity of the 1868 ruling inevitably raised an obvious question: Did a "layman" have to be literally male, or might the term refer to church members of either sex? When four women came to the General Conference in 1888 demanding to be seated, they were quickly turned away. But instead of ending the issue, this summary dismissal brought the women question resoundingly to the surface. The General Conference's 1880 decision to rescind all preaching licenses held by Methodist women also fueled denominational acrimony.[34]

The issue was not women's inferiority. As the leading conservative in the Methodist debate, *Christian Advocate* editor James M. Buckley declared, "All objections to the admission of women into the General Conference come at last to this, — that they are *women* and not men." "That each sex is endowed with qualities fitting its members for a peculiar kind of influence and work," he argued, was "the grounds of doubt and opposition."[35] The fundamental issue was the fact of women's spiritual difference. In a 1909 anti-suffrage tract he was still arguing that "there is a feminine, as well as a masculine, soul; a spiri-

32. William M. Cox, "The Social and Civil Status of Woman," *Presbyterian Quarterly Review* 9 (1895): 592.

33. Haven, "Introduction," *The Harvest and the Reaper. Reminiscences of Revival Work of Mrs. Maggie N. Van Cott, The First Lady Licensed to Preach in the Methodist Episcopal Church in the United States* (New York, 1853), xxx-xxxi.

34. Carolyn DeSwarte Gifford, "Introduction" to *The Defense of Women's Rights to Ordination in the Methodist Episcopal Church* (New York: Garland Publishing, Inc., 1987), n.p.; Gifford, "Introduction" to *The Debate in the Methodist Episcopal Church Over Laity Rights for Women*, n.p.

35. James M. Buckley, *"Because They Are Women" and Other Editorials from "The Christian Advocate" on the Admission of Women to the General Conference* (New York: Hunt and Eaton, 1891), 26.

tual sex, as well as a corporeal."[36] Buckley did not, however, sentimentalize women. In his view, they were unfit to exercise church leadership because their emotions were simply too instantaneous to allow for normal conduct of denominational business. "Men may debate in apparent rage and tremendous vehemence of manner," he explained, "and five minutes after it is over — whether in the courts or in ecclesiastical bodies — they can usually resume their former relations. The intensity of woman's feelings makes such a thing impossible with her."[37]

The problem, of course, was that in terms of consistency an essentialist argument worked both ways. "Our records of crime show which sex is chief among sinners," Methodist laywoman Kate Tannatt Woods remarked in 1891. "Surely, the purest should preach the gospel of purity."[38] Indeed, Methodism's most famous purity reformer, Woman's Christian Temperance Union president Frances Willard, was one of the four women denied a seat at the 1888 General Conference. In a book entitled *Woman in the Pulpit*, she declared that "[t]he strongest argument in favor of a woman minister is found in woman herself, in her sympathetic and intuitive nature, in her high moral sense, in her deep and fervent religious spirit." Feminine moral influence was determined "not by what woman *does*," as Willard told a temperance gathering, but by "what she *is*."[39]

But women's maternal role ultimately qualified them for church leadership. "The mother-heart of God will never be known to the world until translated into terms of speech by mother-hearted women," Willard insisted. Though unmarried and childless, she also hinted that only women who had experienced the rigors of childbirth could truly understand the incarnation. "The more it is studied, the more it will be proved," she argued, "that our holy faith can have no human ally so invincible as she who, with strong crying and tears, has learned the sublime secrets of pain and pathos that only mothers' hearts can know."[40]

Willard also believed that women's faith, grounded in unmediated experience, was the best defense against modern skepticism. "Men preach a creed," she wrote; "women will declare a life. Men deal in formulas, women in facts." While masculine logic created empty legalisms, women offered "compassion,

36. Buckley, *The Wrong and Peril of Woman Suffrage* (New York: Fleming H. Revell, 1909), 40.

37. Buckley, *"Because They Are Women,"* 28.

38. Woods, "Woman in the Pulpit," *Transactions of the National Council of Women*, 291.

39. Willard, *Woman in the Pulpit* (Chicago: Woman's Christian Temperance Publication Association, 1889), 97; Willard, "Woman Represents the Home."

40. Willard, *Woman in the Pulpit*, 66.

forgiveness, and sympathy." "Men's preaching has left heads committed to a cat-echism," Willard declared, "and left hearts hard as nether millstones."[41] The celebration of women's religiosity, echoed in the more radical declarations of Elizabeth Cady Stanton and Charlotte Perkins Gilman, seemed to support not only woman's claim to the pulpit, but the very authenticity of religious belief. Unable to compartmentalize behaviors or admit to doubt, woman "became a symbol of nonalienated, and hence nonmodern identity."[42]

Masculine logic, however, quickly returned Willard's challenge. Writing in the *Homiletic Review*, Henry Van Dyke angrily denied that women had any particular qualifications for the work of the ministry. "They are not holier by nature than men, and if they were this would not make them better ministers," he groused. "There are multitudes of men who preach a life and deal in facts, and there are women who can understand and use a syllogism." The Bible itself, Van Dyke reminded his readers, contained at least as many examples of female sinners as male ones.[43]

Science backed him up. In the decades leading up to the turn of the century, empirical research on brain chemistry had begun to challenge not only the truth of the supernatural, but the assumption that women enjoyed any kind of immediate or special access to the divine. What religious people called the "soul" or the "mind," skeptics argued, was really the end result of a series of chemical processes, the "subjective experiencing of objective bodily phenomena."[44] Under this empirical lens, sentimental notions about women's greater propensity for religious belief withered quickly. Writing in 1900, Methodist educator George A. Coe commented that "Women are commonly said to be more religious than men, but I think it can be shown that the real difference is less in the degree of religiousness than in the general make-up of the mind. Sex is certainly a fact of mental as well as of physical constitution, and the mental peculiarities of each sex naturally and necessarily appear in religion as well as elsewhere."[45] Psychologist of religion Edwin Starbuck similarly argued that the sexes were equally open to religious belief, but in different ways and for different reasons. Men tended to be moralistic and "self-regarding" in their approach to conversion, Starbuck concluded, and usually motivated by personal feelings

41. Willard, *Woman in the Pulpit*, 97, 46-47.

42. Felski, *The Gender of Modernity* (Cambridge: Harvard University Press, 1995), 18.

43. VanDyke's reply in the January 1888 *Homiletic Review* is reprinted in Gifford, *The Defense of Women's Rights to Ordination in the Methodist Episcopal Church*, 116, 121.

44. James Turner, *Without God, Without Creed: The Origins of Unbelief in America* (Baltimore: The Johns Hopkins University Press, 1985), 177.

45. George A. Coe, *The Spiritual Life: Studies in the Science of Religion* (New York: Eaton and Mains, 1900), 236.

of guilt. In contrast, the women he had interviewed were driven to God mostly by social pressures to conform or to do good in the world. This model seemed a clear reversal of Victorian assumptions about gender and religion; by most measures of authenticity, women's religion seemed a less true reflection of the self than did men's.[46]

The very fact that women were immune to doubt seemed, for some, reason enough to be wary of their belief. By the turn of the century, both agnostics and fundamentalists were proclaiming themselves more "manly" — that is, more heroically individualistic — than those who believed out of "idle respectability."[47] Excoriating the tendency toward "infidelity among women," St. Louis Presbyterian James H. Brookes found female skeptics "as common and offensive as dog-fennel in a barren field." The root sin of these "silly women" chasing after unorthodox doctrines was not genuine doubt but vapid insincerity. "They understand from the books and book notices they have read," Brookes wrote, "that 'people of culcha' have outgrown faith in the Bible, and they are determined to keep up with the times, particularly when they find that they can live without prayer, without watchfulness over their conduct, without the necessity of listening to dull and orthodox sermons, without a thought of eternity." Other conservative Protestants shared Brookes' dislike for Victorian sentimentalism and its uninspected assumptions about women's character. Downplaying the claims of suffrage advocates that female voters would usher in a new age of moral uplift, a premillennial Baptist publication reminded its readers that "there are vicious and incompetent women as well as vicious and incompetent men."[48]

In the end, Methodists found that the best way out of controversy was to simply dismiss the notion of a "female nature" in the first place. Citing Galatians 3:28, that "in Christ there is no male nor female," A. J. Kynett asked, "what has sex to do with such service?" The question was really one of "Church organization and life," he argued, and in that respect, there was no legal way to

---

46. Edwin Diller Starbuck, *The Psychology of Religion: An Empirical Study of the Growth of Religious Consciousness* (New York: Charles Scribner's Sons, 1899), 53, 62-67.

47. Lester Ward quoted in James Turner, *Without God, Without Creed*, 235. Similar assumptions about women's religiosity appeared among Freethinkers. See Evelyn Kirkley, *Rational Mothers and Infidel Gentlemen: Gender and American Atheism, 1865-1915* (Syracuse, N.Y.: Syracuse University Press, 2000), 29-50.

48. Brookes, "Infidelity Among Women," *Truth; or Testimony for Christ* 12 (August 1886): 385-88; "Woman Suffrage," *Watchman*, March 7, 1895, 1-2. On fundamentalists and women, see Betty A. DeBerg, *Ungodly Women: Gender and the First Wave of American Fundamentalism* (Minneapolis: Fortress Press, 1990); Margaret Bendroth, *Fundamentalism and Gender, 1875 to the Present*.

"to justify the exclusion of women from the councils of the Church." In 1891 a series of articles in the *Methodist Review* likewise denied that the question of women's eligibility had anything to do with either the interpretation of the Bible or with gender. The so-called "woman question" was really just a matter of Methodist polity, in which sex had never been a condition of church membership. The entire matter might best be decided on purely procedural grounds.[49] In 1900 the denomination quietly accepted this logic, allowing women full laity rights; twenty-four women attended the General Conference of 1904 with very little fanfare. In the ensuing decades, discussion among Methodists and most other Protestant denominations largely ceased.

## God and the "New Woman"

By the end of the nineteenth century, in some denominations and areas of the country, a woman in the pulpit had become "an unquestioned commonplace." In 1898 Methodist Anna Howard Shaw estimated the number of female preachers at around 2,000, most of them entering the ministry in the decade previous.[50] Even the most cynical observers of orthodox Protestantism found reason for hope. "The night of ignorance, credulity, and despair is nearly at an end," freethinker Matilda Joslyn Gage told a religious symposium at a meeting of suffragists, reformers, and religious leaders in 1888. "Man has lost his power over woman."[51]

The evidence was mounting by the turn of the century. The rising generation of the educated middle class seemed genuinely undaunted by old ideas of women's proper place. The "new woman" was delaying marriage, going to college, even campaigning for suffrage. She could also aspire to a career in one of the new professions open to women, in librarianship, social work, or nursing. Shedding her cumbersome skirts and corsets, she rode a bicycle, played tennis, even dared to smoke a cigarette in public.[52] "No, woman is not handicapped ex-

49. A. J. Kynett, *Our Laity: And Their Equal Rights Without Distinction of Sex in the Methodist Episcopal Church* (Cincinnati: Cranston and Curtis, 1896), 29, 31. (Legal tack also in "Eligibility of Women Not a Scriptural Question," *Methodist Review* 73 [1891]: 287-91; "The Ground of Woman's Eligibility," *Methodist Review* 73 [1891]: 456-63; Willis Palmer, *Are Women Eligible as Lay Delegates to the General Conference?* from Gifford.)

50. Shaw, "Women in the Ministry," *Chautauquan* 28 (1898): 489.

51. Tupper, "Present Status of Women in the Church," 106; Gage, "Women in the Early Christian Church," *History and Minutes of the National Council of Women, Organized in Washington, DC, March 31, 1888*, ed. Louise Barnum Robbins (Boston, 1898), 406, 407.

52. Nancy F. Cott, *The Grounding of Modern Feminism* (New Haven: Yale University Press,

cept by tradition and habit," as one commentator rejoiced in 1926; "yes, her nature is almost interchangeable with that of man; certainly, she is fitted to share the full work of the world."[53]

These outward changes in women's status corresponded with a new round of questions about gender and transcendence. But this time the issue was one of freedom from restraints imposed not by nature, but by culture. Thus, as one feminist argued, the old canard about the lack of "female geniuses" derived not from an "inherent lack in the make-up of the sex," but "the oppressive, restrictive cultural conditions under which women have been forced to live." The real problem was with the environment, not women themselves. "Conventions are, doubtless, always rather ridiculous," the bohemian writer Floyd Dell agreed, "inevitably a shackle upon the free motions of the soul."[54]

Still, the idea that gender identity was somehow negotiable introduced the unsettling possibility that under certain conditions, men might lose their masculinity and women might cease to be truly feminine.[55] This new sense of personal malleability drove the growing popularity of body-building and physical sports among young men, and the parallel interests of young women in dieting and dress. For good or ill, the outward form increasingly defined the inward person. Thus, in her study of young Danish women in the 1920s, Birgitte Soland notes the importance they attached to "style." They became "modern," she explains; they "used their bodies in special ways. They walked in particular ways. They sat in particular ways. They even shook hands in particular ways."[56] Early-twentieth-century technology further underlined the defining role of the outer self, as "men's and women's bodies were displayed and dramatized as never before in popular theater, sports, photography, fiction, film, and advertisements."[57]

By the turn of the century, middle-class Americans were also coming to

---

1987), 20-23; Sheila Rothman, *Woman's Proper Place: A History of Changing Ideals and Practices, 1870 to the Present* (New York: Basic Books, 1978), Chs. 1-3.

53. Elisabeth Woodbridge, "The Unknown Quantity in the Woman Problem," *Atlantic Monthly* 113 (1914): 514. See also Zelphine Humphrey, "The Modern Woman's Home," *Woman Citizen* (June 1926): 22.

54. Sylvia Kopold, "Where Are the Female Geniuses?" in *Our Changing Morality: A Symposium*, ed. Freda Kirchwey (New York: Albert and Charles Boni, Inc., 1924), 121; Floyd Dell, "Can Men and Women Be Friends?" in Kirchwey, ed., *Our Changing Morality*, 186.

55. Laura Behling, *The Masculine Woman in America, 1890-1935* (Urbana: University of Illinois Press, 2001); Gail Bederman, *Manliness and Civilization: A Cultural History of Gender and Race in the United States, 1880-1917* (Chicago: University of Chicago Press, 1995), 5-10, 16-20.

56. Soland, *Becoming Modern: Young Women and the Reconstruction of Womanhood in the 1920s* (Princeton, N.J.: Princeton University Press, 2000), 15.

57. John F. Kasson, *Houdini, Tarzan, and the Perfect Man; The White Male Body and the Challenge of Modernity in America* (New York: Hill and Wang, 2001), 18.

understand that the self was far from transparent or knowable. The discovery of the subconscious had ushered in what historians often refer to as the "modern self," no longer a single fixed entity but a complex web of subconscious drives and motives. In contrast to the traditional Victorian notion of an internally formed character, the modern personality was shaped by external events and driven by desire.[58]

All of this posed difficult new possibilities for women's religious role. The "new woman" was a different kind of being than her Victorian predecessor. No longer a unity of soul and body, she was in fact multiple: a sexed body, an ungendered brain, and an unfettered individual personality. The new formulation promised much, for as diverse individuals, women could argue more effectively for social equality. But they could also be genuinely selfish. Remarking on the past example of Victorian womanhood, one woman wondered a bit shamefacedly, "Can we remember that selflessness, and see no difference between it and the present feminine individualism?"[59] And they were also capable of introspection and doubt. "It has always been carelessly assumed," the *Christian Century* editorialized in 1920, "that the church need give no attention to women — that it would hold them as a matter of course." But now, the author admitted, women were no longer Christians just "because they happen to be women. They pause and question here as in all things else."[60]

In the early twentieth century, therefore, the woman and religion question became both more pressing and less interesting. Two brief episodes among northern Presbyterians offer a good case in point. In 1919 and again in 1929-30, the denomination debated opening various church offices — elder, licensed preacher, and ordained pastor — to women. The presenting issue in both cases was female discontent over the reorganization of denominational boards and agencies, a move which consolidated all of the mission agencies into one and summarily ended the existence of the independent women's missionary work. Those pushing for ordination were intensely aware of the growing frustration among Presbyterian laywomen, and of the many competing opportunities

58. On the "discovery of the subconscious," see Ann Taves, *Fits, Trances, and Visions: Experiencing Religion and Explaining Experience from Wesley to James* (Princeton, N.J.: Princeton University Press, 1999), 254-55. See also David Riesman, Nathan Glazer, Reuel Denney, *The Lonely Crowd: A Study of the Changing American Character* (New York: Doubleday, 1954); Warren Susman, *Culture as History: The Transformation of American Society in the Twentieth Century* (New York: Pantheon Books, 1984), 271-85; Anthony Giddens, *Modernity and Self-Identity: Self and Society in the Late Modern Age* (Stanford: Stanford University Press, 1991).

59. Margaret Deland, "The Change in the Feminine Ideal," *Atlantic Monthly* 105 (March 1910): 292.

60. "What Shall Be Done With the Women?" *Christian Century,* 1 April 1920, 6.

opening up to them in secular arenas. They feared, quite appropriately, that churches were falling hopelessly behind the times.

But the women who pushed for the denominational overtures were hardly radical people. In a key discussion of the pending proposals for ordination in 1929, one observer reported that "Every one felt that . . . she personally did not want to be a pastor or an elder, and would doubtless vote against a woman pastor in her local church." Many confessed to worrying more about the "growing demands of young people that all sex bars in ecclesiastical matters be removed."[61] The stakes were genuinely high, as were the possibilities for success, but Presbyterian women did not rally behind the cause. When the overture for women's ordination failed in 1930, it "hardly occasioned a murmur"; the decision to allow women to be elected as elders "was received with only feeble applause."[62]

Part of the reason for the silence was an underlying confusion about what Presbyterian women might demand from their denomination. In the mid-1920s the General Assembly commissioned two major studies of "unrest" in the church, one focusing on the fundamentalist-modernist controversy and the other on women's response to the restructuring of the mission boards. In their report detailing the "causes of unrest," the authors, Margaret Hodge and Catherine Bennett, concluded simply that "Woman asks to be considered in the light of her ability and not of her sex."[63] The confusion of categories — the mythical nineteenth-century "woman" demanding treatment as a modern independent individual — illustrates the liminal state of the discussion. In 1928, a round-table conversation between church executives and "Fifteen Representative Women" dealt with the problem more explicitly. Noting that "the change in the status of women in the last fifty years is the most significant thing that has happened in twenty centuries," Emma Speer admitted that "the Church's attitude toward the place of women is only in the most dim way understood both by women themselves and by the men in the church."[64] Yet another participant argued that the women of the denomination were simply not interested in public debate over their right to leadership. "I think there is nothing we would deprecate so much as any controversy presented to any body on the basis of sex," she said. "We do not wish that that issue shall be brought up in any action

61. "Women's Meetings in St. Paul," *Women and Missions* 6 (July 1929): 126.

62. Mary E. Moore, "Women at the General Assembly," *Women and Missions* 7 (July 1930): 123.

63. *Causes of Unrest Among the Women of the Church* (1927), 27.

64. "Conference of the General Council with Fifteen Representative Women at the Fourth Presbyterian Church, Chicago, Ill., November 22, 1928," 12 [Presbyterian Historical Society, Philadelphia].

which should be taken."[65] Though the emerging consensus in the discussion was, as one denominational official put it, "the complete equality of men and women as members of the Church," a great deal of the talk concerned the institutional survival of women's separate missionary societies. In the end Robert Speer concluded, "We started out with the theory of absolute equality. We have come to the point of deepening distinctions." By the end of the discussion, the committee seemed convinced that, in Speer's words, "The only differences inside Christianity are differences of ability and capacity." No one on the committee, however, could offer any clear rationale for changing, or maintaining, women's present status in the church.[66]

Opponents of the ordination measures also struggled to frame their complaints. The *Presbyterian* affirmed, somewhat vaguely, that "the majority of men and women" felt that there was "something abnormal in a woman addressing a mixed public assembly." Another contributor agreed that the prospect was "offensive" and "indecent," arguing that "Nature seems to object to this as well as Scripture."[67] Increasingly, however, opponents of the overtures turned to more ad hominem attacks, linking the ordination questions to a liberal conspiracy for control of the mission boards. Others invoked the dubious example of Mary Baker Eddy as a warning that women were more easily deceived into false doctrines. Seattle pastor Mark Matthews denounced the "female pulpiteeress" as an "ecclesiastical freak," a human absurdity with no right to speak in church.[68]

Not surprisingly, fewer and fewer people had the stomach for this kind of controversy. After the 1920s, women's ordination simply dropped from the Presbyterian agenda, as it did from most of the major Protestant denominations. It quietly resumed in the late 1950s, but for the next decade or so the number of women entering the ministry remained low. Thus, a debate that had endlessly riled nineteenth-century Protestants hardly made a mark on their early-twentieth-century successors. And so, the question: Why did women drop the fight for equal rights in the church in the midst of a clearly dynamic time of change in their political, educational, and economic status? Why did they have so little to say about religion?

In the history of American women, the early twentieth century was a para-

65. "Conference of the General Council with Fifteen Representative Women," 10-11.
66. "Conference of the General Council with Fifteen Representative Women," 13, 16, 32.
67. "Paul's Teaching About Women," *Presbyterian*, July 15, 1920, 4; Daniel Williams, "Three Articles on Women Speaking in Church," *Presbyterian*, August 5, 1920, 7. See also "Women and the Order of God's House," *Presbyterian*, September 23, 1920, 1.
68. Matthews, "Why Women in the Pulpit?" *Presbyterian*, January 16, 1930, 7. See also Bendroth, *Fundamentalism and Gender*, ch. 3.

doxical time. It marked the emergence of the new woman in all of her frank, open spirit, but also, as many historians have noted, a surprisingly muted feminine voice of social protest. In contrast to the robust gender politics of the late nineteenth century, women in the latter period struggled to emerge as subjects with their own view and volition. The esoteric New Thought movement, which emphasized the force of female mind over matter, sought unsuccessfully to re-envision women as dynamic, desiring selves.[69] Even the frank sexual banter of New York's bohemian couples was dominated by the language of male desire and, in some cases, became a soapbox for men's grievances against women. The goal of sex talk was honesty, but as Christine Stansell notes, too often it became "an early contribution to the annals of 'men talk, women listen.'"[70]

## Conclusion

For women, traditional Christian understandings of the soul are a valuable but complicated resource. Feminist critics, for example, have pointed out the misogynist consequences of the dualistic soul-body model, as well as the stereotypical implications of imagining soul and body into a single gendered whole. Moreover, after decades of effort to reclaim "our bodies, ourselves," modern women do not require spiritual transcendence to escape from physical inferiority. Nor can they affirm the Victorian ideal of womanhood, which imagined bodies and souls in a tight unity. Though in some sense, this model resembles the contemporary idea of "wholeness," it denied women the opportunity for introspection or growth. One-dimensional, "self-less" women could not doubt God, nor could they fully believe. Despite these difficulties, the soul question can't be lightly cast aside as just another means of essentializing women into a single mold or denigrating their physical bodies. As the nineteenth-century debate over women's ecclesiastical role clearly shows, ensoulment — whether understood dualistically or not — has been closely tied to matters of spiritual authority, specifically women's right to speak.

Perhaps the Victorian model suggests some benefit in revisiting not the feminine soul, but the place where the inner and outer person meet. Certainly in the broad flow of Christian tradition the intersection between spirit and flesh has been the most dynamic angle for understanding personhood. In

69. Satter, *Each Mind a Kingdom*.

70. Christine Stansell, "Talking About Sex: Early-Twentieth-Century Radicals and Moral Confessions," in *Moral Problems in American Life*, ed. Karen Halttunen and Lewis Perry (Ithaca, N.Y.: Cornell University Press, 1998), 305.

Christian thought the two are separate and distinct aspects of what is often termed human nature — the apostle Paul describes them in a constant war for supremacy. But they are also indispensable to each other; awareness of their conflict is, in some way, essential to becoming a mature person. Though terms like flesh and spirit are a bit arcane for present-day speech, the ideas they are meant to convey might not be completely obsolete. Contemporary awareness of the complex, often mysterious interplay between body chemistry and individual motivation certainly leaves room for seeing personhood as something more than a simple addition of a body plus a soul. And in women's case, given the longstanding tendency to overestimate the purity of the soul or the fallenness of the body, this more nuanced understanding of embodiment is genuinely well warranted. But this also means that for women there is no luxury — or necessity — of being sinless in the older nineteenth-century sense. It means, in the end, that they have the opportunity to be both thoroughly flawed and authentically human.

# Me, Myself, and Inc.: "Social Selfhood," Corporate Humanism, and Religious Longing in American Management Theory, 1908-1956

EUGENE MCCARRAHER

It is axiomatic that over the course of the twentieth century the structure of the American economy was transformed by the dominant influence of a relatively small number of large, heavily capitalized, nationally organized, and bureaucratically managed business corporations. What is less well understood, though, is the effect that these changes would have on the beliefs and ethos of managers and other white-collar salaried employees who labored within the new corporate world. What would become of such individuals, mere figures in a complex carpet of massive structural change? And indeed, what would become of individuality itself? For much of American history, selfhood had been defined in terms appropriate to a world of small-scale proprietary enterprise and culturally dominant Protestantism. But such assumptions would not suffice for the brave new corporate dispensation. As the controlling conditions of business and labor departed dramatically from those of the past, it seemed that the optimal forms of selfhood for this new corporate environment would also have to be redefined.

There has been no scarcity of perceptive American writers in the past century who have contributed to our outlook on this phenomenon; one thinks immediately, for example, of such gifted social observers as Thorstein Veblen, Robert Lynd, David Riesman, C. Wright Mills, Vance Packard, and William H. Whyte. Yet Eugene McCarraher's vivid and imaginative essay, which examines the efforts of a series of American management writers to reconfigure the concept of selfhood in terms

Thanks to Wilfred M. McClay for his friendship, encouragement, and invitation to join a remarkable team of scholars. Among them, Kurt Berends, Casey Blake, Tom Cole, Daniel Walker Howe, Betsy Lasch-Quinn, and John McGreevy have been especially helpful with criticism and advice. For conversations about earlier drafts or their contents, I also thank Howard Brick, Michael Hanby, Stanley Hauerwas, Seth Koven, Jackson Lears, John Milbank, Jeffrey Sklansky, Lauren Winner, and Paul Wright.

more compatible with the needs of the corporate milieu, breaks new ground. It does so precisely by taking careful notice of something previous critics have declined to take seriously: the religious, or quasi-religious, language and aspirations that animate such authors and texts. Unlike previous critics, McCarraher genuinely respects the needs that are met by religion, while also being unusually attentive to the cultural power of ideas — particularly false ideas that nevertheless are used to address real human yearnings. Through an examination of the work and influence of Simon Patten, Frederick Taylor, Mary Parker Follett, Peter Drucker, and Steven Covey, McCarraher casts a critical eye upon the prescriptive ideals and disciplines these writers offered as ways of addressing the personal and religious longings produced by the world of corporate business, and of thereby recalibrating selfhood itself. Indeed, when considered in the light of older religious traditions of belief about human personhood, traditions that these management writers freely borrowed from and traded upon for their own purposes, the appropriation of such religious ideals for commercial and managerial purposes takes on a truly sinister and totalizing aspect. From the standpoint of religion it represents a profanation every bit as lamentable and dangerous as the melding of religion and state — the confusion of church and counting house. Among its other ambitions, then, McCarraher's essay seeks to protect the temple from the moneychangers — an undertaking for which there is admirable precedent. Eugene McCarraher is Assistant Professor of Humanities at Villanova University, and the author of *Christian Critics: Religion and the Impasse in Modern American Social Thought* (Cornell, 2000).

When Henry James walked through the Waldorf-Astoria, he saw the marriage of heaven and hell. The Waldorf became, in James' account, an epitome of a new America, a site betokening the impending arrival of "a perfect human felicity." With its visitors, clerks, and shop-owners mingling in vivid and delightful promiscuity, the Waldorf heralded a consummation of history that James rendered, at first, in religious terms. Embracing its milling guests as "the serene faithful," the Waldorf was "a temple builded, with clustering chapels and shrines, to an idea," that of "a wondrous complexity" whose "every wheel . . . was on the best terms with all the rest." And yet, though enchanted by this "earth and its heaven," James paused to reflect on the love that moved "this general machinery," and he segued slowly from admiration to foreboding. While admiring the play of people and business, he could not distinguish the "ingenuous joy below" from the "consummate management above," so easily and completely had they "melted together." Indeed, James discerned in the Waldorf's harmony the "absolute presiding power" of "the master-spirits of management," who impressed James as "the intensest examples of American character." "Waving the magical baton of some high-stationed orchestral leader," the exemplary manager understood his "material" and played it "like a master indeed." Indeed, for all their lightness of being, the hotel's visitors and employees danced like "an army of puppets" on strings manipulated by the manager-spirits. For the managerial character possessed "innumerable ways of pulling," subtle and almost undetectable means of disguising control as freedom. Though unable to see the master-spirits "more intimately at work," James suspected a managerial ruse in the "apparently ingenuous agitation" of the Waldorf's faithful.[1] So in the Waldorf's managerial temple, among the anonymous technicians of community, James discerned an eschatology of expertise, a paradise convened in the corporate merger of self and organization.

James' prophecy of panoptical blessedness anticipated many a vision of "the air-conditioned nightmare." We are all familiar with the gray-flannelled fiends in the demonology of twentieth-century cultural criticism: the "other-directed character," the "organization man," the "cheerful robot," the "one-dimensional man," the "narcissist" or "minimal self." Whatever the variations, the usual suspects in this critical lineage raise the specter of a happy but orchestrated self, convinced of its freedom as it moves in a cage without bars. This specter has haunted not only critics but also historians of American culture, who see in modern selfhood the "triumph of the therapeutic," the conquest of bureaucratic rationality, or the victory of consumer culture. This figure of consumer selfhood is secular, morally elastic, and insistent on personal freedom, all the while indentured to the corporation, mesmerized by mass culture, and dependent on credentialed expertise.[2]

---

1. Henry James, *The American Scene*, intro. Leon Edel (Bloomington, 1968 [1904]), 102-107.

2. Henry Miller, *The Air-Conditioned Nightmare* (New York, 1945); David Riesman, *The Lonely Crowd: A Study of the Changing American Character* (New Haven, 1950); William H. Whyte, *The Organization Man* (New York, 1956); C. Wright Mills, *White Collar: The American Middle Classes* (New York, 1951); Herbert Marcuse, *One-Dimensional Man: Studies in the Ideology of Advanced Industrial Society* (Boston, 1964); Christopher Lasch, *The Culture of Narcissism: American Life in an Age of Diminished Expectations* (New York, 1979); Lasch, *The Minimal Self: Psychic Survival in Troubled Times* (New York, 1984); Jackson Lears, *No Place of Grace: Antimodernism and the Transformation of American Culture, 1880-1920* (New York, 1981); Lears, "From Salvation to Self-Realization: Advertising and the Therapeutic Roots of the Consumer Culture, 1880-1930," in Richard Wightman Fox and T. J. Jackson Lears, eds., *The Culture of Consumption: Critical Essays in American History, 1880-1980* (New York, 1983), 1-38; "The Ad Man and the Grand Inquisitor: Intimacy, Publicity, and the Managed Self in America, 1880-1940," in George Levine, ed., *Constructions of the Self* (New Brunswick, NJ, 1992), 107-41. Whereas Lears

While this pedigree of indictment remains formidable and indispensable, its historical veracity and critical power have come under increasing scrutiny. Some see in the attack on the therapeutic ethos a skinflint dismissal of the real victories over misery and repression enabled by technical and psychological prowess. Others discern in the vilification of modern selfhood a covert nostalgia for the rule of the bourgeois male, the steely, "inner-directed" man who knew his own mind and counted his own money. Those in search of more nuanced accounts of modern therapeutic discourse contend that the rhetorics of "personality" have been resonant forms of social criticism, moral reflection, and religious aspiration. More recently and most contentiously, some historians have argued that consumer culture and corporate capitalism fostered the emergence of a "social selfhood" or "postmodern subjectivity" rich in personal and political possibilities.[3]

Since they focus so often on "consumer culture," both detractors and celebrants of consumer subjectivity seem to take for granted that modern American selfhood is either unanchored, or anchored only tenuously, in the realm of labor and production. When cultural historians do take note of the fact that most adults still spend most of their weekly waking hours at a job of some sort, they often rehearse familiar assertions about the "monotony" or "degradation" of modern work — indisputable assertions, I would hastily agree, but also, I suspect, as lacking in nuance and sympathetic insight as crude rejections of "the therapeutic." If, like Richard Hofstadter, we acknowledge the injustice and indignity of the modern workplace while feeling that there is "something else

---

concentrates on the Ad Man, I look in the present essay at the Grand Inquisitor as Corporate Manager, who orchestrates not only the production of goods and services, but the creation of a corporate self.

3. A representative of the first sort of criticism is Peter Clecak, *America's Quest for the Ideal Self: Dissent and Fulfillment in the 60s and 70s* (New York: 1983), esp. 232-35, 266-71; of the second, Andreas Huyssen, "Mass Culture as Woman: Modernism's Other," in *After the Great Divide* (Bloomington, 1987), 47-57. The third line of criticism includes Casey Nelson Blake, "The Young Intellectuals and the Culture of Personality," *American Literary History* 1 (Fall 1989): 510-34; Blake, *Beloved Community: The Cultural Criticism of Randolph Bourne, Van Wyck Brooks, Waldo Frank, and Lewis Mumford* (Chapel Hill, 1990); Richard Wightman Fox, "The Culture of Liberal Protestant Progressivism, 1870-1925," *Journal of Interdisciplinary History* 23 (Winter 1993): 639-60; Doug Rossinow, *The Politics of Authenticity: Liberalism, Christianity, and the New Left in America* (New York, 1998), esp. 53-84; Eugene McCarraher, "Heal Me: 'Personality,' Religion, and the Therapeutic Ethic in Modern America," *Intellectual History Newsletter* 21 (1999): 31-40; and McCarraher, *Christian Critics: Religion and the Impasse in Modern American Social Thought* (Ithaca and London, 2000), esp. 112-46. The fourth line is represented best by James Livingston, *Pragmatism and the Political Economy of Cultural Revolution, 1850-1940* (Chapel Hill, 1993), and Livingston, *Pragmatism, Feminism, and Democracy* (New York and London, 2002).

even in white collar life," then perhaps it is time for cultural historians to leave the department stores and make appointments in boardrooms, suites, and offices.[4] The *producer* cultures of corporate America deserve urgent and overdue attention, and among the essential stories of those corporate cultures will be those of the laboring self — a self constructed, at least in part, by the "master-spirits of management."

In examining the spiritual mastery of management, I advance two related claims. First, corporate management theory is a neglected but pivotal discourse of selfhood in modern American culture. Arising from the collapse of the proprietary-Protestant moral economy that prevailed in the nineteenth century, management theory has been a form of moral philosophy and a vision of "social selfhood" for the corporate capitalist order. Created by a business intelligentsia of academics, journalists, and corporate professionals, it has remained, since the 1910s, one of the most articulate and systematic vehicles of the corporate moral economy — "corporate humanism," as I dub it. In corporate humanism, the corporate manager has been what Alasdair MacIntyre has called a "moral character," a "social role which provides society with its moral definitions" — what James considered an "intense example of American character."[5] This managerial archetype has been tied to a new conception of agency and labor — "corporate selfhood" — which partially supplanted the proprietary-Protestant ideal of the autonomous individual.

My second claim is that corporate selfhood has been bound up with a sacralized ideal of the corporation. Managerial conceptions of the laboring self have contained — in both senses of the word — aspirations to a skillful and beloved community of production, a place of "perfect human felicity." The literature of corporate humanism abounds with evidence of moral and religious concerns, and many of the managerial theorists of corporate selfhood thought the realm of production necessary for the fruition of moral personality and even for contact with divinity. Even if, as I believe, this corporate clerisy has

4. Richard Hofstadter to C. Wright Mills, January 19, 1952, cited in Irving Louis Horowitz, *C. Wright Mills: An American Utopian* (New York, 1983), 251. An excellent start toward reclaiming the cultural history of the corporate middle classes is Burton J. Bledstein and Robert D. Johnston, eds., *The Middling Sorts: Explorations in the History of the American Middle Class* (New York and London, 2001).

5. Alasdair MacIntyre, *After Virtue: A Study in Moral Theory* (South Bend, 1981), 31. I would contend that, even when studied as a form of moral philosophy, management thought is also what Michel Foucault would call a "technology of the self" or a "political technology of individuals"; see Foucault, "The Political Technology of Individuals," in Luther H. Martin, Huck Gutman, and Patrick H. Hutton, eds., *Technologies of the Self: A Seminar with Michel Foucault* (Amherst, 1988), 144-62.

helped to desecrate the sacramentality of human labor, their ideological mission deserves respect even — perhaps precisely — in its perversity.

As my language now makes clear, theology will play a major role in this essay. Because corporate humanism and management theory have exhibited unmistakable traces of religious aspiration, the history of selfhood fashioned in the crucible of the business corporation offers an auspicious opportunity to make a theological contribution to historical writing. One of the purposes of the Christian Scholars Program's project on "The Nature of the Human Person" is to "contribute to current topics of conversation in [our] disciplines," and one of the aims of the historians is to trace the development of the "fragile concept" of the human person. Anyone who considers theology a truthful account of the human condition must accord it a central (but by no means exclusive) place in the historical imagination. To be sure, theological commitment might seem to open an impassable chasm between historians convinced of the relevance of theology and scholars who consider it irrelevant, incomprehensible, or misleading. While I concede the difficulty of bridging this gulf, I do not believe that a theological approach to history has to be arcane, hermetic, or exclusionary. Skeptical historians should consider such a project akin to Marxist scholarship, a rich and indispensable lineage with a vision, anthropology, and lexicon in which adherents formulate problems, encounter other traditions, and engage in criticism. (Indeed, it will be apparent that I see considerable affinity between Marxism and Christian theology.)[6] Much of what I argue

6. George M. Marsden, *The Outrageous Idea of Christian Scholarship* (New York, 1997), has been the most cogent (if also unsatisfying) statement of the argument that religious, and particularly Christian, historians must reassert the importance of theology to their craft. While I heartily endorse his call upon religious historians to demand a "seat at the table" of the contemporary academy (51-59), I would think that a more important task — unaddressed by Marsden, in my view — is having something worth saying at that table. Marsden offers salutary advice about what *not* to say in "What Difference Might Christian Perspectives Make?" in Ronald A. Wells, ed., *History and the Christian Historian* (Grand Rapids and Cambridge, 1998), 13-14, where he explains what should be meant by "distinctively Christian scholarship": Christian historians will, like Marxists or feminists, ask distinctive kinds of questions, but they will not always arrive at conclusions *only they* can reach. I think this formulation guards against a fetishism of historiographical "difference."

I endorse John Milbank's all-too brief but enormously suggestive reflections on the relationship of theology to history. The church, he writes, "was only constituted, historically, by a particular theoretical perspective upon history . . . a certain history, culminating at a certain point, and continued in the practice of the Church, interprets and 'locates' all other history." A Christian historian, he continues, "'reads' all other history as most fundamentally anticipation, or sinful refusal, of salvation." Especially concerned to define theology's relationship to Marxism (a project botched, he argues, by "liberation theologians"), Milbank maintains that while Marxism offers "a better reading of the 'logic' and 'grammar' of capitalism," theology "would

about corporate selfhood will be comprehensible (and I hope convincing) to historians without theological commitments. Some of my terms — ecclesial bodies, sacramentality — will seem, at first (and maybe last), as hard to credit as reification or penis envy. But, in my view, theology — and particularly Augustinian theology — provides terms in which historians can *describe* historical reality, not simply pontificate about its "ultimate meaning." So to believing historians, I offer this essay as an experiment and a model; to others, I offer it in the spirit of experiment and invitation.

Because I want to reformulate some of the issues involved in the history of modern American selfhood, this article will feature an extended historiographical and conceptual reflection. I begin with a broad discussion of the historical literature on economy and selfhood in America, focusing on the recent imbroglio over the emergence of "social selfhood" and corporate capitalism from 1890 to 1930. Historians have yet to credit and grapple with the religious questions — acknowledged as such by the historical actors themselves — that were raised by the appearance of corporate enterprise. I then link this discussion to reflections on selfhood in the work of MacIntyre; the sociologist Philip Rieff; the theologians John Milbank and Graham Ward; and the philosopher, anarcho-syndicalist, and quasi-Christian mystic Simone Weil. I argue that the retrieval of an Augustinian account of selfhood in the "earthly" and "heavenly" cities, together with Weil's exploration of the spiritual nature of work, shed the most illuminating theological light on the laboring self in corporate modernity. I then turn to an array of business and managerial writers who espoused — and at times critiqued — the conventions of corporate selfhood from the 1910s to the 1950s, the Fordist epoch of corporate capitalism. (Because I am interested in management theory as a language of legitimation, I will *not* be discussing the ways in which this language has been employed, modified, or ignored by actual managers and executives. The daily use of this language is itself the subject of a small but suggestive literature.)[7] Throughout the unfinished history of corpo-

claim to say — in fully historical terms — more precisely what it is that capitalism prefers, and what it refuses"; *Theology and Social Theory: Beyond Secular Reason* (Oxford, 1990), 246-47; for Milbank's critique of Marxism and liberation theology, see 177-255; see also Milbank, "'The Body by Love Possessed': Christianity and Late Capitalism in Britain," *Modern Theology* 3 (March 1986): 35-65, and Milbank, "On Baseless Suspicion: Christianity and the Crisis of Socialism," *New Blackfriars* 69 (January 1988): 4-19. For a more detailed theological engagement with Marxism, see Nicholas Lash, *A Matter of Hope: A Theologian's Reflections on the Thought of Karl Marx* (Notre Dame, 1982 [1981]).

7. This literature includes studies by students of management and by sociologists critical of managerial ideology. For examples of the former, see Christopher Nock and John Milliman, "Thought Self-Leadership: Finding Spiritual Fulfillment in Organizational Life," *Journal of Management Psychology* 96 (January 1994): 5-23, and Peter Ackers and Diane Preston, "Born

rate capitalism, the management vistas of social selfhood have always perverted persistent longings, not only for control and fulfillment in labor, but for celestial felicity, for a workplace recast, in James's words, as part of "this earth and its heaven."

## "A school of character": Moral Economy, Selfhood, and Religion in American Historical Writing

Obviously, historians don't readily consider capitalism a perverse "celestial city." Taking as an implicit standard the pre-capitalist world described by Karl Polanyi in *The Great Transformation* (1944) — one in which "man's economy, as a rule" was indissoluble from "custom and law, magic and religion" — historians continue to write about capitalism as an *amoral* economy energized by a "possessive individualism" unimpeded by moral or religious strictures. (And they do so despite a wealth of insights into the "Protestant work ethic," the "humanitarian sensibility" of the nineteenth century, and the "corporate liberalism" of the twentieth.) But if we return to E. P. Thompson's introduction of the term "moral economy" into historical writing, we can identify a capitalist moral imagination. The pre-capitalist moral economy of eighteenth-century England was, in Thompson's words, "a consistent, traditional view of social norms and obligations, of the proper economic functions of several parties within the community," a view which rested on "definite and passionately held notions of the common weal." Although Thompson later claimed that "moral economy" meant something only in the specific context of the food riots he was discussing, he also conceded that while he had "father[ed] the term . . . upon current academic discourse," it had "long forgotten its paternity."[8] I take

Again? The Ethics and Efficacy of the Conversion Experience in Contemporary Management Development," *Journal of Management Studies* 32 (September 1997): 680-96; for the latter, see Paul Heelas, "The Sacralization of the Self and New Age Capitalism," in Nicholas Abercrombie and Alan Warde, eds., *Social Change in Contemporary Britain* (Cambridge, 1992), 139-66, and Catherine Casey, *Work, Self, and Society: After Industrialism* (New York and London, 1995), esp. 89-117.

8. Karl Polanyi, *The Great Transformation* (Boston, 1957 [1944]), 43-55, quotes on 46, 55. See also "The Place of Economies in Societies" (1957) in *Primitive, Archaic, and Modern Economies: Essays of Karl Polanyi*, ed. George Dalton (Garden City, N.Y., 1968), 116-38. On the "Protestant work ethic," see the classic source, Max Weber, *The Protestant Ethic and the Spirit of Capitalism*, trans. Talcott Parsons (New York, 1958 [1904]), as well as Stephen Innes, *Creating the Commonwealth: The Economic Culture of Puritan New England* (New York, 1995), 5-159; on the "humanitarian sensibility," see Thomas Haskell, "Capitalism and the Origins of the Humanitarian Sensibility," pts. 1 and 2, *American Historical Review* 90 (April and June 1985): 339-61, 547-66; on

this as a license to shelter and employ Thompson's orphan child. Since capitalism clearly possesses "norms," defines "obligations," and affirms "passionately held notions of the common weal," it also thereby articulates ideals of moral selfhood.

Historians have crafted an enormous body of scholarship on the moral economy of nineteenth-century America that ties together political economy, selfhood, and religion. The broad picture that emerges from this work appears with various titles: "producerism," "free labor," "proprietary capitalism," "populism," "modern subjectivity." This constellation of work, selfhood, democracy, and salvation — what I will call the "proprietary-Protestant moral economy" — combined craft labor, patriarchal proprietorship, and Protestant religion. Figured in the yeoman farmer or the leather-aproned artisan, popularized in periodicals, almanacs, sermons, and dime novels, and theorized in classical political economy, this moral economy embodied several interrelated propositions. Work or "productive labor" was the design and creation of goods for the market. This productive labor was performed by a proprietor, an independent farmer or artisan who both owned his own tools and productive space and exercised the requisite mental and manual energies. The proprietor was also the white male patriarch whose participation in the market mandated both his dominion over household production and his subordination of females, who were assigned the duties of reproduction and nurturance that sustained and counterbalanced the conflicts of economic life. Productive labor presupposed a cognitive order of epistemology and representation — the "plain-speech" tradition, faculty psychology, "evangelical rationality" — that distinguished rigidly between knower and known, objectivity and subjectivity, truth and opinion, reality and its symbolic rendering. As the nexus of productive labor, legal ownership, rational will, and representational fidelity, the independent proprietor signified genuine moral selfhood, possession of which sanctioned both consumption of goods and participation in democratic politics. Finally, this moral economy was leavened by a religious faith, mainly evangelical Protestantism, whose work ethic and sense of "calling" constituted the covenant theology of proprietary America.

---

"corporate liberalism," see James Weinstein, *The Corporate Ideal in the Liberal State, 1900-1918* (Boston, 1968); R. Jeffrey Lustig, *Corporate Liberalism: The Origins of Modern American Political Theory, 1890-1920* (Berkeley, 1982); and Martin J. Sklar, *The Corporate Reconstruction of American Capitalism, 1890-1916: The Market, The Law, and Politics* (Cambridge and New York, 1988), esp. 333-441.

On "moral economy," see E. P. Thompson, "The Moral Economy of the English Crowd in the Eighteenth Century" (1971), in *Customs in Common* (New York, 1991), 188. Thompson fretted over the fate of his conceptual progeny in a 1991 essay, "The Moral Economy Reviewed," in *Customs in Common*, 259-351.

This "soul's economy," in Emerson's words, fostered what Daniel Walker Howe has termed "the autonomous self" of rational will and proprietary labor. As a writer in the *Atlantic Monthly* eulogized in a 1904 homage to small business, the small proprietorship had been "a school of character second in importance only to the Church."[9]

Historians also agree that the industrial and cultural revolutions of the 1870s to the 1940s posed fatal challenges to this proprietary-Protestant dispensation. The corporate form of industrial capitalism entailed the separation of ownership from effective control of the enterprise — a solvent, administered mainly by the "visible hand" of corporate management, of the fusion of legal proprietorship and productive labor. At the same time, the visible hands of corporate managers and technical professionals effected the shotgun divorce of mental and manual labor by appropriating the craft knowledge and organizational prowess once possessed by artisan-proprietors. Meanwhile, the transformation of the independent male proprietor into a waged or salaried worker, together with the growing exodus of women from the household into the wage labor force, precipitated the prolonged "gender trouble" or "sexual revolution" that unsettled the Protestant moral economy's conventions of reproduction, gender, and sexual conduct. Evangelical Protestantism reeled under the demographic assault of Jewish and Catholic immigrants, as well as the intellectual bombardment of evolutionary biology, biblical scholarship, and a liberal theology that ascribed enormous redemptive significance to scientific investigation and professional knowledge. Because

---

9. Henry A. Stimson, "The Small Business as a School of Manhood," *Atlantic Monthly* 93 (March 1904): 337. My description of this "proprietary-Protestant moral economy" relies on a vast literature which includes Eric Foner, *Free Soil, Free Labor, Free Men: The Ideology of the Republican Party before the Civil War* (New York, 1970); Herbert G. Gutman, *Work, Culture, and Society in Industrializing America* (New York, 1976); Ann Douglas, *The Feminization of American Culture* (New York, 1977), 44-117; Daniel Rodgers, *The Work Ethic in Industrial America, 1850-1920* (Chicago, 1978), esp. 1-29; Jean Bethke Elshtain, *Public Man, Private Woman: Women in Social and Political Thought* (Princeton, 1981), 100-146; John P. Diggins, *The Lost Soul of American Politics: Virtue, Self-Interest, and the Foundations of Liberalism* (Chicago, 1984); David Roediger, *The Wages of Whiteness: Race and the Making of the American Working Class* (New York, 1991), esp. 43-64; Lears, *Fables of Abundance: A Cultural History of Advertising in America* (New York, 1994), 82-85; Lears, *Something for Nothing: Luck in America* (New York, 2003), 61-62, 168-78; Stephanie McCurry, *Master of Small Worlds: Yeoman Households, Gender Relations, and the Political Culture of the Antebellum South Carolina Low Country* (New York, 1995); Wilfred M. McClay, *The Masterless: Self and Society in Modern America* (Chapel Hill, 1994), 40-73; Daniel Walker Howe, *Making the American Self: Jonathan Edwards to Abraham Lincoln* (Cambridge, Mass., 1997); Howe, *The Political Culture of the American Whigs* (Chicago, 1979), 96-122, 150-80; and, most recently, Jeffrey Sklansky, *The Soul's Economy: Market Society and Selfhood in American Thought, 1820-1920* (Chapel Hill, 2002), 13-31.

the first generations of the professional-managerial class were trained largely in still strongly religious universities, liberal Protestants officiated at the ordination of technical and managerial experts.[10]

This corporate reconstruction of American capitalism has been labeled "Fordism," an industrial regime which originated in the early 1900s, reached its apogee in the two decades after World War II, and eroded over the 1970s and 1980s. The Fordist political economy mandated standardization of design and production; mechanization of assembly; a high degree of division of labor, with a corresponding routinization of the worker's tasks; the spread of managerial expertise in production and marketing; and the concentration of all these activities in a single plant. Politically, Fordism faced what Ellis Hawley has called "the problem of monopoly," the question of who would define the productive, social, and political powers of corporate capital. Fordism accommodated, at least in key industrial sectors, labor unions capable of bargaining with corporate management over wages, benefits, and conditions. Because unions also acquired some capacity to enlist state power, and because corporate capital needed similar access on its own behalf, Fordism eventually featured a more or less interventionist state, which attempted to stabilize the business cycle, foster economic growth, and temper class conflict. This solution was the "New Deal order."[11]

10. Here I am encapsulating another vast body of literature, including Alfred D. Chandler, Jr., *The Visible Hand: The Managerial Revolution in American Business* (Cambridge, Mass., 1977); David Montgomery, *The Fall of the House of Labor: The Workplace, The State, and American Labor Activism, 1865-1925* (Cambridge and New York, 1987), esp. 9-57, 214-56; Harry Braverman, *Labor and Monopoly Capital: The Degradation of Work in the Twentieth Century* (New York, 1974), esp. 85-168; Angel Kwollek-Folland, *Engendering Business: Men and Women in the Corporate Office, 1870-1930* (Baltimore, 1994); Olivier Zunz, *Making America Corporate, 1870-1920* (Chicago, 1990); Susan Porter Benson, *Counter Cultures: Saleswomen, Managers, and Customers in American Department Stores, 1890-1940* (Urbana, 1986); Sharon Hartman Strom, *Beyond the Typewriter: Gender, Class, and the Origins of Modern Office Work, 1900-1930* (Urbana, 1992); Clark Davis, *Company Men: White-Collar Life and Corporate Cultures in Los Angeles, 1892-1941* (Baltimore, 2000); John Bodnar, *The Transplanted: A History of Immigrants in Urban America* (Bloomington, 1985), esp. 30-84; David Hollinger, "Justification by Verification: The Scientific Challenge to the Moral Authority of Christianity in Modern America," in Michael J. Lacey, ed., *Religion and Twentieth-Century American Intellectual Life* (New York, 1989), 116-35; Julie A. Reuben, *The Making of the Modern University: Intellectual Transformation and the Marginalization of Morality* (Chicago, 1996), 61-187.

11. Antonio Gramsci, "Americanism and Fordism," in David Forgacs, ed., *The Antonio Gramsci Reader* (New York, 1988), 275-99; David Harvey, *The Condition of Postmodernity* (Oxford, 1990), 125-40, is a nice summary of the characteristics of "Fordism." On the "problem of monopoly," see Ellis Hawley, *The New Deal and the Problem of Monopoly: A Study in Economic Ambivalence* (Princeton, 1966); "Herbert Hoover, the Commerce Secretariat, and the Vision of

Because mechanized production undermined proprietary conceptions of personal agency and selfhood, the Fordist regime confronted doubts about the moral legitimacy of the corporation. The corporation often figured in popular (and especially populist) culture as a soulless leviathan, destructive of the creativity and moral agency once located among artisan-proprietors and local communities. As Antonio Gramsci realized in his celebrated essay "Americanism and Fordism," the attempt to make "the whole life of the nation revolve around production" entailed the necessity of creating "a new type of worker and of man." "Hegemony is born in the factory," he asserted flatly. The creation of this new laboring self required "breaking up the old psycho-physical nexus" of proprietary artisanship which had, he admitted, engaged the worker's "intelligence, fantasy and initiative." True to Marxist teleology, Gramsci did not weep at the grave of the artisan, whose demise he refused to consider "the spiritual death of man." Fordist mechanization released subjectivity from production, enabling a freedom of mind which held revolutionary promise — even as, Gramsci recognized, "the industrialists are concerned about such things."[12]

So far, American historians have downplayed Gramsci's emphasis on the workplace origins of Fordist cultural hegemony by focusing on the realm of consumption. The crisis of American moral economy becomes the problem of "culture and commitment," in Warren Susman's formulation, the desire to foster "participation and belonging" by discovering "a special collective relationship in which all Americans might share." That collective relationship has been understood as a "consumer culture" — a "Republic of Goods," in Roland Marchand's words — which accompanied what Warren Susman labeled a shift "from character to personality." In their landmark 1983 collection of essays, Richard Fox and Jackson Lears described "the culture of consumption" as "an ethic, a standard of living, and a power structure," an "ideology and a way of seeing." Dispossessed from proprietary labor, unbound from Protestant hegemony, and increasingly reliant on expertise, the consumer self sheds the virtues associated with "character" — hard work, sobriety, self-denial — and follows a "new gospel of therapeutic release" which "subordinate[s] the old goal of transcendence to new ideals of self-fulfillment and immediate gratification." But this surrogate gospel of "personality" imprisons the self in a carceral culture of advertising, marketing, professional advice, and public relations. Under the cheerful aegis of "personality" — and under the political aegis of the corpora-

---

an 'Associative State,' 1921-1928," *Journal of American History* 61 (June 1974): 116-40. On the "New Deal order," see Steve Fraser and Gary Gerstle, eds., *The Rise and Fall of the New Deal Order, 1930 1980* (Princeton, 1989).

    12. Gramsci, "Americanism and Fordism," 278, 290, 295-96.

tion — the commodity form extends its reach from the purchase of material objects to the transformation of human consciousness into a storehouse of qualities for sale. Consumer subjectivity arises as well from an incessant identification with qualities attributed to commodities, and thus becomes the selfhood of commodity fetishism. The recovery of the self from consumer culture depends, accordingly, on the transcendence of consumer culture, whether in the form of socialism, artisanal labor, or populist politics.[13]

A growing number of historians, especially James Livingston, are eager to modify or discard this inherited wisdom. To Livingston, as to Gramsci, the rise of the corporation augured both a humane and democratic socialism and a rich and capacious selfhood. Joining in the rediscovery of pragmatism by historians and philosophers, Livingston sees in the work of William James and John Dewey a moral and intellectual matrix through which we can identify the possibilities residing in corporate capitalism. James and Dewey offer a "postrepublican frame of acceptance" through which Americans can view the demise of the proprietary republic and the ascendance of a corporate order as "the necessary condition of a passage beyond class society." The modal figure of this corporate order is a "social self" which, though sinfully conceived in corporate capitalism, will eventually incorporate and redeem its parent. Unanchored in male property ownership and released from artisanal "productive labor," this social self embraces new kinds of subjectivity and new forms of politics unrelated to class relations. Aware of its social origins and divested of the proprietary need to accumulate, this "postmodern moral personality," rather than being the demon of consumerist nihilism, is actually "a more promising bearer of an intelligible morality than the progeny of Enlightenment."[14] Often feared for its bright satanic offices, the corporation becomes, for Livingston, a new school of character.

Livingston often invokes Dewey as the prophet of social selfhood, exploring his portentous reflections in *The Public and Its Problems* (1927) and *Individualism Old and New* (1930) on "the change in social life from an individual to a

13. Warren Susman, *Culture as History: The Transformation of American Society in the Twentieth Century* (New York, 1985), 105-21, 150-210, 271-85; Roland Marchand, *Advertising the American Dream: Making Way for Modernity, 1920-1940* (Berkeley, 1985), 218; Fox and Lears, "Introduction," *Culture of Consumption,* xii.

14. Livingston, *Pragmatism and the Political Economy of Cultural Revolution,* 158-294, quotes on 215, 275; *Pragmatism, Feminism, and Democracy,* 17-83; see also "Corporations and Cultural Studies," *Social Text* 44 (Fall 1995): 61-68. For similar arguments, see Walter Benn Michaels, *The Gold Standard and the Logic of Naturalism: American Literature at the Turn of the Century* (Berkeley, 1987), esp. 183-213, and Alec Marsh, *Money and Modernity: Pound, Williams, and the Spirit of Jefferson* (Tuscaloosa and London, 1998), esp. 165-73.

corporate affair" — that is, the rise of a "corporateness" that determines and sanctions a "new individualism." Acknowledging the crisis of traditional moral agency that attended the metamorphosis of proprietary into corporate capitalism, Dewey trusted that individuals would discover the conditions of a new moral agency and selfhood "only," in his words, "as their ideas and ideals were brought into harmony with the realities of the age in which they act." Technological and organizational interdependence were foremost among these realities, and once Americans recognized their irreversibility then a democratic socialism was conceivable, even inevitable. "We are in for some kind of socialism," Dewey predicted. Livingston's Dewey could already see the socialist child gestating in the womb of corporate capitalism, as "modes of private business become 'affected with a public interest' because of quantitative expansion." Moreover, by uncoupling personal identity from production, corporate society "broaden[s] the terrain of political struggle," in Livingston's words, by enabling what we call cultural politics, the "expression and legitimation of subject positions" unrelated to male proprietorship. (Beholden to Gramsci on this point, Livingston often points to feminism and "the New Woman" as envoys of post-pecuniary selfhood.) In Dewey's view, corporateness mandated a "choice between a socialism that is public and one that is capitalistic"; as Livingston glosses it, Dewey saw the choice before Americans as one between "a pecuniary measure of subjectivity and a 'social self.'"[15]

But by ignoring the reference to a socialism that is "capitalistic," Livingston subtly misrepresents the choice Dewey posed. Dewey's odd conception of a "capitalistic" socialism indicates his own ambiguity about the demise of the pecuniary self. For one thing, if, as Dewey conceded, labor remained under the direction of "the business mind" — and if, as he also admitted, managers would always have "the more active and leading share in the intellectual direction of great industrial undertakings" — then "corporateness" portended not so much the transcendence of the proprietary self as the creation of a pecuniary social self.[16] Because Livingston equates the death of proprietary capitalism with the withering of the rage to accumulate, he cannot entertain the possibility that the "social self" can be driven by the imperatives of capital. Thus, Dewey's oracular prophecy about "some kind of socialism" offers no support for Livingston's contention that the "social self" is non-pecuniary, and that its presence heralds the extinction of corporate capitalism.

15. John Dewey, *Individualism Old and New* (New York, 1930), 41-42, 70, 119-20; *The Public and Its Problems* (Athens, Ohio, 1954 [1927]), 48; Livingston, *Pragmatism, Feminism, and Democracy,* 54, 82; on feminism as harbinger of post-pecuniary subjectivity, see especially 171-82.

16. Dewey, *Individualism Old and New,* 41, 58, 134.

Moreover, as Dewey noted in *The Public and Its Problems,* those sources of the self that had traditionally mitigated pecuniary desire — family and religion in particular — had been weakened or pulverized by industrialization. As a result, the identification of "cultural possibilities" would be the work, Dewey concluded in *Individualism Old and New,* of "sociologists, psychologists, dramatists, and poets." That is, "corporateness" supplied productive labor for workers in corporate-sponsored institutions whose cultural and moral power — the new "seat of intellectual authority," as he put it in *A Common Faith* (1934) — still depended heavily on their utility to capital accumulation. So when Livingston glosses Dewey's remark that "crisis becomes a habit" in corporate society by observing that "nothing, not even habit, is exempt from scientific scrutiny and method," he fails to consider that the most powerful arbiters of "scrutiny and method" have been the very pecuniary cadres of market researchers and corporate managers. Thus, dispossession from the means of material and cultural production — that is, membership in the political economy marked by "corporateness" — goes a long way in explaining why, as Livingston himself observes, pragmatists and other heralds of a brave post-pecuniary subjectivity "didn't notice what now seems obvious, that a 'social self' could be *more* susceptible than its predecessors to external manipulation."[17]

Still, more skeptical students of social selfhood do not, I think, offer a completely satisfying historical and critical alternative to Livingston. Recasting the history of nineteenth-century social thought as a prolegomena to "social selfhood," Jeffrey Sklansky maintains that social thinkers from Emerson and George Fitzhugh to Dewey and Charles Horton Cooley gradually "shifted the stakes of social struggle . . . away from proprietary claims upon productive resources and toward cultural claims upon selfhood and moral agency." Unlike most other students of social selfhood, Sklansky acknowledges the intractable realities of labor and class, and insists that political economy remains indispensable to any account of modern selfhood. Yet even Sklansky's wide-ranging and penetrating study leaves unreconciled those oppositions between culture and economy, consciousness and material life, desire and labor, that "social selfhood" and its antecedents were designed to resolve. Though admiringly wary of attempts by Dewey and James to "reconceive the bond between labor and will, or body and soul," Sklansky himself only gestures, however suggestively, to the shadow of classical political economy or the prospect of democratic socialism.[18]

17. Dewey, *Individualism Old and New,* 131; Dewey, *A Common Faith* (New Haven, 1934), 31; Livingston, *Pragmatism, Feminism, and Democracy,* 76, 78.

18. Sklansky, *Soul's Economy,* 208, 139. See also "Corporate Property and Social Psychology: Thomas M. Cooley, Charles H. Cooley, and the Ideological Origins of the Social Self," *Radical History Review* 76 (Winter 2000): 90-114.

More important, Sklansky's salutary insistence on the relevance of political economy to identity works to obscure the religious penumbra around social selfhood. Despite his reference to Emerson and the proprietary "soul's economy," Sklansky (like Livingston) pays scant attention to the unmistakable religious residue in Dewey's notion of "corporateness." Yet Dewey's discussion of "corporateness" in *Individualism Old and New* must be read as a secular prologue to his outline of "a common faith" four years later. The great challenge for modern Americans, he argued in *Individualism,* was to find vital replacements for the "older creeds" and "magic formulae" of the Protestant proprietary past. Fortunately, the capacity to identify possibilities for shared belief and achievement — the "prophetic aspect" of the new individualism, its pragmatist prowess for "perceiv[ing] the meaning of what exists only as we forecast the consequences it entails" — lay in a "new psychological and moral type" (akin to Gramsci's "new type of worker and of man"?) attuned to the social ensemble of modern selfhood.[19]

Dewey himself poured the old wine of religion into the new wineskin of corporateness in *A Common Faith.* Before modernity, he argued, faith — "the unification of the self through allegiance to inclusive ideal ends" — had been fostered through the disparate, contentious creeds and rites of "religious" institutions oriented toward the supernatural. But with the cultural ascendancy of science and the proliferation of activities considered "secular," the "religious" elements of selfhood "more and more oozed away . . . from the guardianship and care of any particular social institution." Rather than consign the religious to the unenlightened prehistory of the species, Dewey discerned the possibility that the religious could be "emancipated" from particular religions and re-embedded in the "actual connections of human beings with one another" — that is, in "the enormous expansion of associations formed for educational, political, economic, philanthropic, and scientific purposes." Dewey reasoned that since these "human relationships are charged with values that are religious in function," these institutions marked not the death but the renewal of faith on "a new basis and a new outlook." The common faith of a new individualism would flourish with the "development of social intelligence" akin to what was formerly called a "gospel of salvation" and its articulation in theology.[20] Anchored in corporate modernity and apprehended by "social intelligence," Dewey's new individualism — the "new psychological and moral type" — would reconcile

19. Dewey, *Individualism Old and New,* 9, 16.

20. Dewey, *A Common Faith,* 33, 62, 65, 67, 72, 77, 80, 83. The best historical discussions of Dewey's religiosity are Robert Westbrook, *John Dewey and American Democracy* (Ithaca and London, 1991), 418-28, and Bruce Kuklick, "John Dewey, American Theology, and Scientific Politics," in Lacey, *op. cit.,* 78-93.

economy, selfhood, and religion. But if we recall the possibility of a capitalist "corporateness," then that new individualism might well turn out to be a common faith in accumulation as the "inclusive ideal end."

Dewey's opaque allusion to "social intelligence" as the heir to theology indicated the transferal, oft-noted by historians, of cultural authority once held by Protestant intellectuals to mostly academic social scientists. But his acknowledgement that the cultural "center of gravity" had shifted to, among other venues, the "direction of great industrial undertakings" pointed to an arguably more significant passage of ministerial influence to a corporate intelligentsia of management writers and other business intellectuals — a managerial or corporate clerisy, so to speak, for the moral economy of social selfhood. Walter Lippmann, once Dewey's fellow Progressive and, by the 1920s, his antagonist in the pages of the *New Republic*, expressed the earliest and most expansive perception of corporate management's clerical status. Musing in *Drift and Mastery* (1914) that partisans of proprietary enterprise were "pilgrims to an empty shrine," Lippmann declared that the modern corporation and its salaried managers had dispelled the "old sanctities of private property," loosened the shackles of possessive individualism, promoted technological and organization innovation, and fostered a cosmopolitan sensibility. Although corporate managers were still capable of doing "brutal and stupid things," their reliance on salaries rather than proprietorship permitted them to "revolutionize the discipline, the incentives, and the vision of the business world." They were achieving what Lippmann called "modern communion" — what he would call "high religion" in *A Preface to Morals* (1929) — the recovery of that "old sense of cosmic wonder" to which "the old religions could point as their finest flower."[21]

Lippmann drew a mandarin portrait of the new corporate manager. If Thorstein Veblen's "soviet of technicians" was unmistakably technocratic, Lippmann's managerial cadre combined the expertise of the specialist with the wisdom of the humanist. If patriarchal avarice had driven "the old-fashioned chop-whiskered merchants," he wrote in *Drift and Mastery*, the "civilizing passions" of science and public service inspired managers, who tempered "the primal desire to have and to hold and to conquer." Indeed, the manager was "a rel-

---

21. On the social-scientific inheritance of theology's cultural authority, see R. Laurence Moore, "Secularization: Religion and the Social Sciences," in William R. Hutchison, ed., *Between the Times: The Travail of the Protestant Establishment in America, 1900-1960* (New York, 1989), 236-39; Susan Henking, "Sociological Christianity and Christian Sociology: The Paradox of Early American Sociology," *Religion and American Culture* 3 (Winter 1993): 49-67; and McCarraher, *Christian Critics*, 40-45. Walter Lippmann, *Drift and Mastery: An Attempt to Diagnose the Current Unrest* (Madison, 1985 [1914]), 42-43, 45, 154-55; Lippmann, *A Preface to Morals* (New York, 1929), 191-210.

atively disinterested person," beholden to "stubborn and irreducible facts" and less dominated than his mercantile and industrial predecessors by "the acquisitiveness of immaturity." For now, the manager's cultural authority was restrained by the lingering strength of the proprietary sanctities of yesteryear. But when fully released from the bondage of proprietary orthodoxy, the corporate manager could finally achieve "a more permanent place in the higher reaches of the imagination."[22] While every bit as ambiguous as Dewey about any "transcendence" of capitalism, Lippmann realized that the corporate manager was a new moral figure, a victor over drift, in his terms, and a paragon of mastery.

## The Manager and the Heavenly City:
## Philosophy, Theology, and the History of Laboring Selfhood

With its moral import and religious aura, Lippmann's portrait of the corporate manager was what Alasdair MacIntyre would call a "moral character," an ideal of personal conduct, a moral self. Lippmann and Dewey's convergence on the status of managers in the new corporate society suggests that, rather than look to pragmatist philosophers as the framers of a post-republican order, we should turn to MacIntyre's exploration of the managerial moral character in *After Virtue* (1981) for direction in the history of social selfhood. In what he calls his own "social history," MacIntyre traces a direct line from the Enlightenment desire for a science of society to the management theory utilized by state and corporate organizational leaders. Rooted in the fact/value distinction endemic to modern moral thought since Hume, managerial rationality — the bureaucratic rationality studied in the classic work of Max Weber — appears as morally neutral knowledge accountable only in terms of "effectiveness." Thus, the managerial moral character derives and even creates his own status from his possession of certain skills that he can deploy for a variety of ends. Equipped with this social expertise, corporate and government administrators are virtuosi of power who invoke their "competence as scientific managers of social change."[23]

MacIntyre's critical genius and historical limitation lie in his demolition of management's "scientific" status. When a manager displays "skill" in manipulation, his success is no different, MacIntyre maintains, from that of a clergyman "fortunate enough to pray for rain just before the end of a drought." Like "God" in analytic philosophy, managerial effectiveness is a "believed-in reality, appeal to which disguises certain other realities." Thus,

---

22. Lippmann, *Drift and Mastery,* 35, 39, 44; Lippmann, *Preface to Morals,* 256-57.
23. MacIntyre, *After Virtue,* 74, 86.

managerial expertise is a "moral fiction," in his words, a social performance that cannot exist outside of the quality's attribution to certain individuals. Still, if, as MacIntyre implies, managerial expertise is an *enacted* fiction, then it remains a historically significant form of cultural authority, regardless of its counterfeit intellectual claims. But even this dismissal of management theory as intellectually vacuous cannot be too facile or even cynical. If, as MacIntyre contends, we cannot "separate the history of the self . . . from the history of the language which the self specifies and through which roles are given expression," then a discovery of moral or religious language in management literature might indicate that managerial expertise is about much more than "effectiveness."[24] Indeed, Lippmann's appeal to the "civilizing passions," as well as his perception of a passage from an "empty shrine" to "modern communion," suggest that the formation of a managerial character entailed more than the deployment of a bogus and amoral expertise.

In linking the managerial character and the therapist as virtuosi of technique and effectiveness, MacIntyre gestures to the sociologist Philip Rieff, whose formulation of "the triumph of the therapeutic" has done a lot of heavy lifting for cultural critics and historians. At first, Rieff's amoralist portrait of the modern therapist might seem akin to MacIntyre's managerial character. The therapist possesses a "technology of the inner life" which can be used for a variety of ends, and the therapeutic ethos sanctions a plenitude of moral options, extending to adherents "permission to live an experimental life." These experiments depend, however, on lines of psychic and moral credit that bind the therapeutic self to statistical norms and cultural fashion. But Rieff's broad (and widely misunderstood) conception of "therapy" also suggests the irreducibly religious character of selfhood. As Rieff explains, "all cultures have a therapeutic function insofar as they are systems of symbolic integration." The crucial differences lie not between therapeutic and non-therapeutic cultures but between rival therapeutic communities, their ideals of health and methods of cure. "Positive" communities link self-fulfillment to commitments outside the self, defining the healthy self as a moral self whose desires have been transformed and aligned with some larger communal order, whether political, religious, or both. (Recall Dewey's definition of "faith" as the self's allegiance to "inclusive ideal ends.") On the other hand, "negative" communities — "purely therapeutic" cultures, as Rieff rather confusingly dubs them — lack integrating symbols, eschew communal purposes, and register rather than transform desire.[25]

24. MacIntyre, *After Virtue*, 35, 75-76, 107.
25. Rieff, *Triumph of the Therapeutic*, 26, 66-75, 93.

Although these differences may seem clear-cut and even polarized, Rieff identifies a persistence of religious forms and concerns in what he considers our secular, managerialist, "negative" communities of the West. While he observes that positive therapies "tend to take on a sacramental symbolism" while negative ones exhibit an "anti-sacramental bias," he also notes that "every science has its canon"; that science has a "cadre of men empowered to organize ideas into dogma"; and that "every science, like every teaching church, must have its dogmatists."[26] If management theory is one such "science" — or even if, to follow MacIntyre, it impersonates one — it is, in Rieff's terms, a historical heir of theology. This would imply that the capitalist corporation is not exactly a "negative community" but rather a simulacrum of a positive community, and that it is characterized not so much by an "anti-sacramental bias" as by a surrogate religiosity. We could then say that the business corporation is the nucleus of a new "positive community," namely, corporate capitalism; that management theory is a key therapeutic and quasi-theological lexicon of this "corporate society"; and that Rieff's "purely therapeutic" self is the "new individual" or "social self," whose misdirected and managed religious aspirations are indispensable, even central, to corporate cultural hegemony.

If management theory, like Deweyan "social intelligence," provides a moral discourse and even a surrogate theology for "social selfhood," then historians might want to look to theology to understand the laboring self engendered in corporate capitalism. I would propose that the Augustinian tradition, along with the meditations on work of Simone Weil, together provide the most compelling historical perspective on selfhood in the corporate moral economy. Among theologians, John Milbank and Graham Ward have performed the most sophisticated reconstruction of Augustinian thought. In Augustinian theology, the fundamental truth about the human person is its status as the *imago dei*, the reflection of the triune God. From this truth stems not only the sanctity of human life but an "ecstatic" conception of selfhood in terms of desires and commitments outside the self. In Trinitarian anthropology, the self's most basic and insistent desire is to love and worship God, who always desires and fulfills the self. Love and worship, when rightly directed, become *caritas*, love of other human beings and of all creation, whose perfect communal incarnation is in the "heavenly city," or *civitas Dei*. Thus, all of our desires — for attractive surroundings, for delicious foods, for abundant knowledge, for steadfast friends, for beautiful bodies — partake of desire for union with God. On earth, the church or *ecclesia* is the community through which desires are educated, transformed, and conducted toward their proper fulfillment. Thus, the Trinitarian

26. Rieff, *Triumph of the Therapeutic*, 76, 81.

self *is* a "social self," but one in which the social matrix of personality is neither proprietary nor corporate, but ecclesial.[27]

This Trinitarian conception of the person entails a sacramental conception of labor and the laboring self. Since human personality reveals the *imago dei,* human labor possesses a sacramental character. When performed for the love and worship of God, human labor becomes "an aesthetic and liturgical work offered to God," in Milbank's words, a portal onto divinity which "open[s] up our awareness of the sacred in the presentation of compelling forms." Thus, proletarianization — the *sine qua non* of capitalism and, we should recall, secular socialism — marks the subordination of *poesis* to accumulation and its perversion into "productivity." While artisanal in its affirmation of *poesis,* the Trinitarian view of labor is anything but "possessive individualist." For a motley lineage of non-Marxist anti-capitalists — John Ruskin, Eric Gill, Simone Weil, to name a few — and for many French, British, and American radicals — republican artisans, guild socialists, "personalists" — this sacramental conception of labor animated the search for what Christopher Lasch termed "modern forms of proprietorship" that would combine advanced technology with direct workers' management. This quest was for more than, but also never for less than, social and economic justice. The acolytes of sacramental labor believed that it anticipates, on this side of paradise, the final consummation and redemption of human history. "Eschatology," Ward asserts, "is both not yet and is being realised in our midst, through our labourings."[28]

As an intellectual who labored in the Paris Renault plant during the 1930s, Weil was the keenest theological student of modern work. Along with art and science, labor, Weil wrote, was a way of "entering into contact with the divine order of the universe." Just as God united thought and action, so the perfection of the *imago dei* wedded consciousness with physical life. Weil saw the divine likeness most clearly in the medieval artisan — Gramsci's "demiurge," marked

27. Ward, *Cities of God* (London and New York, 2000), 97-116; Milbank, *Theology and Social Theory,* 380-438; See also Michael Hanby, "Desire: Augustine beyond Western Subjectivity," in Milbank, Ward, and Catherine Pickstock, eds., *Radical Orthodoxy: A New Theology* (London and New York, 1999), 109-26. The human self, Hanby writes, possesses a "doxological character which it cannot escape, but can only pervert" (115).

28. Milbank, "Socialism of the Gift, Socialism by Grace," *New Blackfriars* 77 (December 1996): 545; Milbank, *Theology and Social Theory,* 193; Lasch, *True and Only Heaven,* 317-44 *passim*; Ward, *Cities of God,* 94. Examples of the sacramental tradition I am invoking are John Ruskin, *Unto This Last: And Other Writings,* ed. Clive Wilmer (London, 1985); Eric Gill, *Work and Leisure* (London, 1935); Simone Weil, *Oppression and Liberty,* trans. Arthur Wills and John Petrie (Amherst, 1973), esp. 37-124. Milbank discusses the theological and political character of this lineage in "On Complex Space," in *The Word Made Strange: Theology, Language, Culture* (Oxford, 1999), 268-92.

for extinction by progressive industrialization — but also wherever skilled workers, educated and seasoned by experience, were "obliged to think while acting." "The full skilled worker, trained in modern technical methods . . . resembles most closely the perfect workman." When skilled workers associated for a task, it was "a fine sight," she marveled, to see them "ponder the problem each for himself, make various suggestions for dealing with it, and then apply unanimously the method conceived by one of them, who may or may not have any official authority over the rest." At such moments, she concluded, "the image of a free community appears almost in its purity." In such a free association, where mental and manual labor were fused and no distinct managerial cadre reigned, a sacramental social self would appear, in and among the workers. Each worker "would see in every work-fellow another self occupying another post, and would love him in the way that Gospel maxim enjoins." Over and above freedom workers would possess "a still more precious good . . . friendship," or *caritas*.[29]

On this basis, Weil proposed that such a "sacramental" analysis of work in capitalism would, like Marxism, begin from the relations of production, but would continue "in terms of the relationships between thought and action." Because it took *poesis* rather than productivity as its standard of labor, such a social analysis would both affirm the indissoluble unity of soul and body and avoid the trap of "progress" that ensnared both liberal and Marxist historical thinking. Of course, unlike G. K. Chesterton, Dorothy Day, Wendell Berry, or other critics of modern industry, Weil never longed for a restoration of agrarian life or pre-industrial technology. Even after her days in the Renault complex, she could affirm that "a plant or factory could fill the soul through a powerful awareness of collective life." Still, where Gramsci (antedating celebrants of the "socialist" promise resident in the corporation) saw emancipatory possibility in the uncoupling of mind from action, Weil saw the opportunity for management to conscript the disembodied soul through the mystification of managerial expertise. Because modern science and technical education had become "a corpus of knowledge closed to the working masses," they comprised an "outstanding mystery" analogous to theology or the occult. The mystification of managerial expertise facilitated the entrusting of management, not to workers as freely associated individuals, but to "a curious machine, whose parts are men, whose gears consist of regulations, reports and statistics," and which tried

29. Weil, "Fragments, London 1943," in *Oppression and Liberty*, 168; Weil, "Theoretical Picture of a Free Society," in *Oppression and Liberty*, 85-108, quotes on 100-01, 108. Hannah Arendt claimed that Weil's writings on work were the only essays "in the huge literature on the labor question which deal with the problem without prejudice or sentimentality": *The Human Condition* (Chicago, 1958), 131 n. 83.

to "imitate the effort of thought to life." In its fracturing of the laboring self and its construction of a spurious social selfhood, Fordist capitalism constituted a massive desecration of sacramental labor, because only in the unity of thought and action could work afford "a certain contact with the reality, the truth, and the beauty of the universe and with the eternal wisdom which is the order in it." This is why Weil could warn that "it is sacrilege to degrade labor in exactly the same sense that it is sacrilege to trample upon the Eucharist."[30]

Such a sacrilege was possible, contemporary Augustinians would say, because the sacramental laboring self shares in the distortion of personality wrought by sin. Sin, for Augustine, is not the opposite but the perversion of our desire for God, an errant love in which, lacking trust in God, we attribute to earthly goods, and especially to ourselves, the power and goodness possessed only by God. Bereft of confidence in the bounty of creation, *caritas* becomes lust for dominion *(libido dominandi)* and the communities we build in this grotesque desire constitute the "earthly city." Because we still bear the *imago dei*, our art, technology, commerce, and politics — evidence, Augustine wrote, of "the blessings we enjoy" from God — stand as distorted representations of the heavenly city, illustrious but disfigured products of our longing. All the institutions of the fallen world — state, family, university, corporation, even the church — are, even at their best, caricatures of celestial communion. Sin is predatory on paradise; and just as, in Marxist terms, ideology cannot succeed without the beguiling allure of Utopia, so sin and perversion cannot enslave without offering some promise of heaven. But if we make the theological assertion that the "materialist" metaphysics fundamental to Marxism does not provide an adequate account of matter itself — more precisely, of its sacramental and revelatory character — then our history and criticism can both incorporate and transcend the Marxist critique. If Marxist "demystification" purports to uncover the material roots of ideology, an Augustinian "demystification" exposes the perversely ecclesial and sacramental roots of injustice.[31]

---

30. Weil, "Theoretical Picture," *op. cit.*, 100, 110; "Factory Work," *Politics* 3 (December 1946): 369; "Human Personality," in Richard Rees, ed., *Simone Weil: Selected Essays, 1934-1943* (New York and Toronto, 1962), 18.

31. The classic starting point remains Augustine, *City of God*, trans. Henry Bettenson and ed. John O'Meara (London and New York, 1984), 5-75; see also Milbank, *Theology and Social Theory*, 389-92, and Ward, *Cities of God*, 227-37.

Augustine's views on evil are ably summarized in Andrew Delbanco, *The Death of Satan: How Americans Have Lost the Sense of Evil* (New York, 1995), 46-51, esp. 48-49. Although Delbanco interprets the Augustinian conception of sin as one of "privation" rather than perversion, his remarks do not, I think, conflict with my own account. Before Delbanco, the last interpreter of Augustine to American historians was, of course, Perry Miller, especially in *The New*

In his remarkable *Cities of God* (2000), Ward searches through the utopian imagery of modern urbanism — "cities of eternal aspiration" — and concludes that the modern city has been envisioned by architects, engineers, advertisers, and artists as the consummation and transcendence of ecclesial longing, "a city without a church" in which "all a human being's desires might be met and potentially realized." These cities of incessant production and consumption are perverse "communities of desire, dreamt and engineered by modernity, parodies of the Christian *ecclesia*."[32] What Ward suggests about the modern city I will suggest about the modern corporation, management theory, and the corporate laboring self. Unlike other critics of the "culture of consumption," I see not a simple rejection of transcendence in favor of self-fulfillment, but a search for transcendence — that is, for self-fulfillment — in a historical variation of the earthly city, a perverse community of desire. Unlike celebrants of "corporate society" who see the incubation of a humane socialism, I see an enchanting and beleaguered simulacrum of the heavenly city. In this view, corporate humanism, distilled in management theory, is an imitation of moral theology, and the modern corporation and its corporate selfhood are grotesques of beloved community, parodies of the earthly *ecclesia*. They "fill the soul," to borrow Weil's words, through a fraudulent but "powerful awareness of collective life."

## "The modern corporation specializes in personality": Corporate Humanism, Corporate Selfhood, and the Birth of American Management Theory

Historians are beginning to realize that corporations were attempting to "fill the soul." As Lears has demonstrated, corporate advertising developed in part as a

---

*England Mind: The Seventeenth Century* (Boston, 1961 [1939]), 3-34. As central as it remains to American cultural and religious history, Miller's notion of an "Augustinian strain of piety" looks very Protestant (and very Niebuhrian) to any Catholic observer.

Drawing heavily on the work of George Lukacs, Marxist intellectuals have begun to recognize the resemblances, even the continuities, between the concept of reification and the Christian theological notions of sin, sacrament, and redemption. (Marshall Berman has called Lukacs "Communism's St. Augustine": *Adventures in Marxism* [New York and London, 1999], 193.) See, for instance, Fredric Jameson, *The Political Unconscious: Narrative as a Socially Symbolic Act* (Ithaca, 1981), 247-52, 284-85; Slavoj Zizek, *The Fragile Absolute: Or, Why the Christian Legacy Is Worth Fighting For* (London and New York, 2000); and Timothy Bewes, *Reification: Or the Anxiety of Late Capitalism* (London and New York, 2002). I am indebted to Casey Blake, Jackson Lears, and Wilfred McClay for challenging me to clarify the distinction between Marxist and Augustinian forms of "demystification."

32. Ward, *Cities of God*, 27-51 (quote on 40-41), 125.

way to "fetishize" or "enchant" commodities produced by firms that were the starkest embodiments of bureaucratic, disenchanted reason. In an increasingly impersonal marketplace, advertisers attempted, through a variety of aesthetic strategies, to effect "the reanimation of the inanimate world under the aegis of major corporations." At the same time, the profession of public relations emerged, as Marchand has shown, as the vehicle through which business conjured a "corporate soul," a vision of the corporation as the friendly neighborhood behemoth. Exemplified in Bruce Barton's unequalled "talent for fusing the methods, aspirations, and languages of religion and business," the search for a corporate soul reached a point, by the 1940s, where the moral legitimacy of the corporation had been accepted, however ambivalently, by most Americans.[33]

As students of consumer culture, both Lears and Marchand focus on the *external* effects of corporate imagery, paying little attention to the *internal* symbolic universe of the corporation, especially of the managerial ranks. Indeed, Marchand goes so far as to assert that corporate executives "remained only vaguely aware" of one of their key hegemonic activities, "that of fostering morale and shaping company culture on their own, executive, level."[34] Marchand is wrong about this, I think, but his concentration on the "soulful" aspirations of corporate PR, together with Lears's insights into corporate "reanimation," point to the religious longings that have pervaded corporate culture. If we introduce a theological vocabulary into the study of cultural history, we can redescribe these quests for soul and reanimation as longings for the heavenly city. The search for a corporate soul and the wish for re-enchantment, together with the need for "participation and belonging" and the pursuit of the good monopoly — all of these reflected desires not just for a new moral economy, but for an ecclesial body, a sacramental community. And if we pay attention to the internal verbal and visual imagery of corporate life, we might see that the "soul" of the corporation was conjured not only in advertising and public relations, but in a moral philosophy of corporate humanism and a moral theology of management theory. In these bodies of doctrine, we can study the alchemy through which a corporate clerisy attempted to transfigure the autonomous self of proprietary capitalism into the corporate self of the Fordist order.

The initial round of these moral experiments was inseparable from the construction of a managerial moral character who combined expertise with sagacity. From the 1890s to the 1910s, the first generation of corporate industrial-

---

33. Lears, *Fables of Abundance*, 292; Marchand, *Creating the Corporate Soul: The Rise of Public Relations and Corporate Imagery in American Big Business* (Berkeley, 1998), 130-63 on Barton, quote on 136.

34. Marchand, *Corporate Soul*, 363.

ists pioneered "welfare capitalism" by erecting what Sanford Jacoby has called "modern manors" on the collapsing estate of the Protestant moral economy. Entering what Andrea Tone has called "the business of benevolence" — company-sponsored benefits and programs, efforts to improve factory conditions and compose class relations — welfare capitalists created a new class of managers equipped with new forms of social expertise: "welfare work," "vocational guidance," "personnel management." These technologies of benevolence originated in daily corporate practice; in professional networks such as the American Management Association; and in the new business schools such as Wharton (1881) and Harvard (1908). From these business schools, the philanthropist Joseph Wharton hoped, professional managers would bring "the solution of the social problems incident to our civilization" and emerge as "a class of men likely to become pillars of the State." Students of early corporate culture have detected these moral aspirations among the first managers and executives. Olivier Zunz has described their "utopian impulses," their self-conception as a liberating vanguard of "innovation, profit, and order," while David Nye has seen in General Electric's publicity and advertising a managerial character, staring into "infinite executive space," whose station was "olympian, outside petty concerns."[35]

At the same time, these corporate moral visions broadened into a fairly self-conscious moral discourse — "corporate humanism" — that pervaded the work of business journalists, pundit-executives, and management theorists. Precursors of later businessman-philosophers such as Bill Gates and George Soros, these writers commenced a long tradition of visionaries who saw in corporate capitalism a new form of moral economy and personality. The inaugural document of corporate humanism was, arguably, *The New Basis of Civilization* (1908) by Simon Patten, a professor of political economy and management at the Wharton School. While Patten's tidings of an impending "economy of surplus" have been rightly identified as pivotal in the moral legitimation of con-

---

35. Sanford Jacoby, *Modern Manors: Welfare Capitalism since the New Deal* (Princeton, 1997), 3-5, is an overview of welfare capitalism before the New Deal; see also *Employing Bureaucracy: Managers, Unions, and the Transformation of Work in American Industry, 1900-1945* (New York, 1985), 39-97, 126-89, on the variety of management practices and ideologies; Andrea Tone, *The Business of Benevolence: Industrial Paternalism in the Progressive Era* (Ithaca and London, 1997), esp. 140-71; on business schools, see Steven A. Sass, *The Pragmatic Imagination: A History of the Wharton School, 1881-1981* (Philadelphia, 1982) (Wharton quote 22-23), and Robert M. Smith, *The American Business System and the Theory and Practice of Social Science: The Case of the Harvard Business School, 1925-1945* (New York, 1986); Zunz, *Making America Corporate*, 67-101, quote on 65; David E. Nye, *Image Worlds: Corporate Identities at General Electric, 1890-1930* (Cambridge, Mass., 1985), 93-111, quotes on 104, 106.

sumer culture, his work also heralded a sacralized social selfhood that would flourish through managerial expertise. Surpassing the scarcity and hardship which had defined moral character, not only in the proprietary order but throughout history, the new economy of surplus — figured in the corporation, or the "socialized capitalist" in Patten's words — enabled the creation of a character whose goodness inhered not in sacrifice but in generosity, showering "gifts without conditions." With its technological and organizational resources, socialized capitalism promised to usher in the *eschaton* that unified *caritas* and character. As Patten made clear in a later but neglected book, *The Social Basis of Religion* (1912), the advent of a surplus economy was the annunciation of a new "social religion" in which "the Holy Spirit [Jesus] promised is with us as the social spirit."[36] As "social religion," socialized capitalism was the earthly city of Fordism, and the character of surplus was a self redeemed.

Under the sign of "social religion," Patten's corporate humanism infused managerial talent with religious import, envisioning the end of traditional faiths and their replacement with benevolent expertise. If historians have emphasized his acknowledgement that consumer pleasure was a compensation for unsatisfying labor, Patten believed that managerial cultivation of a new religious spirit would rejuvenate the laboring character. Prophesying "the new basis of character," Patten balanced his account of purchasing and generous dispersal by observing that the character of surplus was still a laboring self capable of augmenting "the superabundance of general goods." The task for the socialized capitalist was utilizing "the workingman's latent vitality." In *The Social Basis of Religion*, Patten solved this problem with a managerial psychology that doubled as religious faith. Rejecting the faculty psychology of proprietary Protestantism — the mind, he asserted, "is not a unit with definite, predetermined expressions" — Patten endorsed a pragmatist view of mental life as "a series of developing functions" whose consuming and producing energies would reach their highest consummation, as he put it in *The New Basis of Civilization*, in "modern trained generosity." The fullest vigor of these energies was "the psychical expression of the new birth sought by religion." This resolutely psychosomatic conception of religion entailed the eradication of existing religious differences, since a "socialized world can no more have a dozen religions than it can have a dozen sciences in one field."[37] Patten's corporate humanism antici-

36. Simon Patten, *The New Basis of Civilization* (Cambridge, Mass., 1968 [1907]), 79, 86; *The Social Basis of Religion* (New York, 1912), 193-205, quote on 204. On Patten, see Daniel M. Fox, *The Discovery of Abundance: Simon N. Patten and the Transformation of Social Theory* (Ithaca, 1967), who considers Patten's psychological remarks "pseudoscientific gibberish" (94), and Lears, *Fables of Abundance*, 113-17.

37. Patten, *New Basis of Civilization*, 123, 155; *Social Basis of Religion*, 151, 155, 229.

pated Dewey's "common faith" with a clearer recognition of its eschatology of expertise.

Patten's vaguely liberal Protestant brand of corporate humanism coincided with Progressive confidence that corporate enterprise was a new chapter in the moral and spiritual history of American selfhood. Indeed, Progressive intellectuals put such faith in the possibilities of corporate organization and managerial selfhood that Progressivism itself might be interpreted as a variant of corporate humanism. Lippmann's vision of a managerially orchestrated "modern communion," as well as Dewey's "common faith" in "corporateness," partook of the expansive hopes articulated by Herbert Croly and Josiah Royce. Croly saw the new corporate era as an arduous but liberating "pilgrimage," as he put it in *Progressive Democracy* (1914), toward a "holy city" or "consummate community" — a Puritan, but more strikingly Augustinian, account of the moment — while Josiah Royce considered the corporation a prefiguring of the "Beloved Community," the modern solution to *The Problem of Christianity* (1913). In *War and Insurance* (1914), Royce marveled at the corporation's fusion of mortal material assets with an identity, legally conferred but nonetheless forceful, which marked an immortal social selfhood, an "essentially intangible soul." Croly, too, beheld in the corporation a new vessel of religious selfhood — a "constructive individualism" as he called it in *The Promise of American Life* (1909) — which would reach its apotheosis in the holy city of corporate consolidation. Croly's social self relied on the expertise of social sciences. Observing that "individuality cannot be dissociated from the pursuit of a disinterested object," Croly believed that the new America was precisely that way and truth. This "common faith sanctifies those who share it," he wrote in *Progressive Democracy*, and that modern sanctity depended on the conservation and enlargement of a "fund of virtue," a "spiritual heritage" of intellectual resources, invested by a modern clerisy of "learned or holy men" who included the "democratic administrator" and the "scientific manager" — moral characters for the coming Holy City.[38]

In the decade after World War I, many intellectuals, reformers, and corporate leaders looked more directly to the corporation and its managerial cadres as the builders of the Holy City. Walter Lippmann, for instance, considered corporate leaders more innovative and disinterested than liberals or socialists. The ideas and activities of businessmen, he declared in *Men of Destiny* (1927), were

---

38. Herbert Croly, *Progressive Democracy* (New York, 1914), 191-93, 353, 399-401, 409-10, 414-15; *The Promise of American Life* (New York, 1909), 411, 444-46; Josiah Royce, *The Problem of Christianity*, 2 vols. (New York, 1913), vol. 2, 163-213; *War and Insurance* (New York, 1914), xxvii-xxviii.

"more novel, more daring, and more revolutionary than the theories of the progressives." Corporate executives and business writers certainly agreed. In his treatise on *Successful Living in This Machine Age* (1931), the merchandising mogul Edward A. Filene augured "the oneness of all humanity" through the corporate pursuit of profit. Mass production and consumption repealed the old laws of proprietary Protestant economics and allowed Americans to focus on "distinctly human problems." Filene echoed J. George Frederick, managing editor of *Printer's Ink*. In *Humanism as a Way of Life* (1930), Frederick invoked a cavalcade of "great thinkers" from Aristotle to . . . Filene. Sensing that modern industry prompted "new questions of destiny and meaning" — especially in the midst of a worsening economic depression — Frederick convened a symposium of business leaders and writers to produce *A Philosophy of Production* (1930). Frederick summarized the wisdom of the participants (who included GE's Owen Young, AT&T's Walter Gifford, and U. S. Steel's Myron Taylor) as a call for "a new humanism" in industry whereby corporate leaders, in their deployment of labor and technology, would create an ecclesial laboring body, spreading "the ideality of the human spirit" through "our vast mechanism of production."[39]

Declaring in *Business the Civilizer* (1928) that Americans were entering a "business millennium," the advertising executive Earnest Elmo Calkins expressed the corporate humanist moral imagination with the most unabashed and telling grandiloquence. Because of its sponsorship of science, technology, and art, the corporation offered "the glory that in the past was given to the crusader, the soldier, the courtier, the explorer, and the martyr." Most successful businessmen toiled not for the money, Calkins maintained, but because "there are no longer any long, slimy, green dragons holding captive maidens in durance vile, no holy sepulchers to be reft from the infidel, no Pacifics to be viewed for the first time." As the most auspicious modern venue for romantic adventure and personal achievement, corporate business, Calkins rhapsodized, was "our Field of the Cloth of Gold." Calkins concluded with a bold assertion of corporate moral and sacral ambition. "That eternal job of administering this planet must be turned over to the business man," he wrote. "The work that religion and government have failed in must be done by business."[40] Anticipating Francis Fukuyama's more highbrow declaration of the end of history, Calkins implied a historical trajectory that moved from *corpus Christi* to the corporation.

39. Lippmann, *Men of Destiny* (New York, 1927), 228; Edward A. Filene, *Successful Living in This Machine Age* (New York, 1931), 1, 87, 96; J. George Frederick, *Humanism as a Way of Life* (New York, 1930); "Humanism as the Emerging American Philosophy," in Frederick, ed., *A Philosophy of Production* (New York, 1930), 258-59.

40. Earnest Elmo Calkins, *Business the Civilizer* (New York, 1928), 118, 232-33, 272, 294-95.

This *mission civilisatrice* of corporate humanism found its moral theology in management theory. From its inception in scientific management, the enormous body of twentieth-century management theory has constituted more than a "social technology of production," in David F. Noble's words, or the "Marxism of the professional middle class," as Steve Fraser has characterized it. Progressives such as Croly considered Frederick W. Taylor's handiwork "the great critical and regenerative influence in business organization," a utopian discourse that would specify "the relation between scientific business and economic democracy" — the pilgrim road, we might add, to what Croly himself called the Holy City. Lacking Progressive rhetorical flourish, Taylor certainly said so. Musing in *The Principles of Scientific Management* (1911) that "a life which is one continuous struggle with other men is hardly worth living," Taylor argued that his new form of managerial expertise would replace class war with "close, intimate, personal cooperation between the management and the men." In a visionary gesture to the end of alienation, Taylor imagined a social self, a moral personality constructed on the bases of corporate labor and scientific knowledge. In a scientifically managed workplace, "each man possesses his own individuality and loses none of his originality and proper personal initiative," while at the same time agreeing to be "controlled by and . . . work harmoniously with many other men."[41] By erasing the line between democracy and expertise, Taylor's corporate humanism envisioned corporations as sites of democratic social selfhood as well as productive efficiency.

Though the master himself seemed indifferent to conventional religion, Taylor's "disciples" bore the ark of the covenant with clerical demeanor and evangelical zeal. H. L. Persons cast Taylor as a moral character, even a prophet, a "Seeker of Truth." H. L. Gantt concluded *Organizing for Work* (1919) by tracing a direct line from Christ — "the first great Economist" — to scholastic philosophers — whose "intellectualism" had obscured Christ's managerial wisdom — to Taylor, whose intellectual ancestry, in Gantt's account, made scientific managers the heirs of medieval clerical authority. Tying both Masters together more

41. David Noble, *America by Design: Science, Technology, and the Rise of Corporate Capitalism* (New York, 1977), 257-320; Steve Fraser, "'The Labor Question,'" in Fraser and Gerstle, op. cit., 59-62; Croly, *Progressive Democracy*, 399; Frederick W. Taylor, *The Principles of Scientific Management* (New York, 1911), 7, 26, 52, 140-41. Examples of the enormous literature on scientific management include Samuel Haber, *Efficiency and Uplift: Scientific Management in the Progressive Era, 1890-1920* (Chicago, 1964); Daniel Nelson, *Frederick W. Taylor and the Rise of Scientific Management* (Madison, 1980); Robert Kanigel, *The One Best Way: Frederick Winslow Taylor and the Enigma of Efficiency* (New York, 1997); see also Montgomery, *House of Labor*, 229-56, and John M. Jordan, *Machine-Age Ideology: Social Engineering and American Liberalism, 1911-1939* (Chapel Hill, 1994), 36-67.

directly, Morris Cooke enthused that Taylor had taken the Sermon on the Mount and made it "a practical, profitable, working formula." Cooke fondly quoted a French priest who had sermonized that "the love of God is the Taylor system of the inner life."[42]

Given the ferocious conflict over Taylorism then underway in Europe and the United States, Cooke's French priest was voicing one side of a debate whose counter was expressed by another Catholic, Jacques Maritain, who maligned scientific managers in *Art and Scholasticism* (1920) for their reduction of artisanal movement to the "chronometrized and taylorized gesture."[43] Still, Cooke's *cure* had underlined the catechetical purpose that informed not only scientific management, but the subsequent canon of management theory. Historians could (rightly) interpret the religious parlance of the Taylor circle as the discursive residue of the proprietary-Protestant order, and thus amend the historical record of managerial ideology as a shift from cold scientific management to warm (if not fuzzy) "human relations." But if we recast this more secular historical account in terms of Augustinian theology, we could see the work of post-Taylorist management writers as elaborations of what was often explicit in the original gospel: a corporate social self, congregating in the *ecclesia* of the Fordist corporation, spiritually disciplined in the rhythms of Fordist production, and overseen by an episcopate of manager-clerics.

Wartime struggles over Taylorism and "industrial democracy," as well as the fears of labor unrest generated by the Bolshevik Revolution of 1917, forced management writers to recognize the limitations of the founder's original vision. Even as labor capitulated reluctantly in the 1910's and 1920's to the corporate-sponsored "American Plan" of welfare capitalism and open shops, the desire to avert further class conflict prompted business leaders and ideologues to concentrate more studiously than ever on what the Harvard Business School's Elton Mayo called "the human problems of industrial civilization" — those quandaries of soul, belonging, and participation rooted in the

---

42. H. S. Persons, "Frederick W. Taylor as a Seeker of Truth," *Journal of the Efficiency Society* 4 (April 1915): 8; Morris Cooke, "Forward," *Annals of the American Academy of Political and Social Science* 85 (1919): xi; H. L. Gantt, *Organizing for Work* (New York, 1919), 15, 70, 108. Historians have not been completely inattentive to the religious character of scientific management. Haber, ix, opens his study by describing the "efficiency craze" as "a secular Great Awakening." Jordan, 53-55, briefly discusses the religiosity of Taylor's followers, noting the "sacerdotal overtones" of Taylorite publications. Kanigel, 412, writes that religious words "dog any account" of scientific management, but never stops to ponder their significance.

43. On the controversy over Taylorism in Europe, see Anson Rabinbach, *The Human Motor: Energy, Fatigue, and the Origins of Modernity* (New York, 1990), 244-70; Jacques Maritain, *Art and Scholasticism*, trans. J. F. Scanlon (New York, 1949 [1920]), 16.

passage from proprietary-Protestant to Fordist corporate capitalism.[44] In the three decades after World War I, several members of the corporate intelligensia — John R. Commons, Mayo, Mary Parker Follett, and Peter Drucker — drew up new managerial blueprints for the social self, which doubled as doctrine for the Fordist earthly city.

In *Industrial Goodwill* (1919) and *Industrial Government* (1921) (a collection of reports by industrial researchers), Commons and his colleagues provided an ecclesial account of corporate selfhood. Although "a corporation is said to have no soul," Commons replied that its soul resided in its "goodwill." Commons insisted that "goodwill" was much more than the backslapping boosterism soon to be excoriated as "Babbitry" by Sinclair Lewis. Goodwill — which Commons used interchangeably with "soul" and "personality" — seemed to signify the ensemble of social and emotive relationships within the corporate workplace. A "multiple of all the different personalities that keep the business going," goodwill or corporate personality was a "spirit of brotherhood" that united workers and employers in the consciousness of a common project. This corporate selfhood depended on its "distinguish[ing] the true and the false" — an eminently dogmatic power — and on its pursuit of "the grand purpose of promoting public welfare." From this exalted workplace, corporate selfhood projected "personality" into its products, advertising, service to customers, even its stocks and bonds. Indeed, Commons wrote, "the modern corporation specializes in personality." Acknowledging that this corporate personality no longer rested on direct worker control over production, one of Commons's researchers asserted that it now resided in "zeal for progress and pride in a great enterprise," in a consciousness that lit up "the most menial and stupefying task with the rays of a great industrial vision." While to a skeptic this might have seemed quite a bit to expect from pushing a broom or feeding a machine, Commons and his colleagues believed that, through the imaginative vistas opened up by corporate production, the modern firm and its corporate selfhood afforded "more chances for personality than ever were known before in industry."[45]

This corporate self was exemplified for Commons in the professional-managerial worker, the moral and clerical character of the modern corporation. Allegedly liberated from the pressures of survival and accumulation, profession-

44. On "industrial democracy," see Joseph A. McCartin, *Labor's Great War: The Struggle for Industrial Democracy and the Origins of Modern American Labor Relations, 1912-1921* (Chapel Hill, 1998); Elton Mayo, *The Human Problems of an Industrial Civilization* (New York, 1933).

45. John R. Commons, *Industrial Goodwill* (New York, 1919), 19-20, 147, 151-67; Jennie McMullin Turner, "Thinking and Planning," in Commons, ed., *Industrial Government* (New York, 1921), 7. On Commons, see Dorothy Ross, *The Origins of American Social Science* (Baltimore, 1991), 202-204.

als and managers "look for the approval of others in the profession." Moreover, this "new personality in industry" had as his productive labor not only technical and bureaucratic work but the moral education of the corporate self. Mental workers "do what is 'right,' not what they are ordered to do," and they "issue orders, even to the employer." With a broad and scientific awareness of corporate possibility, this new class would increasingly "lay down the law, not of coercion, but of goodwill" and harmonize "all the relationships of capital and labor." Trained in the social sciences, these managers represented a new "humanism in management" that meant, for Commons, the reformulation, not the rejection, of the Taylorist inheritance. In its primitive, Taylorist version, scientific management displayed "the defects of autocracy," the narrow and ruthless self-regard of the proprietary personality. But in the growth of welfare work and personnel management, Commons perceived a movement among corporate leaders from "business to humanity." As one of his researchers put it, management was shifting "from figures to feelings as instruments of control."[46] Thus, humanity consisted in the credentialed orchestration not only of physical movement, but of emotional and spiritual life as well. The corporate self, the soul of the corporate ecclesia, would flourish in accordance with managerial objectives.

Although the moral and ecclesial ambitions of corporate leaders still had to respect and compete with the conventions of more traditional religious bodies, the Commons researchers had identified a powerful current of corporate self-understanding, one that would grow stronger over the twentieth century. The figure of the manager as a moral character soon became a lightning rod for this moral and religious energy. Henry P. Kendall, president of the Kendall Corporation (a conglomerate of manufacturing and service companies) and a contributor to the 1930 Frederick symposium, reflected that the true executive lived "in the realm of the spirit," a "humanistic spirit" leavened by a "passion for precision and excellence." "Our ultimate objectives" as managers, Kendall thought, "are found in the intangible, rather than the tangible realm." Wallace B. Donham, dean of the Harvard Business School, maintained in a number of articles published in the mid-1920s that the quotidian wisdom and professional training of corporate managers afforded them a special "depth and perspective on vital social problems." Chester Barnard, president of New Jersey Bell Telephone and a respected management writer between the wars, explained that "the necessity of creating moral codes" was among *The Functions of the Executive* (1938).[47]

46. Commons, *Industrial Goodwill*, 19, 161; Turner, op. cit., 10.

47. Henry P. Kendall, "Change and the Common Sense of Industrial Management," in Frederick, *A Philosophy of Production*, 182; Wallace B. Donham, "The Social Significance of

This Fordist humanism took three forms in the most significant management literature before and a bit after World War II. All of this literature recognized, in varying degrees, the religious character of the workplace. The work of Elton Mayo and Fritz Roethlisberger, professors at the Harvard Business School best known for their study of Chicago's Hawthorne Works of Western Electric, represented the most forthrightly technocratic brand of corporate selfhood. Mayo's work in particular doubled as industrial research and corporate humanist social criticism. Calling for a "wide research into the nature of man" in a series of *Harper's* essays over 1924 and 1925, Mayo derided the "uncivilized reason" of most business leaders and held out the promise of scientific management to quell worker unrest and cultivate "morale" — a quality akin to Dewey's "common faith." Accordingly, in *The Human Problems of an Industrial Civilization* (1933), Mayo concentrated not on the material working conditions of his Hawthorne subjects but on their "mental preoccupations," their ambivalent feelings toward Western Electric. Suffering from what might be described as a sickly corporate selfhood, the Hawthorne workers considered Western Electric "an almost mythical entity," one whose perceived combination of power, solicitude, and indifference produced "a sense of human defeat." Mayo's perception of the corporation as a "mythical," quasi-divine entity dovetailed with Roethlisberger's insight in *Management and Morale* (1941) that the "system of sentiments" among factory workers bore a telling resemblance to tribal moral economies. Drawing on the work of Bronislaw Malinowski, Roethlisberger argued that "the forces which make collaboration possible [in tribes] are only in part economic," and that tribal productive life was "essentially social and religious," governed by numerous "ceremonials and rituals." In a previous study conducted with William J. Dickson, *Management and the Worker* (1939), Roethlisberger had emphasized the meanings attributed by workers to the means and relations of production. Wages, conditions, technology, and personal ties were, he concluded, "carriers of social value" — sacramental, we might say, reflecting a divinity obscured by accumulative and instrumental perversity.[48]

---

Business," *Harvard Business Review* 5 (July 1927): 417-18; Chester Barnard, *The Functions of the Executive* (Cambridge, Mass., 1938), 247.

48. Mayo, "The Great Stupidity," *Harper's* 151 (July 1925): 233; the other essays in the series were "Uncivilized Reason," *Harper's* 148 (March 1924): 527-35, and "Civilization: The Perilous Adventure," *Harper's* 149 (October 1924): 590-97; *Human Problems*, 100, 120-21, 188; Fritz Roethlisberger, *Management and Morale* (Cambridge, Mass., 1955 [1941]), 33, 52, 66; Roethlisberger, with William J. Dickson, *Management and the Worker* (Cambridge, Mass., 1939), 374. The only biography of Mayo is the relatively uncritical R. C. S. Trahair, *The Humanist Temper: The Life and Work of Elton Mayo* (New Brunswick, 1984). Critiques of Mayo include Daniel Bell, "Work and Its Discontents" (1956), in *The End of Ideology: On the Exhaustion of Political*

Mayo realized that, despite the mechanization and routinization of labor, "the desire for continuous and intimate association in work with others remains a strong, possibly the strongest, human capacity." But in Mayo's view, science and technology had discredited or displaced the traditional social and religious sources of the laboring self, and so the moral vacuum could be filled only by a "logic of understanding" articulated by "an administrative elite" equipped to handle "the concrete difficulties of human collaboration." The fundamental task for this managerial cadre was enabling workers to "obtain human satisfactions," in Roethlisberger's colorless prose, that would make them "willing to contribute their services to the economic objectives of cooperation." Like the manager-paragon of Lippmann and Frederick, Mayo's "New Administrator" was a moral character trained to supervise the corporate self from "the critical posts of communal activity." Far more than a sleek and proficient technocrat, the New Administrator became, in Mayo's hopes, a secularized cleric, just as corporate capitalism, like Dewey's "corporate society" and its "common faith," inherited the religious aura of a believing age. As Mayo told a Harvard Business School audience in May 1947, the social consciousness promoted by social science could replicate "the strong and simple religious feeling of medieval times." Thus, William H. Whyte was not far off the mark when he observed that Mayo and his students were "evangelists as well as researchers."[49] In Mayo's corporate vision, the religious desire for sacramental labor would be consummated in an eschatology of expertise.

If Mayo's conception of corporate selfhood was overtly elitist and faintly religious, that of Mary Parker Follett was more ostensibly democratic and more avowedly sacral. Follett's career as a managerial theorist began as a student of political philosophy at Radcliffe and Cambridge. She soon became a fixture of Boston's thriving women's civic culture, and promoted the city's first public school vocational guidance program. Based on these experiences, her first book, *The New State* (1918), is a now obscure but under-appreciated classic of Progressive political thought. After World War I, Follett's work in vocational guidance piqued an interest in industrial relations, and she quickly joined the ranks of Boston's business elite. Moving easily among Filene, manufacturer Henry A.

---

*Ideas in the Fifties* (New York, 1960), 245-49, and C. L. R. James, *American Civilization* (Cambridge, Mass., 1993 [1950]), 181-84. Loren Baritz argues that Mayo's work was an attempt to "make possible the re-creation of Agrarian Virtue": *The Servants of Power: A History of the Use of Social Science in American Industry* (Middletown, Conn., 1960), 110-11.

49. Mayo, introduction to Roethlisberger, *Management and Morale*, xxi; *Human Problems*, 172, 185; *The Political Problems of an Industrial Civilization* (Division of Research, Graduate School of Business Administration, Harvard University, 1947), 23; Roethlisberger, *Management and Morale*, 192.

Dennison, and personnel management specialists Meyer Bloomfield, Frank Parsons, and Henry C. Metcalf, Follett soon became a force in American and British industrial relations circles. In numerous addresses to the Taylor Society, the Bureaus of Personnel Administration in Boston and New York, the Harvard Business School, and the London School of Economics — as well as in *Creative Experience* (1924), a tome that combined religion, philosophy, psychology, and management — Follett articulated a corporate humanist conviction that, as she told a management conference in 1926, "industry is the most important field of human activity, and management is the fundamental element in industry."[50] Recycling Taylorism through pragmatism, psychology, and a misty religious sensibility, Follett created a managerial lexicon of selfhood that both promised sacramental labor and veiled subordination to the imperatives of capital.

With more vivid religious fervor and imagery than Mayo or the Taylorists, Follett espoused a form of corporate humanism in which the workplace became a portal onto aesthetic, metaphysical, moral, and spiritual truths. "Our daily living may itself become an art," she wrote in *Creative Experience*. "In commerce we may find culture, in industry idealism, in our business system beauty, in mechanics morals." Providing more than commodities, profits, and paychecks, the corporate workplace offered "our greatest spiritual nourishment," she wrote, a "sacrament of life." In Follett's view, corporate managers and executives epitomized this moral and sacramental economy. "The real service of business" to the community, she asserted in a typical 1925 talk, was "the better organization of human relationships." The manager was the moral character of the sacramental corporate order. "Long after the clerks have departed from the office of a big corporation you can see lights burning in the rooms of the executives." Their overtime reflected not an obsession with money or a crackpot devotion to work, but "the craftsman's love of doing a job well." Echoing Lippmann and Calkins, Follett lauded the loyalty of managers and executives to "the soul of [their] work," a dedication which was "the highest romance as it is the deepest religion." Indeed, the "high adventure of business," Follett waxed, was its cultivation of "the deeper thing within every man, transcending every man, which you may call your ideal, or God, or what you will." "No occupation," she concluded, "can make a more worthy appeal to the imagination."[51]

50. Pauline Graham, "Mary Parker Follett: A Pioneering Life," in Graham, ed., *Mary Parker Follett, Prophet of Management: A Celebration of Writings from the 1920's* (Boston, 1995), 11-16; Strom, *Beyond the Typewriter*, 117-19; Follett, "The Illusion of Final Authority," paper given to the Taylor Society, New York, December 10, 1926, in *Freedom and Organization: Lectures in Business Organization* (London, 1949), 8.

51. Follett, *Creative Experience* (New York, 1924), 87, 132; "How Must Business Management Develop in Order to Become a Profession?", paper given to the New York Bureau of Personnel

In *Creative Experience,* Follett advanced a phenomenology of management that mixed pragmatism, Gestalt psychology, and shards of theology. Her writing was replete with the keywords central to pragmatist and Gestalt vocabulary: "experience," "experiment," "process," "total" or "evolving situations," all of which conveyed the mutability of the world and the self. Since "reality" existed, she intoned, "in the relating, in the activity-between," then selfhood was relational, arising from "the reciprocal influence of subject and object." Like Dewey portraying the new individual of a common corporate faith, Follett captured this fluid and expansive conception of human identity in the "crescent self," a "soul at home" who lived from that "sacrament of life" ritualized in corporate labor and embodied in corporate commodities. For if the crescent self was a relational self, then its creation and flourishing were the "real service of business." And if the crescent self was realized in corporate labor, then Fordist "manufacture" enabled "those manifold, interweaving activities of men by which spiritual values are created."[52] For Follett, the social self was born and redeemed in an ecclesial community of production.

This "crescent," corporate, ever-expanding self required a new managerial philosophy of "dynamic administration" or "progressive integration" which Follett espoused in numerous talks to corporate leaders in the 1920s. If the proprietary autocrat had practiced "coercive power" or "power-over," the "progressive integrator" attuned to crescent relationships would practice, or rather share, "coactive power" that brought managers and workers together in a genuine industrial democracy. More than collective bargaining or adjustment of in-

Administration, November 5, 1925, in *Dynamic Administration: The Collected Papers of Mary Parker Follett* (New York and London, 1941), 135, 137, 140-41. On Follett, see Henry S. Kariel, "The New Order of Mary Parker Follett," *Western Political Quarterly* 8 (September 1955): 425-40; Haber, *Efficiency and Uplift,* 126-28; Jean B. Quandt, *From the Small Town to the Great Community: The Social Thought of Progressive Intellectuals* (New Brunswick, 1970), 36-50; William Graebner, *The Engineering of Consent: Democracy and Authority in Twentieth-Century America* (Madison, 1987), 71-73; and James Hoopes, *Community Denied: The Wrong Turn of Pragmatic Liberalism* (Ithaca and London, 1998), 145-63, who relates Follett to James, Lippmann, and Reinhold Niebuhr, claiming that she "surpassed their work in acuteness and originality."

52. Follett, *Creative Experience,* 54-55, 63, 91-116, 132, 203; "The Psychology of Control," paper given to Boston's Bureau of Personnel Administration, March 1927, in *Dynamic Administration,* 183-209. On pragmatist psychology see Hoopes, *Consciousness in New England: From Puritanism and Ideas to Psychoanalysis and Semiotics* (Baltimore, 1989), 190-233, and Livingston, *Pragmatism and Political Economy,* 263-73. On Gestalt psychology, see Katherine Pandora, *Rebels Within the Ranks: Psychologists' Critique of Scientific Authority and Democratic Realities in New Deal America* (Cambridge and New York, 1997), 36-40. Follett's ideas resembled the "social plant politics" theorized in Weimar Germany by Fritz Giese, whose *Philosophie der Arbeit* (1932) is described by Rabinbach as a "romantic philosophy of work": Rabinbach, *The Human Motor,* 282-84.

terests, "dynamic" or "integrated" solutions to problems arose from "constructive conflict" through which "both sides found a place, and neither side . . . had to sacrifice anything." If this sounded too good to be true, Follett's oracular rhetoric often suggested that dynamic, coactive industry augured the erasure of class lines. Because, in her view, "the distinction between those who manage and those who are managed [was] fading somewhat," she dismissed the conventional dichotomy that set "that modern beneficent despot, the expert" against a "muddled, befogged 'people.'" She noted that reliance on experts could be an evasion of personal and political responsibility, and that technical and social specialists were assuming roles once assigned to clerics. "The expert," she warned, was becoming "to many what the priest is."[53] Beckoning to the prospect of a priesthood of crescent producers, Follett's vision of corporate selfhood seemed to anticipate the sacramental anarcho-syndicalism of Weil.

Yet the corporate selfhood Follett envisioned in "dynamic administration" also, and more directly, pointed in the direction of managerial hierarchy. Speaking to a conference of personnel administrators in the spring of 1927 — "pioneers," she flattered her audience, "working out something new in human relationships" — she observed that "business men are quietly . . . working out a system of organization which is not democratic in our old understanding of the word, but something better than that." This new corporate system was based "neither on equality nor on arbitrary authority, but on functional unity." The new manager leader was "the man who can energize his group, who knows how to encourage initiative, how to draw from all what each has to give." Even Follett's ostensibly mutualist conception of coactive power could end up meaning, as she explained to a conference of managers in the winter of 1925, that non-managers manage when they "use their own judgment in regard to the manner of executing orders."[54]

Follett's nebulous account of "coactive power" and "integration" suggests that the lissome parlance of pragmatism and psychology both veiled the managerial orchestration of social selfhood and relied on appeals to ecclesial and sacramental longing. She certainly avoided the open technocracy of a Mayo, affirmed the moral and spiritual significance of labor, and provided a language, however opaque, in which social selfhood could be defined in democratic and religious terms. Still, when Follett mused that corporate businessmen trained in the social sciences now have "a richer idea of the meaning of control than we

53. Follett, *Creative Experience,* xiii-xix, 3-29, 163-87; "Constructive Conflict" and "Business as an Integrative Unity," papers given to Boston's Bureau of Personnel Administration, January 1925, in *Dynamic Administration,* 30-49, 71-95.

54. Follett, "Business as an Integrative Unity," op. cit., 81, 88; "Leader and Expert," in *Dynamic Administration,* 247, 249.

have ever had before," she underscored the inequities of the corporate moral economy. When she informed the Bureau of Personnel Administration in 1925 that "you can be *for* labor without being *against* capital," she signaled (in a manner reproduced later, almost verbatim, by Bill Clinton and other "New Democrats") that the class division of labor and capital would remain, albeit shrouded in the mist of "integration." Then and now (as the recent resurgence of interest in her work attests) Follett offered to corporate ideologues a benign but perverse language of manipulative domination. Her managerial moral character who gave "neither orders nor advice" presaged the "facilitator" or "team leader" of today, who, as Richard Sennett observes, "has mastered the art of wielding power without being held accountable." Likewise, the "crescent self" and "coactive power" anticipated the parlance of "participation" that marks our "post-Fordist" regime of "flexible" labor practices and decentralized capital accumulation.[55] And the openly religious cast of Follett's language — "sacrament of life," "soul at home," "deepest religion" — suggested that this managerial ruse depended on the enlistment of desires for a liturgical community of labor.

One student of management well-acquainted with Follett's work was Peter Drucker, whose prolific writings, according to a recent profile, have been "read by more managers than those of any single author, living or dead." (Not that Drucker was always sanguine about the penchant among managers to seek philosophical raiment for their naked *libido dominandi*. In a refreshing lament, he once rued that the word "philosophy" was being "tossed around with happy abandon these days in management circles.") Indeed, Drucker's frequent description as a management "guru" underlines the moral and spiritual concerns which have leavened his work, and which also explain his reputation outside corporate business. In the 1940s, W. H. Auden recommended Drucker's work to friends as, in Edward Mendelson's words, "an example of Christian thought applied to the practicalities of management." In the 1950s, Erich Fromm appealed to Drucker's corporate studies as evidence of worker alienation, and Clinton Rossiter included him among "the thankless persuasion" of American conservatism. More devout than Mayo and less ponderous than Follett, Drucker has been the consummate corporate humanist, gliding easily through the corridors connecting finance, journalism, academia, and management. His résumé reflects a transatlantic career more lucrative and influential than those of many mid-century émigré intellectuals: financial reporting in Europe in the early 1930s; commentary for *Harper's*, the *New Republic*, and the *Saturday Evening*

---

55. Follett, "The Illusion of Final Authority," op. cit., 15; "Business as an Integrative Unity," op. cit., 82; Richard Sennett, *The Corrosion of Character: The Personal Consequences of Work in the New Capitalism* (New York, 1998), 115.

*Post;* editorial stewardship at the Luce manors of *Time* and *Fortune;* teaching in economics and the humanities at Bennington; consulting work for General Motors and other corporations. Ignored by cultural historians, he has arguably had a far greater impact than Theodor Adorno, Paul Tillich, Hannah Arendt, or other postwar luminaries in the "intellectual migration" occasioned by fascism.[56] For in his theologically denatured way, Drucker has been the most accessible theorist for the corporate humanist perversion of sacramental labor and selfhood.

Drucker began his managerial theorizing at a time when corporate business — shaken by the Great Depression, the reforms of the New Deal, and the militance of the CIO — was scurrying to find "a new vocabulary of business leadership," in William Bird's words, that would revalidate its moral and political claims. One strategy emerged in talk of a "managerial revolution" proclaimed by Adolph Berle and Gardiner Means in *The Modern Corporation and Private Property* (1932) and by James Burnham in *The Managerial Revolution* (1941). While Burnham believed that the new managers would be as exploitative as the old capitalists, Berle and Means placed their hopes in a "purely neutral technocracy" that resembled Mayo's "New Administrators." Another strategy — borrowed from Popular Front culture and honed in public relations and advertising departments — translated the mandarin corporate humanism of Filene, Fredericks, and Calkins into the idiom of "the American Way of Life."[57]

56. Drucker hails Follett as a "prophet of management" in his introduction to *Mary Parker Follett,* 1-9; his remark on "philosophy" is in *The Practice of Management* (New York, 1954), 136. William Clarkson, "Drucker: Closing the Theory/Practice Gap," *New Management* 2 (Winter 1985), 23; Edward Mendelson, *Later Auden* (New York, 1999), 151; Erich Fromm, *The Sane Society* (New York, 1955), 161-62; Clinton Rossiter, *Conservatism in America: The Thankless Persuasion* (New York, 1962 [1955]), 224.

Drucker discusses his early life and career in *Adventures of a Bystander* (New Brunswick, N.J., 1994 [1978]), 9-82, 123-35, 158-86, 223-43. Secondary studies of Drucker include Berthold Freyberg, "The Genesis of Drucker's Thought," in Tony H. Bonaparte and John E. Flaherty, eds., *Peter Drucker: Contributions to Business Enterprise* (New York, 1970), 17-22; Steven Waring, *Taylorism Transformed: Scientific Management Theory since 1945* (Chapel Hill, 1991), 78-103, and "Peter Drucker, MBO, and the Corporatist Critique of Scientific Management," in Daniel Nelson, ed., *A Mental Revolution: Scientific Management since Taylor* (Columbus, Ohio, 1992), 205-36; Jack Beatty, *The World According to Peter Drucker* (New York, 1998). On the intellectual migration, see Donald Fleming and Bernard Bailyn, eds., *The Intellectual Migration: Europe and America, 1930-1960* (Cambridge, Mass., 1969). The only critique of Drucker I've discovered — a penetrating one, I might add — is by the French sociologist Georges Friedmann, who considered Drucker's social vision "a technician's Utopia": *The Anatomy of Work: Labor, Leisure, and the Implications of Automation* (New York, 1961), 117-20.

57. William Bird, *Better Living: Advertising, Media, and the New Vocabulary of Business Leadership, 1935-1955* (Evanston, Ill., 1999); Marchand, *Creating the Corporate Soul,* 202-48; Adolf

This more populist form of Fordist humanism stressed the "participation and belonging" afforded by consumer culture — a parodic *ecclesia* of consumption.

Drucker intervened in this crisis of corporate hegemony by emphasizing the moral economy of production in a way that synthesized Christian theology, Fordist political economy, and "human relations" managerial ideology. From the outset of his career in the turbulent Austrian Republic of the late 1920s, Drucker sought a way to reconcile corporate enterprise with Christian (in his case, Catholic) standards of economic and personal conduct. Drawing on the work of Austrian Catholic "corporatists" in search of an alternative to both capitalism and socialism, Drucker affirmed their "Christian" understanding of "authority," their insistence on the "duties" incumbent on property owners, and their promotion of an economic system that would combine "personal responsibility" and social "commitment" in "organic" economic institutions — in our terms, their conception of a "social selfhood." In his first book, a 1933 study of the right-Hegelian philosopher Friedrich Stahl, Drucker contended that Catholic corporatists needed to accept the institutional realities of corporate capitalism and concentrate their efforts not on restoring small proprietorship, but on "Christianizing" corporate firms, especially their managers and executives. Alluding to Joseph Schumpeter's celebratory account of the old-style industrial capitalist, Drucker argued that the most urgent task facing corporatists was to find a way to combine the entrepreneurial spirit of innovation with the Christian requirement to seek the common good.[58]

In portentously titled books such as *The End of Economic Man* (1939) and *The Future of Industrial Man* (1942), Drucker sketched both a thesis of moral declension and a hope that corporate managers could save Western civilization from both pagan fascism and undisciplined democracy. In their different ways, fascism, communism, and unbridled democracy reflected both the apotheosis and the disintegration of "Economic Man." Western society was no longer a "community of individuals bound together by a common purpose" but rather a

---

Berle and Gardiner Means, *The Modern Corporation and Private Property* (New York, 1932), esp. 345-57, quote on 356; James Burnham, *The Managerial Revolution: What Is Happening in the World* (New York, 1941). Drucker described Burnham's book as "the Bible of the next generation of neo-Marxists": "The Rulers of Tomorrow," *Saturday Review* 24 (May 10, 1941): 9. On the corporate appropriation of "the American Way of Life," see Robert Griffith, "The Selling of America: The Advertising Council and American Politics, 1942-1960," *Business History Review* 57 (Autumn 1983): 388-412, and Michael Denning, *The Cultural Front: The Laboring of American Culture in the Twentieth Century* (New York, 1996), 47.

58. Drucker, *Friedrich Julius Stahl: Konservative Staatslehre und Geschichtliche Entwicklung* (Tubingen, 1933); on Austrian corporatism, see Alfred Diamant, *Austrian Catholics and the First Republic: Democracy, Capitalism, and the Social Order, 1918-1934* (Princeton, 1960), esp. 99-207.

"chaotic hubbub of purposeless isolated monads" impelled by "demonic forces." Fascism, Bolshevism, and consumer culture were all bogus "creeds," in his view, upholding "false gods" for worship. Disillusioned by the feckless responses of church and business leaders, Drucker called on a new generation of corporate managers to become, in effect, a clerisy, and to create a corporate moral economy permeated by a refurbished Christian ethic, a "new order and creed" to replace Economic Man. "There has never been," he insisted, "a more efficient, a more honest, a more capable and conscientious group of rulers than the professional management of the great American corporations today." These corporate clerics were the main repositories of the "Christian concept of man's nature: imperfect, weak, a sinner, and dust destined unto dust; yet made in God's image and responsible for his actions."[59]

On the strength of his books and reportage, Drucker received an invitation from General Motors in the fall of 1943 to assess the company's management structures and policies. (GM's president, Alfred P. Sloan, already considered himself something of a philosopher-manager. In *Adventures of a White-Collar Man* [1941], Sloan had informed his fellow executives, in classic corporate humanist fashion, that "industrial management must expand its horizon of responsibility" to embrace "the social and economic welfare of the entire community.") Over the next two years, Drucker completed his report and reworked his findings into *Concept of the Corporation* (1946), a corporate case study which doubled as corporate humanist social criticism. Drucker depicted GM's social ecology as an ecclesial ideal of production, a felicitous convergence of freedom and efficiency, Fordist routinization and craftsmanship. GM emerged as a quasi-syndicalist community, a "federal union," in his words, in which a "two-way flow" of information enabled both "a division of powers and of functions" and a "unity of action." Drucker also lauded the overt indifference to "title, rank, and formal procedure" on the line and in the office.[60]

But the ecclesial character of Drucker's GM was strikingly manifest when

59. Drucker, *The End of Economic Man* (New York, 1939), 22, 44, 85-111; Drucker, *The Future of Industrial Man* (New York, 1942), 99, 148-50. James, *American Civilization*, 185-89, perceptively links Drucker to Robert Maynard Hutchins, Mortimer Adler, and other advocates of "Catholic humanism." The religiosity of Drucker's early work belies his claim that he "never had much use for theology": *Adventures of a Bystander*, ix.

60. Alfred P. Sloan, *Adventures of a White-Collar Man* (New York, 1941), 145; Drucker, *Concept of the Corporation* (New York, 1946), 59-71. Drucker discusses his relationship with GM in *Adventures of a Bystander*, 256-93. Drucker recalled that Sloan "never accepted my study, never thought it worthwhile," and that GM executives thought his book overly critical, even hostile (279-80, 288). Sloan does not mention Drucker's report in *My Years with General Motors* (Garden City, N.Y., 1964).

he celebrated the business corporation's unprecedented prominence in the nation's moral imagination. Hoping that his book would contribute to the postwar rehabilitation of business in American culture, Drucker called upon executives and managers to hold out "the promise of adequately fulfilling the aspirations and beliefs of the American people." The managerial elite could undertake this mission because the corporation was now "our representative social institution," having supplanted the family, the church, and even the state as the main agent of social identity, cohesion, and vitality. It provided both "the standard for the way of life and the mode of living" and "the symbol through which facts are organized in a social pattern."[61] Clearly the corporation embodied the "new order and creed" for which the declining West had been longing.

Although, in the 1940s, Drucker paid more attention to the corporation as a social ideal than to corporate work as a new form of personal identity, he made gestures toward an account of corporate selfhood. During and directly after the 1945-46 strike at GM by the United Auto Workers, Drucker foreshadowed the uneasy, two-decade truce between management and organized labor by addressing obliquely the problems of "human relations" in corporate industry. Acknowledging the "unease, fear, and resentment" that fuelled postwar labor unrest, Drucker advised that, rather than make the worker into "an expert engineer or a production man" — that is, rather than fully democratize technical and administrative skills in a manner that Weil would have considered sacramental — managers should cultivate an appreciation for "what the product is, what it is being used for, and how it is being made."[62] As if in some corporate eucharistic liturgy, workers could participate vicariously in the design, execution, and consumption of their products. In this way, Drucker both signaled his future interest in corporate selfhood and augured the postwar eclipse of industrial democracy in which organized labor ceded claims to managerial prerogatives.

Drucker's more pronounced interest in "human relations" did not stem solely from his concerns as a management consultant. In the first wave of prophecy against the "air-conditioned nightmare," American social criticism after World War II abounded in ambivalent or hostile portraits of corporate life: David Riesman's "other-directed character in *The Lonely Crowd* (1950); C. Wright Mills' incarnation of "the managerial demiurge" in *White Collar* (1951); William H. Whyte's conformist paragon of the "Social Ethic" in *The Organization Man* (1956). Against these stains on the gray-flannel archetype,

61. Drucker, *Concept of the Corporation,* 6-7.

62. Drucker, "What to Do about Strikes," *Collier's* 119 (January 18, 1947): 13, 26-27; Drucker, *Concept of the Corporation,* 191-99. On the "Treaty of Detroit," see Nelson Lichtenstein, *The Most Dangerous Man in Detroit: Walter Reuther and the Fate of American Labor* (New York, 1995), 154-298.

Drucker offered an unambiguous affirmation of the managerial moral character and the promise of corporate selfhood in *The New Society* (1950) and *The Practice of Management* (1954). *The New Society* was a managerial manifesto, an account of a revolution whose vanguard was "the new industrial middle class: technicians, engineers, supervisors, accountants, statisticians, and branch managers." Having secured a "victory of the secretariat" over stockholders and corporate directorates, these cadres of expertise stood poised to carry the West "beyond Capitalism and Socialism." With their "very high, almost unprecedentedly high, degree of imaginative and intellectual ability," the new managers in particular deserved the respect once conferred upon the nobilities and clerisies of old. Echoing Lippmann, Mayo, and Follett, Drucker asserted in *The Practice of Management* that if "vision and moral responsibility define the manager," then "perhaps," as he reflected in *The New Society,* management merited "the standing of a genuine 'aristocracy,' such as the Confucian scholar in China, the Senatorial Class in Republican Rome, or the 'gentleman' in eighteenth- and nineteenth-century England."[63]

With no apologies to Alexander Pope, Drucker asserted in *The New Society* that "the proper study of mankind is organization," and that the moral lexicon of the managerial society was "Human Relations." (Perhaps only half-unwittingly conveying the perversely ecclesial nature of the corporation, Drucker at one point compared a company's organization manual to a volume of church canon law.) Following Mayo and Follett, Drucker maintained that "human relations" was not only an indispensable "diagnostic tool" in the workplace, but a lingua franca for American society, "the whole area of the social life of the industrial society." Unlike his predecessors, however, Drucker rooted human relations in a vague Christian theology. "In hiring a worker," he wrote in *The Practice of Management,* "one always hires the whole man," an indivisible human personality whose "relationship with his Creator," together with his "relationship to his work . . . underlies all of [a] man's life and achievements."[64]

Yet while this language might recall Weil's personalist, sacramental view of work, which entailed direct and collaborative workers' control, in Drucker's usage it rehearsed Follett's subtly manipulative paradigms of the "crescent self" and "coactive power." Unsatisfied with mere "acquiescence" to corporate imperatives, Drucker argued that managers needed to inculcate a "managerial attitude" in the worker — by which he meant not a directive capacity but an identi-

---

63. Riesman, *The Lonely Crowd,* 218-24; Mills, *White Collar,* 77-111; Whyte, *The Organization Man,* 14-167; Drucker, *The New Society: The Anatomy of the Industrial Order* (New York, 1950), 25-26, 348, 351; Drucker, *Practice of Management,* 350.

64. Drucker, *New Society,* 105, 157-67, 266; *Practice of Management,* 262.

fication with the goals of managers, a conception of "his job, his work, and his product the way the manager sees them." Through this "management by objectives," managers could, he insisted, induce workers to "convert objective needs [of the firm] into personal goals" and foster an "aggressive *esprit de corps.*" Though technically and managerially disenfranchised, all workers, right "down to the last sweeper and wheelbarrow-pusher," could internalize a "'managerial attitude' toward their work and toward the enterprise" and embrace the corporation as a democracy of industrial citizenship. In this cameo of corporate selfhood — reminiscent, with its Fordist resonance, of Huxley as much as Orwell — Drucker corroborated Mills' contention that the modern manager could "relax his authoritative manner and widen his manipulative grip."[65] Much more than an urbane and erudite exception to an otherwise dullard genre, Drucker's management writing crowned a generation of corporate humanist literature, bringing into clear and troubling view its moral and religious ambitions.

These ambitions were apparent to Whyte, Drucker's colleague at *Fortune,* whose anatomy of "the organization man" is one of the keenest and most misconstrued documents of American social criticism. Often associated with a motley chorus against "conformity," Whyte (*Fortune's* managing editor) was an Erasmus of corporate humanism, a humane and erudite member of the business clerisy who knew the follies of the corporation, lavished praise on its achievements, and wrote not as a revolutionary but as a reformer. To be sure, Whyte is justly remembered for his portrait of the scrambling hypocrisy behind the ranch-house sublime, and for his tough-minded rejection of the personal compromises he berated as "conformist." But Whyte refused to disdain or demonize the residents of Park Forest because he knew, better than more facile critics, that the Organization life was, in his words, "a moral quest," a search whose authenticity made it all the more compelling, desperate, and perverse. The suburban quest of the laboring self was a peculiar spiritual problem, Whyte thought, because what the old authoritarian industrialist wanted "primarily . . . was your sweat. The new man wants your soul."[66]

One of the unremarked features of *The Organization Man* is Whyte's frequent resort to religious metaphors to describe the corporate self and its career. On the very first page, Whyte observed that the management student at a business school, poised to take "the vows of organization life," was "blood brother" to the seminarian. (Whyte later compared the same fledgling manager to a young medieval man "off to join holy orders.") Indeed, when Whyte interviewed college seniors majoring in business administration, he discovered that

65. Drucker, *Practice of Management,* 121-36, 158, 267; Mills, *White Collar,* 235.
66. Whyte, *The Organization Man,* 381, 397.

the typical image of a personnel manager combined "YMCA worker, office Solomon, and father confessor" — a figure that might have made Lippmann and Drucker proud. These earnest clerics-to-be soon learned the corporate moral theology of Human Relations, whose "quasi-religious overtones" both impressed and worried Whyte. Impressed by the unfeigned devotion of the organization men in Park Forest — somewhat to his own surprise, Whyte found that corporate life provided "a great deal of real brotherhood" at the office and at home — Whyte worried that the broader "Social Ethic" sanctioned by managerial social science was "almost a secular religion."[67]

Stripped of the overtly Protestant theology of rugged, proprietary individualism, the Social Ethic of corporate capitalism was the ecclesial code of corporate selfhood. As a "secular faith" that reshaped even suburban churches and synagogues, the Social Ethic embraced a triune doxology: the group is the source of creativity (Whyte likened one management conference to a "convocation of believers"); "belongingness" or "togetherness" is the highest good; and social science — modeled after management — is the way to the *summum bonum*. Whyte concluded that management theory and practice were only "superficially" about directing employees. Likening firms and suburban neighborhoods to antebellum Owenite and Fourierist communities, Whyte dubbed the Social Ethic a "utopian faith," a religious desire for a prosperous harmony. Of course, as in any faith, the Organization had many who doubted the truth of the covenant. But without a clear alternative to the creed and rites of the Social Ethic, the communicants of the Organization's ecclesial parody continued in their appointed tasks, however "hesitant and unsure, imprisoned in brotherhood."[68]

It is only by respecting and reclaiming the religiosity of Whyte's remarks — not by disarming them as "metaphorical" — that we can appreciate the quandary of corporate selves "imprisoned in brotherhood." If we recall Whyte's dismissal of an easy and empty "non-conformity" as an antidote to the Social Ethic,[69] we might recycle his insight through Augustinian theology to restate its full significance, one that is arguably all the more imperative in these allegedly more libertarian times. The carceral power of corporate brotherhood — the panoptical felicity of corporate selfhood — derives from its ecclesial character, its capacity to mobilize the desire of the laboring self for a sacramental relation to the world. Far more penetrating than assaults on "conformity" that are by now among the most predictable banalities, Whyte's insight points to some of the deepest recesses of the human person.

67. Whyte, *The Organization Man*, 3, 44, 74, 98, 361.
68. Whyte, *The Organization Man*, 6-58, 365.
69. Whyte, *The Organization Man*, 10.

It is a point worth pondering as we, in our post-Fordist age, must deal with a corporate order unprecedented in its material and cultural power. As Thomas Frank has demonstrated, a good deal of that power has come from the very critical energy directed at corporate life by "counter-cultural" partisans of "non-conformity": the "conquest of cool" has provided high-octane fuel for the consumer culture of contemporary capitalism. And in forms such as "liberation management" that Whyte could never have imagined, "non-conformity" has been incorporated and trademarked in the lexicon of management theory. But in "total quality management"; in the proliferation of corporate "mission statements" and assertions of "social responsibility"; in the network of inspirational seminars that comprise the Chautauqua circuit of corporate culture; in the best-selling works of Steven Covey, Peter Senge, Laurie Jones, Ken Blanchard, and other advocates of the "soulful corporation" — in all of these guises and venues, we see an accessible and lucrative fund of cultural capital for investment in the popular business imagination.[70] Adding to an already well-stocked ideological portfolio, these visions of the ecclesial corporation and its corporate social self represent the newest and farthest horizons of corporate cultural authority. Any historical account or political defiance of corporate power must take the measure of these religious aspirations, recognizing in their very distortion the immortal desire for "perfect human felicity."

---

70. Thomas Frank, *The Conquest of Cool: Business Culture, Counterculture, and the Rise of Hip Consumerism* (Chicago, 1997); on "liberation management," see Tom Peters, *Liberation Management: Necessary Disorganization for the Nanosecond Nineties* (New York, 1992); on "total quality management," from among numerous examples, see Eric Anschutz, *TQM America: How America's Most Successful Companies Profit from Total Quality Management* (Bradenton, Fla., 1995); Steven Covey, *The Seven Habits of Highly Effective People: Restoring the Character Ethic* (New York, 1989); Peter Senge, *The Fifth Discipline: The Art and Practice of the Learning Organization* (New York, 1990); Laurie Jones, *Jesus CEO: Using Ancient Wisdom for Visionary Leadership* (New York, 1995); Ken Blanchard, *The Heart of a Leader* (Tulsa, 1999); see also James Autry, *Business Lessons from the Tao Te Ching* (New York, 1999). I discuss some of the cultural and theological features of this literature in "'Jesus is My CEO': American Christianity, Corporate Business, and 'Theologies of the Corporation,' 1975-2001," report to the Louisville Institute for the Study of American Religion, January 2003. Following Livingston, Mary Britton King has argued (unconvincingly, in my view) that contemporary management literature and practice signal the advent of a progressive "social selfhood," a "connected or distributed individuality" which is in "constant experimental collective inquiry within a social realm that is not civic, but corporate": "New Management Theory and the Social Self," *Radical History Review* 76 (Winter 2000): 18, 20. Hope springs eternal.

# A Stranger's Dream:
# The Virtual Self and the
# Socialization Crisis

Elisabeth Lasch-Quinn

Elisabeth Lasch-Quinn's essay poses a question that is both fascinating and terrifying to contemplate. Is it possible that the human person as we have known it is in the process of vanishing under the multiple influences of modernity? If so, it would be the most bitter of historical ironies. What else has the revolution of modernity been about, after all, if it has not been about the progressive liberation and empowerment of the individual self, making possible a life free from the sorrows and constraints of material necessity? Yet the absolute triumph of the will turns out to be a ghastly and unstable concept, antithetical to the very happiness it so ardently seeks. An individualism that gets precisely what it wants soon loses its savor, and even its reason for being. Deprived of the hardness and intractability of the very nature it struggles against, deprived of a world whose form and pressure it needs in order to thrive, the will dies of enervation. Or what is nearly the same thing, it seeks solace, as so many romantics did, in fantasies of self-annihilation, or of immersion in that "oceanic" feeling in which the problem of individuation itself is absorbed and thereby disposed of. What forms the soul and makes it interesting, and capable of work and love and responsibility and happiness, is not the triumph of the will, but the triumph over self-absorption and narcissism — a triumph that always entails the defeat of the will, achieved under the forceful tutelage of family, society, and the school of hard knocks. The human person turns out to be larger, much larger, than the human will, for it cannot find happiness and wholeness without in some sense incorporating the social context from which it originates, and within which it moves. This is what we really mean when we speak of "socialization"; it is another word for "humanization," for the fullest formation of human personality.

Where, though, will those educative hard knocks — those authoritative messages from reality about where we end and where the world begins, and about the limits that are appropriate to our nature, even if they do not come naturally to our wills — come from, for the children of today and tomorrow? Particularly if they live in a world in which experience is increasingly mediated by technologies of the will which erase nearly all the limitations of time and space, and there is no normative standard available beyond that of a therapeutic worldview which eschews any possibility of judging the status quo on terms other than its own? Today's child grows up in a world almost wholly different from that of her grandparents, or even that of her parents. New technologies, and the willingness of absent parents and diffuse families to employ them freely, create a virtual world in which our children immerse themselves. What effect do these changes have on the process of social-ization? How have these historical and cultural developments affected the forma-tion of moral conscience in the young? What are they missing, and what will be the consequences? At this point, we have more questions than answers, but the questions must be asked. Elisabeth Lasch-Quinn is Professor of History in the Maxwell School of Citizenship and Public Affairs at Syracuse University and the au-thor, among many other works, of *Black Neighbors: Race and the Limits of Reform in the American Settlement House Movement, 1890-1945* (North Carolina, 1993), which won the annual book award of the Berkshire Conference of Women Historians.

It is possible that the self, or the human person, we know — or once knew — will soon be a relic from the past. At least in the United States, the forces of moder-nity — including industrial mass production and consumption, the reification of electricity and new technology, population growth and clustering around ur-ban centers and their periphery, the rise of vast bureaucracies, radical individu-alism, auto-mobility, the triumph of market practices and values, moral uncer-tainty and loss of faith, the waning of civil society and small communities, the compartmentalization of daily activities, the commodification of even intangi-ble aspects of human existence, the replacement of a religious with a therapeutic worldview — have already produced a new culture and new behaviors. This is perhaps nowhere more apparent than in the realm of children's induction into the social order, where the issues of culture and behavior figure prominently. A brief foray into the impact of modern media culture (specifically television, which lies at its heart) on children's socialization raises vital questions about how the human person might be changing in response to modernity.

Corporate capitalism and the electronic media technologies have emerged as two of the most pervasive institutions of modern life, now playing a central role in the upbringing of American children, if not transforming childhood al-

together. The new technologies — television, computers, cell phones, video re-
corders, computerized games — have increased the dominance of popular culture over children's lives as never before. Many parents, politicians, and
reformers have raised their voices in alarm to such a degree that new cultural
forms have arisen, from home-schooling to publications monitoring the popular culture, ratings systems for music CDs, character education programs, and
television cutback campaigns and organizations. While the extent and nature
of the media's impact on children remain a matter of dispute, few would deny
that the modern media technologies are changing daily life as we know it. But
the political polarization of the contemporary moment has prevented any far-
reaching and collective questioning of these forces' consequences for the human person. With the political left blaming the market for some of the vicious-
ness and hyper-individualism we see, but protective of the media under the
auspices of free speech, and the right blaming the media but protective of the
market under the auspices of economic freedom, arguments break out over
particular policy issues and media content but not over the broader questions:
What is the fate of the human person if the media-saturated consumer culture
continues to hold sway, especially over children, who lack any acquaintance
with a social world beyond its influence? Do the actual forms of modern media
technologies, and not just the popular culture content, play a role in the observ-
able changes in the modern self?

At worst prone to vicious fits of aggression and at best suffering from unprecedented levels of depression, anxiety, loneliness, and distraction, the new
human person — or perhaps more accurately, human sans personhood —
could well be modernity's most unfortunate legacy and democracy's greatest
threat. At the heart of democracy has always lain a certainty that the apotheosis
of humanity is individual freedom — both the freedom from dictatorial or any
other illegitimate or abusive form of power and the freedom to give assent to
the social contract and participate in civil society and governance. In early
democratic thinking, the enjoyment of these freedoms (only belatedly thought
to extend to all adults) demanded the moral virtue necessary for the responsible exercise of free will. Literacy and learning were deemed the foundation
stones for a self-governing citizenry that could act beyond selfish interests.[1]
Only the vision of a good and just society — seen as the common good —
could reconcile the imperatives to secure the bonds of community and ensure
the freedom and inviolability of the human person.

How this reconciliation between individual and community is to be

---

1. Bernard Bailyn, *The Ideological Origins of the American Revolution* (Cambridge, Mass.:
Harvard University Press, 1967).

achieved is, of course, one of the most crucial questions facing any individual or polity.[2] The Judeo-Christian tradition informed democratic assumptions about the human person from the start, with its notion of a transcendent good that infused human endeavors. As certainty and consensus about transcendence has waned with secularization and social pluralism, so has the notion of the human person as both guided and fulfilled by a moral community with a higher end than self-interest. Instead, the prevailing cultural ideal became, by the late twentieth century, the autonomous individual. As many have observed, American culture now glories in a vision of the individual as no longer bound or restricted by duties or obligations. In response, communitarian thinkers have launched an impressive critique of atomistic individualism and its threat to community sentiment and solidarity. But it is not just duty to others that has been sacrificed. Ironically, individualism itself has suffered from its own triumph. This is not just because the individual receives endless blows from others in the anti-social climate of hyper-individualism, although he or she surely does. It is also because we have become alienated from our own best interests by thinking of nothing but them. We cannot easily mine the sources of individual satisfaction and flourishing if our sights are fixed on them alone and our experience is confined to them. Ironically, modern media technology often serves to limit our horizons in this way, rather than expanding them as promised.

## Liberated from the Self

Cultural historians have delineated a basic change in the concept of the self over the long sweep of modernity. Their portraits, when taken together, show not just the heightening but also the distortion of individualism. Warren Susman, synthesizing the ideas of writers like Thorstein Veblen and Jacob Burckhardt, described the essence of modernity as the "development of consciousness of self." The Protestant Reformation, capitalism, and the rise of nation-states broke down old habits and loyalties, yielding a newly autonomous, fragile, and inward-looking individual. The notion of character, the root of which was self-control, underlay the new social relations of competitive capitalism, informing both manners and morals. Particularly evident in the nineteenth century, a veritable "culture of character," Susman argues, guided individuals in their search for both "a moral and social order and a freely developing self." By the early twentieth

---

2. In *The Masterless: Self and Society in Modern America* (Chapel Hill, NC: University of North Carolina Press, 1994), Wilfred M. McClay shows that individual and community have been perpetually in tension in American social thought.

century, this gave way to the "culture of personality" with the shift from "a producer to a consumer society, an order of economic accumulation to one of disaccumulation, industrial capitalism to finance capitalism, scarcity to abundance, disorganization to high organization," work to leisure, and "self-sacrifice" to "self-realization." Performance replaced accomplishment as the path to success. Nebulous qualities such as likeability, uniqueness, and self-confidence edged out duty, right action, and moral courage. A central contradiction arose between the need for self-expression and self-improvement, both of which emphasized uniqueness, and the need to please and fit in. The cult of celebrity represented a departure from the older notion of fame as rooted in accomplishment rather than personal magnetism or display.[3]

Susman's typology fits portraits drawn by other writers. David Riesman's description of the shift from the inner-directed individual required by market capitalism (who consulted an inner "moral compass" instilled through parental upbringing) to the other-directed one (who sought direction from his peer group as represented in the media) agrees with Susman's characterization.[4] Susman himself associated his "culture of personality" with Philip Rieff's "psychological man." Rieff observed that a cultural revolution had transformed an older culture based on religious faith and revelation to a modern one based on the self and its perceived needs. Since the late eighteenth century, the West experienced a wholesale deconversion. Culture, which Rieff defines as a set of sanctions and interdictions made meaningful by a commitment to a higher end, coalesces around "a design of motives directing the self outward, toward those communal purposes in which alone the self can be realized and satisfied." The waning of religious faith and its embodiment in social institutions led by the middle of the twentieth century to a cultural vacuum, replacing "religious man" with "psychological man," who lacked any notion of transcendent purpose and thus viewed others as mere instruments of his own self-gratification.[5]

With this change, older notions of morality based on a commitment to communal purposes emphasized the importance of the channeling of the vast force of human desire into a set of "fixed wants." In the absence of this culture, a doctrine of "impulse release" elevated "an infinite variety of wants to the status of needs." All older sources of authority, no matter how legitimate they were once thought, lost their resonance as people denied the primary human need to

3. Warren I. Susman, *Culture as History: The Transformation of American Society in the Twentieth Century* (New York: Pantheon Books, 1984), 271-85.

4. David Riesman, *The Lonely Crowd: A Study of the Changing American Character* (Garden City, N.Y.: Doubleday, 1953).

5. Philip Rieff, *The Triumph of the Therapeutic: Uses of Faith after Freud* (New York: Harper and Row, 1966), 4.

"have something in common, as an end, to love." Instead, they confined their pursuits to their "secondary needs" for sensual and material gratification, mistaking quantity for the quality of experience. "Religious man was born to be saved; psychological man is born to be pleased," Rieff concluded. The result was cultural disorganization and individual alienation. "Crowded more and more together, we are learning to live more distantly from one another, in strategically varied and numerous contacts rather than in the oppressive warmth of family and a few friends," was his poignant assessment.[6]

While other-direction and the culture of personality are still very much in evidence, the second half of the twentieth century has brought, if not a whole new personality type, then a greatly exaggerated version of the self as obsessed with image or presentation to the exclusion of much else.[7] Portraits drawn by social observers in the late twentieth century, ranging from Tom Wolfe and Christopher Lasch to Philip Slater and Robert Bellah, suggested that attendant on individual grandiosity was a strange emptying of the self. Lasch insisted, in *The Culture of Narcissism,* that narcissists were not so much characterized by inordinate self-love, which "implied a strong, stable sense of selfhood," but by "a feeling of inauthenticity and inner emptiness." They lacked a sense of connection with the world around them, exhibiting "a certain protective shallowness, a fear of binding commitment, a willingness to pull up roots whenever the need arose, a desire to keep one's options open, a dislike of depending on anyone, an incapacity for loyalty or gratitude."[8]

Lasch hammered home the idea that many Americans were not just unduly dependent on the views of others for self-definition, but that they lacked the very basis for a secure self or integrated personality. Modern life was arranged in such a way as to discourage the necessary process by which the individual distinguished between self and the rest of the world. The boundlessness of individual desire — untamed by the realization of its coexistence with the desires of others and devoid of means of reducing desire to manageable proportions — left the narcissist perpetually unsatisfied.[9]

More recently, critics and defenders alike have spoken of a new postmodern self as fragmented, decentered, multiple: in sum, an anti-self. Shorn of any solid self-concept, the postmodern human type seems to be captured neither by the concept of character nor by that of personality.

Some theorists champion the new type, in part for unseating what they

6. Rieff, *The Triumph of the Therapeutic,* 17, 24-25, 243.

7. Susman, *Culture as History,* 278.

8. Christopher Lasch, *The Culture of Narcissism: American Life in an Age of Diminishing Expectations* (New York: W. W. Norton, 1979), 239-40.

9. Lasch, *The Culture of Narcissism.*

consider the outmoded notion of the bourgeois self. In *The Postmodern Condition*, Jean-François Lyotard, for example, echoed a common theme when he defined postmodernism as "incredulity toward metanarratives," including those of the self: "The grand narrative has lost its credibility, regardless of what mode of unification it uses, regardless of whether it is a speculative narrative or a narrative of emancipation." Jacques Derrida, Michel Foucault, and others portrayed all such narratives as exercises in power and domination. While this doubt (associated as much with modernism as with postmodernism by many of its critics) sounds nihilistic, Lyotard denied that it had to give rise to "disenchantment" or "delegitimation," but thought instead that it raised the possibility for new levels of dissent, which could in turn lead to invention. Even without consensus or unity, justice can remain in sight if politics based on metanarratives (which represent the imposition of power) give way to "language games" about "metaprescriptives" — games that allow for a multiplicity of voices and operate only by "local" rules (i.e. those agreed on by the immediate participants in a given argument).[10] As one scholar characterizes postmodernists, "Influenced by the hitherto suspect anti-philosophies of Nietzsche and Heidegger, they showed human interiority split apart, fragmented beyond the simple conscious/unconscious dichotomy of Freud into a decentered, dispersed and fluid subject, not so much speaking as being *spoken by* language. Without a 'genuine' or essential being, individuals were seen as constructed by the texts surrounding them."[11]

Postmodernists disagree — and indeed, often contradict themselves. In postmodern theory, therefore, modern media technology sometimes appears as an egregious misuse of power and sometimes as the source of resistance. In the case of the latter, postmodernists are indistinguishable from, and provide the intellectual justification for, Robert Reich's "symbolic analysts" who see themselves as pushing the frontiers of the "information revolution."[12] As early as 1984, Lyotard waxed effusive about the promises of "computerization":

> Give the public free access to the memory and data banks. Language games would then be games of perfect information at any given moment. But they

10. Jean-François Lyotard, *The Postmodern Condition* (Minneapolis: University of Minnesota Press, 1984). Great disagreements exist about what constitutes postmodernism. See Andreas Huyssen, "Mapping the Postmodern," *New German Critique* 33 (1984), reprinted in Jeffrey C. Alexander and Steven Seidman, *Culture and Society: Contemporary Debates* (Cambridge: Cambridge University Press, 1990), 355-75.

11. Peter Hanson, "Postmodernism," in Richard Wightman Fox and James T. Kloppenberg, eds., *A Companion to American Thought* (Oxford: Blackwell, 1995), 534.

12. Robert B. Reich, *The Work of Nations* (New York: Knopf, 1991).

would also be non-zero-sum games, and by virtue of that fact discussion would never risk fixating in a position of minimax [sic] equilibrium because it had exhausted its stakes. For the stakes would be knowledge (or information, if you will), and the reserve of knowledge — language's reserve of possible utterances — is inexhaustible. This sketches the outline of a politics that would respect both the desire for justice and the desire for the unknown.[13]

Media guru Marshall McLuhan, who also made bold, if sometimes contradictory, claims about the power of the media that at times struck a utopian chord, famously characterized the new electronic media as the basis for a new resurgence of tribalism. In *The Gutenberg Galaxy* and *Understanding Media*, published in 1962 and 1964 respectively, he argued that society does not just produce technological innovations, but is in turn shaped in fundamental ways by them. Prior to literacy, which gave precedence to the sense of sight, he contended, tribal humanity enjoyed the harmonious balance of all the senses. However, literacy fragmented human experience by emphasizing sight above all, interrupting the more holistic interplay of the senses and the group unity of some early human societies. McLuhan saw the electronic age as bringing an end to the era of specialization, fragmentation, and hyper-individualism, together with the linear thinking he thought accompanied it.

At different times neutral observer, virulent critic, and technological triumphalist, McLuhan in his most sanguine mood spoke of a unification of experience enabled by the new electronic media which had the potential to make "the entire human family into a single global tribe." McLuhan trumpeted the revival of a kind of group consciousness, or "synesthesia," which he defined as a "unified sense and imaginative life." The transition from mechanical to electrical technology struck him as key: "Mechanization depends on the breaking up of processes into homogenized but unrelated bits. Electricity unifies these fragments once more because its speed of operation requires a high degree of interdependence among all phases of any operation." This technological shift in turn shapes human understanding and social relations, emphasizing interdependence and unity at the same time as allowing for decentralization and diversity: "Men are suddenly nomadic gatherers of knowledge, nomadic as never before — but also involved in the total social process as never before; since with electricity we extend our central nervous system globally, instantly interrelating every human experience."[14]

13. Lyotard, *The Postmodern Condition*.

14. Marshall McLuhan, *The Gutenberg Galaxy: The Making of Typographic Man* (1962; Toronto: University of Toronto Press, 1967), 8; McLuhan, *Understanding Media: The Extensions of Man* (New York: McGraw-Hill Book Company, 1964), 315, 352-53, 358.

Those who view the changing nature of selfhood with less than equanimity raise fundamental concerns about the future of everything from private life and civil society to democratic politics. Rather than seeing the current era as one in which fragmentation or erosion of the self brings creative multiplicity or unconscious unity, numerous social critics have depicted western society "at the breaking point," in Philip Slater's phrase. A growing number of writers have described what postmodernists celebrate as the decentering of the self as a moral crisis of vast proportions. That this moral crisis is at root a problem of socialization has only recently gained extensive consideration.

## Liberated from Meaning

Two contemporary writers, both inspired by Lasch and Rieff, see these developments as responsible for interfering with the very process of self-formation, which has at its heart the search for meaning in life. In *The Death of Character*, James Davison Hunter traces the socialization crisis to the collapse of civil society and in particular of local religious communities. He sees the purpose of socialization as the formation of moral character, which requires the exercise of virtue. Held as sacred by those properly socialized, virtue possesses a legitimate authority transcending the self, and its exercise presupposes a moral framework for understanding the world. This framework can be conveyed with any complexity or depth only by "concrete and particular moral communities that define the parameters of benevolence and justice." In modern America, tolerance of diversity, while a worthy ideal, has led to a decline of traditional religious communities and beliefs. Only a watered-down and abstract list of virtues can gain general consensus, and even that has no real meaning when taken out of a particular social context.[15]

Hunter argues that several groups dominate moral discourse today. On the one hand, conservative character education programs seek to instill a set of virtues they deem self-evident, and on the other, communitarians stress the importance of a sense of community. Still another set of education reformers, self-professed liberals or progressives, also embrace character education, but conceive of it as involving virtues such as empathy and tolerance for diversity instead of those associated with older notions of character such as courage, self-sacrifice, and humility. But none of these groups, according to Hunter, fully acknowledges the extent to which a deep understanding of morality requires

15. James Davison Hunter, *The Death of Character: Moral Education in an Age Without Good or Evil* (New York: Basic Books, 2000).

something more than theoretical moral argument or instruction alone. What is lacking is the inculcation of an overarching justification for good behavior.[16]

Therapeutic liberalism insinuates itself into nearly all current discussions of morality. Perhaps as a response to modern bureaucratic society's frustrations of our basic human needs, this doctrine looks to individual self-expression as the only explanation for the existence and meaning of social life, and thus interferes with self-development.

A "normative universe that constrains us within the boundaries of what is permissible," morality rests on both affirmation and interdiction, and is conveyed not just by a set of rules but by a whole culture that gives meaning to them.[17] This universe, conveyed to children in the process of socialization, consists, in the usage of Pierre Bourdieu and others before, of a "habitus," which

> refers to the taken-for-granted assumptions that prevail in a particular society or civilization that make our experience of the world seem commonsensical. At the most basic level of experience, habitus operates as a system of dispositions, tendencies, and inclinations that organizes our actions and defines our way of being. Socialized as children into this habitus, we live with an intuitive feeling about the nature of the world around us.

Alongside therapeutic notions of the preeminence of individual gratification as a guide for how to behave, the breakdown of families and faith-based communities has removed the infrastructure in which our moral vocabulary takes on concrete meaning. The embeddedness of moral prescriptions in everyday settings makes them palpable. It is at this mundane and local level that mere abstractions become concrete and "inwardly compelling."[18]

Like Hunter, Kay Hymowitz sees the selfish individualism encouraged by late-twentieth-century economics and culture as a major reason for moral decline and shows that we cannot grasp the moral crisis without understanding the profound problems inherent in the way children are now socialized. In her most recent book, *Liberation's Children,* Hymowitz explores the central paradox that while many American children have an unprecedented degree of opportunity, leisure, and freedom, they seem to lack the basic requisites for good or moral lives. In her view, children do not want for values or even virtues, for their often overscheduled lives now involve numerous activities and much hard work. Instead they lack any larger view of the world that would give this frantic activity any purpose other than self-aggrandizement. The result is that their

16. Hunter, *The Death of Character.*
17. Hunter, *Death of Character,* 16.
18. Hunter, *Death of Character,* 222-23.

liberation — modernity's most highly touted accomplishment — constitutes a form of alienation.[19]

Hymowitz traces the life course of today's children, showing how the current dominance of market values, or "ecstatic capitalism," affects their upbringing from early childhood through adolescence to adulthood. For one thing, the embrace of daycare even by families not driven to work by economic necessity has helped alter the whole process of socialization, radically changing childrearing norms and ideals. Advanced capitalism's cult of paid work (and the consumption it allows) as the main goal of life, together with modern feminism's overemphasis on careers as the expression of identity for women, has given rise to a "having-it-all script" for women.[20]

In addition, today's emphasis on children's cognitive development as the most important aspect of socialization, assumed to be vital for children's later success in the job market, has played a major role in justifying and directing this change. This appears in defenses of daycare based on new research in neuroscience that emphasize early childhood development to justify very early "schooling" for months-old children. A widely publicized 1997 study showed slightly higher cognitive development in good quality daycare over any poor quality care. Hymowitz points out that the same study showed that daycare also brought a decline in children's affection for their mothers at thirty-six months.[21] She thinks this emphasis on cognition alone denies the importance of other aspects of children's development:

> Yes, the problem-solving brain grows exponentially during early childhood, but so does the conscious self, the individual person with an identity that is larger than cognitive skill. Selfhood of the sort Americans have long prized implies a personal history — with its unique places and people — and a distinctive way of viewing the world that evolves in large measure out of an experience within a family and a home with its own character.[22]

Other trends conspire to weaken our understanding of the necessity of discipline in childrearing. The deeply antisocial attitudes and behaviors so often apparent today stem in part, Hymowitz thinks, from the failure to appreciate the importance of the home and parents' role in it. Today's childrearing experts draw on development psychologists like Lawrence Kohlberg, who see children's

19. Kay S. Hymowitz, *Liberation's Children: Parents and Kids in a Postmodern Age* (Chicago: Ivan R. Dee, 2003).

20. Hymowitz, *Liberation's Children*, 12-13.

21. Hymowitz, *Liberation's Children*, 7.

22. Hymowitz, *Liberation's Children*, 14-15.

moral development as an autonomous process of maturation through stages leading to the capacity for moral reasoning. Mistaking reasoning for the sum of forces leading to the exercise of moral conscience, this approach has an air of inevitability and trivializes the role of parents in the formation of children's moral character. It also downplays the importance of the early years of childhood in instilling moral reflexes and feeling. A new "American Child Pastoral" celebrates the expression of the "authentic" self of the child rather than active exercise of parental authority. When children do not receive ongoing reinforcement in the form of parental love and discipline, however, they do not internalize self-control or its rationale. The irony is that this therapeutic style, with its "exaggerated respect for the authentic self," thus deprives children of the moorings necessary for a solid sense of self.[23] As Lasch argued in *The Culture of Narcissism,* one upshot is the narcissist: someone who lacks an appreciation of the limits on his or her desires — the very limits that tame desire and lead to its satisfactions in a life with others.[24]

In light of this situation for children — the scarcity of the very environments most conducive to their formation as moral selves — the increasing dominance of the media and popular culture becomes all the more worrisome. By no means the sole cause, television does play an undeniable — but underappreciated — role in the socialization crisis. In the "void left by the weakening influence of the family," Hunter writes, popular culture, and television in particular, "operates, as never before, as an independent and even dominant source of moral pedagogy." Hymowitz sees television as one of the main purveyors of the market culture, which casts the purpose of experience as personal achievement and material gain. She takes to task the popular PBS children's show "Sesame Street," widely considered an exemplar of high-quality children's television. While "Sesame Street" presents itself as an educational show, it furthers the superficial and instrumental view of education as a path to success in a world of despised competitors and prized possessions rather than exploration and self-betterment for moral ends. The program uses a skills-based curriculum that actually works in concert with the techniques of commercial television to promote television and popular culture itself. A flashy barrage of images grabs the attention of the viewer; guest appearances keep the celebrity world ever in view; letters and numbers appear only as deracinated consumer items in ad jingles; and the viewer is understood as an "energetic, sophisticated hipster" while teachers and others come off as dull and irrelevant. "However well-intentioned," she writes, "by worshipping at television's glowing

---

23. Hymowitz, *Liberation's Children,* 62-63.
24. Christopher Lasch, *The Culture of Narcissism.*

altar Sesame Street effectively ensures the conversion of the next generation to TV's beliefs and gods." The show's "enthrallment to the world of television and stardom" is clear.[25]

Influenced from an early age by the pressures to perform and compete in a ruthless economy and denied the guidance and nurture necessary for secure self-development, children increasingly take their cues from the media. This has come to the attention of the public in the form of the firestorm of controversy about the content of popular culture. In the 1990s, debates and lawsuits over the lyrics of rap songs and the explicit violence and sex displayed on television and in movies led to incremental reforms such as the V-chip, music CD ratings, and other guides to the age-appropriateness of particular shows or movies.[26]

Concerns about the content of television go back at least to its growing popularity in the 1950s. Such concerns have been met by defenses and reassurances from those involved in the media and their supporters in the social sciences and among the public. Defenders have argued that television merely mirrors the culture rather than inventing it, that viewers can and do choose what to watch, that the market determines content, and that there is no direct connection between violence witnessed on television and the commission of violent acts in real life. But there is another strain of media criticism that is easy to overlook given the dominance of today's concerns over content. Disagreements about artistic and educational standards, and the relationship between viewing and behavior, help stall the public debate over the role of the media in children's lives and keep attention on particular scenes or programs and on parents' responsibility to oversee their children's viewing selections. It is worth remembering that alongside the ongoing debates about media content have long arisen criticisms about the form itself. In the current public discourse about the drastic increase in childhood diabetes and obesity, television sometimes draws concern as a contributor to children's lack of physical health. But besides the concern over particular content, that is the only widespread public acknowledgement that there is an underside to today's media culture. Only a few dissenters — isolated individuals, families, critics, and grassroots groups — seem very disturbed about the forms in which popular culture is disseminated.[27]

25. Hymowitz, *Liberation's Children*, 35-45.

26. Diane Ravitch and Joseph P. Viteritti, *Kid Stuff: Marketing Sex and Violence to America's Children* (Baltimore: Johns Hopkins University Press, 2003).

27. An exception is Robert D. Putnam, *Bowling Alone: The Collapse and Revival of American Community* (New York: Simon and Schuster, 2000). Despite the massive attention the book received, however, his conclusion that television was one of the main culprits for the decline of community has been widely overlooked.

## Liberated from Dreaming

To consider fully the impact of the television culture on the self, it is illuminating to return to the writings of some of the most outspoken earlier critics. In the 1970s, for instance, a few voices offered devastating analyses of the way in which television distorted basic human activities of thought, feeling, and perception. While the works of critics like Neil Postman, Marie Winn, and Jerry Mander found many readers, their warnings have been largely ignored.

These critiques illustrate just how drastically their authors thought immersion in television was changing American culture, and allow us to consider its effects, in turn, on selfhood. Jerry Mander's *Four Arguments for the Elimination of Television* is worth special consideration here because Mander's objections to television were concentrated on its influence on the inner life of individuals and thus help us consider the state of the human person in a media-saturated society. Mander agrees with McLuhan that mankind's relationship with technology is mutual: while humans initially create technology, it also ends up affecting them. But there the agreement between McLuhan and Mander ends. Instead of celebrating the new media technology's great potential, as McLuhan did at points, Mander sees it as entirely destructive and anti-democratic. Mander's overarching political message is that, far from a neutral device that can purvey information for good or bad ends, television technology intrinsically lends itself to the exploitation of the majority by the powerful few. Beneath that argument, which overreaches predictably at points and romanticizes cultures Mander deems more ideal because of their lack of technological sophistication, there is still an attempt to call attention to specific, but often hard to identify, ways in which television impinges on the inner life.

Mander presents an array of problems. Although he does not blame television for all of them, he does consider it both a symptom and a contributor. In particular, he stresses the way television interferes with real life by allowing for the "mediation of experience." As modern Americans have increasingly moved work and play to artificial environments, we have lost insight into natural processes because we no longer have personal knowledge of them. Without the firsthand experience of the natural world, we find it increasingly difficult to care about it.[28]

The artificial environments in which we now find ourselves — modern office buildings with sealed windows, bland colors, white noise, and fluorescent lights — starve our senses. While McLuhan rhapsodizes about television's abil-

---

28. Jerry Mander, *Four Arguments for the Elimination of Television* (New York: William Morrow and Company, 1978), 51-58.

ity to stimulate the senses as never before, Mander argues that artificial environments literally resemble those of sensory deprivation (or at least "sensory-reduction") experiments. In those experiments, environments stripped of all sources of distraction lend themselves to heightened human suggestibility. In the case of television viewing, competing light sources are often eliminated, so that the sole illumination derives from the television. Mander cites studies that show that viewers' heartbeats slow, bodies stay abnormally still, and eye movement decreases, leading to "a condition akin to unconscious staring." Even the type of brainwave employed in television viewing appears to differ from that involved in reading and other more active pursuits. In order to keep viewers watching, given that this low level of physical activity produces oft-cited feelings of lethargy and boredom, television producers have developed a repertoire of "tricks." Fast-moving images, loud volume, attention-grabbing imagery: everything aims at the stimulation of the viewer. The result is a kind of "tease," with viewers constantly stimulated but action always repressed. As early as his writing of *Four Arguments*, Mander suggested the connection between television viewing and hyperactivity (since then, childhood hyperactivity has risen to epidemic proportions) and suggested a connection between this repression of stimulus and violent actions.[29]

Mander argues that the form in which television content is conveyed thus lulls viewers into a state of consciousness that makes them especially receptive not just to television's particular messages but the entire artificial world it represents. Citing Jacques Ellul on how propaganda works, Mander is disturbed by the way in which the image itself replaces those the individual would have generated. Because of the particular form of television, images can enter the brain, which has slowed its functioning to a semi-conscious state, without the usual editing, analysis, and imagination that accompanies reading or immediate experience. Today's entrenchment in the culture of media technology may make Mander's description of the process seem a bit literal, but it still rings true:

> The retina collects impressions emanating from dots. The picture is formed only after it is well inside your brain. The image doesn't exist in the world, and so cannot be observed as you would observe another person, or a car, or

29. Mander, *Four Arguments for the Elimination of Television*, 167. This is a little-discussed possibility. The usual reply to those worried about the chance a viewer will mimic a violent act is that there is no scientific correlation. The response, in turn, has been that there is a general numbness to violence that causes viewers to be less prone to assist those victimized by violence and the like. The idea that television exacerbates frustration by simultaneously stimulating and repressing impulses is certainly plausible.

a fight. The images pass through your eyes in a dematerialized form, invisible. They are reconstituted only after they are already inside your head.[30]

This idea finds an echo in the writings of Joseph Chilton Pearce, who points out that "television floods the brain with a counterfeit of the response the brain is supposed to learn to make to the stimuli of words or music." When children hear stories told to them by other people, they receive a stimulus to which their brains respond by forming a mental image. By offering a barrage of pre-formed images, television "feeds both stimulus and response" and "floods the infant-child brain with images at the very time his or her brain is supposed to learn to make images from within."[31] Mander's phrasing poetically captures the cost of this intrusion: "Television viewing may then qualify as a kind of wakeful dreaming, except that it's a stranger's dream, from a faraway place."[32]

Not only does television draw us into an artificial world and replace our mental imagery with its own, but it creates a confusion about reality. It pretends to offer up three-dimensional reality but actually presents a severely skewed version, given that it can only provide a microscope's perspective on a small slice of life — real or imagined — and that that slice is a human creation, often designed with profit in mind. Before the video revolution, humans had some sense of the relation between the world and our senses. With the advent of modern technology, a basic disjuncture occurred. No longer do we think "seeing is believing," for instance. Instead, our senses are provoked by artificial images that are removed from any real source:

> In the modern world, information from the senses cannot be relied upon as before. We attempt to process artificial smells, tastes, sights and sounds as though they could reveal planetary reality, but we cannot make anything of them because we are no longer dealing directly with the planet. The environment itself has been reconstructed into an already abstracted, arbitrary form. Our senses are no longer reacting to information that comes directly from the sources. They are reacting to processed information, the manifestation of human minds. Our information is confined in advance to the forms that other humans provide.

30. Mander, *Four Arguments for the Elimination of Television,* 201.

31. Quoted in Barry Sanders, *A is for Ox: The Collapse of Literacy and the Rise of Violence in an Electronic Age* (1994; New York: Vintage Books, 1995), 41.

32. Mander, *Four Arguments for the Elimination of Television,* 201. Of course television does not just offer images, but a constant barrage of them. This leads to a sensory overload on the only senses employed in passive viewing: hearing and sight. Like sensory deprivation, the over-burdening of the senses is another technique that has been used to wear down humans' resistance to outside domination.

> Now, with electronic media, our senses are removed a step further from the sources. The very images that we see can be altered and are. They are framed, ripped out of context, edited, re-created, sped up, slowed down and interrupted by other images. . . . Meanwhile, the images proceed inward as though they were the same as natural, unprocessed imagery.[33]

The new technology has forced a new preoccupation with the distinction between reality and artifice, requiring a kind of "sensory cynicism" that tells us we cannot rely on our senses and must let the intellect dominate. While we think our intellect protects us from confusing the two, we cannot defend ourselves completely against the images, and we end up incorporating them into our reality. People often act on what they see on television, regardless of the source, and the real human world is shaped by the televised world in a multitude of ways.[34]

Mander sees the content of television programs as intrinsically connected to the technology itself. It is easier to convey extremes of life given the limits of the television screen, which helps explain why "anti-social" or "one-dimensional joyfulness" dominates and the subtleties of human thought and experience rarely appear. Exaggerated facial expressions and gestures, as well as physical movement, are more eye-catching than quiet, mundane moments of everyday life:

> While it may be possible to show friendship in a dramatic context, it cannot be explored very far visually, because expression of such feelings exists in an inward rather than outward realm of experience. Love is simply not as easy to demonstrate through coarse imagery as anger or competition. The heights of intimate feeling — between lovers, or parents and children, or among children — are actually experienced in life's quietest moments.[35]

Mander, who began as an advertising executive and became wary of media manipulation, found through experience that using television to promote the cause of environmentalists particularly brought home its limitations. It turned out that nature could not be conveyed successfully by video technology, which "cannot transmit information that comes in the form of smell, touch, or taste." Attempts to depict the natural world, even those that record it firsthand, actually reduce rather than enhance the viewer's understanding or appreciation. Television has trouble bringing a place to life, as it has no way to capture what it

33. Mander, *Four Arguments for the Elimination of Television*, 248.
34. Mander, *Four Arguments for the Elimination of Television*, 248-55.
35. Mander, *Four Arguments for the Elimination of Television*, 270-71.

is to be in a place. Thus it cannot provoke one to care about a place — only to recognize intellectual arguments for why one should care. Televised portraits thus objectify a place and offer only a very limited aspect of it. This abridged portrait can deaden rather than arouse our sense of wonder. In the case of televised depictions of human beings or other living things, they too are rendered into object form in the process of recording and thus lose their essence, which is based precisely on their *not* being objects. "The human being loses humanness itself," Mander concludes.[36]

Mander's far-reaching perspective raises particularly searching questions in light of the socialization crisis. Perhaps the most important point here is the degree to which immersion in the world created by the electronic media marks a repudiation of reality. In the case of children, whose very selves are in the process of formation and whose ties to reality are just being established, the results may well be devastating.

## Liberated from Love

Writing around the same time as Mander, Marie Winn presented worries along these lines, raising more than just the question of content. Winn wrote that the frequent viewing of television — still a striking cultural innovation when she wrote in the 1970s — should be judged above all as an experience. Supplementing scientific studies with numerous personal interviews, Winn concluded that children's mental state while watching television was indeed often "trancelike," akin to that of "drug-induced states of consciousness." Winn showed how television viewing came to replace a range of other kinds of activities, particularly within the family. In a bold and disturbing analysis, she de-

---

36. Mander, *Four Arguments for the Elimination of Television*, 2/5-86. Mander's book, and works like it that take seriously the way the virtual reality of television threatens the very connection between us and our surroundings, has naturally been received with skepticism and ridicule. The reviewer for *The New York Times Book Review* said it was "one of the smugger, more irritating books I've ever read on any subject, and surely the most hysterical and feebly argued attack on television ever published." While he called Mander's central claims "unarguable," he argued that this does not add up to "a case for television's elimination" but simply calls for reform. In a 2001 article in *Reason,* another writer rightly points to the flaws in the neo-Luddite program (Mander is part of a minute group of organized neo-Luddites who oppose globalization and modern technology) for tendencies toward simplistic causation, visionary posturing, and romanticizing of the underdeveloped world. Yet the argument here, that because technology has brought many advances we cannot debate its uses and desirability in different contexts, is baffling. Richard Schickel, "Two Cheers for Television," *New York Times Review of Books,* April 23, 1978, 13, 38; Ronald Bailey, "Rage Against the Machines," *Reason* 33, no. 3 (July 2001): 26-35.

clared that a combination of the disruption of family life and permissive childrearing left parents at a loss about how to rear their own children. For those parents who resorted to television as an "electronic babysitter," the television only made matters worse, encouraging a self-perpetuating cycle of estrangement of family members from one another.[37]

Winn's analysis centers on the commonsensical observation that children's television viewing, which on average consumes more of their day than "any other single activity," necessarily replaces other experiences they could have. In the case of very young children, whose first years comprise their introduction to the natural and social worlds, and whose first experiences engrave themselves permanently on their personalities, replacement of real-life experiences with television is catastrophic. At the very time of life when children should experience most strongly the bonds of affection in the family, children find themselves in the company of a machine that conveys animated images or recordings of real people instead of a real-life human being. In the "television-dominated family life" of many Americans, watching television may not entirely edge out special activities that draw the family together, such as family vacations, but it does edge out a fuller range of activities in which family members could participate. "Their ordinary daily life together is diminished — " she writes, "those hours of sitting around at the dinner table, the spontaneous taking up of an activity, the little games invented by children on the spur of the moment when there is nothing else to do, the scribbling, the chatting, and even the quarreling, all the things that form the fabric of a family, that define a childhood."[38]

In interviews, parents readily admitted to feeling at a loss about childrearing, often unable to control their children or stop them from arguing without resorting to television. Winn thought the adoption of the medium as an aid or a crutch thus reflected not just children's own demands but parents' needs. As twentieth-century families have encountered an array of challenges — divorce, working mothers, decline of the extended family and community — parents have found the task of childrearing increasingly daunting. Though touted as the great unifier in the 1950s when it first became widespread and when boosters celebrated the ideal of family viewing, television instead allowed parents to "withdraw from an active role in the children's upbringing." And as parents ducked the pressures and unpleasantness of raising their children by sitting them down in front of the screen, their children became even harder to control. Since the physical effect of television is to lull viewers into a temporary

37. Marie Winn, *The Plug-In Drug: Television, Computers, and Family Life* (1977; rev. ed. New York: Penguin Books, 2002), 17, 25, 121-62, 298.

38. Winn, *The Plug-In Drug*, 3-15, 154-56.

state of calm, when parents use television to cope with toddlers and growing children, the strategy often backfires by making them irritable and poorly behaved afterward.[39]

Forced into the regimentation of television viewing, children's innate energies and restless need to explore the world around them is stifled. Television, Winn writes, suppresses just "those explorations, manipulations, and endless experiments in cause and effect" that make raising small children both demanding and rewarding. Addressing the challenges by placing youngsters before a television set "is not all that different from suppressing a child's natural behavior by threat of physical punishment. It is surprisingly similar to drugging a child into inactivity with laudanum or gin."[40] As a result of over-exposure to television, children miss out on the very experiences with the real world they need if they are to develop as full human beings. Another critic helped drive home how much is at stake in what might otherwise seem like an insignificant detail of domestic life:

> The primary danger of the television screen lies not so much in the behavior it produces — although there is danger there — as in the behavior it prevents: the tasks, the games, the family festivities and arguments through which much of the child's learning takes place and through which his character is formed. Turning on the television set can turn off the process that transforms children into people.[41]

Winn points out that this modern response to the rigors of childrearing is hardly the only available choice. Since childrearing is indeed such a demanding task, parents at all times have had to find ways of keeping children busy so as to have time for their own rest or work. One of the ways they achieved this was through intimate knowledge of their children's needs and interests. A mother, for example, might observe her young children "with an eagle eye to obtain a subtle picture of their changing development" as "the pathway to success in getting children to entertain themselves successfully and reliably." For example, she might determine whether her three-year-old was ready for blunt scissors: "If this activity amused the child, it would be worth the mother's time to work on it a bit, to help the child learn how to cut properly, to provide a supply of colored papers or magazines, a jar of paste perhaps, because once the skill was acquired her reward would be a self-entertaining child." Next might come buttons, dough, or blocks, or having the child help around the house. The upshot

---

39. Winn, *The Plug-In Drug*, 206.
40. Winn, *The Plug-In Drug*, 151.
41. Urie Bronfenbrenner, quoted in Winn, *The Plug-In Drug*, 8.

is not only moments of free time for the parent and the development of the child's skills and interests, but better relations and "greater opportunities for shared pleasure." The omnipresence of the television not only helps erode parenting skills, but also lets the skills parents would ordinarily teach their children in the normal course of their upbringing slip away. Winn's scissors example hints at the range of other skills — sewing, knitting, carpentry, farming — once taught to children which the passivity required by television viewing puts at risk.[42]

Further, in nineteenth- and twentieth-century America, functions once performed by the family were transferred to other institutions. The media and the school, for instance, have taken up much of the role of educating children. As a result, many parents have lost their intimate, firsthand knowledge of their children — just the kind of knowledge that makes it possible to enjoy the company of children. In the family, once responsible for everything from economic production to character-building, "All that seems to be left is love, an abstraction that family members know is necessary but find great difficulty giving each other since the traditional opportunities for expressing it within the family have been reduced or eliminated."[43]

Not the least of the activities that are sacrificed when television takes up so much of the waking day is simply conversation with other people. In *A is for Ox,* Barry Sanders draws on scholarship in neuroscience and linguistics that shows that a crucial stage of literacy is that of orality, which refers to the telling and hearing of stories. In the crucial acts of talking and listening, children become acquainted with the rhythm of conversation, the development of a story, including its climax and resolution, and the sound of their own voice. Hearing this voice is part of their very constitution of a self, as they draw on their inner life for things to say. In turn, talking with others is the foundation of their connection with others. "Young people thus talk themselves into a whole and con-

---

42. Winn, *The Plug-In Drug,* 126. In another context, writing about the tragedy of the Indian-white encounter in early America, Francis Jennings wrote poignantly of the speed at which crafts and skills carried on by Native Americans for hundreds of years could be lost within a single generation as they became involved in fur-trade with Europeans. See his *Invasion of America: Indians, Colonialism, and the Cant of Conquest* (1975; New York: W. W. Norton, 1987). Later on, the loss of this rule-of-thumb knowledge of a whole range of activities once performed in the household struck progressive-era reformers as one of the main casualties of the industrial age. The early settlement houses, for instance, held classes in crafts and ran museums of craftwork precisely to keep time-worn skills alive even as the economy was undergoing a drastic change to factory production and away from hand-made products. See Jane Addams, *Twenty Years at Hull House* (New York: Macmillan, 1910). Winn's portrait suggests just this kind of deskilling is going on in the realm of childrearing.

43. Winn, *The Plug-In Drug,* 162.

summate life: they hear out loud how they feel," he writes. Without this experience of orality, "the inner life never fills out and takes shape." When children go on to read, they have "nothing, no substance, for literacy to embrace." They can learn the skill of deciphering letters, but they lack the ability to generate images and make intellectual and emotional connections with their own experiences, essentially because they lack the engaged way of being in the world that orality brings. Overexposure to television at an early age thus silences children at a crucial stage of their development and removes one of the major sources of intimate and meaningful connections with other people.

> Speaking sentences to another human being, listening for a response, marshalling thoughts in order to respond again . . . encourages a person to care about other people. . . . In the exchange of stories, the hope arises, as the poet Robert Browning writes, that the other will "rap and knock and enter in our soul."[44]

## Liberated from Nature

Just as the experience of television viewing takes children away from the experience of real human connection in the family, and the range of activities that reinforces this connection, it takes children away from another central aspect of reality, nature and the outdoors. In his recent book, *Reclaiming Childhood*, William Crain argues that the combination of over-zealous, achievement-oriented child-rearing and modern media technology marks a heavy-handed intrusion into children's early experiences, threatening the very sources of selfhood. Eager to spur on children's cognitive development, parents often interrupt children's exploration of their surroundings, even when they are merely trying to encourage them. By prematurely describing children's experiences in words and applauding their discoveries, parents detract from the immediacy of the experience, and the benefits of uninterrupted exploration. Crain thinks there are many natural propensities children have that parents risk in their focus on future success and accomplishment.[45]

Crain writes in the romantic vein, drawing on William Wordsworth and others who have written of young children's "love affair with the world."[46] At

44. Barry Sanders, *A is for Ox: The Collapse of Literacy and the Rise of Violence in an Electronic Age* (1994; New York: Vintage Books, 1995), 34.

45. William Crain, *Reclaiming Childhood: Letting Children Be Children in Our Achievement-Oriented Society* (New York: Henry Holt, 2003).

46. Phyllis Greenacre and Margaret Mahler, quoted in Crain, *Reclaiming Childhood*, 25.

one time, children might spend their time in "quiet contemplation" of the world around them and at another, "they are the boldest of explorers. . . . A flower, a bird, a puddle of water — the world is full of new wonders." Crain notes that when left to themselves, children may spend vast amounts of time simply observing their natural settings, experiencing a kind of "sensory awakening" at their encounter with plants, animals, and the elements that often provokes deep contemplation and creative expression. This is reflected in children's poetry, in which natural imagery is omnipresent. Nature often provokes a "daydream-like state" of reverie, as in one study in which children played at the edge of a New England frog pond. "In these moments of quiet," he writes, children seem "to feel a fluid connection between themselves and the water — a oneness with the world."[47] In their poems, children often express this unity by imputing human-like feelings and consciousness to animate and inanimate elements of the natural world, as in a poem he quotes by two-year-old Thomas Broadbent:

Bu'fly, bu'fly
Fell in a pond
Why spider, why spider, why?[48]

Crain also points out that this sense of oneness also comes up in some adults' memories of their childhood experience of nature. He refers to the description by Howard Thurman, an African American minister, of the prominent role nature played in his early experiences. The simple coming of night "seemed to cover my spirit like a gentle blanket. . . . I felt embraced, enveloped, secure." A walk by the sea gave him an overwhelming feeling of connection with the world: "I had the sense that all things, the sand, the sea, the stars, the night, and I were one lung through which all life breathed. Not only was I aware of a vast rhythm enveloping all, but I was part of it and it was part of me." Thurman said that these childhood experiences and feelings gave him "a certain overriding immunity" to the travails that followed as he made his way in life: "I felt rooted in life, in nature, in existence."[49]

Intolerant of the romantic view, Wendell Berry sees this unity between mankind and nature as the reality of the human condition. The entry into the untamed wilderness — both literally and figuratively — is crucial to our understanding of what it means to be human, to possess human limitations and live

---

47. Crain, *Reclaiming Childhood*, 25, 56-57.

48. Thomas Broadbent, "Bu'fly, Bu'fly," in T. Rogers, *Those First Affections: An Anthology of Poems Composed by Children Between the Ages of Two and Eight*, quoted in Crain, 96.

49. Howard Thurman, *With Head and Heart*, quoted in Crain, 58.

as a biological being in the world. Our literary tradition delivers many examples of a man becoming restored by a retreat into the natural world:

> Seeing himself as a tiny member of a world he cannot comprehend or master or in any final sense possess, he cannot possibly think of himself as a god. And by the same token, since he shares in, depends upon, and is graced by all of which he is a part, neither can he become a fiend; he cannot descend into the final despair of destructiveness. Returning from the wilderness, he becomes a restorer of order, a preserver.[50]

Berry sees nature as mankind's source of sustenance not just for food and a place to live, but for spiritual renewal. Critical of the over-specialization of expertise in all realms, he thinks that its role in medicine has narrowed our understanding of health to mean an "absence of disease." Instead, health presumes wholeness and thus entails the restoration of the "convergences and dependences of Creation." It is impossible to sever the soul and the body, for they are interdependent; disruption of one affects the other. Further,

> Our bodies are also not distinct from the bodies of other people, on which they depend in a complexity of ways from biological to spiritual. They are not distinct from the bodies of plants and animals, with which we are involved in the cycles of feeding and in the intricate companionships of ecological systems and of the spirit. They are not distinct from the earth, the sun and moon, and the other heavenly bodies.[51]

## Liberated from the Sublime

Although their assessments of modernity diverge dramatically, two of the most perceptive of current-day observers agree that what is most lacking today is a basis for morality and meaning that transcends the individual's wants and needs. In their great works of philosophy *qua* cultural history, Charles Taylor and Alisdair MacIntyre identify the rise of secular modernity as a cultural revolution of massive proportions. To MacIntyre, what is lacking about the modern world is any coherent moral framework or vision that gives meaning to human life beyond the individual's urges and preferences. The modern "emotivist self," for whom his or her own inclinations possess the status of moral claims, has re-

---

50. Wendell Berry, *The Unsettling of America: Culture and Agriculture* (1977; San Francisco: Sierra Club Books, 1986), 99.

51. Berry, *The Unsettling of America*, 103.

placed the traditional or pre-modern "social person," whose membership in social groups constituted the "substance" of the individual, yielded a set of obligations, and inculcated a shared vision of a moral life fitting that substance and transcending particularistic claims. Current notions of individual happiness and self-fulfillment have replaced the Aristotelian commitment to a purposeful completion of "a journey with set goals," and modern bureaucratic society exists to keep the peace among competing subjectivist claims in the absence of any shared moral understanding. In the emotivist culture, other people become to the individual mere obstacles to or instruments of the individual's drive for self-satisfaction. The result is the loss of "any genuine distinction between manipulative and non-manipulative social relations." Lacking the ability to draw on "impersonal criteria" for defining good and bad reasons to influence another person, the individual views all social relations as means to an end — his or her desired end — rather than an end in themselves.[52]

Taylor has a much brighter view of what modernity has to offer than does MacIntyre, but he still raises searching questions about where the commitments of modernity have led. In *Sources of the Self*, he argues that it is not so much the modern focus on the individual's rights, happiness, freedom, and fulfillment at the expense of social obligations and devotion to a higher moral end that is the problem, but the loss of any transcendent moral and spiritual purpose that makes those goods more broadly meaningful.[53]

Seeking to reconcile Christianity with secular humanism, which makes human flourishing its preeminent goal, Taylor sees the "affirmation of ordinary life" as one of the most compelling commitments of modern life. Secular humanism's view of human flourishing, freedom, and diversity as "radically unconditional" and the "cultural revolution" in Christianity in the early modern period brought a "spiritual outlook that our first concern ought to be to increase life, relieve suffering, and foster prosperity." Reformers attacked what they saw as the self-absorption, pride, and elitism of monastic life, with its exclusionary vision of the good life, and instead thought that "the really holy life for the Christian was within ordinary life itself, living in work and household in a Christian and worshipful manner."[54]

This form of Christian piety, exemplified in the beliefs of the Puritans, "exalted practical *agape*," and presented "an earthly — one might say earthy" cri-

52. Alasdair MacIntyre, *After Virtue* (1981; Notre Dame: University of Notre Dame Press, 1984, second edition), 31-36, 23-24.

53. Charles Taylor, *Sources of the Self: The Making of the Modern Identity* (Cambridge, Mass.: Harvard University Press, 1989).

54. James L. Heft, ed., *A Catholic Modernity? Charles Taylor's Marianist Award Lecture* (New York: Oxford University Press, 1999), 22-23; Taylor, *Sources of the Self*, 211-33.

tique of religious practices that adhered to "elite paths of superior dedication," Taylor writes. This critique of religious elites was taken further by secularists or anti-religionists who associated all religious belief with a repudiation of "the real, sensual, earthly human good for some purely imaginary higher end." As a result of the depiction of all religious belief as purist or superstitious, alternative forms of piety that locate the sources of spirituality within everyday life were obscured.[55]

The loss of any view of spiritual transcendence left only "exclusive humanism," Taylor shows, which contains within it the seeds of its own destruction. In the absence of a commitment to moral purpose beyond human ends, human ends themselves are compromised. This is because an emphasis on human flourishing alone has no way of accounting for destruction, death, and human failings — "the immense disappointments of actual human performance." Confronting such disappointments, those driven by a single-minded belief in human life and potential often react with "anger and futility." In the absence of a metaphysical grasp of transcendence, the practical dedication to human flourishing can thus become its opposite:

> . . . modern humanism is full of potential for disconcerting reversals: from dedication to others to self-indulgent, feel-good responses, from a lofty sense of human dignity to control powered by contempt and hatred, from absolute freedom to absolute despotism, from a flaming desire to help the oppressed to an incandescent hatred for all those who stand in the way. And the higher the flight, the farther the potential fall.

The "way out," Taylor thinks, is faith in the transcendent, an entity that can be seen "either as a love or compassion that is unconditional — that is, not based on what you the recipient have made of yourself — or as one based on what you are most profoundly, a being in the image of God." This appreciation of the transcendent source of the self gives us "our standing among others in the stream of love." "Acknowledging the transcendent" thus "means being called to a change of identity" — "a radical decentering of the self, in relation with God." This recognition that "something matters beyond life, on which life itself originally draws" provokes gratitude and humility and allows for the full appreciation of the sanctity of life itself.[56]

This brings us back to Berry, for whom the ideal of "autonomy" is the antithesis of the profound embrace of ordinary life he deems necessary for any full selfhood. The denial of the basic fact of our interdependence with all of

---

55. Heft, ed., *A Catholic Modernity?*, 22-23.
56. Heft, ed., *A Catholic Modernity?*, 32-34, 21, 20.

"Creation" keeps us in a state of profound isolation and alienation both from others and from our very natures. Organized religion has largely not addressed this malady because it too often treats body and soul as two distinct entities, as though only the soul can make legitimate claims on our attention. The idea that the soul must await the withering of the body to be fulfilled holds great dangers. "Contempt for the body," he writes, reappears in "contempt for other bodies — the bodies of slaves, laborers, women, animals, plants, the earth itself." As a result, "relationships with all other creatures become competitive and exploitative rather than convivial."[57]

On the other hand, the supposed celebration of the body seen everywhere these days is actually a sham. Lacking a sense of the interconnection between body and soul, the dominant culture actually degrades the body while trying to elevate it above all else. "One of the commonplaces of modern experience," Berry writes, "is dissatisfaction with the body — not as one has allowed it to become, but as it naturally is." Measuring themselves against a model of supposed physical beauty, and believing this model to possess "exclusive desirability," individuals lose all other ideals by which to consider their physical selves, such as health or wholeness. They view their bodies as objects, severing them from their connections and roles, their place in the household and community, their contribution to production and reproduction, their spirits and minds:

> To think of the body as separate from the soul or as soulless, whether to subvert its appetites or to "free" them, is to make an object of it. As a thing, the body is denied any dimension or rightful presence or claim in the mind. The concerns of the body — all that is comprehended in the term *nurture* — are thus degraded, denied any respected place among the "higher things" and even among the more exigent practicalities.[58]

In the case of sexuality, this "anguish of the body" caused by its treatment from without as object instead of from within as subject is particularly noticeable. Marriage is modeled on the capitalistic marketplace, with spouses treating themselves and each other as objects to be possessed and all others as threats or competitors. This view of sexual love as a competition requires, in turn, the "pretense of the exclusiveness of affection." Romantic love is seen as the private province of two people, having nothing to do with others. The generality of love — love for others, not just one's spouse — must be denied. To Berry, this creates the narrowest possible definition of a household, one that shuts its

57. Berry, *The Unsettling of America*, 105.
58. Berry, *The Unsettling of America*, 113.

members off from the community rather than opening it up to renewal at its source.[59]

This situation — in which both soul and body are severely compromised by separation — has proven disastrous for the modern self, as manifested in what Berry calls a "strange disease of the spirit — the self's loss of self." The modern obsession with identity is rooted in the failure to see the connection between "the immaterial part of one's being — also known as psyche, soul, spirit, self, mind, etc." — and the body and the particular place in which both dwell. Berry calls the identity crisis a "conventional illusion, one of the genres of self-indulgence . . . a way to construe procrastination as a virtue." Rather than restoring broken connections, the modern solution to this crisis is personal freedom, "another illusory condition" that denies our interdependence and the constraints of our particular circumstances. An excuse for "indifference to the opinions and feelings of other people," autonomy has no practical basis in the reality of the human condition. Frustrated by efforts to attain the impossible, "the modern self-seeker becomes a tourist of cures, submitting his quest to the guidance of one guru after another."[60]

Although a searing indictment of modernity, Berry's portrait of modern selfhood is not without hope. This is because he locates the sources of renewal in everyday life. The various aspects of nature and experience need to be brought together, "restoring the ultimate simplicity of their union":

> The lost identity would find itself by recognizing physical landmarks, by connecting itself responsibly to practical circumstances; it would learn to stay put in the body to which it belongs and in the place which preference or history or accident has brought it; it would, in short, find itself in finding its work.[61]

Television is hardly responsible for the state of affairs in which we find ourselves, but its prominent role in the lives of the young may well serve as a substantial obstacle to the recovery of lost selfhood as envisioned by Berry. Perhaps what the world of television does above all is create a competing reality — a "counterpart economy" — that obscures our own. It is undeniable that in rare instances particular programs can be masterpieces of human creativity, and an occasional work of drama, instruction, or reportage adds to our cultural riches like any other work of art or craft. But as a replacement for other experiences — of real people and places — immersion in television has the potential not only

---

59. Berry, *The Unsettling of America*, 112, 116-20.
60. Berry, *The Unsettling of America*, 111.
61. Berry, *The Unsettling of America*, 111.

to sever connections that are vital to the experience of being human, but when it comes to children, also to prevent those connections from being made in the first place. The television and its electronic offshoots invade and transform the tenor of the household, the place Berry sees as the place where nature and civilization are reconciled. The household, with its commitment to nurture and fellowship, is the place where our vast practical and spiritual demands may find satisfaction.

Berry sees our view of the land as inextricable from our way of living in the social world, distinguishing between the appreciation of nature at a remove, in the manner of the tourist, and the gentle use and inhabiting of the land, in the manner of the small farmer. The first sees the world as an object to be exploited at one's will, the second as an organic whole, of which the farmer is a small but significant part. The farmer's role is one of steward, not gawker. Television epitomizes the view of the tourist, suggesting that life is there to be watched, not lived. In his *Making of the American Self,* Daniel Walker Howe shows that in the early years of this nation, Americans' very definition of freedom rested on the notion of self-construction.[62] Rather than the freedom to participate in the building — and the living out — of their own characters within given constraints, Americans now seem to enjoy freedom from precisely that role. It remains to be seen whether this will amount to freedom from any kind of selfhood, but it certainly amounts to freedom from any kind of democratic selfhood.

Children today, by nearly all reports, experience shocking levels of anxiety, depression, hyperactivity, and stress. Confusion abounds: confusion about morality, reality, meaning. Can it be any wonder, given that children spend vast portions of their waking hours immersed in a world that is, as Mander says, inherently artificial, premised on distrust of the senses, cut off from nature and other people, aimed simultaneously at stimulation and repression, and comprised of a barrage of unrelated images designed to draw attention only to themselves? The virtual world of our television culture is now a primary agent of socialization.[63]

Given its widespread abuse as a substitute for living in the world, rather than as merely a source of occasional entertainment or information, television belittles the importance and sacredness of the household, which is the child's introduction to the rest of the world. The household, in any society but partic-

62. Daniel Walker Howe, *Making the American Self: Jonathan Edwards to Abraham Lincoln* (Cambridge, Mass.: Harvard University Press, 1997).

63. Steven Dworetz, "Before the Age of Reason: Liberalism and the Media Socialization of Children," *Social Theory and Practice* (Social Philosophy) 13, no. 2 (Summer 1987): 187-218.

ularly in one as dominated by market values as our own, is one of the only places in which children experience the non-manipulative social relations Mac-Intyre holds dear. Only through such relations do we experience what it means to love — and coexist in the world with — others as ends in themselves rather than means to our own ends, as well as to be loved — and lived with — in this way. Certainly personhood begins here.

The overuse of television capitalizes on our precious waking dream-state, luring us into its virtual reality, helping us mistake its world for our own. Though we may resort to it out of frustration, it does not solve our confusion about meaning and purpose; it only adds to it. A sham world, promising sham goods, its incoherence and deceitfulness threaten our quest for coherence and sources of trust. As Hymowitz and Hunter show, personal liberation has freed us from what we need the most: the discovery in family, friendship, and community life of meaning and purpose. To the loneliness and isolation we feel, television only adds more, fostering the deception that we can have access to a social world, satisfy the basic human need for sociality — for the sounds of human conversation and laughter — by ourselves. As Berry writes, "Healing is impossible in loneliness; it is the opposite of loneliness. Conviviality is healing."[64]

What modernity has wrought is an obfuscation of things that should be simple and clear, that the path to personal satisfaction can be only faintly glimpsed when personal satisfaction becomes the end in itself, severed from the communal realities of our condition and the appeal to a sense of sacredness that gives our own life value and meaning. The concept may be difficult to grasp, but without doing so we may lose sight of what it means to have a self: only in losing ourselves — in love, work, art, music, reverie, divinity — to something beyond us do we become ourselves. The Irish bard Van Morrison — like many of those mentioned in this essay, one of the few holdouts for a counter-tradition of understanding — often captures this simple truth in his lyrics. In a song titled "Oh the Warm Feeling," he evokes the paradoxes that seem to escape so many in our sped-up cyber-world: it is the seemingly most limited, ordinary, concrete situations that deliver the sense of the infinite we so crave — through our interest in or attraction for one another and our setting — and the loss of self, the humbling of the self, in the face of something larger than us, can produce the most intense gratification the self can know. The singer describes a scene in which he and another person sat tranquilly together by the ocean, evoking a climax of feeling through the simple repetition of the title line and restatement of the simple reality of the situation, in which two companions live as one through a magical moment that somehow encompasses

---

64. Berry, *The Unsettling of America*, 103.

all moments: "Oh the warm feeling as I sat by you/. . . And it filled me with devotion. . . ."[65]

Our best hope for recovery of this or any greater value to life beyond the
flourishing of the autonomous individual lies, as it always has, in our everyday
encounters with the world. Television's competing reality — and that of the
computer, the cell phone, and the other electronic mediators of experience —
distorts our perception of what it is to live in the world we have. The unintended consequences of a technologically-driven popular culture stand in
where a real culture should be. Much to the liking of the champions of
postmodernism, the anti-culture, in Rieff's terms, has become the culture.[66] Although Americans claim to be the first to cry out against cruelty to children,
stripping children of the very possibility of living in a real world must be one of
the greatest cruelties of all.

Total immersion in a virtual world makes our connection to the things and
people around us more and more tenuous. We have forgotten that the sources
of human goods — faith, hope, awe, joy, wholeness, love, unity, humility, dignity, sacredness — are discovered one at a time, everyday, close to home. The
mentality of television belittles ordinary experiences in the daylight world of
concrete times, places, people, and things, a daylight world which is our sole access to the sacred. This mentality has nearly overtaken us. If it is not tempered,
we lose touch not just with the significance of something beyond life, but with
the significance of life itself.

65. Van Morrison, "Oh the Warm Feeling," *No Guru, No Method, No Teacher,* published by
Exile Publishing Ltd/Universal Music Publishing Ltd, 1986.
66. Rieff, *Triumph of the Therapeutic.*

# III. SEEKERS

# The Uses of Faith After Rieff:
## A Personal Response to
### *The Triumph of the Therapeutic*

THOMAS R. COLE

When we inquire after the traces of "the human person" in the past, we are trying to catch glimpses of a perennial problem, one of the profoundest of subjects. But that subject is an elusively protean quarry that never shows itself *sub specie aeternitatis,* but instead darts in and out of sight, always in the garb of a particular historical moment and location. Indeed, making sense of the changeableness and plasticity of man is itself chief among the perennial problems. One way that modern historians and social scientists have sought to do this is by positing the existence of modal personalities, ideal types of human character structure that correspond to particular societies, epochs, and socioeconomic structures. Hence, what men or women of a particular time, place, economic class, and social milieu feel to be "natural" may in fact be nothing more than the complex set of thoughts, habits, and expectations that have been deposited in them, and in the people around them, by the relentless transmission belt of culture. Hence, too, the hinges of history come at those moments of transformation, when the modal personality that has dominated a culture is in the process of being superseded by another.

That such a change has been the most consequential development of our own era was precisely the contention of Philip Rieff's enormously influential 1966 study, *The Triumph of the Therapeutic: Uses of Faith After Freud,* a book whose importance seems only to grow with each passing year. A formidably learned and powerfully argued book, deeply committed to the validity and authority of Freud's insights into the human condition, *Triumph* argued that the West has now passed into the age of "psychological man," a new and post-religious form of modal character which is defined by the assumptions of the psychotherapeutic worldview. What has made *Triumph* one of the most haunting texts of its era, however, is its deep ambivalence about the very things it describes — this emerging character type, and the world it would inhabit. Although Rieff seemed to take it as given that henceforth all religious assertions were reducible to psychological functions that were in turn susceptible to therapy, at the same time he seemed fearful that the resulting men and women would be pale shadows of what their less enlightened forebears had been. His insistence upon the inevitability of the "analytic attitude" in all things sat poorly with his acknowledgment that the triumph of the therapeutic might well mean the impoverishment of Western civilization and the diminution of the human prospect. Although he thought the religious faiths of the past to be untenable, he could barely disguise his contempt for the cultural forms that seemed to be emerging in their absence.

The existence of such unbearable tensions ought to call into question the adequacy of the formulation itself, which is precisely the gravamen of Thomas Cole's unusual and courageous essay. It is a sustained intellectual and personal encounter with Rieff's classic work and the analytic assumptions behind it, offering a reinterpretation and revaluation of "the therapeutic" based on the recent rapprochement between psychoanalysis and mystic spirituality. Breaking out of the narrow frame of scholarly exposition, it recounts an experience of psychoanalysis with a classical Freudian, a "struggle of souls" leading Cole to the conclusion that an adequate account of the "self" or "person" in psychotherapy must acknowledge a unique, ineffable, and precious quality of spirit. Such a reengagement with religion, not through a Kierkegaardian "leap of faith" or romantic yielding to the irrational, but through an honest and conscious encounter with the limitations of modernist rationality, may well be a pattern for the future. Cole's encounter, and his subsequent reflections upon it, open the prospect that there may be unsuspected room for the recovery of faith on the other side of the analytic attitude. Thomas R. Cole is Director and Grossman Professor of Spirituality and Health at the McGovern Center for Health, Humanities, and the Human Spirit at the University of Texas Health Science Center in Houston. A pioneer in the field of medical humanities, he is the author of many articles and books on the history of aging and humanistic gerontology, including his book *The Journey of Life: A Cultural History of Aging in America* (Cambridge, 1992), which was nominated for the Pulitzer Prize.

## Pt. 1: Re-reading *The Triumph of the Therapeutic*

I've been reading, re-reading, and teaching Philip Rieff's *The Triumph of the Therapeutic* (1966) for almost thirty years. Sometimes in awe, sometimes in puzzlement, sometimes in disagreement or resentment, but always with a sense that this is a central work for understanding modern culture and reflecting on the conduct of daily life. The book is addressed to "those fellow readers in whose minds and hearts one culture is dying while no other gains enough power to be born."[1] The following essay offers a response and includes reflections on my own experience in psychotherapy, the recovery of my identity as Jew, and my intellectual evolution toward a postmodern religious humanism.[2]

*Triumph* is difficult to classify and even more difficult to read (which perhaps explains why there are so few reviews).[3] By training Rieff is a professional sociologist. But he is better understood as a grand social theorist in literary critic's clothing, writing an extended philosophical essay on a big and provocative idea:

> We live in an era when the "inherited aspirations of the Greek, Christian, and Humanist past [have] gone stale, when both Athens and Jerusalem, not to mention Paris, Oxford, and the Italian Renaissance cities, have become tourist spots rather than shrines of pilgrims in search of spiritual knowledge."[4] The West has come to the end of a long period of "deconversion," characterized by the decline of a unitary system of common belief. "There seems little likelihood of a great rebirth of the old corporate ideals. . . . By this time men may have gone too far, beyond the old deception of good and evil, to specialize at last, wittingly, in techniques that are to be called, in the present volume, 'therapeutic,' with nothing at stake beyond a manipulatable sense of well-being. . . ."[5]

1. Philip Rieff, *The Triumph of the Therapeutic: The Uses of Faith After Freud* (New York: Harper and Row, 1966), 2, 13.

2. For earlier thoughts along these lines, see Thomas Cole, "On the Possibilities of Spiritual and Religious Humanism in Gerontology," in *Aging, Spirituality, Religion*, Volume 2 (Minneapolis: Fortress Press, 2003), pp. 434-48, and Thomas Cole and Faith Lagay, "How the Medical Humanities Can Help Revitalize Humanism and How a Reconfigured Humanism Can Help Nourish the Medical Humanities," in *Practicing the Medical Humanities: Forms of Engagement* (Frederick: University Publishing Group, 2003), pp. 157-77.

3. Book reviews are surprisingly few. See Yiannis Gabriel, "Freud, Rieff, and the Critique of American Culture," *Psychoanalytic Review* 69, no. 3 (Fall 1982): 341-66; Robert Coles, "Freud: the First and the Last," *New York Times Book Review,* February 6, 1966, 8, 39; Perry LeFevre, "A Penultimate Ethic of Honesty," *The Christian Scholar* 43 (1959): 329-34; James N. Lapsley, "Book Review: Triumph of the Therapeutic: Uses of Faith After Freud," *Theology Today* 23, no. 4 (January 1967): 573-75; William F. Lynch, "Psychological Man," *America*, November 25, 1967: 635-37; Jerry Z. Muller, "A Neglected Conservative Thinker," *Commentary*, Feb. 1991, 49-52. Excellent overviews of Rieff's work include Richard H. King, "From Creeds to Therapies: Philip Rieff's Work in Perspective," *Reviews in American History* 4, no. 2 (1976): 291-96; Richard H. King, "A Precious Commodity," *Virginia Quarterly Review* 68 (1992): 586-93; and Jerry Z. Muller, "Philip Rieff," in David Murry, ed., *American Cultural Critics* (Exeter, UK: University of Exeter Press, 1995): 193-205.

4. Rieff, *The Triumph of the Therapeutic*, 59.

5. Rieff, *The Triumph of the Therapeutic*, 2, 13.

Rieff's previous book, *Freud: The Mind of the Moralist* (1959), established him as one of the leading twentieth-century observers of Freud. Unlike Herbert Marcuse or Norman O. Brown,[6] who saw in Freud a potentially radical and liberating critique of repressive society, Rieff's Freud is the conservative realist who insists on the irreconcilable conflict between social demands and individual desires. As Richard King observes, Rieff's work in this area revolves around three central themes: (1) Freud's influence on American intellectual and cultural life; (2) the historical-cultural shift from religious and political ideals and explanations to psychological ones; and (3) the implications of this shift for contemporary culture.[7]

It is important to grasp the irony in Rieff's use of the word "triumph."[8] He is more a critic than an advocate of the therapeutic, arguing that it reflects and contributes to the "impoverishment of Western culture." Rieff's thought converges with a stream of cultural history and criticism that warns of the dark side of America's optimistic pursuit of individual happiness and personal freedom.[9] As Eugene McCarraher writes in this volume, the "therapeutic" takes his or her place alongside the "other-directed character," the "organization man," the "cheerful robot," the "one-dimensional man" or the "narcissist." Each of these versions of the modern self is "secular, morally elastic, and insistent on personal freedom, all the while" conforming to the power of the corporation, consumer culture, or credentialed expertise.[10]

*Triumph* picks up where *Freud* left off — analyzing the new character ideal[11] (the "therapeutic" or "psychological man") which he detects in the increasingly permissive culture of the 1960s. Rieff argues that every historical era generates a character ideal that molds individuals to its particular values and institutions. Such character ideals are not to be understood literally; they are

6. Herbert Marcuse, *Eros and Civilization: A Philosophical Inquiry into Freud* (Boston: Beacon Press, 1974); and Norman O. Brown, *Life Against Death: The Psychoanalytical Meaning of History* (Middletown: Wesleyan University Press, 1986).

7. King, "From Creeds to Therapies," 291.

8. Not all reviewers (especially Gabriel) appreciate this irony.

9. David Reisman, *The Lonely Crowd, Revised Edition: A Study of the Changing American Character* (New Haven: Yale University Press, 2001). See also Herbert Marcuse, *One-Dimensional Man: Studies in the Ideology of Advanced Industrial Society*, 2nd ed. (Boston: Beacon Press, 1992); Don S. Browning, *Generative Man: Psychoanalytic Perspectives* (Philadelphia: Westminster Press, 1973); William H. Whyte, *The Organization Man* (New York: Doubleday, 1956); C. Wright Mills, *White Collar: The American Middle Classes* (New York: Oxford University Press, 1951); Christopher Lasch, *The Culture of Narcissism* (New York: Norton, 1978).

10. Eugene McCarraher, "Me, Myself, and Inc." in this volume, p. 187.

11. Philip Rieff, *Freud: The Mind of the Moralist*, 3rd ed. (Chicago: University of Chicago Press, 1979), 356.

heuristic myths of social theory, which aim to identify central tendencies in the relationship between culture and personality. In Rieff's eyes, the West has previously been dominated by three successive character ideals: the ideal of "political man" formed in classical antiquity; the ideal of "religious man" handed down from Judaism and Christianity; and the ideal of "economic man" embodying the rationalism and acquisitive individualism of the Enlightenment.[12]

Psychological man — the newest modal personality on the block — "lives neither by the ideal of might nor by the ideal of right, which confused his ancestors, political man and religious man. Psychological man lives by the ideal of insight — practical, experimental insight leading to the mastery of his own personality."[13] "It may be too early," writes Rieff, "to squeeze my fragile conception dry between the hard covers of a book. I am merely announcing his presence, fluttering in all of us, a response to the absent God."[14]

The book's subtitle, *Uses of Faith After Freud,* hints at Rieff's central concerns. Can modern Western culture hold itself together without a common faith? Can the Freudian ideal of insight help sustain a healthier balance between the repressive demands of authority and the individual desire for pleasure? What dangers accompany new faiths proclaimed by prophets anxious to fill the space vacated by the death of God? Do sexual permissiveness and focus on the self signal cultural decadence and decline?

If I can speak of a "method" in such an idiosyncratic work, it lies in the interpretation of specific texts from which Rieff conjures this new character ideal taking shape in the petrie dish of modern culture. His style of analysis verges on the Talmudic: Freud provides the sacred proof texts; post-Freudians (Jung, Reich, and Lawrence) provide the commentary or secondary texts, and Rieff interprets them against one another, in the light of contemporary circumstances. The first half of *Triumph* lays out a theory of culture, paints a broad picture of the "impoverishment of Western culture," and issues a "defense of the analytic attitude." The second half of the book critiques the post-Freudians C. G. Jung, Wilhelm Reich, and D. H. Lawrence, each of whom offered some new faith or myth in place of the dying Christian myth.

12. Since Rieff obviously meant to include women in his new character ideal, I have decided not to add quotation marks around the word "man." Analyzing gender as a hidden dimension of the "therapeutic" (and of ideal types in general) would be a fruitful exercise — but one I leave to others.

13. Rieff, *Freud: The Mind of the Moralist,* 356.

14. It occurs to me that "psychological" or "therapeutic" man even bears some resemblance to the "golem" — that ghost-like figure of Eastern European Jewish folk culture who comes to life with magical powers that can be used for good or for evil; Rieff, *The Triumph of the Therapeutic,* 40.

Why does Rieff turn to the Freudian corpus for his proof texts? Not because Freud was a great doctor or critic or reformer or even the founder of a new system for treating mental health problems. Rieff admires Freud chiefly as a diagnostician of the mechanisms and pathologies of civilization, the great scientist of humanity who declared us permanently rent by the eternal struggle between individual desire and social demand. Freud accepted the traditional dualisms of spirit and flesh, individual and society, and he warned against the illusions of any ideal of permanent healing. Rieff endorses this stance in the name of tragic realism: "we are not unhappy because we are frustrated . . . we are, first of all, unhappy combinations of conflicting desires. Civilization can, at best, reach a balance of discontents."[15]

Rieff's theory of culture attributes explanatory power not to social forces (bureaucratization, urbanization, etc.) but to ideas, in particular the ideas of dominant elites. "Civilization" is based on "culture" — the symbolic system of "restraints" and "permissions" that regulates society and community. Against the grain of most contemporary theorists who emphasize the aesthetic or symbolic dimension of culture, Rieff identifies culture by what it *forbids*. A culture is constructed by elites who invent and advocate its moral demands. Beneath the elites is a cadre of functionaries who administer the system of restraints and permissions and console people by recommitting them to some communal system as a whole. Beneath the therapeutic functionary is a social system of institutions, life patterns, and all the more mundane beliefs, justifications, restraints, and satisfactions that make up everyday life.[16] A culture is functioning well when its system of moral demands is internalized and sinks into the character structure of ordinary people. Such affective internalization, which goes much deeper than cognitive belief, is what Rieff refers to as "faith."

The decline of Christian culture therefore brings with it a long process of "deconversion" — uprooting of more and more people from a moral demand system culminating in salvation or damnation, hope or despair. The ascetic who sacrifices on behalf of higher ideals gives way to the therapeutic who focuses on everyday well-being. The lost symbolism of shared religious aspirations and commonly accepted moral demands is what Rieff refers to as the "impoverishment of Western culture."

What remains to control and channel the instinctual drive for pleasure? Rieff looks to Freud as a potential bulwark against nihilism and decadence. For all his pessimism, Freud continued to believe that science, with its rigor-

---

15. Rieff, *Freud: The Mind of the Moralist,* 343.
16. Browning, *Generative Man,* 36.

ous methods for creating reliable knowledge, could guide humanity into a somewhat more harmonious and enlightened future. Psychoanalysis originated as a scientific system of psychotherapy that did not offer a new saving faith but promised to ease suffering and strengthen the individual's rational capacities.

In an era dominated by an obsolete (but still internalized) cultural system of inhibitions, Freud created a system of therapy rooted in analysis rather than faith or moral guidance — a rational, secular form of spiritual guidance. Psychoanalysis helps people choose without telling them what to choose. In Rieff's words, it aims "to wean the ego away from either a heroic or a compliant attitude toward the community."[17] By contrast, what he calls traditional "therapies of commitment" rely on faith — "some compelling symbolic of self-integrating communal purpose" — to reintegrate the individual into the community.[18] The classical therapist (shaman, priest, philosopher, physician) uses whatever sacramental techniques (ritual, magical, rational) are available to re-anchor individual identity in communal identity.

Rieff admires Freud for refusing to take sides in the internal battle between authority and instinct, between *being* good and *feeling* good. Freud proposed no doctrine of the good, no religious promise of salvation, no historical march of progress. Instead, he offered a personal apprenticeship in the "analytic attitude," an educational re-training that helps patients entertain tentative opinions about the "inner dictates of conscience."[19] They would grow healthier by learning to feel and interpret hidden conflicts between personal desires and internalized moral demands. By placing the clear light of reason ("where *id* was *ego* shall be") between impulse and action, psychological man gains the power to choose unencumbered by inherited religious illusions. In cultural terms, "Where theologies once were, there therapies will be."[20]

An unmistakable tone of loss and decline moves beneath the ironic and seemingly irenic surface of the *Triumph of the Therapeutic* — a tone that becomes stronger and more explicit in Rieff's later work. In *Fellow Teachers* (1973/ 1985), he mourns the "second death of culture" (the moral and spiritual void in academic life). In "For the Last Time, Psychology" (1987), he stridently condemns the therapeutic while invoking an unspecified "sacred order" and its interdictions.

In spite of his obvious leaning toward a culture of religious authority,

17. Rieff, *Freud: The Mind of the Moralist*, 329.
18. Rieff, *The Triumph of the Therapeutic*, 5.
19. Rieff, *The Triumph of the Therapeutic*, 31.
20. Philip Rieff, "For the Last Time, Psychology: Thoughts on the Therapeutic Twenty Years After," *Salmagundi* 74-75 (Spring-Summer 1987): 105.

Rieff never challenges Freud's view of religion as illusion or his one-sided reliance on a hermeneutics of suspicion.[21] He writes: "I, too, aspire to see clearly, like a rifleman, with one eye shut; I, too, aspire to think without assent."[22] In later work, he retreats farther and farther into writing that intentionally disguises as much as it communicates.[23] It is clear that Rieff — the epitome of high culture in the Western humanist tradition — believes theoretically (and passionately) in the moral centrality of sacred order.[24] But since he never reviews the debate within psychoanalysis about religion,[25] or ventures onto the terrain of theology, Rieff offers no genuine alternative to "the ultimate violence" of the "modern intellectual" — destroying illusions in the name of science.[26]

But modern science has its own illusions, and these are embedded in Freud's answer to the central question, "how are we to live without divine sanction?" The classical psychoanalytic answer — by overcoming self-deception and coming to terms with the tragic Truth of the human condition — suffers from the objectivism of modern science. It assumes that "Reality" — both internal and external — is relatively fixed and essentially knowable by cognition alone.[27] This assumption stands behind Rieff's dazzling rhetorical performances, and the effect is to distance him from the lived truths of psychotherapy. The attempt to understand human experience by standing entirely apart

21. Freud (and Rieff) occupy only one end of the spectrum of interpretation. As Paul Ricoeur, *Freud and Philosophy: An Essay on Interpretation,* trans. Denis Savage (New Haven: Yale University Press, 1970), puts it: "Hermeneutics seems to me to be animated by this double motivation: willingness to suspect, willingness to listen; vow of rigor, vow of obedience. In our time we have not finished doing away with *idols* and we have barely begun to listen to *symbols*" (27).

22. Rieff, *The Triumph of the Therapeutic,* 13.

23. His prose, as Richard H. King in "From Creeds to Therapies" observes, becomes ever more "knotty, convoluted, opaque, allusive, pedantic, arrogant, and dazzling" (294).

24. In Philip Rieff, *Fellow Teachers: Of Culture and Its Second Death* (Chicago: University of Chicago Press, 1985), he writes, "In this book, by 'culture' I intend whatever was, is and ever shall be, the form of address, in its specifics as art, science and conduct, to sacred order. . . . In its every sift, our lives are entirely symbolic. Life exactly represents, in its moments, where we stand in sacred order" (xiv).

25. See, for example, W. W. Meissner, *Psychoanalysis and Religious Experience* (New Haven: Yale University Press, 1984); William B. Parsons, *The Enigma of the Oceanic Feeling: Revisioning the Psychoanalytic Theory of Mysticism* (New York: Oxford University Press, 1999); Michael Eigen, *The Psychoanalytic Mystic* (London: Free Association Books, 1998).

26. Rieff does appear in his later work as a clandestine religious apologist, but without a dogma or a defense of any religion or culture in particular; see Jerry Z. Muller, "Philip Rieff," 201-203; King, "A Precious Commodity," 591-92.

27. Irvin Z. Hoffman, *Ritual and Spontaneity in the Psychoanalytic Process* (Hillsdale: Psychoanalytic Press, 1998), 7.

from it is like trying to jump over our own shadows.[28] Important truths in life cannot be understood by logical or empirical methods alone; they must be experienced holistically. Grappling with existential questions — in the classroom, in the polis, in the church or on the couch — requires that we affirm and live our limited answers with both eyes open and in dialogue with others. That is, as vulnerable persons, not as disembodied intellects.

## Pt. 2: Fragments of an Analysis

*"In most hearts there is an empty chamber waiting for a guest."*

Nathaniel Hawthorne

*"Either the psychoanalyst thinks he knows the best stories, and therefore should convince his patients of their viability; or . . . he thinks of himself as an expert listener, someone who can bear and process what is called up in him when people talk about their urgent preoccupations and predicaments; someone who, by definition, traffics in the provisional and doesn't need to be believed."*

Adam Phillips

When I was studying American cultural history at the University of Rochester in the mid-1970s, *Triumph* possessed the aura of a sacred text. I absorbed it through the eyes of my mentor, Christopher Lasch, who used it as a touchstone to understand the decline of a religiously based communal culture and the emergence of a medicalized culture in which professional elites preached the gospel of individual well-being and health. I lived, in a way, under the paternal spell of these ideas: the ideas of a detached modern intellectual, who accepts nothing on faith and prides himself on being undeceived by illusion, falsehood, ideologies, pious hopes, or romantic wishes.

Throughout the 1970s and into the 1980s, I was inspired by Rieff's stern warning about the dangers of a remissive culture, his call for scientific analysis and clear-eyed thinking, his dismissal of the search for new gods to replace the fallen God of Christian culture. I admired his insights, his aphoristic and literary gifts, the staggering breadth of his knowledge. But I was increasingly troubled by his *ex-cathedra* pronouncements, his reduction of religion to its social function, his seeming indifference to individual suffering, and by the contempt

---

28. I believe that this image is from Hannah Arendt, *The Human Condition* (Chicago: University of Chicago Press, 1958).

that seeps into his analysis of the therapeutic. During the 1990s, my own emotional and spiritual needs led me into psychoanalysis and into a renewal of my Jewish identity. In the process, I confronted my own psychic limits as well as the limits of Rieff's point of view.

I made my first visit to Dr. Banquer in late 1991. I was really hurting. Every morning, I woke up dreading that something awful was going to happen. Simple daily life seemed to require more energy or confidence than I possessed. My first book, *The Journey of Life: A Cultural History of Aging in America*, had just appeared. Rave reviews appeared in the *New York Times*, the *Boston Globe*, the *Houston Post*, the *New England Journal of Medicine*. Cambridge University Press nominated it for a Pulitzer Prize. Yet I felt black and empty, immobilized.

Dr. Banquer came highly recommended as one of the city's most accomplished analysts. He was trained as a physician at Oxford, highly published, and had recently joined the psychiatry faculty of the University of Texas Health Science Center in Houston. After some initial sessions in December 1991, Banquer concluded that he could help me. His tone was authoritative and businesslike. This would be serious psychoanalytic work, not cuddly supportive psychotherapy designed to help me feel better about myself. Three times per week, a hundred dollars per session. I'd be responsible for any missed sessions, except for two weeks of vacation per year and days when he'd be out of town. He'd work from the assumption that my recurrent depression was rooted in the death of my father when I was four years old.

Beginning in January 1992, I left my house before dawn every Monday, Wednesday, and Friday morning at 6:40 AM and headed for Banquer's office. Down University Boulevard under a tunnel of live oak trees, to the edge of the Rice University Campus. Across Fannin and into the bowels of the Texas Medical Center. My body stiffened as I got off the elevator and headed to his office. I'd glance at the readings on his desk: *The New Yorker, New England Journal of Medicine, Journal of the American Psychoanalytic Association*, his own writings on autism, pictures of the current class of UT psychiatry residents.

At our first session, Dr. Banquer asked if I'd like to lie down. I walked across the room and lay down on the blue couch next to the wall of windows. The couch pitched like a sailboat in a stiff wind. Any moment, I could fall overboard. I constantly worried about what he was doing behind me, out of sight, where I couldn't see him. I could not shake the feeling that he might harm me at any moment. I needed to sit up, so that I could keep him in my sights.

So we began working face to face. In a corner formed by two book-lined walls, we sat at the opposite sides of a triangle lit by a corner lamp sitting on a circular table. Blue stuffed chairs. He wore thick black glasses and often folded one leg underneath the other; I usually crossed one leg over the other, mimicking the way my childhood rabbi sat on the stage at Temple Mishkan Israel in Connecticut. In those first few months, I came to see that my professional accomplishments, wonderful though they were, could not erase the sense of abandonment and emptiness that followed my father's death in the autumn of 1954. Humbled, I came to know the bereft child that lived inside my forty-three-year-old self, the ongoing grief that seemed to have no end.

Once my initial depression lifted, I began talking about my spiritual life, which involved an increasing commitment to Jewish study and prayer. Like Rieff, Banquer considered himself a "Jew of culture" rather than a religious Jew.[29] Like Freud, he saw religion as an illusion, a childish collective wish for an all-powerful Father. Yearning for *my* lost father was indeed a powerful theme in my psychic life. And Dr. Banquer made no bones about his views: idealizing rabbis, yearning for connection with God, and obsessive prayer and study would never satisfy the wish to have my father back. The sooner I renounced these yearnings and accepted "reality," the happier I'd be. The problem, of course, was that Banquer had now become the unconscious focus of my yearning for a perfect father. My fragile sense of well-being depended on identifying with him, seeing the world through his omniscient eyes. Accepting his judgments about my inner life. If I disagreed with him, I risked feeling abandoned, empty, bereft — the very things that brought me to him in the first place.

"Do you know that Freud opened a clinic for obsessive-compulsive Orthodox Jews? Their religion was making them sick. Your own obsessionality has very *particular* Jewish roots. A four-year old child has no grasp of cause and effect. Your father disappeared one morning and never came home. You assumed that you had done something wrong, that you had, in effect, killed him. If you could do everything exactly right — that is, become perfect — then you could atone for your sin and bring him back. Like the cargo cult rituals of the South Sea Islanders who first encountered Europeans with sailing ships and amazing powers.

"Midway on their trips to the Far East, Europeans would drop anchor and come ashore — loaded with spices and silk and big guns, which they traded for food, shelter, and fresh water. These primitive islanders had never seen such wealth and power. The Europeans would then set sail again, and the Islanders never knew when these great white men would return. They assumed that their actions before the Europeans arrived magically caused the white men to come ashore. So they created new rituals repeating their prior actions in order to bring back the Europeans. Like a rain dance or fertility ritual. That's what your

---

29. See Philip Rieff, *Fellow Teachers: Of Culture and Its Second Death* (Chicago: University of Chicago Press, 1985), 46, 51, 83, 95, 162, 198, 206.

obsessiveness is like, a magic ritual designed to bring your father back. That's why, after you throw yourself headlong into a major project, you become depressed after the task is completed. And I can guarantee that you won't find your father by becoming a more observant Jew, no matter how often you pray."

I spent many hours in Banquer's office feeling cloudy and stuck: I was furious with him for trivializing my spiritual life; and I was furious with him because he was right. I have almost no memories of my father. But I remember being wrapped with him under a large prayer shawl, swaying together before the open ark at New Haven's orthodox Orchard Street synagogue. As an adult, I would often choke up or cry when the rabbis and congregation prayed before the open ark. My family was so accustomed to this that they came to expect the tears trickling down my cheeks. "What's wrong, Daddy?" my eight-year old daughter Emma asked during a High Holy Day service. "Are you thinking about your father?" For weeks I felt foggy-headed and immobilized. I desperately wanted Banquer to be all-knowing, yet I felt wounded and angry at his arrogance. And I fiercely resisted the idea that my feelings and ideas about God were still shaped by the four-year-old child within me.

Banquer loved to tell stories, and he had a favorite story about God. It was drawn from Lion Feuchtwanger's novel *Josephus* (1932), which tells the life story of Flavius Josephus, the first-century Jewish historian who chronicled the Roman war against the Jews and the sacking of the Temple in Jerusalem in 70 C.E. Banquer liked to recount the novel's climactic moment. Jerusalem lay in ruins and the Jews had almost been routed from the great Temple of Solomon, the sacred center of Jewish ritual life.

"The Roman centurions had finally entered the Temple," said Banquer, "and they wanted to behold the great God of the Jews, whose dwelling place was the Holy of Holies — that innermost sanctuary into which none dared enter except the High Priests. They marched into the center of the Temple, right up to the veil that separated the Holy of Holies from the courtyard. With great trepidation, the lead centurion took hold of that veil and pulled it back," said Banquer. "And do you know what he saw? . . . Nothing. Nothing but a dark, empty room, with a cold, damp floor." Banquer sat back in his chair with a satisfied look on his face, as if the story's meaning was so obvious that there was no need to interpret it.

I did not know how to interpret the story, but I felt as if I had stepped into an elevator that wasn't there. It was a fall into not-knowing. I felt humbled and frightened. If I gave up the magical thinking in my prayer life and in my yearning for God, what was left? Meanwhile, 7 AM sessions had become my psychoanalytic ritual, and Banquer had become my great white father. He saw in my uncertainty an opportunity to see the Truth and renounce the illusion of religion altogether. I was bewildered. Was there a difference between unconscious wishes and a mature, post-critical faith? Could I learn and live an answer?

"I don't think that all religious beliefs and feelings can be simply reduced to a childish wish for security and comfort," I said one day.

"Well then, what is this thing you call your spiritual journey?"

"It's hard to say. I think the goal of becoming a self is to give up the self. I think I'm trying to bring my self into alignment with what's ultimately real."

"Ultimate Reality?" he asked bemusedly.

"Yes," I said, "I want to open my self to the mystery of existence. I know this sounds silly to you. But in spite of my Jewish self-hatred and lack of Hebraic learning, I am a Jew. I cannot not be a Jew. I can be a secular Jew. Or I can be a committed, practicing, and evolving Jew. So I have a large task ahead of me — learning to live inside Jewish texts, symbols, myths, and rituals, learning mystical and meditative practices."

"I see. You think you can achieve some kind of 'oceanic feeling,' some Nirvana beyond the flesh and blood reality of this world. Well, you're free to try, but I think you'll only become depressed and disappointed when it doesn't happen. I have a much more modest worldview: give up religious illusions and fantasies of spiritual transformation. And *carpe diem*. The clock is ticking."

These sessions were very difficult for me. I loved Banquer in spite of his arrogance, and I felt dependent on his support and guidance. But he wasn't fulfilling my wish for the perfect father; so I hated him. I needed his support of my confused and anxious desire to grow and heal. But we seemed to founder on the rocks of religion. Sometimes our sessions felt more like intellectual sparring than therapy sessions. One day I said that his comments seemed based on his counter-transference (i.e., his personal reaction to me) rather than on my emotional needs. "Counter-transference is everywhere," he responded, evading the issue. We both wanted to win. Banquer told the Josephus story again and again. I still didn't know what to make of the story, and I wondered why he kept repeating it. So I decided to read the novel for myself.

As Feuchtwanger describes this climactic moment, Roman troops have stampeded through the Temple gates in a fury. General Titus wavers between destroying the Temple and preserving it. Fire rages through the outer rooms as Titus and his officers move into the central court.

> The sacred room rose lofty and cool, cut off from the heat and the savage tumult outside. The candlestick stood there, the table with the shewbread, the altar where the incense was burnt. Slowly and hesitatingly Titus advanced to the veil behind which lay the mystery, the Holy of Holies. . . . What was behind the veil? Was it perhaps only some silly idol, an ass's head, a monster

half animal and half human? . . . Titus seized the veil . . . and tore it aside. A shadowy room, square, not very large, revealed itself, and Titus entered. There was a smell of earth and very old wood. The bare hewn rock, the topmost peak of the hill on which the Temple stood, rose there; the room was filled with a great and oppressive isolation; and that was all. "Well, well," said [the centurion] Pedanus, shrugging his shoulders, "it's just silly."

*Titus breathed freely when he was back again in the lighter hall adjoining the Holy of Holies. He recognized the noble simplicity and symmetry of the room, and eyed the austerely beautiful sacred vessels. . . . "We dare not let all this be destroyed." . . . Already tongues of fire were shooting in through the doors; . . . It was too late.*[30]

Reading this passage was an electrifying moment for me. I was transported to the ancient Temple as a Jew, feeling the despair, the death and destruction that sent our people sprawling into the Diaspora. I was there as the conquering General, trying too late to preserve the most sacred ritual space of these conquered Jews and their God. And I was here as a contemporary reader, a committed Jew, wondering who or what and where God is, whether God is, and why these questions matter.

Like a Reformation Protestant reading the Bible in the vernacular, I was liberated from the authority of a priest. I was free to read the text for myself, to wrestle with innumerable questions and interpretations. What is the meaning of the emptiness, the "great and oppressive isolation"? Perhaps the Holy of Holies was not empty at all but filled with God's presence. Why did the Roman general Titus want to preserve it?[31] Did he fear the wrath of this God of the Jews? Did he hear the call?

30. Lion Feuchtwanger, *Josephus,* transl. Willa and Edwin Muir (New York: Viking Press, 1932), 438.

31. I have come to see three major options to interpret the emptiness inside the Holy of Holies: the Wizard of Oz, the Death of God, and the Infinite Nothingness. In the Wizard of Oz view, we project our greatest human qualities onto an image called God. Once we remove the veil of illusion, there is nothing there, nothing to worship. Hence we can reappropriate the best of our own humanity. The Death of God perspective acknowledges the power of our longing for the Absolute, an Archimedean God. The Death of God calls us to the painful acknowledgement that these longings can never be fulfilled. And after God is dead, this perspective warns against idolatry. The most important thing is to keep empty the space God once occupied, to avoid the oppression that follows when any group claims special access to the Absolute. And finally, the perspective of the Infinite Nothingness. Judaism has always prohibited graven images, sculptures — any attempt to represent the Holy One. God is infinite, beyond all human categories and powers of understanding. As Maimonides argued, we can only describe God using negative attributes — by saying what he/she/it is not. In Jewish mysticism, the highest aspect of God is known as the "Ayn Sof," the Infinite Nothingness. For these reasons, any attempt to name, describe, or symbol-

I had freed myself from Banquer's control over the story, but I had not freed myself from his transferential spell. I was angry and disappointed: not only had he misremembered the novel, he had failed in the most basic responsibility of the analyst: to be open to the play of interpretation in support of the patient's growth.[32] I eventually left Dr. Banquer's care, managing the difficult work of leaving an unfinished analysis. Not until a decade later did I have the occasion to call him again — this time he was dying.

It took a long time to find 8265 Bernadino Street. He and his wife lived there in a little circle of townhouses on a large lot near Braes Bayou. Since the number 8265 was not visible from the street, I drove past it a few times, breathing deeply, wondering what I would say, trying to gather myself for this encounter.

Mrs. Banquer came to the door and let me in.

"No more than fifteen minutes," she said in a whisper. "He's around to the left and I'll be in the kitchen."

"I'm in here," Dr. Banquer called weakly. I imagined him lying down in bed.

I turned the corner and walked into a small family room with an eastern exposure. It was about 5:30. I remembered that early New England families often gave older parents a western exposure to soak up warmth from the setting sun — not a good idea in Houston. Dr. Banquer was sitting at the end of a couch, walker in front of him, blue towel under his bottom and upper legs. He looked like an upright cadaver, but his right hand was warm. He grasped my hand with some force. I had forgotten that his left hand had been mangled in Germany during the Battle of the Bulge.

"Hello," I said, trying to figure out where I should sit. "It's good to see you."

This time, he was on the couch. There was a small square table to his right. I sat down in a chair next to the table and faced him from a 45-degree angle.

"Don't ask me how I am," he said. "Tell me how you are. Are you still working in Galveston?"

"Yes. I'm fine. This is a very good time for me. I want to thank you for the help you gave me. It made many things possible."

---

ize God is merely a finite means of approaching the Infinite. Since God is utterly Other, everything and no-thing, perhaps it was wise to put no thing inside the Holy of Holies. After the destruction of the Temple in Jerusalem, rabbinic Judaism emerged and eventually placed the Torah — the word of God — inside the Ark of the Covenant. For the most part, the rabbinic tradition has opposed the mystical quest for direct experience of God or the "Ayn Sof."

32. At its best, psychoanalysis is a "unique form of *not already knowing*"; Jonathan Lear, *Open Minded: Working Out the Logic of the Soul* (Cambridge: Harvard University Press, 1998), 33.

"Thank you. It's very gratifying to have so many people come by and visit. It makes me feel that I've lived a good life and been productive."

"What are your days like?"

"Well, after I get up and eat a bit, I mostly nap. It's not a happy time. My eyes have gone south. I listen to books on tape sometimes."

"What do you think about?"

"Well, Tom," he said, leaning backward and looking as if I had asked an inappropriate question. "It's amazing how apathetic you can be." A small wave of sadness passed through him.

I hurt inside. Here I was, in the presence of my analyst, now a blind and dying patriarch. I wanted to express my appreciation. I wanted to say goodbye. And I wanted a final blessing. I thanked him again for the years of mornings we spent together. "It was very hard work for me," I said. "I don't know what it was like for you."

"Well, let me talk shop for a minute," he said, pointing his index finger somewhere between me and the door. "The problem you presented" — he coughed to clear his throat and then blew his nose — "the problem you presented was . . . a very selfish . . . a very selfish and narcissistic mother, and I think you came to see that."

"Yes," I nodded, thinking that he had not helped me much on that front. "I've recently been reviewing my notes — the notes I wrote after our sessions in a little coffee shop on Fannin Street. And I think what really helped was when you told me that I was carrying a secret — the secret that I hated the Jew in me. I was amazed, wouldn't hear of it. But it was in my mother's milk."

"Well, that about sums it up," he said, checking me off his list of cases. A diagnosis, a problem solved — not a blessing. "I'm glad you came by and gave me a chance to see how you are coming along." I recognized my exit cue. Smiling, I stood up and took his right hand again. It felt warm between my two hands. "I'd better let you rest now," I said, walking slowly toward the door. He stared straight ahead, unseeing through those thick black-rimmed glasses.

"Goodbye."

I got into my car and leaned my head against the steering wheel, wilting in the summer heat, an ancient sadness running down my spine. I had come bearing gifts: the gifts of gratitude and of love, willingness to share in his suffering. I wanted to be present in the dying of my analytic father. I had come to be of comfort, to open the empty chamber in my heart and invite him in. He declined to be a visitor. Yet again, I was disappointed and hurt.

I started the engine and turned on the news. And then it dawned on me. Banquer was my analyst, not my father. He had granted my request to see him because he knew I needed to say good-bye. And because it was my final opportunity to learn that he could never be the perfect father that never was.

## Pt. 3: Reclaiming the Therapeutic

*"Suspicion is no respecter of persons."*

Merold Westphal

*"The contrary of suspicion, I will say bluntly, is faith. What faith? No longer, to be sure, the first faith of the simple soul, but rather the second faith of one who has engaged in hermeneutics, faith that has undergone criticism, postcritical faith. . . . It is a rational faith, for it interprets; but it is a faith because it seeks, through interpretation, a second naivete."*

Paul Ricoeur

Dr. Banquer died a few weeks after I visited him. He was the perfect incarnation of what Rieff calls the "analytic attitude." There was no room for faith in Dr. Banquer's therapeutic arsenal, only room for reason. To the end, he practiced within the orthodox Freudian tradition, whose remedy is to expose, master, and renounce infantile longings. I have learned much from my long encounters with Banquer and Rieff. In a spirit of gratitude, I sketch the following response to *The Triumph of the Therapeutic.* I begin with a highly compressed discussion of recent psychoanalytic theory and suggest that it renders Rieff's depiction of the "therapeutic" untenable. Then, I turn to the philosopher Charles Taylor, whose work on authenticity and the modern self undermines Rieff's blanket condemnation of the therapeutic. Next, I turn around and emphasize the limitations of authenticity, invoking Rieff against Taylor. Rieff's notion of the "Jew of culture" (developed in later work) functions as a necessary counterweight to morally unanchored versions of authenticity or the therapeutic. Finally, I acknowledge my need to speak as a Jew *of faith* as well as a Jew *of culture* — and as a humanist scholar who thinks that we can no longer afford the false dualisms between the "therapeutic" and the "religious," or between "faith" and "reason."

Since Freud's death, psychoanalytic theory and practice have been transformed in ways he could scarcely have imagined. In a masterful summary of recent psychoanalytic thinking, Stephen Mitchell notes a primary shift away from renouncing infantile longing toward a broadly conceived therapy that involves reclaiming and revitalizing "the patient's experience of self, the healing of disordered subjectivity." Freud's emphasis on cognitive knowledge is seen as interfering with the emotional, intersubjective truth of therapy. (This orientation is consistent with Gadamer's notion of truth not as ahistorical correspondence but as an event, a "happening" of Being located in human historical experience.)[33] Whereas Freud sought to make the unconscious conscious, contemporary analysts (and psychotherapists in general) hope to enhance this kind of experiential truth — in Mitchell's words, to make "personal experience more real and deeply meaningful."[34]

When postclassical analysts discuss the self, they think in terms of some relational model rather than Freud's structural model (of id, ego, and superego). We learn to become a person by interacting with different others and through different kinds of interaction with the same other, in different relational contexts. The self is seen not as unified and continuous but rather as an elusive composite of multiple images of self and other, images derived from different relational contexts.[35]

On the question of "faith" and psychoanalysis, it seems clear that Rieff's notion of faith (as an internalized cultural symbolic) is too narrow and idiosyncratic to handle the multiple issues involved. For one thing, he fails to acknowledge the possibility of religious faith construed as a psychologically mature choice. For another, he misses the importance of faith (understood as trust grounded in hope) as a key element of personality and psychological growth.[36] Something like this kind of faith occupies an important place in the work of Winnicott, Lacan, and Bion.[37] Perhaps the most radical of these psychoanalytic thinkers, Bion uses the term "O" to refer to an ultimately unknowable and constantly changing emotional truth toward which analyst and analysand reach out together. For Bion, "faith is the very heart of the psychoanalytic attitude, a radical openness through which one aims at the ultimate emotional reality of the moment."[38]

It is no longer tenable, then, to conceive the therapeutic in terms of knowledge and individual choice-making or to maintain the ideal of complete analytic neutrality. As Irwin Hoffman points out, "truth-seeking and the expansion

---

33. Hans-Georg Gadamer, *Truth and Method*, 2nd rev. ed., trans. J. Weinsheimer & D. G. Marshall (New York: Crossroad, 1990), 484.

34. Stephen Mitchell, *Hope and Dread in Psychoanalysis* (New York: Basic Books, 1993), 31, 32. The initial instigators of this revolution are D. W. Winnicott, Wilfred Bion, Heinz Kohut, and Jacque Lacan, followed more recently by Hans Loewald, Thomas Ogden, Jessica Benjamin, and Christopher Bollas.

35. Mitchell, *Hope and Dread,* 104.

36. Eigen, *The Psychoanalytic Mystic,* 124-26.

37. Michael Eigen, "The Area of Faith in Winnicott, Lacan, and Bion," *International Journal of Psychoanalysis* 62 (1981): 413-33.

38. Eigen, *The Psychoanalytic Mystic,* 124.

of the individual's range of freedom" are not "the only moral imperatives underlying the analyst's endeavors."[39] Since the work of Winnicott, Kohut, and Loewald, there is a growing sense that "love and respect for the individual and individual development" (Loewald, 1960) is an essential element in successful psychotherapy. Most psychoanalytic writing today sees the real work of psychotherapy involving the mutual exploration of a patient's existential choices along with critical reflection on the limits and distortions created by transference and persisting childhood prototypes.[40]

I continue to think that Rieff's analysis of Freud and his cultural influence is still the most accurate and most penetrating portrait we have. But I have come to believe that Rieff's conception of the therapeutic is distorted, his cultural critique too harsh, and his assessment of our moral and spiritual prospects too bleak.[41] The antidote to personal and cultural loss lies not in restoring absent authority but in pursuing identity, meaning, and connection. I think we need to move beyond blanket condemnation and attempt to reclaim the cultural work of the therapeutic. One way to do this is by retrieving the important moral ideal behind the search for identity. Another is by attending to the uncertain, ambiguous, and dialogical work of re-envisioning the sacred in a pluralist culture.

First, what is moral about searching for the self? Here I turn to the work of philosopher Charles Taylor, who places this question in the context of the moral landscape of modernity. Taylor argues that the key to understanding the "moral world of moderns" lies in the way it construes respect for human life. In contrast to heroic and religious hierarchical cultures, modernity places special emphasis on three things: respect for the dignity of each individual, the affirmation of everyday life, and relief of suffering. This emphasis, he notes, generates a deep and ongoing cultural confusion: how do we "hold on to a vision of the incomparably higher, while being true to the central modern insights about the value of ordinary life?"[42] Taylor (himself a Catholic) envisions a way to hold these tensions together, at least in theory. Despite moral philosophy's protests to the contrary, he believes that biblical values continue to underwrite modern ideals of reason, universality, and benevolence. And he argues that the moral re-

---

39. Hoffman, *Ritual and Spontaneity*, 6.

40. Hoffman, *Ritual and Spontaneity*, 9.

41. For a more sociologically grounded account of the "self as a reflexive project" and the place of therapy as a methodology of life-planning, see Anthony Giddens, *In Modernity and Self-Identity: Self and Society in the Late Modern Age* (Stanford: Stanford University Press, 1991), chs. 1-3, pp. 179-80.

42. Charles Taylor, *Sources of the Self: The Making of Modern Identity* (Cambridge: Harvard University Press, 1989), 11, 24.

sources for living a good life after the Death of God can be found in a deeper, historically informed understanding of the modern self.

In his magisterial *Sources of the Self* and a series of less technical books,[43] Taylor has steered a middle course between unfettered individualism of capitalism and communitarianism of the left or the right — between what he calls the "boosters" and the "knockers" of contemporary culture. When he looks closely at the "modern notion of what it is to be a human agent, a person, or a self," [44] Taylor discerns moral resources that are largely overlooked by critics of liberal individualism. In a nutshell, he argues that selfhood or identity is inextricably bound up with some historically specific (yet often unarticulated) moral framework or notion of "the good." The quest for becoming oneself, therefore, need not degenerate into self-indulgence, emotivism, or moral relativism. It can (and logically does) entail becoming aware of and articulating the implicit moral framework of one's family, community, or religious tradition, which provide standards of conduct against which the fully developed person must measure herself.[45]

Taylor acknowledges the fear of Tocqueville, Kierkegaard, and Nietzsche, among others, that without "larger social and cosmic horizons,"[46] the individual comes to lack a sense of higher purpose in life and seeks merely personal pleasures. As Rieff puts it, "With no place to go for lessons in the conduct of contemporary life, every man must learn, as Freud teaches, to make himself at home in his own grim and gay little Vienna."[47] But he questions the blanket condemnation of the "me generation," "the permissive society," the "culture of narcissism."[48] These terms stack the ethical deck, implying that there can be no legitimate moral dimension to the search for the self. Taylor, on the other hand, sees the subjective turn of modern Western culture as a continuation, extension, and

43. Charles Taylor, *The Ethics of Authenticity* (Cambridge: Harvard University Press, 1992); Taylor, "The Dialogical Self," in *The Interpretive Turn: Philosophy, Science, Culture,* ed. David R. Hiley, James F. Bohman, and Richard Shusterman (Ithaca: Cornell University Press, 1991); Taylor, *Varieties of Religion Today: William James Revisited* (Cambridge: Harvard University Press, 2002).

44. Taylor, *Sources of the Self,* 3.

45. Taylor's notion of identity and the good cannot be squared with Freud's notion of the eternal conflict between personal desire and social demand. But it is entirely consistent with Winnicott's understanding of childhood and moral education. See Adam Phillips, "Winnicott: Moral Surprises," *Raritan* 7, no. 1 (Summer 1998): 139.

46. Taylor, *Ethics of Authenticity,* 3.

47. Rieff, *The Triumph of the Therapeutic,* 59.

48. Harold Bloom, *The Closing of the American Mind* (New York: Simon and Schuster, 1987); Daniel Bell, *The Cultural Contradictions of Capitalism* (New York: Basic Books, 1976); Lasch, *The Culture of Narcissism.*

secularization of Augustine's notion that the way to God moves through a reflexive awareness of oneself. In *The Ethics of Authenticity* (1991), he argues that there is a powerful moral ideal at work here, however debased or travestied it has become. The ideal of "authenticity" that we see informing contemporary psychoanalytic thought is richer and more complex than its critics allow.[49]

Taylor sees authenticity arising in the eighteenth century out of what he calls the "massive subjective turn of modern culture . . . in which we come to think of ourselves as beings with inner depths."[50] Tracing a philosophical history of authenticity through Shaftesbury, Hutcheson,[51] and Rousseau,[52] Taylor credits Herder with the idea that each person has an original way of being human. As Taylor puts it, "There is a certain way of being human that is *my* way. I am called upon to live my life in this way, and not in imitation of anyone else's. . . . [T]his gives a new importance to being true to myself. If I am not, I miss the point of my life, I miss what being human is for *me*."[53] Differences between unique individuals come to take on a new moral significance. But what prevents authenticity from becoming pure solipsism and navel gazing?

In Taylor's view, human life and identity are fundamentally dialogical.[54] We become full, self-aware, and responsible human persons by engaging with others. Our identities must be confirmed or recognized in dialogue and negotiation with others. Self-definition is not possible in isolation, apart from social forms of expression and the expectations, needs, and values of others.[55] Taylor agrees that the contemporary culture of authenticity often encourages a purely personal understanding of self-fulfillment, and that it fosters a view that makes relationships subservient to self-realization. But he calls on us to retrieve the full moral potential of authenticity.

A person in search of identity always exists within a "horizon of important questions" which transcend the self. Attempts at self-definition and self-fulfillment that ignore questions and demands outside the self suppress the very conditions of significance. As Taylor writes, "Only if I exist in a world in which history, or the demands of nature, or the needs of my fellow human be-

49. On authenticity in psychoanalysis, see Mitchell, *Hope and Dread,* ch. 5; see also Lionel Trilling, *Sincerity and Authenticity* (Cambridge: Harvard University Press, 1972).

50. Taylor, *Ethics of Authenticity,* 26.

51. Taylor, *Sources of the Self,* ch. 15.

52. Taylor, *Sources of the Self,* 356-67.

53. Taylor, *Sources of the Self,* 28-29.

54. Taylor, "The Dialogical Self."

55. For a recent psychoanalytic statement of this perspective, see Robert M. Galatzer-Levy and Bertram J. Cohler, *The Essential Other: A Developmental Psychology of the Self* (New York: Basic Books, 1993).

ings, or the duties of citizenship, or the call of God, or something else of this order *matters* crucially, can I define an identity for myself that is not trivial."[56]

The search for authentic experience plays a central role in the wave of spirituality that has engulfed American culture since the 1970s. The New Age movement, as it has come to be called, has been appropriately criticized for its intellectual shallowness, blatant commercialism, lack of spiritual discipline, and encouragement of narcissism. My beloved mentor Christopher Lasch, for example, interpreted New Age spirituality as a degenerate form of ancient Gnosticism, a form of "nihilistic despair" that retreats from the ethical and public demands of genuine religious traditions. New Age healers, he argued, reduce religion to therapy and offer little more than a spiritual high, "another drug in a drug-ridden society."[57]

There is much truth in this portrait. But like Rieff, Lasch oversimplifies the therapeutic, and he seems blind to its potential for personal healing and social transformation. Perhaps, as Philip Wexler suggests, the bull market in spirituality and the reemergence of mystical and esoteric practices are part of a larger tendency toward revitalization, resacralization, and reconnection of the personal, the social, and the cosmic.[58] Perhaps, as Jorge Ferrer suggests, we can work to transcend the misuse of spiritual practices or experiences for self-centered purposes.[59]

On the other hand, Lasch and Rieff rightly understand the danger: if authenticity has the potential to point us toward fuller and more responsible forms of life, it also has a profound moral weakness. Authenticity alone cannot provide reasons to restrain the person who authentically chooses selfishness or evil. It contains no intrinsic moral norms or prohibitions. At this point, we must invoke Rieff against Taylor. Rieff would have us look to "culture" — a symbolic system of prohibitions and permissions regulating community and society. But which culture can we turn to in a multicultural, pluralist world? While Rieff does not offer an explicit response, I suggest that a Rieffian answer can be developed from his notion of the "Jew of culture" — a figure who dances fleetingly across the pages of *Fellow Teachers* (1973).

*Fellow Teachers* originated as an extended response to questions from faculty and students at Skidmore College.[60] Here, Rieff extends the argument in

56. Taylor, *Ethics of Authenticity*, 40-41.

57. Christopher Lasch, "The New Age Movement: No Effort, No Truth, No Solutions: Notes on Gnosticism — Part V," *New Oxford Review*, April 1991, 12.

58. Philip Wexler, *The Mystical Society*.

59. Jorge Ferrer, *Revisioning Transpersonal Theory* (Albany: State University of New York Press, 2002), 37.

60. An early version appeared in *Salmagundi* 20 (Summer-Fall 1972).

the *Triumph of the Therapeutic* and drops his former neutrality, even suggesting provocatively that teachers must now perform the repressive work no longer accomplished by the church.[61] Rieff seems to offer the Jew of culture as an ideal type — a potential counterweight to the therapeutic.[62] The Jew of culture makes seven brief cameo appearances in *Fellow Teachers*.[63] I suggest that this ambiguous figure embodies a shifting blend of three elements: secular Jewish identity, canonical textual interpretation, and universal moral law.

- The Jew of culture is an assimilated, secular Jew (or a "non-Jewish Jew") who accepts the bargain that allowed Jews to enter the mainstream of modern society. Beginning in the late eighteenth century, European Jews were accepted (at least in theory) as *individuals* with full rights of citizenship; but the price of admission was to renounce the public authority of Jewish ritual practice and tradition.[64] This variant of the Jew of culture carries

61. Rieff, *Fellow Teachers*, 94.
62. Richard King first made this observation in "From Creeds to Therapies," 293.
63. Rieff, *Fellow Teachers*, 46, 51, 83, 95, 162, 198, 206.

> "A universal culture is a contradiction in terms. We Jews of culture are obliged to resist the very idea." (46)

> "I have not the slightest affection for the dead church civilization of the West. I am a Jew. No Jew in his right mind can long for some variant (including the Party) of that civilization. Its one enduring quality is its transgressive energy against the Jew of culture." (51)

> "A great scholar and teacher, a true Jew of culture, Huizinga understood the enemy now deep within our sacred precinct." (83n)

> "Do you think the illiterate sons and daughters of the ethnics are inferior to the condescending swine before whom our gentleman-servant predecessors dared cast their false pearls?" Footnote: "The old and rich Americans appear a forgetful people. Jews of culture grow more helpless against the purse strings of the state the less private purses support their traditions of public policy." (95)

> "In the absence of a supreme interdictory figure, another Moses, with his disciples, a defense by Jews of culture against our democratic orgiasts may be reordered . . . by a revival of severe codes of law." (162)

> " . . . the figure under siege in our culture is not Johnny Carson, but Lionel Trilling, superior teacher and leading American Jew of culture. For us pedagogically inclined Jews of culture, England was Zion, the fantasy fatherland; perhaps it was only the Pax Britannica, seen from the top of the Hawksmoor towers." (198)

> "The most original figure of lightness and play is the satyr of Reason, who opposes the Jew of culture." (206)

64. Arnold Eisen, *Rethinking Modern Judaism* (Chicago: University of Chicago Press, 1998), ch. 1.

forth Judaism's normative stance, welcomes the marriage of Athens and Jerusalem, and strives for success in the secular world.

- The Jew of culture is an elite university teacher — the kind of teacher Rieff found missing from academic life in the 1960s and 1970s. The sacred duty of the Jew of culture, according to Richard King, "lies in exploring with his students the inner spaces of the culture's authoritative texts. The ideal teacher seeks not to galvanize students into action . . . but to reestablish the awareness of the 'presiding presences' of the past."[65]
- The Jew of culture is an individual — *not necessarily a Jew* — who lives by laws that are binding on all men. Rabbinic tradition holds that even before the revelation at Sinai, there were certain laws binding on all men.[66] In Genesis 8:15-9:17, God enters into a covenant with Noah. He promises no more floods on the condition that his descendants (that is *all human beings* in the future) abide by seven commandments that the rabbis described as Noahide Law: (1) the setting up of courts of justice; (2) the prohibition of blasphemy; (3) the prohibition of idolatry; (4) the prohibition against killing innocent human life; (5) the prohibition of incest, adultery, homosexuality, and bestiality; (6) the prohibition of robbery; and (7) the prohibition of tearing a limb from a living animal for food.[67]

One or more of these elements is present during each appearance of the Jew of culture. For example, all three are present when Rieff refers to Lionel Trilling (whose liberalism he strongly opposed) as "superior teacher and leading American Jew of culture."[68] Characterizing the Dutch cultural historian Johan Huizinga (a non-Jew who was jailed for resisting the Nazis) as "a great scholar and teacher, a true Jew of culture" highlights the dimension of moral law.[69] Noahide law is clearly the most important element of the Jew of culture, and it represents Rieff's answer to Taylor.[70] The rabbis of the Talmud judged Gentiles and Jews alike by these universal commandments, which they considered a form of natural moral law, available and applicable to all humankind.[71]

65. King, "From Creeds to Therapies," 293.

66. I want to thank Arnold Eisen for suggesting this idea in conversation. For his earlier thinking on Rieff's Jew of culture, see *Rethinking Modern Judaism*, 66-69. Thanks also to Greg Kaplan for helping me further explore these issues.

67. I am relying on David Novak's summary in "Mitzvah" (commandment) in Tikva Frymer-Kensky et al., eds., *Christianity in Jewish Terms* (Boulder: Westview Press, 2000), 117.

68. Rieff, *Fellow Teachers*, 198.

69. Rieff, *Fellow Teachers*, 83n.

70. Rieff may not have been thinking specifically of Noahide law.

71. David Novak, "Mitzvah," 119.

Rieff's Jew of culture represents a fascinating, poignant, and enigmatic turn to his own ethnic and religious roots. But it is crucial to recognize that none of the three elements — secular Jewish identity, canonical textual interpretation, Noahide law — requires a commitment to the covenant of Abraham, to the Jewish people, or to Torah.[72] Rieff and other Jews of his generation each made their own peace with the forced choice between an explicitly Jewish identity and American-style success in the academy, business, and the professions. And we who are Jewish understand all too well the potential self-hatred and other forms of psychological and spiritual dis-ease entailed in this historic bargain. The ground rules of Jewish Emancipation remain in force; each generation, as Eisen points out, works out a "familiar and oft-practiced Jewish calculus of assimilation, acculturation, and distinctiveness."[73]

I have struggled for many years to find my own way through this calculus. Changes in contemporary life and changes in my inner life have made possible a new balance. The establishment of the state of Israel, the ascent of American Jewry, establishment of Jewish Studies Departments, and the renewal of Jewish learning in general have restructured the calculus. And postmodern culture has made it possible to see that identity is not a unitary thing that one simply finds and wears like a suit of clothes; rather, identity is an unstable, relational process, a story negotiated in difference and relationship.[74] In Bill McClay's terms (see introduction), I understand myself not as an unencumbered self but as an embedded person, living in multiple life-worlds. I was the last person in my family to be circumcised by a "moyel" — a nonmedical orthodox practitioner. And I may be the first person in my family to return to the covenant as a freely chosen obligation. I am a Jew of faith, who sees the personal reappropriation of Judaism as a lifelong task. And I am a scholar committed to the educational tradition of *humanitas* — rooted in fellow feeling, knowledge, and compassionate action in the world. In pain and in love, I have turned to the therapeutic *and* the religious to carry forward the legacies of all my fathers.

72. For a call to such commitment by a former student of Rieff, see Arnold M. Eisen, *Taking Hold of Torah: Jewish Commitment and Community in America* (Bloomington: Indiana University Press, 1997).

73. Eisen, *Rethinking Modern Judaism*, 245.

74. Joan Scott, "Multiculturalism and the Politics of Identity," *October* 61 (Summer 1992): 12-19.

# Wendell Berry and the Agrarian Recovery of the Human Person

Allan Carlson

From his home on an eighty-five-acre hillside farm in an obscure corner of Kentucky, the farmer-writer Wendell Berry has become one of the most influential intellectuals of our time, developing an international following of readers who find in his many poems, novels, stories, and essays a powerful vision of the human prospect that stands in confident and defiant opposition to the most unsettling and despoiling aspects of modernity. At the core of all his work is advocacy for a certain form of agrarian traditionalism, a comprehensively different approach to life that would seek to restore the human sense of connection to the life-giving cycles and limits of nature, and to natural forms of family and community. It is not easy to categorize Berry's outlook in the usual left-right or liberal-conservative binary opposites, since his outlook is, in many respects, both socially conservative and economically radical, espousing a commitment to local economies and institutions that is dramatically different from either of the chief political alternatives now on offer. His uncategorizability reflects the fact that he is insisting upon a different way of thinking about the human person, and of thinking about "what humans are for." That new way is, in most respects, a recovery of the old way, a way that existed before the Industrial Revolution, a way so old as to seem radically new to our globally wired and technology-besotted world. Hence its challenge is just as threatening to the political left as to the political right. If we accept Berry's vision, Carlson argues, we can come to only one conclusion: "The human person is conditioned for life in the village or on the small farm. For thousands of years . . . this has been humankind's normative way." If that is so, what then does that say about the way we now live — and the way we should live? Small wonder that Carlson labels Berry as a prophet, for, like the prophets of Biblical times, he has dared to hold modern society up before a more enduring standard — and dared to find it sadly wanting. Allan Carlson is President of The Howard Center for Family, Religion, and Society. His many publications include *Family Questions: Reflections* on the American Social Crisis (Transaction, 1991); *The Swedish Experiment in Family Politics* (Transaction, 1990); *The New Agrarian Mind: The Movement Toward Decentralist Thought in Twentieth Century America* (Transaction, 2000); and *The 'American Way': Family and Community in the Shaping of the American Identity* (ISI Books, 2003).

Standing athwart the main currents of American life for the last forty years, the poet, novelist, and essayist Wendell Berry has fairly gained the label "prophet." In the era of the globalizing economy, Berry has forcefully rejected the essentials of market capitalism, urging instead a return to small economies built on productive households. At the dawn of the Second "American Century" guided by the world's last superpower, Berry has all but rejected American nationhood, embracing instead a local patriotism celebrating his small corner of rural Kentucky. In an age of unprecedented scientific and technological advances, Berry has renounced it all, from computers and cloning to industrialization and the scientific method. In a culture increasingly devoted to individual self-fulfillment, he has summoned his readers back to the burdens and responsibilities of wifery, husbandry, marriage, and community building. Underscoring the disastrous hubris of modern science and the dangers of a modern economy resting on "creative destruction," Berry has rejected incremental solutions and compromises. He has urged instead the building of an alternate culture: anti-materialist, self-sufficient, localist, communal, familistic, and agrarian.

Berry's worldview has also shown a distinctive understanding of the human person. He has denied *homo economicus,* or "Modern Economic Man" as celebrated by twentieth-century liberal capitalists: a person individualistic, rational, competitive, and yet constrained in family relations by bourgeois sensibilities. Berry has also scorned the "New Soviet Man" of the last century's Marxists: a creature self-denying and altruistic and yet experimental in human and sexual bonds. Implicitly, Berry has rejected as well the "Third Way" of Scandinavian Social Democracy, complete with its own vision of re-engineered human nature: "Modern Cooperative Human," combining moral individualism and gender egalitarianism with social obligation.[1]

Rather, Berry's understanding of human nature has been closer to that of

---

1. See Allan Carlson, *The Swedish Experiment in Family Politics: The Myrdals and the Interwar Population Crisis* (New Brunswick: Transaction, 1990), ch. 3.

another reputed "Third Way": the Distributist society outlined eighty years ago by the English journalists G. K. Chesterton and Hilaire Belloc. This construct had twentieth-century peasants and craftsmen living traditional family lives in radically decentralized economic and political structures; a vision of "Propertied and Devout Village Man."[2] Berry has also built on the legacy of a distinct band of American writers who crusaded to create "The New Agrarian Man." Their vision was rooted in a mythology of the Agricultural Republic founded in 1776. They sought to reinvigorate a rural civilization in America, with its own culture and traditions. Distrustful of both capitalism's tendency toward monopoly and socialism's thrust toward bureaucratic centralization, they looked for ways to protect and expand small property, especially general and subsistence farms. Socially conservative, they viewed small farms as the nurseries of the nation and the natural home of the family. Wrestling openly with modernity, they theorized about ways to turn new technologies and new methods of education into servants of rural tradition. The New Agrarians included the Cornell University horticulturalist Liberty Hyde Bailey, the Harvard University sociologist Carle Zimmerman, the renegade economists Ralph Borsodi and Troy Cauley, the popular novelist Louis Bromfield, the "Twelve Southerners" at Vanderbilt University who produced the 1930 volume *I'll Take My Stand*, the historian Herbert Agar, and the Iowa priest and rural activist Luigi Ligutti. Their work gained momentum during the first three decades of the century and won wide national attention and some policy influence during the 1930s, only to be overwhelmed by the economic and social upheaval of the Second World War.[3]

Berry stands as their most prominent heir. Born in Kentucky in 1934, he published his first short story in 1955, his first poem in 1957, and his first novel in 1960, and remains active to this day. Berry has acknowledged his intellectual debt to and kinship with the Vanderbilt Agrarians, Liberty Hyde Bailey, Louis Bromfield, and others involved "in the familial and communal handing down of the agrarian common culture."[4] And yet he has been different in two important ways.

First, Berry was direct witness to the failure of the early-twentieth-century New Agrarian dream. The farm population in the United States — still 30 million strong in 1940 (the same as in 1900) — had fallen sharply thereafter: to 23

---

2. See G. K. Chesterton, *What's Wrong With the World*, in *Collected Works*, Vol. 4: *Family, Society, Politics* (San Francisco: Ignatius, 1987); and Hilaire Belloc, *The Restoration of Property* (New York: Sheed and Ward, 1936).

3. A story told in Allan Carlson, *The New Agrarian Mind: The Movement Toward Decentralist Thought in Twentieth Century America* (New Brunswick, N.J.: Transaction, 2000).

4. Wendell Berry, *What Are People For?* (San Francisco: North Point Press, 1990), 105.

million by 1950, to 7 million by 1970, and to about 4 million at century's end. Technocratic and educational strategies (such as creation of the Extension Service) for agrarian renewal had failed. It sometimes seemed that nothing was left. Running through all of Berry's work would be descriptions of the vanishing rural life, as found in his novel *Jayber Crow:*

> [The farmers] would talk quietly, humorously, anxiously about what was happening to them. They were going to die, most of them, without being replaced. . . . Poor old Luther Swain was dead, alone for days, lying on his face in the barn lot. (To his grandchildren wherever they were, if they could have known him, he would have been no less strange than Abraham.)

Berry's fictional village of Port William suffered as well: "In 1964, acting on the certified best advice, the official forces of education closed The Port William School. . . . I know that closing the school just knocked the breath out of the community. . . . It gave the [village] a never-ending wound." As Jayber Crow, town barber, mused nearer to the century's end: "The now wooded, or rewooded, slopes and hollows hereabouts are strewn with abandoned homesteads, the remains of another kind of world."[5] Berry's tasks became those of capturing in words that which had been real and transforming these images into a vision of an alternate agrarian future.

Berry is also unique among the American Agrarians in the comprehensive nature of his vision. Berry would, without doubt, be disturbed by the labels "systematic" or "philosophy." The easy flow of his poetry, prose, and narratives also belies the ponderous weight of those words. All the same, in a way almost unique to contemporary American authors, a common worldview permeates all of Berry's work — poetry, fiction, and essays — from his earliest products to the present. Although the material reality of Berry's agrarian world is today radically diminished, the clarity of his vision of the true and good human life remains both to haunt and give hope for a new and uncertain century.

Berry's work holds a particular attraction for young adults, who find in it a powerful critique of the dehumanizing forces apparent in contemporary American life and arguments that transcend the usual political boundaries. In these qualities, his appeal resembles that held by Henry David Thoreau among earlier American generations. But while the two share a passion for Nature, an appreciation for the wisdom and beauty in small things, and a tendency toward political iconoclasm, there are large differences as well. Notably, Thoreau was first and foremost a radical individualist, in civic philosophy as in matters of sexual

5. Wendell Berry, *Jayber Crow* (Washington, D.C.: Counterpoint, 2000), 276-77, 356.

morality. Berry, in contrast, is a localist communalist, and traditionalist in matters of marriage and sex. Moreover, Berry's work is richer, more humane, and more coherent than that of the Sage of Walden Pond.

Agrarianism seems an unlikely candidate for success in this commercialized, globalizing age. But the idea refuses to die. At its contemporary core lies Berry's portrait of the human person, brought to fullness in his most recent work. It can be understood through nine qualities:

## To be human is to be tied to a specific place, a spot on the earth.

In one respect, Wendell Berry holds a very modest view of the individual. In the story "Making It Home," the author has the World War II veteran Art Rowanberry musing about combat: "You got to where you could not look at a man without knowing how little it would take to kill him. For a man was nothing but just a little morsel of soft flesh and brittle bone inside of some clothes." His fictional persona Andy Catlett, flying in a jetliner above the nation's midsection, saw reality "as it might appear to the eye of Heaven, and afterwards was obliged to see himself and his life as small, almost invisible, within the countryside and the passage of time." In the essay, *Life Is a Miracle*, Berry declares that "No individual life is an end in itself" and that the notion of "personal liberation" is destructive.[6]

Instead of "who am I?" Berry says that the proper questions are "where am I?" and "where have I been?" The individual is not the building block of human society, as liberal theory would have it. Rather, the social order is composed of "the planet's millions of human and natural neighborhoods, each on its millions of small pieces and parcels of land, each one of which is in some precious way different from all the others." These "humble households and neighborhoods" form the fabric of human existence.[7] Individual identity comes only as persons merge their personalities with their small places on earth and with their families and neighbors. As Jayber Crow explains, "I don't remember when I did not know Port William, the town and the neighborhood. My relation to that place, my being in it and my absences from it, is the story of my life."[8]

Human nature, Berry argues, is both inborn and learned, with his empha-

---

6. Wendell Berry, *Fidelity: Five Stories* (New York and San Francisco: Pantheon, 1992), 88; Wendell Berry, *Remembering* (San Francisco: North Point Press, 1988), 107; and Wendell Berry, *Life Is a Miracle: An Essay Against Modern Superstition* (Washington, D.C.: Counterpoint, 2000), 8, 133.

7. *What Are People For?* 200.

8. *Jayber Crow*, 11.

sis clearly on the latter.[9] True life begins with "a motion of the heart" toward one's place. Jayber Crow again: "Far from rising above [my origins], I was longing to sink into them until I would know the fundamental things."[10] Indeed, the person becomes truly self-aware only in the place "where people of his lineage and history" have lived for generations "in an indecipherable pattern of entrances, *minds into minds, minds into places, places into minds.*"[11] As Berry explains in *Life Is a Miracle:* "We all are what we are partly because we are here and not in another place."[12]

The purest model of this blending of human personality and place occurs on the small farm, where farmer and farmstead flow into one:

> . . . it is who you are
> And you are what it is.
> You will work many days
> No one will ever see;
> Their record is the place.[13]

In the story "It Wasn't Me," Berry has the country lawyer Wheeler Catlett explain to Elton Penn that "the farm" had actually chosen him as its farmer: "The land expects something from us. The line of succession, the true line, is the membership of people who know it does."[14] Indeed, the *place* took precedence over the individual: "[He] was the farm's farmer but also its creature and belonging. He lived its life, and it lived his; he knew that, of the two lives, his was meant to be the smaller and the shorter."[15]

These bonds are stronger than those of kin. In the short story "The Wild Birds," an aging Burley Coulter recalls the return of those who have left Port William for life in a "better" place: "I see them come back here to funerals — people who belong here, or did once, looking down into coffins at people they don't have anything in common with except a name. They come from another world." Disturbed by a cold sky filled with "lonesome stars" and by a science that tells "about these little atoms and the other little pieces that things are made out of, all whirling and jiggling around, and not touching, as if a man could reach his hand right through himself," Burley finds peace only when he

9. *Life Is a Miracle,* 111.

10. *Jayber Crow,* 73.

11. *Remembering,* 65. Emphasis added.

12. *Life Is a Miracle,* 44.

13. Wendell Berry, *A Timbered Choir: The Sabbath Poems, 1979-1997* (Washington, D.C.: Counterpoint, 1998), 146.

14. Wendell Berry, *The Wild Birds* (San Francisco: North Point Press, 1986), 68.

15. *Jayber Crow,* 82.

turns his thoughts to his place on earth: "I think of all the good people I've known, . . . all of them dead, and you three here and the others still living. And I think of this country around here, . . . better than we deserve. . . . [W]e are members of each other. All of us. Everything."[16]

## To be human is to be part of a web of memory.

In his essay, "The Work of Local Culture," Berry defines a "good local culture" as "a collection of the memories, ways, and skills necessary for the observance, within the bounds of domesticity, of this natural law" of renewal. To survive, a culture "must exert a sort of centripetal force, holding local soil and memory in place."[17] As Jayber Crow reports, Port William had scant written history: "Its history was its living memory of itself."[18] One of Berry's Sabbath Poems explains:

> Past Life
> Lives in the Living.[19]

Local memory, local history, and local names provide continuity and purpose to human life: "This living procession through time in a place is the record by which such knowledge survives and is conveyed. When the procession ends, so does the knowledge," with immeasurable loss to humanity.[20] The web of memory includes the distinct accent found in every locality: "the old broad speech of the place . . . my native tongue." It also includes the music that is native to the place. And it includes the spirits of those who have passed on but who come back in the mind through sights and sounds: "I saw that, for me, this country would always be populated with presences and absences, presences of absences, the living and the dead. The world as it is would always be a reminder of the world that was, and of the world that is to come."[21] As another of the Sabbath Poems explains:

> . . . In time
> this place has come to signify

16. *The Wild Birds,* 135.
17. *What Are People For?* 154-55.
18. *Jayber Crow,* 3.
19. *A Timbered Choir,* 6.
20. *Life Is a Miracle,* 138.
21. *Jayber Crow,* 130, 132.

the absence of many, and always
more, who once were here.
Day by day their voices
come to me, as from the air.
I remember them in what I do.[22]

In one respect, Berry rejects here the idea of a universal human nature. Ties of *place* and *memory* mean that the nature of the human person will take on different characteristics in different places. To be *human* is to be in one of these local, particular settings. But different settings will produce different group characters, resistant to homogenization. An earlier Agrarian, Donald Davidson, summarized the matter well in the title of his 1933 essay: "Still Rebels, Still Yankees."[23] Universalist notions of "human rights" would also intrude on local mindsets, characteristics, and institutions; better that "rights" and "duties" find face-to-face reconciliation in less formal language and actions.

Berry's focus on memory also contains an implicit psychology. He objects to the confinement of the human mind to the brain in "the hard shell of the skull," seeing this as an indirect way of exiling mind to "the dry circuits of machines," and so enslaving consciousness. Rather, the human mind also exists in the whole body, in relationships, and in places, which give it true freedom:

. . . Once the mind is reduced
to the brain, then it falls within the grasp
of the machine. It is the mind incarnate
in the body, in community, in the earth
that they cannot confine.[24]

Holding on to the children as they grow becomes the critical challenge for a place, for if "the children depart, generation after generation, the place loses its memory of itself, which is its history and culture."[25] When this occurs, the place withers; in another way, so do the lost children, and it "becomes possible to foresee a human child as unrecognizable to its forebears as a new species, unable to recognize them, having no past which is not forgotten." The old, too, are dehumanized by this loss of memory. Schoolhouses are remodeled into nursing homes, where "the old, useless, helpless, or unwanted s[i]t like monuments, gap-

---

22. *A Timbered Choir*, 161.
23. Donald Davidson, "Still Rebels, Still Yankees," *American Review* 2 (Nov. 1933): 58-72; 2 (Dec. 1933): 175-88.
24. *A Timbered Choir*, 117-18.
25. *What Are People For?* 165.

ing into the otherworldly light of a television set."[26] As Berry summarizes: "[t]here must be no institutionalized 'child care' and 'homes for the aged.' The community knows and remembers itself by the association of old and young."[27]

## To be human is to be a member of a local community.

"Community" is the word perhaps most abused in recent decades, and also the word most often associated with Wendell Berry. In his essays, he gives it formal definition as "the commonwealth and common interests, commonly understood, of people living together in a place and wishing to continue to do so"; and as "a locally understood interdependence of local people, local culture, local economy, and local nature."[28] Berry gives more depth to the word in his fiction, where the residents of the village of Port William see their bond as a "membership":

> It was a community always disappointed in itself, . . . always failing and yet always preserving a sort of will toward good will. I knew that in the midst of all the ignorance and error, this was a membership; it was the membership of Port William and of no other place on earth.[29]

The "beloved community" makes claims that commonly trump the freedom of the individual. It embodies common experience, shared effort, and common ground "to which one willingly belongs."[30] Individual rights and the satisfaction of individual desires "are limited by human nature, by human community and by the nature of the places in which we live."[31] This membership is "that company of friends" that gives pleasure and meaning to individual lives.[32] Even the landscape becomes marked by paths connecting households, a commerce of shared affection, trust, bounty, and work.[33] Indeed, the true community becomes an almost living thing, a network for communicating news and gossip, part of "the town's ever-continuing conversation about itself."[34]

---

26. *Remembering,* 115-16.
27. Wendell Berry, *Another Turn of the Crank* (Washington, D.C.: Counterpoint, 1995), 20.
28. Wendell Berry, *Sex, Economy, Freedom and Community* (New York and San Francisco: Pantheon Books, 1992, 1993), 119-20.
29. *Jayber Crow,* 205.
30. *What Are People For?* 78, 85.
31. *Another Turn of the Crank,* 84.
32. *The Wild Birds,* 144.
33. *Fidelity,* 74.
34. *Jayber Crow,* 104, 121.

Most good communities have shared characteristics. They live by a "precarious interplay of effort and grace."[35] They can "enforce decency without litigation," using techniques such as shunning and emotions such as shame to influence individual behavior.[36] Living communities also create people of superior moral worth: "Persons of character are not [governmental] products. They are made by local cultures, local responsibilities."[37] The vital community also rests on the natural economy of altruism, solving its challenges "by non-monetary exchanges of help, not by buying things," for no community can survive "under the rules of competition."[38] True art and science also merge in the good community, with the latter understood as "knowing" and the former as "doing." To have a real conversation, the artist and the scientist must leave the university for a community that knows "the ancient human gifts of reverence, fidelity, neighborliness, and stewardship."[39] The beloved community evidences a depth of knowledge. Jayber Crow again, on his friend Athey: "He knew more of the history and geography of the country between Bird's Branch and Willow Run than most people know of the United States."[40] The healthy community also conforms its tools and artifacts "to the local landscape, local circumstances, and local needs."[41] Berry summons up the powerful metaphor of the Dance to describe the good community, where the members would gather "in the immortal ring, the many-in-one." As the fictional Andy Catlett explains: "He has heard the tread of his own people dancing in the ring, the fiddle measuring time to them, a voice calling them, through the steps of change and absence, home again, the dancers unaware of their steps, with only the music, older than memory, remembered."[42]

Berry's vision of community grants few claims to nationhood, while offering a fresh conception of pluralism. One fictional voice finds no connection between Port William and war overseas except in senseless death and suffering. "No more can I think of Port William and the United States in the same thought," he continues. "A nation is an idea, and Port William is not."[43] Berry's poetic persona, "The Mad Farmer, Flying the Flag of Rough Branch, Secedes

---

35. Wendell Berry, *Watch with Me: And Six Other Stories of the Yet-Remembered Ptolemy Proudfoot and His Wife, Miss Minnie, Nee Quinch* (New York: Pantheon Books, 1994), 210.

36. *Sex, Economy, Freedom and Community,* 120.

37. *What Are People For?* 26.

38. *What Are People For?* 135.

39. *Life Is a Miracle,* 124, 127, 132.

40. *Jayber Crow,* 218.

41. *Life Is a Miracle,* 141.

42. *Remembering,* 94-95.

43. *Jayber Crow,* 143.

from the Union" and summons "all ye conservatives and liberals/. . . into the dance of the community. . ./the dance of the eternal/love of women and men for one another/and of neighbors and friends for one another."[44] In place of the nation-state and a national culture, Berry envisions "a mosaic of cultures, based upon every community's recognition that all its members have a common ground, and that this ground is the ground under their feet."[45] Crafted in this manner, community cultures would clearly differ, and sometimes radically so, because locations differ: "This is the true and necessary pluralism."[46]

On every side, though, the modern world threatens and corrupts true community. Berry cites the commercial order as a most sinister force: "As the salesmen, saleswomen, advertisers, and propagandists of the industrial economy have become more ubiquitous and more adept at seduction, communities have lost the loyalty and affection of their members." Neither conservative nor liberal defends any longer "the economic integrity of the household or the community," which are the mainstays of family life. Under a "conservative" President [Ronald Reagan], he notes, the American economy, "which once required the father to work away from home — a development that was bad enough — now requires the mother to work away from home, as well." Meanwhile, the global economy fails to help the millions of little cultures around the globe. Rather, it exists "to siphon the wealth of those communities and places into a few bank accounts."[47] Modern war, too, erodes true community. As Jayber Crow describes World War II: "This new war, like the previous one, would be a test of the power of machines against people and places; whatever its causes and justifications, it will make the world worse. . . . The dark inhuman monstrous thing comes and tramples the little towns and never even knows their names." The true world of vital communities is "a mosaic of little places invisible to the powers that be." Indeed, "much of the doing of the mighty has been the undoing of Port William and its kind." Cleverly, the powerful have even convinced the little communities "to approve and support" their undoing through the propaganda of war.[48]

The consequences, Berry maintains, are vast. As communities fail, so do the tasks that *only* true communities can provide: "the care of the old, the care and education of children, family life, neighborly work, the handing down of memory, the care of the earth, respect for nature and wild creatures."[49] Small

44. Wendell Berry, *Entries* (Washington, D.C.: Counterpoint, 1997), 40.
45. *Life Is a Miracle*, 95.
46. *Sex, Economy, Freedom and Community*, 171.
47. *Sex, Economy, Freedom and Community*, 121-25, 129.
48. *Jayber Crow*, 139-43.
49. *Sex, Economy, Freedom and Community*, 133.

towns wither, leaving the debris of abandoned villages, boarded-up storefronts, and decaying houses. The "local succession of the generations" breaks, impossible to reclaim. As the country lawyer Wheeler Catlett explains:

> He does not forget . . . that he is making his stand in the middle of a dying town in the midst of a wasting country, from which many have departed and much has been sent away, a land wasting and dying for want of the human names and knowledge that could give it life.[50]

## To be human is to resist the dominion of science and the machines.

Berry's complaint is not with the excesses or errors of science. He finds the very nature of scientific inquiry wanting. In *Life Is a Miracle*, Berry deconstructs the work of the eminent Harvard entymologist E. O. Wilson, and implicitly of the whole of modern science. For example, Berry rejects all attempts at biological categorization. At this stage of his argument, the individual actually becomes paramount. "I don't think creatures can be explained," he writes. "I don't think lives can be explained" by the generalizations of science. He views modern existence as "a daily mockery of our scientific pretensions. We are learning to know precisely the location of our genes, but significant numbers of us don't know the whereabouts of our children." The universities turn out scientists, he says, who can detail the construction of atoms or genomes or galaxies, "but who do not know where they are geographically, historically, or ecologically." Berry objects to standards of behavior increasingly set by the capabilities of science and technology, rather than by "the nature of places and communities." He agrees with Erwin Chargaff that "all great scientific discoveries . . . carry . . . an irreversible loss of something that mankind cannot afford to lose." And he affirms with agriculturalist Sir Albert Howard that scientific authority "has abandoned the task of illuminating the laws of Nature, has forfeited the position of the friendly judge. . . : it has sunk to the inferior and petty work of photographing the corpse." As this type of knowledge grows globally, wisdom is lost locally.[51]

The crimes of science reach humans as technological innovation. "What I am against," Berry reports, "is our slovenly willingness to allow machines and the idea of the machine to prescribe the terms and conditions of the lives of creatures." He wants "to quit using our technological capability as the reference point and standard of our economic life." He also rejects the heroic quest for

---

50. *The Wild Birds,* 129.
51. *Life Is a Miracle,* 113, 33, 35, 12, 70, 75, 90-91.

discovery that lies at the heart of scientific inquiry. Where E. O. Wilson sees this as "basic to human nature," Berry warns that a person might "trade one's life — all the ordinary satisfactions of homeland and family life — for the sake of a hope not ordinarily realizable." Innovation pursued for its own sake, and especially for the marketplace, "is disruptive of human settlement."[52]

Born out of science, industrial standardization of all sorts — even of gender and race — destroys humanness in its quest of "the objective":

> The races and the sexes now intermingled perfectly in
>     pursuit of the objective.
>
> The once-enslaved, the once-oppressed were now free
> to sell themselves to the highest bidder
> and to enter the best-paying prisons
> in pursuit of the objective, . . .
> which was the destruction of all obstacles, . . .
> which was to clear the way to victory, which was to clear
>     the way to promotion, to salvation, to progress,
> to the completed sale. . . .[53]

Berry points to Monsanto Corporation's "aptly named 'terminator gene'" — which causes the next generation of seed to become sterile — as an example of "the tyranny of technological and genetic monoculture" and "as grave an indicator of totalitarian purpose as a concentration camp."[54] The whole of human life, he charges, has been corrupted by technology and its poisons:

> In early morning we awaken from
> The sounds of engines running in the night
> And then we start the engines of the day;
> We speed away into the fading light. . . .
> This is the promised burning . . .
>     And blessed are
> The dead who died before this time began.
> Blessed are the dead who have escaped in time
> The twisted metal and fractured stone,
> The technobodies of the hopeless cure.[55]

---

52. *Life Is a Miracle*, 54-56, 140.
53. *A Timbered Choir*, 208-09.
54. *Life Is a Miracle*, 132.
55. *A Timbered Choir*, 105.

The Machine looms as Berry's Terrible Dragon or White Whale: this time, the product of a technology that knows no limits. In the novel, *Remembering,* his fictional persona Andy Catlett loses his hand in a cornpicker: "The machine took his hand. . . . He heard the long persistence of the noise of the machine that did not know the difference between a cornstalk and a man's arm."[56] More concretely, Berry points to the coming of tractors and combines to the farms after 1940 as the end of community. "Did the machines displace the people from the farms, or were the machines drawn onto the farms because the people already were leaving . . . ? Both, I think."[57] The result was a remnant of "Premier Farmers," top operators with massive machines whose "ambition had made common cause with a technological power that proposed no limit to itself, that was, in fact, destroying [them] as it had already destroyed nearly all that was natural or human around [them]."[58]

Berry holds out alternatives: what he calls "small answers." In place of scientific categories, he urges a return to pictures, stories, songs, and dances, where creatures and lives can be explained.[59] In place of abstract innovation, he urges "revelations of familiarity" — appropriate tools and ways — that draw from and elaborate on local cultural patterns.[60] Berry also urges a very different approach to work: praise for manual labor and hard work that is "necessary to the long-term preservation of the land." As fictional Elton Penn tells his friends during a tobacco harvest: "Boys, all I want is a good day and a long row."[61] Berry criticizes the segregation of children and the elderly from work as well. In viable household and local economies, they would have meaningful tasks to do, actions "useful to themselves and to others."[62]

Appropriately, Berry's distrust of the machines carries into his own work as a writer. He crafts all of his manuscripts by hand, arguing, "I don't want to deny myself the pleasure of bodily involvement in my work, for that pleasure seems to me to be the sign of an indispensable integrity." Rejecting the word processor, he adds: "I have the notion . . . that the longer I keep a piece of work in longhand, the better it will be."[63]

---

56. *Remembering,* 14.

57. *Jayber Crow,* 183.

58. *Remembering,* 73.

59. *Life Is a Miracle,* 113.

60. *Life Is a Miracle,* 114.

61. Wendell Berry, *Two More Stories of the Port William Membership* (Frankfort, Ky.: Gnomon Press, 1997), 36.

62. *What Are People For?* 128.

63. *What Are People For?* 192-93.

## To be human is to fit one's work into the rhythms of nature.

A great conceit of modern humankind, Berry holds, is belief that one can escape the rhythms of the natural world. All life yearns to return to nature. He notes that even the good farm is an endless effort to impose some human purpose on land seeking a way back to primeval order:

> And so you make a farm
> That must be daily made
> And yearly made, or it
> Will not exist.

The farmer finds his place in "the Dear Opening between What was and is to be,"[64] when he submits to the natural flow and special needs of his place. As Berry describes the character Burley Coulter: "He learned to do what his place asked of him. He became the man it asked him to be. . . . [H]e knew he'd become the farm's belonging, necessary to it."[65]

Berry contrasts this quest for agrarian harmony with the waste and ruthlessness of most modern American agriculture, seen in its ravaging of the land:

> I go from the woods into the cleared field,
> A place no human made, a place unmade
> By human greed. . . .
> The growth of fifty thousand years undone
> In a few careless seasons, stripped to rock
> And clay. . . .[66]

Free from submission to nature's rules and timing, lives grow dehumanized as well. Berry points to the terrible anonymity of the airport, as "the wingless are preparing to fly." Passengers stand in line to board the aircraft, alien to each other, "observing scrupulously the etiquette of strangers, careful lest by accident they should touch." When they take flight, "they do so clumsily, with a ludicrous hooferaw of noise and fire."[67] Estranged from nature's rhythm, Americans — "all of us" — exist as "a kind of human trash, living our lives in the midst of a ubiquitous damned mess of which we are at once the victims and the perpetrators."[68]

Sanity is regained only as individuals strive to bring human life back into

64. *A Timbered Choir*, 146.
65. *The Wild Birds*, 54.
66. *A Timbered Choir*, 16.
67. *Remembering*, 99.
68. *What Are People For?* 127.

harmony with the natural order. Berry praises the anarcho-environmentalist Edward Abbey, who fought "for the survival not only of nature, but of *human* nature, of culture, as only our heritage of works and hopes can define it."[69] The fictional characters portrayed as offering hope are those who reject the industrial order in favor of a more natural existence: "Danny never had belonged much to the modern world, and every year he appeared to belong to it less. Of them all, Danny most clearly saw that world as his enemy — as their enemy — and most forthrightly and cheerfully repudiated it." In the story "Fidelity," Danny covertly frees his father, Burley, from the life-sustaining machines of a modern hospital, so that he might die a natural death surrounded by the woods that he cherished.[70]

Indeed, the forest stands for Berry as the final locus of respite and release, a place independent of human plans, where the soul reconnects with nature:

> To rest, go to the woods
> Where what is made is made
> Without your thought or work.[71]

This return to the woods means willing submission to its rules and flow, bringing both freedom and inner peace:

> Whoever wants me now must hunt me down
> Like something wild, and wild is anything
> Beyond the reach of purpose not its own. . . .
> Lost to all other wills but Heaven's — wild.[72]

## To be human is to enter into the mysteries, wonders, and agonies of marriage.

Berry underscores the communitarian nature of sex and marriage. The good community, Berry contends, includes "a set of arrangements between men and women" that govern marriage, family structures, a division of labor and authority, and responsibilities for teaching children and youth. He notes that these arrangements exist in part "to reduce the volatility and the danger of sex — to preserve its energy, its beauty, and its pleasure." Importantly, he adds that these arrangements also exist to bind the couple as "parents to children, fami-

---

69. *What Are People For?* 40. Emphasis added.
70. *Fidelity*, 134-37.
71. *A Timbered Choir*, 148.
72. *A Timbered Choir*, 188.

lies to the community, [and] the community to nature."[73] The bride and groom "say their vows to the community as much as to one another, and the community gathers around them to hear and to wish them well, on their behalf and on its own." All else depends on the success and endurance of these vows. They bind the lovers to each other, "to forebears, to descendants, . . . to Heaven and earth." Marriage stands as "the fundamental connection without which nothing holds."[74] Even the touch of one lover to another:

> feelingly
> persuades us what we are:
> one another's and many others' . . .
> How strange to think of children
> yet to come, into whose making
> we will be made. . . .[75]

Sexual love, mediated through marriage, "is the heart of community life," the force that connects persons most intimately to the Creation, to the earth's fertility, and to farming. Returning to a favorite metaphor, Berry says that it "brings us into the dance that holds the community together and joins it to its place."[76]

Berry weaves a remarkable tapestry of images of marriage. For example, he gives the old language of two-becoming-one-flesh new power in the story "A Jonquil for Mary Penn":

> That she was his half, she had no doubt at all. He needed her. At times she knew with a joyous ache that she completed him, just as she knew with the same joy that she needed him and he completed her. How beautiful a thing it was, she thought, to be a half completed by such a half! When had there ever been such a yearning of halves toward each other, such a longing, even in quarrels, to be whole? And sometimes they would be whole. Their wholeness came upon them as a rush of light, around them and within them, so that she felt they must be shining in the dark.[77]

Marriage bore a vast power. As Jayber Crow thought about it: "I would have been asking for her life, for the power to change her into what could not be foreseen."[78] Andy Catlett remembered Flora as his new bride, one as "innocent

---

73. *Sex, Economy, Freedom and Community,* 120-21.

74. *Sex, Economy, Freedom and Community,* 133, 139.

75. *A Timbered Choir,* 99.

76. *Sex, Economy, Freedom and Community,* 133.

77. *Fidelity,* 79.

78. *Jayber Crow,* 197.

as himself of the great power they were putting on." They were not making a marriage so much "as being made by it," where "time and their lives flowed over them, like swift water over stones, rubbing them together, grinding off their edges, making them fit together, fit to be together, in the only way that fragments can be rejoined."[79] Marriage marked the renewal of life and hope and served as a bridge between Heaven and earth:

Again, hope dreams itself
Awake . . .
        . . . We know
That hearts, against their doom,
Must plight an ancient troth. . . .
Now come the bride and groom,
Now come the man and woman
Who must begin again
The work divine and human
By which we live on earth.[80]

Berry insists that a marriage, like a friendship, cannot survive demands for strict justice or equality. The marriage bed cannot tolerate the rhetoric of "rights." Such efforts quickly descend into anger, feud, and divorce.[81] Contemporary demands by women for equal involvement in the industrial economy also produce little good: "[w]hat are we to say of the diversely skilled country housewife who now bores the same six holes day after day on an assembly line? What higher form of womanhood or humanity is she evolving toward?"[82]

The good marriage rests instead on mutual help and the integration of children into a working household. Children, Berry says, need a daily association with both parents; they need to see their parents at work, ideally through the return of productive tasks to the home.[83]

Berry also skewers the idea of "sexual revolution." He labels as "pretentious, fantastical, and solemn idiocy" the use of the phrase "sexual partner." This utilitarian monstrosity denies all the richness found in the labels *husband, wife,* and even *lover.* He calls "sexual liberation" as great a fraud and failure as the "peaceful atom." Sex education classes give to the young "an illusion of thoughtless freedom and purchasable safety," which leads to premature and dangerous experimenta-

79. *Remembering,* 34, 113.
80. *A Timbered Choir,* 153.
81. *Sex, Economy, Freedom and Community,* 139-40.
82. *What Are People For?* 184.
83. *What Are People For?* 180-82.

tion with an extraordinary force. Dismissing still another popular phrase, Berry concludes: "Sex was never safe, and it is less safe now than it has ever been."[84]

And yet, Berry also suggests that "legal" marriage and "true" marriage are not always the same thing: you might have one without the other. His novel *The Memory of Old Jack* traces the failure of Jack Beechum's formal marriage to Ruth. Unable to complete each other or to build a working home, their relationship ended in tragedy: Jack "had not united farm and household and marriage bed, and he could not."[85] In the story "The Wild Birds," meanwhile, Berry describes the long relationship of Burley Coulter and Kate Helen Branch as a real, if never regularized, marriage. He had loved her, cared for her, and fathered a child by her, without ever standing before an altar. Long after her death, Burley went to his lawyer, seeking to pass his farm on to his out-of-wedlock son: "What Burley is performing, asking him to assist in, too late but nonetheless, necessarily, is a kind of wedding between himself and Kate Helen Branch."[86] *Jayber Crow* is, in plotline, a novel about the "strange marriage" of the town barber to Mattie, from her time as a school girl through her life as another's wife. Jayber was "the keeper of a solemn, secret vow"; he "was married to Mattie Chatham, but she was not married to him." The power of this book lies in Berry's success in convincing the reader that *this* marriage was nonetheless real, and good.[87]

## To be human is to be a generalist in the skills of life.

Berry rejects the competitive industrial economy and its driving force, the division of labor. Both, he says, demean human nature.

As he forcefully explains in the essay "Economy and Pleasure," "perhaps the best beginning would be in understanding the falseness and silliness of the economic ideal of competition, which is destructive both of nature and of human nature." Where classical liberal economic theory sees most market exchanges, even simple trades, as "win/win" situations (each trader increases his or her "marginal utility"), Berry insists that "[e]very transaction is meant to involve a winner and a loser." Competition readily destroys the life of a family, just as the existence of a community. "[F]or this reason," Berry says, "the human economy is pitted without limit against nature."[88]

84. *Sex, Economy, Freedom and Community,* 140-42.

85. Wendell Berry, *The Memory of Old Jack* (San Diego and New York: Harcourt Brace Jovanovich, 1974), 51, 165-66.

86. *The Wild Birds,* 137.

87. *Jayber Crow,* 191, 193, 248, 258.

88. *What Are People For?* 130-31.

*Jayber Crow* offers concrete examples of the process. The town barber notes how small chicken flocks had been a "mainstay" of each small farm's household economy. Yet under the press of competition, these flocks dwindled away. Small dairy operations of two to six cows also disappeared. The farm wives, who formerly came to town with produce to sell and went home with money, now came to some more distant town "with only money and went home with only groceries." He concludes, "The Economy no longer wanted the people of Port William to produce . . . eggs. It wanted them to eat eggs without producing them. Or, more properly, it wanted them to buy eggs."[89]

It was the modern division of labor that arrayed the economy against human nature. Berry acknowledges the appropriate specialization of work implied by the ancient labels *husbandry* and *wifery*. Man and woman both labor on their place, sorting out their tasks according to relative strengths and skills. The industrial order promises the liberation of husbands and wives from these old ways, "but one can be thus liberated only by entering a trap . . . the ideal of industrialism." The result is the loss of the skills — carpentry, gardening, animal husbandry, food preparation, spinning, weaving, and sewing — that preserve true independence. Berry ponders the effect that even a mere two days without electricity would have on Americans. Such a disaster would show how far removed most persons are from local, natural economic relations.[90] Their real status is not that of free workers in a free economy, but as a new kind of slaves. As Jayber Crow explains it, the "new slavery" has improved on the old kind by "giving the new slaves the illusion that they are free." Freedom is not taken away by force. Rather, the economy "buys their freedom, pays for it, and then persuades its money back again with shoddy goods and the promise of freedom."[91]

Berry also rejects the idea that modern government acts to shelter persons and families from the excesses of "The Economy." Particularly when embodied as "The War," he holds that the state actually joins in sustaining the new slavery. Jayber Crow again becomes Berry's voice. "it seemed that The War and The Economy were more and more closely related. They were the Siamese twins of our age, ready at any moment to merge into a single unified Siamese. . . . The War was good for The Economy."[92]

What is the alternative? "Resist classification!" Berry declares. "[L]et us have/no careers," he writes to follow Kentuckian Hayden Carruth, "lest one day we be found dead in them."[93] Learn and maintain the skills needed for inde-

89. *Jayber Crow,* 275.
90. *What Are People For?* 149, 160.
91. *Jayber Crow,* 332.
92. *Jayber Crow,* 273.
93. *Entries,* 53.

pendent living. Reject the modern disciplines "which are increasingly conformable to the aims and standards of industrialism." Deny "oversimplifying, feelingless utilitarianism" and its "destruction of the living integrity of creatures, places, communities, cultures, and human souls."[94] Learn to live with less: "We must achieve the character and acquire the skills to live much poorer than we do." Understand that authentic economy "exists by the willingness to be anonymous, humble, and unrewarded."[95] Recognize that the best work is done in community, where each person understands what the others are good at and where not much needs to be explained.[96]

## To be human is to maintain a true home economy.

Building a viable home economy serves as the most complete alternative. The foundation of this economy is marriage, where lovers "'die' into their union with one another as a soul 'dies' into its union with God." At the very heart of community life lies "this momentous giving,"[97] around which the couple build "a wonderful provisioning: the kitchen and garden, hogpen and smokehouse, henhouse and cellar . . . ; the little commerce of giving and taking that spoke[s] out along the paths connecting [one] household to the others."[98] This home economy rests on an inherited moral capital, building on the principles of thrift and trust. Crafting a home economy is a form of art as complex and beautiful in its way as poetry, painting, and musical composition.[99] Berry also stresses how the viable home economy serves as the foundation of liberty and order. As he explains in the poem "The Farm":

> But don't neglect your garden.
> Household economy
> Makes family and land
> An independent state.
> Never buy at a store
> What you can grow or find
> At home — this is the rule
> Of liberty. . . .[100]

94. *Life Is a Miracle*, 15, 76, 136.
95. *What Are People For?* 200.
96. *Fidelity*, 68.
97. *Sex, Economy, Freedom and Community*, 138.
98. *Fidelity*, 74.
99. *Life Is a Miracle*, 150.
100. *A Timbered Choir*, 139.

Maintaining household economic autonomy also brings an inner peace:

> In time of hate and waste,
> Wars and rumors of wars,
> Rich armies and poor peace
> Your blessed economy,
> Beloved sufficiency
> Upon a dear, small place,
> Sings with the morning stars.[101]

Even Jayber Crow, living alone, finds meaning and dignity within his little economy: "I have food to harvest and preserve in the summer and fall, firewood to gather and saw up and split in the fall and winter, the garden to prepare and plant in the spring. . . . I have the endless little jobs of housekeeping and repair."[102]

Berry notes that modern Americans "have made a social ideal of minimal involvement in the growing and cooking of food":[103]

> . . . nowadays,
> A lot of people would
> Rather work hard to buy
> Their food already cooked
> Than get it free by work.[104]

The result, he argues in the essay "The Pleasure of Eating," has been "industrial eating" which, like "industrial sex," is a "degraded, poor, and paltry thing." This leaves both "eater and eaten . . . in exile from biological reality." In encouraging the rebirth of a household food economy, Berry urges readers at a minimum to participate in food production as much as they can, prepare their own food, buy from local producers, study the best farming and gardening techniques, and learn the life histories of the food species.[105]

More expansively, Berry celebrates the kind of eating that a rich and full home economy can produce. He describes the meals found at the big table in the kitchen of fictional Minnie Branch:

> The mornings would have begun there with a great commerce between kitchen and garden and smokehouse and chicken house and cellar. Even the

---

101. *A Timbered Choir*, 148.
102. *Jayber Crow*, 323.
103. *What Are People For?* 128.
104. *A Timbered Choir*, 144.
105. *What Are People For?* 28, 147-50.

young children would be put to picking and plucking and fixing. The result would be a quantity of food that you would be surprised at when you saw it laid out on the table, and surprised again to see how quickly it was eaten up.[106]

At still another level, Berry points to the wonderful provisioning provided by nature itself: blackberries from the fencerows; strawberries from the forest floor; wild cherries and grapes; persimmons and blackhaws; walnuts and hickory nuts:

> Of all your harvests, those
> Are pleasantest that come
> Freest . . .
> In your wild foragings
> The earth feeds you the way
> She feeds the beasts and birds.[107]

Lyda and Danny Branch embodied this integrity of country life, for they "ate what they grew or what came, free for the effort, from the river and woods."[108]

## To be human is to be in communion with the God of Nature.

Wendell Berry is a Christian, but not of a discernable orthodoxy or denomination. Again, he lets Jayber Crow speak for him: "I liked the church [building] when it was empty"; "The more my affections and sympathies had got involved in Port William, the more uneasy I became with certain [Scripture] passages, not just in the letters of Paul, . . . but even in the Gospels"; and "I am, maybe, the ultimate Protestant, . . . for as I have read the gospels over the years, the belief has grown in me that Christ did not come to found an organized religion but came instead to found an unorganized one."[109]

Unlike some of the earlier twentieth-century agrarians, Berry does hold to key Christian doctrines: *original sin* ("And I recall myself/more innocent than I am/gone past coming back/in the history of flaw"); *the judgment day* ("except Christ dead and risen . . ./shall judge/condemn, and then forgive");[110] *faith* (". . . religious faith *begins* with the discovery that there is no 'evidence'");[111]

---

106. *The Wild Birds,* 36.
107. *A Timbered Choir,* 144-45.
108. *Two More Stories of the Port William Membership,* 50.
109. *Jayber Crow,* 163, 250, 321.
110. *A Timbered Choir,* 97.
111. *Life Is a Miracle,* 28.

*grace* ("For we are fallen like the trees, our peace/Broken . . . And must await the wayward-coming grace/that joins living and dead . . .");[112] *apocalypse* (". . . how/ shall we pray to escape the catastrophe . . . ?");[113] *and life after death.*[114] He also holds that persons can live fully "only by making ourselves as answerable to the claims of eternity as to those of time."[115]

Berry's personal theology builds on his reversal of the usual dichotomy between body and soul and on his view of the natural and workaday world as holy. While studying for a time at a seminary, Jayber Crow grew disturbed by the way his teachers laid everything bad on the body, and credited everything good to the soul: "It scared me a little when I realized that I saw it the other way around."[116] Man was the fallen creature, his *soul* scarred by greed, lust, and the quest for power. But the Creation, including the human body, was God's handiwork. Absent the intrusions of corrupted human souls, the natural order was — and remained — good.

Indeed, human persons could find Holiness in everyday life. Labor, for example, could become a true communion with God:

> Work done in gratitude
> Kindly, and well, is prayer.[117]

The creation work of the Spirit continues to animate the physical world: "I could see that I lived in the created world, and it was still being created. I would be part of it forever."[118] The cycle of birth, maturity, death, decay, and rebirth draws all creatures into the great pageant of life and resurrection. As a Sabbath poem explains,

> . . . I lie down in the deer's bed
> and . . . sleep a sleep as dark
> and vast as the deer slept, or as the dead sleep,
> simple and dreamless in their graves,
> awaiting the dawn that will stand them
> timeless as they stood in time. . . .[119]

---

112. *Life Is a Miracle,* 74.
113. *A Timbered Choir,* 110.
114. See Wendell Berry, *A World Lost* (Washington, D.C.: Counterpoint, 1996), 151.
115. *Life Is a Miracle,* 8.
116. *Jayber Crow,* 49.
117. *A Timbered Choir,* 140.
118. *A Timbered Choir,* 83.
119. *A Timbered Choir,* 90.

Nature itself sings out in praise of the Creator, particularly in wilderness and forested places, where the human presence is small:

> Great trees, outspreading and upright
> Apostles of the living light. . . .
> Patient as stars, they build in air
> Tier after tier a timbered choir,
> Stout beams upholding weightless grace
> Of Song, a blessing on this place.[120]

In these respects, Berry's theology might be labeled "post-Augustinian"; he blurs the boundary between the City of God and the City of Man. Can Berry's views also be labeled "Christian pantheism"? Such a label would mislead, for Christ the Redeemer looms larger in his thought than pantheism would allow. Berry understands Christ as God *and* Man, the one called "to bring together sky and earth, like a stalk/of corn."[121] This Christ is a personal God, too, whom one might meet, together with virgin mother and earthly father, even while doing one's chores:

> That we ourselves, opening a stall
> (A latch thrown open countless times
> Before), might find them breathing there,
> Foreknown: the Child bedded in straw,
> The mother kneeling over Him,
> The husband standing in belief
> He scarcely can believe, in light
> That lights them from no source we see,
> An April morning's light, the air
> Around them joyful as a choir . . .
>     . . .our place
> Holy, although we knew it not.[122]

Berry's vision of Heaven is also too human to bear the label *pantheistic.* In *Remembering,* the novelist describes this life and place to come, where "one great song sings," answered by every leaf, flower, and blade of grass: "And in the fields and the town, walking, standing, or sitting under the trees, resting and talking together in the peace of a sabbath profound and bright, are people of

---

120. *A Timbered Choir*, 83.

121. "The Birth (Near Port William)," in Wendell Berry, *Collected Poems, 1957-1982* (San Francisco: North Point Press, 1984), 127.

122. *A Timbered Choir*, 94.

such beauty that he weeps to see them. He sees that these are the membership of one another and of the place and of the song or light in which they live and move."[123]

CONSIDERING THESE VIEWS, modern economists might retort that Wendell Berry completely misunderstands human interaction, where self-interest translates into the creation of wealth. Scientists could say that Berry is ignorant of the true scientific method, which rests not on hubris but rather on the effort to disprove one's own hypothesis. Social biologists might scoff at his emphasis on the power of environment over personality. Historians might warn that appeals to "localism" and "agrarianism" have sometimes been prelude to ethnic cleansing. Modernist critics could sum up Berry's qualities of the human person in an unflattering way, as being bound to one place, enslaved by inherited ways, locked into the community of one's birth, crimped by pre-scientific biases, threatened by the rigors of nature, captive to an unbreakable marriage, condemned to poverty, endangered by the risks that go with self-reliance, and restrained by a capricious religion. Logicians might underscore the tension between Berry's call to think small or local and the obvious enormity of his social, economic, and political project. Others might ask: Is not Berry himself merely another social engineer, this time one looking dangerously backward? Where earlier ideologues sought to create *Homo Economicus* or "New Soviet Man," perhaps Berry's project is a latter-day effort using creative destruction to forge "New Neolithic Man"?

To embrace these criticisms would be to miss the larger problem that Berry confronts. His work resonates with readers today in part because he exposes the actual novelty and frailty of modern industrial life. Whether one sees human nature as the product of Divine creation or of socio-biological evolution, a common historical conclusion remains: the human person is conditioned for life in the village or on the small farm. For thousands of years, and hundreds of generations, this has been humankind's normative way. The small farm is the ideal place for the human family, where husband and wife work together to advance their small enterprise without rancor over gender roles, where children are welcomed as products of love, as little workers, and as heirs, where the old find useful work, and where economic independence makes a broader liberty possible. For only a few generations has the great mass of persons tried to live as industrialized, urbanized, autonomous creatures. Human nature and the human family are alien to such a life. The strains are obvious, and inevitable. And they show no signs of healing.

123. *Remembering*, 123.

Berry's work underscores another possibility regarding this circumstance: incremental solutions will no longer suffice. To choose one example: perhaps the need is not for higher quality day care for the children; perhaps the need is for a social and economic revolution that will undo the industrialization of human life and restore both parents to the home, re-forging the necessary human bond of household, work, and children. Perhaps we need the social equivalent of the scientific paradigm shift described by Thomas S. Kuhn: a metamorphosis where "one conceptual worldview is replaced by another."[124] This is not the work of ordinary analysts and politicians; prophets are necessary.

Not surprisingly, Berry points his readers to the Old Order Amish as the best example of an alternate reality. "They alone," he relates, "have carefully restricted their use of machine-developed energy, and so have become the only true masters of technology."[125] They subordinate the push for efficiency to the preservation of certain kinds of human labor. Their tools remain bound to the ideal of craftsmanship, and their technological innovations are subsumed to the preservation of community. They sell their farm products, quilts, and furniture in the marketplace, yet avoid becoming creatures of the great corporations. Not only their existence, but their growth in America as well (from 5000 souls in 1900 to 150,000 today), testifies that humankind is not condemned to industrialized life by the inevitable force of history.

In Texas, Heritage Homesteads on the Brazos de Dios River is a vital Christian community that has drawn direct inspiration from Wendell Berry. Started in 1973 in a storefront church in Manhattan's "Hell's Kitchen," the ethnically diverse Homesteaders now number about a thousand. They discovered "home births" in the 1970s, followed by "home schools" and "family gardens." The congregation migrated to rural locations in Colorado, then Texas. The majority now earn their living through crafts such as furniture making, pottery, and weaving organized on a guild model. This is supplemented by homegrown produce and collective agriculture and animal husbandry. The Homesteaders mix horse-drawn plows and modest clothing with air conditioners and pickup trucks. Their marriages appear to be strong and their children are numerous. Importantly for the future, their young adults are now marrying within the community.[126]

The Old Order Amish, the Heritage Homesteaders, and similar communi-

---

124. Thomas Kuhn, *The Structure of Scientific Revolutions* (Chicago: University of Chicago Press, 1962), 10.

125. Wendell Berry, *The Unsettling of America: Culture and Agriculture* (New York: Avon, 1977), 95, 210.

126. *A Glimpse of Brazos de Dios* (Elm Mott, Tex.: Heritage Homesteads, n.d.); and Lana Robinson, "Simple Gifts," *Texas Highways* 43 (Nov. 1996): 36-41.

ties (e.g., the Hutterites of Montana and Canada) not only survive but thrive once they psychologically escape from the mental trap of industrialism. If Wendell Berry is right, they live lives more closely attuned to the true nature of the human person. And they hold the promise of a different, more natural, and more satisfying human future.

# The Politics of Suffering:
# Ivan Ilich's Critique of Modern Medicine

CHRISTOPHER SHANNON

As our present-day debates over new medical procedures and biotechnological innovations show, there are few points upon which modern Americans are more likely to be in agreement than the desirability of relieving human suffering — and the likelihood that any effort promising progress toward that goal will deserve nearly unquestioned support. There is not, and never will be, an advocacy group lobbying the Congress "for" suffering *per se*. And yet there is a shadow side to this seemingly overwhelming cultural consensus. For the profound and soul-shaping character of suffering is one of the most powerful and recurrent themes in the religious and literary traditions of the West. In the life of Christ and the saints and martyrs of the church, in the works of authors from Sophocles to Dostoyevsky and Camus, one sees again and again an insistence that suffering, far from being meaningless, is absolutely essential in the apprehension of the truth and the deepening of the soul. In this view, suffering is an important factor in the making and refining of our human personhood, and a world without it would leave our souls deeply impoverished. It would seem that, culturally speaking, our right hand knows not what our left hand is doing. Our own most cherished moral and spiritual traditions from the past warn us against the very assumptions that motivate our commitment to the most unquestioned causes of the present.

The late Ivan Illich, like Wendell Berry, spent his career warning against the political and technological erasure of the order of nature, which meant in his case a radical, and often quixotic, critique of some of the most automatically revered institutions of the modern West: chiefly its institutions of education and medicine, and the professions that sustain and control them. As Christopher Shannon argues in this provocative essay, Illich's willingness to argue for the rightness in the natural order of things extended to his understanding of the meaning in human suffering. The contrast Shannon draws between the isolation and dehumanization brought about by the medicalization of suffering on the one hand, and the vibrant

318

sense of community made possible by the sharing of suffering, and the integration of that suffering into communally shared narratives, on the other, suggests how central the experience of suffering is to our fundamental humanity. And Shannon's connection of the politics of suffering with the ideal of cultural diversity — an ideal that, he believes, is honored more in the breach than the observance — suggests that our full personhood is inseparable from the integrity of the particular small communities and subcommunities in which our sufferings are seen and shared and taken up by others. Christopher Shannon is Assistant Professor of History at Christendom College, and author of *Conspicuous Criticism: Tradition, the Individual, and Culture in American Social Thought, from Veblen to Mills* (Johns Hopkins, 1995) and *A World Made Safe for Differences* (Rowman & Littlefield, 2000).

> *. . . the term 'suffering' has become almost useless for designating a realistic human response because it evokes superstition, sadomasochism, or the rich man's condescension to the lot of the poor. Professionally organized medicine has come to function as a domineering moral enterprise that advertises industrial expansion as a war against all suffering. It has thereby undermined the ability of individuals to face their reality, to express their own values, and to accept inevitable and often irremediable pain and impairment, decline, and death.*
>
> Ivan Illich, Medical Nemesis

The modern West prides itself on promoting a historically unprecedented commitment to the relief of human suffering. It also prides itself on a similarly un precedented commitment to the tolerance of cultural diversity. Deflecting ideological challenges from the anti-modern right and the postmodern left, defenders of modernity routinely turn to these two values as unquestionable bases for the moral and political legitimacy of the modern age.[1] Suffering, however, is itself a cultural phenomenon. The overwhelming majority of peoples,

---

1. I would like to thank Thomas R. Cole, whose essay in this collection reminded me of Charles Taylor's assessment of the three enduring virtues of modernity: the dignity of each individual, the affirmation of everyday life, and the relief of suffering. For a critique of modernity's supposed commitment to cultural diversity, see Christopher Shannon, *A World Made Safe for Differences: Cold War Intellectuals and the Politics of Identity* (Lanham: Rowman & Littlefield, Inc., 2001).

throughout the East and the premodern West, have understood suffering as not simply a problem to be solved, but a story to be lived. Suffering has long held a special place in human cultures as somehow intimately connected to the deepest truths of the human person, society, and the cosmos.[2] For the past two hundred years, the spread of Western modernity across the globe has waged total war against traditional cultures, not simply as a consequence of social and economic modernization, but through the deliberate imposition of "universal" humanistic norms — not the least being the commitment to relieve human suffering, whatever the cultural consequences.

The career of Ivan Illich from the 1950s through the 1970s sheds much light on the largely ignored connections between suffering, modernization, and cultural diversity. One of the most significant radical thinkers of the 1960s, Illich's countercultural star faded in the 1970s as the traditionalist basis of his critique of modern society became more apparent. Illich's traditionalism drew inspiration not simply from a romantic longing for the Middle Ages, but from his encounter with the still vital traditional practices of Latino Catholicism among Puerto Rican immigrants in New York City and the *campesinos* of Latin America. Illich's efforts to synthesize traditional practice and critical theory bore its fullest fruit in his 1976 book *Medical Nemesis: The Expropriation of Health.* At one level, Illich presented this work as an anarchist critique of the medical profession; at a deeper level, he sought to challenge the modern West's very definition of health. The radical nature of this challenge is best captured by Illich's attempt to recover some notion of virtuous suffering. Illich's moral rehabilitation of suffering proceeded from an understanding of the human person as the inhabitant of a broken universe whose limitations are not technical but ontological. Uncomprehending mainstream intellectuals largely rejected Illich's critique as at best politically irresponsible, at worst morally sadistic. Decades later, the Latino popular Catholicism that originally inspired Illich would vindicate his critique. Fusing traditional ontology with modern politics, Latino rituals of suffering continue to offer an alternative model of political action directed less toward the achievement of social justice than realization of communal solidarity.

The modern Western understanding of suffering as simply a problem to be solved is a minority view in world cultures and human history. Clifford Geertz long ago noted that in traditional cultures, "the problem of suffering is, paradoxically, not how to avoid suffering but how to suffer." Traditional healing ceremonies, such as the Navaho "sing," do not cure illness so much as they "give the stricken person a vocabulary in terms of which to grasp the nature of his

2. Ariel Glucklich, *Sacred Pain: Hurting the Body for the Sake of the Soul* (New York: Oxford University Press, 2001), 20.

distress and relate it to the wider world." In the sing, the healer or singer places the body of the afflicted on a sand painting depicting the figures of various gods. Illness seeps out through purification rites of vomiting and sweating, while health seeps in through physical contact with a mythic story of divinity.[3] The individual sufferer comes to understand the pain as a moment within a larger cycle of chaos and order. Sickness becomes an occasion to reconnect to a cosmic story of death and rebirth.

Traditional Christianity in the West provided a particularly nurturing environment for the cultivation of this general attitude toward suffering. In the Christian story, Jesus came to heal the sick, feed the hungry, preach the Word — and to suffer. Premodern Christianity understood suffering as evil, in the sense of being a consequence of the Fall from Eden, yet also redemptive, in the example of Jesus' sacrifice on the Cross. With the Cross as the central act of redemption, the key to the salvation of humanity, suffering came to be understood as in many ways the highest, most sublime value.[4] The ritual and liturgical life of premodern Christianity provided the general community with an ordered hierarchy of concrete practices that served to relieve guilt, console suffering and situate particular human persons in the cosmic story of Jesus' death and resurrection.[5] Traditional Christianity did not exclude so much as subordinate other values in a hierarchy of virtues that privileged suffering above all others. Within and beyond the context of illness, suffering in imitation of Christ provided a general model for Christian sainthood well through the medieval period.

The Reformation shattered the institutional unity of Western Christianity and initiated a retreat from the traditional positive evaluation of suffering. Medieval social and religious life proceeded from an assumption of the material immanence of God in civil law and religious worship.[6] Martin Luther followed certain developments in late-medieval Catholic philosophy in positing a sharp break, an unbridgeable gap, between the physical and the metaphysical worlds. This philosophical dualism issued in Luther's political doctrine of the Two Kingdoms, which posited a strict separation between the church and the state; at the same time, Luther's immaterialization of God, his denial of divine immanence and rejection of natural law, rendered both spiritual and political notions of justice and right action arbitrary, subjective, and ultimately meaningless. Suffering

3. Clifford Geertz, "Religion as a Cultural System," in Geertz, *The Interpretation of Cultures: Selected Essays* (New York: Basic Books, 1973), 104-105.

4. Joel James Shuman and Keith G. Meador, *Heal Thyself: Spirituality, Medicine, and the Distortion of Christianity* (New York: Oxford University Press, 2003), 29.

5. Cynthia Halpern, *Suffering, Politics, Power: A Genealogy in Modern Political Theory* (Albany: SUNY Press, 2002), 54.

6. Cynthia Halpern, *Suffering, Politics, Power*, 43-44.

suffered, if you will, the fate of all human action in the wake of Luther's *sola fide* and Calvin's doctrine of innate depravity: if human "works" had no role in salvation, than suffering in imitation of Christ had no more efficacy than the devotional practices and acts of charity that Reformers routinely attacked as vain efforts to merit entrance to heaven.[7] The new doctrine of salvation by faith alone did not, of course, diminish the presence of suffering as a part of everyday life; it simply removed the institutional — which is to say the ritual and narrative — remedies that had previously invested suffering with meaning.[8]

The radical dualism of certain aspects of the Reformation reformulation of Christianity proved impossible to institutionalize in its purest form. In the wake of the assault on works and merit, the Reformers did not abandon human action so much as they developed new models of activity based on modes of living marginal to the medieval Catholic understanding of the human person — the most notorious of these being the instrumental rationality of the Protestant work ethic. The retreat from ritual and narrative elicited two new, and seemingly contradictory, responses to suffering. On the one hand, the privatization of faith led to a certain privatization of suffering; Christians turned from the heroic model of Jesus' public suffering to the comfort and consolation afforded by a newly emotionalized understanding of family life. On the other hand, the reconstruction of the public sphere as a "neutral" space for the exercise of instrumental rationality rendered suffering, along with all other traditional constraints on human action, a problem to be solved by rational state policy.

The social contract tradition provided the primary locus for the early modern political engagement with the problem of suffering. In *Leviathan*, Thomas Hobbes rewrote the origins of human society as a necessary response to one kind of suffering, the war of all against all in the state of nature; the social contract would not redeem suffering, but rather relieve and regulate it through the imposition of authoritative procedural norms. Jean-Jacques Rousseau differed from Hobbes in idealizing nature and locating the cause of human misery in society itself, yet in his writings he still imagines an ideal social contract as the political form that would transcend the corruption of the present age and bring relief to the suffering of humanity. By questioning the foundations of the social order, early modern social contract theory dramatically challenged traditional understandings of necessary and unavoidable suffering in political life.[9]

A significant social and cultural distance remained, however, between the

7. Cynthia Halpern, *Suffering, Politics, Power,* 35-45.
8. Cynthia Halpern, *Suffering, Politics, Power,* 45-46.
9. Cynthia Halpern, *Suffering, Politics, Power,* 58, 72-73, 86, 132, 147.

attack on the suffering caused by social inequality and the humanitarian ideal of a life free from pain. At the most practical level, this distance was a function of persistent technical limitations. Despite its theoretical advances, Enlightenment science had little impact on the material conditions of everyday life for people in Western Europe and the North American colonies; Francis Bacon's utopian vision of the total control of nature in the service of man remained science fiction through the eighteenth century. Nobles and peasants alike continued to accept a certain degree of pain as natural and inevitable. In his *Preliminary Discourse to the Encyclopedia of Diderot,* Jean d'Alembert proclaimed "exemption from pain" the highest goal of philosophic and scientific inquiry, but the rising bourgeoisie that would lead the democratic revolutions in America and France saw the reduction of physical suffering as at most a by-product of liberty, rather than a legitimate goal in its own right.[10] As a matter of principle, the republican tradition harbored a deep suspicion of "luxury" and feared that too much physical comfort would undermine moral virtue.

Developments in the history of medicine reveal the persistence of something like a traditional acceptance of pain despite the utopian ideals of political revolution. The Hippocratic tradition of Greek medicine bequeathed to the Christian West an enduring tension between the concern to relieve suffering and the imperative to preserve life.[11] Through the early modern period, this tension generally resolved itself in favor of life, but the Christian story generally counseled acceptance of both pain and death as simply in the natural order of things. With respect to duty to care for the sick, the fourth-century saint Basil the Great spoke for the premodern Christian view: acknowledging that "the medical art was given to us to relieve the sick, in some degree at least," he cautioned that whatever "requires an undue amount of thought or trouble or involves a large expenditure of effort and causes our whole life to revolve, as it were, around solicitude for the flesh must be avoided by Christians."[12] Despite Francis Bacon's attack on the Hippocratic/Christian tradition, even enlightened, post-Christian thinkers continued to accept pain as an essential part of life. Dr. Benjamin Rush, a signer of the Declaration of Independence and founder of the first medical school in the new republic, believed that the efficacy of the cure was directly proportional to the harshness of the treatment, and his "heroic" use of bloodletting and other purgative measures held sway over medical practice in America well

10. Jean d'Alembert, *Preliminary Discourse to the Encyclopedia of Diderot* (Chicago: University of Chicago Press, 1995), 10. I would like to thank Christopher Blum for pointing me to this quote.

11. Martin S. Pernick, *A Calculus of Suffering: Pain, Professionalism, and Anesthesia in Nineteenth-Century America* (New York: Columbia University Press, 1985), 104.

12. Shuman and Meador, *Heal Thyself,* 107.

through the 1830s.[13] Even as the American medical community — and after 1847, the medical profession — turned away from Rush's extreme measures, it continued to accept a positive role for pain in the healing process. Doctors and lay people alike saw pain as a sign of life, a trigger for the system to react; the absence of pain signaled the coming of death.[14]

The controversy surrounding the first successful use of ether as a surgical anesthetic in 1846 reflects the enduring cultural meaning of pain through the middle of the nineteenth century. Beyond the traditional associations of pain and life, many objected to the new technology as a threat to the patient's autonomy. At one level, it deprived the patient of the collaborative, supervisory power that had been an essential part of pre-anesthetic surgery; further, it clashed with the common-sense assumption that people would want to be conscious when facing death, if only to be able to put their spiritual and temporal affairs in order.[15] Some radical democrats attacked anesthesia as a threat to the autonomy of rational economic actors seeking to contract for medical care now understood as simply one of many services for hire in the free market; some radical reformers even equated it with chattel slavery.[16] Martin Pernick has argued, however, that underlying all these historically particular objections to anesthesia, "there remained a strong residual feeling that pain was something more elemental — something simply inherent in the essential nature of the human flesh. To lose the ability to feel pain was to become less than human, to be literally a vegetable or a brute."[17] During the second half of the nineteenth century, doctors balanced traditional values and modern technology through a policy of selective anesthesia. Though the medical profession never developed comprehensive criteria for when and when not to apply anesthesia, it remained firm in its insistence that anesthesia was not to be used indiscriminately to alleviate pain.

In its ambivalence, however, the American Medical Association was fighting something of a rearguard battle. The decades before the discovery of anesthesia saw cultural and technological developments that worked to undermine traditional positive evaluations of pain. Traveling through Jacksonian America in the 1830s, Alexis de Tocqueville noted that "In America the . . . effort to satisfy even the least wants of the body and to provide the little conveniences of life is upper-

---

13. Pernick, *A Calculus of Suffering*, 42, 112, 113-14. Francis Bacon's oft-quoted revision is as follows: "I esteem it the office of a physician not only to restore health, but to mitigate pain and dolors; and not only when such mitigation may conduce to recovery, but when it may serve to make a fair and easy passage" (112).

14. Pernick, *A Calculus of Suffering*, 42, 43.

15. Pernick, *A Calculus of Suffering*, 58, 59.

16. Glucklich, *Sacred Pain*, 184, 186, 187.

17. Pernick, *A Calculus of Suffering*, 48.

most in every mind." Tocqueville interpreted this new "love of well-being" as a distinctly middle-class phenomenon that, in democratic America, "sweeps everything along in its course."[18] Not all Americans were economically middle class, but it was this class that established comfort and convenience as a legitimate aspiration for all. In 1845, Perry Davis's "Celebrated Pain Killer" became the first nationally advertised product directed toward the relief of pain in general, rather than any specific illness.[19] As the medical profession dithered, patent medicine pain killers rode the wave of a general humanitarian revulsion against pain and violence in all its forms, including slavery, corporal punishment, dueling, and the traditional blood sports now seen as animal cruelty.[20] By the late nineteenth century, these cultural pressures combined with increasing professional consolidation and the availability of a broader range of anesthetics (free from the taint of patent medicine) to bring an end to the practice of selective anesthesia among licensed physicians. In medical practice, the doctor gradually lost his role as the special bearer of a certain shared, received wisdom with respect to understanding pain, and increasingly derived his authority from his command of the technical information needed to eliminate pain. Anesthesia, and the general rejection of the idea of "good pain," transformed the patient from a person in a community to a consumer and/or object of technology.[21]

This attitude was ascendant, yet hardly universal. The Roman Catholic Church, the main institutional repository of premodern traditions in the West, provided the most articulate dissent from this new anesthetic ethos. Nineteenth-century popes, generally quick to condemn anything that smacked of modernity, surprisingly withheld their anathema from anesthesia. Still, in the face of modern science and medicine, the church continued to sacralize pain. As Ariel Glucklich has commented, the church accepted the goodness of alleviating pain but continued to understand pain within a broader "ecology of community and Christ." Pain was to "be taken as a meaningful sign of something," not "mere biological damage or dysfunction, but psychic alienation from the end (telos) of the person's being."[22] At the level of popular practice,

---

18. See "The Taste for Physical Comfort in America," chapter 10 in volume 2 of Alexis de Tocqueville, *Democracy in America* (Garden City: Doubleday, 1969), 530-32.

19. Pernick, *A Calculus of Suffering*, 72.

20. For the rise of the humanitarian sensibility, see James Turner, *Reckoning with the Beast: Animals, Pain and Humanity in the Victorian Mind* (Baltimore: Johns Hopkins University Press, 1980).

21. Glucklich, *Sacred Pain*, 195. Glucklich has summed up this transformation as follows: "What remains for the patient is not ontological (his being in the world) but juridical — the right to feel better, or not to hurt."

22. Glucklich, *Sacred Pain*, 204.

these theological ideals fostered the cult of the "victim soul." Catholics understood suffering as a sign of sanctity, of a life lived in imitation of Christ. Like Jesus, the victim soul suffered not for his or her own sins, but for the sins of others. Within the spiritual economy of the church, individual sanctity conferred merit to the whole community.[23] This positive ideal of suffering profoundly shaped international Catholic culture well into the 1950s.

In America, this theological tradition carried with it a particular cultural valence. Despite growing power and influence through the early decades of the twentieth century, Catholicism remained a minority faith in a predominantly Protestant country. Attitudes toward suffering served as a powerful reminder of Catholic difference: many Protestants understood it as yet another symptom of backwardness, while Catholics saw it as a mark of their spiritual superiority. A predominantly working-class church lacking the inherited power and privilege of its European counterpart, the American Catholic church saw suffering as both a universal lot and their special duty. In purely material terms, they may not have suffered more than their co-religionists in Europe and Latin America, but American Catholics certainly felt they suffered more than American Protestants, whom they equated with the ruling class. Even as American Catholics accepted modern democracy and struggled to equalize power in political and economic life, they remained committed to a certain premodern ideal of powerlessness in their religious life. Jesus' surrender on the cross remained the highest spiritual ideal, and the church institutionalized this theological proposition through a variety of devotional practices that focused on Jesus' redemptive sacrifice. The high, neo-medieval ritualism of these practices provided a tangible, material expression of Catholic difference.[24]

---

23. On the victim soul and the place of suffering in American Catholic culture, see Robert A. Orsi, "'Mildred, Is It Fun to Be a Cripple?': The Culture of Suffering in Mid-Twentieth-Century American Catholicism," in Thomas J. Ferraro, ed., *Catholic Lives, Contemporary America* (Durham: Duke University Press), 19-64; and Paula M. Kane, "'She Offered Herself Up': The Victim Soul and Victim Spirituality in Catholicism," *Church History* 71 (March 2002): 80-119. It should be noted that the middle-class Protestant "cult of sentimentality" had its rough equivalent of the victim soul, usually an innocent mother or child suffering to redeem the heartless masculine world (see Pernick, *A Calculus of Suffering*, 117-18). Still, this tradition is more deeply rooted in Catholic practice, and survived in American Catholicism for a good half-century longer than its Protestant equivalents.

24. On the role of suffering in promoting communal identity among American Catholics, I am deeply indebted to Joseph P. Chinnici, OFM, "From Sectarian Suffering to Compassionate Solidarity: Joseph Cardinal Bernardin and the American Catholic Language of Suffering," talk delivered at the Cushwa Center for the Study of American Catholicism, University of Notre Dame, March 9, 2000. On the role of devotions in modern Catholicism, see Emmet Larkin, "The Devotional Revolution in Ireland, 1850-75," *American Historical Review* 77, no. 3 (June 1972): 625-52.

By the mid-twentieth century, this synthesis of medieval European culture and modern American society was proving increasingly unstable. Restrictive immigration legislation during the 1920s worked to dilute the European character of the church in America. A significant and influential faction of Irish-American clergy took this development as an opportunity to realize their long-standing goal of a unified, post-ethnic, American Catholicism: distinctly Catholic beliefs and practices would provide a kind of firewall against total assimilation to 100 Percent Americanism, but clerical leaders emphasized, or in some cases created, devotions and rituals that would transcend, and thus help to weaken, particular ethnic traditions. This newly achieved cultural unity soon faced an unprecedented material challenge: prosperity. Concentrated in the urban industrial centers, American Catholics benefited disproportionately from the postwar economic boom. Catholics followed middle-class Protestants in the flight to the suburbs, and the breakup of the ethnic ghettos undermined the geographic basis for communal solidarity. Clerical leaders looked to devotional practices to pick up the communal slack at a time when those practices, particularly rituals of suffering, seemed increasingly removed from the everyday experience of American Catholics. In the context of prosperous middle-class suburbia, rituals that once provided a basis for authentic community now functioned more as sectarian badges of identity, strained and increasingly unconvincing markers of difference for Catholics in most respects indistinguishable from non-Catholic Americans.[25]

In 1951, Father Ivan Illich arrived in New York City and quickly developed his own particular take on the American Catholic struggle to reconcile tradition and modernity. Born in Vienna in 1926 to a minor Dalmatian Catholic noble and a Jewish mother, educated in the highest European tradition, Illich was hardly an immigrant priest in the typical nineteenth-century mold. Still, Illich's academic training only immersed him more deeply in the triumphant medievalism that the Vatican had been promoting across all educational levels of priestly formation. At the University of Salzburg, where he received a doctorate in the philosophy of history, Illich was profoundly influenced by Albert Auer, an old Benedictine monk whose scholarly specialization focused on the twelfth-century theology of suffering. Illich developed this medieval sensibility further through the liturgical studies that provided the focus for his priestly, as

25. Chinnici makes this argument in his talk, "From Sectarian Suffering to Compassionate Solidarity." The literature on postwar assimilation and conformity is voluminous, but the starting point for the discussion with respect to religion remains Will Herberg, *Protestant, Catholic, Jew* (Garden City: Doubleday & Company, Inc., 1955).

distinct from his scholarly, formation. As scholar and priest, Illich came to see the decline of rituals capable of embodying the grand cosmology of the Christian story — not the moral (i.e. sexual) laxity routinely scapegoated by the clergy in the American church — as the greatest threat to the survival of the faith in the modern world.[26]

Cosmopolitan and urbane, theologically orthodox, Illich found himself being groomed for service in the Vatican diplomatic corps. He decided instead to go to New York City. Stories circulated that he went to New York on a dare from his American fellow seminarians in Rome; for all his intelligence and erudition, they teased, Illich would never survive in a tough, urban American parish. Illich himself later insisted that he came to America primarily to flee a career in the Vatican bureaucracy. In 1951, he received an invitation to postdoctoral study in medieval philosophy at Princeton University; as a condition for the freedom to pursue his studies, Illich accepted an assignment to Incarnation Parish, a historically Irish-American enclave in the Washington Heights section of Manhattan.[27] Illich quickly discovered that his assignment had placed him at the center of the single most significant ethno-demographic upheaval in postwar America: the massive influx of Puerto Rican immigrants into New York that would come to be known as the Great Migration. Between 1946 and 1964, over a half million Puerto Ricans came to New York. As the American clergy tried to incorporate Puerto Ricans into the church according to models of assimilation developed through the pastoral care of earlier European immigrant groups, Illich looked to the indigenous traditions of Puerto Rican Catholicism as the basis for an alternative not simply to Americanization, but to modernization in general.

The firmly ensconced Irish, not the newly arrived Puerto Ricans, presented Illich with his initial pastoral challenge. "Ivan sounds Communist. We'll call you Johnny." Thus declared Monsignor Casey, pastor of Incarnation, upon meeting his new priest. "What in heck did you come here for?" asked his parish colleague Father Joseph Connolly.[28] For centuries, people of Illich's class have

---

26. David Cayley, *Ivan Illich in Conversation* (Concord, Ontario: House of Anansi Press Limited, 1992), 65, 81. Lee Hoinacki, "Reading Ivan Illich," in Lee Hoinacki and Carl Mitcham, eds., *The Challenges of Ivan Illich: A Collective Reflection* (Albany: State University of New York Press, 2002), 4.

27. Cayley, *Ivan Illich in Conversation,* 84. Illich also had more personal reasons for going to America: his mother and sister, Jewish refugees from Hitler's Europe, had relocated in New York. See Ana María Díaz-Stevens, *Oxcart Catholicism on Fifth Avenue: The Impact of the Puerto Rican Migration Upon the Archdiocese of New York* (Notre Dame: University of Notre Dame Press, 1993), 125.

28. Quoted in Francine du Plessix Gray, *Divine Disobedience: Profiles in Catholic Radicalism* (New York: Knopf, 1970), 241, 243.

sought spiritual redemption in serving the poor; few have sought it by working for the lower middle class. Most men of Illich's breeding would have been hard-pressed to imagine a spiritual fate worse than submitting to the authority of the grandsons of the famine Irish; fortunately, Illich was not like most men. Personally charming and extremely adaptable to unfamiliar surroundings, Illich quickly overcame the suspicions of his fellow parish priests. Indeed, whereas French missionaries in nineteenth-century America looked down on the Irish, Illich envied their impeccable working-class roots. Connolly had grown up in Hell's Kitchen and left school after the fifth grade to work in a slaughterhouse. Illich once turned to him and said, "I wish like you I had been a slaughterhouse butcher, because I could be closer to the other priests." Connolly answered, "You were not cast for the role of shepherd, but for empire."[29] In Cardinal Francis Spellman, archbishop of New York, Illich found the most powerful empire builder in American Catholicism.

At first glance, Spellman and Illich would appear the strangest of bedfellows. Spellman, the archconservative anticommunist whom some have accused of personally engineering the Vietnam War; Illich, the leftist intellectual who would later criticize the Marxist-inspired liberation theology movement for being insufficiently radical. Illich nevertheless came to New York highly recommended by Spellman's contacts in Rome, and Spellman saw Illich's Vatican connections as a way to expand his own power and influence. Illich was, moreover, impeccably orthodox in his theological orientation. Personally ascetic, committed to traditional devotions such as the rosary, he impressed and intimidated his more easygoing Irish-American colleagues. Connolly, for one, feared his zeal was inspiring *too many* women to join the sisterhood: "Lay off that stuff," he would tell Illich. "You're pushing them in."[30]

Still, Illich would perform his most valuable service to Spellman less through his theological rigor than his simple ability to master Spanish. When Spellman was not preaching the need to protect Catholics from communist oppression in the Third World, he focused his energy on the plight of Third World Catholics in America. In New York during the 1950s, Puerto Ricans provided the face of the Third World; in America, the danger was not communism, but a certain kind of modernism understood in terms of secularism, materialism, and of course, Protestantism. This consensus on antimodernism obscured serious ideological differences, but proved sufficient for Spellman to place Illich in charge of the Puerto Rican apostolate.

Despite certain similarities with earlier immigrant groups, the Puerto Ri-

29. Gray, *Divine Disobedience*, 244.
30. Gray, *Divine Disobedience*, 244.

cans presented special challenges. The earlier model of Catholic Americanization succeeded largely because immigration restrictions had cut ethnic Catholics off from the contact with their culture of origin. In contrast, Puerto Ricans
were American citizens with access to cheap air travel that enabled them to
move freely back and forth between Puerto Rico and America, thus reinforcing
ties to their native cultural traditions. Spellman's initial efforts to Americanize
Puerto Rican Catholics had been perfectly consistent with the integrationist
ethos of the emerging civil rights movement; however, while African Americans
conceived their struggle as an effort to reclaim a four-hundred-year-old birthright, Puerto Ricans saw America primarily as a place to work and had no particular interest in integrating or assimilating into American culture, or even
into the American Catholic subculture. Spellman's initial efforts at outreach,
including the futile attempt to have the Irish-American sons of hog butchers
learn Spanish, were stymied by an inability to recognize or accept this cultural
reality. By the early 1950s, Spellman realized the need for new strategies.

Illich came to this situation with several advantages over his Irish-American
counterparts. First, and perhaps most important, he could learn Spanish
quickly. His education and general cosmopolitan upbringing certainly helped,
but so too did his general ease with and openness to people different from himself. After quickly mastering the Berlitz Spanish language program that Monsignor Casey had struggled with in vain for years, Illich took to mastering Spanish
by standing on street corners and simply asking questions of Puerto Ricans he
would encounter in Washington Heights. Second, Illich understood that effective ministry required a commitment not simply to help the poor, but to be
poor. To help break down the physical distance between the institutional church
and its Puerto Rican congregation, Illich rented an apartment in a tenement and
turned it into El Cuartito de Maria (The Little House of Mary). As a service project, El Cuartito provided free child care for the women of the tenement, but
Illich saw the primary purpose of the apartment as simply the establishment of a
neighborly presence for the church in the Puerto Rican community.[31]

For Illich, ministry to Puerto Ricans required a complete surrender of his
own cultural values. He understood this surrender in explicitly Christian terms,
equating it with the surrender of the will that precedes the reception of grace in
traditional Christian theology. Familiar with modern social theory, Illich nonetheless understood this surrender of cultural assumptions not in terms of objectivity or tolerance, but as "a beatitude of cultural poverty."[32] Illich spent va-

---

31. Joseph P. Fitzpatrick, S.J., "Ivan Illich as We Knew Him in the 1950s," in Hoinacki and
Mitcham, *The Challenges of Ivan Illich*, 36.
32. Díaz-Stevens, *Oxcart Catholicism on Fifth Avenue*, 133.

cations in Puerto Rico, walking and hitchhiking across the country, performing priestly duties and soaking up the peasant culture of the people; he became convinced that the future vitality of Puerto Rican Catholicism depended on the maintenance of Puerto Rican cultural traditions.[33] One commentator on Illich has claimed that, "if he had had his way he would have totally transferred the church of the *campesinos,* with its unpunctuality, its semi-pagan rituals, its great community feast days, to the streets of New York."[34] The appeal to tradition provided Illich with a language through which to subvert Spellman's Americanization goals without appearing subversive.

Unable to transfer the culture whole, Illich began with a part. In 1955, he organized a *Fiesta de San Juan* to serve as a day for Puerto Rican Catholics to celebrate their religious and cultural heritage. Naming the event after the patron saint of Puerto Rico, Illich conceived of the event on the model of traditional *fiestas patronales,* which freely mixed religious processions and a solemn high mass with picnicking, card playing, music, dance and theatre.[35] If the Irish could have St. Patrick's Day on March 17, Illich reasoned, the Puerto Ricans should have St. John's Day on June 24. Spellman could hardly argue with that logic, and agreed to allow the use of the great quadrangle at Fordham University for the event — with himself as the guest of honor.[36] Illich took charge of promotional efforts, placing ads in Spanish language newspapers and eliciting support from slick Madison Avenue executives. On June 23, the eve of the feast, the police estimated they would need officers to control a crowd of about 5000; the next day, 35,000 people descended on Fordham for a celebration of ethnic cultural identity unprecedented in postwar America.

The success of the fiesta convinced Spellman that Illich was the man to take control of the church's ministry not simply to Puerto Ricans in New York, but to Catholics throughout Latin America. In 1956, Spellman loaned out Illich to the diocese of Ponce to serve as Vice Rector of the Catholic University of Puerto Rico. Illich was to oversee the creation of an Institute of Missionary Formation, whose goal was to train American priests in Latin American cultures so as to serve Latinos better in America and in their home countries. In 1959, the institute changed its name to Institute of Intercultural Communication. Incorporated in the state of New York, the institute remained housed at the University of Puerto Rico, yet operated largely to serve the needs of the archdiocese of New

---

33. Jaime R. Vidal, "Puerto Rican Catholics," in Jay P. Dolan and Jaime R. Vidal, eds., *Puerto Rican and Cuban Catholics in the U.S., 1900-1965* (Notre Dame: University of Notre Dame Press, 1994), 89-90.

34. Gray, *Divine Disobedience,* 245.

35. Vidal, "Puerto Rican Catholics," 101.

36. Gray, *Divine Disobedience,* 246.

York. Each year Spellman would send half his ordination class to the institute for training.

Despite the financial and moral support of Spellman, Illich's time in Puerto Rico was short. His overtures to Puerto Rico's leading secular political party brought him into conflict with local church authorities. In the fall of 1960, the Irish-American bishop of Puerto Rico James McManus ordered him off the island.[37] Even more distressing, Illich began to see his theory of intercultural communication fall before the institutional inertia of Americanization. Catholic missionaries continued to try to export the American urban parish model, complete with brick rectories and parish schools, to the slums of Latin America. With the continuing support of Cardinal Spellman, Illich searched for a new base of operations. Drawn by good weather and a liberal bishop, Illich gravitated to Cuernavaca, Mexico. In the spring of 1961, Illich introduced himself to Bishop Sergio Mendez Arceo with a pronouncement: "I would like to start, under your auspices, a center of de-Yankeefication."[38] Bishop Mendez Arceo enthusiastically embraced Illich's project, which would become the "Center of Intercultural Documentation," or CIDOC.

This rather inelegant title belies the institute's dynamic role as a center for radical thinking in the 1960s. Initially conceived as another intercultural training center for priests, the CIDOC quickly became a clearinghouse for a wide range of countercultural thinkers searching for alternatives to modern industrial society. Described by one chronicler as "part language school, part conference center, part free university, part publishing house," the CIDOC defied established institutional and ideological categories.[39] Illich clearly took delight in this outsider role, yet in resisting efforts to link the CIDOC to any specific political movement he never fell into the trap of purely negative criticism. His ideal of detachment was priestly rather than critical, rooted in the Christian tradition that affirms the goodness of creation while counseling indifference to the world. Illich himself described the CIDOC as "in its deepest sense a contemplative place, not a conspirational place," and recognized, with more than a little pride, that contemplation "is scandalous to both the left and the right."[40]

Illich would alienate many not simply by his worldly indifference, but by the conspiratorial vision emerging from his contemplative ideal. At Cuernavaca, he continued to speak out against the missionary efforts to remake Latin America in the image of the American church. Illich saw the priest short-

---

37. Vidal, "Puerto Rican Catholics," 104.
38. Gray, *Divine Disobedience*, 252.
39. Gray, *Divine Disobedience*, 253.
40. Gray, *Divine Disobedience*, 275.

age in Latin America as an opportunity, not a crisis, and argued for the need to envision a less clerical model of the church. Catholic liberals and radicals who warmed to his affirmation of the laity were puzzled by his insistence that the church keep its distance from politics. Deeply aware of the need for social change in Latin America, Illich nonetheless rejected the idea that the church should be in any direct way at the vanguard of a new social order. Illich declared it "blasphemous to use the gospel to prop up any social or political system," and opted for a more detached, prophetic role for priests and religious leaders.[41] Viewing some sort of Christian consciousness as essential to any meaningful alternative social vision, he nonetheless guarded against the reduction of religion to politics that he saw in the rising Latin American movement of liberation theology. These subtleties were lost on church officials who saw any criticism of its clerical vision as incipient heresy. Called to Rome to give an account of his activities at Cuernavaca, Illich decided simply to withdraw from active priestly service. He remained a priest until his death in 2002, but from 1969 onward his inactive status enabled him to speak on political matters with the freedom of a Catholic layman.

Illich's critique of the excessive clericalism of the Roman Catholic Church provided the model for his critique of all modern bureaucratic institutions. Illich continued to operate CIDOC through the mid-1970s, and quickly broadened his focus to include the full range of social issues related to industrial development. During what he later referred to as his pamphleteering period, CIDOC's method of operation was as follows: Illich would periodically announce a theme or topic for discussion; by invitation or their own volition, interested intellectuals, famous and obscure, would gather in Cuernavaca for an extended (anywhere from one to two years) discussion of the topic; Illich would then produce a book laying out his own views in light of the seminar discussion. He began this period by tackling the issue of education, and moved on to technology, the environment, and the so-called helping professions, particularly medicine.[42]

Illich proved just as frustrating to his secular (though equally obtuse) interlocutors as he had to church officials. Opposition to the Vietnam War and an uncompromisingly critical stance toward capitalism made Illich a darling of

41. Ivan Illich, "The Seamy Side of Charity," in Illich, *The Church, Change and Development* (Chicago: The Urban Training Center Press, 1970), 30.

42. John L. Elias, *Conscientization and Deschooling: Freire's and Illich's Proposals for Reshaping Society* (Philadelphia: Westminster Press, 1976), 20, 22, 28. Illich's major works from this period are *Deschooling Society* (New York: Harper and Row, 1971); *Tools for Conviviality* (New York: Harper and Row, 1973); *Energy and Equity* (New York: Harper and Row, 1974); and *Medical Nemesis: The Expropriation of Health* (New York: Pantheon Books, 1976).

the political left for a brief period, but by the early 1970s it became clear that Illich did not fit into conventional political categories. Student radicals who saw themselves as the new vanguard of human liberation were troubled by Illich's argument that the ideal of universal education, from the multiversity to the humble public school, was the problem, not the solution. Against those who placed their hopes for social transformation in properly radical, consciousness-raising education, Illich argued that the very idea of schooling creates invidious social hierarchies by devaluing traditional knowledge and certifying one type of intelligence — book learning — and one type of discipline — the Protestant work ethic — as a universal requirement for all citizens.[43]

Radicals attracted to Illich's critique of liberal capitalist programs for Third World uplift were perplexed by his assessment of Marxist and nationalist revolution as simply capitalist economic development by another name.[44] Illich greatly admired the Vietnamese resistance to U.S. imperialism, yet saw the war as an object lesson in the limits of technological "superiority" rather than a vindication of any Marxist logic of history. At a time when enlightened opinion focused on how to bring the material benefits of modern Western society to the rest of the world, Illich called on the West to embrace poverty as both a moral and environmental imperative.[45] For Illich, the acceptance of the material limits imposed by a subsistence economy was the precondition for human freedom.[46] At the height of Illich's influence, his views nonetheless elicited charges of nostalgia, utopianism, irrationality, and statistical inaccuracy. They still do today.[47]

Illich never let his critique of modernity descend to a mere numbers game.

43. Ivan Illich, *Celebration of Awareness: A Call for Institutional Revolution* (Garden City: Doubleday, 1970), 126, 127, 187. Gray, *Divine Disobedience*, 315.

44. Illich, *Celebration*, 174.

45. Illich, *Celebration*, 110, 180, 24.

46. Elias, *Conscientization and Deschooling*, 32-33.

47. In a seminar discussing an earlier draft of this essay, I was surprised to find Illich's insistence that it is materially impossible, not to mention environmentally suicidal, to export the Western middle-class standard of living to the rest of the world to be a point in need of further statistical verification. Those in need of numbers should consult J. R. McNeill's irresponsibly balanced survey of the consequences of the last one hundred years of industrial development, *Something New Under the Sun: An Environmental History of the Twentieth-Century World* (New York: W. W. Norton & Company, 2000). According to McNeill, the human race has used more energy in the last one hundred years than in all the previous years of recorded human history. He acknowledges that "our current ways are ecologically unsustainable." Much like Illich, McNeill realizes that any meaningful solution to this problem would require a new creed of drastic economic restraint; much like Illich's critics, he sees such a creed as unrealistic, perhaps even undesirable, and places his hope in technological progress and population control (see 15, 358-360).

He understood the debate over modernization to be less about realism than about the nature of reality. Illich called for "a new language, a language that speaks not of development and underdevelopment but of true and false ideas about man, his needs, and his potential." The contours of this language of human nature became clearer as Illich turned from education to the other sacred cow of development theory, medicine. True to his earlier critiques, he continued to rail against high-tech solutions, now calling for clean water and aspirin rather than surgery. In seeming defiance of humanist compassion, Illich approved of Third World doctors who let patients die of cancer rather than incur the risks of surgery, and argued against medical programs designed to minimize those risks.[48] Declaring himself "for those who want to deepen life rather than lengthen it," Illich argued that immediate needs should not be allowed to shape long-term plans for achieving meaningful health in the Third World.[49]

For most of Illich's opponents in the international development community, however, words such as "meaningful" were meaningless. Depth of meaning does not lend itself to the quantitative measurement; qualitative judgments are personal and arbitrary, and therefore inadmissible to public debate. Illich wrote *Medical Nemesis* (1976) as a challenge both to modern medical practice and to the illusion that such practice could be debated apart from questions of truth about the nature of the universe.

The last book to grow out of the Cuernavaca seminars, *Medical Nemesis* follows the polemical strategy of Illich's earlier studies. That is, it proceeds via both internal and external critique. Technically, modern medicine fails to live up to its own standards of effectiveness; politically, the medical profession claims for itself the immunities of a private organization, yet commands coercive state power to impose a single definition of health on all citizens; philosophically, the medical community's stated humanist commitment to the elimination of suffering proceeds from a deeper, technocratic worldview that reduces humanism to mere utilitarianism. Against these internal contradictions, Illich offers an alternative view of health based on a non-technical relation between the human person and the world, a relation in which meaningful pain exists as an essential part of a meaningful life.[50]

Illich was not alone in his critique of the technical and political dimensions of modern medical practice. He drew on a substantial body of historical and sociological studies that called into question the previously unquestioned au-

---

48. Illich, *Celebration,* 180, 159.

49. Quoted in Gray, *Divine Disobedience,* 288. Illich, "The Seamy Side of Charity," 29.

50. Illich, *Medical Nemesis.* All further references to specific pages in this work will be in parentheses following the quotation or paraphrase.

thority of the medical profession. Through the nineteenth and early twentieth centuries, industrial and humanitarian leaders increasingly turned to the narrowly technical understanding of healing bequeathed by the Enlightenment as the medical ideal appropriate to a rational, progressive social order; however, the ideal of technical control gained social and political authority completely apart from demonstrated technical effectiveness (159, 194). Most of the epidemics that twentieth-century medicine claims to have cured were in fact a consequence of "progress" — the rise of industrial society — and declined well before the introduction of medical cures; tuberculosis, cholera and typhoid all "peaked and dwindled outside the physician's control" (16). Improvements in diet and environment were much more decisive than any medical "magic bullet" in the conquest of the diseases of the industrial era. At the same time, industrialism has bequeathed a new set of diseases, including heart disease and hypertension, emphysema, obesity, and cancer, equally environmental and similarly resistant to medical intervention (24).

Illich rereads the history of modern medicine as a story of the creation, rather than the cure, of disease. He labels this a process of "iatrogenesis," from the Greek words for "physician" and "origin" (3). At the most basic physical level, hospitals, the defining institution of modern medicine, hurt people. At the time of Illich's writing, the U.S. Department Health, Education, and Welfare estimated that 7 per cent of all patients suffer compensable injuries, an accident rate higher than any industry except mining and high-rise construction. One in five patients admitted to a typical research hospital acquires a disease, with one case in thirty leading to death (31-32). At a subtler level, the medical profession has been able to create disease by redefinition. Illich notes that medieval craft guilds reserved the right to determine *who* could work and *how* the work was to be done, but the modern medical profession claims the authority to determine *what* its work shall be, medicalizing whole areas of life previously never considered to be occasions for medical intervention; the medicalization of childbirth and old age are but the most obvious examples of this larger process (46, 81). For Illich, preventative care simply expands the scope of professional power, and European-style socialized medicine simply increases the coercive power behind the enforcement of this iatrogenic regime (222).

In the roughly thirty years since the publication of *Medical Nemesis,* such muckraking has become part of our medical culture. Exposés of malpractice or incompetence by doctors or hospital staff appear routinely in newspapers and evening television magazine programs; anyone who has lived through cancer with a loved one has wondered whether the treatments might be worse than the disease. The medical profession itself concedes the provisional nature of many of its high-tech breakthroughs. Still, with a broader cultural commitment to what one physician recently called "medicine's progress, one setback at a time," medical authority has steadily expanded despite its seeming newfound humility.[51] Illich warned that such superficial housecleaning would only serve to naturalize the existing state of affairs. He realized that modern medicine draws its authority less from its ability to conquer disease, eradicate suffering, and prolong life than from the absolute value assigned to the pursuit of these goals regardless of their attainment (166). He distinguished himself from mainstream liberal and radical critics by insisting that modern medicine is a threat not only to health, but to culture.

Like so many of Illich's other works during this period, *Medical Nemesis* was profoundly shaped by his experiences with development programs in Latin America. Mainstream critics looked at the Third World and saw the failure of the West to distribute scarce yet desperately needed medical resources; Illich, in contrast, saw primarily the destruction of ancient healing practices and traditional understandings of sickness and health. In *Medical Nemesis*, Illich decries the encroachment of a universal ideal of "health" over "the ideal of concrete and specific patterns of functioning characteristic of each tribe or *polis*." The introduction of modern pharmaceuticals into peasant societies quickly destroys "the historically rooted patterns that fit each culture to its poison," and replaces relatively stable systems of meaning with an ever-changing system of techniques (63, 133). Medicine, as much as economic dislocation, has fostered the "breakdown of the family as a cocoon, of the neighborhood as a network of gift relationships, and of the environment as the shelter of a local subsistence community" (132, 86).

Refusing nostalgia and pastoral lament, Illich defends traditional cultures in that aspect that even the most sympathetic moderns find most repulsive: the acceptance of pain as not only inevitable, but meaningful (149). Pain and suffering have different meanings in different cultures, but all traditional and non-Western cultures distinguish themselves from Western modernity by having a place for something like an art of suffering and dying. In declaring war on pain and suffering, modern medical civilization thus stands "in opposition to every single cultural health program [it] encounter[s] in the process of progressive colonization" (132). In declaring war on modern medicine, Illich attempts to revive the art of suffering.

In declaring war on modern medicine, Illich was attempting to revive the art of suffering. He acknowledges that in the modern West, "the advocacy of a renewed style in art of suffering . . . will inevitably be misinterpreted as a sick desire for pain," the moral equivalent of sadism (153-54). Against this charge, he distinguishes pain as mere physical sensation from suffering as the physical sen-

51. Lisa Sanders, M.D., "Medicine's Progress, One Setback at a Time," *The New York Times*, March 16, 2003.

sation of pain given meaning by culture. Traditional cultures make pain tolerable "by integrating it into a meaningful setting"; they "confront pain, impairment, and death by interpreting them as challenges soliciting a response from the individual under stress" (133-34). The traditional response begins where the modern ends, with the recognition of pain as a problem:

> When I suffer pain, I am aware that a question is being raised. . . . Pain is the sign for something not answered; it refers to something open, something that goes on the next moment to demand What is wrong? How much longer? Why must I/ought I/should I/can I/ suffer? Why does this kind of evil exist, and why does it strike me? (142).

Modern medicine claims there is no answer to these questions, only the need to minimize or eliminate pain. In contrast, within the framework of the traditional questions Illich invokes, pain is less a problem to be solved than a question to be answered. The appropriate response is moral or spiritual, and only incidentally technical.

The major religious traditions have generally counseled resignation to pain, yet they have also provided "a rationale, a style, and a community setting" in which pain could be transformed into meaningful suffering. Each great religious tradition places pain in a larger story: for Hinduism, pain is the result of karma accumulated through past incarnations; for Islam, it is an invitation to surrender to God; for Christianity, it is an opportunity for a closer association/identification with a crucified savior (108-109). These stories are cosmological, not personal; they do not explain individual suffering so much as they relocate it in the structure of the universe. Illich's account of the understanding of pain in premodern Europe may stand for his characterization of the general attitude of "traditional" cultures toward pain: "pain was man's experience of a marred universe, not a mechanical dysfunction in one of its subsystems" (149).

Illich sees acceptance of this truth as the basis for a "poetic interpretation" of pain. The appropriate response is neither passive resignation nor active defiance, but a search for appropriate models of heroic behavior:

> . . . cultures always have provided an example on which behavior in pain could be modeled: the Buddha, the saint, the warrior or the victim. The duty to suffer in their guise distracts attention from otherwise all-absorbing sensation and challenges the sufferer to bear torture with dignity. The cultural setting not only provides the grammar and technique, the myths and examples used in its characteristic "craft of suffering well," but also the instructions on how to integrate this repertoire (145).

These models mediate between the general cosmological story and the particular suffering of individuals; they provide instruction in proper conduct, yet just as importantly draw the individual out of himself through association with a community of those who have endured great suffering.

The narrative and performative dimensions of the art of suffering co-existed with technical practices more recognizable as antecedents of modern "pain killing." Alcohol, coca leaf, peyote, and other popular, low-tech analgesics have always had a place in traditional health practices. The art of suffering requires not the pursuit of maximum pain (that *is* masochism), but merely a recognition that alleviation of pain is only one mode — and not the most important one — of our response to the reality of suffering:

> The medicalization of pain . . . has fostered a hypertrophy of just one of these modes — management by technique — and reinforced the decay of the others. Above all, it has rendered either incomprehensible or shocking the idea that skill in the art of suffering might be the most effective and universally acceptable way of dealing with pain. Medicalization deprives any culture of the integration of its program for dealing with pain (145).

Illich notes that the evidence from anthropology suggests that the modern West is unique in allowing technical efficiency to set the limits for the use of tools: "in all other societies, recognizing sacred limits to the use of sword and plow was a necessary foundation for ethics" (267). Recognizing and accepting something like sacred — rather than merely practical — limits to medical technology is the necessary first step toward the realization of a meaningful alternative to modern medical nemesis.

Curiously, the conclusion to *Medical Nemesis* renders this first step a dead end. Illich would not be the first critic to come up short on a positive program, but his program for political action seems to work against the most provocative elements of his critique. Illich titled his book after the Greek myth of Nemesis — the divinity who punished *hubris,* understood specifically as the mortal aspiration to divinity — in part to capture the dynamic of iatrogenesis, but also to distinguish his analysis from "the explanatory paradigm now offered by bureaucrats, therapists, and ideologues for the snowballing diseconomies and disutilities that, lacking all intuition, they have engineered" (35). Illich suggests that ancient myth trumps modern expertise for understanding the clinical, social, and cultural dynamics of modern medicine. He consistently invokes the mythic structures of traditional healing as viable alternatives to modern medical technique. Still, when Illich looks to the future, he falls into the same kind of rationalist paradigm he so often criticizes in his work: traditional cultures have passed away; the old taboos and myths can no longer guide our conduct; appeals to the sacred have no place in modern, pluralistic democracies; "inherited myth" must give way to "respectful procedures" and universal moral principles. Illich's rationalism is, admittedly, of a distinctly anarchist variety. Illich envisions the overthrow of the medical profession's monopoly on health followed by the flourishing of a variety of non-technical health cultures. Still, by dismissing myth he appears to turn away from the only cultural resource capable of providing non-technical models.

Is this a case of critical nemesis? Illich's invocation of procedural liberalism reflects a longstanding commitment to nonviolence and the rule of law, as well as the more specific influence of the great liberal political theorist John Rawls, who participated in CIDOC seminars in the early 1970s.[52] Still, his rejection of inherited myth certainly also reflects his growing stature as a universalist, critical intellectual, as well as the continued critical distance he kept from his own mythic community, the Roman Catholic Church. Fearing that his vision would be co-opted by the liberal establishment or become yet another left movement, he closed CIDOC following the publication of *Medical Nemesis*. His subsequent writing returned to more explicitly Christian mythic language, yet he maintained a critical distance from the institutional church. To be fair, the post–Vatican II church would not have been the most hospitable institutional base for Illich's brand of orthodoxy. Ascendant liberal Catholics were in flight from just the sort of truths Illich looked to in the art of suffering; indeed, for a whole generation of Catholic intellectuals, rejection of the victim soul tradition stood as a badge of intellectual and spiritual maturity.[53] By the late 1970s, Illich's idiosyncratic brand of critical orthodoxy left him without a party or a church.

Colleagues and admirers often expressed frustration with Illich's anti-institutionalism, but few questioned his intellectual integrity and consistency.[54] Even as his anarchism led him to trust no social grouping beyond a small, close circle of friends, he continued to see all his intellectual work as proceeding from the Western-Christian tradition of the Incarnation, the belief that in the person of Jesus, God became fully human and remained fully divine.[55] The divine affirmation of the flesh, with all its limitations, points inevitably to the Cross, the

52. Elias, *Conscientization and Deschooling*, 94-95.

53. For an insightful yet ultimately symptomatic account of this transition, see Orsi, "'Mildred, Is It Fun to Be a Cripple?'"

54. See Fitzpatrick, "Ivan Illich as We Knew Him in the 1950s," 41.

55. For Illich's vision of community, see Ivan Illich, "The Cultivation of Conspiracy," in Hoinacki and Mitcham, *The Challenges of Ivan Illich*. On his intellectual debt to the theology of the incarnation, see Cayley, *Ivan Illich in Conversation*, 280.

ultimate symbol of the limits inherent in embodied existence.[56] Illich continued to see modern medicine as a fundamental denial of the truth of the Cross. Looking back on *Medical Nemesis* a decade after its initial publication, he conceded only that he had overestimated the importance of the medical profession proper: the movements for self care and so-called alternative medicine proceed from an understanding of "health" in basic accord with the medical establishment's utilitarian/instrumental ideal of well-being apart from communal story.[57] Medical and environmental humanisms substitute the notion of life as a biological process for the ideal of the human person in relation to other persons. This biological notion of life is a perversion of the Life spoken of in the gospels. That Life, in turn, "was given to us on the Cross, and . . . we cannot seek it except on the *via crucis*."[58]

THE VIA CRUCIS is a story. Drawing on the gospels and folk traditions of various Catholic cultures, it recounts the events surrounding the death of Jesus: his acceptance of the cross; his encounters with his mother, friends, and strangers; his stumbles on the road to Calvary; and finally, his crucifixion. The Via Crucis is theology. The cross as a model of Christian discipleship demands a self-giving love that leads to death; as such it resists translation into the more familiar modern language of social responsibility and political justice.[59] The Via Crucis is a practice. For centuries the Roman Catholic Church disseminated its theology through its official liturgies and support for popular para-liturgical devotions. The Via Crucis has inspired some of the most enduring spiritual practices in the history of Catholicism, including the Stations of the Cross and the Passion Play; it has provided the name for a kind of street theatre reenactment that has been particularly significant in the Mediterranean Catholicism that the Spanish brought to the New World in the sixteenth century. It remains a vital practice among many of the Catholic cultures of Latin America.

The story of Jesus' sacrifice has parallels among a wide range of premodern cultures, yet from the beginnings of Christianity the cross has for many proved to be, in the words of St. Paul, at best a stumbling block, at worst an absurdity. Enlightenment modernity has presented its own special obstacles to compre-

---

56. Barbara Duden, "The Quest for Past Somatics," in Hoinacki and Mitcham, *The Challenges of Ivan Illich*, 220. Cayley, *Ivan Illich in Conversation*, 49.

57. Ivan Illich, "Twelve Years after *Medical Nemesis*: A Plea for Body History," in Illich, *In the Mirror of the Past: Lectures and Addresses, 1978-1990* (London: Marion Boyars, 1992), 211-17.

58. Ivan Illich, "The Institutional Construction of a New Fetish: Human Life," in Illich, *In the Mirror of the Past*, 220, 225.

59. For a representative example of this tradition, see Arthur Chute McGill, *Suffering: A Test of Theological Method* (Philadelphia: Geneva Press, 1968), 55-56.

hension: the very act of crucifixion violates the prohibition against cruel and unusual punishment; the notion of a blameless man dying for the crimes of others violates liberal notions of justice; and the paradoxical ideal of triumph through surrender stands as a rebuke to all modern notions of freedom as autonomy and control. For those seeking to reconcile Christianity and modernity, these obstacles have often proved insurmountable. After Vatican II, the hard sayings of the crucifixion began to recede from mainstream Catholic theology and popular religious practice. In Latin America, Catholic promoters of a new theology of liberation looked with suspicion on popular rituals of suffering as fatalistic, death-obsessed, and consequently politically retrograde.[60]

The failure of conventional political liberation in Latin America has led in recent years to a renewed engagement with popular ritual on the part of politically progressive theologians. Some of the leading theologians working out of a liberationist framework have turned to the Via Crucis, particularly as practiced by Mexican immigrants in the United States, as the locus of a new politics capable of reconciling traditional belief and practice with modern social justice. The popularity of the Via Crucis and other practices such as the Days of the Dead seems to confirm the stereotype of Mexico as a death-obsessed country. The theologian Roberto Goizueta has argued that these practices reflect not obsession — which suggests psychological dysfunction — but rather a distinct popular epistemology that understands death as part of life and refuses to accept the modern view of the two as mutually exclusive.[61] Goizueta's sense that this alternative epistemology provides the basis for a truly alternative politics grew out of his experience of the Via Crucis enacted by the working-class Mexicano community in the Pilsen district of Chicago. A brief look at the history of this community, along with a deeper consideration of Goizueta's reflections on the Via Crucis, suggests the contours of a postmodern politics of suffering.[62]

On Christmas Eve of 1976, a fire broke out at a children's Christmas party in a Pilsen apartment building just two blocks from the St. Vitus Catholic Church. By the time the fire trucks arrived, adults were dropping children out

---

60. Roberto S. Goizueta, "The Symbolic World of Mexican American Religion," in Timothy Matovina and Gary Riebe Estrella, eds., *Horizons of the Sacred: Mexican Traditions in U.S. Catholicism* (Ithaca: Cornell University Press, 2002), 137.

61. Goizueta, "The Symbolic World of Mexican American Religion," 120.

62. My account of the Pilsen *Via Crucis* relies almost exclusively on Karen Mary Davalos's ethnographic study, "'The Real Way of Praying: The *Via Crucis, Mexicano* Sacred Space, and the Architecture of Domination," a paper presented at the University of Notre Dame on March 11, 2000, at the conference "Catholicism in Twentieth-Century America." A published version of this study has recently appeared in Timothy Matovina and Gary Riebe Estrella, eds., *Horizons of the Sacred: Mexican Traditions in U.S. Catholicism* (Ithaca: Cornell University Press, 2002).

of windows. The fire fighters could not speak Spanish and did not understand that there were still children trapped in the building. Ten children and two mothers died in the blaze. News spread throughout Pilsen and neighbors quickly packed the midnight mass at St. Vitus to hold a memorial service for those who had died. After the funerals, the people of St. Vitus held a community meeting with the parish of St. Pius V and other Pilsen churches. They issued a statement to the press placing responsibility for the fire and the deaths on the overcrowded housing, the general neglect of city services, and the lack of Spanish-speaking fire fighters. St. Vitus parish had a long history of social activism, yet the fire affected the community in ways more profound than any social program could address. The people of Pilsen turned to the Via Crucis not simply to secure better housing, but as an act of solidarity, affirming their shared cultural and spiritual heritage in remembrance of those who had died in the fire.

In conjunction with other parishes in the area, St. Vitus parish decided to enact the stations in public places so as to link the suffering of Christ to the specific historical suffering of the community in Pilsen. The stations moved from parish to parish, stopping at places with specific social and political significance to the community. At the thirteenth station, in which Jesus is taken down from the cross, the procession passed by the apartment building that had burned on Christmas Eve. Participants paused to reflect on the deaths of the members of the community and symbolically link those deaths to the death of Christ. The particular location of each station has varied from year to year, but always serves as a symbolic or literal landmark of either social injustice or social solidarity. Some locations are points of community pride, such as a branch library named after a political activist murdered in his home for his attempts to unionize workers. Other locations have been selected because of their status as sites of violence perpetrated within the community itself, particularly violence related to gangs and drugs. The prayers and songs recited at these stations incorporate these sites into the larger spiritual story of Christ's suffering, death, and resurrection.

Since 1977, the Via Crucis has grown from a local community ritual to one that draws over 10,000 participants from throughout the city of Chicago. It has been the vehicle for many tangible, practical reforms; however, like Illich's art of suffering, it must be judged not simply in terms of technical effectiveness, but in terms of the relationships it creates and sustains. The story of the Via Crucis ends in death, in Jesus' crucifixion on Calvary. The onlookers do not rescue Jesus; they accompany him. Roberto Goizueta has argued that this act of accompaniment, the public display of communal support for the suffering, itself stands as the triumph of life over death; in many Latino communities, the resurrection of Easter Sunday is redundant, an epilog to a drama essentially completed on Good Friday.[63] Within the terms of this symbolic politics of suffering, cleaning up a drug corner is ultimately less important than the public expression of solidarity on the part of a community struggling against drugs.

The critique of conventional liberation implicit in Goizueta's ideal of accompaniment is but one aspect of his broader critique of the social and epistemological assumptions of modernity. Traditional and deeply organic, the social ideal embodied in Latino popular Catholicism stands as the most profound alternative to both the liberal and communitarian/socialist variations of modern social organization. Goizueta emphasizes that the worldview underlying the Via Crucis "reflects a particular notion of the human person, a particular 'theological anthropology.'" Life is not a right, but a gift given to us by those who have come before us. As a consequence, "personal identity is not so much achieved through an individual's choices and decisions as it is received from one's family, one's community, and above all, from God." Against the Tocquevillean tradition to which many American communitarians appeal, Goizueta insists that for Latino Catholics community is never a voluntary association. Individuals do not make community; rather, the community provides the foundation for human persons, who live in largely involuntary relationships with one another. Such an understanding of the human person does not deny the possibility of creative human agency, but it subordinates meaningful human agency to the authority of the community.[64]

Tradition and community can be oppressive. By the same token, from the enslavement of Africans and the extermination of Native Americans to the gulag, modernity has waged much terror in the name of human liberation. One significant strain of modern social thought has sought to transcend the classic sociological stalemate between tradition and modernity by shifting the debate from an either/or to a both/and; however, that such dialectics quickly descend to a kind of cost-benefit analysis already skews the balance in favor of modernity. For Goizueta, the issue is ultimately not balance, but priority:

> Social and personal improvement are certainly desirable goals. Paradoxically, however, if we view human life as but a means to those noble goals, we will never attain them. If our goal is a just society, where all human persons are valued, affirmed, and loved as ends in themselves, as genuine 'others,' we cannot arrive at that goal through an instrumentalization of persons which contradicts the very goal itself. At its most basic level justice, like happiness, is

63. Goizueta, "The Symbolic World of Mexican American Religion," 130, 131. For a more detailed treatment of this theology of accompaniment, see Roberto Goizueta, *Caminemos con Jesús: Toward a Hispanic/Latino Theology of Accompaniment* (Maryknoll: Orbis Books, 1995).

64. Goizueta, "The Symbolic World of Mexican American Religion," 121, 122.

not a product but a concomitant, or byproduct, of human life when that life is lived and valued as an end in itself. Like human happiness in general, social justice and personal growth or transformation are not directly-intended 'products' of the 'work' the individual person undertakes respectively 'on' society, or 'on' himself or herself. Rather, these are but byproducts of the person's interaction with *others*. In short, the only justice and the only true self-improvement or personal growth is that which is the unintended (directly, at least) consequence of the person's active *love* of others. This is simply another way of expressing the paradox of the cross.[65]

Truth — that is, the truth of suffering — is prior to justice. It does not exclude justice, but contains it within a story of radical injustice that leads to redemption. It is a story in which, as Goizueta has written elsewhere, love is more important than life.[66]

Many who live outside of this story may find it repulsive, and even those more sympathetic may still remain unconvinced. The politics of suffering is ultimately a politics of story — not the imposition of one story on all citizens, or the constant critical dialog across stories in search of some hermeneutic fusion of horizons, but simply the survival of the alternative stories bequeathed by premodern and non-Western cultures.

A simple appeal to diversity skirts the issue of political power. Despite, or perhaps because of, its dominant utilitarian calculus, modernity has generated its own stories of suffering. Soap operas and support groups are but two of the most obvious ways in which our medicalized culture has tried to reclaim some notion of meaningful pain; both, in distinct yet increasingly interrelated ways, substitute psychology for cosmology and naturalize the emotional network of family and friends — Tocqueville's social world of individualism — as the only refuge from cold rationality. The hegemonic power these stories exercise in civil society (that is, popular culture) is at least as coercive as the legal authority granted the medical profession by the state. The strength of the Via Crucis among Mexican Americans is in part a function of their marginality to mainstream Anglo-American culture; the historical record suggests that assimilation, or at best the subordination of one's tradition to middle-class ideals, is the price of overcoming this marginality. Middle-class European-American Catholics were for a time able to sustain something like a traditional view of suffering largely due to the creation of an extensive network of parallel social institutions that enabled them to maintain a distinct cultural identity. The American Cath-

---

65. Goizueta, *Caminemos con Jesús,* 107.
66. Goizueta, "The Symbolic World of Mexican American Religion," 119.

olic example suggests that cultural integrity depends to a significant degree on cultural isolation.

Ironically, a meaningful commitment to diversity requires a willingness to live without it. True diversity will only flourish when people are allowed to live primarily within one culture, encountering only the diversity allowed by geographic proximity in a world in which geographic mobility is relatively limited. Illich's positive evaluation of suffering grew out of a deeper understanding of limits as the condition for the possibility of meaning; restricting access to cultures may be understood as one instance of the broader subsistence ideal Illich saw as necessary for environmental survival. As with Goizueta's treatment of love and life, it is a question of priority rather than mutual exclusion. Traditional cultures must be allowed to engage modernity from a position of strength something like that from which the Amish decide whether a new invention will disrupt community life. Amish communalism is as marginal to mainstream America as the Via Crucis, but the vitality of these kinds of cultural practices is a much truer measure of cultural diversity than, say, the proliferation of ethnic autobiographies. Like all politics, the politics of diversity is a zero-sum game. If modernity is to maintain its commitment to cultural diversity, it must relinquish its claims to universalism, even if that means allowing people to "suffer." In this way, modernity may yet bear its own unique witness to the paradox of the cross.

# Pilgrim to an Unknown Land:
# Christopher Lasch's Journey

Eric Miller

More than just a political philosophy, modern liberalism has constituted itself as a worldview and a way of life, one that has had the pervasive effect in American culture of exalting the rights and liberties of the unconstrained and unencumbered individual, and offering the widest possible range of individual choice as the highest political good. Any serious movement from "self" to "person," then, will necessarily have to face up to a wrenching rethinking of many of the presumptions underlying this liberalism. Few thinkers of the latter half of the twentieth century undertook that struggle more valiantly, and with more passion and honesty, than the historian Christopher Lasch, whose life journey from a Progressive to radical to post-liberal is the subject of Eric Miller's fascinating essay. Lasch's dissatisfaction with so many elements of modern American culture — its rootlessness and thoughtlessness, its crumbling families and dissociated communities, its violent cities, its exploitative economy, its disconnection from nature, its devaluation of work — led him naturally to the political Left, as the only plausible force for large-scale reform. But Lasch was soon equally unhappy with the Left, particularly for its embrace of cultural radicalism and personal liberationism, commitments he considered symptomatic of the very diseases needing to be cured. Such discontent led Lasch to revisit some of the discarded ideas of the past, and in particular to reconsider the moral effects of traditional religious faith — effects that he had hitherto, like much of his generation, dismissed. Miller's account of Lasch's intellectual journey is, in some respects, more a story of deconversion than conversion, an account of a critical intelligence that refused to be satisfied with any of the conventional wisdom on offer — very much including the conventional wisdom of the post-secular Left. He was never a religious believer in any straightforward sense, and his story gives the reader no easy and unambiguous answers in that department. He is better described, as in Miller's title, as a restless pilgrim, animated more by a moral critique of modern American life than by a precise sense of ultimate destination. That ambiguity may be precisely why his story is so valuable. Among other things, it suggests why Lasch's influence on the rising generations of writers and thinkers remains strong, and why the power of both his work and his example is likely to continue to grow in the years ahead. Eric Miller is Associate Professor of History at Geneva College, and a frequent contributor to such journals as *First Things, Christianity Today, Books and Culture,* and *The New Pantagruel.* The present essay is drawn from his ongoing work on a book-length biographical study of Christopher Lasch.

"The Soul of Man Under Secularism." It's a safe bet that not even the most astute observers of Christopher Lasch in the 1960s would have seen this, the last chapter of his last book, coming.[1]

In it Lasch returned to the subject he had taken up some thirty years earlier in *The New Radicalism in America, 1889-1963: The Intellectual as a Social Type,* the book that launched him into intellectual stardom in 1965. *The New Radicalism* was an interpretive history of twentieth-century radicalism wrapped in a bracing call for intellectuals to resist the allure of political power and return to their birthright as exemplars of "the life of reason." Intellectuals, positioned uneasily in "a world in which the irrational has come to appear not the exception but the rule," would on this vision chart the way forward with critical analyses of contemporary society that would yield more rational directions for the nation to take.[2]

Three decades later, Lasch in "The Soul of Man Under Secularism" was still monitoring the intellectuals, but from a quite different vantage. Intellectuals were still compromised, but now he declared their failure to be rooted not in their rejection of "the life of reason" but rather in their embrace of a "seductive vision of selfhood unconstrained by civic, familial, or religious obligations." Whereas in *The New Radicalism* Lasch had blamed the intellectuals' longing for political power on their devotion to "the religion of experience," he now saw their political preoccupations as the fruit of their submission to another religion: "the religion of art," a "secular religion" that had emerged from "the tradition of romantic sub-

1. "The Soul of Man Under Secularism" appears as chapter thirteen of *The Revolt of the Elites and the Betrayal of Democracy* (New York: Norton, 1995), 230-46.
2. Lasch, *The New Radicalism in America, 1889-1963: The Intellectual as a Social Type* (New York: Knopf, 1965), xvii.

jectivity." This new "ideal of personal freedom" had triumphed both politically and culturally, Lasch noted: it was in key respects the defining element of what by the 1990s had come to be known as "postmodernity."[3]

The distance between these perspectives on twentieth-century intellectuals reflects significant shifts in Lasch's understanding of human personhood. One way to frame these shifts is to state simply that Lasch moved from being an arch defender of the liberal tradition to being a severe critic of it. Coalescing as an intellectual and political tradition during the eighteenth century, liberalism has championed a vision of human progress in which the exponents of a rational, scientific apprehension of the world remake that world in such a way that human rights are protected and the related ends of equality, freedom, and material prosperity triumph. As the United States diversified ethnically and industrialized economically throughout the nineteenth century, the liberal vision gained cultural footing; in the twentieth century, it emerged triumphant. As the political theorist Michael Sandel puts it, "The public philosophy of contemporary American politics is a version of this liberal tradition of thought, and most of our debates proceed within its terms." Liberalism's triumph has increasingly meant that a primary responsibility of the state is to ensure that each individual enjoys the legal freedom to pursue his or her desired ends, apart from any normative communal or civic morality. Defining personal choice as the highest political good, the modern liberal state has cast aside the responsibility of guiding the citizenry by means of its legal structures toward a more collective, encompassing moral vision.[4]

For Lasch, liberalism, far from being a mere political philosophy, was a worldview, a tradition, a *mentalité*, a way of life that by the twentieth century had gained cultural dominance in the United States, especially among what he termed "the educated classes."[5] As over the years his unease with the liberal tradition mounted, he engaged in a sustained effort to pare away its assumptions about history and the human person, while dissecting its untoward political, cultural, and psychic effects.

It was this effort to reveal the human toll of liberalism's triumph that led to Lasch's eventual fame — or to some, infamy. By the end of his career he had earned the scorn of critics such as Louis Menand and Stephen Holmes, who took him to task for what Holmes with derision called his "anti-liberalism"; for such, Lasch, with his fierce condemnation of the political tradition that had done so much to protect and promote the formerly oppressed, was simply odd,

---

3. Lasch, *Revolt of the Elites*, 233, 231, 234, 233, 234.

4. Michael Sandel, *Democracy's Discontent: America in Search of a Public Philosophy* (Cambridge, Mass.: Harvard University Press), 5.

5. Lasch, *Revolt of the Elites*, 239.

in a faintly dangerous sort of way.[6] Strangely enough, other critics included Lasch in the very tradition that Holmes and Menand saw him as attacking; for them, any attacking of liberalism Lasch was doing was coming from within. He was, essentially, still a liberal.[7]

Lasch himself acknowledged this tension. In an interview given the summer before his death in February of 1994, he admitted that inasmuch as he had been raised a liberal he was "unavoidably" a part of that tradition; at the same time, he noted, "Some people would probably say I was more of a renegade from it." "If I seem to spend a lot of time attacking liberalism and the Left, that should be taken more as a mark of respect than one of dismissal," he stressed. "You don't bother to argue against positions that aren't worth arguing with."[8]

Lasch certainly proved unable to simply dismiss liberal modernity, and his richly provocative and deeply personal engagement with it makes his life an optic of rare worth for probing the perplexing fate of the human person in modern times.

TOWARD THE END of his life Lasch mentioned to an interviewer that he had grown up in "a very political household," a simple fact that explains much about his life and work.[9] His father, Robert Lasch, was an editorial writer for newspapers in Omaha, Chicago, and St. Louis, and his mother, Zora Schaupp Lasch, did social work, taught philosophy, and was an officer in the League of Women Voters. They were, in no uncertain terms, Democrats. They rallied to the left side of the New Deal in the 1930s, criticized the Democrats' hawkish conduct in the mid-century decades, and cheered on the Ted Kennedy wing of the party in the 1970s and 1980s. Robert Lasch was himself a distinguished presence in American political life, winning the Pulitzer Prize in 1966 for his editorial writing on Vietnam. As late as 1980 he protested President Carter's handling of the Afghanistan crisis in *Newsweek* magazine.[10]

---

6. See Stephen Holmes, *The Anatomy of Antiliberalism* (Cambridge, Mass.: Harvard University Press, 1993); Louis Menand, "Christopher Lasch's Quarrel with Liberalism," in John Patrick Diggins, ed., *The Liberal Persuasion: Arthur Schlesinger, Jr., and the Challenge of the American Past* (Princeton: Princeton University Press, 1997), 233-50.

7. Christopher Shannon, *Conspicuous Criticism: Tradition, the Individual, and Culture in American Social Thought, from Veblen to Mills,* in New Studies in American Intellectual and Cultural History series, ed. Dorothy Ross and Kenneth Cmiel (Baltimore: Johns Hopkins University Press, 1996); Eugene B. McCarraher, *Christian Critics: Religion and the Impasse in Modern American Social Thought* (Ithaca, N.Y.: Cornell University Press, 2000).

8. Casey Blake and Christopher Phelps, "History as Social Criticism: Conversations with Christopher Lasch," *Journal of American History* 80, no. 4 (March 1994): 1311.

9. Blake and Phelps, "History as Social Criticism," 1311.

10. See Robert Lasch, "Lessons of Korea and Vietnam," *Newsweek,* 18 February 1980, 23.

By the time Lasch entered Harvard as a freshman in 1950, he was already an experienced activist, having made "impassioned speeches" in school assemblies for 1948 Progressive Party presidential candidate Henry Wallace, an activity of a piece with his "flaunting" of his "atheism" at his classmates, most of whom were, he recalled, "avid young Republicans."[11] He arrived in Cambridge a self-conscious liberal, and continued the family tradition there, campaigning for Stevenson in 1952 and writing his honors thesis on the late-nineteenth-century anti-imperialists, those turn-of-the-century Americans who had the good sense to resist "the mad and uncontrollable longing after identity and adventure and power and glory" then poisoning American politics.[12]

For all of the liberal rhetoric of his college papers, though, Lasch left Harvard having begun in earnest his lifelong reckoning with the political and intellectual world of his parents. His correspondence with friends and family reflected a sustained grappling with what in one letter he called "the unforgettable heritage of a liberal upbringing."[13] An aspiring novelist (like his roommate, a young Pennsylvanian named John Updike), he wrote numerous short stories and started several novels in which the youthful protagonist seethes at the smothering certitudes of his parents and what he sees as their smug and shallow way of seeing.[14] Early on at Harvard Lasch had discovered that to his own truly great surprise, he, the young atheist who had been raised by parents whom he later described as "militant secularists," had a taste for theology.[15] When he began cautiously to express this interest to his parents, they greeted it with concern and eventually disdain. Still, the neo-orthodox flavor of the era spoke to him, and theologians like Karl Barth, Reinhold Niebuhr, and Søren Kierkegaard opened up for him an angle of vision, both on the self and on the world, that remained with him throughout his life; he remembered years later the course he took with Sydney Ahlstrom on Pauline theology as one of the "most important" of his senior year.[16] He made no religious confessions, but a gap was beginning to open up between his parents' intellectual and moral frameworks and his own maturing worldview.

---

11. Blake and Phelps, "History as Social Criticism," 1311, 1313.

12. Christopher Lasch, "Imperialism and the Indpendents: A Conflict of Allegiance" (senior honors thesis, Harvard College, 1954), 53. This thesis is housed in the Christopher Lasch Papers, Department of Rare Books and Special Collections, Rush Rhees Library, University of Rochester, Rochester, New York. Unless otherwise noted, all correspondence cited is from this collection. This collection will be referred to as CLP.

13. Christopher Lasch to Naomi Dagen, 22 January 1954, box 0, folder 34.

14. See especially box 58, CLP.

15. Blake and Phelps, "History as Social Criticism," 1313.

16. Richard Wightman Fox, "An Interview with Christopher Lasch," *The Intellectual History Newsletter* 16 (1994): 5.

Still intent on becoming a writer but unsure how or when that might happen, Lasch upon graduation enrolled in a Ph.D. program in American history at Columbia University in the fall of 1954, married Nell Commager, the daughter of Columbia historian Henry Steele Commager, in 1956, and studied the history of twentieth-century American politics with William Leuchtenburg. His dissertation, published in 1962 as *American Liberals and the Russian Revolution*, began his long public argument with the liberal tradition with a sharp-edged analysis of the intellectual history of the Progressive era. Liberalism, he explained, was fundamentally "a set of assumptions about human affairs," rooted in what he scorned as "the benevolent assumptions of the eighteenth-century Enlightenment." Especially misplaced, to him, was the confidence World War I–era liberals had in the "moral progress of the human spirit," manifested in their "refusal, under the greatest imaginable stress, to give up the optimism on which liberalism rested." Four decades on, the era had changed but the posture of American liberals remained the same. Still inspired by their lingering hope that "human reason could ultimately order the world so as to eliminate poverty, disease, discomfort and war," liberals in the 1950s were bungling their way through a time when the failure to see history and humanity clearly could well lead to unspeakable human tragedy. He faulted liberalism for being like communism in this one crucial respect: it too was "a messianic creed" that foolishly "staked everything" on its "ultimate triumph."[17]

In this line of argument Lasch was following the historian, diplomat, and architect of the doctrine of containment, George F. Kennan, in his well-publicized effort to correct the moralistic liberalism of the early part of the twentieth century with a "realism" that seemed all too necessary by the century's middle decade. But Lasch's turn toward political realism did not last long. In the early sixties, soon after beginning his teaching career, he began to distance himself from the realism of Kennan and a host of lesser cold warriors, seeing it more and more, as the decade unfolded, as an abdication to despair and cynicism as a way of life, a disquieting refusal to work toward the realization of the most central American ideals — including, especially, democracy itself. Having loosened himself from his native progressivism, he found himself gravitating not toward Kennan's Calvinism but, along with so many others, toward Marxism and the left, in search of a deeper understanding of his seemingly doomed world and a renewed hope for it.

Lasch's first serious break with liberalism, then, was his rejection of progressive politics and the political economy that had grown up with it, liberal

---

17. Lasch, *American Liberals and the Russian Revolution* (New York: Columbia University Press, 1962; reprint, New York: McGraw-Hill, 1972), vii, xvi, vii, xv, vii, xvi.

capitalism. To Lasch by the mid-sixties this political system had removed power from the people and permitted those to have it who held little regard for them or their world. Beneath this critique, he was, in moving toward Marx, embracing a different view of humanity and history than the one the progressive narrative of his youth had taught him, one in which a taste of bitter despair in the present commingled with a transcendent vision of future freedom. Marxism explained far more adequately for him than had liberalism "the human capacity for collective self-deception," as he put it in his 1969 volume *The Agony of the American Left*, but also held out hope that in the course of redistributing power "an alternative culture and vision" might emerge, one in which humans could flourish. By the late 1960s Lasch was urging socialists to embrace a "long-term effort to create a mass consciousness of the moral superiority of a socialist order," which he hoped would give birth to "a new culture, absorbing but transcending the old."[18]

This conviction of the moral necessity of a "new culture" predated Lasch's Marxist turn, and in key ways prepared the way for it. His steadily growing sense of disaffection with the culture of modernity had been building at least since his years at Columbia in the 1950s, where he had developed an almost immediate disdain for life in Manhattan. "You know what I hate most about New York?" he wrote to a friend six months into his career as a graduate student. "You can go there and not look up anybody you know." "Everybody has a furtive look as if he were likely at any moment to run smack into a friend," he continued, in a sarcastic bombast. "The man without friends is lucky. He just has to avoid strangers. But woe to the man with friends! He can never be sure that some of his friends, instead of avoiding him, may actually be looking for him."[19]

Lasch's distaste for the modern American setting and for the estate of humans within it deepened steadily in the next ten years. Immersed in the sociological literature of the postwar period, he began to decry what he in *The New Radicalism in America* termed the lack of "cohesive influences that make a society into a community," noting that "placelessness" had become one of the primary attributes of the "youth-culture."[20] In an article published in *The New England Quarterly* in 1963, he and co-author William R. Taylor portrayed this "placelessness" as a central feature of American life even in the antebellum period, and they acidly described its effects. Ordinary folk had become "victim[s] of the relentless American environment, which ripped men and women from

18. Lasch, *The Agony of the American Left* (New York: Knopf, 1969), 7, 212, 9, 212.
19. Lasch to Naomi Dagen, 28 January 1955, 0:36, CLP.
20. Lasch, *New Radicalism in America*, 69, 73, n. 5.

the safety of a predefined social context and cast them out into a world where a man was defined only by his own efforts — where every man and woman was obliged to become, in a sense more profound than those who coined the phrase may have intended, 'self-made.'"[21]

In his leftist guise Lasch tapped into a powerful explanatory framework for probing the "relentless American environment" and its social and psychic effects. A "manipulative and managerial" form of liberalism had won out in the twentieth century, he explained in 1969, fashioning a society "characterized by a high degree of uniformity which nevertheless lacks the cohesiveness and shared sense of experience that distinguish a truly integrated community from an atomistic society." Noting the "pervasive anomie of the contemporary world," and the fact that "democratic values show so little vitality," he suggested that the United States "might better be described as an empire than as a community."[22]

It was not a place he wished to live. By the late sixties he had developed a deep and sustained yearning for a world of intergenerational continuity, coherence, and stability: these elements, rapidly receding from his own world, must be at the heart of any "new culture" worth working toward; it was only under these conditions that any sort of human flourishing could take place. Returning to his own suburban Chicago high school to give a commencement address just a few days after the assassination of Robert Kennedy in June 1968, he traced the upsurge in violence at all levels of American life back to "the destruction of tradition and continuity, the forcible destruction of people's lives." "The culture is violent," he charged, "because it is a culture in which machines take precedence over people" — machines that served the less than charitable interests of a small and powerful minority: "Certain affluent white people derive tangible benefits from guns, bombs, napalm, cars, superhighways, bulldozers, and supersonic transports which impoverish the rest of the culture and make life in America for people who don't happen to be affluent and white, increasingly insupportable." Americans were thus living in a world

21. William R. Taylor and Christopher Lasch, "Two 'Kindred Spirits': Sorority and Family in New England, 1839-1846," *New England Quarterly* 36 (March 1963): 41.

22. Lasch, *Agony of the American Left*, 10, 27, 27, 29, 27. In one of his most illuminating essays from this period, Lasch argued that African Americans had developed the means to battle for civil rights precisely because of their (forced) separation from the dominant liberal culture. "The civil rights movement, in its Southern phase," he noted in 1969, "rested on the indigenous Negro subculture which has grown up since the Civil War under the peculiar conditions of Southern segregation — a culture separate and unequal but semiautonomous and therefore capable of giving its own distinctive character to the movement for legal and political equality" (*Agony of the American Left*, 119-20). He would build on this insight in the coming years, culminating in a more intricate articulation of the same thesis in *The True and Only Heaven: Progress and Its Critics* (New York: Norton, 1991).

in which "the bulldozer" had become "one of the prime instruments of official violence."[23]

This politics of intergenerational continuity made for uneasy relations with the New Left, whose general critique of the destructive dominance of white elites was of a piece with Lasch's, but whose program of revolutionary liberationist freedom grated against his own longing for what can only be called "tradition." Despite his ongoing efforts to make common cause with the student radicals during his years of teaching at Iowa (1961-1966) and Northwestern (1966-1970), he found himself, as the sixties moved along, increasingly critical of them (especially as they became increasingly critical of anyone "over thirty"). They had an "obsession with authenticity," Lasch noted, and failed to understand that "authority and discipline are not necessarily instruments of oppression." "Until it solves the problem of continuity," he contended, "the student left will be a force for disruption but not, except indirectly, for major social change." That sort of change could only come as leftists sought to connect themselves to those on the left who had gone before, probing their thinking, their triumphs, and their failures in order to develop a full-orbed political-cultural movement, one that might prove by its very example that "life under socialism would be preferable to life under corporate capitalism."[24]

Given his rejection of political liberalism and indeed the general liberal drift of twentieth-century American culture that he had already done much to make manifest, it is curious, and illuminating, that Lasch in the sixties and early seventies continued to see what he termed "liberal culture," preserved imperfectly but most fully in the university, as a crucial ingredient in the "new culture" to come.[25] He thought, for instance, that what he described as "the liberal values of self-reliance, sexual self-discipline, ambition, acquisition, and accomplishment" were still culturally and psychically necessary but in need of a radically new political and economic context that could augment and amplify them.[26] Lasch,

---

23. Lasch, commencement address given at Barrington High School, 9 June 1968, in CLP, box 12, folder 23.

24. Lasch, *Agony of the American Left*, 181, 185, 188, 199, 200. With acuity Lasch noted that even amid the violence of the sixties it was "the inscrutable sullenness of their own children," the "radical dissociation of the young from the adult world" that many citizens feared most. The "institutional links between generations" had, he sadly noted, "broken down" (*Agony of the American Left*, 30-31).

25. See Lasch's fascinating reflections in the "Notes and Bibliography" section of *The World of Nations: Reflections on American History, Politics, and Culture* (New York: Knopf, 1973), where he describes the attempt of which he was a part "to construct an ad hoc defense of liberal culture . . . that would still be distinguishable from a defense of liberalism as a political ideology" (334).

26. Lasch, *Agony of the American Left*, 209.

temperamentally cautious and conserving, was trying to preserve what he saw as best in his native liberalism: its rationalist epistemological starting point (what in a 1969 essay he termed "the rationalist tradition"), its valuing of the individual, and its belief in the necessity and possibility of a sweeping, nation-wide renewal of society and culture.[27]

Still confident in what he in *The New Radicalism* termed "the rock of rationalism," still convinced that the pursuit of "the life of reason" was central to the good life, Lasch continued to bear the imprint of his political and intellectual formation.[28] Progressivism's optimism about human nature may have been misguided and its political structures inadequate, but the essential liberal confidence in human rationality remained. It was still the last, best hope on earth. Rational, free-thinking humans could yet come together to conquer "the relentless American environment."

THE COLLAPSE OF THE LEFT in the late sixties and early seventies sent Lasch into dark retreat, from which he would emerge by the end of the decade in a very different position in American intellectual life.

"Surveying the wreckage of the sixties," he wrote his parents in the spring of 1970, "one is amazed at how little has been accomplished. Just in the last two years the outlook has changed completely." He recalled how in 1968

> Paris, Columbia, McCarthy's candidacy, Johnson's withdraw, and the emergence of Kennedy all seemed to give hope that the monolith was really beginning to break up, and that the intense political activity of the sixties, however chaotic and discordant, was going to produce important changes.

But nothing enduring had happened. After having devoted himself to various forms of activism in the sixties to the point of intellectual and psychic exhaustion — including leading teach-ins and trying to help launch a new socialist party — he sensed that the seventies might be a time for more thinking and less agitating.[29] In a telling confession in 1973 to a professor at the University of Vir-

27. Lasch and Eugene Genovese, "The Education and University We Need Now," *New York Review of Books*, 9 October 1969, 27.

28. Lasch, *New Radicalism in America*, 11, xvii.

29. Christopher Lasch to Robert Lasch and Zora Schaupp Lasch, 26 March 1970, 0:38. In this letter Lasch added, "In my case the occasion seems to call for an abandonment of political activities and occasional political writing and an effort to get down to fundamentals . . . undistracted by political alarums and excursions." See also his opening statement in a *New York Review* essay in the fall of 1971: "An interminable war in Indochina; the revolutionary movement elsewhere in disarray; the American left fragmented and driven on the defensive; Nixon acting belatedly but with apparent success to disarm his opponents; public services in decline; the

ginia, he admitted that he felt not only distanced from the left "but from the modern world in general — the same way I always felt, only more so."[30]

It was the liberationist direction that post-sixties America took with such gleeful haste that had heightened Lasch's disaffection and shifted his attention from politics to culture, in concert with thousands of other activists and intellectuals. If the sixties radicals had been in the vanguard of anything, the seventies were proving, it wasn't national politics but personal morality. Lasch found himself in the uneasy and unusual position of having been in agreement with the radicals regarding the former but in opposition regarding the latter, and for him this was no inconsequential difference. Writing to one defender of the counterculture in 1969, he opined that "Hedonism, self-expression, doing your own thing, dancing in the streets, drugs, and sex are a formula for political impotence and a new despotism, in which a highly educated elite through its mastery of the technological secrets of a modern society rule over an indolent population which has traded self-government for self-expression."[31] Democracy, in Lasch's view, demanded of the citizenry a discipline and a posture that the counterculture had declared passé. Personal "liberation" would lead only to the continued entrenchment of the manipulative and managerial liberal capitalism he had long been decrying.

For Lasch, these broadsides against what he began to call "cultural radicalism" were not simply abstract concerns driven by ideological ends. He later revealed that his turn in the 1970s toward the study of culture, the family, and personhood was rooted most deeply in his "experience as a husband and father"; he referred especially to "the unexpectedly rigorous business of bringing up children" amid the spectacular moral upheaval of the age.[32] He and Nell, like so many of their generation, had married young and had four children in rapid succession; by 1970 their oldest was twelve, and the youngest five. His sense of discouragement as a father led him to vow, in a moving letter to his parents

quality of public discussion lower than ever; demoralization and drift on every side — the political scene has seldom looked more dreary. Only three years ago the glacial rigidity of American politics appeared to be breaking up . . . . Columbia, Paris, the dumping of Johnson seemed so many proofs that the diverse strands making up the new left had finally coalesced as a movement, a political force." But he continued, "Now it appears that the new left, even in the moment of its apparent triumphs, has already passed the peak of its influence. The Chicago convention was an end rather than a beginning." Lasch, "Can the Left Rise Again," *New York Review of Books*, 21 October 1971, 36.

30. Lasch to Dante Germino, 9 June 1973, 3:12.

31. Lasch to Martin Duberman, 20 May 1969, 2:14. Duberman had expressed his hope in the counter culture in his review of *Agony of the American Left* in the *New York Times Book Review*, 23 March 1969, 34.

32. Lasch, *True and Only Heaven*, 31, 33.

written in 1970, that he was "determined to try to provide my children with some inner resources against the contemporary madness, the youth culture, and the enormous temptations to cynicism and despair."[33] The foundations of family life in America were shaking, giving a tense, edgy quality to all familial relations. In a deceptively breezy letter written in 1972 to John Updike, he expressed with a telling anecdote his growing unease: "Because almost everyone I know has been divorced at least once, I have taken to calling mine, with an arrogance that as always provides rich satisfaction but does not amuse the other members of the family, 'the last marriage.'" He supposed that "Others who cling to this obviously archaic mode of reproduction doubtless experience similar feelings of historical obsolescence."[34]

Groping for ways to understand and counter the liberationist direction of the 1970s and searching for "inner resources," he, somewhat surprisingly, turned back in the direction of the Protestant theology he had encountered at Harvard; this time the author he found himself reading was Jacques Ellul, the Protestant sociologist, theologian, and leftist whose book *The Technological Society* had won a broad readership in the United States upon its publication in English in 1964. In an article published in 1970, Lasch followed Ellul in arguing that what radicals — and Americans in general — most needed was a fundamentally different understanding of freedom. Whereas the "cultural radicals" were determined to "seek salvation in drugs, sexual liberation, and communal arrangements," Lasch noted, Ellul proffered a different vision of freedom, one that by necessity included such elements as "privacy, order, and continuity," the centrality of "the family," and the "belief that institutionalized tension should be clearly present in human affairs." Ellul's understanding of liberty, sourced in what Lasch termed "Christian humanism," enabled him, on Lasch's reading, "to see the modern obsession with personal liberation as itself a symptom of pervasive spiritual disorder." It was the "*creation* of order," rather than mere "revolutionary violence," that radicals must pursue. No radical shift in political economy could ipso facto create the good society that revolutionaries had in mind; just social structures were impossible apart from properly ordered selves. The fate of the person and the fate of the society were intricately intertwined.[35]

Unlike Ellul, Lasch was not a Christian, making the conceptual frameworks and ecclesiastical traditions of Ellul of limited worth to his own project. Searching for the means to develop an understanding of human freedom rich

33. Lasch to Robert Lasch and Zora Schaupp Lasch, 26 March 1970, 0:38.

34. Lasch to John Updike, 6 November 1972, 3:10.

35. Lasch, "The Social Thought of Jacques Ellul," in *World of Nations*, 274, 276, 292. In a 1974 letter he mentioned, cryptically, that he considered this piece one of his best essays. See Lasch to Linda Smithson, 4 December 1974, 3:19.

enough to sustain both a communal way of life and the dignity of the person within the community, he continued to probe the rationalist tradition, looking for a counterpoint to the regnant liberationist individualism. Eventually, it was Freud, a towering presence in the modern rationalist tradition, who seemed along with Marx to hold out the most promise. Melded together in Lasch's mind, Marx and Freud yielded a somewhat quixotic and perplexing combination: a social vision that was intensely communal but a human psychology that was anything but utopian.

Lasch was no stranger to Freud in the 1970s. Indeed, to be educated in the humanities and social sciences at Harvard and Columbia in the middle decades of the century was to be influenced by both Freud and Marx. In particular, Lasch, along with so many other young radicals in the 1960s, had fallen under the influence of the Frankfurt School, whose synthesis of Freud and Marx had provided Marxism, as he later wrote, "with a serious theory of culture," one that emphasized the baleful dominance of industrial capitalism in western nations even as it pointed hopefully toward the possibility of a psychologically satisfying human liberation emerging dialectically from the heart of the dominated cultures.[36] In the midst of his leftward turn, Lasch took seriously this body of social thought; in a strenuous course in "Twentieth Century Social Theory in the U.S." offered at Iowa in 1964 he had students read Frankfurt philosopher and New Left hero Herbert Marcuse, along with Thorstein Veblen, Randolph Bourne, C. Wright Mills, and others.[37]

In his post-sixties quest to find cultural and psychic rooting for "the new culture," the Frankfurt School's analytic method and vision of domination continued to influence him, even as he began to reject the liberationist elements of its worldview. Lasch continued to believe that humans require a deeply communal experience to achieve personal and social freedom, but it was Freud's insight into the fundamental limits that plague humans in their questing for that freedom that he ended up seizing on most fiercely. As Americans in the 1970s were enthusiastically embracing an array of pathways to freedom — pop psychology, sexual liberation, revolutionary politics, therapeutic religion — Lasch sought to take Freud's more stoic vision of the human prospect to the masses. Freud, he carefully instructed in the *New York Times Magazine* in 1976, had defined "the human mind as the product of an unrelenting struggle between instinct and culture." Since on this view "the miseries of existence" were unavoidable, it only followed that those who denied the fundamentally divided condition of the self

36. Lasch, *True and Only Heaven*, 29.

37. Syllabus for "History 16-273, Twentieth Century Social Theory in the U.S.," dated September 1964, in box 44, folder 1, CLP.

would end up groping toward the sorts of "sweeping spiritual consolations" that would make them the easy objects of corporate and state manipulation. In the face of such shallow and dangerous hopes, Lasch championed Freud's "skepticism about spiritual transformation and about psychoanalysis as its agent."[38] The tensions inherent in human experience and responsible for a good measure of our pain and suffering needed to be not dissolved but embraced for any true personal, political, and cultural advance to take place. America's progressive optimism about the human condition was actually regressive.

Of course, progressive assumptions of all sorts underlay much of what Lasch saw as malign in the 1970s, and so with seasoned, simmering prophetic verve, he emerged from his quiet years to meet modern, progressive America head-on. The two books he published at the end of the seventies were among the most potent salvos in the culture wars that had begun to convulse American life in the wake of the sixties.

*Haven in a Heartless World: The Family Besieged,* published in 1977, had, according to Lillian Rubin's review in *Society,* become "a verbal Rorschach test" for intellectuals and activists, uncovering "a special place where rage and fear hide."[39] Savaged by the left for his traditionalist perspective on the family (one reviewer dismissed *Haven* as "a crusty example of male backlash"[40]) and applauded uneasily by conservatives (who were not sure what to do with his contention that capitalism worked *against* their traditionalist vision[41]), Lasch had become a true maverick in the polarized world of late-twentieth-century America.

The controversy surrounding *Haven* prepared the way for an even more heady response to 1979's *The Culture of Narcissism: American Life in an Age of Diminishing Expectations.* Within weeks of its publication *Time* and *Newsweek* had each devoted articles to it; *Time* even featured a picture of a grim Lasch leaning against a fence outside of their newly purchased house in Pittsford, New York, just south of Rochester, where he was teaching at the time. The picture matched the tone of the article: "Like a biblical prophet," the author began, "Christopher Lasch appears at the gates of our culture with dire pronouncements."[42] In two months the book sold 26,000 cloth-bound copies, and paper-

38. Lasch, "Sacrificing Freud," *New York Times Magazine,* 22 February 1976, 71, 72.

39. Lillian B. Rubin, review of *Haven in a Heartless World: The Family Besieged* (New York: Basic Books, 1977) in *Society* (March/April 1979): 98.

40. Adrienne Harris and Edward Shorter, "Besieging Lasch," *Theory and Society* 6, no. 2 (September 1978): 279, 291-92.

41. See George Gilder, "The Therapeutic State," *National Review,* 17 February 1978, 220; Robert Crunden, "Enemies of Civilized Life," *Modern Age* 22, no. 3 (Summer 1978): 330.

42. Valerie Lloyd, "Me, Me, Me," *Newsweek,* 22 January 1979, 75; R. Z. Sheppard, "The Pursuit of Happiness," *Time,* 8 January 1979, 76.

back rights were almost immediately auctioned off. Less than two months later cloth-bound sales had reached 45,000.[43]

What had he said? He launched *Haven* with a timely but disarming question: "Why has family life become so painful, marriage so fragile, relations between parents and children so full of hostility and recrimination?" His answer formed a thesis both simple and alarming: Democratic freedom depends on tightly knit families that consist of a husband, wife, children, and, ideally, a larger kinship network; without these relationships, children never develop sufficient psychic strength to resist the powerful forces of state and economy and actually become citizens. By the 1970s, Lasch argued, the basic structures of family life in America had collapsed, due largely to corporate capitalism's relentless invasion of the home. Fathers and mothers were abandoning the home for both work and play, and their children were left to be formed by others far less able: the university-trained elites working in what he scathingly termed "the helping professions," marketers and advertisers, and the youth culture. This was not the pathway to maturity for either parents or children. Both mothers and fathers needed to be at home *making* a home — for their sake and for the sake of democracy.[44]

In *The Culture of Narcissism*, Lasch continued with a starkly etched psychological portrait of the new non-citizen that the liberal capitalist state was yielding. Capitalism's "new kind of paternalism," he contended, had by the 1970s weakened dramatically the ability of Americans to act as individuals; lacking the "inner resources" that could be nurtured only in the family, the typical American desperately turned to persons and institutions beyond the family to prop up his or her own neglected and underdeveloped self. The result was the "narcissist": one whose "apparent freedom from family ties and institutional constraints" merely "contributes to his insecurity, which he can overcome only by seeing his 'grandiose self' reflected in the attentions of others, or by attaching himself to those who radiate celebrity, power, and charisma." Perniciously, the widespread narcissistic tendency quashed the very elements democratic renewal required, including the inner strength and clarity of vision that might make possible a collective attack against capitalism's destructive social structures. Fragile, delicate, and weaker than they believed themselves to be, humans needed just the right conditions in order to thrive, conditions that capitalism certainly could not produce, as evidenced by the emergence of the narcissist, with his repressed rage against authority and inability to touch and shape the

43. Lasch to Robert Lasch and Zora Schaupp Lasch, 6 March 1979; Lasch to Robert Lasch and Zora Schaupp Lasch, 22 April 1979.

44. Lasch, *Haven in a Heartless World*, xvi.

actual world of culture and politics. Locked within himself, the narcissist was unable to break loose from his solitary cell, and so had nothing to offer to the building of "the decent society." Diabolically, this was the only kind of person the liberal capitalist state was capable of forming.[45]

While the public bought tens of thousands of copies of these books, critics took turns taking shots at them, with the usual mixture of applause, envy, and insight. They came at Lasch from widely varying points of view, but they made one salient point over and over: for all of his keen perception of the American circumstance, Lasch had little to point *toward*. In the succinct judgment of one reviewer, Lasch was "very long on acid distaste for our time, and very short on transforming visions."[46]

In the aftermath of his remarkable achievement in these two books, Lasch found himself confronted with a looming question: was his morally conservative variant of Freudian Marxism sufficient philosophically, politically, or personally? Did this tradition furnish him with a worldview sufficiently capacious and rich to underpin his vision of human flourishing? Jean Bethke Elshtain, who in later years would become one of Lasch's closest friends and allies, thought not. In her review of *Haven*, published in 1979 in *Commonweal*, she disdained the overwhelming presence of "culprits and malefactors" in the book, and incisively underscored her quarrel with his overarching worldview: in his account of the forces besieging the family, democracy, and humanity itself, Lasch, remarkably, "could not go on to proffer any hope that private virtue might flourish despite all and the beleaguered family might survive." The strange irony, she thought, was that those who were "credulous" enough to accept Lasch's depiction of the family in contemporary America would actually abet a "further erosion of the family's normative significance coupled with the extension, paradoxically, of precisely that brutalization of social life Lasch himself indicts as characteristic of our age."[47]

What he most fundamentally needed, Elshtain and other critics seemed to suggest, was a more satisfying solution to the problem of *goodness:* a more convincing elaboration of the moral possibilities of the age and race, one that moved beyond pathology toward health. Lasch could not abide what he termed the "hedonism" of the "cultural radicals"; the good life, whatever it was, certainly did not abide in unrestrained submission to base impulses. He supported this belief by recourse to Freud; yet for all of his immersion in Freud, Marx, and

45. Lasch, *The Culture of Narcissism: American Life in an Age of Diminishing Expectations* (New York: Norton, 1979), 218, 210, 10, xv.

46. Allen Lacy, "Visions of Narcissus in a Decadent World," *The Chronicle of Higher Education,* 22 January 1979, R-12.

47. Jean Bethke Elshtain, "Under the Lasch," *Commonweal,* 16 March 1979, 155.

others in their train, he still found himself searching for adequate ways to underpin his vision of the good life. But where could he go for help?

In an effort to spur him to reconsider the nature of the human person, Elshtain in her review had commended to Lasch the work of the prolific Harvard psychologist Robert Coles, who, she noted, possessed the virtue of "treating us to complex, thickly textured portraits of real human beings, men, women, and children in real social locations, living in and through genuine political and moral crisis."[48] As it turns out, Lasch was already reading Coles; one year before Elshtain's *Haven* review appeared, Lasch's review of Coles's *Privileged Ones: The Well-Off and the Rich in America* had been published in *Psychology Today*. Among other things, Lasch found in Coles's research evidence for his own understanding of human maturity as essentially a struggle. "I can think of no other book that demonstrates so vividly why growing up, under any circumstances, has to be regarded as above all a process of accommodation, compromise, and renunciation," Lasch wrote approvingly.[49]

Lasch had struck a chord with Coles as well. Coles was among the reviewers who had found much to heed in *Narcissism*, and he published a long, meditative review of it in *The New Yorker* in August of 1979. Stressing that the argument for pervasive narcissism was indeed rooted in "a growing psychoanalytic literature," he commended Lasch as "one who has looked back hard and looked around keenly," and he added his voice to Lasch's. "We possess no larger, compelling vision that is worth any commitment of energy and time," Coles lamented. "We shun the elderly, reminders of our own mortality. We worship super-athletes, promoted by endless and sometimes corrupt schemes. We cultivate postures — ironic cynicism, skeptical distance — meant to keep us from the inevitable difficulties of human involvement." In short, wrote Coles, "We play it cool, play it fast, and, in the clutch, place our faith in lotions and powders and soaps and dyes and surgical procedures so that we can stay — we hope, we pray — in the game as long as possible." Did Coles have a cultural and moral corrective to offer that might move beyond Lasch? He suggested, softly, that religion, far from being "a joke," or "inconsequential," or just "a mere ritual," provided a means of combating the prevailing narcissistic direction.[50]

It was a view Lasch was beginning to warm up to. In the face of the attacks of left-wing reviewers who viewed with alarm Lasch's seeming affection for aspects of the "bourgeois" American Protestant past — his advocacy for the tra-

48. Elshtain, "Under the Lasch," 156.

49. Lasch, "To Be Young, Rich, and Entitled," *Psychology Today,* March 1978, 124, 126.

50. Robert Coles, "Unreflecting Egoism," *New Yorker,* 27 August 1979, 98, 104, 103. For Coles's account of the friendship that later developed between Lasch, Elshtain, and himself, see his "Remembering Christopher Lasch," *New Oxford Review* (September 1994): 16-19.

ditional family, for instance, and his antipathy toward "hedonism" — Lasch had found himself, curiously, unable to dismiss it. In fact, in the aftermath of *Narcissism* he ended up enlarging its place in his social vision. Invariably, this turned him toward a more careful consideration of the religious roots of the civilization that he was trying, idiosyncratically, to defend.[51]

As he was pressed on the matter of "religion" and its connection to the cultural crisis he was describing, Lasch more and more began to speak in favor of it — something he had not done in any significant way in *Haven* or *Narcissism*. Invited to participate with the British author Henry Farlie in a "National Town Meeting" on "The Me Decade: Narcissism in America" in 1979 at the John F. Kennedy Performing Arts Center in Washington, Lasch took part in a question-and-answer session that followed their presentations. When a member of the audience asked Farlie, who had just published *The Seven Deadly Sins Today,* whether the "elimination of a supreme being" had helped to foster the current narcissism, Farlie responded that indeed, "Western civilization without its god is a very anchorless, drifting thing." Lasch, surprisingly, professed that he agreed, and added that for all of the wisdom that the great nineteenth-century thinkers like Freud and Marx had brought to bear on human history, they displayed what he referred to as a "blind spot" by disregarding religion. Their failure to find a place for religion in their understanding of the human prospect "begins to look very old-fashioned," remarked Lasch, and "exposes the limits" of their thought. He made it clear that he was not urging a return to the Christian church, though, so much as a "new worldview" that might enfold the insights of Christianity within a more critical framework. But religion, he insisted, was indispensable for cultural and political health: "Religion is the substitute for religion," he averred; to be rid of it was both impossible and undesirable.[52]

In the aftermath of the *Narcissism* phenomenon Lasch stood uneasily by his rationalist conception of human experience, even as he enlarged it to include a more self-consciously religious component. He criticized the sociologist Philip Rieff's "resort to religious categories" in a 1979 lecture at Columbia University that he had attended. Rieff's use of religion, he wrote to a friend in dismay, was "not backed up by any sensitivity to the sociology and psychology of religion." He continued, interestingly, by acknowledging the bind he found himself in. "In stating these objections," mused Lasch, "I suppose I am merely falling into the

51. See especially Norman Birnbaum's 1975 interview with Lasch, in which Lasch remarked that the "personality" that had been developed in the West, notwithstanding its "pathological side effects," was "irreplaceable." Lasch and Norman Birnbaum, "America Today: An Exchange," *Partisan Review* 42, no. 3 (1975): 365.

52. Audio tape, "The Me Decade," in the Library of Congress, in the Recorded Sound Reference Center of the Madison Building, Washington, D.C.

critical style that Rieff deplores, not without reason." But he was at a loss to discern how to move beyond critical rationalism's way of framing and explaining religion, and life in general: "I don't see any alternative short of a full-scale restoration of Christian theology that is intellectually untenable." He was stymied.[53]

LASCH, IT TURNS OUT, wasn't done with religion, due in part to shifts that were taking place in his thinking; as he later put it, by the early 1980s his "politics were in the course of changing." Preparing to give the Freud lectures at the University of London in 1981, he discovered that he was "sick of psychoanalysis."[54] And as Freud fell, so fell Marx. Through his writings in journals such as *Salmagundi* and the short-lived but historically significant journal *democracy* in the early eighties, he sought for ways to maintain fidelity to what he continued to see as indispensable in the tradition of the left while rejecting "cultural radicalism" and a rather singular commitment to Marx.

The ways in which his politics were changing were subtle, but of a piece with the larger shifts taking place in American intellectual life in the 1980s, as postmodern assumptions and sensibilities began to alter whole disciplines and rearrange alliances. Having been a defender and exponent of the "rationalist tradition" throughout the 1970s, Lasch in the eighties began to rethink the basic epistemic assumptions that lay beneath his worldview; he was especially affected by his reading of two looming figures of the decade, Richard Rorty and Alasdair MacIntyre. Both argued persuasively that the Enlightenment's foundationalist project was dead, which helped Lasch understand his own waning confidence in figures such as Freud and Marx. Rorty spoke for a secular pragmatism, while MacIntyre wrote as an ex-Marxist turned Thomist; Lasch listened intently to both. What he seemed mainly to take away from them and others was an increasing desire to listen to past human perceptions of the world, rather than to turn so confidently to "analysis" of it, as had been his usual method. His writings began to focus not so much on the "conditions" that might lead to cultural and personal transformation as on the actual people to whose political and moral traditions he found himself attracted. In effect, this led to his moving in the direction Elshtain had urged him to take, one that probed with more nuance and even respect the historical particularities of human experience, focusing less on abstractions like "society" and more on the lives of those who comprised societies.[55]

53. Lasch to Robert Boyers, 27 February 1979, 5:3.
54. Fox, "An Interview with Christopher Lasch," 13.
55. For Lasch's mid-1980s perspective on MacIntyre and "communitarianism," see Lasch, "The Communitarian Critique of Liberalism," *Soundings* 69, nos. 1-2 (Spring/Summer 1986): 60-76.

This postmodern moment, gaining strength in the eighties, brought with it a neo-traditionalism that splashed across American society and culture, including the academy but extending well beyond it. A genuine (if mild) longing among Americans to restore their rapidly eroding connections to their own past surfaced at large, as seen in instances as varied as the nostalgia-soaked rhetoric of Ronald Reagan, the self-consciously traditional jazz of Wynton Marsalis, the popularity of Ken Burns's documentaries on the Civil War, and books like E. D. Hirsch's *Cultural Literacy,* Robert Bellah's *Habits of the Heart,* and Allan Bloom's *The Closing of the American Mind.* Following in train, American academics, in the process of abandoning universal categories of human experience for the particularities of place and time, began embracing with a certain ardor the analytic category of "tradition." Scholars began to see in the past not fodder for analysis so much as a body of experience to absorb; consequently, the words spoken (and written) by a people became the object of more intense scrutiny. As confidence in scientific approaches to apprehending human behavior diminished, scholars began directing their inquiries (with their wildly varying philosophical starting points) toward the ways in which humans have used language to construct "meaning." What people *said* became central, once more, to understanding what they *did.*[56]

In the midst of this seismic shift, Lasch ended up deepening his own sense of connection to a movement and a people about which he had written with a sense of affinity almost from the start of his career: the Populists. In rediscovering the Populists, he found a way to expand and advance his quest for a culture more nourishing of human ideals and ends. While in the rationalist guise of the objective critic, Lasch had at the height of the sixties attempted to point leftists toward the Populists as a sort of case study, in the hope that they might avoid the Populists' errors and build upon their virtues.[57] Now he moved off his analytic perch and actually embraced them (at least in his writings), connecting himself in a self-conscious way to what he began to describe as the "populist tradition." In the 1980s Lasch became both a student and an advocate of this "populist tradition," which he now understood as emerging from the republicanism of the early modern period and continuing on into the twentieth century in the culture of the lower middle class, with its native wariness of the lifestyle of the placeless, careerist, professional classes, and its deeply embedded

56. For an essay that illumines how this general postmodern critique affected the practice of intellectual history, see John E. Toews, "Intellectual History After the Linguistic Turn: The Autonomy and the Irreducibility of Experience," *American Historical Review* 92 (October 1987): 879-907. See also Eric Miller, "Intellectual History After the Earthquakes: A Study in Discourse," *History Teacher* 30, no. 3 (May 1997): 357-371.

57. Lasch, "The Decline of Populism," in *Agony of the American Left,* 3-31.

consciousness of the abiding presence of goodness at the center of the uni-verse.[58] Over against either the left or right species of liberal individualism he, as populist, proposed a politics rooted in long-term membership in particular communities, in opposition to a rootless society defined merely, in his words, by "individual rights, contractual relations, and the primacy of justice." Both left and right, he believed, failed to understand that the self gains its sense of identity and strength by being "situated in and constituted by tradition," by ex-periencing "membership in a historically rooted community." For those with this understanding of the good life, populism, he contended, was the tradition to which to appeal for communal support and a usable past.[59]

In embracing the Populists Lasch took their religious thinking and experi-ence seriously, understanding it to be integral to that which was drawing him to their politics. In his 1984 volume *The Minimal Self: Psychic Survival in Troubled Times* he had tentatively suggested that "psychoanalysis recaptures some of the deepest insights of the Judaeo-Christian tradition," including "the definition of selfhood as tension, division, and conflict."[60] He now found within this popu-list tradition thinkers (among them, per Lasch, Jonathan Edwards, Thomas Carlyle, Orestes Brownson, and Martin Luther King Jr.) whose meditations on these themes stood in striking opposition to the wishful and finally futile incli-nations of progressives to try to dissolve the fundamental tensions of human existence through means technological, economic, chemical, or therapeutic. In his last books, *The True and Only Heaven: Progress and Its Critics* (1991) and *The Revolt of the Elites* (1994) Lasch went so far as to root his convictions on self-hood and human history in metaphysical confession. Glossing Edwards, for in-

58. Lasch summarizes his new vantage point in the preface to *True and Only Heaven*, 13-17. It was this broader populist tradition that had helped to foster what in a memorable 1975 essay he had termed "the plebeian revolt against modernity," in which ordinary Americans had re-sisted by a variety of means what he termed "cultural modernism" and its way of life "based on technique, critical self awareness, and the refinement of exact knowledge." Lasch contended that the "cultural civil war" taking shape in the mid-seventies was simply the latest development in this long conflict that had its roots in the nineteenth century, when the Populists raised their timely protest of the industrial capitalists' destruction of their way of life. See Lasch, "The De-mocratization of Culture: A Reappraisal," *Change* 7, no. 6 (Summer 1975): 14-23.

59. Lasch, "What's Wrong with the Right," *Tikkun* 1, no. 1 (1986): 27, 29; Lasch, "A Reply To My Critics," *Tikkun* 1, no. 2 (1986): 94, 95, 96, 97. As he put it in a letter to *Tikkun* editor Michael Kazin, trying to convince him to take the magazine in a self-consciously populist (and not "pro-gressive") direction, populism had "always put more emphasis on restoration and renewal, on the fulfillment of old promises, old covenants, than on 'making it new.' It doesn't endorse the il-lusion that the past doesn't count, that individuals or societies can start all over again whenever they feel like it." Lasch to Michael Lerner, 25 July 1987, 7a:18.

60. Lasch, *The Minimal Self: Psychic Survival in Troubled Times* (New York: Norton, 1984), 301, 258.

stance, Lasch remarked that "Man has no claim to God's favor, and a 'grateful good will' has to be conceived, accordingly, not as an appropriate acknowledgement of the answer to our prayers, so to speak, but as the acknowledgment of God's life-giving power to order things as he pleases, without 'giving any account of his matters,' as Edwards put it."[61] But unlike Edwards and other orthodox Christians in this lineage, and much like post-Protestants Ralph Waldo Emerson and William James, whom he discussed with subtlety and admiration, Lasch in the end, despite his deepening appreciation of religion and even his own emerging religious beliefs, stood outside of a historical, ecclesiastically embodied religion.[62] While advocating "religion" in general and, as one critic noted, displaying a sense of affinity for Calvinism, he continued to remain distant from any sort of creedal or confessional identity.[63]

Still, he got as much critical leverage as possible from this long-emerging religious stance for his continued assault on the destructive effects of the liberal capitalist order on human flourishing. Amidst the triumph of corporate capitalism, he had argued in 1984, Americans had executed a widespread "emotional retreat from the long-term commitments that presuppose a stable, secure, and orderly world." This retreat, he believed, had jeopardized "selfhood" itself, since much of what selfhood requires — including "a personal history, friends, family, a sense of place" — had become increasingly difficult to maintain.[64] By the early 1990s he had concluded that Americans had acquiesced in this retreat with less than admirable motives. The emergence of suburbia offered a telling example. "Suburban life, organized around the shopping mall rather than the neighborhood, eradicated the last vestiges of reciprocal obligation, neighborly or familial; and it is important to see that this was precisely what made it attractive. It was not just the lure of green lawns and open spaces that drew people to the suburbs but the dream of perfect freedom." Americans, captive by this time to the liberal "equation of freedom with choice," were bent on escaping a way of life rooted in the necessity and desirability of "trust and mutual obligation."[65]

61. Lasch, *Revolt of the Elites*, 245.

62. In the bibliographical essay of *True and Only Heaven*, Lasch calls Emerson "the central figure" of the book (546).

63. In his review of *True and Only Heaven*, Richard Wightman Fox surmised that Lasch "has vigorously rejected Marxism, has gratefully embraced Judeo-Christian (read 'Calvinist') wisdom about human nature and destiny, and is enthusiastically devoted to the democratic 'populist' tradition in American thought and life" ("Lasching Liberalism," *Christian Century*, 11 March 1992, 281-82).

64. Lasch, *Minimal Self*, 15, 16.

65. Lasch, *Women and the Common Life: Love, Marriage, and Feminism*, ed. Elisabeth Lasch-Quinn (New York: Norton, 1997), 104, 105, 103.

This "suburban ideal," of a piece with so much else that was troubling in modern liberal society, was not just barren, Lasch warned, but dangerous. Dissolving and deferring obligations with unsettling ease, it was perpetrating a way of seeing that failed to apprehend a vast and looming psychological and ecological devastation. Rather than understanding themselves to be creatures with inherent limitations living on a planet whose fragility required studied care, the more "educated" (and thus powerful) of westerners were living with a lonely recklessness that both denied and defied their nature as humans and the habitat upon which all — rich and poor — were dependent. Speaking in a self-consciously prophetic vein, in the religious language that lay at the heart of the West, Lasch proposed the need for a "politics of limits" in *The Daily Telegraph* of London in December 1986. "We need to impose limits not only on economic growth and technological development," he wrote, "but on human pretensions and pride. A politics of limits entails the abandonment of the whole ideology of progress and the recovery and restatement of old religious insights, ones that stress the finitude of human powers and intelligence."[66]

In his journey from critical rationalism toward Christian tradition, Lasch had come to believe that of the many conceits that plague moderns, the most insidious was the smug confidence that they had evaded their basic state of dependence: dependence upon one another, dependence upon the earth, dependence upon a creator. Convinced now that "rebellion against God is the natural reaction to the discovery that the world was not made for our personal convenience," Lasch in that final essay, "The Soul of Man Under Secularism," suggested that autonomous, independent moderns "find it galling to be reminded of their dependence on a power beyond their own control or at least beyond the control of humanity in general." Taking their dependent estate as an offense rather than as a touchstone, moderns had developed an economic-technological apparatus that made dependence on anything else seem unnecessary, unreal, even blasphemous. It was this illusion — "the illusion of mastery" — that was proving to be so tenacious, and so deadly. "If the whole world now seems to be going through a dark night of the soul," he wrote, "it is because the normal rebellion against dependence appears to be sanctioned by our scientific control over nature, the same progress of science that has allegedly destroyed religious superstition."[67]

By the time he wrote this passage, such "superstition" had, for Lasch, become anything but. Rather, the religious heritage of his civilization had become

---

66. Lasch, *Women and the Common Life,* 119; Lasch, "The Politics of Limits," *The Daily Telegraph* (London), 16 December 1986, 16.

67. Lasch, *Revolt of the Elites,* 244, 245, 246.

a source of spiritual and intellectual ballast, a means of discerning our deepest identity and guiding us toward more satisfying ends. "If progressive ideologies have dwindled down to a wistful hope that things will somehow work out for the best," he wrote in 1991, "we need to recover a more vigorous form of hope." The message Lasch delivered as he pointed toward that recovery inspires precisely the vigor and hope he spent his life pursuing. For any seeking to move beyond modern, liberal conceptions of personhood, a study of that message is a promising place to begin.[68]

68. Lasch, *True and Only Heaven*, 530.

# IV. STRUCTURES

# Religion and Education
# in the Young Republic

Daniel Walker Howe

Education, if it is to be more than mere vocational training, must always be an instrument of character formation. And character formation can never be procedural or neutral; it always presumes a particular set of virtues and vices, goods and evils, excellences and deficiencies, which in turn reflect certain generally approved social ends. Small wonder that so many of the greatest Western philosophers, from Plato to Dewey, have concerned themselves directly with educational issues, since our ideas about the optimal formation of the human character cannot help but be of central importance in any effort to understand the proper means and ends of human existence. Small wonder, too, that questions of educational philosophy and objectives have so often proven to be political flashpoints in modern American history, particularly insofar as these questions involve the equally conflicted issue of the proper place of religion in public life. This essay by Daniel Walker Howe brings together both matters. It serves to underscore how important questions of education were to political and cultural leaders in the formative years of the American republic. And it also shows how differently the proper relationship between religion and education was conceived of in those years. Should education be provided by a free public system operating under strictly secular state-sponsored auspices? Do religious institutions have any role to play in the education of citizens? As Howe shows, the answers to these questions in antebellum America were almost exactly the opposite of the answers that would be given today. It is no simple matter, however, to discern what this fact means. Is it simply another example of the many ways that the American experiment had to outgrow its origins in order to achieve a fuller maturity? Or does it suggest how

This essay is a revised and expanded version of "Church, State, and Education in the Young American Republic," *Journal of the Early Republic* 22 (Spring 2002): 1-24.

difficult it is for the nation's public educational systems to flourish in isolation from, or even in opposition to, its other character-forming institutions? How then should American educational institutions proceed, if they are to produce citizens capable of continuing America's great experiment in self-governance? Howe's essay is a powerfully evocative slice of evidence from the American past, bearing on that very question. Daniel Walker Howe has recently retired from his position as the Rhodes Professor of American History at Oxford University, and is the author of numerous distinguished works of American history, including *The Political Culture of the American Whigs* (Chicago, 1979) and *Making the American Self* (Harvard, 1997).

Thomas Jefferson's tombstone bears the inscription he composed for it, identifying him as "Author of the Declaration of American Independence, of the Statute of Virginia for religious freedom, & Father of the University of Virginia." Of the great man's many achievements and services to his country, he selected these three as the ones by which "I wish most to be remembered."[1] Self-government, religious freedom, and public education: all were fundamental to American republicanism as he defined it. Jefferson believed that the disestablishment of religion, freeing the mind from "monkish ignorance and superstition," would firmly ground "the blessings and security of self-government" in "the unbounded exercise of reason."[2] He fought hard to create tuition-free secular elementary schools in Virginia and to keep his infant university free from any religious presence. But the general history of American education to the mid-nineteenth century did not confirm Jefferson's hopes and expectations; in practice, state-sponsored secular education did not provide the foundation for American republicanism. In principle, the Enlightenment presupposed a state strong enough to take responsibility for popular education. In American practice, the state significantly defaulted on this obligation.

On the other hand, organized Christianity continued to play a much more active role in American life than Jefferson had expected. Often religious freedom turned out to mean freedom *for* religion rather than freedom *from* religion. Indeed, religious institutions sometimes proved more effective means for Americans to exercise their self-government than did political ones. Religion

1. Thomas Jefferson, "Epitaph" (1826), *Writings*, ed. Merrill D. Peterson (New York: Library of America, 1984), 706.
2. Thomas Jefferson to Roger C. Weightman, 24 June 1826, *Writings*, ed. Peterson, 1517.

figured prominently in defining both the curriculum and the objectives of education at all levels in the young republic, not only in private but also in publicly supported institutions of learning.

## Education in the Formation of a Person

Most of the leaders of the American Revolutionary generation, both Republicans and Federalists, believed strongly in state-supported education. Besides Jefferson, these included Benjamin Franklin, James Madison, George Washington, John Adams, and Benjamin Rush. Their attitude was hardly surprising: the two principal fountainheads of Revolutionary ideology, Enlightenment liberalism and classical republicanism, converged in agreement that free institutions would depend on a well-informed, educated citizenry. John Locke concurred with the ancient philosophers that education was a matter of central importance, although both he and they had assumed that education, like political power, would be confined to an elite. In the new context of American liberty, the necessity for the education of a broad public assumed an unaccustomed urgency.[3]

In classical political thought, going back through the Renaissance to Aristotle, republican institutions could only rest on the virtue of the citizenry, that is, on their unselfish devotion to the common good. Early modern liberal political thought began the legitimation of self-interest as a political motive and offered another rationale for an educated citizenry. Anglo-American liberals taught that an enlightened populace must keep a sharp watch on political power, lest it be corrupted to tyrannical ends. Yet in practice a substantial degree of overlap remained between classical and liberal political ideals, particularly with regard to education. Both classical virtue and liberal vigilance presupposed education for citizenship; they also shared a common sense of what the educated person's character should be like. In both philosophies, education aimed at forming a "balanced" character, that is, one in which morality and reason predominated over passion and appetite. Republican thinkers — ancient and modern alike — believed that the individual personality constituted a commonwealth in microcosm, requiring a balance among the component faculties. A proper balance, only achieved through a disciplined education, enabled a person to reach sound decisions and avoid the usurping tyranny of the

---

3. See Richard D. Brown, *The Strength of a People: The Idea of an Informed Citizenry in America, 1650-1870* (Chapel Hill: University of North Carolina Press, 1996); and Lorraine Smith Pangle and Thomas L. Pangle, *The Learning of Liberty: The Educational Ideas of the American Founders* (Lawrence: University Press of Kansas, 1993).

passions. A person possessed of such a balanced character possessed an empowered reason, the faculty essential for meaningful autonomy. Only a fully rational and autonomous person was capable of functioning as a citizen, judging issues on their merits, voting, and serving on juries. Indeed, only such a person could give that rational assent which alone legitimated government and constitutions. The balanced character of the good citizen was the individual analogue to the balanced institutions of a good government.[4]

But political participation did not constitute the only goal of education in the early republic. Often education took place under Protestant religious auspices. The goals of the religious educators included civic responsibility and harmonized with those of classical and liberal citizenship, yet went beyond them to encompass the entire formation of a moral person. Protestant educators too aimed at the creation of a balanced character. They invoked the same authorities on human nature that Enlightenment thinkers did, namely the Scottish moral philosophers of common sense, in particular Thomas Reid and his followers. The common sense that Scottish moralists like Reid celebrated was a sense common to all humanity. (*Common,* meaning *shared,* was a powerful word at the time, used in such important ways as common law, common land, common prayer, and as we shall see, common schools.) Education prepared individuals not only to be autonomous moral agents but also to live responsibly with others. Unanimously, Christian moralists warned that without conscientious training, the baser impulses of perverse human nature would overcome the nobler faculties.[5] A person with a strong, carefully nurtured moral sense and reason would be capable of studying the Bible and taking its lessons to heart. This person could rise superior to vices and temptations and conduct the business of life honestly. Such a sturdy person could own the covenant in a Protestant congregation. Because Protestant educators took an interest in the *whole* person, not just the decision-making self, experiments in manual labor, diet, and communal living sometimes took place within the context of religious education. And precisely because the religious educators took an interest in broader issues than training for citizenship, their concerns could extend beyond the white male electorate to include the education of women and people of color.

4. See, for example, Stephen Macedo, *Liberal Virtues: Citizenship, Virtue, and Community in Liberal Constitutionalism* (Oxford: Clarendon Press, 1991); Daniel Walker Howe, *Making the American Self: Jonathan Edwards to Abraham Lincoln* (Cambridge, Mass.: Harvard University Press, 1997); and Holly Brewer, "Beyond Education: Thomas Jefferson's Republican Revision of the Laws Regarding Children," in *Thomas Jefferson and the Education of a Citizen,* ed. James Gilreath (Washington: Library of Congress, 1999), 48-62.

5. See Donald H. Meyer, *The Instructed Conscience: The Shaping of the American National Ethic* (Philadelphia: University of Pennsylvania Press, 1972).

Among Enlightened commentators on education in the new nation, some like Jefferson wanted to break away from the traditional curriculum based on classics and theology, while others like John Adams did not.[6] Christian educators, on the other hand, generally supported the classical curriculum, at least for all males. Although Protestants differed among themselves in their attitudes toward child discipline, they agreed entirely on what constituted appropriate school and college subject matter.[7] And whatever curricular innovations were discussed, in practice the central educational importance of classical learning remained. Educators prized the classics not only because of the value attached to the precepts of ancient philosophy and the moral lessons to be learned from ancient history, but also because of the character-building "mental discipline" achieved through the study of Latin and Greek. At least to the middle of the nineteenth century, the classical basis of a liberal education held up remarkably well. The Yale Report of 1828 provided it a firm vindication. This report, expressing the collective judgment of the faculty of the largest and most influential American college at the time, affirmed the utility of classics as the core of a liberal education in forming a balanced character.[8]

The importance of classics in the educational system had significant consequences for American culture and political life. As long as classical learning formed the backbone of all formal education, classical republicanism would remain a major component of American political thought and action. Classical learning glorified the rivalry of oratorical contests and the emphasis placed on rhetoric and elocution even in English-language studies. Children learned to read aloud, to memorize poetry and perorations, and to deliver them with stylized gestures. Political orators like Daniel Webster and John C. Calhoun saw themselves as Roman senators. The classical rules of rhetoric provided practical information for prospective political leaders who needed to master the arts of persuasion. Finally, because of the universality with which it was taught, classical learning provided a common culture shared by all educated people, who could understand each other's references in a way that we, with our fragmented culture, can only appreciate with a sense of loss.[9]

---

6. See Linda K. Kerber, "Salvaging the Classical Tradition," in her *Federalists in Dissent: Imagery and Ideology in Jeffersonian America* (Ithaca: Cornell University Press, 1970), 109-34.

7. On the variations in attitudes toward discipline among Protestants, see Philip Greven, *The Protestant Temperament: Patterns of Child-Rearing, Religious Experience, and the Self in Early America* (New York: Knopf, 1977).

8. The Yale Report is conveniently reprinted in Richard Hofstadter and Wilson Smith, eds., *American Higher Education: A Documentary History,* Vol. 1 (Chicago: University of Chicago Press, 1961), 275-91.

9. See Daniel W. Howe, "Classical Education and Political Culture in Nineteenth-Century

Classics-based popular education claimed to create a virtuous citizenry and to shape responsible individual characters. These were much the same justifications that had long been offered on behalf of state establishments of religion.[10] Jefferson wanted state-supported education to substitute for the social purposes of state-supported religion in a free republic, but effecting this substitution turned out to be a slow and complicated process. As a matter of practical politics, much of the support for American public education came from religious people, who favored education for religious reasons. Ironically, therefore, Jefferson's dual project turned out to harbor an internal conflict: his goal of disestablishing religion in practice hampered his goal of promoting education.

## The Strange Passivity of the American Enlightenment

One of the striking anomalies of American history is the discrepancy between the founders' grand plans for education and the paucity of their actual accomplishments. This is nowhere more evident than in the failure of the project for founding a national university in the District of Columbia. George Washington had conceived the idea. As president, Washington proposed the university to Congress in his first annual message, worked on various plans for its establishment, and commended it strongly in his famous farewell address — but all in vain. In a final gesture, the Father of His Country willed a portion of his large estate to form a core endowment for a future national university. But Congress ignored the bequest, until in 1823 the fund finally became worthless when the company in whose shares it was invested went bankrupt.[11]

Opposition to a national university came partly from doubts about its constitutionality, partly from the jealousy of existing colleges that feared being overshadowed, and partly from sheer parsimony. Washington evidently envisioned the national university as a mixed public-private corporation analogous to Hamilton's national bank, so the university inherited some of the enemies of the bank. Originally, Jefferson supported Washington's plans for a national university and

---

America," *Intellectual History Newsletter* 5 (Spring 1983): 9-14; Carl J. Richard, *The Founders and the Classics: Greece, Rome, and the American Enlightenment* (Cambridge, Mass.: Harvard University Press, 1994); Walter J. Ong, S.J., *Rhetoric, Romance, and Technology: Studies in the Interaction of Expression and Culture* (Ithaca: Cornell University Press, 1971).

10. See Peter S. Onuf, "State Politics and Republican Virtue: Religion, Education, and Morality in Early American Federalism," in *Toward A Usable Past: Liberty Under State Constitutions,* ed. Paul Finkelman and Stephen E. Gottlieb (Athens: University of Georgia Press, 1991), 91-116.

11. David Madsen, *The National University* (Detroit: Wayne State University Press, 1966), 15-34; Pangle and Pangle, *Learning of Liberty,* 146-52.

had advised him to staff it with *émigré* professors from the University of Geneva. As president, however, Jefferson came to the conclusion that, although a national university would be welcome, a constitutional amendment would be required to authorize it.[12] Given his belief that the national bank had been unconstitutional, Jefferson thus protected himself against a charge of inconsistency. Only one portion of Washington's plans for national higher education was fulfilled by Jefferson's Administration: the founding of the United States Military Academy at West Point in 1802. Even then, the academy was kept starved for funds. It took the disasters of the War of 1812 to prompt Secretary of War John C. Calhoun, in the years after 1817, to ensure that West Point became an institution of the first rank. For years the Military Academy and Rensselaer Polytechnic (1824), further up the Hudson, were the leading American schools of engineering; Rensselaer's founding was prompted by the needs of the Erie Canal. The Naval Academy at Annapolis was not founded until 1845, by Secretary of the Navy George Bancroft during the Polk Administration's buildup to war against Mexico.[13]

All of the first six presidents supported a national university one way or another, but the one who worked the hardest for it was James Madison. Three times — in 1810, 1815, and 1816 — Madison urged a national university in his annual message to Congress. The university formed a part of Madison's legislative program of Republican nationalism, along with internal improvements, a protective tariff, and a second national bank. Within this framework, the president seemed to encourage young Congressman John C. Calhoun's "Bonus Bill," a plan to use the federal dollars generated by rechartering the national bank to fund internal improvements throughout the Union. Then, just before leaving office, Madison surprised the political community by vetoing the Bonus Bill on grounds that it was unconstitutional. Madison's last-minute failure of nerve made it hard for his successor Monroe to continue to press the cause of a national university, which, like internal improvements, depended on Congress exercising implied, rather than expressly enumerated, powers. Once again, Jeffersonian principles of strict construction got in the way of a positive national program.[14]

12. Thomas Jefferson to George Washington, Feb. 23, 1795, in *The Writings of Thomas Jefferson*, Vol. 19, ed. Andrew Lipscombe and Albert Bergh (Washington, D.C.: Thomas Jefferson Memorial Association, 1903), 108-14; Thomas Jefferson, "Sixth Annual Message to Congress" (December 2, 1806), *Writings*, ed. Peterson, 524-31.

13. See George S. Pappas, *To the Point: The United States Military Academy, 1802-1902* (Westport, Ct.: Praeger, 1993); and Jack Sweetman, *The U.S. Naval Academy* (Annapolis, Md.: Naval Institute Press, 1979).

14. The Bonus Bill and Madison's veto of it are brilliantly analyzed in John Lauritz Larson, "'Bind the Republic Together': The National Union and the Struggle for a System of Internal Improvements," *Journal of American History* 74 (1987): 363-87.

The final repetition of Washington's call for a national university came in the first annual message of John Quincy Adams in December 1825. Adams linked his eloquent plea for the university with the promotion of applied knowledge in all its aspects: the founding of a national astronomical observatory, geographical exploration to follow up the Lewis and Clark expedition, adoption of the metric system of weights and measures, improvement of the patent laws to encourage inventions, and an ambitious program of public works to provide a commercial infrastructure. As an agenda for the advancement of knowledge, Adams's message embodied a summary of the American Enlightenment. But as legislation, it was far ahead of its time. Secretary of State Henry Clay had warned his chief that the national university would be dead on arrival in Congress, and this proved to be the case with the President's entire program.[15]

Even more surprising than the fate of Washington's planned national university is the fate of Jefferson's ambitious plans for education in Virginia. The conflict between Jeffersonian commitment to an informed citizenry and laissez-faire political principles was nowhere posed more starkly than in the Old Dominion. Jefferson's "Bill for the More General Diffusion of Knowledge" (1778) is considered a landmark in the history of American thinking about education. Its elaborate preamble justified a Statewide system of primary schools on two grounds: (1) the creation of an informed electorate who could guard against the encroachments of tyranny, and (2) the recruitment of political leaders on the basis of "genius and virtue" rather than "wealth, birth or other accidental condition."[16] But the same Virginia legislature that passed Jefferson's bill for religious freedom rejected his bill for education. Virginia republicans, suspicious of government, preferred to leave schooling to the marketplace of private enterprise. Soon thereafter the invasion of the British army distracted the attention of Governor Jefferson and the legislature. Finally, in 1796, the legislature authorized counties to adopt Jefferson's educational scheme on a voluntary basis, but none of them chose to do so.[17]

15. John Quincy Adams, "First Annual Message, December 6, 1825," *Messages and Papers of the Presidents,* Vol. 2, ed. James D. Richardson (Washington, D.C.: Library of Congress, 1900), 299-317; John Quincy Adams, diary entry for November 26, 1825, in *Memoirs,* Vol. 7, ed. Charles Francis Adams (Philadelphia: J. B. Lippincott, 1874-77), 62-63.

16. Thomas Jefferson, "A Bill for the More General Diffusion of Knowledge," *Writings,* ed. Peterson, 365-73. Written in 1778, the bill was introduced into the Virginia legislature in 1779. See Jennings Wagoner Jr., "Thomas Jefferson's Concept of Utility in the Education of Republican Citizens," in *Jefferson and the Education of a Citizen,* ed. Gilreath, 115-33.

17. Lawrence A. Cremin, *American Education: The National Experience, 1783-1876* (New York: Harper & Row, 1980), 109.

For a number of years, events drew Jefferson away from Virginia politics to the national arena, where he served as secretary of state, vice president, and president. Not until 1817 did he recur to the subject of state-sponsored education. In his draft legislation of that year, Jefferson proposed to provide all free white children with three years of primary education at public cost. He called for subdividing the counties of Virginia into small units called "hundreds" or "wards," modeled on the townships of New England, which would function as school districts. Rather than make primary education compulsory, even for three years, Jefferson added to the 1817 version of his bill a clause taking citizenship away from those of either sex who remained illiterate after age fifteen. This, he believed, would provide incentive for parents to send their boys and girls to school, at least for the three free years. (Punishing the fifteen-year-olds for the negligence of their parents did not seem to bother him.) It all proved hypothetical anyway, since not even the ex-president's personal prestige and political connections could persuade the Virginia legislature to approve this minimal proposal.[18]

The following year, Jefferson shifted his tactics: he focused on higher education, hoping that a comprehensive State educational system could be created from the top down. His Rockfish Gap commission report of 1818, endorsing the founding of a University of Virginia, offered a comprehensive rationale for education, emphasizing its vocational and moral advantages as well as its public function of training citizens.[19] The report included plans for public secondary schools called "grammar schools" as feeders for the university. These schools, as their name implied, would focus on the study of Latin, for even Jefferson, educational "modern" that he was, acknowledged that classical studies retained much real value.[20] This time his bill passed (January 1819), though in truncated form: the university was approved but not the secondary schools.[21]

Long before, as Governor of Virginia, Jefferson had sought to turn the College of William and Mary from an Anglican institution into a secular state school, but while he had effected some changes in his *alma mater* he had not succeeded in either reinvigorating it or transforming it to his liking. Accordingly, Jefferson now preferred to start afresh with a newly created state univer-

18. There is much information in Roy J. Honeywell, *The Educational Work of Thomas Jefferson* (New York: Russell & Russell, 1964).

19. Thomas Jefferson, "Report of the Commissioners for the University of Virginia," *Writings*, ed. Peterson, 457-73.

20. Jefferson's views on the proper place of classics in the curriculum are sorted out in Pangle and Pangle, *Learning of Liberty*, 121-23.

21. The complicated political maneuvering is described in Merrill D. Peterson, *Thomas Jefferson and the New Nation* (New York: Oxford University Press, 1970), 961-76.

sity, one more centrally located than Williamsburg. Working through his network of friends and associates, including Thomas Ritchie, editor of the *Richmond Enquirer,* he was able to get himself named rector of the university and its site located in Charlottesville, close enough to Monticello that Jefferson could conveniently oversee every detail. The University of Virginia was the elder statesman's labor of love. Still truly a Renaissance man even in his seventies, Thomas Jefferson designed the university's architecture as well as its mode of governance, hired the professors, even presumed to prescribe the curriculum — at least in sensitive subjects like politics and religion.[22]

In its architecture, the University of Virginia is a world-class masterpiece. As an institution of higher learning, however, its distinction was not immediately apparent. Funding remained perennially problematic; the recruitment of both faculty and students difficult. The first functioning academic year, 1825-26, the only one the founder lived to see, was not auspicious. The students took advantage of Jefferson's permissive discipline to get drunk, gamble, skip classes, and misbehave; it was not the intellectual and meritocratic ambience the founder had envisioned. Among those who had to be expelled for participation in a riot was the founder's own great-grandnephew.[23] The shortcomings of the student body were in part caused by the legislature's failure to establish a proper system of preparatory secondary schools. Not that such difficulties were peculiar to the University of Virginia — they were widespread in American colleges of the time. And in the years after its founder's death, Virginia came to take a respected place among nineteenth-century state universities.

One must record a certain narrowing of Jefferson's own vision with regard to the purposes of his beloved university. In his struggles against religious influences he alienated many of the Presbyterian clergy, whose support his university needed because they were one of the social groups most favorably inclined to higher education in Virginia.[24] In politics the old man became even more intolerant than in religion. Viewing the Missouri Debates of 1819-21 as a threat to southern political power rather than as an encouraging sign that his own misgivings about slavery

22. Peterson, *Thomas Jefferson and the New Nation,* 976-88; Philip Alexander Bruce, *History of the University of Virginia* (New York: Macmillan, 1920), Vol. 1; James Morton Smith, *The Republic of Letters: The Correspondence between Thomas Jefferson and James Madison* (New York: W. W. Norton, 1995), Vol. 3, 1776-1841 and 1883-1951.

23. Robert McDonald, "Thomas Jefferson's Image in America, 1809-1826" (master's thesis, Oxford University, 1997). Cf. Bruce, *University of Virginia,* Vol. 2, 300.

24. Peterson, *Thomas Jefferson,* 978-80; Dumas Malone, *The Sage of Monticello* (Boston: Little, Brown, 1981), 376-80. For more of Jefferson's attitude toward the Presbyterians, see his letters to Joseph Correa, April 11, 1820, in *Transactions of the American Philosophical Society* 45 (1955): 177-78; and to Thomas Cooper, November 2, 1822, in *Writings,* ed. Peterson, 1463-65.

were shared, Jefferson became worried about sending southern youth north to colleges where they would be exposed to abolitionism and the broad construction of the Constitution. "We are now trusting to those who are against us in position and principle, to fashion to their own form the minds and affections of our youth."[25] Sadly, Jefferson came to define the purpose of his university as the defense of southern sectionalism. His sympathetic biographer Merrill Peterson, after speculating that Jefferson may have been pandering to regional pride to gain political support for the university, concludes, "whether [by] conviction or strategy, Jefferson tended to give a political cast to his conception of the University; and while he did not abandon the ideal of a fountainhead of learning for the entire nation, it slowly receded from view."[26] More recently, Robert Forbes has found reason to suspect that Jefferson's determination to insulate his university from religious influences reflected his intention to isolate it from contemporary antislavery currents in theology and moral philosophy.[27]

The University of Virginia was by no means the only example of a disparity between promise and realization in American education during the early national period. In most states, even less was accomplished. The shortfall was particularly evident in New York, Michigan, and Indiana. The so-called University of the State of New York was created in 1784 as part of a grandiose plan. It was not a teaching institution at all but an administrative system designed to coordinate all levels of education, primary, secondary, and higher, in the state. In practice, however, this "university" exerted little control over the institutions that were nominally subject to it, some of which were actually private and sectarian. Not until after World War II did New York actually create a state university that would function as a teaching and research institution. The case of Michigan presents another glaring contrast between dream and reality. The "University of Michigania" was conceived by Augustus B. Woodward, whom Thomas Jefferson appointed chief justice of Michigan Territory in 1805. Woodward secured territorial legislation establishing this, purportedly a unified system of education at all levels, topped off by a "catholepistemiad" (university) of thirteen "didaxia" (departments) led by thirteen "didactors" (professors). In practice, however, for a long time only the primary and secondary levels of instruction were implemented; the Ann Arbor campus did not open until 1841,

25. Thomas Jefferson to James Breckinridge, February 15, 1821, *Writings,* ed. Peterson, 1452. For such reasons, Jefferson encouraged his grandson Francis Eppes to enroll at South Carolina College in 1820 rather than at any northern institution. Malone, *Sage of Monticello,* 379.

26. Peterson, *Thomas Jefferson,* 981. Cf. Brown, *Strength of a People,* 97.

27. Robert P. Forbes, "Slavery and the Evangelical Enlightenment," in *Religion and the Antebellum Debate over Slavery,* ed. John R. McKivigan and Mitchell Snay (Athens, Ga.: University of Georgia Press, 2001), 87-94.

although the present University of Michigan proudly declares the date of its founding to be 1817. Finally, one might note the 1816 Constitution of Indiana, which called for "a general system of education, ascending in regular gradation from township schools to state university, wherein tuition shall be gratis, and equally open to all." It took more than thirty years for the Indiana legislature to begin to implement this promise.[28] In the meantime, a Presbyterian seminary-turned-college operated in Bloomington.

There are various ways of explaining the strange passivity of the American Enlightenment. Universal public education was not its only failure, of course; another conspicuous one was universal emancipation. In both cases, the optimism of their ideology misled statesmen into procrastination, as they imagined that a future generation would find the hard tasks easier to confront. In the field of education, as in other respects, the Jeffersonian Republicans could never quite make up their minds whether purposeful government action on behalf of the public welfare was justified, or whether it would set the wrong kind of precedent for the strong government of some future tyrant. A letter from Thomas Jefferson to his close political friend Joseph C. Cabell in 1816 illustrates this ideological tension: Jefferson defends his proposal to create small school districts and then launches into an attack upon a competing proposal by Charles Fenton Mercer that would have given the State more authority over the schools. Jefferson warns that Mercer's educational plan exemplifies "the degeneracy of our government, and the concentration of all it's powers in the hands of the one, the few, the well-born or the many." Powerful government, even in the hands of "the many" and even for beneficent purposes like education, was not welcomed by the sage of Monticello.[29]

## The Disestablishment of Higher Education

There were other Americans more willing to use the powers of government: the Federalists. The Federalists believed in synthesizing the Enlightenment with Christianity and had no hesitations about cooperation between church and state.[30] By cooperating with Presbyterian clergy, North Carolina Federalists suc-

---

28. Cremin, *American Education*, 150-53, 160-63, 171-72; Willis T. Dunbar, *Michigan: A History of the Wolverine State*, rev. George S. May (Grand Rapids: William B. Eerdmans, 1980).

29. Thomas Jefferson to Joseph C. Cabell, February 2, 1816, *Writings*, ed. Peterson, 1377-81; Rush Welter, *American Writings on Popular Education: The Nineteenth Century* (New York: Bobbs-Merrill, 1971), 13-14.

30. For one aspect, see Jonathan Sassi, "'To Envision a Godly Society': The Public Christianity of the Southern New England Clergy, 1783-1833" (Ph.D. dissertation, UCLA, 1996).

ceeded in founding a state university as early as 1789. The Federalists were also generally well disposed toward the colleges that had been founded in colonial times and were willing to support them as means for securing the public advantages of an educated leadership. The Federalist vision was predicated on interlocking relationships among church, state, and college. Yet, like the Republicans, the Federalists failed to implement their vision for higher education successfully.

The United States entered upon its independence with nine colleges already in existence: Harvard, William and Mary, Yale, Dartmouth, Brown (originally called the College of Rhode Island), Columbia (originally King's), Rutgers (originally Queen's), Princeton (originally the College of New Jersey), and Pennsylvania. All had religious connections. The status that these institutions would enjoy under independence was not clear at the outset and only gradually achieved definition. The colleges themselves would have welcomed the status of mixed public-private corporations. This tended to align the interests of the colleges with the Federalist political party, which was sympathetic to such corporations in other fields, especially finance and transportation. The Republican Party generally had little sympathy with mixed corporations; an exception was the Clintonian faction in New York with which Columbia College aligned itself. But Republicans did not consistently articulate an ideology of purely public, secular education at the state level. Instead, the presence of the colonial colleges muted the Republican call for alternative institutions in those states where they existed. Jeffersonian Republicans were thrifty above all, and economy generally trumped secularism in defining their educational priorities. Why spend money to meet a need if it was already being met?

The most troublesome problem for the existing colleges in the early national period was neither religious anti-intellectualism nor demand for a secular educational alternative. Their problem stemmed from religious diversity. Harvard, Yale, and Dartmouth were identified with the Congregational religious establishments of Massachusetts, Connecticut, and New Hampshire respectively, just as William and Mary and King's/Columbia were with the Anglican establishments of Virginia and New York. The disestablishment of Anglicanism after independence severely hurt the latter two colleges, and both spent a generation struggling for an alternative identity. The three Congregational colleges were spared the post-revolutionary opprobrium attached to Anglicanism/Episcopalianism, and their religious establishments survived until 1817 in New Hampshire, 1818 in Connecticut, and 1833 in Massachusetts. (The First Amendment as then interpreted prevented only the federal government, not the states, from establishing religion.) The three colleges were nevertheless caught up in the politico-religious controversies of New England Congregationalism and suffered from them.

In colonial times the American colleges had received financial support from public authorities. During the early national period such support became much less dependable. When it came, it often took the form of non-tax revenues, such as land grants or permission to hold a lottery. What made legislative financial support to the colleges especially politically sensitive was their identification with particular denominations or theological factions. Harvard is a case in point. Located in a commonwealth with a religious establishment where Federalists and National Republicans were usually in power, the college in those respects enjoyed advantages. However, after 1805 Harvard clearly identified with the theologically Liberal wing of Congregationalism, and when the religious standing order finally split apart in the years after 1819, it became the intellectual center of the emerging Unitarian denomination. This undercut Harvard's popularity with Trinitarian Congregationalists and led to the founding of Andover Seminary in 1807 as an orthodox alternative. In 1823 the split among Federalists between Unitarians and Trinitarians enabled the Republicans to win the governorship and lower house of the legislature in Massachusetts; they wasted no time in cutting off Harvard's annual appropriation of $10,000 and arranging for the founding of Amherst College (1825) as another orthodox rival.[31] Williams (1793) and Bowdoin (1794) had already been created to provide geographical diversity in Massachusetts higher education (Maine, where Bowdoin is located, was then part of Massachusetts). Similar geographical and religious pressures for new foundations were present in almost all the states; the consequence was a growing number of institutions competing for what little financial aid was on offer.

The most famous confrontation concerning the public or private status of an American college was the Dartmouth College Case decided by the United States Supreme Court in 1819. It originated in a dispute between the president of the college and the trustees. Both sides were Federalist and Calvinist, but a majority of the trustees supported organized revivals and novel moral reforms like temperance. The president of the college did not sympathize with this program, and the trustees dismissed him. The Republican-controlled state legislature intervened, trying to make a mixed public-private corporation more responsive to religious diversity. The state's intervention was intended to be a one-time thing: after the new gubernatorial appointees had taken office, the board of trustees would have recruited further members by cooptation. If the old trustees had accepted this legislation, they would still have had a (bare) ma-

31. See Samuel Eliot Morison, *Three Centuries of Harvard* (Cambridge, Mass.: Harvard University Press, 1936), 187-91, 211-21, 241-45; Morison, *Harrison Gray Otis: The Urbane Federalist* (Boston: Houghton Mifflin, 1969), 437-42.

jority on the board. But they were uncompromising men. The old trustees took their case to court, and they won.[32]

In the case of *Dartmouth College v. Woodward* the two sides reversed their customary positions. The Republicans now defended the legitimacy of mixed public-private corporations; the old trustees' line of argument on behalf of the absolute independence of private education was a novelty, doubly peculiar coming from Federalists. Daniel Webster argued the case for the old trustees in the U.S. Supreme Court: "It is, Sir, as I have said, a small College. And yet, there are those who love it." Webster's famous peroration was an ingenious twist, adapting Republican principles of the defense of private rights against big government to suit the needs of his Federalist clients. Chief Justice Marshall handed down the opinion of a five-to-one majority in favor of the old trustees. The decision set Dartmouth on a course headed for transformation from a mixed public-private institution into a completely private college.[33]

In the long run, Marshall's decision furthered the process of differentiation between public and private institutions of higher learning. But it did not immediately end the claim of the older colleges to be mixed public-private institutions; even Dartmouth itself turned around and requested state appropriations as soon as the case was over. And the New Hampshire legislature, while refusing Dartmouth funding, also decided against founding a rival state university.[34] The Dartmouth College Case illustrates how the legal concept of private institutions emerged in education as a result of particular religious disputes, not as a result of the application of church-state separation as a general principle.

If the Republicans lost their battle against the Dartmouth trustees, they won the war on another front. The same Republican-controlled legislature that tried to alter the Dartmouth charter took advantage of the division among Federalists to strip the Congregational church of its favored status in New Hampshire. In subsequent years, the religious establishments of Connecticut and Massachusetts also fell. Republican secularists allied with Baptists and other pietist dissenters to enact disestablishment. In each case, the Republicans took

---

32. See Steven J. Novak, "The College in the Dartmouth College Case: A Reinterpretation," *New England Quarterly* 47 (1974): 550-63; Donald B. Cole, *Jacksonian Democracy in New Hampshire* (Cambridge, Mass.: Harvard University Press, 1970), 30-41; and Lynn Warren Turner, *The Ninth State: New Hampshire's Formative Years* (Chapel Hill: University of North Carolina Press, 1983), 334-43.

33. *Dartmouth College v. Woodward*, 4 Wheaton 551-624 (1819). Webster's words as reported by a witness are quoted from Albert J. Beveridge, *The Life of John Marshall*, Vol. 4 (Boston: Houghton Mifflin, 1919), 249.

34. See John S. Whitehead, *The Separation of College and State: Columbia, Dartmouth, Harvard, and Yale* (New Haven: Yale University Press, 1973), 53-88.

advantage of religious divisions among the Federalists: revivalists versus Old Calvinists in New Hampshire; Congregationalists versus Episcopalians in Connecticut; Trinitarians versus Unitarians in Massachusetts.[35] The disestablishment of the New England state churches foreshadowed the disestablishment of what we call the Ivy League colleges, though the separation of college and state occurred later and more gradually. Eventually all the colonial foundations became private institutions. When that happened they did not need to fear for their autonomy, but neither could they look to their state governments for financial assistance.

The most successful example of a state-founded, state-supported venture in higher education in the early national period was South Carolina College, founded in 1801. Conceived by Federalists as a way of preserving the values of the tidewater aristocracy, the college was located in the upcountry to enlist Republican support. Although there were early problems with discipline much the same as at the University of Virginia, the college surmounted them to become an integral part of the tight cohesion of South Carolina political culture, supplying leaders for both the state itself and the rest of the Lower South. South Carolina College became the only institution of higher learning in the country to be generously supported by annual legislative appropriations. Since the state did not support public schools, they did not compete with the college for funds.[36]

Thomas Cooper, an expatriate Englishman, became president of South Carolina College in 1821. Cooper combined proslavery politics with anti-clericalism; Jefferson declared him "the greatest man in America, in the powers of mind," and had tried desperately to recruit him to head the University of Virginia.[37] In South Carolina Cooper won popularity with his ardent state-rights rhetoric only to lose it afterwards by his tactless denunciations of Christianity. Under fire from a combination of Presbyterian clergy and political Unionists, Cooper found it necessary to resign in 1834. The one example of successful state-sponsored higher education in the country also illustrated the unacceptability of state-sponsored secularism. With Cooper out of the way, South Carolina College established a professorial chair of "Christian Evidences and Sacred Literature" and resumed its accustomed popularity.[38]

---

35. See William G. McLoughlin, *New England Dissent, 1630-1833: The Baptists and the Separation of Church and State*, Vol. 2 (Cambridge, Mass.: Harvard University Press, 1971), 877-911 (on New Hampshire); 1025-62 (on Connecticut); 1189-1262 (on Massachusetts).

36. See Michael Sugrue, "'We Desire Our Future Rulers to Be Educated Men': South Carolina College, the Defense of Slavery, and the Development of Secessionist Politics," *History of Higher Education Annual* 14 (1994): 39-71.

37. Jefferson to Joseph C. Cabell, quoted in Forbes, "Evangelical Enlightenment," 88.

38. Daniel Walker Hollis, *South Carolina College* (Columbia: University of South Carolina

Neither the Federalist nor the Jeffersonian vision of higher education achieved adequate implementation. In the meantime, however, the churches rushed to fill the gap.

## The Second Great Awakening as an Educational Movement

Writing to the lieutenant governor of Kentucky in 1822, James Madison had to admit that Virginia's educational system was not a fit model for the younger commonwealth to follow; instead, Kentuckians should look to the New England States.[39] New England's township-based system of primary schools was the daughter not of the Enlightenment but of the Reformation; it had been created in response to the Protestant doctrine that all good Christians should be able to read the Bible for themselves. The first legal provision for free public schools had been enacted by Massachusetts in 1647 and Connecticut in 1650. Puritanism was a religion of a book; to practice the religion, one had to be able to read the book. In early national times, American Protestant devotional practices remained largely bible-centered: reading, memorizing, analyzing, and applying passages from Scripture. It was only logical, then, that the multitudinous sects of evangelical Protestantism should remain in the forefront of efforts to promote literacy and schooling. An educated Protestant laity provided the basis for an educated citizenry.[40]

Although the American state remained remarkably limited and passive, American churches were remarkably innovative and energetic. Nowhere is the contrast between them more evident than with regard to education. The outpouring of religious activity contemporaries called a "Second Great Awakening" proved to be an epoch in the history of American education as well as in the history of Christianity itself. Although the great revivals are celebrated in American history, they probably had less in the way of lasting effect than the multitude of educational institutions founded by Presbyterians, Methodists, Baptists, and

---

Press, 1951), 74-119. See also William W. Freehling, *Prelude to Civil War: The Nullification Controversy in South Carolina* (New York: Harper & Row, 1966).

39. James Madison to W. T. Barry, *The Writings of James Madison*, Vol. 9, ed. Gaillard Hunt (New York: G. P. Putnam's Sons, 1910), 103-109.

40. See David Paul Nord, "Religious Reading and Readers in Antebellum America," *Journal of the Early Republic* 15 (1995): 241-72; David Tyack, "The Kingdom of God and the Common School: Protestant Ministers and the Educational Awakening in the West," *Harvard Educational Review* 36 (1966): 447-69; and Kurt Berends, "'Thus Saith the Lord': The Use of the Bible by Southern Evangelicals in the Era of the American Civil War" (D.Phil. thesis, Oxford University, 1997).

others across the land. Perhaps the history of charisma is more exciting than the history of institutions. But the long-term impact of famous revivalists like George Whitefield, Peter Cartwright, or even Charles G. Finney may well have been exceeded by that of the relatively unsung founders of Christian elementary schools, academies, colleges, mission schools, and seminaries.[41]

One such educational initiative was the Sunday school, which provided one day a week of instruction under religious auspices for poor children who might receive no other (and might be employed during the rest of the week on farm, in factory, or in shop). Originating in Britain in the 1780s, the Sunday school movement quickly caught on in America; by 1827 it provided some 200,000 American children with Bible-centered training in literacy. In frontier areas, Sunday schools were often established in advance of the more ambitious, expensive weekday schools. Only after public primary education became more widespread did Sunday schools concentrate exclusively on religious instruction.[42]

In the young American republic, the educational goals of Christian and secular educators converged most conveniently. Religious educators inculcated that unselfishness and respect for the social virtues classical republicanism considered indispensable for the citizenry. Christian and Enlightenment moral philosophy alike taught that conscientious training of young people was necessary to create a properly balanced character in which reason and the moral sense could prevail over baser motives. Ever since the founding of the medieval universities, Christianity had been supportive of classical learning. There was, accordingly, nothing unusual about the mutual support of education and the churches, nothing to surprise contemporaries.

The states where public education was best supported were those that had strong traditions of supporting religious establishments as well. But New Light sectarians cooperated with Jeffersonian liberals to abolish America's religious establishments, beginning with the Anglican ones during the Revolution and then, more than a generation later, those of Congregational New England. In the absence of religious establishments, would the New Lights endorse popular education or declare it superfluous? This was clearly an issue of pivotal importance. To be sure, the left wing of the Reformation had spawned varieties of pietistic reli-

---

41. See T. Scott Miyakawa, *Protestants and Pioneers: Individualism and Conformity on the American Frontier* (Chicago: University of Chicago Press, 1965); Donald G. Mathews, "The Great Awakening as an Organizing Process, 1780-1830," *American Quarterly* 21 (1969): 23-43; Dickson D. Bruce, *Violence and Culture in the Antebellum South* (Austin: University of Texas Press, 1979).

42. Carl F. Kaestle, *Pillars of the Republic: Common Schools and American Society, 1780-1860* (New York: Hill and Wang, 1983), 45; Anne M. Boylan, *Sunday School: The Formation of an American Institution, 1790-1880* (New Haven: Yale University Press, 1988).

gion that based their faith on the immediate action of the Holy Spirit in the hearts of individual believers, not on a learned ministry or its articulated theology. At least as far back as the Great Awakening in the eighteenth century, there had been revivalists in America who were accused of anti-intellectualism. But even the "New Lights" predicated their faith on the Book of books, and their leaders often showed great ingenuity in interpreting it. In truth, the New Lights were not so much opposed to education itself as to its elitist and pretentious corruptions, and to the assumption that education could substitute for the grace of the Holy Spirit.[43] For the most part, the leaders of the American pietist sects embraced public education. Alexander Campbell, a former schoolteacher turned preacher who advocated the restoration of New Testament church practices, voiced sentiments in 1836 that were at once representative of New Light pietism and worthy of the founders of the American republic:

> To transmit to our posterity the rich blessings which we enjoy, it behooves us
> . . . to give not only our suffrage, but our efforts to the cause of education,
> and to use all lawful means to facilitate the diffusion of knowledge and the
> influence of morality and good order.[44]

Campbell's exhortation combined Christian evangelism with an appreciation for the civic virtues of education. Echoed countless times across the land, the combination proved effective. The largest evangelical denomination, the Methodists, turned away from experientially-based class meetings to embrace Sabbath schools. American evangelicals enlisted the Enlightenment in the service of Christ.[45]

Sometimes the support for education came from the previously established denominations, looking for ways to reassert their influence. As New England Yankees moved west, the Congregationalists founded a host of colleges

43. See, for example, Brooks Holifield, *The Gentlemen Theologians: American Theology in Southern Culture, 1795-1860* (Durham: Duke University Press, 1987); Richard T. Hughes and C. Leonard Allen, *Illusions of Innocence: Protestant Primitivism in America, 1630-1875* (Chicago: University of Chicago Press, 1988); Nathan Hatch and Mark Noll, eds., *The Bible in America* (New York: Oxford University Press, 1982). For a different interpretation that seems to me no longer tenable, see Richard Hofstadter, *Anti-Intellectualism in American Life* (New York: Random House, 1963).

44. Alexander Campbell, "Closing Address" to Sixth Annual Meeting of the Western Literary Institute, Cincinnati, Ohio, 1836, reprinted in Welter, *American Writings on Popular Education,* 61.

45. See Mark A. Noll, "The Evangelical Enlightenment and the Task of Theological Education," in *Communication and Change in American Religious History,* ed. Leonard I. Sweet (Grand Rapids: William B. Eerdmans, 1993).

across their band of settlement, including Western Reserve University and Oberlin College in Ohio, Illinois College, Beloit College in Wisconsin, and Grinnell College in Iowa. These institutions became important centers in the propagation of all aspects of Yankee culture and politics across the continent.[46] Often these colleges were founded under joint Congregationalist-Presbyterian auspices; the name of one of them, Union College in Schenectady, New York, commemorates this interdenominational collaboration.

Many of the western colleges were in effect daughter institutions of Yale, not only founded by Yale graduates but imitating the Yale curriculum and loyal to the Yale Report of 1828. Yale's academic imperialism persisted after the Civil War and included the founding of Colorado College (1874), Yankton College in South Dakota (1881), and Pomona College in Claremont, California (1887). Even the University of California can trace its origins to the Yale-sponsored Congregational/Presbyterian College of California founded in Berkeley in 1855.[47] Yale provided centralized direction to the expansion of higher education through its Society for the Promotion of Collegiate and Theological Education at the West (the SPCTEW), which numbered as many as twenty-six institutions at one time. As the Society declared in 1849, "The Ministry is God's instrumentality for the conversion of the world. Colleges and seminaries are God's means of training up a learned and efficient Ministry."[48] The motives that had led the Puritans to found Harvard in 1636 were still operative more than two centuries later.

But in the enthusiasm of the Second Great Awakening, the denominations that had never been established proved even more prolific in founding colleges than did the Congregationalists and Episcopalians. By 1848, the Presbyterians had the most colleges (twenty-five), followed by Methodists and Baptists (fifteen each), Congregationalists (fourteen), and Episcopalians (seven).[49] But since denominational affiliation mattered comparatively little to the college curriculum in most cases, student bodies typically included youths from the area across denominational lines. These numerous little colleges were serving the purposes of their local communities, not just their particular sects.[50]

46. The classic account is Richard L. Power, "A Crusade to Extend Yankee Culture," *New England Quarterly* 13 (1940): 638-53.

47. See Horace Bushnell, *The Movement for a University in California* (San Francisco, 1857).

48. *Sixth Annual Report of the Society for the Promotion of Collegiate and Theological Education at the West* (New York, 1849), 62.

49. Statistics based on Donald Tewksbury, *The Founding of American Colleges and Universities Before the Civil War* (New York: Teachers College Press, 1932, reprinted 1972), 32-46.

50. See David B. Potts, "American Colleges in the Nineteenth Century: From Localism to Denominationalism," *History of Education Quarterly* 11 (1971): 363-80; Potts, "'College Enthusiasm!' as Public Response, 1800-1860," *Harvard Educational Review* 47 (1977): 28-42.

Following the influential example of the New Light Calvinist Presbyterian John Witherspoon of Princeton, Protestant educators of all denominations typically synthesized Christian theology and classical learning with polite culture.[51] The incorporation of politeness into Christian education softened the rough edges of early Methodism and other branches of evangelical piety. The three-way synthesis turned out to be a powerful force in civilizing the American frontier and promoting education in the young republic. The combination of politeness, Christianity, and classical education taught in colleges and academies and disseminated in the new mass circulation magazines, often published by the churches, provided simultaneously a democratization of gentility and a cultural basis for the formation of a new, broadly based middle class.[52]

All told, by 1815 there were 33 colleges in the United States, a figure that climbed to 68 by 1835 and 113 by 1848. Sixteen of these 113 were state institutions, which by then were generally distinguishable from private religious ones. Eighty-eight were Protestant denominational colleges; the remaining nine, Roman Catholic.[53] Catholic educational initiatives in the United States were largely the work of religious orders. They included Georgetown and Fordham (both founded by the Jesuits), Notre Dame (by the Order of the Holy Cross), and Villanova (by the Augustinians). Founded in advance of substantial Catholic immigration, these Catholic colleges aimed at winning converts rather than at serving an existing Catholic constituency. Protestants like Lyman Beecher were correct in interpreting the Catholic institutions as an ideological challenge. The appearance of such Catholic institutions of course excited the Protestants to redouble their own evangelical-educational exertions.[54]

Much of the innovation in secondary education, too, came from religious impulses. In the absence of state-supported high schools, academies under religious auspices flourished. They began with the academies founded by Samuel Phillips in Andover, Massachusetts (1780), and John Phillips in Exeter, New Hampshire (1781), both of whom were devout Congregationalists. Like the colleges of the time, the academies were at first mixed public-private institutions and only gradually came to be considered strictly private. In the early days they were hardly ever boarding schools and usually drew their students from their

51. See Mark A. Noll, *Princeton and the Republic: 1768-1822* (Princeton: Princeton University Press, 1989); and Donald R. Come, "The Influence of Princeton on Higher Education in the South Before 1825," *William and Mary Quarterly*, 3d ser., 2 (1945): 359-96.

52. See Richard Bushman, *The Refinement of America* (New York: Knopf, 1992).

53. Tewksbury, *Founding*, 32-46. These numbers could vary slightly because of the existence of evanescent and marginal institutions.

54. For example, Lyman Beecher, *A Plea for the West* (1835), reprinted in Daniel W. Howe, ed., *The American Whigs: An Anthology* (New York: John Wiley, 1973), 133-47.

own vicinity. Of course, most students had to pay tuition. The generation between 1820 and 1840 represented the peak of the influence of the academies. Only after that did public high schools gradually supplant most of them, with a few remaining academies gradually transforming themselves into selective private boarding schools.[55]

The colonial Puritans had included educational provision for girls as well as boys in their primary schools, for females too needed to practice the religion, and mothers needed to instruct their children. In the early nineteenth century, when formal secondary and even higher education began to open up to girls and women, religious motivations remained important, as illustrated in the Edwardseanism of Mount Holyoke (1836), the evangelical abolitionism of coeducational Oberlin (1834), or the Wesleyan Methodism of Georgia Female College (1836).[56] No individual did more to apply the Second Great Awakening to women's education than Catharine Beecher, eldest daughter of the evangelist Lyman Beecher. Moral philosopher and founder of the Hartford Female Seminary (1820), she pioneered the entry of women into the school teaching profession on a par with men and created home economics as an academic subject in order to recognize the dignity of the domestic role that most women then performed.[57]

For African Americans, most of whom were held in chattel slavery, religion was even more important as a source of education than it was for the whites. The religion of the slave quarters was an "invisible institution" that often did not show up in church records but profoundly influenced African American culture.[58] What little interest the state took in the education of black people could be negative: in four southern states, it was against the law to maintain schools for slaves. (This was to insulate them against abolitionist propaganda and make concerted uprisings more difficult.) However, individual masters

---

55. James McLachlan, *American Boarding Schools* (New York: Scribner's, 1970), 35-48; see also Theodore Sizer, *The Age of the Academies* (New York: Teachers College Press, 1964).

56. See Barbara Solomon, *In the Company of Educated Women: A History of Women and Higher Education in America* (New Haven: Yale University Press, 1985); Linda Kerber, *Women of the Republic* (Chapel Hill: University of North Carolina Press, 1980); Kathryn Kish Sklar, "The Founding of Mount Holyoke College," in *Women of America: A History*, ed. Carol Berkin and Mary Beth Norton (Boston: Houghton Mifflin, 1979), 177-201.

57. See Kathryn Kish Sklar, *Catharine Beecher: A Study in Domesticity* (New Haven: Yale University Press, 1973).

58. See, for example, Thomas L. Webber, *Deep Like the Rivers: Education in the Slave Quarter Community* (New York: Norton, 1978); Albert J. Raboteau, *Slave Religion: The "Invisible Institution" in the Antebellum South* (New York: Oxford University Press, 1978); John B. Boles, *Black Southerners, 1619-1869* (Lexington: University of Kentucky Press, 1984), 153-69; and Paul E. Johnson, ed., *African-American Christianity* (Berkeley: University of California Press, 1994).

sometimes taught their own slaves even in those states. Between five and ten percent of adult slaves must have possessed some informally taught literacy and numeracy, for these were useful in the skilled and supervisory occupations performed by the top echelon of enslaved workers. Some masters and mistresses also felt a religious obligation to teach their slaves to read, as Frederick Douglass recalled learning from the woman who owned him in Maryland.[59] In the free Negro communities there were schools — almost always segregated, even in the North. These schools had usually been created by white religious philanthropy and/or black self-help, seldom by local public authorities. In Connecticut, Prudence Crandall's efforts to provide secondary education for black girls were actually opposed by the authorities.[60]

Religious-sponsored education for Native Americans figured prominently in the most dramatic actual clash between the Second Great Awakening and the government: the long crisis over Cherokee removal, 1828-39. The American Board of Commissioners for Foreign Missions and other Christian missionaries had established schools in the Cherokee Nation. Sometimes the mission schools enjoyed a measure of federal support, one more example of mixed public-private enterprises. Such schools generally sought to assimilate the Indians into Euro-American culture in the process of converting them to Christianity. They taught much the same curriculum, sometimes including Latin, that was taught to white students. A missionary-educated elite emerged in Cherokee society, melding Native achievements like Sequoia's invention of a system for writing the Cherokee language with Western civilization and technology.[61]

The State of Georgia determined to interrupt this process. An educated Indian population, determined to retain their land and develop their resources, could block white expansion all the more effectively.[62] Accordingly, when Geor-

---

59. There are no hard data on slave literacy. The most commonly given estimate is five percent, but the most thorough study to date concludes that ten percent is closer to the truth. Janet Duitsman Cornelius, *"When I Can Read My Title Clear": Literacy, Slavery, and Religion in the Antebellum South* (Columbia: University of South Carolina Press, 1991), 8-10, 62-67. See also Beth Barton Schweiger, *The Gospel Working Up: Progress and the Pulpit in Nineteenth-Century Virginia* (New York: Oxford University Press, 2000), 73.

60. Kaestle, *Pillars of the Republic*, 171-75; Brown, *Strength of a People*, 170-83.

61. For a contemporary source sharing the missionaries' outlook, see Jedidiah Morse, *Report to the Secretary of War of the United States, on Indian Affairs* (New Haven, 1822); for a critical secondary interpretation, see William G. McLoughlin, *Cherokees and Missionaries, 1789-1839* (New Haven: Yale University Press, 1984). See also Michael C. Coleman, "Cherokee Girls at Brainerd Mission," in *Between Indian and White Worlds,* ed. Margaret Connell Szasz (Norman: Oklahoma University Press, 1994), 122-35.

62. Anthony F. C. Wallace, *The Long, Bitter, Trail: Andrew Jackson and the Indians* (New York: Hill & Wang, 1993), 62.

gia unilaterally extended its laws over the Cherokee Nation in 1828, it forbade the missionaries to remain without state licenses. Two missionaries who defied the state, Samuel Worcester and Elizur Butler, were arrested and imprisoned. They challenged the validity of Georgia's action as a violation of the federal treaty of 1785 with the Cherokees and took their case to the Supreme Court. Basing his opinion in *Worcester v. Georgia* (1832) on the federal supremacy clause of the Constitution, Chief Justice Marshall in effect sided with the Awakening against state rights, as he had in the Dartmouth College Case.[63] His decision upheld the legal claims of the missionaries and their Cherokee hosts, but President Andrew Jackson made it clear he would never enforce the Court's ruling and the Cherokees wound up on their infamous forced migration to Oklahoma (the "Trail of Tears") in 1838-39. Similar policies were followed with other tribes. Despite the thin disguise of a professed desire to continue the educational-assimilation process on western reservations, the Jeffersonian/Jacksonian state demonstrated hostility to Native American education whenever its fruits conflicted, even potentially, with the material interests of white would-be settlers.[64]

Of course, schools and colleges are not the only vehicles of education. Many people learned how to read at home. Parents taught their children by candlelight or by the fireside — especially in rural areas where schools were scarce. Beth Schweiger's studies of literacy among the southern yeomanry show that though only 40 percent of southern white children went to school, 80 percent of southern white adults could read. This indicates that a lot of people were acquiring at least rudimentary literacy at home. Why did farm parents, tired at the end of a day's work in the fields, make time to teach their children? The primary motive seems not to have been commercial or political, still less to facilitate the children's upward social mobility. It was religious. Among many other uses, the family Bible served as a primer. Although Protestant piety did not produce free common schools in the rural and individualistic South, the way it did in the villages of New England, Protestantism still promoted literacy in the South.[65]

In its broadest definition, education is the entire process of cultural transmission, as historians like Bernard Bailyn and Lawrence Cremin have made clear to us.[66] The first half of the nineteenth century was a time of rapidly ex-

---

63. *Worcester v. Georgia*, 6 Peters 515-97 (1832).

64. Jeffersonian professions are taken seriously in Ronald M. Satz, *American Indian Policy in the Jacksonian Era* (Lincoln: University of Nebraska Press, 1975). See also Robert Remini, *The Life of Andrew Jackson* (New York: Harper & Row, 1988); and John Ehle, *Trail of Tears: The Rise and Fall of the Cherokee Nation* (New York: Doubleday/Anchor, 1988).

65. Schweiger, *The Gospel Working Up*, 67, 202.

66. Bernard Bailyn, *Education in the Formation of American Society* (New York: Norton, 1972; first pub. 1960); Cremin, *American Education*, ix.

panding communications, enabling people to be better informed about the world than ever before. The distribution of magazines, newspapers, and books benefited from improvements in printing, paper, and transportation; mail service integrated commercial and civic life; by the end of our period telegraphy had been invented. The Second Great Awakening both exploited and fostered these developments.[67] Among the many agencies for the dissemination of ideas and attitudes in the early republic, those of the Awakening were prominent. Voluntary associations to achieve particular purposes, such as the Bible Society, the Tract Society, the Sunday-School Union, and the sabbatarian, temperance, mission, antislavery, and peace movements, often operated under lay leadership and educated a broad public in the issues of the day. Evangelical Christianity was efficiently organized at a time when little else in American society was — when, for example, there was no bureaucracy but the Post Office and no nationwide business corporation save the Bank of the United States. Evangelical voluntary associations socialized individuals to community concerns, dominated the cultural landscape, brought order to the frontier, and at times mobilized voters at the polls.[68]

The educational function of the evangelical associations was particularly important in the case of women. Excluded from political institutions, women found their inclusion in the benevolent societies to be of momentous importance. Countless women were educated in responsible public awareness as well as organizational and publicity skills through the "women's auxiliaries" of evangelical voluntary organizations. When women's rights emerged as a cause at Seneca Falls in 1848, it came out of the womb of religious reform, and in particular the antislavery movement.[69]

---

67. See Richard D. Brown, *Knowledge Is Power: The Diffusion of Information in Early America, 1700-1865* (New York: Oxford University Press, 1989); Richard R. John, *Spreading the News: The American Postal System from Franklin to Morse* (Cambridge, Mass.: Harvard University Press, 1995), esp. chaps. 5 and 7; David Paul Nord, *Evangelical Origins of Mass Media in America, 1815-1835* (Columbia, S.C.: Journalism Monographs, 1984).

68. Among many works, see Richard Carwardine, *Evangelicals and Politics in Antebellum America* (New Haven: Yale University Press, 1993); Donald G. Mathews, *Religion in the Old South* (Chicago: University of Chicago Press, 1977); and Randolph A. Roth, *The Democratic Dilemma: Religion, Reform, and the Social Order in the Connecticut River Valley of Vermont, 1791-1850* (Cambridge: Cambridge University Press, 1987).

69. See Nancy A. Hardesty, *Your Daughters Shall Prophesy: Revivalism and Feminism in the Age of Finney* (Brooklyn: Carlson, 1991); Nancy A. Hewitt, *Women's Activism and Social Change: Rochester, New York, 1822-1872* (Ithaca: Cornell University Press, 1984); Ross Paulson, *Women's Suffrage and Prohibition* (Glenview, Ill.: Scott, Foresman, 1973); and Stuart Blumin, *The Emergence of the Middle Class: Social Experience in the American City, 1760-1900* (Cambridge: Cambridge University Press, 1989).

## Bringing the State Back into Education

The American Enlightenment had made big plans for education in the young republic, but proved unable to carry them out effectively. The Evangelical revival demonstrated more effectiveness in educational initiatives, but had not entirely succeeded in providing education to all, regardless of economic status or sectarian affiliation. What a diverse American society needed at this juncture was a movement capable of synthesizing the civic objectives of the Enlightenment with the energy and commitment of the Awakening. Such a movement appeared in the educational reforms embraced by the Whig party in the 1830s. The Whig party was formed out of a combination of former Federalists who had come to terms with democratic politics and Jeffersonian Republicans who had decided to accept a positive role for the state.[70]

An early exemplar of the advantages of energetic government was New York's Governor DeWitt Clinton. Clinton represented the wing of the Republican Party that had become persuaded of the benefits of economic development, and to this end supported state aid to education as well as to transportation projects ("internal improvements") like the Erie Canal. During his terms as governor (1817-23, 1825-28), Clinton proved a steadfast advocate of popular education, maintained through cooperation between private and public agencies. He also secured legislative appropriations to help the scientific and agricultural societies in his state. The New York (City) Free School Society (after 1825 called the New York Public School Society) a private agency to which were delegated public functions, exemplified the public-private partnership Clintonians approved.[71] DeWitt Clinton also supported women's education; he tried to found a state college of technology for women, but failed to obtain funding for it. In 1821 Emma Willard succeeded in founding Troy Female Seminary, a private secondary school that pioneered the teaching of science to women.[72]

The greatest of the Whig educational reformers was, of course, Horace Mann (1796-1859), who became secretary of the newly created Massachusetts State Board of Education in 1837. From that vantage point Mann tirelessly crusaded on

70. See Daniel Walker Howe, *The Political Culture of the American Whigs* (Chicago: University of Chicago Press, 1979).

71. On the New York Free School Society, see Timothy Smith, "Protestant Schooling and American Nationality," *Journal of American History* 53 (1967): 679-95. Some of DeWitt Clinton's statements on education are reprinted in Wilson Smith, ed., *Theories of Education in Early America* (Indianapolis: Bobbs-Merrill, 1973), 340-60; and in Welter, ed., *American Writings on Popular Education*, 23-25.

72. Edward W. Stevens Jr., *The Grammar of the Machine: Technical Literacy and Early Industrial Expansion in the United States* (New Haven: Yale University Press, 1995), 133-47.

behalf of "common schools" — schools that the whole population would have in common, tuition-free, tax-supported, meeting statewide standards of curriculum, textbooks, and facilities, staffed with teachers who had been trained in state Normal Schools, modeled on the French *Ecole Normale*. In Massachusetts, Mann could build on the strongest tradition of public education in any state. Ever since the seventeenth century, towns (later school districts) had been required by statute to maintain schools, though only gradually had the commonwealth come to provide any financial or other support for localities in meeting this obligation. The important thing was that local communities had become accustomed to taxing themselves to support education (and, for that matter, religion).[73] On the basis of this past history, Horace Mann was able to erect that structure of state-supported public education which had eluded Thomas Jefferson. Mann did not manage to avoid religious conflicts, but he did avoid Jefferson's political error of pitting education against organized religion in general.

Mann shared Jefferson's vision of a democratic republic based on a standardized state educational system, but unlike Jefferson he felt no misgivings about the exercise of state power. A political disciple of John Quincy Adams, Mann succeeded to that ex-president's seat in the federal House of Representatives for the Eighth Congressional District of Massachusetts after Adams's death in 1848.[74] As a follower of Adams, Mann did not have to learn his faith in strong government from overseas. But European examples did illustrate for him what an energetic and enlightened state could achieve. Having toured Europe in 1843, Mann came away impressed by the school system of the Kingdom of Prussia. The Prussian educational system was linked with the state Protestant church in the Ministry of Education and Religious Affairs. Over 80 percent of the school-age population received formal instruction. The Prussian system employed some of the pedagogical innovations of the Swiss educator Johann Heinrich Pestalozzi.[75] Mann admired the Pestalozzian theories and their Prussian implementation, the use of teaching aids like blackboards, and restraint in the application of corporal punishment.[76]

73. On Mann in his context, see Daniel W. Howe, "The History of Education as Cultural History," *History of Education Quarterly* 22 (1982): 205-14.

74. On Mann's Congressional career, see Susan-Mary Grant, "Representative Mann: Horace Mann, the Republican Experiment and the South," *Journal of American Studies* 32 (1998): 105-23.

75. See Marjori Lamberti, *State, Society, and the Elementary School in Imperial Germany* (New York: Oxford University Press, 1989), 13-39; Karl Schleunes, *Schooling and Society: The Politics of Education in Prussia and Bavaria* (New York: St. Martin's Press, 1989), 50-99.

76. See Jonathan Messerli, *Horace Mann* (New York: Alfred A. Knopf, 1972), 392-96, 406-407.

Mann's educational goals were partly humanistic — the balanced development of human nature — and partly civic — the creation of a responsible citizenry. As a result, he articulated a combination of humane, Lockean pedagogy and classical republican preoccupation with civic virtue. On the individual level, his objective was conventional: a balanced character, with the passions under the dominion of reason and the moral sense. People needed such individual characters in order to be fit for freedom; self-government on the psychological level was a prerequisite to self-government on the political level. Mann had little faith in institutional restraints in the absence of moral ones, inculcated by home and school. His goal was the creation of rational, disciplined, autonomous individuals.[77]

As envisioned by Mann and his successors until long after the Civil War, the common schools embodied a common ideology. The distinguished educational historian Lawrence Cremin has called their ideology a *paideia*, that is, a set of integrated cultural ideals together with a program for achieving these ideals through education. *Paideia* was originally an ancient Greek conception, and because of the importance of classical learning and ideals to Mann's generation of Americans it provides a particularly relevant way of understanding their goals. The *paideia* of the American common schools included patriotic virtue, a balanced, responsible character, and democratic participation, all to be developed through intellectual discipline and the nurture of the moral qualities.[78]

It would never have occurred to Mann and his disciples that such an educational program would not include religion, but since they wanted above all to achieve an education common to all, this necessitated a common religious instruction. Following Mann's lead, the Massachusetts School Board prescribed that only those doctrines should be taught on which all Protestants agreed. In the days of more local autonomy, school districts had taught the religion of the local majority. With Horace Mann, a Unitarian Christian follower of William Ellery Channing, the Second Great Awakening took on a generalized form to render it politically acceptable to as broad a base of the commonwealth's electorate as possible. Mann's approach in the common schools constituted a "least common denominator" of Protestant Christianity.[79] On this basis, the state was brought back into an active role in shaping American education.

The Normal Schools that Mann created (beginning with Lexington in

77. Horace Mann, "The Necessity of Education in a Republican Government" (1838), in *Life and Works of Horace Mann*, Vol. 2 (Cambridge, Mass., 1867), 143-188; partially reprinted in Howe, ed., *The American Whigs*, 148-58.

78. Cremin, *American Education;* he borrowed the term from Werner Jaeger, *Paideia: The Ideals of Greek Culture*, trans. Gilbert Highet (New York: Oxford University Press, 1945).

79. See Daniel Walker Howe, *Making the American Self*, chapter 6.

1839) constituted perhaps his most important innovation. The precursors of teacher training colleges, the Normal Schools defined "norms," that is, standard guidelines for prospective teachers. The Normal Schools turned out to be the vehicle through which women in large numbers first entered any profession, fulfilling Catharine Beecher's call in her *Essay on the Education of Female Teachers* (1835). Since they were paid less than men were, women teachers provided a human resource agreeable to legislators worried about the cost of Mann's ambitious plans. The Whig governor, Edward Everett, gave Mann solid support in appointments to the board and helped him overcome opposition from jealous local authorities, doctrinaire Christian groups, and pedagogically conservative schoolmasters. When a Democrat, Marcus Morton, was elected governor by a margin of one vote in 1839, he proved unable to persuade the General Court (as the Massachusetts legislature is called) to abolish Mann's Board of Education and its new Normal Schools.[80]

At the top of Mann's agenda was the education of the immigrants, especially the children of migrant laborers, both to improve their chances in life and to ensure their assimilation into American democracy. But the nondenominational Protestant schools that Mann created proved to be unacceptable to the growing Irish immigrant community and their increasingly self-conscious Roman Catholic clergy. The values of American Catholic leaders differed significantly from those of Protestant educators and were not so easily harmonized with the Enlightenment. Although Catholic educators reposed at least as much faith in a classical curriculum as their Protestant counterparts, they did not share Mann's educational objectives. Unlike the Protestants, the conservative Catholic educators of the time, usually members of religious orders, had not reached an accord with the Enlightenment. Their model of human nature, based like that of the Protestants upon faculty psychology, built on the classical foundation of Aristotle via Thomas Aquinas. But Horace Mann's ideal of the autonomous individual, so typical of nineteenth-century liberalism, was not their ideal. Responding to Ultramontane authoritarianism, the Irish Catholic clergy emphasized the organic unity of society, the risks of anarchy and innovation, the virtues of obedience and resignation, the redemptive value of suffering.[81] Although American Catholics themselves expressed confidence in the compatibility of their goals

80. Messerli, *Horace Mann*, 326-31; Carl F. Kaestle and Maris A. Vinovskis, *Education and Social Change in Nineteenth-Century Massachusetts* (Cambridge, Mass.: Harvard University Press, 1980), 221-28.

81. For the outlook of the Catholic educators, see John T. McGreevy, *Catholicism and American Freedom* (New York: Norton, 2003), chapter 1. For the influence of Ultramontanism, see Dale B. Light, *Rome and the New Republic: Conflict and Community in Philadelphia Catholicism between the Revolution and the Civil War* (Notre Dame: University of Notre Dame Press, 1996).

with American republicanism, Protestants were not so sure of this. (The nineteenth-century papacy, fearful of modernity and democracy, shared the American Protestants' suspicions of such incompatibility and eventually condemned one form of harmonization as the "Americanist Heresy.")

Conflict between Protestant-public schools and the Catholic minority first came to a head not in Massachusetts but in New York in 1839. Bishop (later Archbishop) John Hughes led the New York Catholics through the controversy; a superb administrator, Hughes was also skilled in politics. The clash provoked the downfall of Clinton's New York Public School Society and embarrassed Whig Governor William H. Seward. While Nativists warned of the Catholic menace to democratic values and the Democratic Party seized the opportunity to split the Whigs, Hughes welcomed the chance to place himself at the forefront of a community he feared might otherwise be led by secularist Irish nationalists. Seward tried vainly to bridge the gap between the two sides with an unsuccessful proposal for state subsidies to Catholic schools, as Protestant educational enterprises had so often been subsidized. Instead the legislature stripped the Public School Society of its power and ruled that no public money should go to any school in which religion was taught.[82]

The rest of the country could draw a clear lesson: where public aid to Protestant institutions had been within the bounds of political acceptability, such aid to Catholic institutions was not. The old model of public-private partnership was doomed; a new sense of the distinction between public and private had to be imposed, in schools as in colleges. When faced with a charge of inconsistency, public authorities would cut off aid to Protestants rather than extend it to include Catholics.

To be sure, many public, or common, schools would retain features of nondenominational Protestantism for a good many years to come. Horace Mann hoped that passages from the Bible, read without interpretation, might offer a nonsectarian common religious ground. Although Catholics and even some of the Protestant sects did not find this acceptable, Bible reading in the common schools was a widespread and even increasing practice in nineteenth-century America. The historian Laurence Moore has estimated that over half of American common schools practiced Bible reading at the end of the nineteenth century.[83]

82. See Martin Meenagh, "John J. Hughes, First Archbishop of New York, and the Atlantic Irish" (D.Phil. thesis, Oxford University, 2003); Glyndon Van Deusen, "Seward and the School Question Reconsidered," *Journal of American History* 52 (1965): 313-19; Vincent P. Lannie, *Public Money and Parochial Education: Bishop Hughes, Governor Seward, and the New York School Controversy* (Cleveland: Case Western Reserve University, 1968).

83. R. Laurence Moore, "Bible Reading and Nonsectarian Schooling," *Journal of American History* 86 (March 2000): 1581-99.

However, the common school *paideia* of nondenominational Protestant-ism could not be redefined to a Christianity that would include Catholicism. American Catholics moved, slowly and at great expense, toward the creation of their own parochial school system.[84] The scholastic synthesis of Christianity and the classics that Catholic education perpetuated continued on through most of the twentieth century, proving even more durable than its Protestant counterpart.[85]

## Conclusion

In traditional Western civilization, the church had been in charge of the educational system. After the American Revolution, the question was raised whether the state would replace the church in this role. The principles of the Enlightenment seemed to demand an educated citizenry to be vigilant in protection of its own liberty. In spite of this, the American state accomplished surprisingly little in the realm of education during the first half century of independence. Notwithstanding a generation of discussion, the recently established federal government refused to accept any responsibility for education, even a national university. The attempt by the Federalists to perpetuate the church-state-college alliance of colonial times foundered on the rock of religious diversity. Widespread dislike of strong government and taxation at all levels proved a serious obstacle to initiatives in education.

But if religious diversity was a problem for education, religious energy was an asset. The states aided education more effectively in places like New England where they could build on traditions of religious education than where stricter separation of church and state was enforced. Rising to the opportunities presented by religious disestablishment, the many religious sects proliferated denominational academies and colleges that partially filled the vacuum left by state inaction and met, at least to some extent, the needs of local communities. The methods and objectives of Protestant religious educators, who sought to promote social virtues and disciplined, balanced individual character, broadly coincided with the needs of the civil state for good citizens. In many ways, edu-

84. See Jay Dolan, *The Immigrant Church: New York's Irish and German Catholics, 1815-1865* (Baltimore: Johns Hopkins University Press, 1975), 99-120; and Philip Gleason, "The Schools Question: A Centennial Retrospect," in Gleason, *Keeping the Faith: American Catholicism Past and Present* (Notre Dame: Notre Dame University Press, 1987), 115-35.

85. See Edward J. Power, *Catholic Higher Education in America* (New York: Appleton-Century-Crofts, 1972); and Philip Gleason, *Contending with Modernity: Catholic Higher Education in the Twentieth Century* (New York: Oxford University Press, 1995).

cation in the early republic seemed to owe more to the principles of the Reformation than to those of the Enlightenment.

It was only in the 1830s and 1840s that the political leaders of the Whig party succeeded in synthesizing moral and religious motives for education with civic and economic ones so as to secure state support and sponsorship of education on a large scale. In a sense, the Whig educational reformers reconciled the Reformation with the Enlightenment, instead of pitting them against each other as Jefferson had been wont to do. With the Whigs came the beginnings of school systems, rather than individual local schools, either public or private.

The distinction between the public and the private, in education as in other spheres, was still in the process of definition in the early republic. During the period we have examined, Americans did not practice the separation of church and state as we now understand it.[86] To be sure, Jefferson and some of his followers like Thomas Cooper espoused the principle, which is why Jefferson remains a favorite source of quotations cited by present-day guardians of the separation. But in political terms the secularism of Jeffersonian educational theory constituted a distinct liability and helps explain the widespread failure to implement Jeffersonian educational plans. More successful than Jefferson in sponsoring education in the early republic were National Republicans like DeWitt Clinton and Whigs like Horace Mann, both of whom were willing to accept a place for religion in publicly supported education. The arguments being made in the early republic on behalf of education — the need for a virtuous citizenry and responsible individual characters — were, after all, arguments that also suggested the social value of religion. However, cooperation between church and state on behalf of education became much more difficult after the rise of Roman Catholicism to a position of significance within the American commonweal. Ironically, it was not so much the power of Jeffersonian educational ideals as the estrangement between the Protestant and Catholic branches of Christianity that led to the triumph of secularism in American education.

86. See Philip Hamburger, *The Separation of Church and State* (Cambridge, Mass.: Harvard Univ. Press, 2002), which distinguishes separation of church and state from the free exercise of religion guaranteed in the First Amendment.

# Catholicism and Abolition:
# A Historical (and Theological) Problem

John T. McGreevy

No political and social issue in American history goes more directly or deeply to the question of the human person than the issue of slavery. We have so completely absorbed the implications of the abolition of slavery, and the view of the human person that made it possible, that we can barely imagine today that civilized people tolerated, let alone endorsed, its existence. It takes an enormous leap of the historical imagination, as well as great reserves of charity, to understand how men and women living in an avowedly Christian society, whose foundational political document declared it to be self-evident that "all men are created equal," could have so readily acquiesced in the ownership of, and trafficking in, other human beings. Indeed, the wonder to us is not that there were abolitionists, but that there were so few of them, and that they aroused such antagonism. Nor is that the only surprise. Accustomed to thinking of the Roman Catholic Church's visible social witness in recent decades, modern scholars are astonished to find that such Catholic social activism was next to nonexistent in the great cause of abolition a century before. Why was this so? Why did so few nineteenth-century Catholics became abolitionists? Why did Catholics regard abolitionism in such neutral or negative terms? And why did abolitionists so often return the favor?

It would be simple to answer this question with the very sort of anti-Catholic accusation, exemplified by Theodore Parker's words just below, that antebellum America already abounded in. Catholics, in this view, were conditioned to favor authoritarian, hierarchical, and paternalistic institutions, and to devalue the rights and judgments of free individuals. The whole purpose of Catholic formation was to create servile and unquestioning persons, who would not be fit to be good American republican citizens. But historian John McGreevy believes the answer has to be sought on a deeper level, one that takes into account the dramatic philosophical differences between Protestant and Catholic understandings of the human person, differences that he believes still exist and still matter today. Answering this question requires consideration of the "moral conventions" that separated Catholics from the burgeoning liberalism of that era. Catholics were convinced that the human person must be understood as embedded in networks of family, community and church, while religious and nonreligious liberals, supported by the Protestant tenor of the culture, were equally convinced that the most authentic human person was the autonomous and self-motivating person, and that Roman Catholicism stood as the eternal enemy of that ideal. McGreevy suggests that these contrasting sets of moral conventions formed the intellectual and ideological grid within which the issue of slavery, and other social issues, must be understood. This argument does not exonerate the Roman Catholic Church or explain away its indifference to the abolitionist cause. But it suggests that the sources of opposition were deeper and more complex than has generally been appreciated. It also suggests, surprisingly, that those very sources might prove very useful to us today, to counteract an entirely different set of problems, arising out of the hypertrophy of liberalism. Catholics, he argues, have been much more alert to the limitations of liberal individualism in a society that consistently places individual rights over communal obligations. John T. McGreevy is Chair and Professor of History at the University of Notre Dame, and author of *Parish Boundaries* (Chicago, 1996) and *Catholicism and American Freedom* (Norton, 2003).

# I

Abolitionist Theodore Parker, in a widely noticed 1854 sermon on the dangers threatening the United States:

> The Catholic clergy are on the side of slavery. They find it is the dominant power, and pay court thereto that they may rise by its help. They love slavery itself; it is an institution thoroughly congenial to them, consistent with the first principles of their Church.[1]

Was Parker right? Answering this question requires revisiting a venerable historical problem. Why did some people become abolitionists in the late eigh-

---

1. Theodore Parker, "A Sermon of the Dangers Which Threaten the Rights of Man in America," July 2, 1854, in Parker, *Additional Speeches, Addresses, and Occasional Sermons*, Volume 2 (Boston, 1855), 244.

teenth and nineteenth centuries, and why, more challenging for us moderns, did more people choose not to?

The touchstone for discussion of modern antislavery movements remains the spirited mid-1980s debate between Thomas Haskell and David Brion Davis in the *American Historical Review*.[2] Heat replaced light as the two combatants exchanged blows, but a summary might run as follows: Haskell cast serious doubt on Davis's claim, made in his monumental *The Problem of Slavery in the Age of Revolution, 1770-1823*, that abolitionists, by championing slave emancipation instead of ameliorating the plight of industrial workers, "reinforced or legitimized" capitalist exploitation.[3] But Haskell's tentative explanation for the rise of antislavery sentiment — reformers were inspired by the "widening of causal horizons" associated with the rise of capitalism — seemed aloof from the sources, and unhelpful for countries such as the Netherlands where capitalism flourished and antislavery sentiment did not.[4]

A decade later, Elizabeth Clark advanced the discussion. While the oscillating fortunes of antislavery sentiment after 1750 showed no direct relationship to a steadily expanding market capitalism, the antislavery movement, Clark argued, depended upon the new eagerness of liberal Protestants to alleviate human suffering, especially the suffering of slaves. Rejecting Calvinist understandings of a sovereign God who demanded human suffering as atonement for sin, many nineteenth-century liberal Protestants came to understand pain and suffering as a violation of God's order on earth, a problem to be remedied by social reform.[5]

Extending Clark's insight in the opposite direction, this essay asks the following question: why did so few Catholics, in the United States and around the world, become abolitionists, and why did so many abolitionists remain suspicious of Catholicism?

Answering this question requires consideration of the divide separating liberals from Catholics during much of the nineteenth century, what one histo-

---

2. The Davis and Haskell essays, along with two contributions by John Ashworth, are collected in *The Anti-Slavery Debate: Capitalism and Abolitionism as a Problem in Historical Interpretation*, ed. Thomas Bender (Berkeley, 1992).

3. Bender, ed., *The Anti-Slavery Debate*, 70-71.

4. Seymour Drescher, "The Long Goodbye: Dutch Capitalism and Antislavery in Comparative Perspective," in *Fifty Years Later: Antislavery, Capitalism and Modernity in the Dutch Orbit*, ed. Gert Oostindie (Leiden, 1995), 26-66.

5. Elizabeth B. Clark, "The Sacred Rights of the Weak: Pain, Sympathy, and the Culture of Individual Rights in Antebellum America," *Journal of American History* 82 (September 1995): 463-93. On the theological debate, see David F. Wells, "The Collision of Views on the Atonement," *Bibliotheca Sacra* 144 (Oct-December 1987): 363-76.

rian has recently identified as a "central theme" of modern history.[6] The slavery debate highlights this division, but only a more systematic look at moral conventions makes sense of it. Or as philosopher Michael Sandel puts it, "For all our uncertainties about ultimate questions of political philosophy, . . . the one thing we know is that we live *some* answer all the time."[7] Perhaps Catholics lived one answer to the question of immediate emancipation in the nineteenth century (convinced that the human person must be understood as embedded in networks of family, community and church, convinced that suffering was redemptive) while liberals (convinced that the most authentic human person was autonomous, convinced that Catholicism corrupted autonomy) lived another.

## II

How did Catholics think about slavery? Like almost all Christians, Catholics in the early nineteenth century faced few restrictions on their ability to own slaves. Masters must permit slave marriages, Catholic theologians agreed, and educate their slaves in the rudiments of the faith, but slavery itself, as confirmed by Aristotle and St. Paul, did not violate either the natural law or church teaching. In a theological tradition that distinguished itself from Protestantism by claims of constancy, any shift in the Catholic position on slavery faced formidable hurdles.[8]

6. Raymond Grew, "Liberty and the Catholic Church in Nineteenth-Century Europe," in *Freedom and Religion in the Nineteenth Century,* ed. Richard Helmstadter (Stanford, 1997), 197. Grew refers to modern European history but the point could be extended to North and South America. For example, *The Politics of Religion in an Age of Revival: Studies in Nineteenth Century Europe and Latin America,* ed. Austen Ivereigh (London, 2000); John T. McGreevy, *Catholicism and American Freedom: A History* (New York: W. W. Norton, 2003).

7. Michael J. Sandel, "The Procedural Republic and the Unencumbered Self," *Political Theory* 12 (February 1984): 81.

8. Two new books, published too recently, unfortunately, for discussion in this essay, deepen our understanding of Catholics and the American debate over slavery: Mark A. Noll, *The Civil War as a Theological Crisis* (Chapel Hill, 2006), 125-155; and Matteo Sanfillippo, *L'Affermazione del Cattolicesimo Nel Nord America: Elite, Emigrante E Chiesa Cattolica Negli Stati Uniti E in Canada, 1750-1920* (Viterbo, 2003), 100-115. The most useful and wide-ranging discussion is John Francis Maxwell, *Slavery and the Catholic Church: The History of Catholic Teaching Concerning the Moral Legitimacy of the Institution of Slavery* (Chichester, 1975). For the United States the basic source remains Madeleine Hooke Rice, *American Catholic Opinion on the Slavery Controversy* (New York, 1944). Thomas Murphy, S.J., *Jesuit Slaveholding in Maryland 1717-1838* (New York, 2001) is also useful. For a survey focusing on France, Claude Prudhomme, "L'Église catholique et l'esclavage: une aussi longue attente," in *L'Église et l'Abolition de l'Esclavage,* ed. Guy Bedouelle, O.P., et al. (Paris: Le Centre D'Études du Saulchoir, 1999), 9-20. On slavery and doctrinal development the crucial source is now John T. Noonan, Jr., *A Church*

Still, a handful of European Catholic theologians criticized slavery in the early nineteenth century, and in some ways Catholics seemed more accepting of African Americans than were white Protestants. Both white and African American Protestants chided co-religionists by noting that Roman Catholic churches in the American South rarely segregated worshippers: "her consolations are open alike to black and white, bond and free."[9]

In the early nineteenth century, most Latin American countries gradually abolished slavery with minimal controversy.[10] In 1839, Pope Gregory XVI published an apostolic letter banning Catholic participation in the slave trade. That same year, the French Catholic statesman Charles Montalembert expressed his horror of American slavery, and along with Félix Dupanloup, the liberal bishop of Orléans, Montalembert would lead the Catholic component of the successful campaign to abolish slavery in French colonies in the late 1840s. (And here enthusiasm for abolition among enslaved African Catholics was often vital.)[11] Ireland's Daniel O'Connell attacked Irish-Americans tolerant of American slavery in 1843.[12]

All this made an alliance between Catholics and anti-slavery activists seem possible. In Boston, Wendell Phillips denounced "Prejudice against Catholics among abolitionists" and, after reading Gregory XVI's 1839 letter, the "first papal bull which was ever read in Faneuil Hall," led a crowd of abolitionists in

---

*That Can and Cannot Change* (Notre Dame, 2005), 17-123. For a thorough examination, Joseph Edward Capizzi, "A Development of Doctrine: The Challenge of Slavery to Moral Theology" (Ph.D. dissertation, University of Notre Dame, 1998).

9. "Colour in the Catholic Church," *National Anti-Slavery Standard* 8 (July 1, 1847): 17; James McCune Smith to Horace Greeley, January 29, 1844, in *The Black Abolitionist Papers:* Volume 3, *The United States, 1830-1846,* ed. C. Peter Ripley (Chapel Hill, 1991), 435.

10. Herbert S. Klein, *African Slavery in Latin America and the Caribbean* (New York, 1986), 250-52.

11. Charles de Montalembert to Fr. Jean Baptiste Henri Lacordaire, O.P., September 20, 1839 in *Lacordaire-Montalembert Correspondance Inédite, 1830-1861,* ed. Louis Le Guillou (Paris, 1989), 449; Charles de Montalembert, "Emancipation des Esclaves" (April 7, 1845) and "Emancipation des Noirs dans les Colonies" (March 30, 1847), in Montalembert, *Oeuvres de M. le comte de Montalembert,* Volume 2 (Paris, 1860), 59-62, 461-72. Lawrence C. Jennings, *French Anti-Slavery: The Movement for the Abolition of Slavery in France, 1802-1848* (New York, 2000), 213-46. See also an important new study, Troy Feay, "Mission to Moralize: Slaves, Africans, and Missionaries in the French Colonies, 1815-1852" (Ph.D. dissertation, University of Notre Dame, 2003).

12. Daniel O'Connell, "Daniel O'Connell and the Committee of the Irish Repeal Association of Cincinnati" [1843], in *Union Pamphlets of the Civil War, 1861-1865:* Volume 2, ed. Frank Freidel (Cambridge, 1967), 802-803. On this episode, see Gilbert Osofsky, "Abolitionists, Irish Immigrants and the Dilemmas of Romantic Nationalism," *American Historical Review* 80 (October 1975): 889-912.

three cheers for the pope.[13] One American abolitionist recalled that Catholic opinion on the slavery question seemed open into the early 1850s:

> It was still doubtful which side of the slavery question the Roman church would take. O'Connell was in the zenith of his power and popularity, was decidedly anti-slavery, and members of Catholic churches chose sides according to personal feeling, as did those of other churches. It was not until 1852, that abolitionists began to feel the alliance between Romanism and slavery; but from that time, to be a member of the Roman church was to be a friend of "Southern interests."[14]

## III

In fact, the trend of Catholic opinion was already clear. The Catholics central to the abolition of slavery in early-nineteenth-century Latin America were probably more influenced by Enlightenment thought (Catholic and non-Catholic) than the ultramontane theology and philosophy that would sweep across the Catholic world in the mid-nineteenth century.[15] Montalembert and Dupanloup were liberals on a variety of theological and political issues, and the two men would soon become embroiled in struggles with Pope Pius IX and Vatican officials over religious and academic freedom and papal infallibility. O'Connell died in 1847, but even before his death Irish Catholics in the United States had urged him to reconsider his views on slavery. From Savannah, Georgia, came the lament "that he [O'Connell] has learned his lessons on Southern institutions from Northern Abolitionists, the dire enemies of real liberties, and the notorious enemies of Ireland's religion."[16] A leading American Jesuit, a native of Cork, quietly dismissed O'Connell's "invectives against slavery."[17]

Recent commentary on the O'Connell episode has highlighted Irish American recalcitrance on the slavery issue, emphasizing the desire of working-class Irish immigrants to deflect possible competition from freed African American workers, and to capture the material and psychological benefits of identifying

---

13. "Grand Meeting in Faneuil Hall," *Liberator* 13 (November 24, 1843): 187.

14. Jane Grey Swisshelm, *Half a Century* (Chicago, [1880] 1970), 150.

15. Suggestive on this point is Pamela Voekel, *Alone Before God: The Religious Origins of Modernity in Mexico* (Durham, N.C., 2002).

16. Thomas Paul Thigpen, "Aristocracy of the Heart: Catholic Lay Leadership in Savannah 1820-1870" (Ph.D. dissertation, Emory University, 1995), 591.

17. Thomas Morrissey, S.J., *As One Sent Peter Kenney S.J. 1779-1841: His Mission in Ireland and North America* (Dublin, 1996), 433.

themselves as white. The Catholic church, in this view, did little more than "reflect the racial attitudes of its members."[18]

This argument neglects uneasiness about abolition found among German and French Catholics, as well as opposition to abolition among affluent Catholics not vulnerable to competition from African American labor. Studies of membership lists for American abolitionist organizations in the 1830s find few Catholics, and not one prominent American Catholic urged immediate emancipation before the Civil War.[19] Of course most white Americans rejected the idea of immediate slave emancipation up until the Civil War, although most white northerners endorsed Abraham Lincoln's pledge to block any expansion of slavery. But Methodists, Presbyterians, Episcopalians, and Baptists had important abolitionist or antislavery wings, while Catholics did not.

Catholic opposition to abolition cannot be reduced to the particular American racial dynamic. Instead, many Catholic intellectuals around the world — in France and the French Caribbean in the 1840s, the Dutch colony of Curaçao in the 1850s, Cuba in the 1860s, and Brazil in the 1880s — tended to accept slavery as a legitimate, if tragic, institution.[20] This acceptance rested upon the pervasive fear of liberal individualism and social disorder that so shaped Catholic thought during what historians now term the nineteenth-century Catholic revival. Beginning in full force in the early nineteenth century, the revival affected large regions of France, Belgium, Germany, and Italy, and swept across Ireland and into the United States, Canada, parts of Latin America, and Australia. Mass attendance became more regular, and religious vocations (especially among young women) grew steadily.[21]

---

18. The literature is now large. The most influential formulation is David R. Roediger, *The Wages of Whiteness: Race and the Making of the American Working Class* (London, 1991), 133-86, quotation on 140. Also see Noel Ignatiev, *How the Irish Became White* (New York, 1995), 6-31.

19. John R. McKivigan, *The War Against Proslavery Religion: Abolitionism and the Northern Churches, 1830-1865* (Ithaca, 1984), 38; John W. Quist, "'The Great Majority of our Subscribers are Farmers': The Michigan Abolitionist Constituency of the 1840s," *Journal of the Early Republic* 14 (Fall 1994): 357.

20. See Feay, "Mission to Moralize"; Patricia Motylewski, *La Société française pour l'abolition del'esclavage, 1834-1850* (Paris, 1998), 125; Philippe Delisle, *Renouveau Missionaire et Société La Martinique: 1815-1848* (Paris, 1997), 99-101; Armando Lampe, *Mission or Submission? Moravian and Catholic Missionaries in the Dutch Caribbean during the Nineteenth Century* (Göttingen, 2001), 160-64; Arthur F. Corwin, *Spain and the Abolition of Slavery in Cuba, 1817-1886* (Austin, Tex., 1967), 166-68; Joaquim Nabuco, *Abolitionism: The Brazilian Antislavery Struggle*, ed. and trans. Robert Conrad (Urbana, 1977), 19.

21. Margaret Lavinia Anderson, "The Limits of Secularization: On the Problem of the Catholic Revival in Nineteenth Century Germany," *Historical Journal* 38 (1995): 647-70.

A group of Jesuits, including Germany's Joseph Kleutgen and Italy's Matteo Liberatore and Luigi Taparelli d'Azeglio, provided the revival's philosophical underpinnings. For these scholars, a destructive individualism, or focus on autonomy, beginning with Martin Luther's rejection of church authority and the subjectivity of Descartes, permeated modern thought.[22] The only solution was a return to an Aristotelian, or more properly Thomist, communal vision of church, state, and society. Initially a minority view, even in Catholic circles, this position benefited from papal encouragement after 1848, as Pope Pius IX recoiled from a European liberalism he viewed as hostile to Catholicism, and as his successor, Pope Leo XIII, a pupil of leading Italian Thomists, made Thomism a favored Catholic philosophy.[23]

Particularly troubling for these Catholics was the liberal idea of freedom as freedom to choose, diversity of opinion for diversity's sake. This sort of freedom, without the virtue or character to make proper choices, was dangerous. One Catholic editor bluntly contrasted European liberals and Catholics: "They say that true liberty is a freedom from right as well as from wrong; we assert that it is freedom only from wrong."[24] A Maryland Jesuit entitled an 1852 Fourth of July sermon, "On Liberty," conceding that "human liberty is a great gift," but regretting that "so many to their great injury abuse it."[25]

The particular form of Catholic identification with God is also suggestive. The Catholic Jesus of the mid-nineteenth century was a suffering Jesus, the Jesus of the Passion more than Jesus the teacher or the risen Lord. The usefulness of suffering, the conviction that it served as part of human redemption, sustained a range of devotions associated with the Catholic revival, one reason for their enormous popularity in Ireland and Germany immediately after the famine and economic distress of the 1840s.[26]

The extant body of Catholic sermons is evocative on this point. One German Redemptorist told his New York City parishioners in 1854 to "meditate upon your suffering Jesus. . . . Let us place ourselves, now, my very dear brethren,

---

22. Gerald A. McCool, *Nineteenth Century Scholasticism: The Search for a Unitary Method* (New York, 1989), 17-187; John Inglis, *Spheres of Philosophical Inquiry and the Historiography of Medieval Philosophy* (Leiden, 1998), 62-156.

23. McCool, *Nineteenth Century Scholasticism*, 17-187.

24. "Hungary," *New York Freeman's Journal*, Sept. 1, 1849, 4.

25. Thomas Mulledy, S.J., "On Liberty," July 4, 1852, folder 1, box 4, Thomas Mulledy papers, Georgetown University Special Collections.

26. Jonathan Sperber, *Popular Catholicism in Nineteenth-Century Germany* (Princeton, 1984), 292-93.

27. "Final Discourse: the Agony in the Garden," *New York Freeman's Journal*, March 11, 1854, 5.

by the side of him who is suffering for us in the Garden of Olives. Let us contemplate him in his agony and covered with blood, and ask ourselves, who is this sufferer?"[27] A Boston Jesuit informed his audience that "God can give us no greater proof of His love than by sending afflictions — I am aware that this proposition may seem false or exaggerated but I trust to be able to convince you of its truth." A New York Paulist priest entitled one sermon "Joy Born of Affliction."[28]

The contrast between these emphases in the Catholic revival and developments in Protestant (or secular) liberalism was dramatic. Catholics thought that modern intellectuals placed too much emphasis on individual autonomy, or in the words of one New Orleans priest, that "most misunderstood" word, "liberté." In part because of the slavery debate, liberals on both sides of the Atlantic came to define freedom as an autonomous self, exempt from external constraint.[29] The individual as negotiator of contracts, as voluntary marriage partner and as owner of himself and his labor must serve as the starting point for a progressive social order. Ralph Waldo Emerson extolled "self-reliance" (and would later complain of "Romish priests, who sympathize, of course, with despotism").[30]

Protestant theologians such as William Ellery Channing and Horace Bushnell also rejected the idea that human suffering was a necessary sacrifice to a sovereign God. Instead, Protestants ranging from evangelicals like George Cheever, Gilbert Haven, and Joseph Thompson to liberals such as Theodore Parker increasingly understood suffering as a marker of human failing, a cruelty to be remedied by social reform.[31] Cheever bemoaned the fact that Italian Catholic peasants "seemed to have the idea that their sufferings in this life, if rightly endured, would be considered as a sort of penance, in consideration of which they would gain eternal life in the world which is to come."[32]

Catholic devotional practices seemed a distraction from real Christian work, or as one *North American Review* writer speculated, a hypocritical attempt by church leaders "to obtain [power] through fear of mental or spiritual suffering in this world to come."[33] Catholic crucifixes and paintings of suffering

28. "Edward Holker Welch: The Puritan as Jesuit," in *American Jesuit Spirituality: The Maryland Tradition, 1634-1900*, ed. Robert Emmett Curran (New York, 1988), 300-1; Clarence A. Walworth, "Joy Born of Affliction," in *Sermons Preached at the Church of St. Paul the Apostle New York During the Year 1863* (New York, 1978), 43-57.

29. "De la Liberté," *Propagateur Catholique*, January 30, 1858, 1.

30. Ralph Waldo Emerson to Thomas Carlyle, Sept. 26, 1864, in *The Correspondence of Thomas Carlyle and Ralph Waldo Emerson, 1834-1872*, Volume 2 (Boston, 1883), 286.

31. Clark, "'The Sacred Rights of the Weak,'" *Journal of American History* 82 (September 1995): 470-73.

32. George B. Cheever, *Wanderings of a Pilgrim in the Shadow of Mont Blanc* (New York, 1846), 131.

33. "The Romish Hierarchy," *North American Review* 82 (January 1856): 114.

saints were especially offensive. One visitor to an American convent regretted the "endless pantomimes of pain" decorating the walls, and Charles Eliot Norton noted that "A Protestant is often shocked by representations of the crucified Saviour, carved or painted of the size of life, and in a style which betrays the utmost brutality of conception and the deadness of all true reverence."[34]

## IV

A wariness about liberal individualism, combined with an appreciation for the value of human suffering, predisposed Catholics to resist pleas for immediate slave emancipation. Some of the first European advocates of slave emancipation in the late eighteenth century, such as France's Abbé Henri Grégoire, also confirmed Catholic suspicions that abolition was a misguided radicalism. (Grégoire sent the first American bishop, John Carroll, a copy of one of his attacks on slavery, but many Catholics detested Grégoire for his allegiance to the revolutionary French government that persecuted less conciliatory Catholics.[35]) Even Gregory XVI's 1839 decision to condemn only the slave trade, not slavery itself, stemmed in part from abolitionism's association with a European liberalism that papal advisors considered anti-Catholic and revolutionary.[36]

In the United States, Catholics calculated that social stability outweighed any benefit to be gained from immediate emancipation. Fr. J. W. Cummings argued in 1850 that "Those who talk about the 'rights of human nature and the inalienable rights of man,' ought to consider the evil done by the application of their principles. How far these men have gone in the late revolutions in Europe is now a matter of historical record. They have cut throats, overthrown altars, subverted thrones."[37]

Bishop Francis Kenrick of Philadelphia, author in 1843 of the first textbook in Catholic moral theology published in the United States, shared this point of view. Kenrick's years as a student in Rome alerted him to new currents in Catholic theology and philosophy, and his analysis of slavery seems similar to that of

34. Ryan K. Smith, "The Cross: Church Symbol and Context in Nineteenth Century America," *Church History* 70 (December 2001): 74; Charles Eliot Norton, *Notes of Travel and Study in Italy* (Boston, 1859), 210-11.

35. Abbé Henri Grégoire to John Carroll, February 6, 1815 in Jacques M. Gres-Gayer, "Four Letters from Henri Grégoire to John Carroll, 1809-1814," in *Catholic Historical Review* 79 (October 1993): 703.

36. Claude Prudhomme, "La papauté face à l'esclavage: quelle condamnation?" *Mémoire Spiritaine* 9 (1999): 135-60; François Renault, "Aux origines de la lettre apostolique de Grégoire XVI *In Supremo* (1839)," *Mémoire Spiritaine* 2 (1995): 143-49.

37. Dr. Cummings, "Slavery and the Union," *New York Freeman's Journal*, May 25, 1850, p. 1.

Italian Neo-Thomists such as Luigi Taparelli d'Azeglio. Taparelli noted that slavery in the abstract might be permissible, although he speculated that in lands "where legal slavery has not been done away with" slaveholders rarely adhered to Catholic guidelines. But he also stressed that "certain philanthropic declarations against slavery in its general meaning" had led to a "false idea of an inalienable right to freedom."[38]

Kenrick made similar distinctions when analyzing American slavery. The slave trade was wrong, slaves must be allowed to partake of the sacraments and educated in the faith, and lynching was abhorrent. Nonetheless, Kenrick concluded, slavery existed as part of the social order in the American South, and those who attempted to overturn the social order often made conditions worse.[39] Kenrick's 1851 translation of Saint Paul's letter to Philemon contained a preface that disdained "vain theories of philanthropy to the prejudice of social order" and encouraged the return of fugitive slaves to their rightful owners.[40] Similarly, when a Catholic priest visited abolitionist John Brown in his jail cell after Brown's failed 1859 raid on the Harper's Ferry Armory, the priest urged Brown to recall "an epistle of St. Paul to Philemon, where we are informed that he sent back the fugitive slave Onesimus from Rome to his master."[41]

Many Catholics saw slavery as one among many hierarchical relationships. New York Bishop John Hughes compared the master to the father, emphasizing that the "difference in the relations and obligations of those who own slaves, and those who are masters of hired servants, or the parents of children, is rather one of degree than of kind."[42] A writer for the *Boston Pilot* attacked the argument that "slavery is, in itself, intrinsically evil. This is nonsense, and it is so patent that we have never seen even a respectable attempt to prove it. In itself, slavery simply involves the right of one man to the proceeds of another. The *principle* of slavery is involved in apprenticeship, in imprisonment, in peonage, and in other forms of servitude."[43]

38. Luigi Taparelli d'Azeglio, *Saggio teoretica di dritto naturale appogiato sul fatto:* Volume 1 (Rome, [1855] 1949), 360-62.

39. Rev. Joseph D. Brokhage, *Francis Patrick Kenrick's Opinion on Slavery* (Washington, 1955), 123.

40. Francis Patrick Kenrick, *The Acts of the Apostles, the Epistles of St. Paul, the Catholic Epistles, and the Apocalypse* (New York, 1851), 497. Also see Francis Patrick Kenrick to George Bernard Allen, December 5, 1862, in *Records of the American Catholic Historical Society of Philadelphia* 32 (December 1921): 265-66.

41. Father M. A. Costello to Rev. D. Harrington, February 11, 1860, Archives of All Hallows College, Drumcondra, Ireland. I am grateful to Fr. Gerald Fogarty, S.J. for supplying me with a copy of this letter.

42. "The Archbishop's Sermon," *New York Freeman's Journal,* May 26, 1854, 1.

43. "Free Soilism," reprinted in *Pittsburg Catholic,* June 21, 1851, 113.

The same Catholics also found it difficult to distinguish the suffering endured by slaves from other forms of human agony. One Baltimore Catholic explained in 1856 that while "[slavery] may be an evil, so is sickness, and extreme poverty, and there are other ills in life which flesh is heir to."[44] Fr. John McMullen, educated in Rome and later bishop of Davenport, Iowa, readily conceded that the plight of a child born into slavery was tragic, and he approved of slavery's abolition. But even in the 1860s McMullen compared slave children to poor children, noting that all children suffered in some fashion. In particular he denied that "it is man's free power to select a state of life more or less exempt from the grievances attending human existence."[45]

Catholic acceptance of slavery included racism, but did not wholly depend upon it. In fact, Vatican insistence on the validity of interracial marriages and opposition to rigid segregation laws made Roman authorities relatively tolerant of racial mixing and opposed to biological notions of racial inferiority. Augustin Martin, bishop of Natchitoches, Louisiana, published a pastoral in 1861 that declared African Americans fit for slavery because of the biblical curse of Ham, and not worthy of a "freedom which they are unable to defend and which will kill them." The pastoral made its way to Rome, where in a response approved by the Congregation of the Index, the Vatican informed Martin that several of his assertions were unacceptable. Especially troubling was Martin's supposition of "a natural difference between the Negroes whom he calls children of Canaan, and the Whites, [who] he says . . . are the privileged ones of the great human family." African American slaves, the Vatican insisted, remained an integral part of the human family saved by Jesus Christ, not simply "poor children."[46]

Similarly, Catholics in both the North and the South disdained claims of polygenesis, that African Americans represented not just another race but another species. One Mississippi bishop specifically urged local Jesuits to criticize the "abominable idea of the plurality of races," and Savannah bishop Augustin Verot, a staunch opponent of immediate slave emancipation, would later urge the world's bishops to denounce theories positing a spurious "white humanity" and "Negro humanity."[47]

44. T. Parkin Scott, "An Inquiry into the Principles Involved in the Late Presidential Election: A Lecture Delivered Before the Catholic Institute of Baltimore," *New York Freeman's Journal,* February 7, 1856, 3.

45. Rev. John McMullen, "Bishop England on Domestic Slavery" [1865?], in Rev. James J. McGovern, *The Life and Writings of the Right Reverend John McMullen, D.D., First Bishop of Davenport, Iowa* (Chicago, 1888), xcv.

46. Maria Genoino Caravaglios, *The American Catholic Church and the Negro Problem in the XVIII-XIX Centuries,* ed. Ernest L. Unterkoefler (Charlestown, 1974), 183-200.

47. Bishop William Elder to Archbishop Jean-Marie Odin, March 24, 1862, VI-2-f-4, corre-

A discussion of slavery in the *Propagateur Catholique* in 1862 captures the complexity of Catholic thought on the issue. The New Orleans Catholic paper had already published Bishop Verot's rejection of immediate slave emancipation. Verot exhorted slaveowners to conform their practices to Catholic doctrine, regretted sexual outrages perpetrated by masters, and lambasted "unreasonable, unchristian and immoral" owners willing to tear apart slave families on the auction block and enslave free persons of color. But Verot also ridiculed the "allegation of agrarians and anarchists that 'all men are born free and equal'" and defended slavery using scriptural and ecclesiastical sources.[48]

Another New Orleans newspaper criticized Verot for failing to mention that only Africans, not whites, should be enslaved. A writer for the *Propagateur Catholique* jumped to Verot's defense, and even as Confederate soldiers gave their lives in battle, insisted that if Holy Scripture condoned slavery it surely condoned the "subjection of white to white." Taking a position held only by the most daring white Protestants, the *Propagateur Catholique* declared that the "legitimacy of slavery [is not] uniquely in the color of the skin" because such "fantastic theories" merely "flatter our pride." After all, "the Negroes are men" regardless of skin color and head size.[49]

In short: Catholics dismissed notions that Africans were biologically inferior to other humans, insisted that slaves be permitted to marry and receive an education, frequently expressed grave doubts about the morality of slavery as it existed in the nineteenth century and almost never defended slavery as an unqualified good. But most Catholic intellectuals thought slavery justifiable in theory, with even the occasional twentieth-century Catholic theologian defining slavery as "not in itself intrinsically wrong."[50]

---

spondence collection, Manuscripts and Archives, University of Notre Dame. On polygenesis, George M. Frederickson, *The Black Image in the White Mind: The Debate on Afro-American Character and Destiny, 1817-1914* (Middletown, CT, [1971] 1987), 71-96; Caravaglios, *The American Catholic Church,* 202-203.

48. Rev. A. Verot, "Slavery and Abolitionism: Being the Substance of a Sermon Preached in the Church of St. Augustine, Florida, on the 4th Day of January, 1861," *New York Freeman's Journal,* June 18, 1864, 1. The second part of the sermon was published in the *New York Freeman's Journal,* July 9, 1864, 1-2. Michael V. Gannon, *Rebel Bishop: The Life and Era of Augustin Verot* (Milwaukee, 1964), 37.

49. "De la source légitime de l'Esclavage," *Propagateur Catholique,* January 18, 1862, 1; "De la source légitime de l'Esclavage," *Propagateur Catholique,* February 1, 1862, 1.

50. James J. Fox, "Slavery, Ethical Aspect of," *The Catholic Encyclopedia:* Volume 14 (New York, 1912), 40; Maxwell, *Slavery and the Catholic Church,* 87-88.

## V

Daniel O'Connell's specific appeal to his American brethren suggested another reason for Catholic uneasiness about slave emancipation. O'Connell urged Irish-Americans not to support slavery, even if it was true "that there are amongst the Abolitionists many wicked and calumniating *enemies* of Catholicity and the Irish."[51]

William Lloyd Garrison upbraided O'Connell for giving credence to the claim that abolitionists are "bigoted against Catholicism," and scholars have followed Garrison's lead, highlighting the broadly anti-authoritarian character of American abolition, not its frequently anti-Catholic tone.[52] Certainly abolitionists directed invective toward Protestant as well as Catholic clergy. When Garrison used the term "priestcraft," he included "self-styled 'Evangelical' clergy who are as bigoted, proscriptive, and self-inflated as the Pope himself." [53] When New York Bishop John Hughes attacked Daniel O'Connell, Massachusetts abolitionists regretted that he had shown "the spirit of Popery to be as bigoted, tyrannical and pro-slavery as that of New England Protestantism."[54]

Yet a powerful strain of anti-Catholicism shaped the antislavery movement.[55] Comparisons of Catholicism and slavery were not new — the Earl of Shaftesbury declared in 1679 that "Popery and Slavery, like two sisters, go hand in hand, sometimes one goes first, sometimes the other, in a door, but the other is always following close at hand" — but the intensity of the nineteenth-century American slavery debate and the rapid growth of the Catholic church in the United States made it newly compelling.[56]

By the late 1840s, antislavery activists frequently denounced slavery and Catholicism as parallel despotic systems, opposed to education, free speech, and po-

51. Daniel O'Connell, "Daniel O'Connell and the Committee of the Irish Repeal Association of Cincinnati," in Freidel, ed., *Union Pamphlets of the Civil War, 1861-1865:* Volume 2, 809.

52. William Lloyd Garrison to Daniel O'Connell, December 8, 1843, in *The Letters of William Lloyd Garrison,* Volume 3: *No Union With Slaveholders, 1841-1849,* ed. Walter M. Merrill (Cambridge, 1973), 229-30; Lewis Perry, *Radical Abolitionism: Anarchy and the Government of God in Anti-Slavery Thought* (Knoxville, [1973] 1995), 18-54; Robert H. Abzug, *Cosmos Crumbling: American Reform and the Religious Imagination* (New York, 1994), 183-229.

53. Garrison to Oliver Johnson, April 9, 1873, *The Letters of William Lloyd Garrison,* Volume 6: *To Rouse the Slumbering Land, 1868-1879,* ed. Walter M. Merrill and Louis Ruchames (Cambridge, 1981), 273-74.

54. *Eleventh Annual Meeting of the Massachusetts Anti-Slavery Society* (Boston, 1843), 95.

55. Peter Walker, *Moral Choices: Memory, Desire, and Imagination in Nineteenth-Century American Abolition* (Baton Rouge, 1978), 161-66.

56. Shaftesbury quoted in Michael P. Zuckert, *Natural Rights and the New Republicanism* (Princeton, 1994), 103.

litical liberty in predictable synchronicity. Protestants who tolerated slavery betrayed their principles, abolitionists believed, while Catholics who tolerated slavery applied them. Catholic leaders in Italy forbade distribution of the Bible to their people, just as southern slaveholders stopped the distribution of the Bible to slaves. Catholics relied upon oral instruction in catechism classes just as slaveholders used oral instruction to prevent slave literacy. Slaveholders exerted unlimited control over female slaves, just as priests allegedly exercised sexual and emotional power over female penitents in the confessional. Slave quarters were likened to the "dungeons of the Popish Inquisition."[57] Popular exposés of women (allegedly) attempting to flee convents resembled fugitive slave narratives.[58] One Ohio abolitionist, after comparing himself to Martin Luther, offered this summary:

> In this country, popery finds its appropriate ally in the institution of slavery. They are both kindred systems. One enslaves the mind, the other both mind and body. Both deny the Bible to those under their control — both discourage free inquiry. . . . By its penances, masses for the dead, indulgences etc. popery extorts money without rendering an equivalent; slavery robs men of all their earnings, their wives and children.[59]

The roster of anti-Catholic abolitionists in the first stages of the American movement is impressive. The first abolitionist martyr, Elijah Lovejoy, murdered in 1836 for his opposition to slavery, spent much of 1835 warning of the Catholic menace.[60] George Bourne became, simultaneously, a leading antislavery and anti-Catholic agitator, writing attacks on Romanism and scurrilous convent exposés even as he became a crucial influence on Garrison's *Liberator*.[61]

Widespread antislavery sentiment in the 1850s meshed with heightened anti-Catholic sensitivity. Joseph Thompson and George Cheever, editors for the country's most prominent religious weekly, the *Independent*, switched back and forth from the dangers of slavery to the dangers of Catholicism.[62] In one ad-

---

57. [George Bourne], *Picture of Slavery in the United States of America* (Boston, 1838), 151.

58. Jenny Franchot, *The Antebellum Protestant Encounter with Catholicism* (Berkeley, 1994), 104-106, 171-81: Ronald G. Waters, "The Erotic South: Civilization and Sexuality in American Abolitionism," *American Quarterly* 25 (May 1973): 177-201.

59. *The Life and Writings of Rev. Joseph Gordon, Written and Compiled by a Committee of the Free Presbyterian Synod* (Cincinnati, 1860), 302.

60. "Elijah P. Lovejoy as an Anti-Catholic," *Records of the American Catholic Historical Society* 62 (September, 1951): 172-80.

61. John W. Christie and Dwight L. Dumond, *George Bourne and the Book and Slavery Irreconciliable* (Wilmington, 1969), 83-86, 99-101.

62. Leo P. Hirrel, *Children of Wrath: New School Calvinism and Antebellum Reform* (Lexington, 1998), 93-116, 134-54.

dress Thompson noted that "Freedom is grappling with Slavery" even as he worried that "Romanism is taking advantage of our religious freedom to oust religious instruction from common schools."[63] In 1854, Cheever authored a popular treatise on the importance of keeping the King James Bible in the public schools. That same year he used similar language in attacking slavery. "At the South," he warned, "the slaveholders and slave-laws forbid the teaching of the Bible; at the North, [so do] the Romanists and Romish laws." When Supreme Court Justice Roger Brook Taney announced the *Dred Scott* decision in 1857 Cheever immediately concluded that Taney's Catholicism made him sympathetic to slavery. He also compared the ambitions of southern slaveholders to those of Spain's Philip II, with his "thumb screws and boot for the tortures of the Inquisition."[64]

Foreign abolitionists made similar assessments. The British evangelical and antislavery advocate Hugh McNeile wrote of the "perfect consistency" involved in working for the suppression of "slavery and popery."[65] Richard D. Webb, the Irish correspondent for the *National Anti-Slavery Standard,* compared "the rampant audacious, insolent Ultramontanism of the Romish clergy" with the "kindred system of chattel slavery."[66] The Mexican liberal Matías Romero pondered the "striking similarity which exists between the Church party of Mexico and the Slavery party in the United States."[67] In Canada, editor George Brown helped found the Anti-Slavery Society of Canada, and serialized *Uncle Tom's Cabin* in the country's most influential newspaper, the *Toronto Globe.* In 1855 a *Globe* editorial concluded that "In Canada the Roman Catholic hierarchy is the slave power. It holds us subjects in bondage as slavish as the Southern taskmaster."[68]

63. Joseph P. Thompson, *The College as a Religious Institution: An Address Delivered in Boston, May, 1859, in behalf of the Society for the Promotion of Collegiate and Theological Education at the West* (New York, 1859), 32.

64. George B. Cheever, *The Right of the Bible in Our Public Schools* (New York, 1854); [Cheever], "The New York Tribune and the Bible in Schools," *Independent,* March 19, 1854, 3; Robert M. York, *George B. Cheever: Religious and Social Reformer, 1807-1890* (Orono, Maine, 1955), 148; George B. Cheever, *God Against Slavery: and the Freedom and Duty of the Pulpit to Rebuke It, As a Sin Against God* (New York, 1857), 179-80.

65. Rev. Hugh McNeile, *Anti-Slavery and Anti-Popery: A Letter Addressed to Edward Cropper, Esquire, and Thomas Berry Horsfall, Esquire* (London, 1838), 4.

66. Richard D. Webb, "Letter from Our Dublin Correspondent," *National Antislavery Standard* 19 (January 22, 1859).

67. Matías Romero, *The Situation of Mexico: Speech Delivered by Señor Matias Romero, Envoy Extraordinary and Minister Plenipotentiary of the Republic of Mexico to the United States, At a Dinner in the City of New York, on the 16th of December, 1863* (New York, 1864), 11.

68. J. M. S. Careless, *Brown of The Globe,* Volume One: *The Voice of Upper Canada, 1818-1859* (Toronto, 1959), 102-103; *Toronto Globe* quoted in *Provincial Freeman,* October 13, 1855.

The political crisis of the mid-1850s revealed the overlap between anti-slavery and anti-Catholic activism. The decisive development was the movement of northern Protestants out of the collapsing Whig Party into the anti-Catholic (and in the North generally antislavery) American Party, which first supplanted the Whigs as the main rival to the Democrats in 1854. Almost as quickly, the new Republican Party swept aside the American Party in 1856, taking the first major step toward the election of Abraham Lincoln in 1860.[69]

The brief triumph of the American Party, and then the movement of many of its members into the Republican Party, ensured that a broad array of politicians, ministers, and editors would begin complaining, in the words of Pennyslvania congressman David Wilmot, about "the alliance between an ancient and powerful Church and the slave interests of America. . . ."[70] Or, as New York congressman Bayard Clark explained to his colleagues, "As in the empires of the Old World, Jesuitism allies itself with 'kingcraft,' so in the New, it strikes hands with slavery."[71] A number of antislavery Know-Nothings forced showdowns on the issue at American Party conventions, and one group of Massachusetts lodges resolved that "there can exist no real hostility to Roman Catholicism which does not embrace slavery, its natural co-worker in opposition to freedom and republican institutions."[72]

In Michigan, the state legislature passed a Personal Liberty Law in 1855 aimed at nullifying the Fugitive Slave Law, along with a church property bill checking the power of Catholic bishops. In Massachusetts, the American Party swept the 1854 elections. The newly elected legislators soon began harassing Catholic nuns with convent "inspections," while outlawing racial segregation in Boston schools and making the Fugitive Slave law unenforceable.[73]

Orations given at the height of the political turmoil in Massachusetts incessantly compared Catholicism and slavery, typified by congressional candidate Anson Burlingame's complaint that Catholicism and slavery "are in alliance by the necessity of their nature, for one denies the right of a man to his

69. For the best overview, William E. Gienapp, *The Origins of the Republican Party, 1852-1856* (New York, 1987), 61-237. Also see Tyler Anbinder, *Nativism and Slavery: The Northern Know Nothings and the Politics of the 1850s* (New York, 1992); and Richard J. Carwardine, *Evangelicals and Politics in Antebellum America* (New Haven, 1993).

70. David Wilmot, Answers to Campaign Questions, July 10, 1857, in Charles Buxton Going, *David Wilmot, Free Soiler* (New York, 1924), 736.

71. Speech of Hon. Bayard Clarke, of New York, July 24, 1856, Appendix to *Congressional Globe* (1856): 957.

72. Ray Allen Billington, *The Protestant Crusade* (New York, 1938), 425.

73. Ronald P. Formisano, *The Birth of Mass Political Parties, Michigan, 1827-1861* (Princeton, 1971), 256-57; John R. Mulkern, *The Know-Nothing Party in Massachusetts: The Rise and Fall of a People's Movement* (Boston, 1990), 105-108, 111.

body, and the other the right of a man to his soul."[74] Rev. Eden B. Foster concluded that "Slavery and Romanism [are] a two-edged dagger with which to stab liberty to the heart."[75]

Republican newspapers across the country used the same explosive language. The *Chicago Tribune* warned its readers that "It is not the foreign element" which threatened the republic, but the "papal portion of that element." Understandably the "Republican Party, which is the avowed and mortal enemy of chattel bondage, is not less the opponent of partisan schemes of political Catholicism. It could not as the defender of human rights everywhere be otherwise."[76] In Pittsburgh the editor of the *Post-Gazette* wondered how anyone could allow the "curse of slavery ... to extend over the free territory of Nebraska ... and ... see nothing to oppose in the temporal and spiritual despotism of the Pope."[77]

## VI

In their reluctance to support immediate emancipation, Catholics were not alone. Influential Southern intellectuals defended slavery, unsurprisingly, but defending the virtues of a more organic, less individualist society also pushed some southerners to reassess Catholicism. Henry Hughes became enamored of corporatist thought; George Frederick Holmes flirted with conversion to Catholicism, and worried that the "rejection of spiritual authority" lay at the root of social problems.[78] Virginian George Fitzhugh, the most extreme southern defender of slavery in the 1850s, admired the Catholic refusal to accept divorce and remarriage, and believed that Catholicism had provided a salutary check on laissez-faire economics during the Medieval period.[79] "We have no quarrel with the Reformation," Fitzhugh felt compelled to announce in 1857, before concluding that northerners opposed to slavery "did nothing more than carry into practice the right of private judgment, liberty of speech, freedom of the press and of religion."[80]

74. *Oration of Hon. Anson Burlingame. Delivered at Salem, July 4, 1854* (Salem, 1854), 21.

75. Eden B. Foster, *The Rights of the Pulpit, and the Perils of Freedom. Two Discourses Preached in Lowell, Sunday, June 25th 1854* (Lowell, 1854), 69.

76. "Popery and Slavery," *Chicago Tribune*, February 8, 1856, 2.

77. N.t., *Pittsburgh Post-Gazette*, March 3, 1854, 2.

78. Douglas Ambrose, *Henry Hughes and Proslavery Thought in the Old South* (Baton Rouge, 1996); Neil C. Gillespie, *The Collapse of Orthodoxy: The Intellectual Ordeal of George Frederick Holmes* (Charlottesville, 1972), 153, 211.

79. George Fitzhugh, *Sociology for the South or the Failure of Free Society* (New York, n.d.), 1, 194-195.

80. George Fitzhugh, *Cannibals All!* 131.

After the Civil War, American Catholics accepted slavery's demise, even if speakers on the Catholic lecture circuit, like other Northern Democrats, still criticized "Lincoln's proclamation of emancipation because the negroes were not prepared for freedom."[81] Pope Leo XIII urged Brazil to abolish slavery in 1888, in an encyclical, *In Plurimus,* that lauded Catholics for the elimination of medieval slavery, while gliding over the last one hundred years.[82] At the same time, Algiers Cardinal Charles Lavigerie spearheaded an ecumenical (and hugely popular) antislavery campaign directed at the slave trade in Islamic regions of Africa.[83]

For a time, liberals reminded Catholics (and themselves) of Catholic recalcitrance. In the United States, poet John Greenleaf Whittier explained in 1873 that he was "not blind to the hostility of leading influences in the Catholic Church to republicanism and religious and political liberty. As an abolitionist I have seen the Bishops and priests oppose the abolition of slavery while a large body of their people were persecuting and abusing the poor blacks in our cities."[84] In France, Ernest Havet mocked a papacy which "condemns so easily and so imprudently all things" but is "unable to make up its mind about slavery"; in the Philippines, José Rizal, the leading Filipino nationalist, chastised Spanish Catholics for defending a church which had tolerated, "if not sanctioned," slavery for eighteen centuries.[85] Even the entry on slavery in the *Dictionnaire de Théologie Catholique,* published in Paris in the early twentieth century, instructed readers on how to respond to the accusation that the church did not abolish or "even condemn" slavery.[86]

The frequency of liberal jabs diminished as the slavery debate receded.

---

81. Entry of April 30, 1872, in *The Diary of Rev. Richard L. Burtsell,* Microfilm copy, Reel 1, University of Notre Dame. On the memory of the war, see David W. Blight, *Race and Reunion: The Civil War in American Memory* (Cambridge, 2001), 130-39.

82. *In Plurimus* (1888), in *The Papal Encyclicals 1878-1903,* ed. Claudia Carlen, IHM (Raleigh, 1981), 159-167.

83. François Renault, *Cardinal Lavigerie: Churchman, Prophet and Missionary,* trans. John O'Donohue (London, 1994); Ehud R. Toledano, *Slavery and Abolition in the Ottoman Middle East* (Seattle, 1994), 194; Richard Roberts and Suzanne Miers, "The End of Slavery in Africa," in *The End of Slavery in Africa,* ed. Suzanne Miers and Richard Roberts (Madison, 1988), 16.

84. John Greenleaf Whittier to an unidentified correspondent, December 1873, in *The Letters of John Greenleaf Whittier,* Volume 3: *1861-1892,* ed. John B. Pickard (Cambridge, 1975), 312.

85. Raul J. Bonoan, S.J., *The Rizal-Pastells Correspondence: The Hitherto Unpublished Letters of José Rizal and Portions of Fr. Pablo Pastell's Fourth Letter and Translation of the Correspondence, Together with a Historical Background and Theological Critique* (Manila: Ateneo de Manila University Press, 1994), 186; Ernest Havet, *Le Christianisme et ses Origines,* Volume 1 (Paris, [1871] 1880), xxi-xxii.

86. J. Dutilleul, "Esclavage," *Dictionnaire de Théologie Catholique,* Volume 5 (Paris, 1924), 516.

Time healed wounds, as did the realization that Catholics and liberals might become allies when grappling with the problems faced by workers in the late-nineteenth-century industrial economy. The same communal sensibility that made many Catholics cautious about slave emancipation, after all, also made them dubious about the morality of laissez-faire capitalism. As the slavery debate receded, the plight of workers became more visible. As early as 1844, New York Bishop Hughes had lamented the "mockery of freedom" evident in an economic system that pitted the "starving laborer" against the "bloated capitalist."[87] Pope Leo XIII, in an 1890 letter, urged German Catholics to work against the slave trade, but devoted more attention to the condition of workers and the poor in Germany itself.[88]

This line of analysis received a new impetus one year later, when Leo XIII attacked the "misery and wretchedness pressing so unjustly on the majority of the working class" in *Rerum Novarum,* the papal encyclical that became the foundation of modern Catholic social thought.[89] "The Catholics have some quite strong and pronounced views on various social and economic problems," explained the most prominent reform economist in the United States, Richard T. Ely, with an enthusiasm that would have shocked an earlier generation of liberals, "and these views are of interest to others as well as to Catholics."[90]

## VII

The slavery debate surfaced again in the 1940s, as racial segregation in the United States and fascist aggression in Europe prompted renewed interest in fundamental human rights. John LaFarge, the American Jesuit most responsible for the racial integration of Catholic institutions in the twentieth century, privately regretted that some nineteenth-century bishops had owned slaves, that many Catholics had believed in the "doctrine that slavery *itself* [is] not necessarily evil" and that few Christians had become "martyrs to the injustice of slavery." When Jacques Maritain, the French Catholic philosopher, traveled to

87. John Hughes, "A Lecture on the Importance of a Christian Basis for the Science of Political Economy, and Its Application to the Affairs of Life" [1844], in *Complete Works of the Most Rev. John Hughes, D.D., Archbishop of New York. Comprising His Sermons, Letters, Lectures, Speeches, Etc.,* Volume 1 (New York, 1865), 521.

88. Claude Prudhomme, *Stratégie Missionnaire du Saint-Siège sous Léon XIII (1878-1903): Centralisation romaine et Défis Culturels* (Rome, 1994), 389.

89. *Rerum Novarum* (1891), in Carlen, ed., *The Papal Encyclicals 1878-1903,* 241, 253.

90. Richard T. Ely to Mr. George P. Brett, May 21, 1901, box 19, folder 3, Richard T. Ely Papers, State Historical Society of Wisconsin.

the United States in the late 1930s, LaFarge warned him that he might be asked the following question: "What response should one make to the allegation that the Catholic church justified slavery?"[91]

Leading Catholic historians still applauded the "wisdom" of the American bishops in endorsing neither side in the American Civil War, but LaFarge was less complacent. After reading an essay by a Jesuit seminarian on the subject, LaFarge, who had spent fifteen years in Maryland working with African American Catholics, retorted that the bishops had been far too "politically minded" and unable to develop a "reasoned Christian philosophy of human rights."[92] In France, theologians found themselves forced to respond to a Ugandan politician, "sympathetic to communism," who declared that the church had tolerated the slave trade, an assertion that "caused a great emotion among the indigenous populations."[93]

Claims by twentieth-century Catholics (African American and white) that the gospel required racial integration inevitably prompted reflections on nineteenth-century slavery. As late as 1944, Gerald Kelly, S.J., a prominent Catholic theologian, could (privately) conclude that Catholics might not be *obligated* to integrate Catholic institutions, since "the Church herself has applied this principle of prudence to the solution of such evils as slavery."[94] Within a decade, however, Kelly, like most Catholic theologians in the United States and Europe as well as at the Vatican, had declared compulsory segregation "obviously unjust." By the early 1960s, only southern bishops (privately) defended racial segregation, since "the Church tolerated slavery for many centuries [and] could not have done so if slavery were intrinsically wrong."[95]

The belated nineteenth-century Catholic endorsement of slave emancipation now became a twentieth-century theological problem. How could the church define as truth a statement (slavery is intrinsically wrong) that most Christians in the eighteen centuries since Christ's birth would have found im-

91. "Considerations," n.d., folder 6, box 12, John LaFarge papers, Special Collections, Georgetown University (hereafter JLF); Questionnaire pour M. Maritain, n.d., folder 17, box 17, JLF. On LaFarge, David Southern, *John LaFarge and the Limits of Catholic Interracialism, 1911-1963* (Baton Rouge, 1996).

92. John Tracy Ellis, *American Catholicism* (Chicago, 1956), 92; John LaFarge to Wilfrid Parsons, May 31, 1939, folder 6, box 12, JLF.

93. L. Christiani, "Aperçu Historique sur L'Esclavage," *L'Ami du Clergé* 63 (March 12, 1953): 163.

94. Gerald Kelly, S.J., "Concerning the Article Why Not Christian Cannibalism?" [1944], Kelly file, Missouri Province Archives, Society of Jesus, St. Louis, Missouri.

95. Gerald Kelly, S.J., "Notes on Moral Theology, 1951," *Theological Studies* 12 (January 1952): 68; Francis Connell to Most. Rev. Egidio Vagnozzi, June 23, 1962, Vagnozzi 2 file, Francis Connell papers, Archives of the Baltimore province of the Redemptorists, Brooklyn, New York.

plausible? Theological shorthand for this problem was "doctrinal development," and as early as 1945, the distinguished Italian Catholic politician and exile from Mussolini's Italy, Don Luigi Sturzo, referred to slavery as both a "flagrant contradiction to the spirit of the Gospel," and proof that ethical norms were not "impervious to the dynamism of social development."[96] In 1953 a French theologian noted that the "progress of civilization" prevented Catholics from holding to the view that slavery was a legitimate social institution. The same "social and religious evolution" would not "permit us today to take on the practices of the Inquisition."[97]

The theme of doctrinal development became central at the Second Vatican Council in the mid-1960s, where the assembled bishops, most obviously through the 1965 Declaration on Religious Freedom, implicitly endorsed the idea that doctrines developed in a particular cultural milieu might imperfectly express the mysteries of Revelation. The same bishops, without comment, listed slavery as an unacceptable offense against "human dignity."[98] More recently, the official Catechism of the Catholic Church defined slavery as "against the dignity of persons and their fundamental rights."[99]

Neither declaration is bold. (Philosopher Jeffrey Stout suggests that no contemporary moral claim is *less* controversial than the assertion that slavery is "intrinsically evil."[100]) But with slavery understood as indefensible, Catholics could now deploy the slavery debate in other skirmishes. The most distinguished contemporary student of doctrinal development, University of California legal scholar and Ninth Circuit Court of Appeals Judge John T. Noonan Jr., has lamented Catholic acquiescence in slavery in the nineteenth century. At the same time, Noonan has insisted that pro-choice advocates speaking about the unborn mimic southern slaveholders talking about slaves, willing to deny personhood to an entire category of humans.[101]

96. Luigi Sturzo, "The Influence of Social Facts on Ethical Conceptions," *Thought* 20 (March 1945): 96, 112.

97. A. Michel, "Sur L'Esclavage," *L'Ami du Clergé* 63 (March 12, 1953): 163.

98. *Gaudium et Spes* (1965) in *Vatican Council II: The Conciliar and Post Conciliar Documents,* ed. Austin Flannery, O.P. (Northport, 1975), 928.

99. *Catechism of the Catholic Church* (New York, 1995), number 2414, p. 639.

100. Jeffrey Stout, *Ethics After Babel: The Languages of Morals and Their Discontents* (Boston, 1988), 84.

101. John T. Noonan Jr., "Do Christian Morals Change?" [1968] in Christian Morals file, drawer C-4, Noonan papers, Boalt Law School, University of California, Berkeley; John T. Noonan Jr., *A Private Choice: Abortion in America in the Seventies* (New York, 1979), 13-14, 80-89. On Noonan, John T. McGreevy, "John T. Noonan: A Case for Doctrinal Development," *Commonweal* 127 (November 17, 2000): 12-17. For an interesting contrast to Noonan, see Mario M. Cuomo's famous 1984 speech on Catholic politicians and abortion, where Cuomo defends his

Michael Ignatieff has recently described the eighteenth- and nineteenth-century abolitionist movement as a pivotal moment in modern history, the first human rights campaign. That Catholics (and not Catholics alone) still struggle to absorb the insights (and limitations) of that campaign would seem to confirm the point.[102] Many Catholics proved incapable of recognizing the dignity of the individual person during the slavery debate, incapable of viewing the person as more than an individual fulfilling a particular social role. At the same time, Catholics became unusually alert to the limitations of what Michael Sandel terms the "unencumbered self" in a society valuing individual rights more than communal obligations.[103] Investigating these tensions allows historians to probe the evolving sympathies and sentiments that lie behind policy statements and doctrinal claims. And it may permit them to better understand how clashing understandings of, say, the human person and suffering, undergird our most agonizing divides.

---

reluctance to support challenges to legal abortion in 1984 by referring to the position of the Catholic bishops on slavery in the nineteenth century, describing the bishops as "realists" and not "hypocrites." Mario M. Cuomo, "Religious Belief and Public Morality," *New York Review of Books,* October 25, 1984, 34.

102. Michael Ignatieff, *Human Rights as Politics and Idolatry,* ed. Amy Guttman (Princeton, 2001), 10.

103. Sandel, "The Procedural Republic and the Unencumbered Self," 81-96.

# The Disposal of the Dead:
# And What It Tells Us about
# American Society and Law

CHARLES J. REID, JR.

There is perhaps no more telling indicator of a culture's regard for the human person than the character of its funerary rituals, the complex of beliefs and practices used to acknowledge and remember the dead. These range from the funeral itself to the various monuments, prayers, rituals, and memorials presented in the deceased's honor — and ultimately to the manner in which that culture goes about the disposal of the body. Funeral rites appear to be as old as the human race itself, and whatever their character, they appear always to carry with them some presentiment about the meaning of life and the nature of death, even as they acknowledge the moral obligation to mourn the departed — and to recognize, however dimly, that the fate of the departed is the fate of us all. Indeed, at no other moment in the cycle of life is the notion of human society as a pact between the living, the dead, and the yet-to-be-born so palpably reinforced, and the fact of our individual dependency and helplessness more compellingly stated.

One might have thought that in a culture shaped by the intense spirituality of Christianity, with its invocation of a God whose kingdom is not of this world, one would not see the same elaborate attention paid to the dead body as one sees in non-Christian cultures. But as Charles Reid shows, something closer to the opposite has been the case, particularly when one considers only the relatively short period of modern historical time represented by American society and law. Notwithstanding its undeniable gnostic and ascetic strains, Christianity at its core maintained the high Jewish view of the body, and even intensified it, with the adoption of such doctrines as the resurrection of the flesh at the Last Judgment. Reid's essay, which concentrates upon the evolving legal status accorded the corpse in nineteenth- and twentieth-century legal scholarship and case law, documents a consistent pattern of profound and ingrained respect for the sacredness of the body, a respect that was grounded explicitly in Judeo-Christian precepts. This pattern holds up until the relatively recent past, when an understanding of the body as a form of property and of the corpse as a meaningless "inconvenience" or a resource for body parts has begun to creep into our shared understanding, and increasingly into the law itself. Reid points out that recent Federal court decisions may be opening the way to the treatment of the human body as the object of commercial exchange, governed not by a belief in the sacred inviolability of the human person, even in death — the inviolability of what we significantly refer to as that person's "remains" — but by less exalted notions of "the property rights of next of kin." Reid concludes that the question of the disposal of the dead serves as powerful evidence of the inherently religious basis of American law. He leaves us with a pointed question: When the dignity of the dead has been entirely undermined, can the dignity of the living be far behind? Charles J. Reid Jr. is Associate Professor of Law at St. Thomas University School of Law, and author of *Power over the Body, Equality in the Family* (Eerdmans, 2004).

# I

"Dreary," "obscure," were among the more polite comments I received when I explained my research interest in the way American law has regarded the disposal of the dead. "But," I responded, "anthropologists tell us that among the most important records of a culture are the symbols and artifacts, the ideas and material remains used to commemorate the resting places of the dead. Anthropologists use these records in their reconstructions of societies ancient and modern. There are few more revealing avenues into a society's basic value system, few better windows onto a society's religious beliefs, and its regard for the personhood of those who were once but are no longer members of the community, than to see how those earthly remains are disposed of."

Historically, the Judeo-Christian tradition has had a deep regard for the sanctity of human remains. The first book of the Hebrew Scripture, Genesis, captures the depth of grief the patriarch Abraham felt over the death of his wife Sarah and his efforts to provide her with a proper resting place. The burial site he purchased, the cave at Machpelah, became known as the tomb of the patriarchs when Jacob, living out his days in Egypt, instructed his descendants to bury him with his fathers in their sepulcher.

The later books of the Jewish Bible, and the books of the intertestamental period, add the theme of the resurrection of the dead. Isaiah speaks of the corpses of the righteous dead who shall arise and sing, and Ezekiel prophesies that "I will open your graves and have you rise from them, and bring you back to the land of Israel." Judas Maccabeus is recorded as having prayers said and offerings made on behalf of his fallen troops in hope of the resurrection of the dead. Some rabbinic schools at the time of Jesus taught the resurrection of the dead, and a belief in both the immortality of the soul and bodily resurrection became an important feature of Pharisaic Judaism at about this time.

Christianity subsequently made belief in man's transcendence over death, and the general resurrection of the dead on the last day, central features of its belief system. Jesus Christ, of course, is recorded as miraculously raising the dead to life and himself bodily arising from the dead on the first Easter Sunday. But Jesus' two most important followers, Peter and Paul, also showed their mastery over death by raising the dead. All Christians, furthermore, are given the assurance — and they retain the assurance still — of rising from the dead on the last day.

Christian theology and liturgical practice from an early date assigned transcendent significance to burial. Prudentius, the fourth-century Christian man of letters whom Robert Wilken has compared in importance to Horace or T. S. Eliot, explained to his audience why burials mattered to Christians:

> Bodies that lay long dead and still and mouldering in their tombs will be carried into the flying breezes in company with their former souls. This is why we spend such great care on graves, this is why the last honour that awaits the lifeless frame and the funeral procession graces it, why it is our custom to spread over it linen cloths of gleaming whiteness, and sprinkled myrrh with its Sabean drugs preserves the bodies. What means the chambered rocks, the noble monuments, but that something is entrusted to them which is not dead but given up to sleep. This earnest care the provident piety of Christ's followers takes because they believe that all that are now sunk in cold slumber will presently be alive.

Liturgical texts dating to the fifth and sixth centuries preserve this sense of sacredness. Prayers composed by Caesarius of Arles (470-542) to be recited at graveside called on God to revive the body of the deceased on the last day and allow it to join the order of saints. St. Augustine counseled that funeral exequies were principally for the benefit of the living, not the dead, and assured his listeners that God could reanimate the dead even if the physical body had been utterly destroyed. Such reminders did not, however, diminish the regard Christians held for the burial places of the dead as churchyards were themselves turned into cemeteries in the early middle ages. By the eleventh century, canon law defined a church as the building and the surrounding graveyard.

This sense of the sacredness of the resting places of the dead, this belief in the human person's ultimate transcendence of death itself, was part and parcel of the belief system of the earliest European settlers of North America. The Puritan divines, whose works exercised so much influence on the first English-speaking colonizers of the New World, spoke frequently of death and its transcendence. William Ames (1576-1633) declared that bodily death was in recompense for man's sin, but assured believers that the separation of body and soul was only temporary since Christ, in his "divine omnipotence," will raise both the just and the unjust on the last day so that all might receive their proper recompense.

Isaac Watts (1674-1748), Anglo-Calvinist hymn writer and theologian extraordinaire, addressed the grave itself in a sermon: "We know thee, O grave, to be a . . . devourer," Watts observed. Our "corruptibility, dishonour, and weakness" are there "freely swallowed up forever." But the grave is also cautioned to know that "there is in the body . . . a divine relation to the Lord of life; and this thou must not, thou canst not dissolve or destroy." For the Christian, Watts asserts, the grave has thus "become as a bed of repose to them that are in Him, and a safe and quiet hiding place for His saints till the resurrection."

Cotton Mather carried this theme across the Atlantic. The grave, Mather pronounced, is the proper home of Christians, until Christ should come in glory once again:

> At a Funeral we see, One of our Friends is gone to his long Home. The Grave is our Home, and a Long Home, there we wait all the days of our appointed time, until that Change come, when God will have a desire to the work of His Hands, and Rebuild it with a Resurrection from the Dead.

Funeral practices in England's North Atlantic colonies reflected this commitment to Christian belief in the human person's transcendence of death. By the middle and end of the seventeenth century, New England Puritan funerals came to be celebrated with far more elaborate liturgies than were utilized by an older generation of English Calvinists. New England grave markers, furthermore, came to be known for their stunning richness and variety of eschatological themes. Arches and doors symbolizing entry into the world beyond the grave, winged death's head skulls, smiling faces depicting the assurance of salvation, were among the many depictions one can still find on grave markers in old New England cemeteries. And, indeed, these and other such depictions are common in cemeteries even today.

## II

This belief system, with its commitment to the resurrection of the dead, its solicitude to the sanctity of burial places, its reverence and regard for the body of the deceased human person, did not stand at variance with the law or the writings of American lawyers and judges. Far from it. There are few areas of American law which more clearly reflect the Judeo-Christian heritage of the American nation than the traditional law governing the disposal of the dead and the proper administration of cemeteries.

The Christian vision of the earthly remains of the deceased human person as a temple of the Holy Spirit, expected to revive again upon the Last Day, remained an animating impulse for judges called upon to decide difficult cases. Individual judges may or may not have taken the biblical assurances literally. They may have adhered to the biblical teachings with greater or lesser fervor, or even rejected them altogether. But whether believers or unbelievers, American judges nevertheless moved in a mental universe structured and shaped by Judeo-Christian understandings of the significance of death and transcendence, and their opinions reflected this regard. The body of the human person remained an object of transcendent significance and respect for its resting place an important subject of judicial concern.

### A. Joseph Story and the Rural Cemetery Movement

As Associate Justice of the Supreme Court of the United States, and as an expounder, commentator, and organizer of vast parts of the law, Joseph Story (1779-1845) exercised profound influence. His commentaries on the law of bailments, the Constitution, conflict of laws, equity jurisprudence, equity pleadings, agency, partnership, bills of exchange and promissory notes remain indispensable starting points for understanding the development of American legal principles in these branches of the law.

Although raised a Calvinist, Story, like many of his New England contemporaries, became a Unitarian. His faith, however, was not the contentless commitment to free inquiry that characterizes so much of modern Unitarianism, but a genuinely deep commitment to basic teachings and principles of the Bible. He wrote "that states should 'foster and encourage the Christian religion generally, as a matter of sound policy as well as of revealed truth.'" And he could seek solace in traditional Christian themes at times of personal tragedy. In some verses he wrote on the death of his young daughter, Story reflected:

Farewell, my darling child, a sad farewell!
Thou art gone from earth, in heavenly scenes to dwell;
For sure, if ever being formed from dust,
Might hope for bliss, thine is that holy trust.
Spotless and pure, from God's thy spirit came;
Spotless it has returned, a brighter flame.

In the 1820s and 1830s, Story involved himself in a controversy first aroused by Thomas Jefferson's contention that Christianity was not a part of the common law. Story responded, "It appears to me inconceivable how any man can doubt that Christianity is part of the Common [Law] of England, in the true sense of this expression, which I take to be no more than that Christianity is recognized as true, and as the established religion of England." In a Supreme Court opinion, Story added that Christianity must be accounted a part of the common law, at least in the "qualified sense that its divine origin and truth are admitted."

Among Story's many undertakings in his virtuosic life was the Chairmanship of the Mount Auburn Cemetery Association. Mount Auburn Cemetery, adjacent to Cambridge, Massachusetts, was established in 1831 as the crown jewel of the new "rural cemetery" movement. So called not because of a desire to locate cemeteries in rural areas but because of the impulse to replicate a rural atmosphere of repose and reflection in the midst of urban centers, the rural cemetery movement sought to create safe, sanitary, and peaceful conditions for the burial of the dead. Burial in churchyards had once sufficed in colonial New York and Boston, and other eastern metropolitan areas, but such cemeteries had become overcrowded, disrespectful to the dead there interred, and a threat to the health of the living.

In 1831, a group of Boston luminaries — among them such names as Edward Everett, General H. A. S. Dearbourn, and Joseph Story — resolved to create a cemetery on a new pattern. Story was elected the first president, and the land for the cemetery was acquired. The cemetery itself featured orderly arranged and neatly landscaped sites for burial, as well as richly manicured gardens, wooded retreats, and flowing brooks. The cemetery was consecrated in September 1831, with Joseph Story delivering the dedication address.

Story's address reflected the attitude of the public generally regarding the proper respect and reverence to be shown the dead. It was an address redolent in religious themes. Story took as his starting point the twenty-third chapter of Genesis, in which Abraham searched for a burial site for his deceased wife Sarah. There was, Story assured his audience, "a sure and certain hope of a resurrection of the body and a life everlasting." This much was a "truth, sublime and glorious." Burial was unnecessary, Story conceded, to God's grand design to raise the dead on the last day. God shall vivify us again, "whether our remains are scattered to the corners of the earth, or gathered in sacred urns."

But, Story continued his lesson in theology, the religious impulse that stirs the human spirit nonetheless demanded proper burial. The burial of a loved one brings home to the living the full reality of our brief mortal existence:

> It is to the living mourner — to the parent weeping over his dear dead child — to the husband dwelling in his own solitary desolation — to the widow, whose heart is broken by untimely sorrow — to the friend who misses at every turn, the presence of some kindred spirit — it is to these that the repositories of the dead bring home thoughts full of admonition, of instruction, and slowly, but surely, of consolation also. They admonish us, by their very silence, of our own frail and transitory being. They instruct us in the true value of life, and in its noble purposes, its duties, and its destination.

These impulses, Story observed, were universal, a part of the spiritual heritage of all peoples — "the barbarian and the civilized . . . the inhabitant of the dreary forests of the north, and the sultry regions of the south — the worshipper of the sun, and the worshipper of idols — the heathen, dwelling in the darkness of his cold mythology, and . . . the Christian, rejoicing in the light of the true God." All persons, at all times and places, have shown a due regard for the dead. These impulses are "absolutely universal, and . . . deeply founded in human affection."

Christians, however, stand apart from other peoples in the regard they show their dead. To the pagan peoples of ancient Rome, to the Germanic inhabitants of the medieval forests, "the burying-place was the end of all things. They indulged no hope, at least no solid hope, of any future intercourse or reunion with their friends." Christians, however, know that the grave "is not an everlasting home." "What is the grave to us, but a thin barrier, dividing time from eternity, and earth from heaven?"

In language that might have been familiar to ancient devotees of the cult of saints, and certainly would have been at home with Cotton Mather, Story exhorted his audience to appreciate that cemeteries are places of profound religious experience. They eloquently teach Christian lessons about virtue and duty and the transcendence of death itself. Story concluded his remarks with a prayer. As we stand at Mt. Auburn, he exclaimed, we must remember that "[b]lessed are the dead, that die in the Lord, for they rest from the labors; and their works do follow them."

Story brought these sentiments into his official capacity as judge. In *Beatty v.*

*Kurtz,*[1] Story confronted a dispute among the German Lutherans of Georgetown, then an independent town in the District of Columbia. In 1769, one Charles Beatty had laid out a series of lots comprising an addition to the town. Accommodation was made for a group of German Lutherans. Poor and small in number, the Lutherans were able only infrequently to operate their own house of worship. They nevertheless established a burial ground, despite lacking clear title to the land. Only in the 1820s, when their rights were challenged, did the Lutherans seek a title. Asserting the equitable power of the Supreme Court to protect the dead Lutherans in their repose, Story wrote on behalf of the entire Court:

> The property consecrated [to the Lutherans] is to be taken from them; the sepulchres of the dead are to be violated; the feelings of religion, and the sentiment of natural affection of the kindred and friends of the deceased are to be wounded; and the memorials erected by piety or love, to the memory of the good, are to be removed so as to leave no trace of the last home of their ancestry to those who may visit the spot in future generations.

With such concerns foremost in his mind, Story ruled in favor of the Lutherans and extended the protection of the Supreme Court to the burial places of their ancestors.

### B. The Courts and Biblical Exegesis: Genesis 23, God's Acre, and Hallowed Ground

American courts in the nineteenth and even early twentieth centuries were not afraid to provide a biblical gloss to their decisions concerning the disposition of human remains. A particular favorite of the courts was Genesis 23, Abraham's purchase of the cave of Machpelah as a burial place for Sarah.

A New York case dating to 1850 (*Schoonmaker v. Reformed Dutch Church,* 5 How. Pr. 265) involved a petition to relocate some graves. The Court waxed eloquent about Abraham's intentions. The burial ground at Machpelah, the opinion-writer observed, was "probably the only land [the patriarch] ever owned." It was his "affection for his beloved dead" which prompted Abraham "to secure a place where their mortal remains might repose, undisturbed, until they should again be reanimated at the resurrection." "The inviolability of the last resting place of the dead," the Court noted, "is the last wish of affection, when it renders back to the earth the body of one dear in life, *ut requiescat in pace, usque ad resurrectionem.*"

This sort of exegesis proved an enduring aspect of American jurispru-

1. 27 U.S. 566 (1829).

dence. When the Pennsylvania Supreme Court, in 1879, authorized the relocation of a historic cemetery, containing burials dating from the eighteenth century, Chief Justice Daniel Agnew (1809-1902) objected. A Republican, a Methodist, and a temperance advocate, Agnew appealed to Abraham and Sarah in denouncing the majority's reasoning:

> This sacredness [of the tomb] is evidenced by one of the most touching incidents of Scripture. When Abraham standing by the dead body of Sarah, addressed the sons of Heth, saying, 'I am a stranger and sojourner with you, give me possession of a burial place with you, that I may bury my dead out of sight:' They offered him a choice of their sepulchres; but Abraham, intent upon possession of his own, where the remains of her he had loved might repose in security, purchased the field of Macpelah of Ephron, the Hittite, for four hundred shekels of silver. Even more touching is the reference of Jacob, who, dying in Egypt, surrounded by his wife and children, charged them and said unto them, 'I am to be gathered unto my people, bury me with my fathers in the cave that is in the field of Macpelah. There they buried Abraham and Sarah, his wife, there they buried Isaac and Rebecca, his wife, and there I buried Leah.' Tradition has preserved to this day, the identity of the cave and the tombs of these ancient worthies, undisturbed even by the Moslem, whose mosque covers and protects their resting places.[2]

A few years into the twentieth century, in 1912, the West Virginia high court encountered the question whether to authorize the exhumation of a body of a homicide victim. The Court's answer was obvious in the way it framed the question: "Can [the court] without consent of the kindred of the dead invade the sacred precincts of the cemetery, and tear open the grave, and tear open once again and lacerate afresh the hearts of those that loved him, and to whom his memory is sacred and dear?"[3]

The respect shown by Muslims toward the tomb of the patriarchs was used to justify this conclusion: "It is said that the conquering Moslem respected the graves of Abraham, Isaac, and Jacob, and Sarah, Rebekah, and Leah, their wives, by abstaining from the removal of their bodies from Macpelah when building a mosque."[4]

The Court acknowledged that some have shown disregard for the dead. The ancient Cynic followers of Diogenes "regarded burial with contempt," and "some modern French philosophers descanted upon the 'glorious nothingness'

---

2. See *Craig v. First Presbyterian Church of Pittsburgh*, 88 Pa. 42, 53 (Agnew, CJ, dissenting).
3. *State v. Highland*, 71 W. Va. 87, 88 (1912).
4. *Id.*, at 89.

of the grave and that 'nameless thing,' a dead body."[5] But, the Court concluded, this approach was not justified even by "the secular jurisprudence of the civilized nations in our day."[6] The Court felt some discomfort at this conclusion, since it was denying the defendant access to possibly exculpatory evidence, but minimized the risk of a miscarriage of justice by noting that decomposition had probably destroyed what evidentiary value the corpse might have had.

A second West Virginia case dating to 1912 involved the removal of a cemetery.[7] In rejecting the petition, the Court relied upon Genesis 23:

> If relatives of blood may not defend the graves of their departed who may? Always the human heart has rebelled against the invasion of the cemetery precincts; always has the human mind contemplated the grave as the last and enduring resting place after the struggles and sorrows of the world. When the patriarch Jacob was dying in Egypt he spake unto the Israelites and said: 'I am to be gathered unto my people; bury me with my fathers in the cave that is in the field of Machpelah, which is before Mamre, in the land of Canaan, which Abraham bought with the field of Ephron the Hittite for possession of a burying place. There they buried Abraham and Sarah his wife; there they buried Isaac and Rebekah his wife; and there I buried Leah.'[8]

The Court foresaw the danger of advancing commercialism overwhelming traditional religious sentiment and sought to stand against it: "This commercial age betokens that trade will at some future time forget the dead reposing there."[9] To forestall such forgetfulness, the Court rejected the petition.

Genesis 23 continued to be cited well into the twentieth century. As recently as 1965, the Genesis story was cited to justify a New York statute restricting the right to sell land dedicated to family burial plots.[10]

Not surprisingly, American courts also invoked a variety of other religious terms and symbols when they chose to protect the precincts of the dead. "The sepulture of the dead," the Indiana Supreme Court wrote, "has, in all ages of the world, been regarded as a religious rite."[11] As early as the Anglo-Saxon period, the Court observed, cemeteries were known as "God's acre."[12]

The metaphor of God's acre continued to be invoked into the twentieth

---

5. *Id.*, at 89.
6. *Id.*
7. See *Ritter v. Couch*, 71 W. Va. 221.
8. *Id.*, at 227-28.
9. *Id.*, 225.
10. See *In the Matter of Estate of Bessie Turkish*, 48 Misc. 2d 600, 600-601 (NY).
11. See *Dwenger v. Geary*, 113 Ind. 106, 112 (1888).
12. *Id.*

century. Citing a New Jersey case, the Minnesota Supreme Court approvingly declared: "The burying ground is God's acre."[13] When the owner of a cemetery lot had a pet dog buried in it, the Kentucky Supreme Court ordered the animal's exhumation as something offensive to the other plot-owners and to religion itself: "why might not the owner of a horse or bull, or donkey, also bury his favorite on his lot therein, if his fancy should take this freakish direction?"[14] A cemetery is the resting place of the human dead: "Sorrow, bending over the graves of her loved ones, smiles through her tears and accepts the assurance with Faith that they are not dead, but sleeping."[15] A New York Court, in denying a request to exhume the body of an automobile accident victim, wrote, "The 'night encampment' of the dead has for centuries been deemed 'God's Acre,' and 'hallowed ground,' and the remains of the dead have been permitted to be disturbed only for urgent and sufficient reasons."[16]

Majority and dissenting opinions might even call upon the same patterns of religiously symbolic language to justify their contrasting views of the same case. *Frost v. Columbia Clay Company* (130 S.C. 72 [1924]) involved a claim for the disturbance by an excavation of a family burial plot. In permitting a trial against the excavating company to go forward, the majority wrote,

> From the time of Abraham, the places where the dead were buried have been considered sacred and inviolate. All nations respect the graves of the dead. The graves of ancestors are a subject of idolatrous worship by the heathen. Our literature is full of references to the last or final resting place. In some of our church literature we find the statement that the bodies of the dead "do rest in their graves until the Resurrection." These burial places are sometimes called "God's Acre."[17]

The dissent, focusing on evidence that the burial plot had been effectively abandoned, countered, "It may appropriately have been called 'God's Acre,' for He alone had visited it and hidden with undergrowth the human shame of neglect."[18]

Cemeteries were also characterized as "hallowed ground." The Pennsylvania Supreme Court wrote, in rejecting an action of partition seeking to divide a burial ground between competing religious claimants, "The only form in

---

13. *Brown v. Maplewood Cemetery Association,* 85 Minn. 498 (1902).
14. *Hertle v. Riddell,* 127 Ky. 623, 626 (1902).
15. *Id.*
16. *Danahy v. Kellogg,* 70 Misc. 25, 28 (1910).
17. *Id.,* at 76.
18. *Id.,* at 78 (Cothran, J., dissenting).

which the partition asked for could be made, would be by a public sale; and what would these graves, of inestimable value to surviving relatives, fetch in the market? . . . [T]he resting place of the dead [is] hallowed ground — not subject to the laws of ordinary property."[19]

Of all the religious language and imagery employed by the courts, the notion of "hallowed ground" has proved perhaps the most enduring. The Colorado Supreme Court spoke of cemeteries as "almost universally . . . regarded as a class of property by themselves."[20] This was because "our people generally, as do people in all civilized states, regard the burying places of the dead as sacred or hallowed ground."[21] A New Jersey Court declared, quoting earlier authority: "The place where the dead are buried is regarded generally, if not universally, [as] hallowed ground."[22] Quoting a legal treatise, the Minnesota Supreme Court wrote: "The sentiment of all civilized peoples regards the resting place of the dead as hallowed ground, and requires that in some respects it be not treated as subject to the laws of ordinary property."[23] As recently as 1961, a Kentucky Court could write, in permitting a tort claim for grave desecration to go forward: "[T]he right of next of kin to recover damages for the desecration of a grave is generally recognized as being for a common law tort. It is based upon the reality of an intrusion into tender feelings. The resting places of the dead have been revered and regarded as hallowed ground from the earliest days."[24]

### C. Christian Burial: More Valuable than Money

Standing behind these developments, of course, was the theologically-freighted idea of Christian burial. Courts were unafraid to employ this concept throughout the nineteenth and early twentieth centuries. A Massachusetts case of Civil War–era vintage declared, in terms reminiscent of Prudentius,

> [W]e think the devotion of a piece of ground to the purposes of burial includes much more than the mere interment of the remains of the dead. "To bury our dead out of our sight," a suitable provision for the pressing claims of a decency and health, is the first, but not the only consideration. "Christians," says Sir Thomas Browne, "have handsomely glossed the deformity of death by careful consideration of the body, and civil rites which take off bru-

---

19. See *Brown v. Lutheran Church,* 23 Pa. 495, 500 (1854).
20. *City and County of Denver v. Tihen,* 77 Colo. 212, 219 (1925).
21. *Id.*
22. *Atlas Fence Company v. West Ridgelawn Cemetery,* 110 N.J. Eq. 580, 592 (1932).
23. *State v. Lorentz,* 221 Minn. 366, 370 (1946).
24. *R. B. Tyler Company v. Kinser,* 346 S.W. 2d 306, 308.

tal terminations; and though they conceived all reparable by a resurrection, cast not off care of interment. . . . Since they acknowledged their bodies to be the lodging of Christ, and temples of the Holy Ghost, they devoted not all upon the sufficiency of soul-existence; and therefore with long services and full solemnities concluded their last exequies."[25]

This idea of Christian burial gained acceptance in the legal treatises and, in fact, became a legal fiction of sorts, but one that required the respect of the mortal remains of all persons, Christian or not:

> A dead man has rights, the greatest of which is called Christian burial. It is a universal desire of mankind that some service be had over the remains of every person before their final disposition, and that this rite be of a religious character. The word *Christian* is not a denominational term, as here used, but means some proper recognition of the nature of man and the solemnity of his entrance into the world beyond. Christian burial, in this sense, is a term applicable to the Hindu, Mohammedan, and Jew, as well as to the Christian.[26]

Because of religious sensibilities, courts were reluctant to allow monetary motives to intrude on the sacredness of a burial site. The case of *Thompson v. Hickey*[27] involved tragically sad circumstances. A father, who must have been hard-pressed financially, pledged the family burial plot, which contained the graves of his three children, as collateral on a loan. The Court denied the possibility that the creditors might foreclose on the burial plot and exhume the graves so as to sell the lots to other parties. Even though New York statutes were silent on this precise question, the Court felt that to allow such a remedy offended against basic religious sensibilities:

> The sentiments and feelings which people in a Christian state have for the dead, the law regards and respects, and however it may have been anterior to our legislation on the subject of cemeteries, the dead themselves now have rights, which are committed to the living to protect, and in doing which they obtain security for the undisturbed rest of their own remains.[28]

*Stewart v. Garrett*[29] involved an action of ejectment, apparently brought against the insolvent estate of the decedent, for satisfaction of debts. The Court

25. *Commonwealth v. Viall*, 84 Mass (2 Allen) 512, 514-15 (1861).
26. Sidney Perley, *Mortuary Law* (Boston, 1896), pp. 30-31.
27. 8 Abb. New Cas. (NY, 1880).
28. *Id.*, at 167.
29. 119 Ga. 386 (1904).

resolved the question on formalistic grounds, holding that an action of ejectment could not be brought against the type of title the family owned in a cemetery plot. Sensing, however, the inadequacy of an answer that relied on the narrow logic of the common law, the Court continued:

> It may be added that, while the action of ejectment has its uses, its quaint fictions and devices do not seem appropriate to the ascertainment of any right in a burial lot. If any fiction is pardonable in a case of this kind, it would be fitter to hold that the fee in these sacred premises belongs to the dead. Within these hallowed precincts no court would desire to send the sheriff with a writ of possession. This instinct of humanity is loyalty to a statute impressed upon all hearts. Its influence is not confined to the weak and ignorant. The plaintive appeal which marks the grave of Shakespeare is said to have been inspired by his fear of a removal of his bones to a charnel house: "Good friend, for Jesus' sake forbear, To dig the dust enclosed here."

It was only with great reluctance that courts entertained the possibility that a property interest might vest in the survivors of a deceased loved one. This reluctance was not the product of any failure to appreciate the importance of family members' interest, but rather a concern that property-based claims had no place in light of the sacredness of the duty.

Samuel Ruggles (1800-1881), a dominant figure in the New York bar and a practicing Episcopalian who was a member of that church's General Convention, was appointed by the New York Chancery Court as a special master to apportion compensation in a case involving the removal of graves from an ancient churchyard cemetery on Beekman Street, now north of Fulton Street and south of the Brooklyn Bridge.[30]

The essence of the case involved monetary compensation to surviving family members of those whose graves had to be relocated. Ruggles noted the paradox implicated by the problem he was called upon to resolve. The ordinary means of valuing prime urban real estate — commerce, traffic, the constant hum of activity that accompanied life in the city — had no place in appraising the value of burial vaults. Their value was diminished by such circumstances. Referring to the Greek root of the word cemetery in *koimeterion* — "dormitory" — Ruggles observed that a burial ground "deriv[ed] its primary and principal, if not its only value, from its repose and security from disturbance."[31]

Despite his discomfort at having to do so, Ruggles ultimately assigned a

---

30. *In re Widening of Beekman Street,* 4 Bradf. Surr. 503 (1856).
31. *Id.,* at 512.

monetary value to the graves that had been disturbed. This much was called for by the natural law:

> The establishment of a right [of family members to the peaceful repose of loved ones] so sacred and precious, ought not to need any judicial precedent. Our courts of justice should place it at once, where it should fundamentally rest for ever, on the deepest and most unerring instincts of human nature; and hold it to be a self-evident right of humanity, entitled to legal protection by every consideration of feeling, decency, and Christian duty.[32]

On the whole, courts were reluctant to employ the category of property in analyzing claims implicating the proper treatment and disposition of the dead. Perhaps typical in this respect is an opinion of Justice William Mitchell (1832-1900), author of nearly 1,600 judicial opinions, who can be fairly described as the founder of Minnesota jurisprudence.

The plaintiff in *Larson v. Chase* alleged that her late husband's body had been "mutilated" and "dissect[ed]" without her permission and sought damages on the basis of "mental suffering and nervous shock."[33] Mitchell cited Ruggles's opinion respectfully, as authority for what he was about to say, but then proceeded to reject a property-based claim. He invoked the "general, if not universal doctrine" that spouses or next of kin have responsibility for the care and burial of the dead.[34] This responsibility, and the concomitant rights that flowed from it, were derived from "common custom and general sentiment" as well as "reason."[35] These rights were "in the nature of a sacred trust, in the performance of which all are interested who were allied to the deceased by the ties of family or friendship."[36]

But upon what basis, if any, should damages be awarded? If not property, then how could an award be justified? Mitchell looked to the nature of the act itself. The unauthorized dissection amounted to "indignity to the dead."[37] Such a deprivation of dignity, seemingly a violation of human dignity itself, and the accompanying mental distress, was sufficient basis on which to ground a claim of damages.

---

32. *Id.*, at 529.
33. 47 Minn. 307 (1891).
34. *Id.*, 309.
35. *Id.*, at 309.
36. *Id.*, at 309.
37. *Id.*, at 312.

## III

Today these kinds of heartfelt concerns for the dignity of the dead are rapidly disappearing. In February 2002, several hundred bodies were found strewn about the grounds of a crematorium in rural north Georgia. The *New York Times* described the scene: "Human bones, weathered white, were scattered through the woods like leaves, skulls mixed with leg bones in a ghoulish jumble that one state trooper compared to a Stephen King novel." An op-ed writer for the *Times* blamed the gory scene at Tri-State Crematory on a new phenomenon in American attitudes about the dead: "cremation not as an alternative to burial but as an alternative to bother — a way of avoiding 'all that fuss.'"

More is at stake, however, than simply a decent regard for the dead. The human body itself is becoming increasingly the object of commercial exchange. Fetal tissue is now routinely bought and sold, as are other forms of human tissue — bones, cartilage, and other parts of human remains. Human organ transplants, at least for the moment, remain immune from commercial exchange, but if the criticism of law-review writers is a predictor of the future course of the law, we can soon expect the emergence of markets in kidneys, hearts, lungs, and other organs necessary for sustaining life.

Even judicial decisions that purport to protect the sanctity of human remains give support for the increasing commercialization of the human body. The Ninth Circuit in 2002 considered the constitutionality of a California statute authorizing county coroners to remove corneal eye tissue in the course of autopsies. No permission of next-of-kin was required under the statute. It was felt that medical needs trumped all other concerns. The plaintiffs were parents of deceased children whose corneas had been removed without parental permission.[38] The Ninth Circuit ruled the statute unconstitutional, grounding its decision on the "property" interest of parents in the corneas of their children. The Court linked property and human dignity in a way that would have appalled nineteenth-century courts. Citing California law, the Ninth Circuit declared, "The property rights that California affords to next of kin to the body of their deceased relatives serve the premium value our society has historically placed on protecting the dignity of the human body in its final disposition."[39] In this manner the Ninth Circuit attempted to vindicate, at least in some measure, the right of parents to protect the bodily integrity of their deceased offspring. The reductionism of the Court, however, in premising its holding entirely on the characterization of the parents'

38. See *Newman v. Sathyavagslwaran,* 287 F. 3d 786 (2002).
39. *Id.,* at 798.

interest as a species of property, subverts the Court's own conclusion. If the parents have a property interest in their children's corneas, why may they not sell them? Indeed, why stop at the cornea? Why not sell heart, kidneys, pancreas, and lungs?

Historically, respect for the body of the deceased human person was premised not on property, but on the uniqueness of every person as a creation of God. All persons are made in His image and likeness. The nineteenth-century courts repeatedly insisted, whenever the question presented itself, that the ordinary rules of property did not apply to human burial. In cemeteries, generations past awaited the coming resurrection of the dead. American courts were loathe to dash such an expectation, at least not without very good reason. The operative concepts were dignity and sacredness.

If this essay sheds light on American attitudes about the dead, it also sheds light on some larger concerns as well. It should be clear that the very substructure of American law is irreducibly religious. We who live in a post-*Everson* age[40] have become accustomed to the arguments of strict separationists like Justice Wiley Rutledge, who see in the First Amendment's religion clause "a complete and permanent separation of the spheres of religious activity and civil authority."[41] Rutledge's call to policy-makers "to uproot" the vestiges of religious influence on American public life has become a commonplace of constitutional argument, at least in some circles. Rutledge justified this call to arms by his own selective reading of American legal history.

The solicitude shown by courts and judges throughout the first century and a half of American legal history to the essentially religious character of human burial makes it clear that the strict separationists' view of the constitutional order is simply lacking in historical merit. The Judeo-Christian heritage saturated American law. Judges were not ashamed at all to rely upon the Bible for guidance in determining cases. Genesis 23 became a staple of legal citation. The body of the human person was a temple of the Holy Spirit, laid to sleep in a cemetery, there to await the resurrection of the dead.

The un-self-conscious ways in which courts deployed these sorts of arguments are indicative of how deeply in American jurisprudence these religious sensibilities were embedded. It was taken for granted, even among American elites — lawyers and judges — that the remains of the deceased human person were worthy of respect. And that respect was grounded on a Judeo-Christian vision of the creation of the person in the image and likeness of God and the capacity of the human person to transcend death itself.

40. *Everson v. Board of Education* 330 U.S. (1947).
41. *Id.*, at 31-32, Rutledge, J., dissenting.

Ultimately, it is this regard for the human person as a creature of God, as a being with transcendent capabilities and ends, that is rapidly disappearing along with the courts' regard for the "dignity of the dead." If the dignity of the dead is destroyed, for how much longer can we maintain the dignity of the living?

# Putting Asunder:
# Changing Perceptions of Marriage
# and Personhood in the
# Early-Twentieth-Century United States

CHRISTINE ROSEN

If the structure of our social institutions reflects our assumptions about the human person, then the institution of marriage is perhaps the most intimate mirror of all, since it reflects both our deepest aspirations and our most mundane realities, our desire for autonomy and our acknowledgment of dependency, and in the end, our fundamental beliefs about a life well lived. What emerges from Christine Rosen's examination of the ways marital ideals changed in the early twentieth century is, in many respects, a very tangled picture. Marriage had clearly changed dramatically, from a traditional institution in which young men and women glided into their unions, following the lead of carefully laid-down expectations and sanctions, into a rather different kind of institution, in which the rules were more fluid, more in keeping with the liberal individualism that increasingly held sway in the general culture. But even this change was a paradoxical and confusing one, since at the same time marriage was coming to be understood and regulated by scientific means — and yet was placed ever more securely under the sacred canopy of romantic love. Marriage was both a social function with consequences for the health of society and an individual, autonomous choice, contingent upon nothing but the couple's feelings for one another. Yet Rosen sees a unifying theme in this seeming contradiction, and the theme is individual control — control over one's marital choices, one's childbearing, one's sexual experiences, one's exposure to venereal disease, and so on. In short, modern American marriage became what it was precisely because it corresponded so perfectly with the liberal-individualist understanding of the human person. By the 1940s, marriage had come to be widely understood as a private institution, in which two consenting, autonomous individuals contract with one another for emotional fulfillment. That they also cannot seem to shake the desire to see their marriages as sacred unions and sources of moral meaning, however, tells us something important, too. Christine Rosen is a fellow at the Ethics and Public Policy Center and au-

446

thor of *Preaching Eugenics: Religious Leaders and the American Eugenics Movement* (Oxford, 2004).

> *"Giving advice regarding matrimony is proverbially a hazardous performance, and it is not much safer for the biologist than for others."*

Princeton University professor Edwin Grant Conklin, 1913

Marriage is a mirror, reflecting many things about a culture. It reflects the importance a society places on sexual morality, childbearing, and the status of women. It projects an image of society's preferences for certain economic relationships. It reveals a society's anxieties about the future and reflects its worst conceits about who belongs and who does not. For the individual, it reflects the sanctioning of personal desire, membership in a community, and entry into a socially important arrangement that has lifelong consequences for financial stability and emotional and physical health. The closer you peer into this mirror, however, the more minor imperfections you will find, like the tiniest wrinkles and spots that are all but invisible from a distance but emerge rapidly the nearer you draw your gaze.

In the early twentieth century, marriage in the United States was an institution riddled with imperfections, small and large — at least this is how a growing number of legislators, biologists, sociologists, and intellectuals were apt to describe it. One need only note the kind of subjects paired with the word "marriage" in magazine stories and in book titles to gather that the institution was perceived to be under siege from a host of assailants: *social diseases* and marriage, *syphilis* and marriage, *companionate* marriage, *genetics* and marriage, marriage and *disease,* marriage and *divorce,* marriage and *race death,* marriage and the *sex-problem.* Fissures that were only beginning to appear in the 1870s and 1880s were by now visible and disturbing evidence of serious problems, problems that prompted a series of questions: How democratic should the institution of marriage be? Were certain people more fit than others to enter into it and fulfill its obligations? Would new arrivals to American shores adapt to American standards of marriage, or undermine them? How firmly soldered was the link between sex and marriage, and between marriage and childbearing? What threat did divorce pose to the institution?

For a number of American leaders, the first few decades of the twentieth century witnessed an expansion of the understanding of marriage as an indicator not merely of the *moral* health of the nation, but its *biological* health as well. Marriage became a useful narrows where scourges such as "feeblemindedness" and venereal disease might be better controlled. It became the gatekeeper for preventing those who were permanently marred by physical defects such as epilepsy and tuberculosis from sullying the institution and (by implication) future generations of Americans. And this view of marriage fed a faith in the superiority of state actors and professional experts. American families, it seemed, were failing to train their offspring in their proper civic duty; the state must step in and supplant some of those functions. Less and less often would one find American leaders praising the hoi polloi for its pragmatic wisdom about marriage and parenting; instead, they expressed fears for the country's apparently increasing immorality and irrationality. Reporting on a sermon about marriage preached at the West End Presbyterian Church in New York City in 1913, for example, the *New York Times* relayed how the minister, Dr. Kelgwin, "said with much emphasis that thousands of people in America had lost their sense of the sacredness of the marriage tie."[1] The states had long used the regulation of marriage as a tool for enforcing social norms, discouraging certain behaviors, and branding certain people as outsiders (Mormon polygamists, slaves, and interracial couples, for example). But in the early decades of the twentieth century, the social distance between the fit and the unfit widened, with marriage increasingly serving as a marker of one's place — not merely socially, but biologically — in American society.

Individual Americans absorbed these concerns; at the same time, they were pushing at the boundaries of marriage themselves. "Marriage is the operation by which a woman's vanity and a man's egotism are extracted without an anaesthetic," quipped journalist Helen Rowland in her 1922 romp, *A Guide to Men*.[2] Rowland's remark captures the new sense of openness about discussing marriage in the early twentieth century, and the fact that Americans were beginning to test whether or not they could alter the institution to better suit present realities. In what sense should marriage be understood as a vehicle for personal fulfillment as well as a social institution? What did it mean that an increasing number of Americans expected "true love" to extend past courtship and into marriage itself? How realistic were demands for fewer barriers to exiting marriage (divorce), and calls, albeit on the fringes, for reimagining or abolishing the institution altogether through "free love" arrangements? More importantly, how

1. "Wedlock Commercialized," *New York Times*, May 19, 1913, 2.
2. Helen Rowland, *A Guide to Men: Being Encore Reflections of a Bachelor Girl* (New York: Dodge Publishing Co., 1922).

strongly would the public's increasing demands for more information about sex in general and greater sexual fulfillment in marriage in particular impact the institution? Pressure points on marriage increased exponentially as sex was seen as something potentially separate from both marriage (via increased extramarital sexual experimentation) and childbearing (through birth control).

But individual Americans also made use of biological and scientific arguments in their examination of marriage. The demand for marriage advice bearing the imprimatur of scientific, expert opinion increased in these years, as did scientific justifications for new practices such as birth control. Fears about venereal disease encouraged individual Americans to accept state restrictions on marriage and more intrusive public health campaigns, and the heightened pressure to find and maintain "true love" itself eventually spawned a mini-industry: the marriage counseling movement. Although at times they resisted state and "expert" efforts to shape the institution of marriage, many individual Americans swiftly and with little fuss accepted the scientific arguments that supported many of these efforts. In the process, their understanding of themselves as individuals changed to include a host of biologically-fueled assumptions about what it meant to be American — assumptions that focused largely on marriage and childbearing — that would endure well past the particular regulations and crises of the period.

By the 1930s, in popular and professional discourse, marriage had become the reassuringly familiar vehicle for discussing some very unfamiliar ideas — abolishing the sexual double standard, frank accounts of sex and venereal disease, the usefulness of contraception and divorce, the appeal of eugenics, and the society-wide effort to winnow unfit candidates for citizenship. The simple narrative of marriage as an institution, wherein young men and women, with little effort, experienced courtship, formalized their feelings with a legal license and a religious ceremony, and proceeded to live productive lives and bear healthy citizens, all within the happy confines of state law, still retained its appeal in theory. In practice, however, something far different had emerged: a sense that marriage could be understood and regulated as a science, and that threats to it — whether from feeblemindedness or divorce — must also be understood in this more rational, more modern context. It was during these first few decades of the twentieth century that Americans made the transition from an older form of marriage — one suited to the demands of the nineteenth century — to a more modern form of marriage, a form that could endure in a heterogeneous, technologically advanced, urban society.

During this transition period, with its calls for science to trump emotion and the state to supplant more traditional arbiters of marriage, Americans did not wholly relinquish their deeply held desire for marriage as a union of genuine emotional connection and an institution that required legal and sacred sanction. Marriage did change as a result of outside pressure from the state, and, internally, through greater individual control over reproduction and divorce. But these changes took place within the context of a broader advance of liberal individualism, one that has meant no end to demands that marriage, as an institution, continue to reflect the often-competing desires of different groups of Americans.

# I

It is the state governments, not the federal government, that regulate marriage in the United States. With a few minor variations based on which state you lived in, at the beginning of the twentieth century, you were not fully accepted into the fold of marriage if you were a black person who wanted to marry a white person, or vice versa; if you were feebleminded, epileptic, or tubercular; if you were chronically poor or chronically drunk; if you were accorded insane; or if you were under a certain age. Protecting the purity of marriage was, at least rhetorically, the motivation behind many of these restrictions. In 1888, for example, the U.S. Supreme Court, in the case of *Maynard v. Hill*, described marriage as more than merely a contract; it was "an institution, in the maintenance of which in its purity the public is deeply interested."[3]

Nearly half of the states forbade marriage between the insane or feebleminded, but they did so on the basis of their inability to make a contract, not because of a belief in their inherent biological weakness. Connecticut made the first explicitly hereditarian foray into marriage restriction in 1896, when it passed a law stating that "no man and woman either of whom is epileptic, or imbecile, or feebleminded" could marry "when the woman is under forty-five years of age," thus explicitly linking marriage to a woman's procreative window. The penalty for violating this stricture was three years in prison. Kansas, New Jersey, Ohio, Michigan, and Indiana passed similar laws in the first few years of the twentieth century. Their impact on the average American was minimal, however, since states rarely enforced the laws.[4] Age of marriage was also regulated by the states, but it too was amenable to changes in public opinion; by 1910, the age at

---

3. *Maynard v. Hill*, 125 U.S. 190, 211 (1888), case quoted in Nancy F. Cott, *Public Vows: A History of Marriage and the Nation* (Cambridge: Harvard University Press, 2000), 102-103.

4. See Mark Haller, *Eugenics: Hereditarian Attitudes in American Thought* (New Brunswick, N.J.: Rutgers University Press, 1963), 142-43, 47; see also Philip R. Reilly, *The Surgical Solution: A History of Involuntary Sterilization in the United States* (Baltimore: Johns Hopkins University Press, 1991), 26-27.

which minors were allowed to marry had risen in most states from twelve to sixteen years old for girls and from fourteen to eighteen years old for boys; most states also had requirements for girls under the age of eighteen and boys under the age of twenty-one to obtain parental consent for marriage.[5]

On the boundaries of the institution, however, things were not entirely settled. Like the sudden gusts of wind that herald the arrival of a storm, free love advocates in the early years of the twentieth century began arguing for a different form of marriage, one based on "natural" laws and freedom from religious and state intrusion. "The attempt to make people conform to *any* given standard of marital or conjugal ethics is the cause of nearly all the failures, the crimes and miseries of moral life," said radical marriage reformer Moses Harman. Only liberty for each individual would stop the "evils of our present marriage system."[6]

Free love advocates found in science a more appealing basis for their cause. "The greatest need of sex is to release it from religion and law and let it be free for science to observe," wrote one correspondent in a free love journal in 1907. "Scientific investigation is content to see all the investigators' ideas of life and ethics demolished if untrue."[7] Science was appealing to these self-described radicals because it stood in for objectivity and rationality — two things they felt the law and the churches had abandoned. But this supposedly radical notion was quickly becoming mainstream. As historians John D'Emilio and Estelle Freedman have argued, by 1907, free love's "once-threatened message of sex education, birth control, and the romantic union of love and sexuality was about to become the dominant middle-class sexual ideology."[8]

Arguably nothing hastened this turn to scientific solutions more than the growing concerns about venereal disease and fears about the future biological health of the nation. As the nation's prime crusader against the "social diseases," dermatologist Prince Morrow described a vast campaign in the preface to his 1880 translation of the text *Syphilis and Marriage:* "There is scarcely a subject in the entire domain of medicine of greater practical importance to the profession and to the public, not only on account of the nature of the pathological questions presented, but also on account of the family and society interests

5. R. Newton Crane, "Marriage Laws and Statutory Experiments in Eugenics in the United States," *Eugenics Review* 2 (April 1910): 65.

6. Moses Harman, "Yesterday, Today, Tomorrow," *The American Journal of Eugenics* 1 (July 1907): 28-31.

7. M. Florence Johnson, "The Scientific Method and Eugenics," *American Journal of Eugenics* 1 (July 1907): 22-24.

8. John D'Emilio and Estelle B. Freedman, *Intimate Matters: A History of Sexuality in America* (New York: Harper & Row, 1988), 165-66.

involved, and which it is the physician's manifest duty to protect."[9] This was not merely a medical issue; the institution of marriage and the integrity of the American family were implicated in the spread of disease. As a result, reformers such as Morrow whittled away at the notion of romantic love as the basis for sound marriage, seeing in it a dangerous delusion for women and a harbor for impure men: "Young women should know that marriage is not all romance and sentiment," Morrow wrote, "that dissipated men make unsafe husbands and unsound fathers, and that the halo of romantic interest thrown around the man with a profligate past by fiction writers is a symbol of shame, a signal of danger for his wife and children."[10]

Similar concerns bothered promoters of the eugenics movement. Eugenicists, who hoped to improve the human race through better breeding, tended to talk about "matings" and "breeding" rather than marriage and childrearing.[11] They also exhibited a general facility in deploying other tropes — including motherhood, "Americanism," and various versions of race pride — to further their cause. But like venereal disease crusaders, eugenicists had found a clear villain: feeblemindedness. The feebleminded included not merely victims of epilepsy and tuberculosis, insanity and alcoholism, but also a more general group of people, those with hereditary skeletons in their family closets, who were viewed as incapable of performing their duties as members of society, duties which included those of spouse and parent.

Charles Davenport, a Harvard-trained biologist and head of the Carnegie-endowed Eugenics Record Office, echoed Morrow in his impatience with Americans' sentimental focus on finding "true love" and happiness through marriage: "The success of marriage from the standpoint of eugenics is measured by the number of disease-resistant, cultivable offspring that come from it," Davenport wrote. "Happiness or unhappiness of the parents, the princip[al] theme of many novels and the proceedings of divorce courts, has little eugenic significance." The law, Davenport felt, was a "cheap device" for preventing the marriage of "defectives."[12]

This did not mean that intervention in marriage wasn't useful; indeed, Davenport found it "grounds for reproach" that "marriage should still be only

---

9. Morrow quoted in Allan Brandt, *No Magic Bullet: A Social History of Venereal Disease in the United States since 1880* (New York: Oxford University Press, 1987), 11.

10. Brandt, *No Magic Bullet*, 19.

11. See, for example, Charles Davenport, *Eugenics: The Science of Human Improvement by Better Breeding* (New York: Henry Holt & Co., 1910).

12. Charles Davenport, *Heredity in Relation to Eugenics* (New York: Henry Holt, 1911), 1; "cheap device" quoted in Edward J. Larson, *Sex, Race, and Science: Eugenics in the Deep South* (Baltimore: Johns Hopkins University Press, 1995), 22-23.

an *experiment* in breeding, while the breeding of many animals and plants has been reduced to a science." And eugenicists shared with venereal disease crusaders a sense of where the individual fit in this society: "The commonwealth is greater than any individual in it," Davenport wrote. "Hence the rights of society over the life, the reproduction, the behavior and the traits of the individuals that compose it." Society can "restrict liberty in a hundred ways."[13]

A resigned sense that legally altering marriage might not be feasible infused some eugenics rhetoric. Francis Galton, the British scientist, cousin to Charles Darwin and founder of the eugenics movement, recognized early in his work "that human nature would never brook interference with the freedom of marriage."[14] Lewellys Barker, a professor of medicine at Johns Hopkins University, offered a similar assessment: "The cultivation of a healthy public opinion regarding marriage and parenthood will, it seems probably, be more efficient in promoting eugenics than anything that can be done by way of legislation, at any rate at present."[15]

Among the more popular eugenics propagandists (the ones widely read by the average American), however, marriage was viewed as an attractive avenue for pursuing the eugenics program. In several best-selling books, eugenics promoter Albert Edward Wiggam argued for greater control of marriage by scientific experts: "By applying one-tenth as much science in mating human beings as we do in mating animals, we would probably add more to the health and happiness of our children and grandchildren than can be done by all the medical discoveries of the next hundred years. 'We conquer nature by obeying her.' And her declaration is that the root of most evil is not love of money but unwise marriage." So confident was Wiggam that he offered official-sounding statistics to back up his claim: "At least three-fourths of the misery in the world is due to the simple fact that the wrong people get married," he said, although he neglected to explain his algorithm for assessing misery. Like other observers who wanted to see a more active role for the state, Wiggam argued that "marriage, where children are expected, should be a privilege bestowed by society solely upon the fit. Parentage is not a natural right, and it should be withheld from the unfit."[16]

Both anti–venereal disease reformers and eugenicists used marriage as a way of pursuing their particular programs: men like Morrow used marriage to

13. Davenport, *Heredity in Relation to Eugenics*, 7, 267.

14. Francis Galton, *Essays in Eugenics* (London: Eugenics Education Society, 1909), 44.

15. Morton A. Aldrich et al., *Eugenics: Twelve University Lectures* (New York: Dodd, Mead and Co., 1914), xiii.

16. Albert Edward Wiggam, *The Fruit of the Family Tree* (New York: Garden City Publishing Co., 1925), 171.

attack the sexual double standard (and the prostitution industry that was its prime temptation for men), and eugenicists, a bit less optimistically, viewed marriage as a way to control harmful "matings" and to educate the public about the perils of bad heredity. Both movements achieved a victory of sorts with the passage of new marriage legislation in the 1910s.

When he addressed the Indiana state legislature in 1905, the governor of that state expressed a feeling that was beginning to gain adherents among legislators, academics, and scientists: "The state should exercise the right of preventing the contract of marriage between persons manifestly unfit to assume its obligations," he said. To whom did the governor want to turn for assessing that fitness? Science. He called for "medical evidence that the contraction of marriage will not threaten society by the perpetuation of mental or physical deficiency."[17] Narratives of incompetence in marriage licensing began making more frequent appearances in mainstream literature at this time as well. Joseph Sabath, a judge in the Municipal Court in Chicago, refused to marry two couples in the Court of Domestic Relations. In both cases, Sabath deemed the prospective brides incompetent, with the mentalities of children. One of the women evidently had no idea where she was and "made no objection when the physician summoned by the City Psychopathic Laboratory stuck a pin in her forehead." Judge Sabath urged greater oversight of marriage by the state.[18] The churches were awakening to the problem as well; the Social Creed of the Federal Council of Churches in 1912 came out for "the protection of the family, by the single standard of purity, uniform divorce laws, proper regulation of marriage, and proper housing."[19]

By 1914, twenty-four states, plus the District of Columbia and Puerto Rico, had enacted some form of marriage restriction law, most with some element of eugenic or anti–venereal disease rationale.[20] Inherent in these laws was a link between biological (or physical) health and the responsibilities of marriage and parenthood. As one observer noted, "The scope of such Acts as have been passed or such legislation as is proposed, is based upon the requirement that all who enter into the marriage state shall be sound in mind and body, and unlikely to bring offspring into the world who may be tainted by the ailments, disorders and mental weaknesses of their progenitors."[21] The majority of the laws

17. Crane, "Marriage Laws," 66-67.

18. "Need for Eugenics Law," *The Survey* 34 (1915): 532.

19. Quoted in Sidney Ditzion, *Marriage, Morals and Sex in America: A History of Ideas* (New York: W. W. Norton, 1953), 231.

20. Reilly, *The Surgical Solution,* 27.

21. Crane, "Marriage Laws," 66.

required prospective couples to submit a health certificate from a reputable physician attesting to their freedom from venereal and hereditary diseases.

Many observers saw in this rush of enthusiasm for eugenic marriage laws a "new idea of the State." Rather than acting as a mere policeman of the present-day, the State was now taking on the responsibility of protecting future citizens, doing everything in its power to assure their health and fitness. A writer for the magazine *Outlook* praised this effort. Not only would this increased state oversight "save children from coming into this world maimed and crippled in body and brain," but it would also serve as a "moral prop" and a force for society-wide education about the importance of marriage.[22] "Let us not forget," Fabian socialist and eugenics advocate Havelock Ellis wrote, "marriage and divorce are a very real concern of the State, and law cannot ignore either. It is the business of the State to see to it that no interests are injured. . . . A large scope — we are beginning to recognize — must be left alike to freedom of marriage and freedom of divorce, but the State must mark out the limits within which that freedom is exercised."[23] In fact, as Ellis surely knew, the states had always marked out those limits; what Ellis and others were articulating was a desire to add more limits, limits based on the findings of modern science.

The eugenic marriage laws were not merely a response to fears of disease and feeblemindedness; implicit in them as well was a suspicion about parents' ability to regulate the health and behavior of their own children. "The time is ripe for it," the *Chautauquan* editorialized. "Not only churches, but city councils and legislatures should demand health and purity certificates of those wishing to enter into the marriage relation. Parents have been too indifferent and too blind to the welfare of their daughters."[24] Charles Ellwood, a sociologist, agreed: "Hitherto, such education [about marriage] has been mainly left to the family itself, but on account of the fact that many families do not function educationally in this matter, it would seem necessary to introduce, in a wise way, some kind of this instruction in our public schools, from kindergarten up."[25]

Physician Oscar Dowling, President of the Louisiana State Board of Health, described well the tension between the need for state control and the interests of individual Americans' right to marry. "As marriage is an institution absolutely essential to the public welfare," he wrote, "it is a necessity to the permanence of the state; it should be protected by the fundamental laws." Nevertheless, he recognized, "society, the state, is made up of individuals, and the well-being of the

22. "Eugenics Marriage Laws," *The Outlook* 105 (October 18, 1913): 342-43.

23. Havelock Ellis, *Essays in War-Time: Further Studies in the Task of Social Hygiene* (New York: Houghton Mifflin Co., 1917), 185-86.

24. "Marriage, Morals, and Health," *The Chautauquan* (June 1912): 11-13.

25. Aldrich et al., *Eugenics: Twelve University Lectures,* 236-37.

state depends upon the character of the units which make up the sum." Unfortunately, too many of those units had proven unsound; Dowling noted that "in 1913, 10,625 cases of syphilis were reported in New York City" alone. These disturbing facts required a shift in the balance of power between the individual and the state, and left Dowling "assured that the state should no longer fail in its duty to its unborn citizens." He ended his assessment "looking forward to the era of regulation of marriage when science will give positive data as to the fit and the unfit, and the state will put forth its strong arm for race betterment."[26]

That strong arm did meet with some resistance by individual Americans, who voted with their feet against the marriage restrictions. In Wisconsin, passage of a eugenic marriage law in 1913 proved a boon to marriage entrepreneurs in nearby Waukegan, Illinois, who married couples fleeing Wisconsin's health certificate requirement. After Illinois passed its own marriage law, one observer noted that the town of Valparaiso, Indiana, "has become a Gretna Green for bordering states with eugenics laws."[27] In their didactic 1916 book, *How to Live*, Irving Fisher and Eugene Fisk tackled this concern. Just past a forward written by William Howard Taft and eleven pages of starched collar portraits of the Hygiene Reference Board, Fisher and Fisk state matter-of-factly, "It is probably true, for instance, that the man or the woman who is unhealthy is now handicapped in opportunities for marriage, which may be considered an index to the ideal of society." But the authors tried to bridge the divide between understanding marriage as an individual, autonomous choice (divorced from anything save one person's feeling for another) and marriage as the exercise of a social function with consequences for the health of society and of future generations. "As soon as men and women acquire the knowledge that their choices in marriage largely determine whether or not their physical and mental faults and virtues will reappear in children," they argued, "they feel a sacred responsibility in that act of choosing. A little conscious knowledge of what kind of combinations of traits bring about their reappearance in offspring can not help but modify a person's taste, and thus automatically direct the choice of a mate, which choice will still be, rightfully, an instinctive one." They concluded, "Upon the wisdom with which choices in marriage are now made depends in large degree the health and efficiency of all the individuals who will constitute society in the coming generations." But "this can be done without surrendering the general principle of individual freedom." The kind of knowledge Fisher and

26. Oscar Dowling, "The Marriage Health Certificate, a Deeply Rooted Social Problem," *American Journal of Public Health* 5 (November 1915): 1142, 1144.

27. Bernard C. Roloff, "The 'Eugenic' Marriage Laws of Wisconsin, Michigan, and Indiana," *Social Hygiene* 6 (April 1920): 233-34; "Gretna Green" comment quoted in Larson, *Sex, Race, and Science,* 97.

Fisk advocated (and that eugenicists and public health experts were pursuing) "will not reduce but increase the number of natural love-marriages."[28]

The efforts of venereal disease crusaders, eugenicists, and marriage certificate promoters all enlisted state power to achieve their goals; most of them also demonstrated a growing mistrust of the public's ability to choose the right course without the educational efforts of experts. Ben Jonson might once have written "that love comes by chance, but is kept by art," but by the late 1910s, love was increasingly being kept by legislators and by professionals in the sciences and social sciences — kept, dissected, hypothesized, poked and prodded in the hope of divining its peculiarities. By 1916, the editor of a reader on social problems could say correctly that "more recent and rationalistically outspoken views of some sociological writers deal with marriage and divorce in their practical social aspect — as matters, like other social relations and institutions, to be regarded in the light of social, economic, and practical ethical conditions."[29] Other books at the time argued that marriage could be "deepened by a rational understanding of the passion that attracts and unites the sexes. . . . The true votary and venerator of marriage is the man or the woman who strives through knowledge to elevate marriage."[30] Or, as one minister in New York, who had recently created a courting parlor in his church, described the sentiment, "Love, courtship, and marriage have too long been regarded as merely sentimental and accidental matters. Cupid should familiarize himself with the facts of science."[31]

## II

What consequences did this new focus on marriage have for individual Americans? The question of who was and was not fit to marry was on their minds, too, as was a fear of being one of the people whose misfortune it was to marry a diseased or feebleminded person. A letter to the editor of the *New York Times* in 1912 captured this well. "Almost any man, of himself, knows his fitness or otherwise long before the question of marriage becomes urgent to him," this correspondent wrote. "But there is a proportion of women which is absolutely unfit for the duties, to say nothing of the cares, of the wife. And the fact that some of

28. Irving Fisher and Eugene Lyman Fisk, *How to Live: Rules for Healthful Living Based on Modern Science* (New York: Funk & Wagnalls Co., 1916), 2, 166-67.

29. Albert Benedict Wolfe, ed., *Readings in Social Problems* (Boston: Ginn and Co., 1916), 580-81.

30. "The Great Unmarried," *Journal of Heredity* 7 (December 1916): 557-61.

31. See *Survey* 29 (1912-1913): 338; see also "The Crusade for Purity," *Literary Digest* 47 (August 2, 1913): 176-77.

them wish to get husbands, and know many ways to hide their shortcomings, should make . . . the men needing wives pause."[32]

It was this void, this gap in individual Americans' knowledge about the responsibilities of marriage and parenthood, that the marriage advice industry sought to fill. The American appetite for marriage advice was steady and large; one manual, *The Marriage Guide*, published in 1850, had reached its three hundredth edition by 1875.[33] As Nancy Cott has shown, by the late nineteenth century, "a new crop of marriage reformers sprang up among ministers, educators, and publicists." Their fears were largely focused on divorce (and its supposed cause, overly hasty marriages), and they lobbied for an end to common-law marriage.[34] They also churned out books, pamphlets, and magazine articles heralding their solutions. As one observer noted, "if all that has been said or written on [the choosing of a mate] were to be gathered together I suppose that there would not or should not be room for it in all the libraries of the world."[35] "We are always meddling with it and worrying over its health and anxiously trying to bolster it up," Havelock Ellis said.[36]

In many of these essays and books one finds a palpable sense of anxiety about marriage and a need to find some solution to redeem it, protect it, and fortify it against the challenges posed by the modern world. From pseudo-scientific texts on marriage and hygiene to the can-do spirit of religiously themed books and pamphlets, these popular advice manuals betrayed a certain forced quality, like the canned rhetoric of a stump speech, and a fairly consistent reliance on "professional" pronouncements to bolster their prescriptions. Even books that urged reform of divorce laws relied on a higher authority to justify their mildly radical views. In *Let's Civilize the Marriage Laws*, a breezy protest of existing divorce laws, Richard Kathrens urged society to embrace "a new code of ethics" whose "new Messiah" was science. "Science will civilize the marriage laws!" he wrote, echoing the free love message of a decade earlier. "It will concern itself about the *real* salvation of the race — the mental and physical development and perfection of the human animal."[37]

Some observers, not the least of which were social science and science professionals, lamented the lurid overtones of so much "education" about mar-

---

32. Letter to the editor, *New York Times*, June 5, 1912, 10.

33. D'Emilio and Freedman, *Intimate Matters*, 59.

34. Cott, *Public Vows*, 109.

35. Edwin G. Conklin, *Heredity and Environment in the Development of Men* (Princeton: Princeton University Press, 1917), 442.

36. Ellis, *Essays in War-Time*, 181-82.

37. Richard D. Kathrens, *Let's Civilize the Marriage Laws* (New York: Broadway Publishing Co., 1913), 176.

riage and sex; education was not supposed to feed the country's prurient impulses, as many believed such didactic novels and magazine narratives did. "The facts should be presented in a more dispassionate, scientific, proportioned, and psychologically sound way," one biologist argued. "Not by cynics, but by competent, experienced, sweet-minded persons."[38] Others expressed concerns about the proliferation of "matrimonial broadsheets," the cheap weekly (or monthly) newspapers that sold space to men and women advertising for a spouse. "Welsh-Scotch, brown eyes and hair, ruddy complexion, in perfect health, born under cancer sign, character will stand the most rigid examination . . . interested in eugenics and physical culture, outdoor life and new thought," read the advertisement of one man seeking "a good loving wife between the ages of 26 and 29." Another warned, "widows with children, Catholics and flirts need not write." Assessing this trend, one critic noted that it was the direct result of the lifting of restrictions on discussing marriage and sex that encouraged such candor. "The influence of the cheap and bogus literature on marriage, parenthood, prenatal influences, crops out everywhere when the lid of tabu [sic] is lifted and people discuss what they know or think they know."[39]

But the public seemed not to mind the melodramatic stories and how-to advice manuals that poured forth from the presses. The solutions these texts offered, with their attractive sheen of expert opinion from objective, scientific investigators, were like glittering paste diamonds — they symbolized goods of a higher order, mined by experts, but within reach of the average American. This desire for expert advice even extended to finding and keeping "true love."

In their 1929 study, *Middletown*, Robert and Helen Lynd described the burg of Middletown (a pseudonym for Muncie, Indiana), in delightfully clinical terms, dissecting common rituals and mores, including marriage, which "consists in a brief ceremonial exchange of verbal pledges by a man and woman before a duly sanctioned representative of the group." These ceremonies had grown more secular over the years: "in 1890, 85 percent of the local marriages were performed by a religious representative and 13 percent by a secular agent," but by 1923 "those performed by the religious leaders had fallen to 63 percent and the secular group had risen to 34 percent." Change was evident in other areas as well: although Middletown outlawed prostitution in 1915, the practice was far from extinct. "As the judge of the juvenile court points out, 'the automobile has become a house of prostitution on wheels.'"[40]

38. Roswell Hill Johnson, "Marriage Selection," *Journal of Heredity* 5 (March 1914): 102-110.

39. A. E. Hamilton, "What to Say about Marriage?" *Journal of Heredity* 7 (February 1916): 79-80.

40. Robert S. Lynd and Helen Merrell Lynd, *Middletown: A Study in American Culture* (New York: Harcourt Brace & Co., 1929), 112, 114.

Yet in Middletown, the Lynds found that "foremost" among the sensibilities of the community regarding marriage was "the demand for romantic love as the only valid basis for marriage." Indeed, "Middletown adults appear to regard romance in marriage as something which, like their religion, must be believed in to hold society together." An overtly sentimentalist popular culture fueled this romantic sensibility. The Lynds noted that "Middletown grows up singing and hearing its fathers sing lustily in their civic clubs such songs as 'It had to be you. . . . It had to be you,'" Gus Kahn and Isham Jones's 1924 ballad about true love. Popular novelist Elinor Glyn furthered the vision in books such as *Philosophy of Love*, where she described, in somewhat lugubrious prose, the ideal marriage as "the infinite bliss of the mating of the soul in peace and freedom from anxiety."[41]

The town's de facto marital sage was syndicated columnist Dorothy Dix, whose work appeared in the local newspaper. By the Lynds' own estimate, Dix's advice to the lovelorn ("Desolate," "A Much Disturbed Young Husband," and similar allegorical sufferers) "is perhaps the most potent single agency of diffusion from without shaping the habits of thought of Middletown in regard to marriage and possibly represents Middletown's views on marriage more completely than any other available source." The wives of Middletown brandished Dix's dictums with regularity during their interviews with the Lynds, and "her remarks were quoted with approval in a Sunday morning sermon by the man commonly regarded as the 'most intellectual' minister in town." (Middletown's affection for the prim but firm matron was widely shared; millions of Americans read Dix's column in their local newspapers.)[42]

This notion of romantic love as the basis for marriage directly challenged the scientific worldview becoming ascendant, which urged a more rational approach to lifelong union. "Approve of 'falling in love' as we may," wrote physician Charles Reed in his text *Marriage and Genetics*, "we must examine it in all of its phases to determine approximately why and how it plays such a large part in the affairs of mankind. . . . We should have the 'falling in love' go on as before, but we would have the motive underlying it broadened, strengthened, exalted by a frank and intelligent understanding of this vital phase of the question."[43]

A physiology professor at Johns Hopkins University agreed. "But so long as we hold to our custom of founding marriage mainly on affection and mutual

41. Lynd and Lynd, *Middletown*, 115; Glyn quoted in Peter N. Stearns, *Battleground of Desire: The Struggle for Self-Control in Modern America* (New York: New York University Press, 1999), 183.

42. Lynd and Lynd, *Middletown*, 115-16.

43. Charles Alfred Lee Reed, *Marriage and Genetics: Laws of Human Breeding and Applied Eugenics* (Cincinnati: Galton Press Publishers, 1913), 12-13.

attractiveness, it is a difficult and delicate matter to influence the direction that fancy may take," he argued. Another academic observer concurred, noting how young men and women fall in love "on the most frivolous and flimsy excuses." What new scientific knowledge offered was not marriage without love, but "the Herculean task of commanding love. It believes that love can, amongst normal people at least, be ordered."[44] Eugenics promoter Albert Wiggam agreed that society's insistence that romantic love was the bedrock of marriage was a disastrous miscalculation. "Can anything more completely blast the romance of love than defective, neurotic, and uncontrollable children?" he asked. The only hope was science. With a deliberate vagueness of tone more suitable for selling toothpaste than science, Wiggam noted, "We know from many actual instances that where young men and women have grown up in the light of this new knowledge of heredity and its influence upon themselves and their future children, it has had a profound influence upon their choice of mates."[45] In hamlets like Middletown, however, Americans sought expertise without the elimination of romance, control without the total abolition of emotion. They sought, in other words, to strike a balance between the rigorously scientific assessment of marriage and the wholly sentimental version presented in popular culture.

"Marriage founded on love ought to bring out all that is best in man and wife, set free energies and powers scarcely guessed before, weld the many sides of their natures into a unified whole, and make each capable of finer living, greater accomplishment, than either could have achieved singly," one contributor to a popular magazine wrote — a view that heartily endorsed the prevailing norm of romantic companionship. But an anonymous young mother, writing in *The Forum*, used that vision to argue for something entirely modern, something that many people feared posed a new challenge to "marriage founded on love": birth control. Noting the significant change in the expectations husbands and wives had of each other, the contributor argued that, far from threatening the institution, birth control was necessary to sustain marriage: "Comradeship is regarded as an essential of marriage nowadays. But comradeship demands some degree of leisure and a margin of energy as well. If babies come fast, neither is possible."[46]

The leaders of the birth control movement had somewhat broader goals in mind for their cause, of course. In her 1920 polemic *Woman and the New Race*, Margaret Sanger argued that "child slavery, prostitution, feeblemindedness, physical deterioration, hunger, oppression and war will disappear from the

---

44. Aldrich et al., *Eugenics: Twelve University Lectures*, 105, 179.
45. Wiggam, *The Fruit of the Family Tree*, 296-97.
46. A Young Mother, "Choosing One's Children," *The Forum* 79 (April 1928): 579-86.

earth," if the country embraced birth control. Oddly, her book says very little about marriage, despite Sanger's frequent mention of her own happy and fruitful union in her public lectures (the frontispiece of the book features an appropriately serious studio portrait of Sanger with her two sons). "Look at it from any standpoint you will," Sanger wrote, "suggest any solution you will, conventional or unconventional, sanctioned by law or in defiance of law, woman is in the same position, fundamentally, until she is able to determine for herself whether she will be a mother and to fix the number of her offspring." For Sanger, nothing less than full autonomy would free women from their biological burden. "It is the essential function of voluntary motherhood to choose its own mate, to determine the time of childbearing and to regulate strictly the number of offspring."[47]

More than any other development in the early twentieth century, birth control promised to transform (or threatened, depending on one's sensibility) the institution of marriage because it effectively severed marriage from reproduction and offered a heretofore unknown level of control to individuals over childbearing. Sanger was surely correct, in 1920, when she declared, "the American public, in a word, has been permeated with the message of birth control."[48] Historians agree that by the late 1920s, most middle-class couples were making use of contraception to control the timing and number of their children.[49]

But they did so in an interesting way. As the remarks of the anonymous married woman above demonstrate, Americans used the language of autonomy in their choice of mate and the narrative of emotional, romantic connection to describe what they were seeking in their marriages, but they began to do so by linking this choice to greater control over their own biological functions. Unlike the crusades against feeblemindedness and venereal disease, which called for restricting entry to marriage, the birth control movement sought to change the landscape of marriage from within, and spoke to the individual desires of a growing number of Americans, especially women, for greater control over reproduction.

Individual fulfillment in marriage included sexual satisfaction as well as control over reproduction. Historian Peter Stearns, who places this new sensibility as developing in the 1920s, argues, "This was the decade in which advice literature began to focus on sex as the primary component of a happy marriage." Margaret Sanger certainly thought so, writing that, "In marriage, as dis-

---

47. Margaret Sanger, *Woman and the New Race* (New York: Truth Publishing Co., 1920), 234, 95, 227.

48. Sanger, *Woman and the New Race*, 225.

49. See Stearns, *Battleground of Desire*, 228; see also D'Emilio and Freedman, *Intimate Matters*.

tinct from every other human relationship, the bedrock of lasting happiness . . . in every respect, lies in a proper physical adjustment of two persons, and a proper physical management of their mutual experiences of [sexual] union." Dr. Isabel Hutton concurred: "No matter how ideal the partnership in every other way, if there is want of sex life . . . marriage cannot be a success."[50]

For individual Americans, then, their sense of personhood in marriage was linked to control — control over the knowledge of what diseases their potential mates might be bringing to the marital bed (and, by implication, control over men who previously had been allowed greater social freedom to indulge in "sowing wild oats"); control over the timing and number of children; and control over the range of sexual experience one expected and desired in marriage. Yet this control did not spark the wholesale abandonment of romantic ideals that many scientists, legislators, and academic experts had hoped for.

Nor did it lead to the wholesale rejection of religious sanction. "The Greeks called marriage *telos*, consecration, and the marriage ritual resembled that of the mysteries," Mircea Eliade has noted.[51] The lure of the sacred remained powerful for Americans as well, despite their tacit understanding that religious leaders no longer exercised the same influence that scientists and academic experts now enjoyed. Americans still wanted religious sanction, as the continuing desire for church weddings attested, but they wanted it without too many limits on their choice of mate and, more importantly, on their own ability (and not that of a priest, minister, or rabbi) to judge when a marriage had failed and should end.

## III

Where did this leave marriage as an institution? Was it, as the experts feared, an institution under siege? Ernest Groves, a sociologist who had published a textbook on marriage, and who is considered one of the founders of the field of marriage counseling, viewed the increase of premarital and extramarital sex, as well as divorce in the 1920s, as cries for help from a beleaguered institution and called for "a revision of norms concerning marriage" in order "to protect the institution from decay."[52]

50. Stearns, *Battleground of Desire*, 193.

51. Mircea Eliade, *The Sacred and the Profane: The Nature of Religion* (New York: Harcourt, Brace & Co., 1957), 185.

52. Groves quoted in Wendy Kline, *Building a Better Race: Gender, Sexuality and Eugenics from the Turn of the Century to the Baby Boom* (Berkeley: University of California Press, 2001), 128; see also Beth L. Bailey, "Scientific Truth . . . and Love: The Marriage Education Movement in the U.S.," *Journal of Social History* 20 (1987): 711-32.

Other experts demonstrated greater facility in adapting to the public's strong desire for romantic partnerships. Eugenicist Paul Popenoe deftly split the difference. The author of a 1925 book, *Modern Marriage,* Popenoe eventually became the country's leading marriage counselor. According to historian Sidney Ditzion, "Popenoe stressed two factors in his study of marriage. The first was its physiological basis, and the second, those personal qualifications which, by experience, husbands and wives found most satisfactory in one another." In 1930, Popenoe founded the American Institute of Family Relations, in Los Angeles, and "in the first eight years of its operation, there was not a single divorce among the thousands of couples to whom the Institute had given premarital advice. The science of marriage seemed to have matured."[53]

But it was critic Walter Lippmann who offered the most incisive assessment of modern matrimony: marriage as a hypothesis. Tossing a bucket of cold water on his era's romantic assumptions, Lippmann argued, "The wisdom of marriage rests upon an extremely unsentimental view of lovers and their passions." But the "prevailing sentimentality about love" ignores this; this sentimentality "assumes that marriages are made in heaven, that compatibility is instinctive, a mere coincidence, that happy unions are, in the last analysis, lucky accidents in which two people who happen to suit each other happen to have met."[54] As for the future survival of marriage, Lippmann presciently wrote, "It will survive not as a rule of law imposed by force, for that is now, I think, become impossible. It will not survive as a moral commandment with which the elderly can threaten the young. They will not listen. It will survive as the dominant insight into the reality of love and happiness, or it will not survive at all." Lippmann himself did not stake a large wager; instead, he concluded, "it means that the convention of marriage, when it is clarified by insight into reality, is likely to be the hypothesis upon which men and women will ordinarily proceed."[55] Or, as British hygienist Havelock Ellis concluded, "As a society is, so will its marriage be."[56]

American society by the 1930s slightly favored scientific over sentimental explanations for marriage, a fact that didn't entirely please all of society's critics. As Joseph Wood Krutch noted with some chagrin, he and many of his contemporaries "were born at a time when the religion of love was all but unquestioned, when it seemed to stand more firmly than even the religion of the church, whose foundations science was already known slowly to have under-

---

53. Ditzion, *Marriage, Morals, and Sex in America,* 389-90; see also Kline, *Building a Better Race.*

54. Walter Lippmann, *A Preface to Morals* (New York: Macmillan Co., 1929), 309.

55. Lippmann, *A Preface to Morals,* 312.

56. Ellis, *Essays in War-Time,* 186-87.

mined." Now, however, "we have seen it rapidly disintegrate. We have seen how works . . . claimed love as a legitimate subject for rationalistic consideration, and how . . . the mystical values lingered as ghosts for only one generation after rationalism had attacked the mythology upon which they rested."[57]

At the individual level, Americans entered the decade of the 1930s having internalized a host of new anxieties about the cultural significance of marriage; they had far more contact with state actors and the health and medical professionals who administered the state laws ensuring health in marriage; their sense of the impermanence of the institution had increased, with the increasing acceptance of divorce; and they entered marriage with a greater degree of control over reproduction.

In the end, both experts and the public had to cede some territory: the legislators and other experts, especially eugenicists, were not able to sustain the restrictions on marriage they erected in the 1910s. By the 1940s, as Nancy Cott has argued, "the view of marriage as a private relationship had become a public value in the United States, enshrined in legal doctrine." In fact, the Supreme Court recognized this view as early as the 1920s in cases upholding the right of parents to send their children to private school and teach them foreign languages.[58] The average American did use insights gleaned from scientific study to consider potential mates and to control birth — just as today they make use of more sophisticated versions of that science to choose their children through artificial reproductive technologies and make use of supposedly scientific matchmaking services to meet their "soul mates." But Americans did not entirely concede the ideal of romantic love.

A somewhat chastened faith in the endless possibilities offered by science survived as well. "Nowadays," sociologist Edward Ross wrote in 1922, "the first thing wise men do when they are face to face with a grave problem, relating, say, to food values or ventilation or juvenile delinquency, or whether animals reason, or the harmfulness of adulterants, is to equip a research laboratory for working it out. We have realized that the old-fashioned reflection and discussion are but a poor method of finding truth."[59] In 1937, *American Magazine*

57. Joseph Wood Krutch, *The Modern Temper: A Study and a Confession* (1929; New York: Harcourt and Co., 1984), 44, 73.

58. The two cases were *Pierce v. Society of Sisters*, 268 U.S. 510 (1925), and *Meyer v. Nebraska*, 262 U.S. 390 (1923). Oddly, Cott cites a 1944 case, *Prince v. Massachusetts*, 321 U.S. 158 (1944), but in this case, involving parents who were Jehovah's Witnesses who had sent their children out to preach on the street, the court affirmed that the state had a right to intervene and that the parents had violated state labor laws by sending their children out to street preach. Cott, *Public Vows*, 1.

59. Edward A. Ross, *The Social Trend* (New York: The Century Co., 1922), 1-2, 169-70.

claimed that "the chances for happiness in marriage may be raised to something approaching a sure bet if courtship and marriage are studied as a science."[60] Individual Americans absorbed decades of teaching about the biological significance of their private choices — and they acted on them, even without state coercion, as rising rates of usage of contraception and abortion (and today, reproductive technologies) demonstrate.

Americans are particularly adept at toppling or replacing old institutions (such as churches or Main Street) and then professing bewilderment and ennui when they are left without something or someone willing to offer endorsements of their personal choices. As well, Americans today ostentatiously avoid encouraging traditional motivations for marriage, such as social ambition or the consolidation of wealth or privilege, despite the many examples of men and women who obviously continue to seek just those things. But if overt demonstrations of enthusiasm for this form of nuptial advancement are treated as crass (Edith Wharton's rapacious Undine Spragg in *The Custom of the Country* still resonates), it is because the ambition that fuels such choices has always lurked just below the supposedly democratic surface of Americans' approach to marriage. No regular reader of newspaper wedding announcements, with their meticulous reporting of couples' academic and social credentials, could believe otherwise.

And so tensions about marriage are never soothed. Today we still question whether marriage should be viewed primarily as a secular or religious institution, and whether its purpose should be the pursuit of traditional markers of status, the rearing of children, the satisfaction of romantic yearnings, or some combination of the above. The adhesive that joins these seemingly contradictory impulses is the liberal-individualist notion of the person, a notion that, despite some cracks in the early twentieth century, was able to incorporate Middletown's starchy pieties as well as increasingly liberationist views of marriage as an institution largely for individual fulfillment.

It is not a surprise, then, that this paradoxical, pragmatic, liberal individualistic impulse continues to encourage new groups of Americans to seek endorsement for their own visions of marriage. What is consistent over time — and, in a way, heartening — is the tendency to do so in a common language. As recent debates over gay marriage have revealed, the leading advocates for gay marriage make an avowedly conservative case for homosexual unions. They employ traditional arguments about marriage, such as the institution's civilizing and stabilizing influence, and link their crusade to America's historical and continuing effort to extend liberty. In this rendering, the pursuit of happiness is

60. Jerome Beatty, "Taking the Blinders Off Love," *American Magazine*, December 1937, 22.

not simply an ideal, a goal, an aspiration. It is a civil right, the exercise of which law, religion, and policy — to say nothing of individual moral qualms — must not be allowed to thwart.[61] Opponents of gay marriage endorse these same traditions, but argue for limits on the excesses of their reinvention, lest we, in our haste to transform, succeed in undermining the liberal interests of the country and its institutions as a whole.[62] Both sides intuitively understand that although the debate often focuses on *legal endorsement* of homosexual unions, it is actually the broader goal of *cultural acceptance* that inspires the fight.

Marriage today looks more like Lippmann's hypothesis than the experts' science, with Americans largely viewing it as a path to individual emotional fulfillment. The institution still bears the mark of the experts' meddling, too; their legacies are birth control, reproductive technologies, and the flourishing professional advice industry, with its armies of therapists and experts. But marriage hasn't entirely lost its power as a source of sacred and moral meaning either, as the heated debates over gay marriage attest. If marriage is an institution, it is one that has always lacked the stony edifice one associates with a permanent structure. It is more like a moat, surrounding a culture, reflecting its values and vices, but constantly changing shape as it responds to the elements.

61. See, for example, Jonathan Rauch, *Gay Marriage: Why It Is Good for Gays, Good for Straights, and Good for America* (New York: Times Books, 2004); Andrew Sullivan, ed., *Same-Sex Marriage: Pro and Con* (New York: Vintage, 1997); and Sullivan, *Virtually Normal: An Argument About Homosexuality* (New York: Vintage, 1996).

62. See, for example, Susan M. Shell, "The Liberal Case Against Gay Marriage," *The Public Interest* 156 (Summer 2004); Stanley Kurtz, "Going Dutch? Lessons of the Same Sex Marriage Debate in the Netherlands," *The Weekly Standard* 9, no. 36 (May 31, 2004); and Kurtz, "The End of Marriage in Scandinavia: The 'Conservative Case' for Same-Sex Marriage Collapses," *The Weekly Standard* 9, no. 20 (February 2, 2004).

# "What Kind of People Are We?":
# The United States and the
# Truth and Reconciliation Idea

RICHARD H. KING

Forgiveness, reconciliation, restoration: the willingness to undertake such tasks needs to be present in any decent and enduring human association. In personal relations, such acts are regarded as marks of healing, of acknowledgment of one's own faults and limitations, of admission that no one can be truly autonomous, and that a high degree of mutuality is an essential element in human flourishing. Even the inmost core of our subjectivity is supported by, and made manifest in, the web of human relationships in which we are involved, and particularly so in those instances when men and women are about the business of claiming, or assigning, or merely assessing, moral responsibility. Nothing is more central to our notions of personhood than such questions of moral agency.

Less clear, however, is the question of how these concepts — forgiveness, rec-

---

I want to acknowledge Wilfred McClay's many suggestions, which have vastly improved the original draft of my essay. Thanks also to the London University American History Group, the Clinton Institute at University College, Dublin, and the American Studies Department at the University of East Anglia (UK) for helping me develop my thoughts on this topic. In particular, I want to thank Mona Frederick and the faculty seminar on "Memory, Identity and Political Action" at Vanderbilt University's Robert Penn Warren Center, where I was visiting Fellow in 2001-2, for providing the impetus to develop several of the ideas contained here.

Though the literature on the TRC and the TRC idea continues to grow, there are three books that represent good places to begin: Robert Rotberg and Dennis Thompson, eds., *Truth v. Justice: The Morality of Truth Commissions* (Princeton and Oxford: Princeton University Press, 2000); Priscilla B. Hayner, *Unspeakable Truths: Confronting State Terror and Atrocity* (New York and London: Routledge, 2001); and John W. de Gruchy, *Reconciliation: Restoring Justice* (Minneapolis: Fortress, 2002). Each contains an extensive bibliography.

The title of the essay "What Kind of People Are We?" is drawn from a sentence in Glen Loury's "Racial Justice: The Superficial Morality of Colour-Blindness," given at the International Council of Human Rights Policy, Geneva, Switzerland, January 24-25, 2001, 6 (www.ichrp.org/paper-files/113-w-04.pdf).

onciliation, restoration — can be applied to the moral life of nations and other multigenerational groups and collectivities. Should their circle be made to extend that widely? Can they play a role in "settling accounts" after centuries of racial injustice and suspicion? If so, how? Who bears the present-day burden for historical wrongs done, and how is that burden assessed and applied? Who is to be made to pay for the past, and how? And who has the authority to decide?

The Truth and Reconciliation Commission (TRC) created in South Africa in the wake of Apartheid's abolition was a notable effort to do something that has almost never been done, or even attempted, in human history — to create a formal process for considering how collective injuries can be made good, and how former enemies can be reconciled and live in peace, even harmony, with the demands of justice satisfied rather than being ignored or papered over.

One can argue over the extent of the TRC's success, but the very attempt excites the admiration of Richard H. King, and causes him to wonder: why have such attempts been so few and so ineffectual, even in societies whose foundational cultural and religious beliefs would seem to mandate gestures of reconciliation? Why, to put a finer point on the question, did it not occur in the United States, which has just such principles and still staggers under the weight of racial enmity and unredressed grievance? Have there been moments in the history of the United States when something like a TRC could have been attempted? If so, when were they, and why were they not attempted? What do our national choices say about us as a people? Has the need for forgiveness and reconciliation ever been openly and frankly confronted in the American past — and if not, why not? What shared cultural presumptions about the nature of moral responsibility and personhood need to be present, if issues of forgiveness and reconciliation are ever to be felt as urgent and compelling ones — and addressed as such? Richard H. King is Professor of American Intellectual History at the University of Nottingham, and author of numerous works, including *Race, Culture, and the Intellectuals, 1940-1970* (Baltimore: Johns Hopkins University Press, 2004) and *Civil Rights and the Ideal of Freedom* (New York: Oxford University Press, 1992).

Though South Africa's Truth and Reconciliation Commission (TRC) consisted of a specific set of processes and institutions, the truth and reconciliation "idea" refers to the general project of exposing violations of civil and human rights and liberties, receiving testimony from the public about such violations, initiating a complex process of apology and forgiveness, considering how collective injury can be made good, and, finally, seeking reconciliation between former racial, religious, or ideological enemies. The questions I want to explore here concern the relevance of the truth and reconciliation idea to race relations in the United States since the Civil War. Could or should there have been something like truth and reconciliation process in the American past or present? Or is it something whose pertinence always lies "somewhere else" — primarily in what was once called the Third World (Africa, Asia, and Latin America) and in the former Soviet bloc? What was until September 11, 2001, a fairly vigorous discussion of reparations for African Americans would suggest, on the face of it, that some aspects of the truth and reconciliation process have relevance to the United States. Yet many feel that reconciliation between white and black Americans can be achieved only if restitution, whether symbolic or material, is foregone by African Americans; and indeed that reviving old memories of past oppression leads to more problems than it solves.

In what follows, I want to address such issues in order to assess the prospects for racial reconciliation in the United States and/or to understand why it is impossible. I will concentrate on three interrelated topics. First, I want to explore the philosophical and conceptual issues involved in political apology, forgiveness, and reconciliation, and suggest what view of the human person or human nature is thereby suggested. Second, I will examine the first and second Reconstructions in the United States in order to determine which factors militated against and which encouraged exposure of the truth about the past, the possibility of something like a political apology, efforts at restitution for past injuries, and reconciliation between the races. Finally, I want to explore an emerging consensus on race, rights, and history in contemporary America that makes the application of the truth and reconciliation idea highly problematic.

## Concepts and Traditions

Neither apology nor forgiveness, restitution nor reconciliation, guilt nor responsibility has been a pressing concern in political thought over the last half century or so. Political philosophy has been concentrated on normative concepts such as rights, equality, liberty, and justice as they relate to the political reality of power, domination, and interests rather than with "action" concepts such as acknowledging, apologizing, and forgiving, or guilt and its relationship to responsibility. If, as conventional wisdom has it, politics is concerned primarily with power and violence, then political thought will obviously have trouble confronting such actions as I listed above, since they arise when someone or some institution gives up power, apologizes for having exercised power in certain ways, or abjures violence. Indeed, such processes can seem hopelessly unrealistic, even apolitical, to those committed to the view that politics is concerned primarily with the exercise of power and the pursuit of interests.

Yet there are exceptions. One of the few post–World War II philosophers to take up the issue of guilt in its various aspects was Karl Jaspers, whose *The Question of German Guilt (Die Schuldfrage)* (1946) also influenced the debate in South Africa in the later years of Apartheid.[1] It is thus no accident that the only modern political thinker who has explicitly explored forgiveness as a political phenomenon is Jasper's (and Martin Heidegger's) one-time student, Hannah Arendt.[2]

Arendt's all-too-brief discussion of forgiveness, *The Human Condition* (1958), makes clear why forgiveness should be of pressing concern in contemporary political thought and why Arendt remains our contemporary, even though she has been dead for just over three decades. There she proposes that forgiving and promising are the two framing "actions" of political life. Making and keeping promises, as exemplified by entering into covenants and contracts, stabilizes the polity by dealing with "unpredictability," while forgiveness, Arendt claims, helps keep open the possibility for "redemption from the predicament of irreversibility."[3] Political forgiveness breaks the cycle of violence and revenge that seems endemic to political life. Though it is not her example, the question of revenge versus forgiveness is also the central theme in Aeschylus's *Eumenides*, a play where the central conflict is the "terror of unending vengeance" by the Furies against Orestes as countered by Pallas Athena's attempt to "inhibit its repetition."[4]

Arendt, an admirer of the Greek polis and a Jew, suggests that the political importance of "freedom from vengeance" (p. 216) was first made evident in the life and teachings of Jesus, though she doubts the political relevance or wisdom of love. According to her, the passion of love seeks to abolish differences be-

---

1. Karl Jaspers, *The Question of German Guilt* (New York: Capricorn, 1946; 1961); John W. de Gruchy, "Guilt, Amnesty and National Reconciliation," *Journal of Theology for Southern Africa* 83, no. 1 (1993): 3-14.

2. More recently, Jacques Derrida has published a short essay, "Forgiveness" (1999), that engages with, but departs from, Arendt's writing on the subject. See Derrida, *On Cosmopolitanism and Forgiveness*, trans. Mark Dooley and Michael Hughes (London and New York: Routledge, 2001).

3. Hannah Arendt, *The Human Condition* (Garden City, N.Y.: Doubleday Anchor, 1958), 212-13. Incidentally, much of Arendt's thought, rather than being time- and culture-bound, seems even more relevant in the wake of the truth and reconciliation experience in South Africa and elsewhere and in the face of the persistence of genocide as an historical fact.

4. Donald Shriver, *An Ethic for Enemies: Forgiveness in Politics* (New York: Oxford University Press, 1995).

tween lovers and, in her terms, is profoundly antipolitical. She looks instead to the Greek concept of political respect, a "kind of 'friendship' without intimacy and without closeness" (p. 218), as the specific source of political forgiveness. Though Arendt, I think, confuses *eros* and *agape,* her larger point is that politics needs the concept of forgiveness in order to break the cycle of vengeance and, more positively, to allow for new initiatives, perhaps the central concept in Arendt's thought. It allows a polity to create a future and a past for itself. This emphasis on the way political forgiveness enables a fresh political start seems quite compatible with Archbishop Tutu's recent assertion that his Christian faith is a "the faith of ever new beginnings."[5] Arendt, however, places two quali-fications on the way forgiveness might work. First, not only does forgiveness not preclude punishment; it may in fact presuppose it. This assumes that pun-ishment is fundamentally different from vengeance, which is counter-violence without legitimacy or limitation. Second, in a formulation that echoes her dis-cussion in *The Origins of Totalitarianism* (1951), she notes in *The Human Condi-tion* that "men are unable to punish what has turned out to be unforgivable," the latter being the "true hallmark" of "radical evil" (p. 217).

While Arendt's contribution is certainly of great importance, there are nev-ertheless gaps in her treatment of the subject. She fails, for instance, to specify whether forgiveness has to do primarily with the relationship between the indi-vidual and the political order or between two roughly equal groups or between a dominant and a dominated group. Only later, in "Eichmann in Jerusalem" (1963), did Arendt explore the problem of whether the unforgivable should be defined in terms of the intentions behind evil actions or in terms of their evil effects. As revealed in her correspondence with Gershom Scholem, Arendt made the point that "banality" applied both to Eichmann's intentions and to evil itself, to which she denied depth or profundity. In other words, she had come to believe that the distinction between willed radical evil and thoughtless banal evil faded in importance in light of the effects of those evil actions.[6]

Nor does Arendt deal with apology, the action often paired with forgiveness. According to Nicholas Tavuchis, an apology between one individual and another differs importantly from that between two groups. In contrast with an interper-sonal apology where indications of sincerity and remorse are looked for, the cru-

---

5. Archbishop Desmond Tutu, Address at Vanderbilt University, April 16, 2003.

6. Arendt, "Eichmann in Jerusalem: Exchange of Letters between Gershom Scholem and Hannah Arendt," *The Jew as Pariah,* ed. Ron Feldman (New York: Grove, 1978), 240-51. See also Susan Neiman, *Evil in Modern Thought: An Alternative History of Philosophy* (Princeton, N.J.: Princeton University Press, 2002) and Richard H. King, *Race, Culture and the Intellectuals, 1940-1970* (Washington, D.C., and Baltimore: Woodrow Wilson Press and Johns Hopkins University Press, 2004), 187-88.

cial point of a collective apology is "to put things on record"[7] as a public event. In our time, public political apology bears on the question of who should apologize for things like crimes against humanity or systematic violations of human rights by one group against another. Those who willfully perpetrate such actions or formulate such policies are rarely willing, much less present, to apologize for them. If this is the case, should the leader of a nation be held responsible for the evil actions his or her nation committed under different leadership at an earlier time? In other words, should the relatively "innocent" be left to apologize for someone else's dirty work? And does a later apology for, say, slavery count for much, if anything? Members of one's own polity or descendants of the former victims may see such an apology as inappropriate or too cheaply arrived at. In the case of slavery in the United States, several generations of descendants of perpetrators and victims have profited and suffered respectively, but no one who was directly responsible for the crime or to whom an apology can be directly addressed remains. "Is there," as Elazar Barkan has wondered, "a statute of limitations on national injustice?"[8] And what is the appropriateness of the language of guilt, apology, and forgiveness in such a context?

One conceptual "solution" here might be to distinguish guilt and responsibility, as Arendt did in her ethical reflections. Whereas one would be *guilty* if he or she directly ordered the enslavement of other human beings or actually participated in crimes against humanity, genocide, or war crimes, those who belong to the perpetrating nation or group might be said to be *responsible* for ameliorating the effects of these crimes and violations, though the actions were ordered and carried out by others. Guilt tends to be associated with intention, initiative, or agency, while responsibility follows effects and implies that an individual or group has benefited from crimes or violations, even if there is a temporal distance from the original and actual violation. Taking responsibility cannot undo what has been done, but it can, through apology and/or restitution, acknowledge earlier violations and take responsibility for them. Overall, guilt has to do with the past, while responsibility is directed toward the future.[9]

---

7. Nicholas Tavuchis, *Mea Culpa: A Sociology of Apology and Reconciliation* (Stanford: Stanford University Press, 1991). Tavuchis identifies three crucial components of apology: "from whom" it should come, "to whom" it should be addressed, and, finally, "for what" an apology should be offered. In addition, he suggests that apology is ideally a part of a temporal sequence that runs from a "call" for apology through the apology itself, the granting of forgiveness, and then "reconciliation." Published before the establishment of the TRC, Tuvachis's book is of great relevance to the whole topic.

8. See Elazar Barkan, *The Guilt of Nations: Restitution and Negotiating Historical Injustices* (New York and London: W. W. Norton, 2000), 288.

9. See Hannah Arendt, "Organized Guilt and Universal Responsibility" (1945), *Essays in*

Here I would suggest that what Jaspers calls "political guilt" in his *The Question of German Guilt* might better be named "political responsibility." For instance, it might be easier for Americans to confront some of the collective issues concerning slavery and segregation if the language of responsibility rather than of guilt were adopted. In such an "Arendtian" way of looking at things, collective guilt but not collective responsibility is ruled out of court. Unlike Nazi Germany, where people were transported to labor and concentration camps or ultimately to extermination centers outside Germany, and the claim of Germans "not to know" had a certain plausibility, the average white U.S. citizen in both North and South prior to 1861 supported, or at least tolerated, slavery. Later, under state-sanctioned segregation, white citizens often voted for and helped enforce measures that mandated the systematic violation of civil and human rights up to and including lynchings. In such a context, the claim not to know the truth of what was going on rings particularly hollow.[10] Overall, if political forgiveness is relatively uncharted territory, then political apology is even more so. Provisionally, we might say that whereas repentance is the ultimate destination of a sense of guilt, responsibility is discharged through action, often over a long period of time.

Finally, in this context, the overlap between political and religious discourses needs addressing. In a (formerly) Christian culture, but generally in cultures where Abrahamic religions are dominant, forgiveness and reconciliation are powerful themes. Indeed, as South African theologian John de Gruchy has pointed out, salvation, redemption, atonement, and reconciliation overlap in meaning and are absolutely central to the Christian faith. Theologically, these conditions are seen to result from human repentance and God's forgiveness, with various theological traditions emphasizing one or the other to a greater or lesser degree. In South Africa, Archbishop Desmond Tutu was largely responsible, given his position, for "Christianizing" the language and ethos of the Truth and Reconciliation Commission. In reaction, South African Jews and Muslims, not to mention those adhering to traditional African faiths, questioned the emphasis placed upon forgiveness over justice.[11] Similar splits were and still are present in the United States. The most readily identifiable leader of

---

*Understanding* (New York: Harcourt Brace, 1994), 121-32, but, more relevantly, see her essays in *Responsibility and Judgment,* ed. and intro. Jerome Kohn (New York: Schocken, 2003).

10. In fact, at the end of World War II, Dwight Macdonald suggested that citizens in relatively open societies could be considered more responsible for crimes perpetrated in their names than German (or Soviet) citizens. See Dwight Macdonald, "The Responsibility of Peoples" (1945), *Memoirs of a Revolutionist* (New York: Meridian, 1958).

11. John W. de Gruchy, *Reconciliation: Restoring Justice* (Minneapolis: Fortress, 2002), 41, 122-23.

the civil rights movement was a Christian minister, the Reverend Martin Luther King Jr., and the institutional core of the movement lay in the southern black Protestant churches, yet the civil rights movement was by no means an exclusively religious movement. John W. de Gruchy tries to resolve the Christian/non-Christian tension by suggesting that, though the "primary expression" of, say, reconciliation derives from the religious sphere, it has historically taken on a secular, "secondary expression" in social and political affairs.[12]

This obvious overlap between sacred and secular meanings of reconciliation has profound implications for a polity in which the separation of church and state is constitutionally mandated and in which cultural and religious diversity is a fact of life. The language of reconciliation and forgiveness may increasingly have less purchase on the commitment of non-Christian citizens in multireligious and multicultural polities. Thus a future task may be to develop new religion-neutral languages to deal with these matters. In the affluent West, one temptation will be to find the alternative to religious language in the various therapeutic discourses that dominate much of the thinking about personal and even group self-scrutiny and transformation. Undoubtedly, the testimony of victims at the TRC hearings was therapeutic insofar as it helped relieve some of the pain of remembering. (One criticism of the TRC has been its failure to provide adequate counseling as a follow-up to former victims' testimony.) The role of survivor and honored victim has come to have considerable cachet in our culture, and thus everyone involved in such processes may face the temptation to exploit the experience for merely personal benefit and to neglect the explicitly political and collective importance of reconciliation.[13]

Finally, the truth and reconciliation idea makes the process of "working through" a painful past absolutely central to both perpetrators and victims. The "truth" at the core of the process concerns what happened in the past, who were perpetrators and who were victims, and how the differences between the two should be sorted out. From this perspective, the truth and reconciliation process implies that facts of the matter exist that need public exposure. Yet this process of establishing the truth of what happened and who was responsible is far more than simply a cognitive process of arriving at true knowledge about the past. It is also a process by which such knowledge is in-

12. Indeed, de Gruchy notes that there are at least four senses in which the term "reconciliation" is used: theological, interpersonal, social, and political (19, 26-27).

13. See Ellen Herman, *The Romance of American Psychology: Political Culture in the Age of Experts* (Berkeley: University of California Press, 1995); Elizabeth Lasch-Quinn, *Race Experts: How Racial Etiquette, Sensitivity Training and New Age Therapy Hijacked the Civil Rights Revolution* (New York and London: W. W. Norton, 2001); and, of course, Philip Rieff, *The Triumph of the Therapeutic* (New York: Harper and Row, 1965).

corporated as integral to oneself and one's group. In sum, not only knowledge but also acknowledgment is involved in accepting the "truth" about the past.[14] It was also a common experience in the TRC hearings that, even where there was an agreement about the facts, their meaning was still by no means obvious. If nothing else, the truth and reconciliation process shows that setting up a facile opposition between facts and interpretation or between public memory and professional history is exceedingly problematic.

But what are the implications of all this for an understanding of human nature and the human person? Can actual historical events and processes such as the truth and reconciliation idea reveal anything very useful about transhistorical and transcultural constants in human thought, feeling, and action?[15] One immediate candidate would be what William James named "the trail of the serpent," that is, the constant presence of individual or group self-interest in human affairs. Beyond that, the centrality of memory to an understanding of what it means to be human is also quite obvious. The consciousness of temporality, and the impulse both to avoid and to come to terms with the past, are constants in human affairs. But memory can work for good or ill. It may allow us to understand what has made us the way we are, but it may also lock us into a view of our past that prevents us from confronting the present (Faulkner's "The past is never dead; it's not even past"). A too-rigid notion of memory can also prevent us from doing what Nietzsche held to be essential — forgetting ("learn to forget"). The third salient trait of the human person revealed by the truth and reconciliation process is that we are always in a condition of relatedness to others. Our identities derive not only from ourselves but also from recognition by others, and morally we are responsible not only for ourselves but for others. This entails, in turn, a strong notion of citizenship that makes us co-responsible for our common political life, a point to which I will return at the end of this essay.

14. This distinction between knowledge and acknowledgment is usually attributed to philosopher Thomas Nagel, though there seems to be no particular piece from which it is clearly drawn. See the opening pages of Lawrence Weschler, *A Miracle, A Universe: Settling Accounts with Torturers* (New York: Pantheon, 1990).

15. For an important effort to defend the notion of human nature (functioning and capability) against poststructuralist and postmodernist skepticism about the notion, see Martha Nussbaum, "Human Functioning and Social Justice: In Defense of Aristotelian Essentialism," *Political Theory* 20, no. 2 (May 1992): 202-46. Nussbaum labels her own position "internalist essentialism" but also suggests the term "historically grounded empirical essentialism" (207-8). She rejects any metaphysical or transcendent grounding for the basic requirements for human functioning and for human flourishing. Though I am sympathetic with Nussbaum's position, I don't see that there is a tight fit between a specific account of human nature and a specific policy, action, or ideology.

## The First Reconstruction: The Road to (Sectional) Reconciliation

Has there been anything in the course of American history that compares with the much heralded truth and reconciliation process in South Africa? Two historical periods come to mind as prime candidates for investigation: the first Reconstruction (1865-77) and, more generally, the 1865-1915 period; and the so-called second Reconstruction period (1954-1968) and its aftermath, including the present. During both periods, the need for black and white Americans to work out ways to live with each other in one society and polity was of high urgency. Moreover, both periods were marked by a reformulation of national memory to accommodate radically new circumstances, particularly in regard to race relations and racial self-consciousness.

Early in his *Race and Reunion: The Civil War in American Memory* (2001), David Blight asserts that "[i]n the wake of the Civil War, there were no Truth and Reconciliation Commissions."[16] Why not? The answer emerges over the whole course of Blight's masterful work, but the Ku Klux Klan Hearings of 1871-72, held in Washington, D.C., as well as in six southern states, yield important clues. Witnesses included blacks and whites, Republicans and Democrats, rich and poor Southerners. As the majority party in Congress, the Republicans dominated the Select Congressional Committee that conducted the hearings. Not surprisingly, rather than rising above partisan, racial, or sectional loyalties, the committee largely reproduced and exacerbated them. According to Blight, the testimony that fills the final 632-page report is strikingly graphic in depicting racial torture, sexualized sadism, and general barbarism directed against the former slaves in the South. Yet the truth about what was happening in the South seemed to shame few white southerners or pro-southern northerners.[17] Worse than that, the pro-white southern minority report from the Democrats depicted, according to Blight, a "victimized and oppressed South, and argued vehemently that most of the alleged Klan violence simply had not occurred" (p. 121). Thus, a pattern was established in which the South represented itself as oppressed by radical Republican occupation and threatened by black aggression. The white South portrayed itself as the real victim, while the former slaves were treated as perpetrators of oppression on behalf of the North and thus fair game for retaliatory violence from whites. Whatever the historical "facts," the reign of Klan terror in parts of the South

16. David Blight, *Race and Reunion: The Civil War in American Memory* (Cambridge, Mass., and London: Harvard University Press, 2001), 3.

17. As later happened in South Africa, witnesses were offered immunity from prosecution, and this obviously encouraged frankness from white southern witnesses before the Congressional committee. Blight, *Race and Reunion*, 420.

was minimized as necessary or as an aberration by the South and eventually faded from active memory in the North.

Though it has become a bit too easy to downplay the difficulties of sectional, intraracial reconciliation after 1865, the nation was in fact reunited after four years of bloody and costly war and twelve more years of intersectional strife. Intraracial and intersectional reconciliation won out over interracial reconciliation. As Blight puts it, "the imperative of healing and the imperative of justice could not, ultimately, cohabit the same house" (p. 57). The transformation of the white South from a slavocracy to a victimized people was remarkable. White racial solidarity arose out of what Blight refers to (in reference to Walt Whitman) as "the mutuality of soldiers' death and the need to mourn, commemorate, and memorialize all of that death on both sides" (p. 23). Or as Robert Meister puts it, what won out was the

> Lincolnian view of national recovery [that] foregrounds national trauma as a unifying experience and seeks to replace the moral logic of victim/perpetrator with the moral logic of common survivorship and collective rebirth.[18]

This is not to say that objections were never raised against the southern case. But in the main, mutual identification rather than sectional enmity was the central theme of the new white national history growing out of the Civil War and Reconstruction. In this reconciliatory narrative, all Americans became victims, participants in a national tragedy that was transformed over time into a national celebration, except for the most victimized, whose losses of over 180,000 men in the war were largely forgotten until the 1960s.

Several factors help explain why the trend toward white racial reconciliation was so powerful, while interracial justice and reconciliation were largely absent. Clearly, folk racism at the popular level and scientific racism among the educated elite were powerful, if blunt, instruments in shaping the narrative of national reconciliation. The dominant scientific understanding of race at the time sanctioned a largely untroubled belief in white racial and cultural superiority, which helped explain alleged black political incompetence during Reconstruction. Indeed, social and/or biological intercourse between the races, it was feared, would lead to deterioration of the superior race and culture. From this perspective alone, racial reconciliation was all but impossible, since reconciliation can take place only between those who acknowledge one another as equals in moral stature or in power. Blight also makes clear that, as of 1915, there was

18. Robert Meister, "Forgiving and Forgetting: Lincoln and the Problem of National Recovery," in *Human Rights in Political Transitions: Gettysburg to Bosnia,* ed. Carla Hesse and Robert Post (New York: Zone, 1999), 137.

an identity between the popular (white) memory and the academic historiography of the Civil War and Reconstruction. Indeed, one effect of late-nineteenth-century disciplinary training in history was to provide an academic version of the popular reconciliationist narrative, according to which, the North (rightly) won the War and the destruction of slavery was seen as an overall good, while the white South's position on Reconstruction and its harsh assessment of black American capability became the standard issue on both sides of the Mason-Dixon line. Third, northern support for anything approaching a genuine racial reconciliation faltered once the generation of abolitionists and Radical Republicans died out. Even while the Radicals were at the peak of their power in the early years after the war, Congress never approved meaningful land reform or a generous enough homestead bill to benefit a significant number of African Americans. Even those who asked God's forgiveness for slavery refused to do the same thing of the former slaves.

Other general tendencies of the culture helped deflect attention from the task of racial reconciliation. Like the rest of us, nineteenth-century Americans wanted to enshrine those aspects of the past that fit their own self-image, which was (and remains) powerfully shaped by the notions of chosenness. William Faulkner's *Absalom, Absalom!* (1936) explores as well as any text the nineteenth-century white American attempt to avoid the realities of race and class. Thomas Sutpen represents Faulkner's answer to Herman Melville's Ahab: both are obsessed with rectifying a deep hurt and humiliation. Yet, as Quentin Compson says of Sutpen, "His trouble was innocence."[19] But that innocence does not derive from his wish to forget the past so much as reflect his desire to deny its reality for the present. A lack of moral imagination, an inability to imagine himself into anyone else's position, marked Sutpen's sensibility just as it did Adolph Eichmann's.

The accelerating urbanization and industrialization of the country gradually shifted the post–Civil War nation's attention from racial and sectional conflict to class and cultural conflict, leaving the white South to manage its own race relations. Northern white elites directed their own nativist ideology against the new immigrants. In turn, the European ethnics had no great investment in the wrenching trauma of Civil War and the failures of Reconstruction. Though few of them wanted to settle in the South, fewer still developed much feeling for the plight of African Americans. Out of all the ethnic groups, only Jewish Americans were to develop a certain solidarity with African Americans. But it is symptomatic of the gap between African Americans and European ethnics that even the

19. William Faulkner, *Absalom, Absalom!* (New York: Vintage International, 1990[1936]), 78.

479

generous vision of cultural pluralism articulated by Horace Kallen and Randolph Bourne was largely silent about African Americans. To a startling degree, Kallen himself shared the white prejudices of his time against people of color such as Alain Locke.[20] Overall, as Louis Menand has suggested about the Progressive period, "The price of reform . . . between 1898 and 1917 was the removal of the issue of race from the table," while Gary Gerstle has suggested that much the same trade-off extended to the end of World War II.[21]

What did African Americans, the "injured party" but also a permanent minority, think about all this? While no single reaction can be attributed to African Americans, the response of the Colored People's Convention in November 1865 captured much of what David Blight refers to when he writes that newly freed African Americans "sought no official apologies for slavery, only protection, education, human recognition, a helping hand" (p. 3). The official resolution of the Convention stated that "we would cherish in our hearts no malice or hatred of those who were implicated in the crime of slaveholding; but we would extend the right hand of fellowship to all." They came, they said, as "friends and fellow-countrymen, who desire to dwell among you in peace, and whose destinies are interwoven and linked with those of the whole American people and hence must be fulfilled in this country."[22] The dignity and the forbearance of the statement are impressive. Slaveholding is unapologetically referred to as a "crime," yet no white apology is called for; and no reparations are threatened.

It is difficult to say how typical such a statement was, but I suspect it expressed mainstream African American thinking, represented by someone like Frederick Douglass. Absent any vision of future interracial harmony, one can only assume that the delegates at the convention were most interested in concrete help from friendly whites or hoped that white people would at least not hinder them in their efforts to forge a life in freedom. In a sense, as Donald Shriver has noted, the fact that the vast majority of black people simply stayed put rather than leaving the country represented a recognition that racial coexistence was to be a fact of life. Most African Americans also rejected overseas migrationist dreams, though the tradition of black nationalism was impressively represented by mid-century figures such as Henry Highland Garnett and Martin Delaney. But it was hard enough to get Kansas and Oklahoma to begin life again, out from under the oppressive conditions in the South. For most black people, Africa was out of the question.

20. Louis Menand, *The Metaphysical Club: A Story of Ideas in America* (New York: Farrar, Straus and Giroux, 2001), 340-49.

21. Menand, *The Metaphysical Club,* 374; Gary Gerstle, "The Protean Character of American Liberalism," *American History Review* 39 (1994): 1043-73.

22. Cited in Shriver, *An Ethic for Enemies,* 171.

Yet, nineteenth-century African American thinking about whites was not always so measured or forbearing. Many commented bitingly on the "hyperaggressive, acquisitive and domineering" nature and "implacable hostility" of the "Angry Saxons."[23] According to one standard trope, the differences between the two races resembled the difference between the (white) "masculine" and (black) "feminine" race. Mia Bay has identified an amalgam of racial science and scriptural lore that made up a kind of nineteenth-century "black ethnology." Though many blacks considered racial differences to be the product of environmental circumstances, significant numbers were also attracted by the view that blacks possessed certain innate qualities that marked them out as different from whites without thereby making them inferior. As Bay puts it, "Racism could be reversed more easily than it could be contraverted" (p. 45). Moreover, a spiritualized sense of racial difference was strong among black intellectuals in the antebellum period. Holding to a "providential" view of black history, such proto-nationalist intellectuals held that African Americans were fighting the Civil War for different reasons than their white counterparts.[24] Overall, it was easier to acknowledge that differences existed and then to reverse their valorization than to refute the nineteenth-century American school of anthropology founded on the belief in polygenesis and racial inequality. Finally, it was but a short step from a belief in the uniqueness of people of African descent to W. E. B. Du Bois' opposition to racial amalgamation and the disappearance of specific black characteristics. Rather, for Du Bois, group differences were to be preserved, even though a common national life with whites was something to be desired. He sought racial coexistence and eventual interracial cooperation rather than some dramatic racial reconciliation.

Finally, one of the most important ideas emerging from nineteenth- and early-twentieth-century African American thought was that black Americans were a "redeemer race." Obviously prefigured both in the Exodus story and the story of Christ's redemptive sacrifice, the persisting theme of black chosenness suggested not only the difference but also the moral superiority of blacks to whites (Bay, 37). This self-characterization fed both the nationalist tradition that questioned black-white coexistence and the integrationist-reconciliationist tradition of black religious thought. However, by World War I, a conservative reconciliationist position forged by Booker T. Washington seemed to have won the day. The Bookerite vision of racial cooperation involved the wager that

---

23. Mia Bay, *The White Image in the Black Mind: African American Ideas about White People, 1830-1925* (New York and Oxford: Oxford University Press, 2000), 77; 7.

24. See John Ernest, *Liberation Historiography: African American Writers and the Challenge of History, 1794-1861* (Chapel Hill: University of North Carolina Press, 2004).

black Americans could make themselves economically indispensable to the South and to the nation. Once this became a realized fact, social and political equality could be achieved in the fullness of time, while reconciliation would entail the melding of interests rather than a meeting of hearts and minds.[25]

## The Second Reconstruction: Things Fall Apart

Historically, second chances are hard to come by, but the United States was lucky, since the "second Reconstruction" was as much an attempt to fulfill the promises of the first Reconstruction as it was a new departure in American race relations.[26] By the mid-1960s, the power of the federal government and the Supreme Court seemed to have taken the side of black political and legal equality. Perhaps the most radical idea in Gunnar Myrdal's *An American Dilemma* (1944) was that the American racial dilemma was a "white man's problem," a judgment that reflected the shift from social and economic to moral and psychological understandings of racial prejudice, now increasingly referred to as "racism." In fact, Myrdal's two-volume study was the cornerstone of the post-1945 universalist consensus on race. Once discriminatory legal impediments to black access to public and private institutions were abolished in the Jim Crow South, all black Americans would then be able to enjoy "equal opportunity" in an increasingly "color-blind" society. As with American ethnics, especially American Jews, upward mobility and assimilation for African Americans would follow in the wake of the dismantling of segregation. If this were hardly the "beloved community" envisioned by some in the Civil Rights movement, it still promised more dignity than the Bookerite idea that black people should work their way into the good graces of white Americans.

Nor was race any longer a topic to be excluded from public debate; rather, it seemed at times to be all people could talk or think about. Between 1944 and 1968, at least three major studies of America's racial dilemma were subject to considerable public discussion. Besides Myrdal's massive two-volume work, a Myrdal-influenced report, *To Secure These Rights* (1947-48), issued by a presidential commission appointed by President Truman, proposed far-reaching re-

25. Blight, *Race and Reunion,* 331.

26. Specifically, the 1954 *Brown v. Board of Education* decision reversed the 1896 *Plessy v. Ferguson* decision; the 1964 Public Accommodations Act revived the 1875 Civil Rights Act that had been ruled unconstitutional by the Supreme Court in 1883; and the 1965 Voting Rights Act put teeth into the Fourteenth and especially the Fifteenth Amendments. See Robert Caro, *The Years of Lyndon Johnson: Master of the Senate* (New York: Vintage, 2003), 916-18, for the use of the term "second Reconstruction" by southern senators.

forms; and in 1968 the Kerner Commission Report, which was produced in the wake of urban rioting and civil disturbances, echoed Myrdal when it identified white racism as the ultimate cause of persisting racial divisions and violence in America's cities. In fact, thirteen commissions dealing with various aspects of race relations and race-related phenomena appeared in the Johnson years alone.[27] Overall, during the second Reconstruction, social science was in is hey-day. American race relations were a problem to be solved rather than a sin to be confessed or a crime to be investigated.

Yet as the 1960s unfolded, the liberal consensus began to disintegrate. While the civil rights movement achieved significant legal and political gains in the South, the social and economic fabric of black life began to unravel as the great migration from the rural South to northern and western urban areas fell to a trickle. Poverty and broken families were increasingly seen as black phenomena. As black political consciousness grew in the increasingly heated atmosphere, black Americans also rediscovered their own cultural roots in Africa and under slavery. No longer was that black heritage one to be ashamed of or a hindrance in the struggle for equality. Indeed, the idea that something called a black or African American culture existed at all was a radical step forward and marked a major difference between the first and second Reconstruction. In this context, it is not surprising that the future of white-black coexistence, let alone reconciliation, was the subject of intense public controversy in the 1960s and early 1970s. Where proto nationalist currents had been largely marginalized during and after the first Reconstruction, Malcolm X and the Nation of Islam, along with secular black nationalists, projected a vision of America that sought black institutional and cultural self-sufficiency as a goal. Since black Americans had a thriving and long-standing culture of their own, asserted black intellectual Harold Cruse, they should take charge of developing their cultural institutions — controlling the means of cultural production, as it were.[28]

With all this in mind, theology and social ethics in the 1960s remain neglected sites for African American discussions of their future in America, including the possibility — and desirability — of racial reconciliation. The reconciliationist position was voiced by older black religious thinkers such as Benjamin Mays and Howard Thurman, along with Thurman's former Morehouse College student, Martin Luther King Jr., and even writer James Baldwin. Like King, Baldwin assumed a mediating role between white and black America in the 1960s. Though he was often caustic in his description of

---

27. Herman, *The Romance of American Psychology*, 232.

28. See Harold Cruse, *The Crisis of the Negro Intellectual* (New York: William Morrow and Co., 1967).

whites, Baldwin concluded that the destinies of the two peoples were joined rather than separated in the United States. Baldwin also spoke of an indeterminate power of love to heal the rifts between the races, as though he had made W. H. Auden's injunction that "we must love one another or die" into his own personal categorical imperative.

By contrast with Baldwin's *eros*, King's concept of love was a politically inflected version of *agape*, a kind of concern for others as children of God. King and his mentor, Howard Thurman, assumed that nonviolence was "one of the great vehicles of reconciliation,"[29] since the latter presupposed a mutual recognition among equals. Indeed, King's basic assumption was that the white oppressor also had a conscience that could be appealed to. But as Thurman suggested, "Before the work of reconciliation can be effective," the oppressor's view of the oppressed must be fundamentally reassessed to determine if the "actual status of a human being as such is denied."[30] For both men, segregation was far more than simply an insulting social arrangement; it symbolized the spiritual state of alienation from the other and even from the self. To Thurman, "segregation, prescriptions of separations are a disease of the human spirit and the body politic."[31] By insisting that "unearned suffering is redemptive," King re-voiced the nineteenth-century notion of blacks as a "redeemer race." The ultimate goal was the "beloved community," a society in which separation had been replaced by wholeness, alienation with reconciliation. Yet neither King nor Thurman called for whites to apologize for slavery or segregation, nor did they take up restitution as a topic of discussion.

Spurred on by James Forman's 1969 Black Manifesto, which did demand reparations for black Americans, a new black theology movement emerged in the 1970s led by theologians James Cone, James Washington, Gayraud Wilmore, and J. Deotis Roberts. Reflecting the accelerating shift from a universalist to a particularist perspective on race among African Americans, Cone conceded the principle to the reconciliationists when he asserted in his *Black Theology and Black Power* (1969) that "Men were not created for separation, and color is not the essence of man's humanity." Yet he also emphasized that black people should refuse the "black self-hatred" whites imposed on them.[32] What was

29. Howard Thurman, "Reconciliation" (1963), in *A Strange Freedom: The Best of Howard Thurman on Religious Experience and Public Life*, ed. Walter Earl Fluke and Catherine Tumber (Boston: Beacon, 1998), 172. Martin Luther King Jr., "Letter from a Birmingham Jail" (1963), in *Why We Can't Wait* (New York: Harper and Row, 1964). The literature on King's idea of nonviolent direct action is, of course, extensive. See my analysis of it in *Civil Rights and the Idea of Freedom* (New York: Oxford University Press, 1992).

30. Thurman, "Reconciliation," 177.

31. Thurman, "Reconciliation," 184.

32. James Cone, *Black Theology and Black Power* (New York: Seabury, 1969), 8.

needed was a "ghetto theology" (p. 32), according to which "the new black man refuses to speak of love without justice and power" (p. 53). This was a Niebuhrian vision with a difference, since Cone's black theology was committed to the twin ideas that "God's revelation in Christ can be made supreme only by affirming Christ as he is alive in black people today" (p. 118) and that "black people have come to know Christ precisely through oppression, because he has made himself synonymous with black oppression" (p. 120). To be sure, Cone spoke of reconciliation as a desirable goal, but only on the condition that "the black community is permitted to do its thing" (p. 144). Ultimately, reconciliation depended on black people's prior acceptance of the fact that "God has reconciled us to an acceptance of our blackness" (p. 149).

Though it was not quite right to claim that Cone was really interested in black liberation rather than racial reconciliation, as Deotis Roberts did, the thrust of Cone's thought was clearly to juxtapose "we" and "they," black and white, as Roberts suggested.[33] Theologically speaking, Cone needed to explain in what ways his theology did not assume a dark-skin chauvinism or idolatry (in secular terms, reification or essentialism), since in practical terms he privileged blackness and demonized whiteness. To his critics, he seemed to have exchanged Christian universalism for a particularist position that saw black people as the exclusive instruments of God's work in contemporary history. In his *A Black Theology of Liberation* (1970), he sought to clarify the meaning of blackness (and whiteness) when he wrote that "blackness is an ontological symbol and visible reality which best describes what oppression means in America."[34] But despite this bow to complexity, he still posited the "satanic nature of whiteness" (p. 290), which he unpacked as "white people's desire to be God in human relations" (p. 193). Overall, the double meaning of color — as a material reality *and* as a sign of a spiritual and moral condition — allowed Cone to have it both ways. He could refer to "Jesus as the Black Christ" (p. 80) and thus seem to make Jesus the exclusive property of African Americans. Or he could be read to be saying that Jesus was the savior of all those who committed themselves to the liberation struggle, no matter what their skin color. In principle, then, white people could be "black," while black people could be "white." In practice, Cone's message gave encouragement to something like a racial Manichaeism.

At the polar opposite of the black theology movement was the theological perspective informing the journal *Katallagete: Be Reconciled!* (1965-1990).

33. J. Deotis Roberts, "Black Theology in the Making" (1973), in *Black Theology: A Documentary History,* 2nd ed., ed. James H. Cone and Gayraud Wilmore (Maryknoll, N.Y.: Orbis, 1993): 117.

34. James H. Cone, *A Black Theology of Liberation* (Philadelphia and New York: J. B. Lippincott, 1970), 27.

*Katallagete* was the publication of the Committee of Southern Churchmen, an interracial group of ministers. Its editor was James Holloway, while maverick theologian Will Campbell was its publisher and spiritual leader. During its existence, it published black writers and intellectuals such as Fannie Lou Hamer, Julius Lester, Vincent Harding, James Bevel, Herbert O. Edwards, and Kelly Miller Smith; Catholic writers and intellectuals such as Walker Percy and Thomas Merton; and lay thinkers such as Jacques Ellul and Christopher Lasch. Its position in its most vital years (1965-1975) was a down-home, southern version of the stringent neoorthodox theology of Swiss theologian Karl Barth.

According to Holloway and Campbell, reconciliation was above all else a question of the relationship between God and humanity and only secondarily a question of human relationships. The biblical basis for reconciliation was found in Paul's message to the Corinthians that God "has reconciled us men to himself through Christ . . . he has entrusted us with the message of reconciliation."[35] The church's main task in a fallen world was to preach the primacy of spiritual over human reconciliation. As Holloway put it: "The reconciliation of which we speak is not the reconciliation, and thus the acquiescence, of the Church to the world, but the reconciliation of the man of the world to God."[36] He qualified this stark claim by asserting that "our work in and for political rights and social integration," whose importance he did not deny, presupposed the priority of spiritual reconciliation.[37] Closely related to this refusal to privilege "worldly" concerns was Campbell's position that liberalism and the civil rights movement had been guilty of "worship of politics," which is to say "the belief that politics is redemptive, that politics is Messiah,"[38] though he and Holloway emphasized that it was not politics as such but its deification that was so pernicious. Political activists, whether liberal or radical, black or white, were guilty of a kind of idolatry that was reminiscent of the way the Israelites had whored after the false god Baal. By attacking the allegedly "liberal" idea that passing laws was the answer to the problem of racism and discrimination, Campbell and Holloway questioned the emphasis upon action in the world as a way to solve the world's problems, much less racial reconciliation. Finally, though distancing itself from blanket support of the Civil Rights movement or the liberal racial agenda (but supporting it in practice), *Katallagete* focused much-needed awareness in the 1970s on the dire economic and social condition of the people in the mountain South.

35. James Holloway, Editorial, *Katallagete* 1, no. 1 (June 1965): 1.

36. Holloway, "For Three Transgressions, and for Four," *Katallagete* 1, no. 2 (December 1965): 7.

37. Holloway, Editorial, 2.

38. Will Campbell, "Repentance and Politics II: Politics as Baal," *Katallagete* 2 (Winter 1966-1967): 9.

Though *Katallagete's* position was creative in all sorts of ways, one might have objected to the way it set God and world in such radical opposition.[39] It was not clear why involvement in the politics of change represented acquiescence to the world, while prioritizing the spiritual over the worldly somehow avoided such an accommodation. Indeed, for all its intellectual cosmopolitanism, *Katallagete* found it hard to shake off the southern white Protestant tradition of holding worldly affairs, particularly economic and social questions, at arm's length. Significantly, the reconciliationist project as developed by South African theologians against Apartheid seems to have arrived at a much more convincing balance between the religious understanding of reconciliation and engagement in the world.

Indeed, *Katallagete* was most interesting when its contributors contained their irritation with the shortcomings of liberalism and concentrated on specific issues. The fact that *Katallagete* remained open to black and white contributors in the Black Power era was a huge point in its favor. Several of its black contributors developed positions considerably at odds with Cone's black theology and more in line with the black reconciliationist position. Herbert O. Edwards's 1971 article argued that the claim that "God was in Christ, reconciling the world unto himself" implies "a relativizing of every institution and institutional pattern of behavior which affected or limited the possibilities of free and open communications between persons within a community."[40] In 1968, civil rights activist Fannie Lou Hamer of Mississippi wrote that "America created this problem. And we forgive America, even though we were brought here on the slave ships from Africa." But, she added, what was needed in return was "our share in political and economic power, so that we can have a great country, together."[41] Julius Lester, on his way from black radicalism to Judaism, took a harder line on Cone's black theology:

39. See Richard King, "Stoking the Fires or Polishing the Pinnacles," in *Perspectives on the American South*, ed. John Shelton Reed and Merle Black (New York: Gordon and Breach Science Publishers, 1984) and, much more recently, Steven P. Miller, "From Politics to Reconciliation: *Katallagete*, Biblicism, and Southern Liberalism," *Journal of Southern Religion* (http://jsr.fsu.edu/Volume7/Millerarticle.htm). Though *Katallagete's* position might be called a Barthian one, John Howard Yoder in "Karl Barth, Post-Christendom Theologian (1995)" suggests that Barth assumed that if one did "theology proper, properly," then the result would provide a valid and powerful perspective on "the principalities and powers of the present evil age" rather than a withdrawal from it (www.nd.edu/~theo/jhy/writings/philsystheo/barth.htm).

40. Herbert O. Edwards, "Racism and Christian Ethics in America," *Katallagete* 3, no. 2 (Winter 1971): 24.

41. Fannie Lou Hamer, "Sick and Tired of Being Sick and Tired," *Katallagete* 1, no. 8 (Fall 1968): 25.

> The same self-righteousness exemplified by black political radicalism is found in Black Theology. . . . Whenever we become absolutists about God and the way He moves in history, we perpetuate violence. . . . Black theology is shameful because its spokesmen want us to believe that blacks are without sin. . . .[42]

Though *Katallagete* exerted little influence in the corridors of power or among national intellectuals, it did demonstrate that creative thought about race and reconciliation was possible even in an atmosphere where the political and psychological lines dividing the races were hardening.

Finally, it is important to note how little the composition of the white political class at the national level changed in response to the Civil Rights movement and the Black Power movement over the course of the second Reconstruction. The comparisons with Vietnam are instructive. Noam Chomsky's "The Responsibility of Intellectuals" (1967) offered a compelling indictment of foreign policy intellectuals — primarily liberal ones — who had been the architects and defenders of intervention in Vietnam, while David Halberstam's *The Best and The Brightest* (1972) did much the same for (or against) U.S. foreign policy elites. But while the war effectively discredited the Democratic foreign policy elite (the "best and brightest"), nothing comparable was published or happened to discredit those white politicians who pursued the politics of racism openly in the years after the *Brown* decision. There were no essays or articles from dissenting conservative intellectuals comparable to Chomsky's causerie against national security intellectuals;[43] no volume that discredited the latter-day defenders of the racial status quo or those who reaped the benefits of the white backlash of the 1960s the way Halberstam's work had done in the area of foreign policy.[44] The Republican Party shamelessly exploited the racial tensions of the decade and was rewarded handsomely for its efforts. No defender of segregation in either house of Congress or either party was expelled from his/her party caucus; nor was anyone denied his committee chairmanship for signing the Southern Manifesto in 1955 or for opposing Civil Rights legislation in that decade or the next. Instead, southern Democrat Strom Thurmond, leader of the Dixiecrat revolt of 1948, was courted as hot political property, not shunned as a political pariah, by the Re-

---

42. Julius Lester, "Be Ye Therefore Perfect," *Katallagete* 5, no. 2 (Winter 1974): 24-25.

43. Richard H. King, "The Struggle Against Equality: Conservative Intellectuals in the Civil Rights Era, 1954-1975," in *The Role of Ideas in the Civil Rights South,* ed. Ted Ownby (Jackson: University Press of Mississippi, 2001), 113-36. One of the very few conservative intellectuals to change his mind on race and Civil Rights publicly was Garry Wills.

44. James Baldwin's *The Fire Next Time* (1964) might have been such a book, but its impact on the political class and opinion makers was more indirect.

publicans in 1968. At the same time, southern moderate and liberal congressmen risked their political lives when they spoke out for obedience to the "law of the land," much less championed desegregation.[45]

All this suggests that both the dismantling of the Jim Crow system and the beginning of significant changes in white racial attitudes were seen by the political class as part of a slow process of historical readjustment rather than an abrupt break with the past or the cutting edge of a sweeping moral revolution. In 1965, President Johnson came closest to announcing a program of radical reform that would help close the gap between white and black Americans, but he was himself the author of that effort's demise.[46] National and southern political elites were able to maintain political continuity to a remarkable degree. This is not to deny that some of the older segregationists gradually fell by the wayside by the early 1970s, while others — like Thurmond — gradually adjusted to the new realities of a biracial southern politics. Nor is it to deny the important, if relatively minor, role that Civil Rights liberals in the North played in the whole drama.[47] But the contrast with South Africa's transformation in the 1990s could hardly have been greater. In fact, the closest thing to a changing of the political guard in American politics after the Civil Rights revolution was what Kevin Phillips described as the "emerging Republican majority." The startling fact is that post-1960s American politics moved to the right rather than to the left after the 1960s. A genuine change in racial attitudes among many white Americans was accompanied, but neutralized, by a growing political conservatism.

## A New Consensus?

Since the 1960s the effort to rethink the relationship between America's troubled racial past and racial reconciliation in the present has by no means been abandoned. The Truth and Reconciliation Commission work itself has exerted an influence on thinking about these matters in certain elite academic and policy circles.[48] The last couple of decades have also seen the emergence of a global

45. See David L. Chappell, *Inside Agitators: White Southerners in the Civil Rights Movement* (Baltimore: Johns Hopkins University Press, 1994), and Tony Badger, "'Closet Moderates': Why White Liberals Failed, 1940-1970," *The Role of Ideas in the Civil Rights South*, 83-112.

46. See Ira Katznelson, *When Affirmative Action Was White* (New York and London: W. W. Norton, 2005), for an account of the potential importance of Johnson's 1965 Howard University address.

47. See Caro, *Master of the Senate*, Part V.

48. Besides Rotberg and Thompson's *Truth v. Justice*, see also Martha Minow, *Between Vengeance and Forgiveness: Facing History after Genocide and Mass Violence* (Boston: Beacon, 1998).

"human rights" culture, whose origins lie in the post–World War II United Nations resolutions defining human rights and genocide.[49] Its trajectory began with the Nuremberg Trials, continued with the Eichmann Trial (1961) and the Auschwitz Trials in Frankfurt am Main in the mid-1960s, and led to the Holocaust trials in France in the 1980s. Since then, an International Court has been established at The Hague to try war crimes in the Balkans, and the ten-year anniversary of the Rwandan genocide (1994-2004) has received considerable attention, including at least two feature films. Once considered too vague to do serious legal duty, notions such as "genocide" and "crimes against humanity" have helped restore a moral dimension to foreign policy debates that normally emphasized the politics of national interest and Realpolitik.[50] Indeed, the term "military humanitarianism" has been coined to describe military operations, such as the one in Kosovo, designed to stop ethnic cleansing and potential genocide.

The record of the United States over the past quarter century has been a mixed one. The 1988 Civil Liberties Act, approved by Congress and signed by President Reagan, contained an official apology for the internment of the Nisei Japanese Americans during World War II and offered monetary restitution of $20,000 per individual survivor.[51] This official U.S. government action obviously lent "the language of restitution a previously unknown prominence," according to Elazar Barkan.[52] In turn, the 1988 Act helped stimulate an intermittent but important discussion about reparations for African Americans, though since September 11, 2001, it has lost whatever momentum it once possessed.[53] But even though the U.S. government authorized reparation payments to the Nisei Japanese, nothing of the same scale has been forthcoming with regard to African Americans on a national level, though in 1994 the Florida state legisla-

---

49. See Michael Ignatieff, *Human Rights as Politics and Idolatry* (Princeton and Oxford: Princeton University Press, 2001).

50. See, for instance, Samantha Power, *"A Problem from Hell": America and the Age of Genocide* (New York: Basic Books, 2002).

51. See Minow, *Between Vengeance and Justice*, 99-100; Tavuchis, *Mea Culpa*, 107; Barkan, *The Guilt of Nations: Restitution and Negotiating Historical Injustice* (New York and London: W. W. Norton, 2000), 30-45.

52. Barkan, *Guilt of Nations*, 31.

53. Lawrie Balfour, "Unreconstructed Democracy: W. E. B. Du Bois and the Case for Reparations," *American Political Science Review* 97, no. 1 (2003): 33-44; Boris I. Bittker, *The Case for Black Reparations*, foreword by Drew S. Days III and new preface by the author (Boston: Beacon, 2003 [1973] ); Randall Robinson, *The Debt: What America Owes to Blacks* (New York: Dutton, 2000); Barkan, *Guilt of Nations*; Minow, "Reparations," *Between Vengeance and Forgiveness*, 91-117; Robert Westley, "Many Billions Gone: Is It Time to Reconsider the Case for Black Reparations?" *Boston College Law Journal* 40 (December 1998): 429-76.

ture approved compensation to survivors (or their families) of the Rosewood Massacre in 1923. Monuments, memorials, and museums, such as the Vietnam War veterans memorial, the National Holocaust Museum, and a National Museum of the American Indian have been built on the Mall in Washington since the 1960s. Only in January 2006 was construction of a national museum of African American life on the Mall approved, while Civil Rights museums of high quality have opened in Memphis and Birmingham.

Why it has been difficult to mount a sustained debate on the history of white-black relations? Besides historical events such as 9/11, the so-called "War on Terror," and more recently the Iraq War, a contemporary consensus on race and the American past has begun to emerge that makes this all more difficult. Not only does this new consensus oppose reparations and (usually) affirmative action, it is also skeptical of the need to scrutinize, much less apologize for, American's troubled past. At its core is what Glenn Loury refers to in *The Anatomy of Racial Inequality* (2002) as "race blindness" and "liberal individualism."[54] Loury's critique of race blindness begins by contending that a society constructed on liberal individualism "cannot cope with the consequences of its own violations" (p. 166). For example, if at the start of a particular historical sequence or at some point along the way, extra advantage is given to one party (individual, group, class, race, etc.) over another, that advantage cannot be overcome by later removing it or by nurturing individual talent and urging superhuman effort. Loury, a one-time conservative, now insists that redress of inequality must take into account racial factors, even if the ultimate goal remains a liberal, color-blind society (p. 152). If it refuses to take into account racial factors, it is incoherent.

Loury's position entails support affirmative action, but not reparations. His objection to reparations is that it makes no political sense for African Americans to advance an "exceptionalist" claim for compensatory aid, since such a move risks alienating political allies.[55] In addition, he considers it a catc-

54. See *The Anatomy of Racial Inequality* (Cambridge, Mass., and London: Harvard University Press, 2002), 112-13; "Reply to J. L. A. Garcia and John McWhorter," *First Things* (May 2002): 15-25 (http://www.firstthings.com/ftissues/ft0205/articles/raceexchange.html); "On Group Identity and Individual Behavior: Thoughts on *The Anatomy of Racial Inequality*," in *Faith and Economics* 41 (Spring 2003): 8-16; and "It's Futile to Put a Price on Slavery," *New York Times*, May 29, 2000 (http://www-personal.ksu.edu/~jbex/repar.htm). By "liberal" Loury refers not to the New Deal–Great Society tradition of the Democratic Party, but rather to a broad position that privileges individual epistemological and moral judgment over socially oriented knowledge and morality. If anything, it is more closely identified with the Republican than the Democratic Party. (Page references for citations from *The Anatomy of Racial Inequality* will be included in the body of the text.)

55. Appearance on C-Span, Dec. 9, 2001.

gory error to use material compensation to rectify moral and psychological damage, what he refers to as the ongoing "stigma" attached to being black in America. Thus he calls for an "interpretive" rather than a "compensatory" approach to the African American past, since "the quantitative attribution of causal weight to distant historical events required by reparations advocacy is not workable."[56] With the example of South Africa's TRC in mind, he concluded a *New York Times* article in 2000 by asserting that "The deepest and most relevant 'reparation' would entail constructing and inculcating in our citizens an account of how we have come to be as we are."[57]

Yet there are problems with this argument. Whatever one thinks about reparations, Loury was wrong about the TRC process in South Africa. It not only instituted public hearings where people could testify about past experiences of injury and insult, and thus help construct a new national narrative, it also included a reparations component — albeit not a large one. Put another way, it is difficult to see why remembering "how we have come to be as we are" and a nuanced form of compensation are mutually exclusive. Still, there are strong reasons for thinking that reparations are impossible in the present political and moral climate. The sheer complexity of determining "who gets what" makes individual compensation all but impossible to imagine. Should it be the experience of slavery only or the century of systematic racial discrimination after the end of slavery — or both — for which reparations should be considered? Finally, it is not clear that it is wise for African Americans to assume the classification of citizen victims, thus perhaps perpetuating rather than annulling the stigma of race in America.

Indeed, when Loury mentions the need to ground political citizenship in historical awareness, he hits upon a second reason why the new consensus makes discussion of compensation so difficult. Many Americans now firmly believe that since discriminatory laws were removed from the statute books in the 1960s, as long as equal opportunity is fairly enforced, then America's racial dilemmas have been effectively resolved. Here the contradictory effects of successful reform become apparent, since the historical conditions that created and perpetuated the Jim Crow system have now been largely forgotten. The concept of "historical aftereffects" seems foreign to American thinking on this matter. Only recently, Ira Katznelson has made clear that, up to the 1960s in the North *and* the South, most liberal-progressive legislation, through a perversely complex process of exclusion and discriminatory implementation, helped widen rather than narrow the economic and social gap between white and

---

56. Loury, *Anatomy of Racial Inequality*, 127; "Reply to Garcia and McWhorter," 19.
57. Loury, *Times on the Web*, 5/29/2000, 3.

black Americans. Thus the American past is sanitized, and the concept of citizenship lacks a historical dimension.

This lack of historical awareness contrasts markedly with the attitudes in present-day Germany toward its troubled history, according to philosopher Thomas McCarthy, who has recently called attention to the serious discrepancy between the transformation of the academic historiography of slavery, Reconstruction, segregation, and race since the 1960s and the existing state of popular American memory about these same historical phenomena.[58] This gap would help explain why many white Americans claim to believe in racial equality and disapprove of slavery, yet are fascinated with Civil War reenactments and identify with the Confederacy rather than the Union when "re-fighting" the war. Contemporary defenders of the Confederate battle flag contend that the Confederacy was not fighting to preserve racial slavery, and that the flag should thus be associated with resistance to federal bureaucracy and local autonomy.[59] Aspects of Ken Burns's much-lauded film "Civil War" (1990) also illustrate this disconnect between historical memory and political morality. Though the series cannot be accused of ignoring race or being racist, the dominant impression the viewer carries away from it, helped along mightily by the seductive charm of Shelby Foote's southern accent, is that the War was a tragic conflict in which bravery and virtue were evenly distributed on both sides. As an up-to-date version of the Lincolnian vision of the Civil War referred to earlier, it all but implies a moral equivalency between the cause of the Confederacy and that of the Union. For all its strengths, the series fails to acknowledge the moral dimension of the most important period of the American past.

Overall, then, the new consensus on race and history is based on a complex, three-stage deflection of moral responsibility for the past. First, most people will accept the basic facts about slavery, the Civil War, and Reconstruction. Second, most people can be brought to admit that these facts taken together suggest that serious wrong was done to African Americans in the past. But, third, it is remarkably difficult for many Americans to accept that any particular people (their ancestors), collective entity (the South), or group (white Americans) was either *guilty* of this in the past or might be *responsible* for dealing with it in the present. The argument that slaveholders and their defenders in the mid-nineteenth century should not be judged by "our" moral standards relativizes and historicizes moral values out of existence and allows us to forget that many

58. Thomas McCarthy, "Vergangenheitsbewältigung in the USA: On the Politics of the Memory of Slavery," *Political Theory* 30, no. 5 (October 2002): 644-46.

59. For an extended exploration of these and related phenomena, see Tony Horowitz, *Confederates in the Attic: Dispatches from the Unfinished Civil War* (New York: Vintage, 1999).

white Americans of both sections did think slavery was immoral, even in 1861. Not surprisingly, similar arguments were heard from those in South Africa who urged blanket amnesty after the end of the Apartheid regime. Overall, this is a bizarre form of historical consciousness. Oppressive, even evil, institutions such as slavery are acknowledged to have existed, but the motives of those who owned slaves or benefited from slavery are sanitized. Crimes against humanity were committed, but the perpetrators should not be considered criminals. Thus what we have is the concept not of "victimless crimes" but of "perpetrator-less crimes." This reflects a profound split between knowledge and acknowledgment — a better explanation, I think, for the discrepancy McCarthy identifies than factual ignorance.

Two more characteristics complete the new consensus on race and the American past. Most white Americans now reject biological racism, but explain black failures by reference to group character or the inadequacies of black culture. This is a tricky matter, since most people, or all people some of the time, fail to perform up to their capabilities. If there is a distinct or semiautonomous African American culture, it has, by definition, characteristics that equip its members to achieve better in some areas than in others. What is objectionable about all this is that blaming black culture for the failure of African Americans to achieve the same rates of success as certain immigrant groups, such as Jews and Asian Americans, makes it very easy to persist in ignoring the real discrimination that still exists and the lingering aftershock of the past. This in turn implies a fourth, more subtle and pervasive characteristic that Loury identifies: an "Ingrained Racial Stigma" or "spoiled collective identity"[60] attributed to African Americans. Racial stigmatization is another of those historical aftereffects of explicit belief in doctrines of black inferiority and "remains yet to be fully eradicated" (p. 70). It is a pervasive yet barely conscious perception, a form of racism without an explicit racial ideology.

Overall the new consensus on race and racism represents an advance on the explicitly racist post-Reconstruction consensus among whites. But it does not provide much reason for optimism regarding the future capacity of Americans to remember, apologize, forgive, and reconcile.

## Conclusion

At several critical historical junctures, the United States has failed to produce the equivalent of the Truth and Reconciliation Commission in South Africa or

60. Loury, *Anatomy of Racial Inequality*, 5-7; 67.

analogous institutional processes. This is not to minimize what has been achieved in public policy; nor is to deny the profound attitudinal changes in white racial views over the last half century. But it is to say that for some complicated reasons, there has never been a concerted effort to come to terms with the nation's racial legacy.

Why not? In long-range terms, demography — that African Americans are vastly outnumbered by white Americans — has been hugely important. Black Americans always have been, and probably always will be, dependent on some sector of the white American population for protection or improvement. This demographic disparity helps explain the historical absence of demands from African Americans for a white apology for segregation or slavery. Within the population of European descent, several other factors have blocked the chances of something like general apology, much less discussion of compensation for African Americans. Historically, white Americans have resisted feeling shame or guilt for slavery simply because they did not acknowledge that African Americans were the same kind of human beings with the same level of culture or the same capacities as white Americans. At work have also been the religiously derived values involving a white sense of national chosenness and a peculiar sort of innocence. Finally, the tradition of liberal individualism has made it difficult to think in terms of collective responsibility for the past or the present. What Michael Sandel has called the "unencumbered" liberal self has been, and still is, alive and well in contemporary America.

Moreover, though both Reconstructions were times of serious racial reassessment, other things "got in the way." In the first Reconstruction, the need for the white nation to be reconciled with itself took precedence over racial reconciliation, while after both Reconstructions large-scale immigration directed the nation's attention elsewhere and diluted the energies that might have been devoted to constructing a society of mutual recognition between white and black Americans. During the second Reconstruction, the Vietnam War contributed mightily to a deep-seated exhaustion with, and alienation from, political and social reform, while the assassination of two white liberal political leaders — President John F. Kennedy and his brother, Robert Kennedy — and two leaders of the black insurgency of the 1960s — Malcolm X and Martin Luther King Jr. — seriously undermined much-needed national leadership on racial issues. Nor, needless to say, did President Lincoln's assassination in April 1865 help further interracial reconciliation in post–Civil War America.

Overall, then, we may look back with a sense of missed opportunities, particularly during and after the 1960s. At present, two areas in particular are in need of patient and careful thought. First, we need to construct a more historically and conceptually sophisticated notion of citizenship based on political language of belonging and responsibility.[61] The issue here is whether a nation of immigrants can create a strong notion of citizenship that entails an assumption of responsibility for the history of the nation antedating their arrival in the country. Put another way, we need to cultivate a Burkean notion of citizenship in which the citizen body is responsible not only to itself but also to those who have come before and those who will come after. As emphasized before, what is at issue is not individual or collective *guilt* for slavery and segregation, but rather a shared commitment to the *responsibility* for remedying economic, social, and political inequalities arising from those historical facts. It is also important to emphasize that this is a political project in which not just white Americans of European descent but all Americans of whatever descent must participate.

The second area for further exploration involves the complex relationship between reconciliation (based on apology and forgiveness) and restitution or compensation. To return to a question mentioned at the beginning: is there a contradiction between the call for apology and forgiveness, on the one hand, and the demand for restitution on the other, where the former seems to involve forgiving an injury and the latter involves collecting something to compensate for that injury? My own sense is that the apology/forgiveness and restitution processes go together rather than being mutually exclusive. Apology of a public sort is already a form of restitution, and often functions psychologically as such. But concrete forms of "making good" *(Wiedergutmachung)* are necessary to show good faith on the part of the collective that is apologizing, particularly when it is a matter of public apology, and also to offer tangible material compensation. Such concrete steps need not involve payments directly to individuals but could take the form of stronger, more exacting forms of affirmative action, as Ira Katznelson has suggested, and significant contributions to long-standing institutions such as predominantly black colleges and universities. Not only government sources but private foundations and philanthropists should be urged to stop thinking in terms of donations to Harvard and Stanford but rather to Fisk and Virginia State. These contributions would benefit not only African Americans but the entire society, including non-African American students who already attend some of these historically black institutions in increasing numbers. Overall, it is important that the effects of targeted and partially symbolic compensations benefit more people than just the historically appropriate recipients. The best form of historical restitution benefits the entire society, thus demonstrating that compensation is not a zero-sum game, but something more.

61. See Michael Ignatieff, *The Needs of Strangers* (London: Chatto and Windus; Hogarth, 1984), 135-42.

# Index

Abolitionism, 406-7; and anti-Catholicism, 418-22; and Catholicism, 405, 407-8, 410-14

Advertising: and corporate America, 208-9; and human depravity, 26

Affirmative action, 491, 496

African Americans: culture of, 491; education of, 394-95; and historical memory, 491, 492-94; on racial reconciliation, 479-82, 483-85, 486-87; and restitution, 469-70, 473, 484, 496

Agrarianism: of Wendell Berry, 294, 315-17; and new agrarianism, 292-94

Allegory, 125

America: and anti-Catholicism, 405, 406-8; innocence of, 20; morality of, 21-23; and South Africa, 469-70

American culture: and human depravity, 24-26; and marriage reform, 457-63; and narcissism, 361-65; and popular culture, 18, 244. *See also* Education in early America; Corporate America

American Medical Association, 324-25

Ames, William, 117, 431

Amherst College, 386

Amish, 316, 346

Andover Seminary, 386

Anesthesia, 324-25

Anselm, 60

Anti-Catholicism: and abolitionism, 418-22; in America, 405, 406-8

Apartheid, 468, 471, 487, 494

Apology and politics, 470-76

Aquinas. *See* Thomas Aquinas

Arendt, Hannah, 471-73

Aristotelianism, 166, 170-78

Art: of Puritans, 72, 74-80, 117-18; and framing, 81-82; and God, 113-14; and gravestones, 94-103

Augustine, 27, 430

Augustinianism: and creation, 29-30; and labor, 207-8; and self, 191, 204-5; and sin, 17-18, 27

Authority: and managers, 201, 203; and women, 166-67, 169

Bacon, Francis, 324

Baldwin, James, 483-84

Basil, the Great, 323

Baxter, Richard, 84-85, 109

*Beatty v. Kurtz*, 434-35

Bellah, Robert, 24

Bendroth, Margaret, 163

Berry, Wendell, 290, 291-93, 315-17; on community, 298-301, 305-6; on home life, 310-12; on industrialization, 308-10; on marriage and sex, 305-8; on memory, 296-98; on nature, 254-55, 260, 303-5; on place, 294-96; on science, 301-3; on selfhood, 257-61; theology of, 312-15

Bible. *See* Scripture